The Fundamentals of
Federal Taxation

The Fundamentals of Federal Taxation
Problems and Materials

FIFTH EDITION

John A. Miller
WELDON SCHIMKE DISTINGUISHED PROFESSOR OF LAW
UNIVERSITY OF IDAHO COLLEGE OF LAW

Jeffrey A. Maine
MAINE LAW FOUNDATION PROFESSOR OF LAW
UNIVERSITY OF MAINE SCHOOL OF LAW

CAROLINA ACADEMIC PRESS
Durham, North Carolina

eISBN 978-1-53101-109-3
ISBN 978-1-5310-1108-6
LCCN 2018944089

Carolina Academic Press, LLC
700 Kent Street
Durham, North Carolina 27701
Telephone (919) 489-7486
Fax (919) 493-5668
www.cap-press.com

Printed in the United States of America

To Maggie, Ben and Alex

— Jack Miller

To My Mother and Father

— Jeff Maine

Summary of Contents

Contents

Preface and Acknowledgments

This edition brings the text current to February 2018 and reflects changes made by recent tax acts, including the Tax Cuts and Jobs Act of 2017 (TCJA). The TCJA is the most sweeping change in the income tax in nearly 30 years, but many of its changes for individual taxpayers are temporary, and the Act merely suspends rather than repeals prior law. Most of those suspensions of prior law are slated to end in 2026, and most of the positive provisions that replaced them are slated to sunset at that same time. This leads to some necessity for the student to appreciate both the present and the suspended law. In this edition we have married our discussion of present law with a description of prior and suspended law as appropriate.

It has been said that the hardest thing about writing a good book is knowing what to leave out. That is certainly true of a book about the law of taxation. The Internal Revenue Code and the regulations interpreting it extend for many thousands of pages. An introduction to its labyrinthian nature must necessarily leave a great deal out. In the materials that follow, we have sought to highlight those parts of federal tax law that are most relevant to the every-day experiences of life in the United States. The level of coverage is not entirely uniform because part of appreciating the law of taxation is seeing its varying depths. Though our approach has been far from encyclopedic, we have tried to make the study of taxation engaging, concrete and specific through examples and problems. By the same token, we have made a consistent effort to delineate the policies that underlie our tax system and to note deviations from generally accepted principles of sound tax policy. Because most people who study taxation do so in order to serve a client, we have also emphasized planning principles.

We have broken the subject matter of this book into many more chapters than is typical of law casebooks. The purpose for this approach is simply to make the book easier for teachers to assign and for students to read. The typical chapter can be covered in one or two class periods. If the instructor chooses to omit a topic, she or he need only direct the student to skip the appropriate chapter. The assignments are structured to make efficient and effective use of student preparation time by segmenting and prioritizing the material.

As is typical of tax law casebooks, this book is intended to be used in conjunction with selected sections of the Internal Revenue Code and the federal tax regulations. Several publishers produce one volume editions that well serve that purpose.

Jack Miller would like to thank Dean Mark Adams for his generous support for this project. He is deeply grateful for the excellent research assistance of Brian Peterson, Jennifer Hedlund, and Jamie Bjorklund.

Jeff Maine would like to thank Dean Danielle Conway for supporting this project. He would also like to thank Corinne Gagnon, Nathan Brown, Ryan Almy, Heidi Gage, Frances Smith, and Deborah Lorenzen for their superb editorial assistance.

The Fundamentals of
Federal Taxation

Chapter 1

Introduction

I. Problems

1. Which of the following items constitute tax expenditures and why or why not?

   (a) A deduction for the interest a taxpayer pays on her home mortgage? See IRC §§ 163(h)(1) & (2)(d).

   (b) A deduction for the interest a taxpayer pays on her business loan? *See* IRC § 163(a).

   (c) An exclusion from income of the value of health insurance provided by the taxpayer's employer? *See* IRC § 106(a).

   (d) A tax deduction for a taxpayer's payment of a reasonable salary to the taxpayer's employee? *See* IRC § 162(a)(1).

   (e) A credit against tax for the cost of adopting a child? *See* IRC § 23(a).

   (f) A tax deduction for a plane ticket to travel to a business meeting? *See* IRC § 162(a)(2).

2. Flagship University employs many pre-doctoral fellows as full-time employees to teach freshman level classes and to do basic research in its laboratories. These predoctoral fellows are also students working on their Ph.D.'s in one of several disciplines including biology, chemistry, engineering, and physics. Their compensation for their teaching and research activities includes tuition waivers for their doctoral studies. Federal law exempts "students" and their employers from paying certain payroll taxes. The statute does not define students. Recently, the Treasury Department issued a regulation categorically providing that anyone who is a full-time employee cannot qualify as a "student" for purposes of the payroll tax exemption.

   (a) Flagship has come to you for advice on whether to contest the validity of the new regulation. What do you think of Flagship's chances to get a court to strike down the regulation?

   (b) Would it make any difference if the new regulation contradicts an earlier repealed but longstanding regulation that allowed exempt status to students who were also full-time employees?

   (c) Would it make any difference in (a) if the new regulation contradicts the legislative history of the statute in question?

II. Overview

The laws of taxation are comparable to the rules of a complex game like poker or chess. You cannot play the game until you learn the rules. Learning the rules is not always pleasant, but playing the game is often great fun. The analogy to poker is especially apt because "playing" tax is about winning, or at least keeping, money. Some people would say that tax is more serious than poker. In truth, the seriousness of either game depends on the size of the stakes and on whether the player can afford to lose. It is, after all, only money. But one important difference is that, unlike poker, one cannot opt out of the tax game. We are all obliged to play. That is why those professionals who serve as financial advisors to taxpayers have no choice but to learn the rules. Ignorance is not a rational option. Hence the need for books like this one.

The players in the tax game are the government and the taxpayer. The government has one great advantage, it writes the rules. However, the government is ultimately answerable to the taxpayer (at least in a democracy such as ours) and this constrains its authoritarian tendencies. Moreover, it is very hard to write rules that contain no loopholes. Lawyers, accountants, and business people often display great ingenuity in exploiting this inherent difficulty. In addition there are multitudes of special interest groups that assiduously lobby the government for tax breaks. Their means of persuasion range from policy arguments to monetary gifts (usually of the legal variety such as campaign contributions and "free" lunches). In the end, the game of tax is probably an even contest if one accepts that the government is entitled to a reasonable share of money in exchange for the services it provides. Most taxpayers agree that the government is entitled to financial support. However, they naturally prefer that it obtain those revenues from someone else. Thus, the game is hard fought and never ending.

As of this writing, the latest round in this tax battle was the enactment of the Tax Cut and Jobs Act (TCJA) in December of 2017. This act made numerous changes to the income tax as it applies to individuals, corporations, and pass-through entities such as partnerships and LLCs. The leading theme of the new law is an across-the-board reduction of tax rates (at least temporarily). The changes wrought by the TCJA are largely effective as of January 1, 2018. Nearly all of the changes to the individual income tax are temporary and expire on January 1, 2026. At this point, it is impossible to predict which, if any, of those changes will continue in effect after that date. Unlike the individual income tax changes, the corporate tax changes are permanent (at least in the sense of having no expiration date).

Over the long term, the TCJA may be seen primarily as a permanent corporate tax cut augmented by temporary individual tax cuts that will ultimately expire or be renewed. It is estimated that the TCJA will add to the federal budget deficit to the tune of about $1.5 trillion over the next decade. Had the individual tax reductions been made permanent, the deficit would have been much greater. The proponents of the TCJA argue that it will ultimately stimulate the economy in ways that are beneficial to workers as well as business owners. The critics of the Act tend toward the view that the primary beneficiaries of the new law are the well-to-do and that the costs of the additional deficit will be borne by present and future workers through higher taxes or reduced government benefits or both. The TCJA amends or repeals (often temporarily) a number of provisions. Some of these changes may be seen as simplification efforts. Other changes are intended to increase revenues in order to offset the revenue losses arising from the rate reductions. As the reader will see, a number of the temporarily repealed provisions are deductions granted to individuals. This means that the overall benefit to any particular person of the tax cuts is only determinable upon a complete analysis of that person's tax situation.

A. Tax Policy

Ideally, certain principles should govern the formation of a tax system. Among the more important of these is that a system should levy taxes commensurately with one's ability to pay those taxes. It is generally thought that income taxes and consumption taxes are best on this count. The first difficulty of both these systems is defining the base. What is income? What constitutes consumption? In general, income is the sum of one's consumption plus one's increase in net worth during a designated period (a calendar year). Consumption is the using up of one's assets for personal satisfaction. From this one can see that the primary difference between an income tax and a consumption tax is that the latter does not tax savings. A consumption tax, therefore, encourages taxpayers to save. For this reason some experts argue that a consumption tax is superior to an income tax. In a capitalist society saving and investing are considered good things. This is because saving leads to capital formation and capital formation generates economic activity leading to profits and jobs.

In the United States the federal government derives the bulk of its revenue from an income tax. The income tax has some of the features of a consumption tax. For example, earnings that are "saved" in retirement accounts are not taxed currently. Instead those earnings are taxed years later when they are distributed from the accounts. In effect taxation is deferred on that income until it is consumed. As you proceed through this book you will encounter many more examples of deferred taxation that cause our income tax to resemble a consumption tax.

After ability to pay, an ideal tax system should also embrace principles of fairness, efficiency, and neutrality. Each of these principles deserves a brief consideration.

1. Fairness

Tax fairness is usually described in terms of the principles of horizontal and vertical equity. Horizontal equity holds that persons who are similarly situated should be taxed in a similar fashion. It has been compared to the constitutional principle of equal protection under the laws. U.S. Const. Amend. XIV, § 1. Vertical equity holds that persons whose situations are different should be taxed differently. The two principles are simply opposite sides of the same coin. For example, under horizontal equity if Person A and Person B each earn $50,000 of income, each should pay the same amount of income tax. It tends to follow (except in the case of a "head" tax) that if A and B earn $50,000 and $75,000 respectively they should pay different amounts of tax. When we add in the ability to pay principle we conclude that B should pay more tax than A.

2. Efficiency

In tax theory, efficiency means various things in various contexts. For present purposes we may think of efficiency as a utilitarian concept requiring that we should seek a balance between maximizing tax revenues and minimizing the social costs of taxation. In other words the tax system should generate enough money for the government to do its job without stifling beneficial economic activity. Fairness and efficiency sometimes may run counter to one another. For example, it may be efficient to tax farmers at a lower rate of tax than other persons of equal income in order to maximize food production. But such an approach violates horizontal equity.

3. Neutrality

The neutrality principle holds that the tax system should avoid unnecessarily shaping economic behavior. This is accomplished by taxing economically equivalent activities in the same fashion even though they may differ in form. For example, under the neutrality principle, an employee who is paid with $50,000 worth of corporate stock should be taxed in the same fashion as an employee who is paid with $50,000 of cash. If this is the case, the decision as to whether to accept stock or cash is "tax neutral" from the employee's perspective. Over the past half century, this neutrality principle has lost ground to what might be termed "social engineering." By this we mean that many tax rules have been enacted to encourage or discourage various behaviors. Thus, for example, a tax rule might be intended to encourage people to go to college or to buy energy efficient appliances. Today, there are many tax rules in place that deliberately attempt to drive such economic decision making. These rules create what are known as "tax expenditures."

B. Tax Expenditures

In the common vernacular a tax expenditure might be called a tax break or a tax loophole. Whatever we call it, a tax expenditure occurs when a rule causes the government to collect less revenue than it would collect under a "normal" income tax. This raises the question of what is a normal income tax? There is a great deal of room for debate on this topic but, in general, we can say that a normal income tax would tax all net accessions to wealth as they arise. Thus, for example, a normal income tax would tax all forms of compensation currently even if some of those forms of compensation are health benefits or pension savings rather than a direct and immediate transfer of cash. Social engineering through tax expenditures is a prominent feature of our current income tax. The federal government maintains what is known as the tax expenditure budget, a compilation of all of the tax expenditures. It is estimated that federal income tax revenues are reduced by hundreds of billions of dollars annually for tax expenditures. *See* https://www.treasury.gov/resource-center/tax-policy/Pages/Tax-Expenditures.aspx. As you proceed through this book keep an eye out for tax expenditure provisions. They are not always easy to recognize and some of them are so well entrenched that they are politically sacred entitlements and are unlikely to be repealed in any event.

There are numerous aspects to tax policy beyond those that are simplistically described above. Many of these aspects will be addressed as we proceed through this book. It is generally helpful in applying a tax rule to understand as much as possible about why it exists and how it fits into or conflicts with sound tax policy. Rules are malleable tools and should be applied purposively.

C. Structure of Current Income Tax System

A taxpayer's federal income tax liability for any given year is determined by applying the appropriate tax rates to the appropriate tax base. The tax base for all taxpayers (individuals, corporations, estates, and trusts) is *taxable income*, which is defined loosely as *gross income* minus allowable *deductions*. IRC § 63. As will be seen, it is not always easy determining what economic benefits and receipts are included in gross income, a statutory term that does not have the same meaning as economic income. In addition, it is not always easy determining what economic outlays and expenditures are allowable as deductions in arriving at taxable income. This book explores the deceptively simple matters of gross income and the allowable deductions which are necessary to determine a taxpayer's taxable income.

Once a taxpayer's taxable income is calculated, the appropriate tax rates are applied. Sections 1 and 11 of the Internal Revenue Code provide the tax rates that apply to different taxpayers—individuals, corporations, estates, and trusts. Section 1 provides the schedule of tax rates for all individuals (single individuals, surviving spouses, married spouses filing jointly, etc.), as well as estates and trusts. Section 11 provides the tax rate for C corporations. Certain privately-held corporations (S corporations), partnerships, and other unincorporated entities (such as limited liability companies) are generally not subject to an entity tax as these business forms are flow-through entities. That is, their income and deductions flow through to the owners of the entities and are reported on their individual tax returns. If the owner is an individual, estate, or trust, section 1 tax rates apply; if the owner is a corporation, the section 11 tax rate applies.

Skimming section 1 reveals that the schedule of tax rates for individuals is progressive or graduated, meaning that as income increases, an individual's tax liability also increases, but at a greater rate. The tax rate at each bracket of taxable income is called the marginal rate of tax. Currently, there are seven rate brackets for individuals, and the highest rate is currently 37%. Thus, a taxpayer who has enough income to be taxed in this bracket has a top marginal tax rate of 37%. The rate for corporations is a flat 21%.

Once the applicable tax rates are applied to the taxpayer's taxable income, *credits* may be available to reduce the amount of tax due. In the table below we offer a federal income tax computation overview. Each component of the overview will be the subject of one or more chapters in this book. Ultimately, we will pull those chapters together by doing some comprehensive problems.

Computational Overview

> Pre-exclusions Gross Income
> − <u>Exclusions</u>
> Gross Income
> − <u>Above-the-Line Deductions</u>
> Adjusted Gross Income
> − Standard Deduction or Itemized Deductions
> − Personal and Dependency Exemptions
> − <u>Section 199A Deduction</u>
> Taxable Income
> × <u>Tax Rates</u>
> Gross Tax Liability
> − <u>Tax Credits</u>
> **Net Tax Liability or Refund**

It is worth noting that the TCJA made the personal exemptions zero in amount, at least temporarily. We left them in the above *Computational Overview* because, as will be seen in Chapter 12, they remain a key structural component of the income tax for purposes of the child tax credit. The TCJA also created a new temporary deduction for certain business owners under new Code section 199A. This deduction is addressed in Chapters 7 and 37.

D. Tax Reference Resources and Authorities

Congress' power to create tax law emanates from Article I, section 8, clause 1 of the United States Constitution (the "tax clause"). Certain technical complexities made it necessary to amend the constitution in order to impose a federal income tax. Thus, the modern income tax only came into existence after the enactment of the 16th Amendment in 1913. We have had a recent illustration of the breadth of the tax power in National Federation of Independent Business v. Sebelius, 132 S. Ct. 2566 (2012). There the Supreme Court relied on the tax clause to uphold the mandate in the Patient Protection and Affordable Care Act of 2010 that individuals must buy health insurance or make a payment to the Treasury in lieu of doing so.

1. Internal Revenue Code

The primary source of federal tax law is the Internal Revenue Code (the "Code"). It can be found at Title 26 of the United States Code. The Code has a reputation of being overly complex and incomprehensible; however, upon closer look, one will find that the Code is structured in an orderly, logical manner. The Code is divided into nine subtitles and each subtitle is divided into smaller units. For example, subtitle

A of the Code contains all the income tax provisions, subtitle B all the gift and estate tax provisions, subtitle C all the employment tax provisions, and subtitle F all the procedure and administration rules.

Each subtitle of the Code is divided into chapters and each chapter is divided into subchapters. For example, subtitle A, chapter 1, subchapter A (§§ 1–59A) contains all the provisions necessary to compute a taxpayer's actual tax liability (e.g., the applicable tax rates and various tax credits); subchapter B (§§ 61–291) contains all the provisions necessary to determine a taxpayer's taxable income (e.g., the receipts and benefits that are included in gross income and the payments, expenditures, and outlays that are allowable deductions). Special tax rules for business entities and their owners can be found in three other subchapters. Subchapter C (§§ 301–385) contains special provisions governing C corporations and their shareholders; subchapter K (§§ 701–777) contains rules governing partnerships and their partners; subchapter S (§§ 1361–1379) contains rules governing S corporations and their shareholders.

Each subchapter is divided into even smaller units, parts. Further, parts may be divided into subparts; and subparts divided into sections.

The "section" is the basic unit in the Code. Sections are numbered sequentially, with breaks in sequence to provide room for new Code provisions to be added. Throughout this book when we refer to a "section" you may assume the reference is to an Internal Revenue Code section unless stated otherwise. Sections are divided into subsections. Subsections are divided into paragraphs. Paragraphs are divided into subparagraphs. Subparagraphs are divided into clauses and even subclauses. Instead of employing all of those terms typically one simply says "section" followed by the full citation. For example, one would simply say "section 1031(a)(3)(B)(ii)" rather than saying "clause ii of subparagraph B of paragraph 3 of subsection a of section 1031."

2. Treasury Regulations

The treasury regulations are the most important administrative interpretation of the Code, and should be part of any tax research. Congress granted general authority to the Treasury Department to promulgate regulations to interpret and give meaning to the Code. *See* IRC. § 7805(a). Congress also delegated specific rule-making authority to the Treasury Department in certain Code sections. *See, e.g.,* IRC § 25A. As a result of the congressional grant of power, treasury regulations generally have the force and effect of law.

In *Mayo Foundation v. United States,* included in the materials below, the Supreme Court clarified the level of deference that courts should grant treasury regulations when faced with an ambiguous Code provision. Specifically, courts will apply the approach in Chevron, U.S.A., Inc. v. Natural Resources Defense Council, Inc., 467 U.S. 837 (1984), and, thus will defer to a treasury regulation if it reasonably resolves a statutory ambiguity. *Chevron* deference will apply to all treasury regulations, whether issued pursuant to the general grant of authority or pursuant to a specific congressional grant of authority, as described above.

Treasury regulations, which the Treasury Department promulgates under the Administrative Procedures Act, are first issued as *proposed* regulations and published for public comment in the Federal Register. Once the comment period expires and revisions are made, regulations are published in final form as Treasury Decisions in the Code of Federal Regulations. On occasion, proposed regulations are also issued as *temporary* regulations. Unlike temporary and final regulations, which are authoritative, proposed regulations in the Federal Register do not have the force and effect of law. Although not authoritative, however, proposed regulations are relevant in tax research since the Treasury has authority to apply final regulations retroactively to the date they first appeared as proposed in the Federal Register. Regulations are numbered the same way as the Code sections to which they relate, but preceded by a numerical prefix which indicates the type of tax (income, estate, gift) involved. For example, the numerical prefix of "1" indicates that the related Code section is an income tax provision.

3. IRS Rulings and Procedures

The Internal Revenue Service issues interpretative pronouncements, called Revenue Rulings, which indicate the Service's official position regarding the application of tax law to a certain set of facts. Revenue Rulings are official interpretations published by the Service for information and guidance to taxpayers. They arise from various sources. For example, a Revenue Ruling may represent the Service's position on issues arising in the audit of a taxpayer's return; a Revenue Ruling may also represent the Service's position on issues decided by various courts. Unlike treasury regulations, Revenue Rulings are not published in proposed form for taxpayer comment and are not approved by the Treasury Department. Accordingly, Revenue Rulings are not as authoritative as regulations. Nevertheless, a Revenue Ruling can be relied upon by any taxpayer whose circumstances are substantially the same as those described in the ruling. It is important to remember that a Revenue Ruling's conclusion is limited in scope to the material facts stated in the ruling. Revenue Rulings are published weekly in the Internal Revenue Bulletin and consolidated semi-annually in the Cumulative Bulletin (cited as C.B.), both of which are official publications of the Service.

For further guidance to taxpayers, the Service also issues Revenue Procedures, which typically are statements of its internal practices and procedures. Like Revenue Rulings, Revenue Procedures are first published in the Internal Revenue Bulletin and later consolidated in the Cumulative Bulletin. These can be very useful to taxpayers when structuring a transaction.

Sometimes, for a fee, taxpayers can obtain private letter rulings from the Service. Private letter rulings are issued by the IRS National Office. They interpret and apply tax laws to specific facts or proposed transactions set forth by taxpayers. Private letter rulings have no precedential value and cannot be relied upon by other taxpayers.

4. Case Law

Three trial courts have original jurisdiction over tax cases: (1) the U.S. District Court; (2) the U.S. Claims Court; and (3) the U.S. Tax Court. The first two courts are known as "refund tribunals." To litigate in these forums, a taxpayer must first pay the asserted tax deficiency and then file an administrative claim for refund. If the taxpayer's administrative claim is denied, the taxpayer may then file an action in either a federal district court or the Claims Court for a refund.

The United States Tax Court is the only forum in which a taxpayer may litigate a disputed tax claim without first having to pay the asserted deficiency. If the Service asserts a deficiency, a taxpayer may refuse to pay and then petition the Tax Court for a redetermination of the deficiency. IRC § 6213. The Tax Court is based in Washington D.C.; however, the court hears cases in several locations throughout the United States. The Tax Court comprises nineteen judges appointed by the President and approximately twenty special trial judges and retired judges who assist with smaller tax cases. The Chief Judge has the responsibility of assigning each case to one member of the court. The judge deciding the case submits a proposed opinion to the Chief Judge, who then decides whether the decision should become the ruling of the court or whether the case should be reviewed by the entire court (this typically occurs if a case presents issues of first importance). If a proposed opinion is not reviewed by the entire court, the Chief Judge designates the opinion as a regular decision or a memorandum opinion. Regular decisions involve significant or novel legal issues and are regarded by the Tax Court as binding precedent on subsequent decisions. They are published officially in the United States Tax Court Reports (T.C.) and published unofficially by commercial sources, such as CCH Tax Court Reporter. Memorandum opinions are generally factual or apply established law to the facts of that case. They are unofficially published by commercial services. In Tax Court cases that the Service loses, the Service will usually either acquiesce or nonacquiesce in the decision. A notice of acquiescence indicates that the Service accepts the decision of the court, whereas a notice of nonacquiescence indicates that the Service may continue to challenge other taxpayers with respect to the issue(s) presented in the case.

In sum, if the Service issues a notice of deficiency, the taxpayer can litigate the matter (1) by paying the tax, filing an administrative claim for a refund, and then filing a suit for a refund in either the district court or the Claims Court; or (2) by filing a petition with the Tax Court for a redetermination of the proposed deficiency. There are several factors a taxpayer should consider in deciding which forum to choose. Factors to consider include: (1) whether the taxpayer has funds to pay the asserted deficiency, which is necessary to litigate in one of the refund tribunals; (2) whether the taxpayer wants a jury trial, which is available only in the district court; (3) the level of discovery required in each trial court; (4) the expertise of the Tax Court judges; and (5) the prior decisions of each of the three possible trial courts and the appellate courts to which an appeal can be taken. *See* Golsen v. Commissioner, 54 T.C. 742 (1970) (holding the Tax Court will follow a court of appeals decision on point from the circuit where an appeal from the Tax Court would lie—the circuit in which the taxpayer resides).

Appeals from each of the trial courts vary. Federal district court decisions may be appealed to the federal court of appeals for the circuit where the district court is located. Decisions of the Claims Court may be appealed to the Court of Appeals for the Federal Circuit in Washington, D.C. Tax Court decisions may be appealed to the appropriate federal circuit in which the taxpayer resides.

5. Legislative History

Legislative history may prove helpful in understanding congressional intent behind a Code provision. The process of enacting tax legislation is similar to that used for other federal laws. In general, a bill is introduced and then referred to the appropriate committee. There are two committees that consider revenue bills—the House Ways and Means Committee and the Senate Finance Committee—although all revenue bills must originate in the House of Representatives. U.S. Cons. Art. I, § 7. These committees may completely ignore a tax bill and never consider it or consider it by substantially rewriting it. They also may hold hearings as well as issue a committee report if a bill is reported out of committee.

Committee reports often form important elements of the legislative history of a tax provision. The reports contain useful information, including statements regarding the bill's purpose, the reasons why the bill should be enacted, and the changes the bill would make to existing law. If the House and Senate versions of a bill differ, a conference committee made up of House and Senate members meets to resolve these differences. This committee generates a third committee report which explains the resolution of the inter-house differences. When an agreement is reached, the bill goes back to each house for passage in the newly agreed upon form.

Tax Research Caveats

- Code headings are not authoritative and can often be misleading. For example, section 1235 is titled "Sale or Exchange of Patents." One might jump to the conclusion that section 1235 applies only to inventions for which a patent has been obtained. Upon further research, however, one would discover that section 1235 may apply even if a patent application for an invention has not been made.

- When researching a particular Code provision, always make sure to use the version of the Code effective for the year(s) in issue. Although it is important to read the Code itself for effective dates and transition rules, it is often necessary to check the underlying legislative acts for such information.

- When reading a particular Code provision, it is important to understand the scope of the provision. Some Code provisions apply to the entire Code, while others apply only to certain portions of the Code. For example, some income tax provisions start out "For purposes of this subtitle …" which indicates that the provision applies broadly to an entire subtitle such as Subtitle A of Title 26 of the U.S.C., and therefore applies to all the income tax provisions of the Internal Revenue Code. Other Code sections begin with "For purposes of this section …" which indicates that the provision is more limited and affects only the particular section at issue, a much smaller unit.

- There may be Code sections for which no regulations exist since Congress enacts new statutes quite frequently and it may take years for the Treasury Department to promulgate regulations. In addition, there may be regulations that fail to reflect the current law since Congress amends Code provisions quite frequently and the Treasury Department does not always react promptly with appropriate regulatory revisions.

E. The Structure of This Book and How to Use It

In this book each chapter is designed to be completed in one or, occasionally, two class sessions. Each chapter after this one is organized into five components: (1) an assignment of Code provisions and treasury regulations that should be read, (2) a problem set, (3) an overview, (4) some cases or rulings, and (5) a section titled "Related Matters." In the related matters section we use bullet points to touch on tax rules that are peripheral to the main points of the chapter. Ideally the reader should read the Code and regulations before reading the problems and the text. The benefit of this approach is that the reader looks at those provisions without preconceptions and is forced to wrestle with the language employed by Congress and the Treasury. We have placed the problems next so that the reader can have them in mind as she reads the overview. Whether to read the problems ahead of the overview is a matter of individual preference. After all the reading is finished the reader should complete the problems. This will help cement one's understanding of the law. The problems are also a way of beginning to play the game of tax.

The overall structure of this book is designed to bring the reader to a series of plateaus of understanding. The first major plateau is an understanding of the basic structure of the income tax. We will pause at this plateau to do one or two review problems that help integrate the material that has been covered. Thereafter we will progress through loose groupings of chapters that address major topics of everyday consequence to taxpayers. These include real estate taxation, intellectual property taxation, family taxation, tax consequences of litigation, retirement resources and deferred compensation, business entity taxation, international income taxation, and estate and gift taxation. The level of coverage varies as appropriate from topic to topic. The effort is to establish a basic but comprehensive tax literacy in the reader. Some of the topics, such as estate and gift taxation, are areas that are addressed more fully in other courses. We include them here for two reasons. First, some students may want nothing more than a general understanding of those topics. Second, others may find that these introductions provide them with the impetus to undertake a more detailed study of one or more of these areas.

III. Materials

Mayo Foundation v. United States

562 U.S. 44 (2011)

CHIEF JUSTICE ROBERTS delivered the opinion of the Court.

[Under the Federal Insurance Contributions Act (FICA), students and their educational employers are exempted from paying Social Security taxes on wages the students earn. IRC § 3121(b)(10) (providing an exemption from taxation for "service performed in the employ of ... a school, college, or university ... if such service is performed by a student who is enrolled and regularly attending classes at such school, college, or university"). In 2004, the Treasury Department issued a new regulation stating that full-time employees (those who work more than 40 hours per week) were not exempt students. The Mayo Foundation filed suit challenging the regulation and seeking a refund of taxes it had withheld and paid on its medical residents' stipends. Mayo argued that its medical residents, who work more than full time but who are still considered students by the medical profession, were exempt under section 3121(b)(10), and that the new regulation was invalid. The District Court ruled in favor of Mayo and held that the regulation was invalid. The Court of Appeals reversed based on Chevron U.S.A., Inc. v. Natural Resources Defense Council, Inc., 467 U.S. 837 (1984), holding that the new regulation is a permissible interpretation of the statute, which is silent on whether a medical resident working for the school full time is a "student." The Supreme Court granted Mayo's petition for certiorari. Eds.]

II. A.

We begin our analysis with the first step of the two-part framework announced in *Chevron,* and ask whether Congress has "directly addressed the precise question at issue." We agree with the Court of Appeals that Congress has not done so. The statute does not define the term "student," and does not otherwise attend to the precise question whether medical residents are subject to FICA. *See* 26 U.S.C. § 3121(b)(10).

Mayo nonetheless contends that the Treasury Department's full-time employee rule must be rejected under *Chevron* step one. Mayo argues that the dictionary definition of "student"—one "who engages in 'study' by applying the mind 'to the acquisition of learning, whether by means of books, observation, or experiment'"—plainly encompasses residents. Oxford Universal Dictionary 2049–2050 (3d ed.1955). And, Mayo adds, residents are not excluded from that category by the only limitation on students Congress has imposed under the statute—that they "be 'enrolled and regularly attending classes at [a] school.'" 26 U.S.C. § 3121(b)(10).

Mayo's reading does not eliminate the statute's ambiguity as applied to working professionals. In its reply brief, Mayo acknowledges that a full-time professor taking evening classes—a person who presumably would satisfy the statute's class-enrollment requirement and apply his mind to learning—could be excluded from the exemption and taxed because he is not "'predominant[ly]'" a student. Medical residents might likewise be excluded on the same basis; the statute itself does not resolve the ambiguity.

The District Court interpreted §3121(b)(10) as unambiguously foreclosing the Department's rule by mandating that an employee be deemed "a 'student' so long as the educational aspect of his service predominates over the service aspect of the relationship with his employer." We do not think it possible to glean so much from the little that §3121 provides. In any event, the statutory text still would offer no insight into how Congress intended predominance to be determined or whether Congress thought that medical residents would satisfy the requirement.

In sum, neither the plain text of the statute nor the District Court's interpretation of the exemption "speak[s] with the precision necessary to say definitively whether [the statute] applies to" medical residents.

B.

In the typical case, such an ambiguity would lead us inexorably to *Chevron* step two, under which we may not disturb an agency rule unless it is "'arbitrary or capricious in substance, or manifestly contrary to the statute.'" (United States v. Mead Corp., 533 U.S. 218, 227 (2001)). In this case, however, the parties disagree over the proper framework for evaluating an ambiguous provision of the Internal Revenue Code.

Mayo asks us to apply the multi-factor analysis we used to review a tax regulation in National Muffler Dealers Assn., Inc. v. United States, 440 U.S. 472 (1979). There we explained:

> "A regulation may have particular force if it is a substantially contemporaneous construction of the statute by those presumed to have been aware of congressional intent. If the regulation dates from a later period, the manner in which it evolved merits inquiry. Other relevant considerations are the length of time the regulation has been in effect, the reliance placed on it, the consistency of the Commissioner's interpretation, and the degree of scrutiny Congress has devoted to the regulation during subsequent re-enactments of the statute." *Id.* at 477.

The Government, on the other hand, contends that the *National Muffler* standard has been superseded by *Chevron.* The sole question for the Court at step two under the *Chevron* analysis is "whether the agency's answer is based on a permissible construction of the statute."

Since deciding *Chevron*, we have cited both *National Muffler* and *Chevron* in our review of Treasury Department regulations.

Although we have not thus far distinguished between *National Muffler* and *Chevron*, they call for different analyses of an ambiguous statute. Under *National Muffler*, for example, a court might view an agency's interpretation of a statute with heightened skepticism when it has not been consistent over time, when it was promulgated years after the relevant statute was enacted, or because of the way in which the regulation evolved. The District Court in this case cited each of these factors in rejecting the Treasury Department's rule, noting in particular that the regulation had been promulgated after an adverse judicial decision.

Under *Chevron,* in contrast, deference to an agency's interpretation of an ambiguous statute does not turn on such considerations. We have repeatedly held that "[a]gency inconsistency is not a basis for declining to analyze the agency's interpretation under the *Chevron* framework." We have instructed that "neither antiquity nor contemporaneity with [a] statute is a condition of [a regulation's] validity." And we have found it immaterial to our analysis that a "regulation was prompted by litigation." Indeed, in United Dominion Industries, Inc. v. United States, 532 U.S. 822 (2001), we expressly invited the Treasury Department to "amend its regulations" if troubled by the consequences of our resolution of the case.

Aside from our past citation of *National Muffler,* Mayo has not advanced any justification for applying a less deferential standard of review to Treasury Department regulations than we apply to the rules of any other agency. In the absence of such justification, we are not inclined to carve out an approach to administrative review good for tax law only. To the contrary, we have expressly "[r]ecogniz[ed] the importance of maintaining a uniform approach to judicial review of administrative action."

The principles underlying our decision in *Chevron* apply with full force in the tax context. *Chevron* recognized that "[t]he power of an administrative agency to administer a congressionally created ... program necessarily requires the formulation of policy and the making of rules to fill any gap left, implicitly or explicitly, by Congress." It acknowledged that the formulation of that policy might require "more than ordinary knowledge respecting the matters subjected to agency regulations." Filling gaps in the Internal Revenue Code plainly requires the Treasury Department to make interpretive choices for statutory implementation at least as complex as the ones other agencies must make in administering their statutes. We see no reason why our review of tax regulations should not be guided by agency expertise pursuant to *Chevron* to the same extent as our review of other regulations.

As one of Mayo's *amici* points out, however, both the full-time employee rule and the rule at issue in *National Muffler* were promulgated pursuant to the Treasury Department's general authority under 26 U.S.C. § 7805(a) to "prescribe all needful rules and regulations for the enforcement" of the Internal Revenue Code. In two decisions predating *Chevron,* this Court stated that "we owe the [Treasury Department's] interpretation less deference" when it is contained in a rule adopted under that "general authority" than when it is "issued under a specific grant of authority to define a statutory term or prescribe a method of executing a statutory provision." Rowan Cos. v. United States, 452 U.S. 247, 253 (1981); United States v. Vogel Fertilizer Co., 455 U.S. 16, 24 (1982) (quoting *Rowan*).

Since *Rowan* and *Vogel* were decided, however, the administrative landscape has changed significantly. We have held that *Chevron* deference is appropriate "when it appears that Congress delegated authority to the agency generally to make rules carrying the force of law, and that the agency interpretation claiming deference was promulgated in the exercise of that authority." *Mead,* 533 U.S., at 226–227. Our inquiry in that regard does not turn on whether Congress's delegation of authority was general or specific.

We believe *Chevron* and *Mead,* rather than *National Muffler* and *Rowan,* provide the appropriate framework for evaluating the full-time employee rule. The Department issued the full-time employee rule pursuant to the explicit authorization to "prescribe all needful rules and regulations for the enforcement" of the Internal Revenue Code. 26 U.S.C. §7805(a). We have found such "express congressional authorizations to engage in the process of rulemaking" to be "a very good indicator of delegation meriting *Chevron* treatment." *Mead, supra,* at 229. The Department issued the full-time employee rule only after notice-and-comment procedures, again a consideration identified in our precedents as a "significant" sign that a rule merits *Chevron* deference. *Mead, supra,* at 230–231; *see, e.g.,* Long Island Care at Home Ltd. v. Coke, 551 U.S. 158, 173–174 (2007).

We have explained that "the ultimate question is whether Congress would have intended, and expected, courts to treat [the regulation] as within, or outside, its delegation to the agency of 'gap-filling' authority." In the *Long Island Care* case, we found that *Chevron* provided the appropriate standard of review "[w]here an agency rule sets forth important individual rights and duties, where the agency focuses fully and directly upon the issue, where the agency uses full notice-and-comment procedures to promulgate a rule, [and] where the resulting rule falls within the statutory grant of authority." These same considerations point to the same result here. This case falls squarely within the bounds of, and is properly analyzed under, *Chevron* and *Mead.*

C

The full-time employee rule easily satisfies the second step of *Chevron,* which asks whether the Department's rule is a "reasonable interpretation" of the enacted text. To begin, Mayo accepts that "the 'educational aspect of the relationship between the employer and the employee, as compared to the service aspect of the relationship, [must] be predominant'" in order for an individual to qualify for the exemption. Mayo objects, however, to the Department's conclusion that residents who work more than 40 hours per week categorically cannot satisfy that requirement. Because residents' employment is itself educational, Mayo argues, the hours a resident spends working make him "more of a student, not less of one." Mayo contends that the Treasury Department should be required to engage in a case-by-case inquiry into "*what* [each] employee does [in his service] and *why*" he does it. Mayo also objects that the Department has drawn an arbitrary distinction between "hands-on training" and "classroom instruction."

We disagree. Regulation, like legislation, often requires drawing lines. Mayo does not dispute that the Treasury Department reasonably sought a way to distinguish between workers who study and students who work. *See* IRS Letter Ruling 9332005 (May 3, 1993). Focusing on the hours an individual works and the hours he spends in studies is a perfectly sensible way of accomplishing that goal. The Department explained that an individual's service and his "course of study are separate and distinct activities" in "the vast majority of cases," and reasoned that "[e]mployees who are working enough hours to be considered full-time employees ... have filled the conventional measure of available time with work, and not study." The Department thus did not distinguish classroom education from clinical training but rather education from service. The Department reasonably concluded that its full-time employee rule would "improve administrability," and it thereby "has avoided the wasteful litigation and continuing uncertainty that would inevitably accompany any purely case-by-case approach" like the one Mayo advocates.

As the Treasury Department has explained, moreover, the full-time employee rule has more to recommend it than administrative convenience. The Department reasonably determined that taxing residents under FICA would further the purpose of the Social Security Act and comport with this Court's precedent. As the Treasury Department appreciated, this Court has understood the terms of the Social Security Act to "'import a breadth of coverage,'" and we have instructed that "exemptions from taxation are to be construed narrowly." Although Mayo contends that medical residents have not yet begun their "working lives" because they are not "fully trained," the Department certainly did not act irrationally in concluding that these doctors—"who work long hours, serve as highly skilled professionals, and typically share some or all of the terms of employment of career employees"—are the kind of workers that Congress intended to both contribute to and benefit from the Social Security system.

We do not doubt that Mayo's residents are engaged in a valuable educational pursuit or that they are students of their craft. The question whether they are "students" for purposes of § 3121, however, is a different matter. Because it is one to which Congress has not directly spoken, and because the Treasury Department's rule is a reasonable construction of what Congress has said, the judgment of the Court of Appeals must be affirmed.

It is so ordered.

[NOTE: In United States v. Home Concrete & Supply, LLC., 132 S. Ct. 1836 (2012), a divided Supreme Court muddied the waters by invalidating a regulation interpreting an admittedly ambiguous statute. The central ground for striking down the regulation was a plurality view that the legislative history was unambiguously counter to the regulation. The regulation in question sought to overrule a pre-*Chevron* Supreme Court decision and this factor was of key importance to the concurrence by Justice Scalia. There was no majority opinion in *Home Concrete*. The IRS appears to interpret *Home Concrete* to mean that pre-*Chevron* holdings cannot be overruled by regulation but that post-*Chevron* holdings can be overruled by regulation where the court's opinion indicates the statute is ambiguous. *See Wilkins, Butler Give Their Take in Home Concrete*, 135 Tax Notes 974 (May 21, 2012). Eds.]

Chapter 2

Gross Income

I. Assignment

Read: Internal Revenue Code: §61. Skim §§74; 274(j)(3)(A); 109; 280A(g)(2).

Treasury Regulations: §§1.61-1, -2(a)(1), -2(d)(1), -2(d)(2)(i), -8(a)–(b), -14(a).

Text: Overview
Commissioner v. Glenshaw Glass Co.
Cesarini v. United States
Old Colony Trust Co. v. Commissioner
Related Matters

Complete the problems.

II. Problems

1. Meriwether Lewis is a successful real estate agent at a well-known real estate company. Which, if any, of the following items must Meriwether report as gross income?

    (a) Meriwether received $75,000 in real estate commissions. As a result of being named "Salesperson of the Year," Meriwether also received from his employer a $1,000 year-end bonus and was allowed to stay for free at his employer's vacation cabin (rental value of $1,500).

    (b) Meriwether borrowed $10,000 from a local bank. Shortly thereafter, Meriwether's employer paid off the loan and paid to the IRS Meriwether's federal income taxes due as a result of the discharge of indebtedness.

    (c) Meriwether purchased unimproved farm land for $100,000 even though it was worth $125,000 at the time of purchase. Because Meriwether acted as agent, he ultimately received a $5,000 commission from the seller.

    (d) Shortly after the purchase in (c), Meriwether discovered on the land a chest of gold relics worth $15,000. In addition, the government designated the farm land a historic landmark which increased its value to $200,000.

    (e) On the farm purchased in (c), Meriwether harvested blueberries with a total value of $3,000. Meriwether ate one-third of the blueberries, sold one-third for $1,000 cash to a local market, and exchanged one-third with a neighbor for a free weekend at the neighbor's beach cottage worth $800.

(f) At a baseball game in Boston, Meriwether caught a record-breaking ball valued at $100,000. A year later, Meriwether sold the ball for $125,000.

(g) Meriwether was selected to be the beneficiary of a home makeover on a new TV show called *Radical Renovation: Home Edition*. Meriwether received, in exchange for letting his home and the makeover be filmed, a major home renovation valued at $250,000. Meriwether also received some cash to cover any taxes that might be owed.

(h) Meriwether withdrew $5,000 from his employer's escrow account to buy a farm tractor. The following year, he restored the funds to his employer's account, and received a manufacturer's rebate of $500 from John Deere.

2. Alice Toklas owns and rents a duplex to local university students. Alice requires tenants to pay up front the first month's rent, the last month's rent, and a security deposit equal to one-month's rent. The security deposits, which are typically deposited in Alice's personal checking account, are required to be returned to the tenants unless the tenants damage the property or fail to pay rent. How should the up-front payments be treated for federal income tax purposes, if:

(a) In practice, 90% of the security deposits are returned to the tenants.

(b) In practice, 90% of the security deposits are retained by Alice to reimburse her for alleged damage to the property.

III. Overview

A. The Definition of Gross Income

The starting point for computing a taxpayer's tax liability is determining what is included in *gross income*. Section 61 of the Code defines gross income broadly as "all *income* from whatever source derived," and then lists types of receipts that are included in gross income. The list is extensive and includes common items, such as compensation for services. However, the list is not exhaustive, and it is necessarily preceded and supplemented by a catch-all clause that includes non-listed items that may be properly defined as *income*.

So, back to the most basic question in our federal tax system, "What is *income*?" For years economists have debated the meaning of income. A widely-accepted definition, known as the Haig-Simons definition, defines income as gains or increases in wealth over a particular period regardless of whether spent on consumption or saved. *See* Robert M. Haig, *The Concept of Income*, in THE FEDERAL INCOME TAX 1, 7 (1921); HENRY C. SIMONS, PERSONAL INCOME TAXATION 50 (1938). Without modification, this economic definition of income would be difficult to apply for tax purposes. For example, it would require taxpayers to pay tax on the mere appreciation in value of their assets each year, which, in turn, would require taxpayers to obtain costly appraisals of assets each year, and would force many taxpayers to sell assets to obtain cash to pay Uncle Sam. Because of these and other practical limitations, courts have searched for a more workable concept of income for tax purposes.

In Eisner v. Macomber, 252 U.S. 189, 207 (1920), the Supreme Court first attempted to define income: "Income may be defined as the gain derived from capital, from labor, or from both combined." This definition of income clearly encompasses receipts derived from personal services and capital investments, but what about items not traceable to labor or to capital, such as windfalls (e.g., prizes, scholarships, or cash found in a taxi)? Should such receipts not be included within the scope of income merely because they are traceable to good fortune and not to labor or capital? In other words, should the source of receipts be relevant? The Supreme Court answered these questions and formulated a different concept of income for tax purposes in *Commissioner v. Glenshaw Glass Co.*, included in the materials. In *Glenshaw Glass*, the Supreme Court defined income as "undeniable accessions to wealth, clearly realized, and over which taxpayers have complete dominion." As can be seen, the *Glenshaw Glass* definition of income is much broader than the *Macomber* definition.

Although the statutory concept of gross income resembles the concept of economic income, the two are not always the same. As discussed below, *realization* is generally a prerequisite to income for tax purposes. Moreover, for various policy reasons, there are statutory rules of exclusion as well as judicial and administrative exceptions which place further limits on the meaning of gross income.

1. The Realization Requirement

Glenshaw Glass defines income as "undeniable accessions to wealth, clearly *realized*." The realization requirement is a principle of accounting that has important tax application. It essentially determines the proper timing of taxation by telling us when income or gain should be recorded. Generally, realization does not occur, and income or gain is not recorded, until a provider of services or a seller of property has fulfilled all the material steps on her side of a bargain. For example, increases in the value of property are not taken into account for tax purposes when they accrue each year, but only when they are realized by a potentially taxable event (when the taxpayer actually sells the property). It is often suggested that the realization requirement rests on the idea that taxing someone on "paper gains" before the conversion of property to cash creates cash flow problems. In any event, the realization requirement gives us consistency, objectivity, and certainty in tax.

2. Statutory Exclusions from Gross Income

The Code contains numerous provisions excluding particular kinds of receipts from gross income, even though such receipts are clearly accessions to wealth. *See* IRC §§ 101–140. For illustrative purposes, three exclusion provisions are summarized below. The details of and the policy behind these statutory exclusions are described more fully in Chapters 4, 5, and 6.

Example 1: Gifts. Assume Taxpayer receives a new car valued at $25,000 from Parent. Must Taxpayer report the value of the car in gross income? The car is plainly an "accession to wealth" under *Glenshaw Glass;* thus, it seemingly falls within section 61's catch-all clause "income from whatever source derived." However, the "except as otherwise provided" language of section 61 tells us to look for statutory exclusions. Section 102, discussed in Chapter 4, specifically excludes "gifts" from gross income. And so the question that must be asked is whether the transfer of the car was a "gift" within the meaning of section 102.

Example 2: Discharge of Indebtedness. Assume Taxpayer borrows $1,000 and the lender subsequently forgives the debt. Must Taxpayer report $1,000 in gross income? Taxpayer has experienced an accession to wealth as a result of the loan cancellation; however, reliance on *Glenshaw Glass* is not even necessary since section 61(a)(12) specifically includes the amount of a taxpayer's discharge of indebtedness in gross income. However, the analysis does not end there since section 108, a more specific statutory provision, excludes discharge of indebtedness income from gross income if the discharge occurs in a bankruptcy case or when the debtor is insolvent. We need more information in this case to determine whether Taxpayer includes the discharge in gross income or benefits from the statutory exclusion.

Example 3: Employee Benefits. Assume Taxpayer receives from her employer numerous employee fringe benefits valued at $5,000, and further Taxpayer receives a check for $1,000 as a result of being named "Employee of the Year." Must Taxpayer include $6,000 in gross income? As in the last example, reliance on *Glenshaw Glass* is unnecessary since section 61(a)(1) specifically mentions "fringe benefits," and section 74(a) specifically includes "prizes and awards" in gross income. However, consider, are there any more specific statutory rules that might exclude such items? Section 132, discussed in Chapter 6, specifically excludes certain enumerated fringe benefits, and section 74(c) specifically excludes "employee achievement awards" as defined in section 274(j)(3)(A). However, the $1,000 check cannot qualify because section 274(j)(3) limits excludable employee achievement awards to non-cash items awarded for limited purposes. We need more information in this case to determine whether Taxpayer can exclude the $5,000 of fringe benefits from gross income under section 132.

3. Long-Standing Administrative Practices

The government (specifically, the IRS) has on numerous occasions chosen to exclude certain items from income even though such items represent clear accessions to wealth and no statutory exclusion applies to them. For example, the IRS has a longstanding policy of excluding from income many government benefits and assistance payments. This is known as the general welfare exclusion. *See* Rev. Rul. 75-271, 1975-2 C.B. 23. "To qualify under the general welfare exclusion, the payments must (1) be made pursuant to a governmental program, (2) be for the promotion of the general welfare (that is, based on need), and (3) not represent compensation for services." Rev. Proc. 2014-35, 2014-26 I.R.B. 1110. Thus, for example, payments under training programs that include reasonable and limited allowances for meals, travel, transportation, and other purposes are excluded from gross income under the general welfare exclusion. From time to time Congress has narrowed or expanded the reach of the general welfare exclusion by specifically addressing the tax treatment of certain government benefits. *See, e.g.,* IRC §§ 85 (unemployment compensation), 86 (Social Security benefits), 139 (disaster relief payments), 139E (Indian General Welfare Benefits).

Arguably the general welfare exclusion arises mainly out of a sense of compassion for the person being helped. But other motivations may also lead to administratively-created exclusions. In each of the examples below, consider the policy reasons behind the administrative practice of excluding from gross income what are accessions to wealth.

Example 4: Imputed Income. Have you ever mowed your own lawn? Painted your own house? Grown your own vegetables? If so, did you report as income the savings that resulted from performing your own services? Whenever a taxpayer performs services for his own benefit or produces goods for his own consumption, the taxpayer has economic gain equal to the amount he saves by not having to pay someone else to provide the services or goods. This type of economic gain is called *imputed income* since the income is attributed to the value of labor or property the taxpayer performs or produces for himself. A rigorous application of *Glenshaw Glass* would require a taxpayer to include imputed income in gross income. However, the government does not attempt to tax imputed income for obvious reasons. The drawback, unfortunately, is the creation of some unneutrality in our tax system. For example, by not taxing imputed income, the tax system favors taxpayers who own their own home over those who rent. Likewise, the tax system favors those taxpayers who decide to stay home to take care of their children over those who work and send their children to day care. Is there any way to avoid this unneutrality?

Example 5: Bargain Purchases. Have you ever purchased something at a bargain, such as a piece of artwork at a flea market that you came to find out was much more valuable than you or the seller thought? If so, is it not fair to say that you experienced an accession to wealth at the time of purchase? The government generally does not require a buyer to report the benefit of a bargain (the true value of the item purchased minus the amount paid for it) at the time of purchase, regardless of whether the buyer knew the purchased item was more valuable than the seller knew. An important exception to this government practice exists when a bargain purchase occurs in an employment setting. *See* Treas. Reg. § 1.61-2(d)(2)(i).

Example 6: Frequent Flyer Trips. Have you ever received benefits under a frequent flyer program, such as a free airline ticket as a result of mileage credits earned for prior travel? If the free trip was received as a result of frequent personal travel paid for by you, there arguably is no income. However, if the free trip was received as a result of prior business travel paid for by your employer, there arguably is additional income. In Announcement 2002-18, 2002-1 C.B. 621, the IRS said that it will not attempt to tax personal benefits received through the use of frequent flyer miles or other in-kind promotion benefits attributable to a taxpayer's business travel, unless the benefits are converted to cash. Why wouldn't the IRS attempt to tax a benefit that is clearly additional compensation for taxpayers?

B. Gross Income May Be Realized in Any Form

The statutory concept of gross income, which resembles but is not the same as economic income, can seem elusive. Fortunately, the Code, the regulations, court decisions, and administrative pronouncements have eliminated much uncertainty, and clarify what is and what is not included in gross income. For example, the definition in section 61 lists specific types of receipts that are included in gross income and the regulations under section 61 lists other items to be included. *See, e.g.,* Treas. Reg. § 1.61-14(a). Several other Code provisions clarify the status of certain items as gross income. *See* IRC §§ 71–90. And, for various policy reasons, several Code provisions specifically exclude certain items from gross income. *See* IRC §§ 101–140. As a result of legislative practice, judicial decisions, and administrative guidance, the statutory concept of gross income has evolved and fewer questions arise.

Glenshaw Glass emphasizes that gross income is a very broad concept, as broad as the Constitution allows. This point is also emphasized in other court decisions, such as *Cesarini v. United States*, included in the materials below. As you read *Cesarini*, think about the following questions: (1) Would the taxpayers have gross income if they discovered after they purchased the piano that it was once owned by Elvis Presley and worth $1 million more than they paid? (2) Would the taxpayers have gross income if, instead of finding cash in the piano, the taxpayers found a rare manuscript worth $5,000?

Section 61 does not make a distinction between cash and non-cash benefits. Indeed, the regulations under section 61 provide that gross income may be realized in any form, whether in money, property, or services. Treas. Reg. § 1.61-1(a). If property is included in gross income (e.g., treasure trove or property received in exchange for services rendered), the fair market value of the property received is the amount of income reported. If services are included in gross income (e.g., services received in exchange for services rendered), the fair market value of the services received is the amount to be included. Treas. Reg. § 1.61-2(d)(1). These principles are especially relevant in barter transactions, such as those presented in Revenue Ruling 79-24, 1979-1 C.B. 60. In Revenue Ruling 79-24, a lawyer and a housepainter were members of a barter club. The lawyer provided legal services to the painter and, in return, the housepainter painted the lawyer's house. The Service held that the fair market value of the services received by the lawyer and the housepainter were to be included in their gross incomes under section 61.

Query: How far should the tax system go in taxing non-cash benefits? Assume, for example, that an employee-taxpayer receives a year-end bonus from her corporate employer consisting of a weekend stay at the employer's beach cottage in Maine. Does the employee have any gross income and, if so, in what amount? If you concluded that the employee must include in gross income the fair rental value of the cottage in gross income, you are correct. In Dean v. Commissioner, 187 F.2d 1019 (3rd Cir. 1951), the taxpayers transferred title to their home to a corporation to satisfy a corporate creditor; however, they continued to live in the home after the transfer. The Third Circuit held that the fair rental value of the residence property was to be included in the taxpayers' gross income as compensation. Query: Would the taxpayers in *Dean* have avoided income if they had retained title and merely pledged the home as security? In answering this question, recall our earlier discussion about imputed income. Clearly, the taxpayers would *not* have to include in gross income the rental value of property owned and occupied by them. *See* Helvering v. Independent Life Ins. Co., 292 U.S. 371 (1934).

Gross income, which includes both cash and non-cash benefits, is usually received directly by the taxpayer. The lawyer in Revenue Ruling 79-24 received painting services directly from the housepainter, and the housepainter received legal services directly from the lawyer. The taxpayer in *Dean* received the use of corporate property directly from the corporation. Gross income, however, does not have to be received directly by the taxpayer. This point is illustrated in *Old Colony Trust Co. v. Commissioner*, included in the materials below. *Old Colony* involves the payment of an employee's taxes by his employer. When reading *Old Colony*, consider the following questions: Would *Old Colony* apply if an employer pays an employee's legal fees directly to the employee's lawyer, or, pays the employee's law school tuition directly to the school?

The principle that the form of income is irrelevant is justifiable. Without it, taxpayers could easily avoid tax by structuring their transactions to receive payment in services or property instead of in cash, or to have payments made to third parties in satisfaction of third-party obligations. Yet the principle introduces a host of valuation, timing, and administrative problems. For example, it is often difficult to value property, services, and other non-cash benefits received and it is difficult for the government to enforce reporting of non-cash receipts (especially in barter transactions). Ironically, these same problems have been used to justify the long-standing administrative practice of excluding certain economic benefits from gross income, such as imputed income and frequent flyer trips, discussed above.

The challenges of administering the income tax continue to grow with the rise of the so-called "sharing economy" exemplified by companies such as Uber and Lyft (ride sharing) and AirBnB and VRBO (residence sharing). In most cases these entities act as online brokers or middlemen between two taxpayers, one of whom is selling a service to the other. *See* Vanessa Katz, *Regulating the Sharing Economy*, 30 Berkeley Tech. L.J. 1067, 1070 (2016). The seller may prefer to keep the transaction "off the books" for tax purposes. In such situations the government's possible response is to require the broker to report the transaction and, perhaps even, withhold and pay tax on the transaction the way an employer is required to withhold and pay income taxes on its employees' wages. *See* Abbey Stemler, *Betwixt and Between: Regulating the Shared Economy*, 43 Fordham Urb. L.J. 1, 36 (2016). One can expect that the brokers, or platforms as they are sometimes called, would prefer not to assume the role of tax collector. This is an evolving area of law with many nuances beyond taxation. *Id.* For more context, *see also* Jordan M. Barry & Paul L. Caron, *Tax Regulation, Transportation Innovation, and the Sharing Economy*, 80 University of Chicago Law Review Dialogue 69 (2015) (addressing taxation and the sharing economy in the context of certain transportation fringe benefits).

C. A Note on "Basis"

If property is included in gross income, it is important to keep track of the "basis" of the property to prevent double taxation upon a later sale of the property. For example, assume that at the end of Year 1, a taxpayer receives as a taxable bonus from his corporate-employer stock valued at $1,000. As discussed above, the fair market value of the stock ($1,000) must be included in the taxpayer's gross income in Year 1. Now, assume that the taxpayer sells the stock in Year 2 for $1,200 in cash. How much gain should the taxpayer report on the sale in Year 2? As we will explore more fully in Chapter 3, the Code provides that the amount of gain is equal to the "amount realized" on the sale ($1,200) minus the taxpayer's cost, the "basis," of the property sold. Although the taxpayer paid nothing for the stock, a zero basis would result in total taxable income of $2,200 for both years ($1,000 compensation income in Year 1 and $1,200 gain in Year 2). To prevent the $1,000 received in Year 1 from being taxed twice, we treat the stock as having a *cost basis* equal to the value included in gross income in Year 1. As a result, the taxpayer has gain of only $200 on the sale in Year 2. In short, by taking the value of the stock into income in Year 1 the taxpayer acquired a $1,000 tax cost basis to offset against any amounts received upon sale of the stock.

D. Impact of Obligations to Repay

If a taxpayer receives money or property, but has a contractual obligation to return it or repay it, the money or property is not considered to be an accession to wealth and thus is not income within the meaning of section 61. For example, if a taxpayer borrows $1,000 from a bank, the borrowed funds are not included in the taxpayer's gross income. The offsetting obligation to return or repay the funds negates any accession to wealth. There has been no change in the taxpayer's net worth. This concept is illustrated by the following fundamental accounting equation:

$$\text{Net Worth} = \text{Assets} - \text{Liabilities}$$
$$\$0 \qquad \$1,000 \qquad \$1,000$$

As with loans, if a taxpayer owns rental property and receives a security deposit from a tenant, the security deposit is not included in gross income if the taxpayer has an offsetting express obligation to return the deposit to the tenant assuming the tenant satisfies the terms of the lease. However, if the taxpayer has unfettered control over whether the security deposit will be applied to the payment of rent, then the deposit will be included in gross income as advance rent. *See* Treas. Reg. § 1.61-8(b). As illustrated by Commissioner v. Indianapolis Power & Light Co., 493 U.S. 203 (1990), all the facts and circumstances must be considered to determine whether payments are nontaxable security deposits or taxable advance rent payments. The most important factor to consider is whether the taxpayer enjoys "complete dominion" over the funds. Although *Indianapolis Power & Light Co.* involved utility company deposits, the decision is consistent with cases involving landlord-tenant leases. *See, e.g.,* J. & E. Enterprises v. Commissioner, 26 T.C.M. at 945–46 ("If a sum is received by a lessor at the beginning of a lease, is subject to his unfettered control, and is to be applied as rent for a subsequent period during the term of the lease, such sum is income in the year of receipt even though in certain circumstances a refund thereof may be required. If, on the other hand, a sum is deposited to secure the lessee's performance under a lease, and is to be returned at the expiration thereof, it is not taxable income even though the fund is deposited with the lessor instead of in escrow and the lessor has temporary use of the money.").

In some circumstances, an obligation to repay is disregarded by the tax system resulting in gross income to a taxpayer. For example, if a taxpayer obtains money or property illegally (such as embezzled funds or insurance proceeds from arson), the taxpayer must include the unlawful receipts in gross income despite the taxpayer's legal obligation to restore the funds. *See* United States v. Sullivan, 274 U.S. 259 (1927); James v. United States, 366 U.S. 213 (1961). Taxpayers may attempt to characterize illegal receipts as "loans" to avoid gross income. However, in most cases, there is no express acknowledgment of an obligation to repay or, even if there is, the taxpayer is most likely lying about his intent to repay. And so, since repayment is unlikely, the receipts must be included in gross income. *But see* Gilbert v. Commissioner, 552 F.2d 478 (2d Cir. 1977) (holding that unauthorized withdrawals of corporate funds were not illegal receipts, but were in the nature of a loan; the taxpayer intended and was reasonably believed to have the ability to repay the funds, the taxpayer thought the corporation would approve the withdrawals, and the taxpayer made an assignment of assets as security). It should be noted that the Supreme Court in *James v. United States* observed that if a wrongdoer included illegal receipts in income and subsequently gave restitution to his victim, he would be entitled to a deduction in the year of repayment. Although the Supreme Court did not cite any statutory authority for such a deduction, the Service has recognized such a deduction in several administrative pronouncements. *See, e.g.*, Rev. Rul. 82-74, 1982-1 C.B. 110 (holding that refund of insurance proceeds when arson is discovered is deductible under section 165); Rev. Rul. 65-254, 1965-2 C.B. 50 (holding that repayment of embezzled funds is a loss deductible under section 165).

IV. Materials

Commissioner v. Glenshaw Glass Co.

348 U.S. 426 (1955)

Mr. Chief Justice Warren delivered the opinion of the Court.

The question is whether money received as exemplary damages for fraud or as the punitive two-thirds portion of a treble-damage antitrust recovery must be reported by a taxpayer as gross income under section 22(a) of the Internal Revenue Code of 1939 [the predecessor of section 61(a)]. The Court of Appeals affirmed the Tax Court's ruling in favor of the taxpayer. Because of the frequent recurrence of the question and differing interpretations by the lower courts of this Court's decisions bearing upon the problem, we granted the Commissioner of Internal Revenue's ensuing petition for certiorari.

The facts of the case were largely stipulated and are not in dispute. So far as pertinent they are as follows: The Glenshaw Glass Company, a Pennsylvania corporation, manufactures glass bottles and containers. It was engaged in protracted litigation with the Hartford-Empire Company, which manufactures machinery of a character used by Glenshaw. Among the claims advanced by Glenshaw were demands for exemplary damages for fraud and treble damages for injury to its business by reason of Hartford's violation of the federal antitrust laws. In December, 1947, the parties concluded a settlement of all pending litigation, by which Hartford paid Glenshaw approximately $800,000. Through a method of allocation which was approved by the Tax Court, and which is no longer in issue, it was ultimately determined that, of the total settlement, $324,529.94 represented payment of punitive damages for fraud and antitrust violations. Glenshaw did not report this portion of the settlement as income for the tax year involved. The Commissioner determined a deficiency claiming as taxable the entire sum less only deductible legal fees. As previously noted, the Tax Court and the Court of Appeals upheld the taxpayer.

It is conceded by the respondents that there is no constitutional barrier to the imposition of a tax on punitive damages. Our question is one of statutory construction: are these payments comprehended by section 22(a)?

The sweeping scope of the controverted statute is readily apparent:

SEC. 22. Gross income

(a) General definition. "Gross income" includes gains, profits, and income derived from salaries, wages, or compensation for personal service ... of whatever kind and in whatever form paid, or from professions, vocations, trades, businesses, commerce, or sales, or dealings in property, whether real or personal, growing out of the ownership or use of or interest in such property; also from interest, rent, dividends, securities, or the transaction of any business carried on for gain or profit, *or gains or profits and income derived from any source whatever*.... (Emphasis added.)

This Court has frequently stated that this language was used by Congress to exert in this field "the full measure of its taxing power." Helvering v. Clifford, 309 U.S. 331, 334. Respondents contend that punitive damages, characterized as "windfalls" flowing from the culpable conduct of third parties, are not within the scope of the section. But Congress applied no limitations as to the source of taxable receipts, nor restrictive labels as to their nature. And the Court has given a liberal construction to this broad phraseology in recognition of the intention of Congress to tax all gains except those specifically exempted. Thus, the fortuitous gain accruing to a lessor by reason of the forfeiture of a lessee's improvements on the rented property was taxed in Helvering v. Bruun, 309 U.S. 461. Such decisions demonstrate that we cannot but ascribe content to the catchall provision of section 22(a), "gains or profits and income derived from any source whatever." Commissioner v. Jacobson, 336 U.S. 28, 49. The importance of that phrase has been too frequently recognized since its first appearance in the Revenue Act of 1913 to say now that it adds nothing to the meaning of "gross income."

Nor can we accept respondents' contention that a narrower reading of section 22(a) is required by the Court's characterization of income in Eisner v. Macomber, 252 U.S. 189, 207, as "the gain derived from capital, from labor, or from both combined." The Court was there endeavoring to determine whether the distribution of a corporate stock dividend constituted a realized gain to the shareholder, or changed "only the form, not the essence," of his capital investment. It was held that the taxpayer had "received nothing out of the company's assets for his separate use and benefit." The distribution, therefore, was held not a taxable event. In that context—distinguishing gain from capital—the definition served a useful purpose. But it was not meant to provide a touchstone to all future gross income questions.

Here we have instances of undeniable accessions to wealth, clearly realized, and over which the taxpayers have complete dominion. The mere fact that the payments were extracted from the wrongdoers as punishment for unlawful conduct cannot detract from their character as taxable income to the recipients. Respondents concede, as they must, that the recoveries are taxable to the extent that they compensate for damages actually incurred. It would be an anomaly that could not be justified in the absence of clear congressional intent to say that a recovery for actual damages is taxable but not the additional amount extracted as punishment for the same conduct which caused the injury. And we find no such evidence of intent to exempt these payments.

Nor does the 1954 Code's legislative history, with its reiteration of the proposition that statutory gross income is "all-inclusive," give support to respondents' position. The definition of gross income has been simplified, but no effect upon its present broad scope was intended. Certainly punitive damages cannot reasonably be classified as gifts, nor do they come under any other exemption provision in the Code. We would do violence to the plain meaning of the statute and restrict a clear legislative attempt to bring the taxing power to bear upon all receipts constitutionally taxable were we to say that the payments in question here are not gross income.

Reversed.

Mr. Justice DOUGLAS dissents.

––––––––––

Cesarini v. United States

296 F. Supp. 3 (N.D. Ohio 1969)

YOUNG, DISTRICT JUDGE.

This is an action by the plaintiffs as taxpayers for the recovery of income tax payments made in the calendar year 1964. Plaintiffs contend that the amount of $836.51 was erroneously overpaid by them in 1964, and that they are entitled to a refund in that amount.

Plaintiffs are husband and wife. In 1957, the plaintiffs purchased a used piano at an auction sale for approximately $15.00, and the piano was used by their daughter for piano lessons. In 1964, while cleaning the piano, plaintiffs discovered the sum of $4,467.00 in old currency, and since have retained the piano instead of discarding it as previously planned. Being unable to ascertain who put the money there, plaintiffs exchanged the old currency for new at a bank, and reported the sum of $4,467.00 on their 1964 joint income tax return as ordinary income from other sources. On October 18, 1965, plaintiffs filed an amended return with the District Director of Internal Revenue in Cleveland, Ohio, this second return eliminating the sum of $4,467.00 from the gross income computation, and requesting a refund in the amount of $836.51, the amount allegedly overpaid as a result of the former inclusion of $4,467.00 in the original return for the calendar year of 1964. On January 18, 1966, the Commissioner of Internal Revenue rejected taxpayers' refund claim in its entirety, and plaintiffs filed the instant action in March of 1967.

The starting point in determining whether an item is to be included in gross income is, of course, Section 61(a) of Title 26 U.S.C., and that section provides in part:

> "Except as otherwise provided in this subtitle, *gross income means all income from whatever source derived*, including (but not limited to) the following items: ..." (Emphasis added.)

Subsections (1) through (15) of Section 61(a) then go on to list fifteen items specifically included in the computation of the taxpayer's gross income, and Part II of Subchapter B of the 1954 Code (Sections 71 *et seq.*) deals with other items expressly included in gross income. While neither of these listings expressly includes the type of income which is at issue in the case at bar, Part III of Subchapter B (Sections 101 *et seq.*) deals with items specifically excluded from gross income, and found money is not listed in those sections either. This absence of express mention in any of the code sections necessitates a return to the "all income from whatever source" language of Section 61(a) of the code, and the express statement there that gross income is "not limited to" the following fifteen examples. Section 1.61-1(a) of the Treasury Regulations, the corresponding section to Section 61(a) in the 1954 Code, reiterates this board construction of gross income, providing in part:

> "Gross income means all income from whatever source derived, unless excluded by law. *Gross income includes income realized in any form*, whether in money, property, or services...." (Emphasis added.)

The decisions of the United States Supreme Court have frequently stated that this broad all-inclusive language was used by Congress to exert the full measure of its taxing power under the Sixteenth Amendment to the United States Constitution. Commissioner v. Glenshaw Glass Co., 348 U.S. 426 (1955).

In addition, the Government in the instant case cites and relies upon an I.R.S. Revenue Ruling which is undeniably on point:

> "The finder of treasure-trove is in receipt of taxable income, for Federal income tax purposes, to the extent of its value in United States Currency, for the taxable year in which it is reduced to undisputed possession." Rev. Rul. 61, 1953-1 Cum. Bull. 17.

The plaintiffs argue that the above ruling does not control this case for two reasons. The first is that subsequent to the Ruling's pronouncement in 1953, Congress enacted Sections 74 and 102 of the 1954 Code, Section 74 expressly including the value of prizes and awards in gross income in most cases, and Section 102 specifically exempting the value of gifts received from gross income. From this, it is argued that Section 74 was added because prizes might otherwise be construed as non-taxable gifts, and since no such section was passed expressly taxing treasure-trove, it is therefore a gift which is non-taxable under Section 102. This line of reasoning overlooks the statutory scheme previously alluded to, whereby income from all sources is taxed unless the taxpayer can point to an express exemption. Not only have the taxpayers failed to list a specific exclusion in the instant case, but also the Government has pointed to express language covering the found money, even though it would not be required to do so under the broad language of Section 61(a) and the foregoing Supreme Court decisions interpreting it.

In partial summary, then, the arguments of the taxpayers which attempt to avoid the application of Rev. Rul. 61, 1953-1 Cum. Bull. 17, are not well taken. While it is generally true that revenue rulings may be disregarded by the courts if in conflict with the code and the regulations, or with other judicial decisions, plaintiffs in the instant case have been unable to point to any inconsistency between the gross income sections of the code, the interpretation of them by the regulations and the courts, and the revenue ruling which they herein attack as inapplicable. On the other hand, the United States has shown a consistency in letter and spirit between the ruling and the code, regulations, and court decisions.

Although not cited by either party, and noticeably absent from the Government's brief, the following Treasury Regulation appears in the 1964 Regulations, the year of the return in dispute:

> "Section 1.61-14 Miscellaneous items of gross income.
>
> "(a) In general. In addition to the items enumerated in section 61(a), there are many other kinds of gross income.... Treasure trove, *to the extent of its value in United States currency, constitutes gross income for the taxable year in which it is reduced to undisputed possession.*" (Emphasis added.)

Identical language appears in the 1968 Treasury Regulations, and is found in all previous years back to 1958. This language is the same in all material respects as that found in Rev. Rul. 61, 1953-1 Cum. Bull. 17, and is undoubtedly an attempt to codify that ruling into the Regulations which apply to the 1954 Code. This Court is of the opinion that Treas. Reg. § 1.61-14(a) is dispositive of the major issue in this case if the $4,467.00 found in the piano was "reduced to undisputed possession" in the year petitioners reported it, for this Regulation was applicable to returns filed in the calendar year of 1964.

This brings the Court to the second contention of the plaintiffs: that if any tax was due, it was in 1957 when the piano was purchased, and by 1964 the Government was blocked from collecting it by reason of the statute of limitations. Without reaching the question of whether the voluntary payment in 1964 constituted a waiver on the part of the taxpayers, this Court finds that the $4,467.00 sum was properly included in gross income for the calendar year of 1964. Problems of when title vests, or when possession is complete in the field of federal taxation, in the absence of definitive federal legislation on the subject, are ordinarily determined by reference to the law of the state in which the taxpayer resides, or where the property around which the dispute centers is located. Since both the taxpayers and the property in question are found within the State of Ohio, Ohio law must govern as to when the found money was "reduced to undisputed possession" within the meaning of Treas. Reg. § 1.61-14 and Rev. Rul. 61, 1953-1 Cum. Bull. 17.

In Ohio, there is no statute specifically dealing with the rights of owners and finders of treasure trove, and in the absence of such a statute the common-law rule of England applies, so that "title belongs to the finder as against all the world except the true owner," Niederlehner v. Weatherly, 78 Ohio App. 263, 69 N.E.2d 787 (1946), appeal dismissed, 146 Ohio St. 697, 67 N.E.2d 713 (1946). The *Niederlehner* case held, inter alia, that the owner of real estate upon which money is found does not have title as against the finder. Therefore, in the instant case if plaintiffs had resold the piano in 1958, not knowing of the money within it, they later would not be able to succeed in an action against the purchaser who did discover it. Under Ohio law, the plaintiffs must have actually found the money to have superior title over all but the true owner, and they did not discover the old currency until 1964. Unless there is present a specific state statute to the contrary, the majority of jurisdictions are in accord with the Ohio rule. Therefore, this Court finds that the $4,467.00 in old currency was not "reduced to undisputed possession" until its actual discovery in 1964, and thus the United States was not barred by the statute of limitations from collecting the $836.51 in tax during that year.

Old Colony Trust Co. v. Commissioner

279 U.S. 716 (1929)

Mr. Chief Justice Taft delivered the opinion of the Court.

The facts certified to us are substantially as follows:

William M. Wood was president of the American Woolen Company during the years 1918, 1919, and 1920. In 1918 he received as salary and commissions from the company $978,725.00, which he included in his federal income tax return for 1918. In 1919 he received as salary and commissions from the company $548,132.87, which he included in his return for 1919.

August 3, 1916, the American Woolen Company had adopted the following resolution, which was in effect in 1919 and 1920:

> Voted: That this company pay any and all income taxes, State and Federal, that may hereafter become due and payable upon the salaries of all the officers of the company ... to the end that said persons and officers shall receive their salaries or other compensation in full without deduction on account of income taxes, State or Federal, which taxes are to be paid out of the treasury of this corporation.

This resolution was amended on March 25, 1918, as follows:

> Voted: that, referring to the vote passed by this board on August 3, 1916, in reference to income taxes, State and Federal, payable upon the salaries or compensation of the officers and certain employees of this company, the method of computing said taxes shall be as follows, viz.:

> The difference between what the total amount of his tax would be, including his income from all sources, and the amount of his tax when computed upon his income excluding such compensation or salaries paid by this company.

Pursuant to these resolutions, the American Woolen Company paid to the collector of internal revenue Mr. Wood's federal income and surtaxes due to salary and commissions paid him by the company, as follows:

> Taxes for 1918 paid in 1919 ....$681,169.88
> Taxes for 1919 paid in 1920 ....$351,179.27

The decision of the Board of Tax Appeals here sought to be reviewed was that the income taxes of $681,169.88 and $351,179.27 paid by the American Woolen Company for Mr. Wood were additional income to him for the years 1919 and 1920.

The question certified by the Circuit Court of Appeals for answer by this Court is: "Did payment by the employer of the income taxes assessable against the employee constitute additional taxable income to such employee?"

Coming now to the merits of this case, we think the question presented is whether a taxpayer, having induced a third person to pay his income tax or having acquiesced in such payment as made in discharge of an obligation to him, may avoid the making of a return thereof and the payment of a corresponding tax. We think he may not do so. The payment of the tax by the employers was in consideration of the services rendered by the employee, and was a gain derived by the employee from his labor. The form of the payment is expressly declared to make no difference. It is therefore immaterial that the taxes were directly paid over to the government. The discharge by a third person of an obligation to him is equivalent to receipt by the person taxed. The taxes were imposed upon the employee, the taxes were actually paid by the employer, and the employee entered upon his duties in the years in question under the express agreement that his income taxes would be paid by his employer. This is evidenced by the terms of the resolution passed August 3, 1916, more than one year prior to the year in which the taxes were imposed. The taxes were paid upon a valuable consideration, namely, the services rendered by the employee and as part of the compensation therefor. We think, therefore, that the payment constituted income to the employee.

Nor can it be argued that the payment of the tax was a gift. The payment for services, even though entirely voluntary, was nevertheless compensation within the statute. This is shown by the case of Noel v. Parrott (C.C.A.) 15 F.2d 669. There it was resolved that a gratuitous appropriation equal in amount to $3 per share on the outstanding stock of the company be set aside out of the assets for distribution to certain officers and employees of the company, and that the executive committee be authorized to make such distribution as they deemed wise and proper. The executive committee gave $35,000 to be paid to the plaintiff taxpayer. The court said:

> In no view of the evidence, therefore, can the $35,000 be regarded as a gift. It was either compensation for services rendered, or a gain or profit derived from the sale of the stock of the corporation, or both; and, in any view, it was taxable as income.

It is next argued against the payment of this tax that if these payments by the employer constitute income to the employee, the employer will be called upon to pay the tax imposed upon this additional income, and that the payment of the additional tax will create further income which will in turn be subject to tax, with the result that there would be a tax upon a tax. This, it is urged, is the result of the government's theory, when carried to this logical conclusion, and results in an absurdity which Congress could not have contemplated.

In the first place, no attempt has been made by the Treasury to collect further taxes, upon the theory that the payment of additional taxes creates further income, and the question of a tax upon a tax was not before the Circuit Court of Appeals, and has not been certified to this Court. We can settle questions of that sort when an attempt to impose a tax upon a tax is undertaken, but not now. It is not, therefore, necessary to answer the argument based upon an algebraic formula to reach the amount of taxes due. The question in this case is, "Did the payment by the employer of the income taxes assessable against the employee constitute additional taxable income to such employee?" The answer must be "Yes."

V. Related Matters

- **Gross Income Considerations.** After determining whether a particular receipt or benefit is included in gross income, and the proper amount of income that must be reported, there are several questions that must be addressed:

- **Proper Timing.** *When* is that amount included in gross income? An item of income must be allocated to the proper taxable year. For instance, if an employee receives her paycheck on December 31, Year 1, but does not deposit it until January 3, Year 2, what is the proper taxable year of inclusion? As discussed in Chapters 13, the proper taxable year is generally governed by the taxpayer's method of accounting (cash versus accrual).

- **Proper Taxpayer.** *Who* must report that amount in gross income? Identifying the proper taxpayer is always important. For example, if a child receives dividends on stock owned by her parent, who must report the dividend income and pay the resulting tax liability? It is governed by the assignment of income doctrine, an issue explored in Chapter 30.

- **Proper Character.** What is the *character* of the item of income? An item of income may be characterized as either "ordinary income" or "capital gain." Ordinary income is taxed at the progressive rates found in sections 1(a)–(e). Certain capital gains, in contrast, are taxed at much lower rates pursuant to section 1(h). The characterization of income is explored in Chapters 17–19.

Chapter 3

Gains and Losses from Dealings in Property

I. Assignment

Read: Internal Revenue Code: §§ 61(a)(3); 109; 1001(a)–(c); 1011(a); 1012; 1016(a)(1)–(2); 7701(g). Skim §§ 165(a), (c); 351(a); 721(a); 1014(a); 1015(a); 1031(a); 1041(a).

Treasury Regulations: §§ 1.61-6(a); 1.1001–1(a), -2(a)–(b); 1.1012-1(c)(1).

Text: Overview
Philadelphia Park Amusement Co. v. United States
Crane v. Commissioner
Related Matters

Complete the problems.

II. Problems

1. Edith Piaf owns a lot on a popular lake that she purchased several years ago for $50,000 but that is now worth $100,000. Which of the following are realization events and, if so, what is the amount of gain or loss realized?

   (a) Edith receives an unsolicited offer to purchase the lot for $100,000, but rejects the offer.

   (b) Edith receives an unsolicited offer to purchase the lot for $100,000, and she accepts it. At closing, she received a check for $95,000 because of selling costs.

   (c) Same as (b) except that Edith purchased the lot several years ago for $125,000.

   (d) Edith gives the lot to her son for the love and affection he has always shown her.

   (e) Edith transfers the lot to Plaintiff in full satisfaction of a $100,000 court judgment.

   (f) Edith transfers the lot to her spouse pursuant to a separation agreement in which he agrees to release all of his claims and marital rights against Edith's property. *But see* IRC § 1041(a).

   (g) Edith exchanges the lot for Bob Hope's lot on the other side of the lake. Bob's lot is worth $100,000 at the time of exchange. *But see* IRC § 1031(a).

(h) Edith exchanges the lot for Bob's RV trailer. Bob's RV trailer is worth $100,000 at the time of exchange.

(i) Edith transfers the lot to a newly formed corporation in exchange for 100% of the company's stock valued at $100,000. *But see* IRC § 351(a).

2. Anne Hathaway, a prominent surgeon, owns a vacation home in Idaho. In the current year, Anne sold the vacation home to an unrelated buyer for $80,000. What are the federal income tax consequences to Anne of the sale in each of the following separate situations?

(a) Anne purchased the vacation home five years ago for $50,000 cash. Three years ago, Anne borrowed on a recourse basis $20,000 from a bank using the vacation home as security for the loan, and used the $20,000 to purchase a boat. This year, Anne sold the home to an unrelated buyer for $80,000, with the buyer paying $60,000 cash and assuming the $20,000 debt.

(b) Same as (a) except that Anne used the $20,000 to make permanent improvements to the vacation home.

(c) Same as (a) except that Anne received the vacation home, unencumbered, five years ago from a client in full payment for a surgery procedure, for which Anne generally charges $50,000.

(d) Same as (a) except that Anne received the summer home (valued at $50,000) five years ago from a fellow surgeon in exchange for her RV trailer (valued at $40,000) and $10,000 in cash. Anne paid $20,000 for the RV trailer ten years ago.

3. Jack Kerouac borrowed $3,000,000 from Bank on a nonrecourse basis and invested $100,000 of his own money to purchase an apartment building for $3,100,000 (its fair market value). Unable to make any payments on the loan, Jack transferred the building to Jill who took the property subject to the nonrecourse liability still at $3,000,000. At the time of this transaction, the building had a value of $2,200,000 and Jack's adjusted basis in the building was $2,000,000 (as a result of claiming a total of $1,100,000 in depreciation during the time he held the property).

(a) What is the amount of gain or loss Jack realizes on the transaction with Jill, and what is Jill's basis in the building?

(b) Would the answer to (a) change if Jack transferred the building by means of a quitclaim deed to Bank?

III. Overview

In this chapter, we begin examining the tax consequences of property transactions. Much of the material in this chapter will serve as the building blocks for material in later chapters. The terminology the Code uses to address property transactions is essential vocabulary for any person who regularly deals with the law of taxation.

Section 61(a)(3) states that gross income includes *gains derived from dealings in property*. To understand this phrase, we turn to section 1001. Section 1001(a) provides that gain from the *sale or other disposition of property* is the excess of *amount realized* over *adjusted basis.* Conversely, loss from the sale or other disposition of property is the excess of adjusted basis over amount realized. To understand the scope of section 61(a)(3), and to perform gain and loss computations under section 1001(a), one must understand the meaning of the terms used in these provisions.

A. Sale or Other Disposition

Increases and decreases in the value of property are not taken into account for tax purposes as they accrue, but only when they are realized by a taxable event. Realization usually does not occur until there has been a dealing in property (to use section 61(a)(3)'s phrase) or a sale or other disposition of property (to use section 1001(a)'s phrase).

Sometimes it is difficult to determine whether a property transaction is a sale or other disposition within the meaning of section 1001(a). For example, the issue may arise whether property has been sold, which is a realization event, or whether property has only been *licensed*, which is not a realization event. The issue also may arise whether a taxpayer has made a gratuitous transfer of property, which is not a realization event within the meaning of section 1001(a), or whether the taxpayer has transferred property in satisfaction of a debt, which is a realization event (i.e., functionally equivalent to a sale of the property for cash followed by use of the proceeds to pay the debt).

The phrase *sale or other disposition* is broad and includes most transactions producing a quid pro quo for the taxpayer. Treas. Reg. § 1.1001-1(a). A taxpayer would clearly experience a realization event if he sold property for money or other property. A taxpayer would also experience a realization event if he (1) transferred property to a creditor in satisfaction of a debt, (2) exchanged property for different property, or (3) was compensated by insurance or otherwise when property is destroyed, stolen, or expropriated. *See* Helvering v. Hammel, 311 U.S. 504 (1941) (holding that a mortgage foreclosure, like a voluntary sale, is a "disposition" within the scope of section 1001); Helvering v. Bruun, 309 U.S. 461 (1940) (listing several events that constitute realization events). A taxpayer would not experience a realization event if he gifted property to a relative or donated property to a charity and did not receive anything in return. In Woodsam Associates, Inc. v. Commissioner, 198 F.2d 357 (2d Cir. 1952), the Second Circuit addressed whether a refinancing transaction was a realization event, and held that no sale or other disposition of property occurred when property was mortgaged as security for a loan.

B. Computation of Gain or Loss Realized

If a transaction is treated as a sale or other disposition within the meaning of section 1001(a), the transferor must determine the amount of gain or loss, if any, realized on the transaction. Section 1001(a) gives us the formulas for gain or loss realized:

Gain Realized

Gain Realized = Amount Realized – Adjusted Basis

Loss Realized

Loss Realized = Adjusted Basis – Amount Realized

1. Amount Realized

The Code defines *amount realized* from a sale or other disposition of property as the sum of any money received plus the fair market value of property (other than money) received in the transaction. IRC § 1001(b). For example, if a taxpayer sells property for $50,000 in cash, and the buyer pays with $50,000 cash, the taxpayer's amount realized is $50,000. Now suppose the buyer pays with $45,000 cash and a motorcycle with a fair market value of $5,000. The taxpayer's amount realized is still $50,000.

Keep in mind that the amount realized in a property transaction is not the amount included in gross income. Rather, it is the gain realized that is included. The reasoning for this is that a taxpayer should be able to recover tax-free his cost or unrecovered investment in the property in order to prevent double taxation. Assume, for example, that Taxpayer earns a salary of $65,000 and pays federal income tax of $15,000. Now assume that Taxpayer takes the after-tax dollars and purchases Blackacre for $50,000. If Taxpayer later sells Blackacre for $50,000, the amount realized on the sale is $50,000, but his gain realized should be zero since he has only recovered his initial investment dollars which were previously taxed. We keep track of a taxpayer's cost or unrecovered investment in property through the tax mechanism of *adjusted basis*. Adjusted basis essentially ensures that the same dollars are not taxed more than once in the same taxpayer's hands.

2. Adjusted Basis

Section 1011(a) provides that the *adjusted basis* of property is the *basis* as determined under section 1012 (or other applicable Code section), *adjusted* as provided in section 1016.

Cost Basis—§ 1012. To determine the adjusted basis of property, basis of the property must first be determined. Basis is determined when a taxpayer initially acquires property. Generally, basis is the amount a taxpayer has invested in a "tax sense" in the property. Section 1012 prescribes that the basis of property is equal to its *cost*. Determining cost is straightforward when a taxpayer invests cash in property. In the example above, if Taxpayer purchases Blackacre for $50,000 in cash, Taxpayer has an initial cost basis of $50,000.

Tax Cost Basis. Property may be acquired in transactions other than cash purchases. What if Taxpayer, in the example above, had not purchased Blackacre, but instead received it in Year 1 from his employer as compensation for services rendered? Would Taxpayer's basis be zero since he did not pay anything for it? Recall from Chapter 2 that compensation for services can take many forms and, regardless of the form, it must be included in gross income. IRC § 61(a)(1); Treas. Reg. § 1.61-2(d)(1). Although it might appear that Taxpayer has no *cost basis* in Blackacre, Taxpayer did have to include the fair market value of Blackacre in gross income in Year 1 as compensation for services rendered. Because Blackacre was included in gross income at its then fair market value of $50,000, Taxpayer has what is called a *tax cost basis* in Blackacre of $50,000. *See* Treas. Reg. § 1.61-2(d)(2)(i). If Taxpayer were not allowed the $50,000 basis and he immediately sold the land in Year 1, he would have $50,000 of gain realized and would have to include it in gross income and therefore would be taxed twice on the same $50,000.

The concept of tax cost arises whenever property acquired other than by cash purchase is included in gross income (e.g., treasure trove, prizes, property received unlawfully). The concept also arises when property is acquired through a taxable exchange. In *Philadelphia Park Amusement Co. v. United States*, included in the materials, the court held that the taxpayer's basis in property received in a taxable exchange is equal to the fair market value of the property received. To understand the holding, assume Taxpayer purchases Blackacre for $50,000 and later exchanges Blackacre, in an arm's length transaction, for Neighbor's yacht worth $80,000.

Taxpayer's Blackacre		Neighbor's Yacht	
FMV	$80,000	FMV	$80,000
AB	$50,000	AB	$45,000

Philadelphia Park tells us that after the exchange Taxpayer's basis in the yacht is $80,000, the fair market value of the property received. This makes sense if we look at the tax consequences to Taxpayer of the exchange. The exchange is a sale or other disposition of property within the meaning of section 1001, and the amount of Taxpayer's gain realized is $30,000, that is $80,000 amount realized (fair market value of the yacht received) minus $50,000 adjusted basis (cost of Blackacre). This $30,000 gain is part of Taxpayer's cost in the yacht. Taxpayer's total cost in the yacht is $80,000 — he gave up Blackacre for which he paid $50,000, plus he reported gain of $30,000 in the exchange. As you read *Philadelphia Park*, think about the following: How would Taxpayer, in the example above, determine the basis of the yacht received if he did not know the fair market value of the yacht?

Gift Tax Basis and Stepped-Up Basis — §§ 1014, 1015. As we will study in Chapter 4, the Code has special basis rules for property received by gift and devise. If Taxpayer received Blackacre from Mother as a gift, Taxpayer's initial basis in Blackacre would be the same as Mother's adjusted basis in Blackacre at the time of gift. Skim IRC § 1015. If Taxpayer received Blackacre after Mother's death pursuant to her will, Taxpayer's initial basis in Blackacre would be the fair market value of Blackacre at the date of Mother's death. Skim IRC § 1014.

Adjustments to Basis — § 1016. Basis, initially determined upon acquisition of property, may later be adjusted as a result of subsequent events to yield the property's adjusted basis. Specifically, the initial basis of property is adjusted upward for the cost of any improvements to the property and adjusted downward for cost recovery deductions (e.g., tax depreciation deductions) that are allowed with respect to the property. IRC § 1016(a)(1)–(2). Improvements and cost recovery deductions are addressed in later chapters.

C. "Recognition" of Realized Gain or Loss

Once a taxpayer has calculated the gain or loss *realized* on a sale or other disposition, the taxpayer must determine whether the gain or loss is *recognized* (i.e., reportable on the tax return for the year of disposition). As a general rule, the entire gain or loss realized on a sale or other disposition of property is recognized for tax purposes, unless an exception is provided in the Code. IRC § 1001(c). The Code provides a number of exceptions commonly referred to as non-recognition provisions. These non-recognition provisions, which are often narrowly defined, are based on the rationale that the taxpayer's economic position has not really changed.

For example, if Taxpayer transferred Blackacre (with an adjusted basis of $50,000) to a corporation or partnership in exchange for an ownership interest in such entity (with a fair market value of $80,000), none of Taxpayer's $30,000 gain realized would have to be recognized. Skim IRC §§ 351(a), 721(a). Likewise, if Taxpayer exchanged Blackacre (with an adjusted basis of $50,000) for similar land Whiteacre (with a fair market value of $80,000), none of Taxpayer's $30,000 gain realized would have to be recognized. Skim IRC § 1031(a). These and other nonrecognition provisions will be dealt with in later chapters.

It should be noted that, in contrast to *exclusion* provisions (e.g., IRC §§ 102, 132), *non-recognition* provisions do not permanently exclude gain or loss. Nonrecognition provisions merely postpone the reporting of gain or loss to a later year when the property received in the transaction is sold or disposed of in a taxable transaction. Gain or loss is preserved by giving the taxpayer the same basis in the property received as he or she had in the property given up in the transaction. *See, e.g.,* IRC §§ 358(a)(1), 1031(d).

Deductibility of Losses. With respect to loss recognition there is an important limitation for individuals established by section 165. This provision disallows the deduction of most losses from dispositions of personal use property such as the taxpayer's home or automobile. Put another way, section 165 only allows loss recognition, with one exception, for losses from dispositions of business or investment property. IRC § 165(c)(1) & (2). The exception is for certain casualty losses and is fully addressed in a later chapter. *See* IRC § 165(c)(3). There are other provisions, including sections 465, 469, and 1211, that overlay section 165 to further limit loss deduction in a variety of circumstances. These provisions are also addressed in later chapters.

D. Impact of Liabilities in Property Transactions

1. General Framework

When a taxpayer purchases property for cash, the property's basis is equal to the amount of cash paid. Many taxpayers, however, finance property acquisitions in whole or in part with debt. Should such debt be included in the property's basis at the time of purchase? Although the Code does not provide an answer, it is well established that a loan is the equivalent of a cash investment and is included in the basis of the asset it finances, regardless of whether the loan is a *recourse* loan (i.e., the borrower agrees to be personally liable for the debt) or a *nonrecourse* loan (i.e., the lender's recourse for default is limited to the asset securing the debt). For example, if Taxpayer borrows $990,000 from Bank and uses the loan, along with $10,000 of his own funds, to buy a $1 million apartment building, Taxpayer's basis in the building is $1 million regardless of whether the loan is recourse or nonrecourse.

When a taxpayer sells encumbered property, the buyer typically agrees to *assume* the debt encumbering the property or to take the property *subject to* the debt. It is well established that the taxpayer must include the relief of outstanding debt, whether recourse or nonrecourse, in amount realized for purposes of determining gain or loss realized. Using the example above, assume that Taxpayer sells the apartment building eighteen months later for $1,200,000 (its fair market value at the time). The buyer will either assume the $990,000 debt or take the property subject to the debt, and will pay Taxpayer $210,000 in cash (i.e., the difference between the property's value and the debt securing the property). The Taxpayer's amount realized is $1,200,000, regardless of whether the loan is recourse or nonrecourse.

For the treatment of debt under current law, read carefully *Crane v. Commissioner*, included in the materials below. *See also* Treas. Reg. § 1.1001-2(a). *Crane* stands for simple tax symmetry. If debt is included in basis, then relief from debt should be included in amount realized, even if the debt is nonrecourse.

Is there any benefit to including debt in "basis" at the time of purchase, if a taxpayer must then include debt relief in the "amount realized" upon an eventual sale or other disposition? After all, the total amount of gain from a property transaction would be the same whether debt is included in both basis and amount realized or excluded from both. As will be explored in Chapter 9, if property is eligible for tax depreciation deductions, including debt in basis allows a taxpayer to enjoy greater depreciation deductions and the time value of such deductions. In the example above, Taxpayer is entitled to an annual depreciation deduction computed by reference to Taxpayer's basis in the property, $1 million (the $10,000 cash investment plus the $990,000 loan). As we will learn in Chapter 9, Taxpayer would be entitled to annual depreciation deductions of approximately $36,000 (annual tax savings of $14,000 assuming Taxpayer is in the 39.6% rate bracket). This is great considering Taxpayer invested only $10,000 of his own funds to purchase the apartment building and may not even be personally liable for the $990,000 debt encumbering the property (i.e., the debt might be nonrecourse). However, Congress has taken steps to limit the amount of depreciation deductions one can take with respect to encumbered property for which taxpayers have little or no putative cost. The *at risk* requirements in section 465 and the *passive activity loss* limitation rules in section 469 are explored more fully in Chapter 27.

2. Specialized Aspects of Debt in Property Transactions

The following examples introduce and illustrate some complexities raised by the use of debt in property transactions.

Example 1. Taxpayer borrowed $1,850,000 from Bank (assume a nonrecourse loan) and used the loan (and no other consideration) to buy a large apartment building at its fair market value of $1,850,000. Unable to make any payments on the loan, Taxpayer later transferred the building to Buyer who took it subject to the mortgage. At the time of the transfer, Taxpayer's adjusted basis in the building was $1,450,000 (as a result of $400,000 in tax depreciation deductions claimed by Taxpayer with respect to the building during the time Taxpayer held the property). The apartment building had a fair market value of only $1,400,000. To determine the amount of gain or loss on this transaction, we must determine Taxpayer's amount realized. The Supreme Court in *Crane* told us that Taxpayer must include in the amount realized any nonrecourse debt taken subject to by Buyer ($1,850,000). This would mean that Taxpayer has gain of $400,000 on the sale. The *Crane* Court, however, raised an interesting question in footnote 37: "Obviously, if the value of the property is less than the amount of the mortgage, a mortgagor who is not personally liable cannot realize a benefit equal to the mortgage. Consequently, a different problem might be encountered where a mortgagor abandoned the property or transferred it subject to the mortgage without receiving boot. That is not this case." Does this mean that Taxpayer's amount realized is no more than the lower $1,400,000 fair market value of the property, which would yield a loss of $50,000 as opposed to a gain of $400,000? The Supreme Court later resolved this question in Commissioner v. Tufts, 461 U.S. 300 (1983), and held that the entire amount of nonrecourse debt must be included in amount realized. In sum, Taxpayer has a gain of $400,000 ($1,850,000 AR minus $1,450,000 AB). It should be noted that if the debt in this example were recourse, as opposed to nonrecourse, the result would be different. The special tax treatment of discharged recourse debt is considered in Chapter 5.

Example 2. Taxpayer purchased an apartment building by giving Seller a nonrecourse mortgage in the amount of $1 million and no additional consideration. Taxpayer agreed to a nonrecourse mortgage that was substantially more than the building's fair market value in order to inflate basis and claim greater tax depreciation deductions at no risk. An interesting question is whether Taxpayer's basis for depreciation purposes should reflect the $1 million nonrecourse mortgage. Courts have answered this question in the negative. In Estate of Franklin v. Commissioner, 544 F.2d 1045 (9th Cir. 1976), the Ninth Circuit disregarded the nonrecourse debt in its entirety for the purposes of determining depreciation. In Pleasant Summit Land Corp. v Commissioner, 863 F.2d 263 (3d Cir. 1988), the Third Circuit took a different approach and recognized the nonrecourse debt for depreciation purposes but only to the extent of the fair market value of the property. The Second and Fifth Circuits have rejected the Third Circuit's approach. *See* Lebowitz v. Commissioner, 917 F.2d 1314 (2d Cir. 1990); Lukens v. Commissioner, 945 F.2d 92 (5th Cir. 1991).

IV. Materials

Philadelphia Park Amusement Co. v. United States

126 F. Supp. 184 (Ct. Cl. 1954)

Laramore, Judge.

[The taxpayer built a bridge, known as the Strawberry Bridge, which it later exchanged for a ten-year extension on a franchise to operate a passenger railway. It later abandoned the franchise and reported a tax loss on doing so. In the ensuing litigation with the tax authority a key question was the amount of the taxpayer's basis in the franchise. Eds.]

This brings us to the question of what is the cost basis of the 10-year extension of taxpayer's franchise. Although defendant contends that Strawberry Bridge was either worthless or not "exchanged" for the 10-year extension of the franchise, we believe that the bridge had some value, and that the contract under which the bridge was transferred to the City clearly indicates that the one was given in consideration of the other. The taxpayer, however, has failed to show that the exchange was one that falls within the nonrecognition provisions of the Code and, therefore, it was a taxable exchange.

The gain or loss, whichever the case may have been, should have been recognized, and the cost basis under section 1012 of the Code, of the 10-year extension of the franchise was the cost to the taxpayer. The succinct statement in section 1012 that "the basis of property shall be the cost of such property" although clear in principle, is frequently difficult in application. One view is that the cost basis of property received in a taxable exchange is the fair market value of the property given in the exchange. The other view is that the cost basis of property received in a taxable exchange is the fair market value of the property received in the exchange. As will be seen from the cases and some of the Commissioner's rulings the Commissioner's position has not been altogether consistent on this question. The view that "cost" is the fair market value of the property given is predicated on the theory that the cost to the taxpayer is the economic value relinquished. The view that "cost" is the fair market value of the property received is based upon the theory that the term "cost" is a tax concept and must be considered in the light of the designed interrelationship of sections 1001 and 1012, and the prime role that the basis of property plays in determining tax liability. We believe that when the question is considered in the latter context that the cost basis of the property received in a taxable exchange is the fair market value of the property received in the exchange.

When property is exchanged for property in a taxable exchange the taxpayer is taxed on the difference between the adjusted basis of the property given in exchange and the fair market value of the property received in exchange. For purposes of determining gain or loss the fair market value of the property received is treated as cash and taxed accordingly. To maintain harmony with the fundamental purpose of these sections, it is necessary to consider the fair market value of the property received as the cost basis to the taxpayer. The failure to do so would result in allowing the taxpayer a stepped-up basis, without paying a tax therefor, if the fair market value of the property received is less than the fair market value of the property given, and the taxpayer would be subjected to a double tax if the fair market value of the property received is more than the fair market value of the property given. By holding that the fair market value of the property received in a taxable exchange is the cost basis, the above discrepancy is avoided and the basis of the property received will equal the adjusted basis of the property given plus any gain recognized, or that should have been recognized, or minus any loss recognized, or that should have been recognized.

Therefore, the cost basis of the 10-year extension of the franchise was its fair market value on August 3, 1934, the date of the exchange. The determination of whether the cost basis of the property received is its fair market value or the fair market value of the property given in exchange therefor, although necessary to the decision of the case, is generally not of great practical significance because the value of the two properties exchanged in an arms-length transaction are either equal in fact, or are presumed to be equal. The record in this case indicates that the 1934 exchange was an arms-length transaction and, therefore, if the value of the extended franchise cannot be determined with reasonable accuracy, it would be reasonable and fair to assume that the value of Strawberry Bridge was equal to the 10-year extension of the franchise. The fair market value of the 10-year extension of the franchise should be established but, if that value cannot be determined with reasonable certainty, the fair market value of Strawberry Bridge should be established and that will be presumed to be the value of the extended franchise. This value cannot be determined from the facts now before us since the case was prosecuted on a different theory.

The taxpayer contends that the market value of the extended franchise or Strawberry Bridge could not be ascertained and, therefore, it should be entitled to carry over the undepreciated cost basis of the bridge as the cost of the extended franchise. If the value of the extended franchise or bridge cannot be ascertained with a reasonable degree of accuracy, the taxpayer is entitled to carry over the undepreciated cost of the bridge as the cost basis of the extended franchise. However, it is only in rare and extraordinary cases that the value of the property exchanged cannot be ascertained with reasonable accuracy. We are presently of the opinion that either the value of the extended franchise or the bridge can be determined with a reasonable degree of accuracy. Although the value of the extended franchise may be difficult or impossible to ascertain because of the nebulous and intangible characteristics inherent in such property, the value of the bridge is subject to more exact measurement. Consideration may be given to expert testimony on the value of comparable bridges, Strawberry Bridge's reproduction cost and its undepreciated cost, as well as other relevant factors.

We, therefore, conclude that the 1934 exchange was a taxable exchange and that the taxpayer is entitled to use as the cost basis of the 10-year extension of its franchise its fair market value on August 3, 1934, for purposes of determining depreciation and loss due to abandonment, as indicated in this opinion.

Crane v. Commissioner

331 U.S. 1 (1947)

Mr. Chief Justice Vinson delivered the opinion of the Court.

The question here is how a taxpayer who acquires depreciable property subject to an unassumed mortgage, holds it for a period, and finally sells it still so encumbered, must compute her taxable gain.

Petitioner was the sole beneficiary and the executrix of the will of her husband, who died January 11, 1932. He then owned an apartment building and lot subject to a mortgage, which secured a principal debt of $255,000.00 and interest in default of $7,042.50. As of that date, the property was appraised for federal estate tax purposes at a value exactly equal to the total amount of this encumbrance. Shortly after her husband's death, petitioner entered into an agreement with the mortgagee whereby she was to continue to operate the property—collecting the rents, paying for necessary repairs, labor, and other operating expenses, and reserving $200.00 monthly for taxes—and was to remit the net rentals to the mortgagee. This plan was followed for nearly seven years, during which period petitioner reported the gross rentals as income, and claimed and was allowed deductions for taxes and operating expenses paid on the property, for interest paid on the mortgage, and for the physical exhaustion of the building. Meanwhile, the arrearage of interest increased to $15,857.71. On November 29, 1938, with the mortgagee threatening foreclosure, petitioner sold to a third party for $3,000.00 cash, subject to the mortgage, and paid $500.00 expenses of sale.

Petitioner reported a taxable gain of $1,250.00. Her theory was that the "property" which she had acquired in 1932 and sold in 1938 was only the equity, or the excess in the value of the apartment building and lot over the amount of the mortgage. This equity was of zero value when she acquired it. No depreciation could be taken on a zero value. Neither she nor her vendee ever assumed the mortgage, so, when she sold the equity, the amount she realized on the sale was the net cash received, or $2,500.00. This sum less the zero basis constituted her gain, of which she reported half as taxable on the assumption that the entire property was a "capital asset."

The Commissioner, however, determined that petitioner realized a net taxable gain of $23,767.03. His theory was that the "property" acquired and sold was not the equity, as petitioner claimed, but rather the physical property itself, or the owner's rights to possess, use, and dispose of it, undiminished by the mortgage. The original basis thereof was $262,042.50, its appraised value in 1932. Of this value $55,000.00 was allocable to land and $207,042.50 to building. During the period that petitioner held the property, there was an allowable depreciation of $28,045.10 on the building, so that the adjusted basis of the building at the time of sale was $178,997.40. The amount realized on the sale was said to include not only the $2,500.00 net cash receipts, but also the principal amount of the mortgage subject to which the property was sold, both totaling $257,500.00. The selling price was allocable in the proportion, $54,471.15 to the land and $203,028.85 to the building. The Commissioner agreed that the land was a "capital asset," but thought that the building was not. Thus, he determined that petitioner sustained a capital loss of $528.85 on the land, of which 50% or $264.42 was taken into account, and an ordinary gain of $24,031.45 on the building, or a net taxable gain as indicated.

The Tax Court agreed with the Commissioner that the building was not a "capital asset." In all other respects it adopted petitioner's contentions, and expunged the deficiency. Petitioner did not appeal from the part of the ruling adverse to her, and these questions are no longer at issue. On the Commissioner's appeal, the Circuit Court of Appeals reversed, one judge dissenting. We granted certiorari because of the importance of the questions raised as to the proper construction of the gain and loss provisions of the Internal Revenue Code.

The 1938 Act, section 111(a), defines the gain from "the sale or other disposition of property" as "the excess of the amount realized therefrom over the adjusted basis provided in section 113(b)...." It proceeds, section 111(b), to define "the amount realized from the sale or other disposition of property" as "the sum of any money received plus the fair market value of the property (other than money) received." Further, in section 113(b), the "adjusted basis for determining the gain or loss from the sale or other disposition of property" is declared to be "the basis determined under subsection (a), adjusted ... for exhaustion, wear and tear, obsolescence, amortization ... to the extent allowed (but not less than the amount allowable)...." The basis under subsection (a) "if the property was acquired by ... devise ... or by the decedent's estate from the decedent", section 113(a)(5), is "the fair market value of such property at the time of such acquisition."

Logically, the first step under this scheme is to determine the unadjusted basis of the property, under section 113(a)(5), and the dispute in this case is as to the construction to be given the term "property." If "property," as used in that provision, means the same thing as "equity," it would necessarily follow that the basis of petitioner's property was zero, as she contends. If, on the contrary, it means the land and building themselves, or the owner's legal rights in them, undiminished by the mortgage, the basis was $262,042.50.

We think that the reasons for favoring one of the latter constructions are of overwhelming weight. In the first place, the words of statutes — including revenue acts — should be interpreted where possible in their ordinary, everyday senses. The only relevant definitions of "property" to be found in the principal standard dictionaries are the two favored by the Commissioner, i.e., either that "property" is the physical thing which is a subject of ownership, or that it is the aggregate of the owner's rights to control and dispose of that thing. "Equity" is not given as a synonym, nor do either of the foregoing definitions suggest that it could be correctly so used. Indeed, "equity" is defined as "the value of a property ... above the total of the liens...." The contradistinction could hardly be more pointed. Strong countervailing considerations would be required to support a contention that Congress, in using the word "property," meant "equity," or that we should impute to it the intent to convey that meaning.

In the second place, the Commission's position has the approval of the administrative construction of section 113(a)(5). With respect to the valuation of property under that section, Reg. 101, Art. 113(a)(5)-1, promulgated under the 1938 Act, provided that "the value of property as of the date of the death of the decedent as appraised for the purpose of the federal estate tax ... shall be deemed to be its fair market value...." The land and building here involved were so appraised in 1932, and their appraised value—$262,042.50—was reported by petitioner as part of the gross estate. This was in accordance with the estate tax law and regulations, which had always required that the value of decedent's property, undiminished by liens, be so appraised and returned, and that mortgages be separately deducted in computing the net estate. As the quoted provision of the Regulations has been in effect since 1918, and as the relevant statutory provision has been repeatedly reenacted since then in substantially the same form, the former may itself now be considered to have the force of law.

Moreover, in the many instances in other parts of the Act in which Congress has used the word "property," or expressed the idea of "property" or "equity," we find no instances of a misuse of either word or of a confusion of the ideas. In some parts of the Act other than the gain and loss sections, we find "property" where it is unmistakably used in its ordinary sense. On the other hand, where either Congress or the Treasury intended to convey the meaning of "equity," it did so by the use of appropriate language.

A further reason why the word "property" in section 113(a) should not be construed to mean "equity" is the bearing such construction would have on the allowance of deductions for depreciation and on the collateral adjustments of basis.

Section 23(l) permits deduction from gross income of "a reasonable allowance for the exhaustion, wear and tear of property...." Sections 23(n) and 114(a), 26 U.S.C.A. Int.Rev.Code, ss 23(n), 114(a), declare that the "basis upon which depletion exhaustion, wear and tear ... are to be allowed" is the basis "provided in section 113(b) for the purpose of determining the gain upon the sale" of the property, which is the section 113(a) basis "adjusted ... for exhaustion, wear and tear ... to the extent allowed (but not less than the amount allowable)...."

Under these provisions, if the mortgagor's equity were the section 113(a) basis, it would also be the original basis from which depreciation allowances are deducted. If it is, and if the amount of the annual allowances were to be computed on that value, as would then seem to be required, they will represent only a fraction of the cost of the corresponding physical exhaustion, and any recoupment by the mortgagor of the remainder of that cost can be effected only by the reduction of his taxable gain in the year of sale. If, however, the amount of the annual allowances were to be computed on the value of the property, and then deducted from an equity basis, we would in some instances have to accept deductions from a minus basis or deny deductions altogether. The Commissioner also argues that taking the mortgagor's equity as the section 113(a) basis would require the basis to be changed with each payment on the mortgage, and that the attendant problem of repeatedly recomputing basis and annual allowances would be a tremendous accounting burden on both the Commissioner and the taxpayer. Moreover, the mortgagor would acquire control over the timing of his depreciation allowances.

Thus it appears that the applicable provisions of the Act expressly preclude an equity basis, and the use of it is contrary to certain implicit principles of income tax depreciation, and entails very great administrative difficulties. It may be added that the Treasury has never furnished a guide through the maze of problems that arise in connection with depreciating an equity basis, but, on the contrary, has consistently permitted the amount of depreciation allowances to be computed on the full value of the property, and subtracted from it as a basis. Surely, Congress' long-continued acceptance of this situation gives it full legislative endorsement.

We conclude that the proper basis under section 113(a)(5) is the value of the property, undiminished by mortgages thereon, and that the correct basis here was $262,042.50. The next step is to ascertain what adjustments are required under section 113(b). As the depreciation rate was stipulated, the only question at this point is whether the Commissioner was warranted in making any depreciation adjustments whatsoever.

Section 113(b)(1)(B) provides that "proper adjustment in respect of the property shall in all cases be made ... for exhaustion, wear and tear ... to the extent allowed (but not less than the amount allowable....)." The Tax Court found on adequate evidence that the apartment house was property of a kind subject to physical exhaustion, that it was used in taxpayer's trade or business, and consequently that the taxpayer would have been entitled to a depreciation allowance under section 23(l), except that, in the opinion of that Court, the basis of the property was zero, and it was thought that depreciation could not be taken on a zero basis. As we have just decided that the correct basis of the property was not zero, but $262,042.50, we avoid this difficulty, and conclude that an adjustment should be made as the Commissioner determined.

Petitioner urges to the contrary that she was not entitled to depreciation deductions, whatever the basis of the property, because the law allows them only to one who actually bears the capital loss, and here the loss was not hers but the mortgagee's. We do not see, however, that she has established her factual premise. There was no finding of the Tax Court to that effect, nor to the effect that the value of the property was ever less than the amount of the lien. Nor was there evidence in the record, or any indication that petitioner could produce evidence, that this was so. The facts that the value of the property was only equal to the lien in 1932 and that during the next six and one-half years the physical condition of the building deteriorated and the amount of the lien increased, are entirely inconclusive, particularly in the light of the buyer's willingness in 1938 to take subject to the increased lien and pay a substantial amount of cash to boot. Whatever may be the rule as to allowing depreciation to a mortgagor on property in his possession which is subject to an unassumed mortgage and clearly worth less than the lien, we are not faced with that problem and see no reason to decide it now.

At last we come to the problem of determining the "amount realized" on the 1938 sale. Section 111(b), it will be recalled, defines the "amount realized" from "the sale ... of property" as "the sum of any money received plus the fair market value of the property (other than money) received," and section 111(a) defines the gain on "the sale ... of property" as the excess of the amount realized over the basis. Quite obviously, the word "property," used here with reference to a sale, must mean "property" in the same ordinary sense intended by the use of the word with reference to acquisition and depreciation in section 113, both for certain of the reasons stated heretofore in discussing its meaning in section 113, and also because the functional relation of the two sections requires that the word mean the same in one section that it does in the other. If the "property" to be valued on the date of acquisition is the property free of liens, the "property" to be priced on a subsequent sale must be the same thing.

Starting from this point, we could not accept petitioner's contention that the $2,500.00 net cash was all she realized on the sale except on the absurdity that she sold a quarter-of-a-million dollar property for roughly one per cent of its value, and took a 99 per cent loss. Actually, petitioner does not urge this. She argues, conversely, that because only $2,500.00 was realized on the sale, the "property" sold must have been the equity only, and that consequently we are forced to accept her contention as to the meaning of "property" in section 113. We adhere, however, to what we have already said on the meaning of "property," and we find that the absurdity is avoided by our conclusion that the amount of the mortgage is properly included in the "amount realized" on the sale.

Petitioner concedes that if she had been personally liable on the mortgage and the purchaser had either paid or assumed it, the amount so paid or assumed would be considered a part of the "amount realized" within the meaning of section 111(b). The cases so deciding have already repudiated the notion that there must be an actual receipt by the seller himself of "money" or "other property," in their narrowest senses. It was thought to be decisive that one section of the Act must be construed so as not to defeat the intention of another or to frustrate the Act as a whole, and that the taxpayer was the "beneficiary" of the payment in "as real and substantial [a sense] as if the money had been paid it and then paid over by it to its creditors."

Both these points apply to this case. The first has been mentioned already. As for the second, we think that a mortgagor, not personally liable on the debt, who sells the property subject to the mortgage and for additional consideration, realizes a benefit in the amount of the mortgage as well as the boot.[37] If a purchaser pays boot, it is immaterial as to our problem whether the mortgagor is also to receive money from the purchaser to discharge the mortgage prior to sale, or whether he is merely to transfer subject to the mortgage — it may make a difference to the purchaser and

---

37. Obviously, if the value of the property is less than the amount of the mortgage, a mortgagor who is not personally liable cannot realize a benefit equal to the mortgage. Consequently, a different problem might be encountered where a mortgagor abandoned the property or transferred it subject to the mortgage without receiving boot. That is not this case.

to the mortgagee, but not to the mortgagor. Or put in another way, we are no more concerned with whether the mortgagor is, strictly speaking, a debtor on the mortgage, than we are with whether the benefit to him is, strictly speaking, a receipt of money or property. We are rather concerned with the reality that an owner of property, mortgaged at a figure less than that at which the property will sell, must and will treat the conditions of the mortgage exactly as if they were his personal obligations. If he transfers subject to the mortgage, the benefit to him is as real and substantial as if the mortgage were discharged, or as if a personal debt in an equal amount had been assumed by another.

Therefore we conclude that the Commissioner was right in determining that petitioner realized $257,500.00 on the sale of this property.

The Tax Court's contrary determinations, that "property," as used in section 113(a) and related sections, means "equity," and that the amount of a mortgage subject to which property is sold is not the measure of a benefit realized, within the meaning of section 111(b), announced rules of general applicability on clear-cut questions of law. The Circuit Court of Appeals therefore had jurisdiction to review them.

Petitioner contends that the result we have reached taxes her on what is not income within the meaning of the Sixteenth Amendment. If this is because only the direct receipt of cash is thought to be income in the constitutional sense, her contention is wholly without merit. If it is because the entire transaction is thought to have been "by all dictates of common-sense ... a ruinous disaster," as it was termed in her brief, we disagree with her premise. She was entitled to depreciation deductions for a period of nearly seven years, and she actually took them in almost the allowable amount. The crux of this case, really, is whether the law permits her to exclude allowable deductions from consideration in computing gain. We have already showed that, if it does, the taxpayer can enjoy a double deduction, in effect, on the same loss of assets. The Sixteenth Amendment does not require that result any more than does the Act itself.

Affirmed.

V. Related Matters

- **Character of Gains and Losses.** A gain or loss is characterized as either *capital* or *ordinary*. The characterization depends on a number of factors, including: the nature of the property, the period the taxpayer has held the property, and whether the taxpayer disposed of the property in a sale or exchange transaction. Individuals generally prefer gains to be characterized as capital gains as opposed to ordinary income since certain capital gains are subject to reduced tax rates. As will be seen in Chapters 17–19, the Code contains general provisions governing the character of gains and losses for most property transactions. The Code also contains some characterization provisions that govern specific types of property and specific types of transactions. In contrast to gains, individuals tend to prefer that their losses be characterized as ordinary losses because of a statutory limitation on capital loss deductions.

- **Timing of Gains and Losses.** A taxpayer typically recognizes gain or loss at the time of sale. However, property is often sold on a deferred payment basis (e.g., payments are spread out over time). Section 453, addressed more fully in Chapter 26, provides that *income* from an *installment sale* is to be reported under the *installment method.* IRC § 453(a), (b)(1). If section 453 applies, the transferor's gain generally is included in income only as payments are received from the transferee. In other words, the gain is spread over the life of the payments. Section 453 provides a formula for determining the income portion of each payment. *See* IRC § 453(c).

- **Virtual Currency.** Virtual currency is a digital medium of exchange. "Bitcoin is one example of a convertible virtual currency. Bitcoin can be digitally traded between users and can be purchased for, or exchanged into, U.S. dollars, Euros, and other real or virtual currencies." Notice 2014-21, 2014-16 I.R.B. 938. One issue concerning this currency is whether it is property for purposes of gain and loss recognition under the Code. The IRS has answered that question in the affirmative. *See id.,* Q&A 6. This means, for example, that a person who buys a bitcoin when it was worth $100 and spends it when it is worth $150 would have $50 of gross income when he or she spends the Bitcoin.

- **Human Egg Donors.** The Tax Court has held that a $20,000 payment received for service as a human egg donor did not constitute an amount realized from sale of property. Nor was it excludable from income as a recovery for personal injuries under section 104(a)(2). Instead the payment was taxable as compensation income. Perez v. Commissioner, 144 T.C. 51 (2015).

Chapter 4

Gifts and Inheritances

I. Assignment

Read: Internal Revenue Code: §§ 102; 1014(a), (b)(1), (b)(6), (b)(9), (e); 1015(a). Skim: §§ 74(c); 274(b)(1).

Treasury Regulations: §§ 1.102-1(a)–(c); 1.1001-1(e); 1.1014-2(a)(5); 1.1015-1, -4; Prop. Treas. Reg. § 1.102-1(f).

Text: Overview
Commissioner v. Duberstein
Wolder v. Commissioner
Related Matters

Complete the problems.

II. Problems

1. To what extent can the recipients in the following situations exclude the amounts received from income?

   (a) In Year 1, Stephen Foster assigns all interests in one of his copyrighted songs to his child, Chuck. In Year 2, Chuck collects $10,000 in royalties from the copyright.

   (b) Pursuant to an irrevocable trust he created, Adam Ant transferred title to his apartment building to Ted, the trustee. The trust agreement instructed Ted to pay the rental income from the building to Adam's child, Betty, for Betty's life. The remainder goes to Betty's children. Ted paid $10,000 in rents to Betty.

   (c) Lotte Lenya is employed as a full-time waitress at a small restaurant owned by her parents. In addition to her regular tips, Lotte receives $500 in cash tips for servicing the tables of family members, $300 more than she typically receives from non-family members. Lotte also receives a $100 check and plaque in recognition of her length of service. Before Thanksgiving, Lotte received, with all other employees, a $15 gift card redeemable at a local grocery-retail store. On Christmas, Lotte received from her parents a $1,000 TV under the tree.

   (d) Movie star, Sarah Bernhardt, is an Oscar nominee for "Best Actress." A well-known jeweler and fashion designer loaned her a $1 million diamond necklace and $200,000 gown to wear at the Academy Awards ceremony (this use was worth $10,000). All nominees, including Sarah, received a "swag bag" worth $30,000 containing a Rolex watch, a mobile phone, and false eyelashes made of mink.

Crier
no longer their
employer
No employee relationship
the congregation
received nothing in re...

(e) John Calvin received $2,000 from a church, of which he had formerly been Pastor for eighteen years. The amount was paid by the congregation pursuant to an adopted resolution "to pay John an honorarium of $2,000 annually with no pastoral authority or duty." John had made no request of the congregation that any amount be paid to him after his resignation, and he has performed no pastoral services for the church since his resignation.

(f) Mother dies and her will provides for the following: (1) $10,000 to Son; (2) $10,000 to Ralph Kramden, her pool boy, "in appreciation of his long and devoted service"; (3) $10,000 to Nephew pursuant to a written agreement under which Nephew agreed to not smoke cigarettes; and (4) $20,000 to Daughter, executrix of her estate, "in lieu of all compensation or commissions to which she would otherwise be entitled as executrix."

2. Catherine de'Medici deeded unimproved land to her daughter, Elisabeth, as a gift. At the time of gift, Catherine's basis was $40,000 and the land was worth $80,000.

(a) A year later, Elisabeth sold the land to a third party for $90,000. What are the tax consequences to Elisabeth upon receipt and subsequent sale of the land?

(b) Same as (a) except that the land was worth only $30,000 at the time Elisabeth received it. What are the tax consequences to Elisabeth upon receipt and subsequent sale of the land for $90,000? For $20,000? For $35,000?

(c) Same as (a) except that instead of giving the land to Elisabeth, Catherine sold it to Elisabeth for $60,000 and, a year later, Elisabeth sold the land to a third party for $90,000. What are the tax consequences to Catherine and Elisabeth.

(d) Same as (a) except that the land gifted to Elisabeth was subject to a $60,000 mortgage which Elisabeth assumed. What are the tax consequences to Catherine and Elisabeth?

(e) Same as (a) except that instead of giving the lot to Elisabeth, Catherine devised the land to Elisabeth when it is worth $80,000. A year later Elisabeth sold the land for $90,000. What are the tax consequences to Elisabeth?

3. Husband and Wife live in Idaho, a community property state. Several years ago, they purchased investment property for $100,000. This year, Husband dies when the property is worth $500,000.

(a) What will Wife's basis be if this is community property and Husband left his one-half to Wife?

(b) What will Wife's basis be if this is community property and Husband left his one-half to his administrative assistant?

(c) What will Wife's basis be if this is joint tenancy property and Wife gets Husband's one-half by operation of law?

III. Overview

Although gross income is a very broad concept, there are limitations on its meaning. As we learned in Chapter 2, Congress decided to exclude (or partially exclude) certain types of receipts or benefits from the income tax base. Skim IRC §§ 101–140. Each statutory exclusion addresses some particular congressional concern or achieves some particular goal. For example, section 104 excludes from gross income damages received in certain tort actions, perhaps reflecting congressional compassion for those who suffer personal physical injury or sickness. Section 121 excludes gain from the sale of a taxpayer's principle residence, promoting the goal of eliminating tax considerations from the decision to move from one home to another. Section 132 excludes certain fringe benefits received from an employer, in part reflecting congressional concern about administrative convenience. These and other statutory exclusions will be addressed in later chapters. This chapter will address section 102, the longstanding exclusion rule for gifts and inheritances and will consider the correlative basis rules that apply when property is acquired by gift or devise.

A. General Exclusionary Rule for Gifts and Inheritances — § 102(a)

1. Exclusion for Inter Vivos Gifts

Assume Parent gives shares of stock of ABC, Inc. to Child. Should the value of the stock be included in Child's gross income? The stock clearly represents an accession to Child's wealth and, absent any administrative or statutory exception, should be included in gross income. Section 102(a), however, specifically excludes the value of property "acquired by gift" from gross income. Although the Code does not define "gift" for income tax purposes, the Supreme Court has established criteria for determining whether a particular transfer is a gift. Review carefully *Commissioner v. Duberstein*, included in the materials. Is the meaning of gift for income tax purposes subjective or objective? To determine whether Child, in the example above, can exclude the value of the stock from income, what additional facts would you need to know?

2. Exclusion for Bequests, Devises, and Inheritances

What if Parent dies and Parent's will leaves shares of stock of ABC, Inc. to Child? Section 102(a) also provides that the value of property acquired by "bequest, devise, or inheritance" is excludable. The phrase "bequest, devise, or inheritance" refers to property "received under a will or under statutes of descent and distribution." Treas. Reg. § 1.102-1(a). The Supreme Court has held that the exclusion also applies to a settlement obtained in a will contest action. Lyeth v. Hoey, 305 U.S. 188 (1938). However, not everything received under a will is excludable. As illustrated in *Wolder v. Commissioner*, excerpted below, *Duberstein* must be taken into account.

3. Policy Reasons Behind Section 102(a)

What is the justification for excluding gifts and bequests from gross income? Some commentators argue that the only justification is a political one. Others believe that the exclusion is a matter of administrative convenience. Life is full of gifting activities, especially within families, and it would be administratively burdensome both for taxpayers, who would have to keep track of all gifts received during the year, and for the IRS, which would have to enforce tax liability. Still others justify the exclusion on the ground that gifts are subject to federal wealth transfer taxes, and so should be excluded from gross income to avoid excessive taxation. The wealth transfer taxes are considered in Chapter 41. *See* IRC § 2001 (imposing on decedents an estate tax on the transfer of property at death); IRC § 2501 (imposing on donors a gift tax on making inter vivos gifts). However, since only a small fraction of taxpayers are subject to gift and estate taxes, this argument is thin.

It should be noted that the *Duberstein* test for determining whether a transfer is excludable from gross income does not apply to transfers between spouses. When property is transferred to a spouse (or to a former spouse if the transfer is incident to a divorce), the property is treated by the Code as received by the transferee spouse as a gift and is excluded from gross income. IRC § 1041(b)(1). The justification for this special statutory rule reflects the congressional view that spouses are a single economic unit and transfers within that unit should not be taxed. With respect to divorcing spouses, the rationale is more appropriately considered a congressional effort to reduce stress in already difficult circumstances by eliminating immediate tax consequences.

It should also be noted that the exclusion for gifts does not apply to prizes, awards, or scholarships, which have their own special statutory rules for inclusion or exclusion. IRC §§ 74, 117.

B. Statutory Limitations on the Exclusion — § 102(b) and § 102(c)

The broad exclusionary rule of section 102(a) is subject to important limitations. The exclusion does not apply to *income* from property received by gift, bequest, devise, or inheritance. IRC § 102(b)(1). Return to the original example above; even if we conclude that the stock Child received is a gift and so is excluded from Child's gross income, the amount of any dividends she subsequently receives from the stock cannot be excluded. Similarly, the exclusion does not apply if the gift itself is only the income from property rather than the actual property. IRC § 102(b)(2). For example, if Parent transfers the stock to a trust and only gives Child the right to income from the trust corpus, the income cannot be excluded. These limitations clearly prevent donees and heirs from living on income from property without paying any tax.

Another limitation on the broad exclusion for gifts applies to gifts given in the employment setting. In fact, the Code clearly denies gift classification to "any amount transferred by or for an employer, to or for the benefit of an employee." IRC § 102(c). Despite the seemingly broad congressional intent to tax all payments by employers to employees, there are a few exceptions. For example, the regulations carve out an exception for "extraordinary transfers to the natural objects of an employer's bounty ... if the employee can show that the transfer was not made in recognition of the employee's employment." Prop. Treas. Reg. § 1.102-1(f)(2). Section 74(c) provides that certain "employee achievement awards" are not included in an employee's gross income. Section 132(e) excludes from an employee's income certain "de minimis" fringe benefits. These specific statutory rules of exclusion override section 102(c)'s broader statutory rule of inclusion. This rule, that specific language controls over general language, is a widely employed canon of statutory construction that exists beyond the area of taxation.

C. Basis of Property Received by Gift, Bequest, Devise, or Inheritance

In Chapter 3, we learned about the importance of determining "basis" in property however acquired. A taxpayer's basis in property dictates the maximum amount of cost-recovery deductions (depreciation deductions) allowed with respect to the property, and also impacts the amount of gain or loss realized upon a subsequent disposition of the property. A taxpayer's basis in purchased property is generally its cost. IRC § 1012. What is a taxpayer's basis in property acquired by gift or inheritance?

1. Property Acquired by Gift

In the case of property acquired by gift, the donee's basis is generally the same basis the donor had in the property (this is called "transferred basis"). IRC §§ 1015(a), 7701(a)(43). Having a donee of gifted property take the donor's basis results in any gain that accrued while the donor held the property being shifted to the donee, and such gain being realized by the donee on a later disposition of the property. While this may seem unfair to donees, the alternative, taxing donors at the time of gift on gain that accrued in their hands, would involve obvious valuation problems and perhaps discourage giving. In addition, donees may be in a more liquid position than donors when they later dispose of the property and realize gain, and so will have the assets to pay the tax on the gain.

Although Congress is willing to shift accrued gain from a donor to a donee through the concept of transferred basis, Congress is unwilling to shift accrued losses from a donor to a donee. Read carefully the "except" clause in section 1015(a). Note the important exception to the general transferred basis rule that applies whenever the value of gifted property (at the time of gift) is less than the donor's basis in the property. In such a case, *for purposes of determining gain* by the donee on a later sale, the general rule still applies and the donee uses the donor's basis. However, *for purposes of determining loss* by the donee on a later sale, the exception applies. The donee's basis is not the donor's basis, but instead is the lower fair market value of the property. The effect of this exception is as follows: If a donee is gifted property that has declined in value in the donor's hands and the property continues to decline in value in the donee's hands, the donee's loss on a later sale of the property is limited to only the loss that accrued in the donee's hands.

To illustrate these basis rules, assume Parent paid $100 for stock in ABC, Inc. and later gave the stock to Child when the stock was worth only $90. If Child later sells the stock for $105, the Child's basis *for purposes of determining gain* would be $100 (the general rule). If, however, Child later sells the stock for $85, the Child's basis *for purposes of determining loss* would be $90 (the exception). These basis rules create an interesting situation if Child later sells the stock between $90 and $100. For example, if Child later sells the stock for $95, there is neither gain nor loss. The basis for determining gain is $100; therefore, there is no gain. The basis for determining loss is $90; therefore, there is no loss. Treas. Reg. § 1.1015-1(a)(2), Example.

2. Property Acquired by Inheritance

Death is the last great tax loophole. The basis of property acquired from a decedent is not the decedent's basis as one might expect. Instead, it is generally the fair market value of the property on the date of decedent's death. *See* IRC § 1014(a) (providing that the basis of property in the hands of a person to whom the property *passed* from a decedent shall be the fair market value of the property at the date of the decedent's death). *See also* IRC § 1014(b)(1) (providing that property shall be considered to have *passed* from the decedent if the property was acquired by bequest, devise, or inheritance).

In the case of *appreciated* property, therefore, an heir takes a *stepped-up* basis in the property equal to its fair market value at the date of decedent's death. This, in effect, wipes out the potential taxable gain lurking in the property. Because potential gain can escape income tax, section 1014 is often an incentive to hold onto appreciated property until death; rather than selling or making an inter vivos gift of such property, the owner feels locked into holding on to it. Despite this "lock-in" effect, section 1014 is justified on several grounds. Some argue that the special basis rule for death transfers is necessary because of the heavy administrative burdens that accompany tracing a decedent's basis. Others argue that subjecting appreciation to the income tax would be excessive in light of the fact that appreciated property is also subject to the estate tax at death. This justification is less plausible in light of the current high threshold level for estate tax, as discussed more fully in Chapter 41.

It should be noted that under section 1014(a), only the portion of property that "passes" from the decedent receives a stepped-up basis. In common-law states, property jointly owned by a husband and wife is treated as half-owned by each. Therefore, a surviving spouse is entitled to a stepped-up basis only in the decedent spouse's half of the property that passes to the surviving spouse. *See* IRC §§ 1014(b)(9) & 2040(b)(1). The basis of the surviving spouse's one-half share is not stepped up. In community property states, each spouse is also treated as owning one-half of community property. However, under section 1014(b)(6), the basis of a surviving spouse's one-half share of community property is stepped up to fair market value on the date of the decedent's death if at least one-half of the community property is included in the decedent's gross estate for estate tax purposes. As a result, if a decedent transfers his half of community property to his surviving spouse, the surviving spouse will have a stepped-up basis in both halves of the community property even though only one-half of the property actually passed and was included in the decedent's estate for estate tax purposes. This special basis rule for community property was enacted in 1948 to equalize the tax treatment of persons in community property states and non-community property states. In common law states, if practically all the wealth of a married couple was the property of one spouse, then the surviving spouse would have a stepped-up basis in most of the property if it passed from the decedent to the surviving spouse. Today the community property basis step up rule lacks any logical foundation since joint ownership by spouses is much more the norm in non-community property states. For further discussion of section 1014(b)(6) and a call for its repeal, see Paul L. Caron & Jay A. Soled, *New Prominence of Tax Basis in Estate Planning*, 150 Tax Notes 1569 (Mar. 28, 2016).

3. Basis and Tax Planning

Tax planning is a term of art that refers to the structuring of a transaction or relationship to maximize its tax benefits. The disparate basis rules for property acquired by gift (section 1015) and property acquired from a decedent (section 1014) create tax planning opportunities. If a person has properties with varying bases and is interested in making some inter vivos gifts, he should consider giving away properties with higher bases and holding onto and passing at death properties with lower bases. This minimizes the total amount of gain taxed to the donees and heirs upon later dispositions of the properties.

Congress foreclosed some tax planning opportunities within the basis provisions. For example, assume Parent gives highly appreciated property to terminally ill Grandparent. Within a year, Grandparent dies and bequeaths the property back to Parent. Is Parent's basis in the property its fair market value at the date of Grandparents death? No. Notice section 1014(e), a very narrow provision that prevents Parent from playing this game to receive a stepped-up basis in the property. The section is narrow in that it is triggered only if the decedent dies within a year of the original transfer and only if the property is bequeathed by the decedent back to the original donor or donor's spouse. So, if Grandparent lived for more than one year after the original transfer, section 1014(e) would not apply and Parent would receive a stepped-up basis in the property. Or, if Grandparent died within one year of the original transfer, but bequeathed the property to Child of Parent, section 1014(e) would not apply and Child would receive a stepped-up basis in the property.

D. Part Sale, Part Gift Situations

Assume Parent owns stock with a basis of $5,000 and a fair market value of $15,000. Parent, out of love and affection, sells the stock to Child for only $7,500 (half of its value). This is a classic part-sale, part-gift situation that produces tax consequences to both Parent and Child.

From the donor's perspective an outright gift of property is not a realization event within the meaning of section 1001 as the donor is not receiving anything. A part-sale, part-gift of property, however, is a realization event for the donor as the donor is receiving some consideration, and has an amount realized. Recall the formula for determining gain realized from the sale or other disposition of property is "amount realized" minus "adjusted basis." IRC § 1001(a). In the part-sale, part-gift example above, Parent's amount realized is $7,500, the amount of money received from Child. What is Parent's adjusted basis for purposes of determining gain? Should it be the full $5,000 basis in the property? Or, should it be only 50% of the full basis since the amount realized is only 50% of the fair market value of the property? The regulations provide that Parent can recover the full $5,000 basis in the property. Accordingly, in this example, Parent has gain realized of only $2,500 ($7,500 AR minus $5,000 AB). Treas. Reg. § 1.1001-1(e). Note that in the case of a part-sale, part-gift to a charitable organization, the result would be different. See section 1011(b), which governs this type of transaction.

It should also be noted that no loss is ever allowed in a part-sale, part-gift situation. Treas. Reg. § 1.1001-1(e). Thus, if Parent sells the stock to Child for less than $5,000, no loss would be allowed to Parent. What do you think is the reason for this loss disallowance rule?

Where a transfer is in part a sale and in part a gift, the transferee has no income. IRC § 102(a). The transferee's basis is the greater of the amount paid by the transferee or the transferor's adjusted basis at the time of the transfer. Treas. Reg. § 1.1015-4. In the example above, the basis of the stock in Child's hands would be $7,500. Notice how this makes sense. If Child sells the stock the next day at its fair market value ($15,000), Child realizes gain of $7,500. Recall Parent's realized gain on the part-sale, part-gift was $2,500; now add this to Child's realized gain on later sale of the stock, $7,500; this sum is the total gain that was lurking in the property in Parent's hands ($10,000)!

IV. Materials

Commissioner v. Duberstein

363 U.S. 278 (1960)

MR. JUSTICE BRENNAN delivered the opinion of the Court.

The taxpayer, Duberstein, was president of the Duberstein Iron & Metal Company, a corporation with headquarters in Dayton, Ohio. For some years the taxpayer's company had done business with Mohawk Metal Corporation, whose headquarters were in New York City. The president of Mohawk was one Berman. The taxpayer and Berman had generally used the telephone to transact their companies' business with each other, which consisted of buying and selling metals. The taxpayer testified, without elaboration, that he knew Berman "personally" and had known him for about seven years. From time to time in their telephone conversations, Berman would ask Duberstein whether the latter knew of potential customers for some of Mohawk's products in which Duberstein's company itself was not interested. Duberstein provided the names of potential customers for these items.

One day in 1951 Berman telephoned Duberstein and said that the information Duberstein had given him had proved so helpful that he wanted to give the latter a present. Duberstein stated that Berman owed him nothing. Berman said that he had a Cadillac as a gift for Duberstein, and that the latter should send to New York for it; Berman insisted that Duberstein accept the car, and the latter finally did so, protesting however that he had not intended to be compensated for the information. At the time Duberstein already had a Cadillac and an Oldsmobile, and felt that he did not need another car. Duberstein testified that he did not think Berman would have sent him the Cadillac if he had not furnished him with information about the customers. It appeared that Mohawk later deducted the value of the Cadillac as a business expense on its corporate income tax return.

Duberstein did not include the value of the Cadillac in gross income for 1951, deeming it a gift. The Commissioner asserted a deficiency for the car's value against him, and in proceedings to review the deficiency the Tax Court affirmed the Commissioner's determination. It said that "The record is significantly barren of evidence revealing any intention on the part of the payor to make a gift. The only justifiable inference is that the automobile was intended by the payor to be remuneration for services rendered to it by Duberstein." The Court of Appeals for the Sixth Circuit reversed. 265 F.2d 28.

The exclusion of property acquired by gift from gross income under the federal income tax laws was made in the first income tax statute passed under the authority of the Sixteenth Amendment, and has been a feature of the income tax statutes ever since. The meaning of the term "gift" as applied to particular transfers has always been a matter of contention. Specific and illuminating legislative history on the point does not appear to exist. Analogies and inferences drawn from other revenue provisions, such as the estate and gift taxes, are dubious. The meaning of the statutory term has been shaped largely by the decisional law. With this, we turn to the contentions made by the Government in these cases.

First. The Government suggests that we promulgate a new "test" in this area to serve as a standard to be applied by the lower courts and by the Tax Court in dealing with the numerous cases that arise. We reject this invitation. We are of opinion that the governing principles are necessarily general and have already been spelled out in the opinions of this Court, and that the problem is one which, under the present statutory framework, does not lend itself to any more definitive statement that would produce a talisman for the solution of concrete cases. The cases at bar are fair examples of the settings in which the problem usually arises. They present situations in which payments have been made in a context with business overtones—an employer making a payment to a retiring employee; a businessman giving something of value to another businessman who has been of advantage to him in his business. In this context, we review the law as established by the prior cases here.

The course of decision here makes it plain that the statute does not use the term "gift" in the common-law sense, but in a more colloquial sense. This Court has indicated that a voluntarily executed transfer of his property by one to another, without any consideration or compensation therefor, though a common-law gift, is not necessarily a "gift" within the meaning of the statute. For the Court has shown that the mere absence of a legal or moral obligation to make such a payment does not establish that it is a gift. Old Colony Trust Co. v. Commissioner, 279 U.S. 716, 730. And, importantly, if the payment proceeds primarily from "the constraining force of any moral or legal duty," or from "the incentive of anticipated benefit" of an economic nature, Bogardus v. Commissioner, 302 U.S. 34, 41, it is not a gift. And, conversely, "[w]here the payment is in return for services rendered, it is irrelevant that the donor derives no economic benefit from it." Robertson v. United States, 343 U.S. 711, 714. A gift in the statutory sense, on the other hand, proceeds from a "detached and disinterested generosity," Commissioner v. LoBue, 351 U.S. 243, 246, "out of affection, respect, admiration, charity or like impulses." Robertson v. United States, *supra*, 343 U.S. at 714. And in this regard, the most critical consideration, as the Court was agreed in the leading case here, is the transferor's "intention." Bogardus v. Commissioner, 302 U.S. 34, 43. "What controls is the intention with which payment, however voluntary, has been made." *Id.* at 45 (dissenting opinion).

The Government says that this "intention" of the transferor cannot mean what the cases on the common-law concept of gift call "donative intent." With that we are in agreement, for our decisions fully support this. Moreover, the *Bogardus* case itself makes it plain that the donor's characterization of his action is not determinative — that there must be an objective inquiry as to whether what is called a gift amounts to it in reality. It scarcely needs adding that the parties' expectations or hopes as to the tax treatment of their conduct in themselves have nothing to do with the matter.

It is suggested that the *Bogardus* criterion would be more apt if rephrased in terms of "motive" rather than "intention." We must confess to some skepticism as to whether such a verbal mutation would be of any practical consequence. We take it that the proper criterion, established by decision here, is one that inquires what the basic reason for his conduct was in fact — the dominant reason that explains his action in making the transfer. Further than that we do not think it profitable to go.

Second. The Government's proposed "test," while apparently simple and precise in its formulation, depends frankly on a set of "principles" or "presumptions" derived from the decided cases, and concededly subject to various exceptions; and it involves various corollaries, which add to its detail. Were we to promulgate this test as a matter of law, and accept with it its various presuppositions and stated consequences, we would be passing far beyond the requirements of the cases before us, and would be painting on a large canvas with indeed a broad brush. The Government derives its test from such propositions as the following: That payments by an employer to an employee, even though voluntary, ought, by and large, to be taxable; that the concept of a gift is inconsistent with a payment's being a deductible business expense; that a gift involves "personal" elements; that a business corporation cannot properly make a gift of its assets. The Government admits that there are exceptions and qualifications to these propositions. We think, to the extent they are correct, that these propositions are not principles of law but rather maxims of experience that the tribunals which have tried the facts of cases in this area have enunciated in explaining their factual determinations. Some of them simply represent truisms: it doubtless is, statistically speaking, the exceptional payment by an employer to an employee that amounts to a gift. Others are overstatements of possible evidentiary inferences relevant to a factual determination on the totality of circumstances in the case: it is doubtless relevant to the over-all inference that the transferor treats a payment as a business deduction, or that the transferor is a corporate entity. But these inferences cannot be stated in absolute terms. Neither factor is a shibboleth. The taxing statute does not make nondeductibility by the transferor a condition on the "gift" exclusion; nor does it draw any distinction, in terms, between transfers by corporations and individuals, as to the availability of the "gift" exclusion to the transferee. The conclusion whether a transfer amounts to a "gift" is one that must be reached on consideration of all the factors.

Third. Decision of the issue presented in these cases must be based ultimately on the application of the fact-finding tribunal's experience with the mainsprings of human conduct to the totality of the facts of each case. The nontechnical nature of the statutory standard, the close relationship of it to the date of practical human experience, and the multiplicity of relevant factual elements, with their various combinations, creating the necessity of ascribing the proper force to each, confirm us in our conclusion that primary weight in this area must be given to the conclusions of the trier of fact.

This conclusion may not satisfy an academic desire for tidiness, symmetry and precision in this area, any more than a system based on the determinations of various fact-finders ordinarily does. But we see it as implicit in the present statutory treatment of the exclusion for gifts, and in the variety of forums in which federal income tax cases can be tried. If there is fear of undue uncertainty or overmuch litigation, Congress may make more precise its treatment of the matter by singling out certain factors and making them determinative of the matters, as it has done in one field of the "gift" exclusion's former application, that of prizes and awards. Doubtless diversity of result will tend to be lessened somewhat since federal income tax decisions, even those in tribunals of first instance turning on issues of fact, tend to be reported, and since there may be a natural tendency of professional triers of fact to follow one another's determinations, even as to factual matters. But the question here remains basically one of fact, for determination on a case-by-case basis.

Fourth. A majority of the Court is in accord with the principles just outlined. And, applying them to the *Duberstein* case, we are in agreement, on the evidence we have set forth, that it cannot be said that the conclusion of the Tax Court was "clearly erroneous." It seems to us plain that as trier of the facts it was warranted in concluding that despite the characterization of the transfer of the Cadillac by the parties and the absence of any obligation, even of a moral nature, to make it, it was at bottom a rec-ompense for Duberstein's past services, or an inducement for him to be of further service in the future. We cannot say with the Court of Appeals that such a conclusion was "mere suspicion" on the Tax Court's part. To us it appears based in the sort of informed experience with human affairs that fact-finding tribunals should bring to this task.

Accordingly, the judgment of this Court is that the judgment of the Court of Appeals is reversed.

It is so ordered.

Wolder v. Commissioner
493 F.2d 608 (2d Cir. 1974)

OAKES, Circuit Judge:

These two cases, involving an appeal and cross-appeal in the individual taxpayer's case and an appeal by the Commissioner in the estate taxpayer's case, essentially turn on one question: whether an attorney contracting to and performing lifetime legal services for a client receives income when the client, pursuant to the contract, bequeaths a substantial sum to the attorney in lieu of the payment of fees during the client's lifetime. In the individual taxpayer's case, the Tax Court held that the fair market value of the stock and cash received under the client's will constituted taxable income under section 61, I.R.C. of 1954, and was not exempt from taxation as a bequest under section 102 of the Code. From this ruling the taxpayers, Victor R. Wolder, the attorney, and his wife, who signed joint returns, appeal.

There is no basic disagreement as to the facts. On or about October 3, 1947, Victor R. Wolder, as attorney, and Marguerite K. Boyce, as client, entered into a written agreement which, after reciting Mr. Wolder's past services on her behalf in an action against her ex-husband for which he had made no charge, consisted of mutual promises, first on the part of Wolder to render to Mrs. Boyce "such legal services as she shall in her opinion personally require from time to time as long as both ... shall live and not to bill her for such services," and second on the part of Mrs. Boyce to make a codicil to her last will and testament giving and bequeathing to Mr. Wolder or to his estate "my 500 shares of Class B common stock of White Laboratories, Inc." or "such other ... securities" as might go to her in the event of a merger or consolidation of White Laboratories. Subsequently, in 1957, White Laboratories did merge into Schering Corp. and Mrs. Boyce received 750 shares of Schering common and 500 shares of Schering convertible preferred. In 1964 the convertible preferred was redeemed for $15,845. In a revised will dated April 23, 1965, Mrs. Boyce, true to the agreement with Mr. Wolder, bequeathed to him or his estate the sum of $15,845 and the 750 shares of common stock of Schering Corp. There is no dispute but that Victor R. Wolder had rendered legal services to Mrs. Boyce over her lifetime (though apparently these consisted largely of revising her will) and had not billed her therefor so that he was entitled to performance by her under the agreement, on which she had had a measure of independent legal advice. At least the New York Surrogate's Court (DiFalco, J.) ultimately so found in contested proceedings in which Mrs. Boyce's residuary legatees contended that the will merely provided for payment of the debt and took the position that Wolder was not entitled to payment until he proved the debt in accordance with § 212, New York Surrogate's Court Act.

Wolder argues that the legacy he received under Mrs. Boyce's will is specifically excluded from income by virtue of section 102(a), I.R.C. of 1954, which provides that "Gross Income does not include the value of property acquired by gift, bequest, devise or inheritance...." *See also* Treas. Reg. § 1.102-1(a). The individual taxpayer, as did dissenting Judge Qualy below, relies upon United States v. Merriam, 263 U.S. 179 (1923), and its progeny for the proposition that the term "bequest" in section 102(a) has not been restricted so as to exclude bequests made on account of some consideration flowing from the beneficiary to the decedent. In *Merriam* the testator made cash bequests to certain persons who were named executors of the estate, and these bequests were "in lieu of all compensation or commissions to which they would otherwise be entitled as executors or trustees." 263 U.S. at 184. The Court held nevertheless that the legacies were exempt from taxation, drawing a distinction — which in a day and age when we look to substance and not to form strikes us as of doubtful utility — between cases where "compensation [is] fixed by will for services to be rendered by the executor and where a legacy [is paid] to one upon the implied condition that he shall clothe himself with the character of executor." 263 U.S. at 187. In the former case, Mr. Justice Sutherland said, the executor "must perform the services to earn the compensation" while in the latter case "he need do no more than in good faith comply with the condition [that he be executor] in order to receive the bequest." The Court went on to take the view that the provision in the will that the bequest was in lieu of commissions was simply "an expression of the testator's will that the executor shall not receive statutory allowances for the services he may render."

But we think that *Merriam* is inapplicable to the facts of this case, for here there is no dispute but that the parties did contract for services and — while the services were limited in nature — there was also no question but that they were actually rendered. Thus the provisions of Mrs. Boyce's will, at least for federal tax purposes, went to satisfy her obligation under the contract. The contract in effect was one for the postponed payment of legal services, i.e., by a legacy under the will for services rendered during the decedent's life.

Moreover, the Supreme Court itself has taken an entirely different viewpoint from *Merriam* when it comes to interpreting section 102(a), or its predecessor, section 22(b)(3), I.R.C. of 1939, in reference to what are gifts. In Commissioner v. Duberstein, 363 U.S. 278 (1960), the Court held that the true test is whether in actuality the gift is a bona fide gift or simply a method for paying compensation. This question is resolved by an examination of the intent of the parties, the reasons for the transfer, and the parties' performance in accordance with their intentions — "what the basic reason for [the donor's] conduct was in fact — the dominant reason that explains his action in making the transfer." 363 U.S. at 286.

Indeed, it is to be recollected that section 102 is, after all, an exception to the basic provision in section 61(a) that "Except as otherwise provided in this subtitle, gross income means all income from whatever source derived, including ... (1) Compensation for services, including fees, commissions and similar items...." The congressional purpose is to tax income comprehensively. Commissioner v. Jacobson, 336 U.S. 28, 49 (1949). A transfer in the form of a bequest was the method that the parties chose to compensate Mr. Wolder for his legal services, and that transfer is therefore subject to taxation, whatever its label whether by federal or by local law may be.

Taxpayer's argument that he received the stock and cash as a "bequest" under New York law and the decisions of the surrogates is thus beside the point. New York law does, of course, control as to the extent of the taxpayer's legal rights to the property in question, but it does not control as to the characterization of the property for federal income tax purposes. New York law cannot be decisive on the question whether any given transfer is income under section 61(a) or is exempt under section 102(a) of the Code. We repeat, we see no difference between the transfer here made in the form of a bequest and the transfer under *Commissioner v. Duberstein, supra*, which was made without consideration, with no legal or moral obligation, and which was indeed a "common-law gift," but which was nevertheless held not to be a gift excludable under section 102(a).

Judgment in the appeal of Victor R. Wolder and Marjorie Wolder affirmed.

V. Related Matters

- **Business Gifts**. A donor may be entitled to deduct business gifts as an expense. IRC § 162 (discussed more fully in Chapter 7). Section 274(b)(1), however, generally limits the deductible amount of business gifts to $25 per donee per year. But note, the $25 ceiling applies only to non-employee business gifts. This is because section 274(b)(1) specifically defines the term gift as an item excludable from the recipient's gross income under section 102. Since employee gifts are includable in gross income under section 102(c), they are not subject to the section 274(b)(1) ceiling.

- **Income Tax Consequences to Donor**. A gift of property is not a realization event within the meaning of section 1001(a). Thus, a donor generally has no *income tax* consequences when making a gift. There are exceptions. First, a donor may have gain on a gift of encumbered property, with the relief of liability treated as amount realized. Recall the *Crane* case from Chapter 3. Second, a donor may have gain on a transfer that is in part a sale and in part a gift, as discussed above. Third, a donor may have gain at the time of gift if the donor previously expensed the property under section 179 and gives the property away before the end of the property's recovery period. IRC § 179(d)(10) (discussed more fully in Chapter 19).

- **Gift and Estate Tax Consequences to Donor.** A donor may have to pay *gift tax* or *estate tax* depending on the size and timing of the gift. The gift tax is an excise tax imposed on the transfer of property by gift; the estate tax is an excise tax imposed on the transfer of property at death. The gift tax definition of the term gift is not the same as the income tax concept of gift. Both taxes, which are imposed on the donor/decedent, are discussed in Chapter 41. The income tax basis taken by the beneficiary cannot exceed the value reported on the decedent's estate tax return. IRC § 1014(f).

- **Ancillary Income Tax Consequences to Donee.** If the donor pays gift tax on the gift, the donee is entitled to increase her basis (but not above fair market value) by the amount of gift tax paid with respect to the gift that arose from appreciation. IRC § 1015(d)(1) & (6).

Chapter 5

Discharge of Indebtedness

I. Assignment

Read: Internal Revenue Code: §§ 61(a)(12); 108(a), (b)(1)–(2), (b)(5), (c), (d)(1)–(3), (e)(1)–(2), (e)(4)–(5), (f), (g); 1017(a), (b)(1)–(3). Skim § 166.

Treasury Regulations: §§ 1.61-12(a); 1.1001-2(a), 2(c) ex. 8; § 1.1017-1. Skim §§ 1.166-1(c), -2(a)–(b).

Text: Overview
United States v. Kirby Lumber Co.
Preslar v. Commissioner
Related Matters

Complete the problems.

II. Problems

1. Will Don Giovanni have any income in the following events? Assume Don is solvent at all times.

    (a) Don made a pledge to give Charity $10,000 and then reneged.

    (b) Don was a defendant in a civil case in which the plaintiff was seeking $100,000 for sexual harassment. Prior to the case proceeding to trial, Don accepted the plaintiff's offer to drop all financial claims in exchange for a signed apology that did not admit legal liability.

    (c) Same as (b) except that the court rendered judgment for the plaintiff, but the plaintiff agreed to ignore the judgment in exchange for a signed apology.

    (d) Don incurred a $5,000 gambling debt at a local casino which he disputed on the basis that the debt was unenforceable under state law. Don and the casino later agreed to settle the dispute for $1,000. Don ultimately paid only $500 to the casino and the casino never sought to collect the rest of the debt.

    (e) Don owed $2,500 to his employees for past services rendered, and had taken no deduction in that amount. The employees agreed to accept $2,000 in full satisfaction of Don's salary obligation.

    (f) Don owed $1,000 to his mother. Don paid off the debt with a painting with a value of $800 and an adjusted basis of $500.

2. Amadeus borrowed $100,000 from First Bank. Later, when Amadeus was insolvent, First Bank accepted a parcel of unencumbered land (with a value of $80,000 and an adjusted basis of $50,000) from Amadeus in full satisfaction of the recourse debt. Prior to the transfer, Amadeus' assets consisted of the parcel of land and some household effects with a total value of $45,000. Amadeus's liabilities included the $100,000 debt to First Bank and $40,000 indebtedness to another bank. In addition, Amadeus has personally guaranteed a $5,000 bank loan that his daughter took out and there is a "50/50 chance" he will have to pay it.

   (a) How much income, if any, must Amadeus report as a result of the settlement of the debt owed to First Bank?

   (b) What are the tax consequences to First Bank upon acceptance of the land in satisfaction of the debt? Specifically, what is First Bank's basis in the land, and is First Bank entitled to any deductions? *See* IRC § 166(a).

III. Overview

In Chapter 2, we learned that borrowed funds are not included in gross income because the borrower has assumed an obligation to repay the debt in full at some point in the future. Since any increase in assets is offset by an increase in liabilities of an equal amount, any accession to wealth is negated. Suppose, however, that the borrower does not pay back the loan, in whole or in part, or the lender subsequently forgives the debt. Is it not fair to say that the borrower has experienced, *at that time*, an accession to wealth that should be taxed? In *United States v. Kirby Lumber Co.*, included below, the Supreme Court held that the repayment of a debt at less than its face amount constituted income to the debtor. This concept was later codified in section 61(a)(12), which expressly includes in gross income the amount of a taxpayer's "discharge of indebtedness."

Different theories have been set forth to rationalize the concept of discharge-of-indebtedness income. Under the *Kirby Lumber* "balance sheet" theory, taxation is appropriate since the taxpayer has an increase in net worth due to the cancellation of an established liability for less than its face amount. Under another theory, discharge of indebtedness is income at the time of discharge since the debtor went untaxed at the time of the borrowing. In other words, borrowed funds were not included in income because of the obligation to repay, and the discharge of the obligation to repay removes the justification for the original borrowing exclusion.

A number of judicial and statutory exceptions to the discharge-of-indebtedness inclusion rule exist. These exceptions address questions such as: Is taxation appropriate if a debtor disputes the enforceability of a debt and subsequently settles the dispute for an amount less than the original debt? Is taxation appropriate if the cancellation of indebtedness is a gift to the debtor? Is taxation appropriate if at the time of discharge the debtor has no assets or wherewithal to pay tax on the discharge-of-indebtedness income?

A. "Contested Liability" or "Disputed Debt" Exception

A judicially-created "contested liability" exception to discharge-of-indebtedness income has evolved. Under the contested liability doctrine (also known as "disputed debt" doctrine), if a taxpayer disputes the original amount of a debt in good faith and later settles that dispute, the settled amount is treated as the amount of recognizable debt for tax purposes. Read carefully *Preslar v. Commissioner*, included in the materials below. Accordingly, if a borrower disagrees with a lender over the amount owed and subsequently settles that dispute for a lower amount, payment of the settled amount does not generate discharge-of-indebtedness income. In other words, the excess of the amount the lender originally said was owed over the amount the borrower paid may be disregarded.

The contested liability doctrine has generated much controversy. In *Preslar*, for example, the Tenth Circuit held that the contested liability doctrine applies only if the original amount of the debt is unliquidated (i.e., the amount of the debt must be disputed before the doctrine is triggered). Notice that the Tenth Circuit in *Preslar* criticized the Third Circuit's decision in Zarin v. Commissioner, 916 F.2d 110 (3d Cir. 1990), which treated liquidated and unliquidated debts alike. In *Zarin*, enforceability of the debt, not the amount of the debt owed, was in dispute. The Third Circuit emphasized that when a debt is unenforceable the amount of the debt is in dispute. Applying the contested liability doctrine, the Third Circuit concluded that there was no discharge-of-indebtedness income.

B. Bankruptcy and Insolvency Exceptions

In 1980, Congress added section 108, which excludes discharge-of-indebtedness income from gross income if the discharge occurs in certain circumstances, such as when the debtor is involved in a bankruptcy case or is insolvent. Section 108 was enacted as a response to the perceived harshness of requiring debtors to pay tax on debt discharge income at a time when they do not have the liquidity to pay the tax.

Section 108(a)(1)(A) provides that gross income does not include discharge-of-indebtedness income if the discharge occurs in a title 11 case. Under section 108(d)(2), a "title 11 case" is defined as any bankruptcy case (under Chapter 7, 11, 12, or 13 of the Bankruptcy Code) if the taxpayer is under the jurisdiction of the bankruptcy court and the discharge-of-indebtedness is granted by the court or pursuant to a plan approved by the court.

Section 108(a)(1)(B) provides that gross income does not include discharge-of-indebtedness income if the discharge occurs when the taxpayer is insolvent. The maximum amount excluded, however, cannot exceed the amount by which the debtor is insolvent. IRC § 108(a)(3). A taxpayer is insolvent to the extent his liabilities exceed the fair market value of his assets determined on the basis of assets and liabilities immediately before the discharge. IRC § 108(d)(3). An interesting issue is whether *contingent* liabilities should be treated as liabilities for purposes of applying the insolvency exception. For example, if a taxpayer has personally guaranteed another person's loan, should the potential obligation to pay the other person's loan be included in the amount of taxpayer's liabilities for purposes of determining the extent to which the taxpayer is insolvent? In addressing this question, the Ninth Circuit in *Merkel v. Commissioner* held that a taxpayer must prove "with respect to any obligation claimed to be a liability, that, as of the calculation date, it is more probable than not that he will be called upon to pay that obligation in the amount claimed." 192 F.3d 844, 850 (9th Cir. 1999).

There is a quid pro quo if income from discharge-of-indebtedness is excluded from gross income under the bankruptcy or insolvency exceptions. Under section 108(b), the taxpayer must reduce certain tax benefits (also known as "tax attributes") by the amount excluded. The tax attributes which must be reduced, and the order in which they must be reduced, are as follows: (1) net operating losses, (2) certain tax credit carryovers, (3) capital loss carryovers, (4) adjusted basis of property, (5) passive activity loss and credit carryovers, and (6) foreign tax credit carryovers. IRC § 108(b)(2). As an alternative to this ordering of attribute reduction, the taxpayer may first elect to reduce the adjusted basis of property by the amount excluded. IRC § 108(b)(5). Although such an election would cause the taxpayer to have more gain or less loss on a later sale of the property, the election preserves the immediate benefits of the other tax attributes, such as net operating loss deductions. Section 1017 and the regulations thereunder provide special rules for making the basis adjustment under section 108. *See* IRC § 1017(b)(1)–(2); *Skim* Treas. Reg. § 1.1017-1.

Other Exceptions: Section 108 contains additional exceptions, some of which are summarized in the Related Matters part of this chapter. Section 108(f) may be of interest to many law students, since it excludes from gross income the forgiveness of student loans. The exclusion, however, is contingent on a student working for a certain period of time in a specified profession such as a position in a public service organization. Section 108(f) was enacted to ensure professional participation in public service organizations. Many educational organizations, such as non-profit law school foundations, have designed loan repayment assistance programs so that loan amounts forgiven fall within the section 108(f) exclusion. Query: Is the section 108(f) exclusion that helpful in light of the fact that most students are insolvent anyway? Note that the Tax Cuts and Jobs Act of 2017 temporarily expanded the exclusion to include discharges of eligible student loans before 2026 due to the student's death or total and permanent disability.

C. Debt Discharge Outside the Scope of Debt Discharge Rules

Income from cancellation of indebtedness does not automatically fall within the scope of the debt discharge rules of sections 61(a)(12) and 108 discussed above. Rather, "debt discharge that is only a medium for some other form of payment, such as a gift or salary, is treated as that form of payment rather than under the debt discharge rules." Rev. Rul. 84-176, 1984-2 C.B. 34 (citing S. Rep. No. 1035, 96th Cong., 2d Sess. 8 n.6 (1980)).

Discharge of indebtedness by an employer may represent compensation income to an employee under section 61(a)(1). For example, if an employer loans money to an employee and later forgives the loan in lieu of paying the employee for a job he completes, that forgiveness would constitute compensation for services rendered under section 61(a)(1). The implication of classifying debt discharge income as section 61(a)(1) income, as opposed to section 61(a)(12) income, is that the bankruptcy and insolvency exclusions under section 108 are unavailable. Section 108 grants a possible exclusion only as to section 61(a)(12) income, and not to other categories of income.

Discharge of indebtedness may be treated as a gift and excluded from income under section 102. For example, if a grandparent loans money to a grandchild and then later forgives the loan, that forgiveness would likely constitute a gift excludable under section 102. If section 102 applies, the requirements of section 108 (e.g., insolvency) do not need to be satisfied, and there is no reduction in tax attributes. Of course, the intent of the lender must be considered before forgiveness is characterized as a gift. A cancellation of debt constitutes an excludable gift only if it proceeds from the lender's "detached and disinterested generosity ... out of affect, respect, admiration, charity or like impulses." Review *Commissioner v. Duberstein*, included in the Chapter 4 materials. Forgiveness of debt in a commercial or business setting will almost never constitute an excludable gift. *See* Commissioner v. Jacobson, 336 U.S. 28 (1949).

D. Discharge of Recourse Debt in Property Transactions

Recall from Chapter 3 that a transfer of property subject to a nonrecourse debt is a realization event, and that the entire amount of the nonrecourse debt must be included in amount realized for purposes of determining gain or loss. This is true even if the value of the property is less than the amount of the nonrecourse mortgage, which was clarified in the case of Commissioner v. Tufts, 461 U.S. 300 (1983).

The rule in *Tufts*, however, does not apply to recourse debt. Consider the following example: Taxpayer, a single individual, owned land subject to a recourse debt. When Taxpayer defaulted on the debt, Taxpayer negotiated an agreement with the bank whereby the bank took possession of the land and released Taxpayer from all liability for the amounts due on the debt. When the land was transferred pursuant to the agreement, its fair market value was $100,000, Taxpayer's adjusted basis in the land was $80,000, and the amount due on the debt was $120,000. It would appear that Taxpayer has $40,000 of *gain derived from dealing in property* under section 61(a)(3) and section 1001 ($120,000 AR minus $80,000 AB). Under these same facts, however, the IRS ruled that Taxpayer had: $20,000 of *gain derived from dealing in property* under section 61(a)(3), and $20,000 of *income from discharge of indebtedness* under section 61(a)(12). *See* Rev. Rul. 90-16, 1990-1 C.B. 12. According to the IRS, the transfer of the land is treated as a sale or other disposition only to the extent of the fair market value of the property transferred ($100,000), and Taxpayer realizes income from the discharge of indebtedness to the extent the amount of the recourse debt ($120,000) exceeds the fair market value of the land ($100,000). The reason this outcome makes sense is because, unlike the nonrecourse debt context, the bank could have sued Taxpayer for the excess of the mortgage amount over the amount it could realize by selling the property. Thus, the bank forgave that excess amount.

You may be wondering if bifurcating the transaction into two categories of gross income — section 61(a)(3) gain and section 61(a)(12) income — makes any difference. After all, Taxpayer still reports $40,000 of gross income. It does for a couple of reasons. One reason is that section 108 grants an exclusion to insolvent taxpayers only for section 61(a)(12) discharge-of-indebtedness income. The exclusion does not extend to any other income, such as section 61(a)(3) gains derived from dealings in property. *See* Gehl v. Commissioner, 50 F.3d 12 (8th Cir. 1995). *See also* Treas. Reg. § 1.1001-2(a)(2). Another reason is that discharge of indebtedness income is treated as ordinary income subject to the regular tax rates of section 1(a), whereas gain from dealing in property may be eligible for the reduced capital gains rates of section 1(h). See Chapter 17.

E. Tax Treatment of the Lender

If a lender discharges, in whole or in part, a borrower's liability, the lender may be entitled to a "bad debt" deduction under section 166. A "business" bad debt, whether partially or entirely worthless, is deductible as an "ordinary" loss to the extent charged off by the lender. A "nonbusiness" bad debt, if entirely worthless, is deductible as a "short term capital loss." *See* IRC § 166. As will be discussed in Chapter 17, capital loss deductions are not as valuable as ordinary loss deductions. In either case, two requirements must be met for a deduction. First, there must be a bona fide debt. Treas. Reg. § 1.166-1(c). Second, the debt must be "worthless within the tax year." Treas. Reg. § 1.166-2(a)–(b).

IV. Materials

United States v. Kirby Lumber Co.

284 U.S. 1 (1931)

Mr. Justice Holmes delivered the opinion of the Court.

In July 1923, the plaintiff, the Kirby Lumber Company, issued its own bonds for $12,126,800 for which it received their par value. Later in the same year it purchased in the open market some of the same bonds at less than par, the difference of price being $137,521.30. The question is whether this difference is a taxable gain or income of the plaintiff for the year 1923. By the Revenue Act of 1921, gross income includes "gains or profits and income derived from any source whatever," and by the Treasury Regulations that have been in force through repeated re-enactments, "If the corporation purchases and retires any of such bonds at a price less than the issuing price or face value, the excess of the issuing price or face value over the purchase price is gain or income for the taxable year." We see no reason why the Regulations should not be accepted as a correct statement of the law.

In Bowers v. Kerbaugh-Empire Co., 271 U.S. 170, the defendant in error owned the stock of another company that had borrowed money repayable in marks or their equivalent for an enterprise that failed. At the time of payment the marks had fallen in value, which so far as it went was a gain for the defendant in error, and it was contended by the plaintiff in error that the gain was taxable income. But the transaction as a whole was a loss, and the contention was denied. Here there was no shrinkage of assets and the taxpayer made a clear gain. As a result of its dealings it made available $137,521.30 [in] assets previously offset by the obligation of bonds now extinct. We see nothing to be gained by the discussion of judicial definitions. The defendant in error has realized within the year an accession to income, if we take words in their plain popular meaning, as they should be taken here.

Judgment reversed.

Preslar v. Commissioner
167 F.3d 1323 (10th Cir. 1999)

BRISCOE, Circuit Judge.

The Commissioner of Internal Revenue appeals the United States Tax Court's decision to redetermine the tax deficiency assessed against Layne and Sue Preslar for underpayment of 1989 federal income taxes. The Tax Court held the Preslars' settlement of a loan obligation for less than the face amount of the loan did not create taxable income because the contested liability/disputed debt exception to the general discharge-of-indebtedness income rule rendered the write-off nontaxable. We exercise jurisdiction pursuant to 26 U.S.C. § 7482(a)(1), and reverse and remand.

I.

Layne Preslar, a real estate agent of twenty-five years, commenced negotiations in 1983 to purchase a 2500-acre ranch near Cloudcroft, New Mexico. On July 12, 1983, after six months of talks, Layne and Sue Preslar agreed to purchase the ranch for $1 million, with the sale to be financed by Moncor Bank. The Preslars executed a $1 million promissory note in favor of Moncor Bank, secured by a mortgage on the ranch. The Preslars were to pay fourteen annual installments of $66,667, with interest at twelve percent per annum, with final payment due September 1, 1998.

The Preslars intended to develop the ranch as a sportsman's resort by subdividing 160 acres and selling one- to two-acre lots for cabins or vacation homes, and permitting lot owners to hunt and engage in other outdoor recreational activities on the remaining 2,340 acres. The goal was to sell each cabin lot for approximately $16,500, with total gross revenues exceeding $1.5 million. The Preslars' 1989 joint tax return indicates several lots sold for substantially higher amounts.

Moncor Bank permitted the Preslars to repay their loan by assigning the installment sales contracts of purchasers of cabin lots to Moncor Bank at a discount. There is no reference to this unique repayment arrangement in the loan documents. The first written description of this repayment method appears in a May 3, 1984, letter from Joseph Ferlo, a representative of Moncor Bank, to Layne Preslar. The arrangement is also discussed in an unsigned 1985 "Dealer Agreement" between Moncor Bank and the Preslars. When each cabin lot was sold, the Preslars assigned and physically transferred the written sales contract to Moncor Bank. In return, Moncor Bank credited the Preslars' debt obligation in an amount equal to 95 percent of the stated principal contract price, regardless of actual payments received from the purchaser. Moncor Bank received a security interest in each lot sold to protect its interests in the event a purchaser defaulted. Between September 1983 and August 1985, the Preslars sold nineteen cabin lots and had assigned most of the contracts to Moncor Bank prior to its declared insolvency. Moncor Bank had credited the Preslars' principal loan balance with approximately $200,000. Funds applied to interest are not included in this amount; thus, the aggregate amount of discounted installment contracts assigned to Moncor Bank exceeded $200,000.

In August 1985, Moncor Bank was declared insolvent and the Federal Deposit Insurance Corporation (FDIC) was appointed as receiver. The FDIC notified the Preslars of the insolvency and advised them to make all future payments on their loan to the FDIC. The FDIC refused to accept further assignments of sale contracts as repayment and ordered the Preslars to suspend sales of cabin lots. The Preslars complied with the suspension directive, but made no further payments on the loan.

The Preslars filed an action against the FDIC for breach of contract in September 1985, seeking an order requiring the FDIC to accept assignment of sales contracts as loan repayment. The parties settled the action in December 1988 after the FDIC agreed to accept $350,000 in full satisfaction of the Preslars' indebtedness. The Preslars borrowed the $350,000 from another bank and, after the funds were remitted to the FDIC, the original $1 million promissory note was marked "paid."

At the time of the settlement, the unpaid balance on the Preslars' loan was $799,463. The Preslars paid a total of $550,537 on the loan ($350,000 settlement plus $200,537 credited for assignment of sales contracts). Therefore, as a result of the settlement, the Preslars' outstanding debt obligation was reduced by $449,463 ($1 million less $550,537).

The Preslars did not include the $449,463 debt write-off as discharge-of-indebtedness income on their 1989 joint tax return. Rather, they opted to reduce their basis in the ranch by $430,000 pursuant to Internal Revenue Code § 108(e)(5). The Preslars' 1989 tax return was audited and they were assessed a deficiency because (1) they had realized $449,463 in discharge-of-indebtedness income, and (2) they were not eligible to treat such income as a purchase price adjustment under § 108(e)(5).

The Preslars sought a redetermination of the deficiency in United States Tax Court, insisting they were free to treat their settlement with the FDIC as a purchase price adjustment pursuant to § 108(e)(5) and/or common law. They supported this theory in part by claiming the FDIC's refusal to honor their repayment agreement with Moncor Bank amounted to an infirmity relating back to the original sale, thereby negating the general prohibition against treating debt reductions as purchase price adjustments.

At no time, however, did the Preslars dispute their underlying liability on the $1 million note.

The Commissioner responded that the Preslars could not invoke § 108(e)(5) because that provision applies only to situations where the *seller* of property agrees to reduce the amount of the purchaser's debt flowing from the property sale. The party responsible for reducing the Preslars' debt was not the seller but was the FDIC (as receiver for Moncor Bank), thereby rendering § 108(e)(5) inapplicable.

The Tax Court ruled in favor of the Preslars without addressing the purchase price adjustment issue. Instead, the court *sua sponte* invoked the contested liability doctrine and held the Preslars' unusual payment arrangement with Moncor Bank caused their liability for the full $1 million loan to be brought into question. The court determined the true amount of the Preslars' indebtedness was not firmly established until they settled with the FDIC; thus, no discharge-of-indebtedness income could have accrued to the Preslars as a result of the settlement.

II.

Decisions of the United States Tax Court are reviewed "in the same manner and to the same extent as decisions of the district courts in civil actions tried without a jury." 26 U.S.C. § 7482(a)(1). We review the Tax Court's factual findings for clear error and its legal conclusions de novo. The Preslars have the burden of proving the Commissioner's determinations are incorrect on factual issues.

Discharge-of-Indebtedness Income

Section 61(a) of the Internal Revenue Code broadly defines "gross income" as "all income from whatever source derived" except as expressly provided otherwise. The phrase is intended to capture all "accessions to wealth, clearly realized, and over which the taxpayers have complete dominion." Commissioner v. Glenshaw Glass Co., 348 U.S. 426, 431 (1955). From its enactment, the "sweeping scope" of this provision and its statutory predecessors has been consistently emphasized by the Supreme Court. *See* Commissioner v. Schleier, 515 U.S. 323, 327–28 (1995); *Glenshaw Glass*, 348 U.S. at 429–32 & n.11.

This case centers around the Commissioner's determination of the Preslars' discharge-of-indebtedness income after they settled their loan obligation with the FDIC in December 1988. The concept of discharge-of-indebtedness income, first articulated in United States v. Kirby Lumber Co., 284 U.S. 1 (1931), and later codified in 26 U.S.C. § 61(a)(12), requires taxpayers who have incurred a financial obligation that is later discharged in whole or in part, to recognize as taxable income the extent of the reduction in the obligation. Two rationales have been identified for this rule:

> This rule is based on the premise that the taxpayer has an increase in wealth due to the reduction in valid claims against the taxpayer's assets. In the alternative it has been suggested that taxation is appropriate because the consideration received by a taxpayer in exchange for [his] indebtedness is not included in income when received because of the obligation to repay and the cancellation of that obligation removes the reason for the original exclusion.

2 Jacob Mertens, Jr., Mertens Law of Federal Income Taxation § 11.01 (1996). Loans ordinarily are not taxable because the borrower has assumed an obligation to repay the debt in full at some future date. *See* Commissioner v. Tufts, 461 U.S. 300, 307 (1983). Discharge-of-indebtedness principles come into play, however, if that assumption of repayment proves erroneous. Otherwise, taxpayers could secure income with no resulting tax liability.

It is undisputed that the Preslars financed their purchase of the ranch in 1983 by executing a $1 million promissory note in favor of Moncor Bank. It is similarly uncontested that when the Preslars settled their lawsuit with the FDIC in 1988, thereby extinguishing all obligations arising from the 1983 loan, only $550,537 had been paid on the loan principal. Nevertheless, the Tax Court ruled the Preslars' underlying debt was disputed and fell within the judicially-created "contested liability" exception to discharge-of-indebtedness income.

Contested Liability/Disputed Debt Exception

The "contested liability" or, as it is occasionally known, "disputed debt" doctrine rests on the premise that if a taxpayer disputes the *original amount* of a debt in good faith, a subsequent settlement of that dispute is "treated as the amount of debt cognizable for tax purposes." Zarin v. Commissioner, 916 F.2d 110, 115 (3d Cir. 1990). In other words, the "excess of the original debt over the amount determined to have been due" may be disregarded in calculating gross income. *Id*. The few decisions that have interpreted this doctrine have generated considerable controversy.

In *Zarin*, the court revers[ed] the Commissioner's recognition of discharge-of-indebtedness income. The state gaming commission identified Zarin as a compulsive gambler and ordered an Atlantic City casino to refrain from issuing him additional credit, but the casino ignored the commission. When Zarin's debt surpassed $3.4 million, the casino filed a state action to collect the funds. Zarin initially denied liability on the grounds the casino's claim was unenforceable under New Jersey law. The parties later settled the dispute for $500,000. After Zarin failed to account for the debt write-off on his tax return, the Commissioner assessed a deficiency for approximately $2.9 million, the amount by which Zarin's underlying debt exceeded his settlement with the casino. The Tax Court affirmed. However, a divided Third Circuit held Zarin had no discharge-of-indebtedness income because, *inter alia*, his transaction with the casino arose from a contested liability. 916 F.2d at 115–16. Citing no authority, the majority reasoned that "when a debt is unenforceable, it follows that the amount of the debt, and not just the liability thereon, is in dispute." *Id*. at 116. Therefore, the $500,000 settlement "fixed the amount of loss and the amount of debt cognizable for tax purposes." *Id*.

The problem with the Third Circuit's holding is it treats liquidated and unliquidated debts alike. The whole theory behind requiring that the *amount* of a debt be disputed before the contested liability exception can be triggered is that only in the context of disputed debts is the Internal Revenue Service (IRS) unaware of the exact consideration initially exchanged in a transaction. The mere fact that a taxpayer challenges the enforceability of a debt in good faith does not necessarily mean he or she is shielded from discharge-of-indebtedness income upon resolution of the dispute. To implicate the contested liability doctrine, the original amount of the debt must be unliquidated. A total denial of liability is not a dispute touching upon the amount of the underlying debt. One commentator has observed:

> Enforceability of the debt … should not affect the tax treatment of the transaction. If the parties initially treated the transaction as a loan when the loan proceeds were received, thereby not declaring the receipt as income, then the transaction should be treated consistently when the loan is discharged and income should be declared in the amount of the discharge.

Gregory M. Giangiordano, *Taxation-Discharge of Indebtedness Income-Zarin v. Commissioner*, 64 TEMP. L. REV. 1189, 1202 n.88 (1991). A holding to the contrary would strain IRS treatment of unenforceable debts and, in large part, disavow the Supreme Court's mandate that the phrase "gross income" be interpreted as broadly as the Constitution permits. *See Glenshaw Glass*, 348 U.S. at 432 & n.11.

This conclusion is underscored by the Supreme Court's holding in *Tufts* that a non-recourse mortgage (i.e., taxpayer has no personal liability upon default) must be treated as an enforceable loan both when it is made and when it is discharged. 461 U.S. at 311–13. The Court reasoned that because the indebtedness is treated as a true debt when it is incurred, it must be treated as a true debt when it is discharged, with all the attendant tax consequences. *Id.* at 309–10. It seems evident from this ruling that if the distinction between the recourse and nonrecourse nature of a loan has no bearing on calculation of gross income, the enforceability of a debt should be of equally minimal importance. Of course, if the debt is unenforceable as a result of an infirmity at the time of its creation (e.g., fraud or misrepresentation), tax liability may be avoided through a purchase price reduction under 26 U.S.C. § 108(e)(5) or an "infirmity exception."

The Tax Court in this case and the court in *Zarin* cited United States v. Hall, 307 F.2d 238 (10th Cir. 1962), in support of their contested liability holdings. In *Hall*, the taxpayer incurred gambling losses at a Las Vegas club in an estimated range of $145,000 to $478,000. One of the owners of the club agreed to forgive the debt in return for a one-half interest in the taxpayer's cattle. Just prior to transfer of the interest in the cattle, which had a base value of $148,110, the parties mutually agreed to assess the taxpayer's losses at $150,000. The Commissioner sought to assess the taxpayer with $1,890 as discharge-of-indebtedness income. Without raising the contested liability doctrine, we rejected the Commissioner's position and held "a gambling debt, being unenforceable in every state, has but slight potential and does not meet the requirements of debt necessary to justify the mechanical operation of general rules of tax law relating to cancellation of debt." *Id.* at 241.

Whether *Hall* has continued viability is questionable in light of the Supreme Court's holding in *Tufts*. The emphasis on a taxpayer's lack of legal obligation to pay a gambling debt in *Hall* is difficult to reconcile with *Tufts'* disregard of the nonrecourse nature of a loan in calculating gross income. Even if parts of *Hall* remain viable, however, the opinion would offer little refuge to the Preslars. The debt in *Hall* was unliquidated. The taxpayer's underlying obligation, therefore, could not be assessed prior to settlement with the club owner. Such a scenario is not present here.

In this case, the Tax Court observed that "the unusual payment arrangement between [the Preslars] and Moncor Bank relating to the Bank loan casts significant doubt on [the Preslars'] liability for the total $1 million stated principal amount of the Bank loan." Tax Ct. Op. at 8. Accepting the Preslars' contention that their $1 million purchase price had been inflated and did not reflect the fair market value of the ranch, the Tax Court suggested the Preslars had agreed to the terms of the financing arrangement only after Moncor Bank assented to a favorable repayment scheme involving assignment of installment sales contracts. The court held when the FDIC refused to honor this payment arrangement, "a legitimate dispute arose regarding the nature and amount of [the Preslars'] liability on the Bank loan." *Id.* Only after the Preslars and the FDIC settled their subsequent lawsuit, the court reasoned, was the amount of liability on the loan finally established.

It is conceivable that two parties could negotiate a loan transaction in which the underlying amount of a debt is tied to the existence or nonexistence of some post-execution event. Indeed, the IRS has defined "indebtedness" as "an obligation, absolute and not contingent, to pay on demand or within a given time, in cash or another medium, a fixed amount." Treas. Reg. §1.108(b)-1(c) (1998). Contrary to the Tax Court's representations, however, there is no evidence of such an agreement here.

The Preslars advanced no competent evidence to support their theory that their loan obligation was linked to the repayment scheme. They maintain that, although they did not state it in writing, their acquiescence in the $1 million purchase price hinged on their being able to satisfy the debt through assignment of installment contracts. Thus, when the FDIC refused to honor the assignments, a concomitant reduction in their liability was necessary. In other words, the "FDIC could not enforce the ranch loan without abiding by the [unsigned] Dealer Agreement. The loan and the Dealer Agreement were two sides of an integrated transaction." Appellees' Br. at 4–5. Neither the May 1984 letter from Moncor Bank to Layne Preslar nor the unsigned 1985 Dealer Agreement, however, contains any statement evincing an intent to link the underlying liability with the repayment scheme. Further, if the parties desired the loan obligation to be inextricably intertwined with the repayment arrangement, that condition should have been memorialized in the loan document and not merely set out in a letter eight months after the loan was formalized. The dissent's protestations notwithstanding, Layne Preslar's own self-serving testimony regarding the intentions of the parties to the original loan agreement is not sufficient to support the Preslars' integrated transaction theory.

In addition, the Preslars' characterization of their dispute with the FDIC as the culmination of their dispute over the ranch loan is not faithful to the evidence. The dispute with the FDIC focused only on the terms of repayment; it did not touch upon the amount or validity of the Preslars' debt. This conclusion is highlighted by the relief sought from the FDIC. As an alternative to accepting assignment of contracts, the Preslars requested that the FDIC "substantially discount the remaining amount due on their loan." Such a position evidences the Preslars' recognition that they had a fixed and certain liability at the time the FDIC took control of their loan from Moncor Bank. In fact, Layne Preslar conceded he understood he was personally liable for the full amount of the $1 million note in the event he could not sell a sufficient number of lots. In sum, the Preslars' underlying indebtedness remained liquidated at all times.

Purchase Price Adjustment

Another method by which taxpayers can avoid discharge-of-indebtedness income is to classify their debt reductions as purchase price adjustments. This rule permits taxpayers to reflect their debt reduction by adjusting the basis of their property rather than recognizing an immediate gain as cancellation of indebtedness. Although this principle had been part of the common law for decades, Congress codified the rule as part of the Bankruptcy Tax Act of 1980, Pub. L. No. 96-589, § 2(a), 94 Stat. 3389, 3389–90 (1980) (codified at 26 U.S.C. § 108(e)(5)).

The Preslars cannot treat their settlement with the FDIC as a purchase price reduction. Section 108(e)(5) applies only to direct agreements between a purchaser and seller. S. Rep. No. 96-1035 at 16 (1980), *reprinted in* 1980 U.S.C.C.A.N. 7017, 7031. "If the debt has been transferred by the seller to a third party (whether or not related to the seller), or if the property has been transferred by the buyer to a third party (whether or not related to the buyer)," the purchase price reduction exception is not available and normal discharge-of-indebtedness rules control. *Id.* The seller in this case was High Nogal. Although Moncor Bank helped negotiate the terms of the sale, it did so only in its capacity as a mortgage holder. The Preslars make much of the fact that one of the signatories to the "Sellers Statement" memorializing the sale was a Moncor Bank representative. However, the vice-president of Moncor Bank testified the bank signed the document at the insistence of the title companies. As neither Moncor Bank nor its receiver, the FDIC, was the seller of the property, the loan settlement the Preslars negotiated with the FDIC does not permit them to invoke the debt reduction as a purchase price adjustment under § 108(e)(5).

III.

We REVERSE the Tax Court's vacatur of the Commissioner's determination of tax deficiency and imposition of untimely filing penalties and REMAND the case with instructions to enter judgment in favor of the Commissioner.

V. Related Matters

- **Section 108(a)(1)(C)** provides that gross income does not include discharge-of-indebtedness income if the taxpayer is engaged in the business of farming, even if the taxpayer is solvent. *See* IRC § 108(g) (providing special rules for "qualified farm indebtedness"). Any amount excluded results in a reduction in the taxpayer's tax attributes, as discussed above. IRC § 108(b)(4).

- **Section 108(a)(1)(D)** provides that a taxpayer may elect to exclude discharge-of-indebtedness income, subject to certain limitations, if the debt was incurred or assumed by a taxpayer in the acquisition or improvement of real property used in the taxpayer's trade or business. Any amount excluded results in a reduction of the basis of the taxpayer's depreciable real property. *See* IRC § 108(c) (providing special rules for "qualified real property business indebtedness").

- **Section 108(a)(1)(E)** provides that certain discharges of indebtedness on a taxpayer's principal residence will not generate discharge of indebtedness income for the years 2007 through 2017. The taxpayer does not have to be insolvent to qualify, but the taxpayer's basis in the residence is reduced (but not below zero) by the amount excluded from income. IRC § 108(h)(1). This provision was in response to the surge in home mortgage defaults and foreclosures.

- **Section 108(e)(2)** provides that gross income does not include the discharge of a liability if payment of that liability would have been deductible had it been paid. For example, the discharge of a liability to pay a supplier (an account payable) will not result in discharge-of-indebtedness income to the taxpayer since payment of that account would have been deductible by the taxpayer as a business expense under section 162.

- **Section 108(e)(4)** treats the acquisition of debt by a person related to the debtor as acquisition of the debt by the debtor himself. For example, assume Child, who is solvent, has outstanding indebtedness to Bank of $1,000. Parent purchases Child's indebtedness from Bank for cash in the amount of $900. Under section 61(a)(12) and section 108(e)(4), Child realizes $100 of income from discharge-of-indebtedness. As noted above, if Parent subsequently forgives Child's indebtedness to him, the forgiveness should be treated as an excludable gift.

- **Section 108(e)(5)** provides that a so-called "purchase money" debt reduction does not create discharge-of-indebtedness income. For example, if the seller of property finances the sale himself and subsequently reduces the buyer's debt, the reduction in the debt does not create income to the buyer. Rather, the reduction in debt is treated as a purchase price adjustment and buyer's basis in the property is decreased by the amount of the debt reduction. As noted by *Preslar*, above, section 108(e)(5) applies only to direct agreements between a seller and purchaser.

Chapter 6

Fringe Benefits

I. Assignment

Read: Internal Revenue Code: §§ 132(a), (b), (c), (d), (e), (h), (j)(1); 119(a).

Treasury Regulations: §§ 1.61-1(a), -2(d)(1), -21(b)(3); 1.132-2(a)(3), -3(a)(4), -4(a)(1).

Text: Overview
J. Grant Farms Inc. v. Commissioner
Charley v. Commissioner
Related Matters

Complete the problems.

II. Problems

1. Stephen Jobs works for Macrohard, a major software developer and computer manufacturer, as a computer designer. Macrohard's aggregate sales for computers are $1,000,000,000 for a representative period. Its aggregate cost of computers is $800,000,000 for that same period. Coincidentally its aggregate sales and costs for software sales are the same as for computers. Determine whether and to what extent the following fringe benefits are excludable from Stephen's gross income.

    (a) Stephen buys a Macrohard computer for personal use as his home computer. The computer normally costs $2,500 at retail but Stephen receives an employee discount of $500 and so only pays $2,000.

    (b) Same as (a) except that Stephen initially pays full price and the discount is received in the form of a $500 rebate check mailed from the home office.

    (c) Same as (a) except Stephen buys Macrohard software that retails for $2,500 but Stephen only pays $2,000.

    (d) Same as (c) except that Stephen is a marketing employee who works in the main office and designs advertising campaigns for both computers and software.

    (e) Same as (a) except that Stephen is president of the company and the discount is not available to non-executive personnel.

    (f) Same as (a) except that the computer is bought by Stephen's son Mac.

2. Amelia Earhart works for TransVandal Airlines as a ticket agent in New York City. Determine whether and to what extent the following fringe benefits are excludable from Amelia's gross income.

    (a) Amelia is permitted to fly standby for free on a half-full TransVandal plane to Las Vegas for a vacation.

    (b) Same as (a) except that Amelia is given a reserved seat and the plane is full. A paying customer is turned away so that Amelia can fly to Las Vegas.

    (c) Same as (b) except the trip to Las Vegas is for airline business purposes.

    (d) Same as (a) except that the passenger is Amelia's Mom.

3. Billy Crystal is a National Basketball Association referee. As part of his compensation Billy is given an allowance to fly first class from game to game. Instead of buying first class tickets, Billy buys coach class tickets, uses his frequent flyer miles to upgrade to first class, and keeps the excess allowance.

    (a) Assuming the allowance would otherwise qualify as an excludable working condition fringe benefit, what is the tax consequence of Billy's approach?

    (b) What if Billy had simply used the allowance to buy two coach class tickets, one for himself and one for his domestic partner and then upgraded both tickets to first class with frequent flyer miles?

4. Leona Helmsley owns all of the stock of Trample Hotel, Inc. The hotel is a destination resort located in the Hawaiian islands. Leona is also the manager of the hotel. Her duties as manager include dealing with drunk and rowdy guests, resolving billing disputes, greeting important dignitaries upon their arrival, being available for emergencies, and hiring and supervising lower management. Her employment contract with the company requires that she live in the penthouse suite of the hotel so that she can be available to address her duties as they arise. She is also obliged to eat her meals in the hotel during her regular working hours. She normally works ten hours a day, five days a week. She is on call 24 hours a day for emergencies. What exclusions, if any, apply to Leona in the following circumstances.

    (a) Leona is unmarried.

    (b) Same as (a) except that Leona's family resides with her in the penthouse.

    (c) Same as (a) except that Leona has assistant managers who actually handle all the matters that are nominally Leona's responsibilities except for Leona's supervision of other executives.

III. Overview

Non-salary employee perquisites ("perks") are commonly called fringe benefits. Typical examples include employer subsidized health and life insurance, retirement benefits, travel expense reimbursements, and education benefits. In theory anything one receives from one's employer as compensation for work performed should be included in gross income. Indeed, as we have seen, even a gift from the employer is income to the employee. IRC § 102(c). Moreover it should not matter whether the payment is in cash or in some other form. It should not matter whether the payment is made directly to the employee or to another person in relief of the employee's obligation to that third party. It is still an accession to wealth that should constitute gross income. Treas. Reg. § 1.61-1(a). But Congress has seen fit to exclude a number of fringe benefits from the employee's gross income while continuing to permit the employer to deduct the costs of those benefits. The continued deductibility of payment by the employer is a crucial aspect of the benefit. Both the deduction for the employer and the exclusion for the employee may serve as opportunities for tax planning. When reading the *Grant Farms* case in the materials consider whether this example of successful tax planning could have any significant disadvantages.

The policy justifications for fringe benefit exclusions vary from exclusion to exclusion but in general we may say that these exclusions arise from a desire to encourage employers to provide the excluded benefit, the difficulty of valuing the benefit, or from the administrative convenience for all parties in not having to account for the fringe benefit. In some cases Congress may have simply acquiesced to customary practices in certain industries that had not been taxed in earlier eras, for example, discounts for department store staff.

It should be recognized that exclusions of fringe benefits encourage employers to offer certain forms of compensation at the expense of regular salaries. This is because the employer gets more bang for its compensation buck by paying excludable compensation than by paying taxable compensation to its employees. Consider for example two employers bidding for the services of the same potential employee. Both employers offer compensation packages worth $100,000 in pre-tax dollars but the first employer's compensation package utilizes $20,000 of excludable benefits and the second employer's package is composed entirely of taxable benefits. If the flat tax rate is 20%, the first package will cost the employee $4,000 less in taxes than the second package (.2 × 20,000 = 4,000). In order to match the post-tax value of the first package to the employee, the second employer has to offer about $105,000 in pre-tax compensation.

The incentives that fringe benefit exclusions create for employers to minimize their costs have the ancillary effect of eroding the tax base. This, in turn, can lead to increased tax rates in order to fund the activities of government. In the end, the exclusions may simply funnel compensation into certain categories without reducing the employee's overall tax burden. One may question whether this leaves the employee better off than if the employee could freely choose how to spend his compensation.

A. The Major Exclusions under Section 132

Section 132 deals with many, but not all, excluded fringe benefits of employment, and is the main focus of this chapter. It establishes seven categories of excludable fringes but we will focus on four: (1) no-additional-cost-services; (2) qualified employee discounts; (3) working condition fringes; and (4) de minimis fringes.

As we delve into this topic it is important to remember that if a fringe benefit is not specifically excluded by the Code, it is gross income under section 61(a)(1). *See* Commissioner v. Smith, 324 U.S. 177 (1945). The amount of gross income is determined by reference to the fair market value of the service or property received. Treas. Reg. §§ 1.61-2(d)(1), -21(b)(3).

1. No Additional Cost Services and Qualified Employee Discounts

A no additional cost service is a service provided to an employee which the employer ordinarily provides to customers and which it is able to provide to the employee at no substantial additional cost, including foregone revenue. IRC § 132(b). The service must be in the line of business in which the employee works. IRC § 132(c)(4). Thus, for example, if a company provides insurance services and financial planning services, an employee who works in the insurance line would not be entitled to exclude from income the value of financial planning services provided at no charge. The exclusion is not available to highly compensated employees unless it is widely available to other employees as well. IRC § 132(j)(1).

A qualified employee discount is a reduction in the retail price given to an employee on qualified services or property not in excess of either the employer's gross profit percentage or, in the case of services, not in excess of 20% of the retail price. IRC § 132(c)(1). Like the no additional cost service it must be provided on a basis that does not discriminate in favor of highly compensated employees. IRC § 132(j)(1). The gross profit percentage is determined by dividing the employer's gross profit (i.e., aggregate sales minus aggregate costs) by the aggregate sales revenue. IRC § 132(c)(2)(A). This calculation is made on a line of business basis. IRC § 132(c)(2)(B). The employee is only entitled to exclude employee discounts for goods or services that are sold in the line of business in which the employee works. IRC § 132(c)(4).

Retired and disabled employees, and the surviving spouses of deceased employees, are entitled to the exclusions for both no additional cost services and for qualified employee discounts. This is accomplished through the legal fiction of defining "employee" to include the persons named above. IRC § 132(h)(1). Spouses and dependent children of employees also get the benefit of those two exclusions. IRC § 132(h)(2). In addition there is a special rule for parents of airline employees allowing the parents to exclude from gross income the value of free or discounted air travel received by the parent if the employee child could have excluded that amount. IRC § 132(h)(3).

2. Working Condition and De Minimis Fringe Benefits

A working condition fringe is a benefit given to an employee which if the employee paid for the benefit would entitle the employee to a deduction under sections 162 (business expenses) or 167 (depreciation expenses). IRC § 132(d). We will look at these sections of the Code later. Typical examples include reimbursements for business travel expenses and depreciation on an employee owned auto used for the employer's business.

A de minimis fringe is a benefit so small that it is not worth accounting for. IRC § 132(e)(1). For example, the Service has announced that an employee's personal calls made on a cell phone provided by the employer for business use are de minimis fringe benefits and will not create income for the employee. *See* Notice 2011-72, 2011-38 I.R.B. 407.

Unlike no-additional-cost services and qualified employee discounts, neither working condition fringes nor de minimis fringes are subject to the non-discrimination rules of section 132(j). But with respect to employer provided eating facilities, see IRC § 132(e)(2).

B. Meals or Lodging for the Employer's Convenience

Many circumstances arise where an employee derives a personal benefit from a condition of employment imposed or offered by the employer. For example, most employees would prefer a corner office to a windowless cubicle. Most business travelers would prefer to fly first class and stay at the finest hotels rather than sit in coach and sleep in flop houses. They usually prefer to take a cab rather than a bus from the airport to the hotel. Those preferences may rest on personal pleasure rather than on necessity, efficiency, or utility. One might conclude that some portion of the things and services that employers provide to employees ostensibly in order to help the employee to do the job should be considered gross income as in kind compensation. There are a number of tax rules that address such issues in a variety of contexts. We will consider just one provision here to give you some flavor for the opposing concerns that shape the debate. But we will return to this topic later when we look at the deductibility of employee related business expenses.

Section 119 excludes from an employee's gross income the value of employer provided meals and lodging when those benefits are provided as a condition of employment for the convenience of the employer. IRC § 119(a). The classic case where this exclusion applies is with respect to firefighters residing at the firehouse in order to be ready to fight fires at a moment's notice. But there are a number of other types of employees to which the exclusion can apply, including funeral home directors, casino workers, hotel managers, ranch workers, and security personnel. Where the exclusion applies it covers the spouse and dependents of the employee as well. The exclusion under section 119 is only available for meals if they are furnished on the business premises of the employer. IRC § 119(a)(1). The Supreme Court has held that cash reimbursements for meals for state troopers (who presumably are always on their employer's premises) do not satisfy this requirement. In other words, the meals must be directly provided by the employer. Commissioner v. Kowalski, 434 U.S. 77 (1977). With respect to employer provided lodging, acceptance of the lodging must be a condition of employment and the lodging must be on the employer's business premises. IRC § 119(a)(2). The business premises of the employer are generally the place of employment of the employee. Treas. Reg. § 1.119-1(c)(1). But an employee's separate dwelling, owned by the employer, has been found to be an employer's business premises where it served an important business function. *See* Adams v. United States, 585 F.2d 1060 (Ct. Cl. 1978).

C. Employment Related Payments from Third Parties

Sometimes businesses confer benefits on persons in order to encourage those persons to do business with them. For example, a book publisher may give out free "examination copies" of its books to professors in order to encourage them to adopt those books in the courses they teach. Or a manufacturer may pay the travel expenses of potential distributors in order to bring them to the manufacturer's plant to see the operation first hand. Do the beneficiaries of such transfers have income? Under the accession to wealth rule of *Glenshaw Glass* one would think so, but the cases do not always agree. With respect to free samples such as the examination copies, the Service seems to accept that no income need be reported as long as the recipient does not seek a charitable gift deduction for any subsequent transfer of the property received. *See* Rev. Rul. 70-498, 1970-2 C.B. 6. Thus, the professor in the above example would have no income unless she sought a charitable deduction for a subsequent gift of the books to a charity such as a library. *But see* Haverly v. United States, 513 F.2d 224 (7th Cir. 1975). With respect to free travel provided by a business in order to induce the traveler to do business with it, there is authority for the traveler excluding the free travel from income. *See* United States v. Gotcher, 401 F.2d 118 (5th Cir. 1968). One rationale for these exclusions might be that had the recipient actually paid for the benefits received, he or she should be entitled to business expense deductions of equal amounts. This would net out to zero. Thus, excluding the payment from income and taking no deduction leads to the same result. One difficulty with this analysis is that the Code sometimes denies deductions for part or all of such expenses. These limitations on deductions are addressed in later chapters.

D. Employer Provided Health Care Benefits

The Code includes an array of provisions that encourage employers to provide health care benefits to their employees. These include income exclusions for employer provided health insurance and disability insurance. *See* IRC §§ 105 & 106. In combination the various tax subsidies for health care represent one of the largest areas of federal government expenditure (running into the hundreds of billions of dollars each year). This system of subsidy is often criticized as inefficient and extravagant. Many commentators note that the United States has the highest per capita health care spending in the world while quality of health care is no better than in many other nations and while still leaving lower income populations seriously underserved. Even so, the elderly in the U.S. do enjoy nearly universal health care protection under Medicare. Does it make sense to make health care more readily affordable for the elderly than for the young?

The debate over whether and, if so, how to subsidize health care is an ongoing topic in American politics. From a policy perspective it might be preferable to eliminate all of the tax preferences for health care spending in order to make government expenditures in this area more explicit and transparent. If the revenue that is currently foregone through health care tax exclusions were being directly appropriated for health care would our expenditures be more rational?

E. The Strange Cases of Frequent Flyer Miles, Free Meals and Other Untaxed Benefits

The tax treatment of frequent flyer miles earned by employees while traveling at the expense of their employers has long posed interesting policy and administrative issues. As noted in Chapter 2, some years ago the Service announced that it will not seek to tax those miles to employees as long as they do not seek to convert them to cash. Announcement 2002-18, 2002-1 C.B. 621. The *Charley* case included in the materials represents a creative variation on that last theme.

The Service's passive approach toward frequent flyer miles may have contributed to an explosion of untaxed benefits for which there is no clear right of exclusion. Currently the most notable examples are the many freebies accorded to employees of Silicon Valley companies. These include meals, fitness classes, concierge services and massages. The non-taxation of these benefits has been widely chronicled and roundly criticized. *See, e.g.*, Jay A Soled & Kathleen DeLaney Thomas, *Revisiting the Taxation of Fringe Benefits*, 91 WASH. L. REV. 761 (2016); Austin L. Lomax, *Five Star Exclusion: Modern Silicon Valley Companies Are Pushing the Limits of Section 119 By Providing Tax-Free Meals to Employees*, 71 WASH. & LEE L. REV. 20177 (2014). *See also* Yehonaton Givati, *Googling a Free Lunch: The Taxation of Fringe Benefits*, 69 TAX L. REV. 275 (2016) (arguing for a partial exclusion). The free meals are of particular concern because of the potential magnitude of the exclusion. How much money could you save if you could get two thirds of your meals for free each year and did not have to report the benefit as income? It certainly does not seem to come within the de minimis fringe benefit category. *See* Treas. Reg. § 1.132-6. We visit the tax treatment of meals again in Chapter 7 when we consider the deduction for business expenses. However, it is worth noting that Congress' most recent response to this area of possible abuse is on the employer side of the equation. In the Tax Cuts and Jobs Act, it modified section 274 to reduce the employer's deduction for meals provided tax-free to employees under section 119 and for tax free meals provided in the employer's dining facility to 50% of the cost. IRC § 274(n)(1). Moreover, the entire cost will be nondeductible after 2025. IRC § 274(o).

IV. Materials

J. Grant Farms, Inc. v. Commissioner

49 T.C.M. (CCH) 1197 (U.S. Tax Court 1985)

GOFFE, JUDGE:

The Commissioner determined deficiencies in petitioners' Federal income tax. After concessions, the issues for decision are: (1) whether the individual petitioners, James A. Grant and M. Jean Grant, may exclude from gross income under section 119 income equal to the fair rental value of the residence they occupied, which was owned by the petitioner employer-corporation, and likewise exclude the cost of utilities of the residence furnished by the corporation for the taxable years 1979 and 1980; and (2) whether petitioner J. Grant Farms, Inc., was entitled to deduct depreciation and utility expenses related to the lodging provided to the individual petitioners for the taxable years ending July 31, 1979, and July 31, 1980, under the provisions of sections 162 and 167, respectively.

FINDINGS OF FACT

James A. Grant and M. Jean Grant, husband and wife (also hereinafter referred to as petitioners or Mr. Grant and Mrs. Grant), were residents of Charleston, Illinois, during the taxable years 1979 and 1980, and at the time the petition in this case was filed. Mr. Grant has resided on what is presently the J. Grant Farms, Inc. farmstead since 1949. In 1976, petitioners incorporated their family-owned farm into J. Grant Farms, Inc. (also hereinafter referred to as the corporation), which is a corporation incorporated under the laws of the State of Delaware, with its principal place of business in Charleston, Illinois. Mr. and Mrs. Grant each own 500 shares of the corporation, representing all of the outstanding shares of J. Grant Farms, Inc.

During the entire period at issue, the corporation was engaged in the farming of grain, which is a business with a low profit margin that requires efficient operation.

The corporation's grain business entailed the planting, cultivation, harvesting, drying, storage, and sale of corn and soybeans. The grain operation begins with planning for the planting of the year's crops; purchasing of seed corn, soybeans, herbicides, and fertilizer; and the maintenance of equipment in preparation for the planting season.

Corn and soybeans are planted during the spring of the year. In planting, soil and weather conditions are carefully monitored in order to plant the crops as close as possible to the optimum planting period. Planting is not carried out on a continual, day-to-day basis because of delays caused by inclement weather. During the planting season, there are days in which only a few hours are available for planting. Under ideal conditions, the acreage owned, rented, or leased by the corporation could be planted in ten 10-hour days, but such conditions seldom occur.

During the growing season, the crops are monitored for insects and weed infestation, with cultivation of the crops, spraying for weeds, and insect control continuing throughout this period. Fluctuating conditions affect cultivation in a fashion similar to the manner in which they affect planting, i.e., cultivation may not be possible for more than a few hours on any one particular day. Under ideal conditions, cultivation of the land worked by the corporation's employees could be accomplished in ten to fifteen 10-hour days. Cultivation, however, follows the inspections and monitoring, and is, therefore, done throughout the growing season.

Harvesting of crops begins in September and ordinarily runs through November, although it may extend for a longer period. After grain is harvested, it is dried in grain storage bins. Soybeans are air dried, while the corn is machine dried. The drying process involves the drying of grain with electric motors pushing air, supplemented with gas or electric heat, through the corn. The temperature is monitored by a thermostat similar to that found in a home heating system. The drying process may last from 6 weeks to 3 months. In the event that the electricity fails, the drying motors in the drying bins do not restart automatically, but must be restarted manually. If the motors stop, the drying process is delayed, but not stopped. During the drying process, the grain bins are monitored several times each day to see whether the optimal moisture content has been attained. If the moisture content is too high, the crops will rot in storage; if too low, the corporation will incur unnecessary drying expense and shrinkage, with consequent reduced sale proceeds. During the drying season, Mr. Grant checked the drying bins several times each day for continued operation and moisture content, with a final check before going to bed. Once the grain is dried, it is stored in a grain elevator or storage bin until sale; in this case, such storage was primarily in the corporation's storage bins.

During the years 1979 and 1980, the corporation was also engaged in the breeding and farrowing of sows and the sale of piglets. The corporation owned an average of eight purebred breeding sows and a purebred boar. During the taxable years ending July 31, 1979, and July 31, 1980, the corporation had gross hog sales in the amounts of $12,593 and $6,613, respectively.

The corporation's hog operation involved 8 to 10 sows and their offspring, which were hand-fed twice a day throughout the year. The sows were farrowed two times per year, normally in January or February and July. During the time of farrowing, the sows and pigs were watched on an around-the-clock basis. There is a substantial annual snowfall in the area of the corporation's farms, making the livestock periodically inaccessible unless there is an on-site manager. In the event of a loss of power and heat, confined hogs and pigs, such as those of the corporation, may freeze to death. Without a manager present to insure that the heaters in the facilities continue to operate, the entire herd could be lost.

During the years in dispute, petitioners' children were actively involved in the local 4-H program, a youth educational program which teaches children how to be farmers. During the years in dispute, two of the Grant children raised 10 of the average herd of 80 to 90 hogs as their 4-H project, and showed the hogs at the county fair. In such a project, the children are expected to do most of the work in raising the hogs.

The corporation employed 11 people during the taxable year 1978, 13 people in the taxable year 1979, and 12 people in the taxable year 1980. The corporation, which was owned entirely by petitioners, employed Mr. Grant as sole manager and operator of the corporation's farm properties under an employment contract dated December 31, 1976, as extended in August 1977, 1978, and 1979. Mr. Grant's responsibilities included making decisions as to the management and operation of the farm and devotion of his "full time, energy, skills and effort to the furtherance of the business of the company." Under the terms of the employment contract, the corporation provided living accommodations to Mr. Grant and his family, and paid all of the expenses of such accommodations. Mr. Grant was required by the contract to occupy the accommodations provided. The reasons provided in the contract for requiring Mr. Grant to live on the premises were so that Mr. Grant could manage the general operations of the farm; manage the feeding, watering, breeding, farrowing, and general supervision of livestock on the farm property; secure equipment owned and leased by the corporation; supervise the drying and storing of grain; and perform all of these duties on a 24-hour-per-day basis.

At all times relevant to this case, petitioners and seven of their children lived on the corporation's land in a residence furnished to them by the corporation. The residence was built in 1977 at a cost of $85,816, to replace a residence that burned in 1976, and contains 2,400 square feet of air-conditioned living space. The corporation's land is located 3 miles from Humboldt, Illinois, 8 miles from Mattoon, Illinois, 8 miles from Charleston, Illinois, and 10 miles from Arcola, Illinois. At all times relevant hereto, there were residences comparable to the one in which petitioners resided available for rental in Charleston and Mattoon.

In Coles County, Illinois, where the corporation's farmstead, rented land, and share-cropped land are located, farmers generally reside on the farm when valuable farm equipment and a grain-drying operation are on the premises. The presence of a manager-operator on the property for 24 hours a day provides security for the equipment; insures continued operation of the grain dryers; and allows for a more efficient operation. Further, a swine operation requires 24-hour-a-day management during farrowing season.

On September 15, 1982, the Commissioner timely issued statutory notices of deficiency to petitioners and the corporation. The Commissioner determined that petitioners received distributions from the corporation equal to the fair rental value of the residence they occupied plus utilities provided for the residence by the corporation. In addition, he determined that petitioners were not entitled to exclude such distributions under the provisions of section 119. The Commissioner determined that the corporation was not entitled to deduct the depreciation and utilities related to the residence occupied by petitioners.

ULTIMATE FINDINGS OF FACT

Petitioner James A. Grant was required to be available for duty at all times in connection with his responsibilities as operator-manager of the corporation's farm operation,

It was both necessary, and a condition of his employment, that petitioner James A. Grant reside upon the farm premises in order to properly perform the duties of his employment.

Petitioners resided on the farm for the convenience of the employer-corporation.

OPINION

After concessions, the issues for decision are: (1) whether the individual petitioners may exclude from gross income under section 119 income equal to the fair rental value of the residence they occupied, which was owned by the petitioner employer-corporation, and likewise exclude the cost of utilities of the residence furnished by the corporation; and (2) whether petitioner corporation was entitled to deduct depreciation and utility expenses related to the lodging provided to the individual petitioners under the provisions of sections 162 and 167, respectively.

The Commissioner's determination in his statutory notice of deficiency is presumptively correct, and petitioners have the burden of disproving each individual adjustment. Welch v. Helvering, 290 U.S. 111 (1933); Rule 142(a).

During the taxable years at issue, the corporation provided lodging to petitioners without charge. The fair market value of such lodging constituted dividend income to petitioners and must be included in their gross income under section 301, unless specifically excluded.

Under section 119, the value of lodging[3] furnished to an employee, his spouse, or any of his dependents by or on behalf of his employer for the convenience of the employer is excluded from gross income, but only if the employee is required to accept the lodging on his employer's business premises as a condition of his employment. Sec. 1.119-1(b), Income Tax Regs., amplifies the requirements for exclusion:

> The value of lodging furnished to an employee by the employer shall be excluded from the employee's gross income if three tests are met:
>
> (1) The lodging is furnished on the business premises of the employer,
>
> (2) The lodging is furnished for the convenience of the employer, and
>
> (3) The employee is required to accept such lodging as a condition of his employment.

The requirement of subparagraph (3) of this paragraph that the employee is required to accept such lodging as a condition of his employment means that he be required to accept the lodging in order to enable him properly to perform the duties of his employment. Lodging will be regarded as furnished to enable the employee properly to perform the duties of his employment when, for example, the lodging is furnished because the employee is required to be available for duty at all times or because the employee could not perform the services required of him unless he is furnished such lodging. If the tests described in subparagraphs (1), (2), and (3) of this paragraph are met, the exclusion shall apply irrespective of whether a charge is made, or whether, under an employment contract or statute fixing the terms of employment, such lodging is furnished as compensation.

The parties agree that the first condition, that the lodging be on the employer's premises, and the second condition, that the provision of such lodging be for the convenience of the employer, are met. The parties disagree, however, on whether the third condition is met. Petitioners assert that Mr. Grant must be available for duty at all times, both to perform his duties under his employment contract, and to obtain the optimum financial return. Respondent contends that it is unnecessary for Mr. Grant and his family to live on the corporation's land on the basis that: (1) many farmers do not live on the property that they farm; (2) few, if any, duties require the presence of a manager for 24 hours a day; and (3) Mr. Grant's duties could be performed just as easily if he commuted from a residence in one of the nearby communities.

---

3. Lodging for purposes of sec. 119 includes all commodities necessary to make lodging habitable including gas and electricity. Harrison v. Commissioner, T.C. Memo. 1981-211.

Respondent attempted, on brief, to contend that alternate grounds for disallowing the exclusion under section 119 were either that the corporation was not an independent entity or that the arrangement described above was, in some fashion, an attempt at tax avoidance under section 269. Neither one of these grounds was contained in either the notices of deficiency or the answers to the petitions. Further, to address these issues at this late date would be to allow respondent, in effect, to change his position subsequent to trial without affording petitioners the opportunity to refute these contentions. We will not, therefore, consider these grounds.

The issue before us is, therefore, whether petitioners were required to accept lodging furnished to them as a "condition of ... employment." The proper inquiry is not whether the employee was contractually required to reside on the employer's premises, or whether housing was available nearby, but whether the lodging was furnished to petitioners because the nature of Mr. Grant's job required that he "be available for duty at all times." Sec. 1.119-1(b), Income Tax Regs. The question is primarily one of fact to be resolved by a consideration of all of the circumstances before us.

Three experts testified on the issue of whether a resident manager was indispensable to the operation of the corporation's farm. Louis Christen, an agricultural extension advisor for Coles County for 26? years, is thoroughly and personally familiar with the particular farm at issue. Coles County is the location of all of the property farmed by the corporation. His opinion was that the constant presence of a manager was both "highly desirable" and "highly necessary" in order to make the maximum profit, particularly in the last several years when good management has made the difference between a small profit and no profit at all. Mr. Christen lives on a farm where he conducts drying operations and stores equipment, and has a tenant farmer who does not live on the property. Mr. Christen stated that if he moved to town, a tenant would be required to live on the farm.

Royce Marble is senior vice-president and trust officer at the Charleston National Bank responsible for the management of approximately 15,000 acres of farm land, most of which is leased on a "share-crop" basis. If a farm has a residence and improvements such as grain bins and machine sheds, the bank routinely requires that the tenant live upon the property. A "courtesy rent" of between $100 and $300 a year is normally charged. He also testified that having a resident farmer improves the bottom line. The bank does not build a residence upon a vacant property if there are no improvements upon it.

Respondent's expert witness, Elmer E. Rankin, has been an agricultural extension advisor for Sangamon County, Illinois, since November of 1980, and testified pursuant to a subpoena served upon him by respondent. He testified that, in general, most land owners do not live on their farms, and that the majority do not require their tenants to live on the farms. Upon cross examination, however, he conceded that he knew of no nonresident farmers who had either grain drying operations or large amounts of equipment and supplies stored on the premises. He also conceded that the presence of a resident manager would make the farm operate more efficiently.

Although he could not recommend a swine operation to a farmer with as large a grain operation as petitioners, such a project would be appropriate because a 4-H project was involved.

This evidence is sufficient to sustain petitioners' burden of proof, thus distinguishing this case from Caratan v. Commissioner, 52 T.C. 960 (1969), revd. 442 F.2d 606 (9th Cir. 1971).

We find as a fact that petitioners were required to reside on the corporation's farmstead in order to properly manage and operate the farm, and that occupying the residence upon the farmstead was a condition of Mr. Grant's employment. A farming operation of the complexity set forth above is not a 9-to-5 business; it requires that a manager be available to make the necessary decisions, solve the necessary problems, and direct the necessary labor. In this case, both the swine operation and the grain-drying operation required constant, if not continuous, monitoring and work. Further, while insurance does, of course, reduce the out-of-pocket cost of replacing expensive equipment, the presence of a manager-operator makes less likely the need to replace stolen or vandalized equipment. We also find, as a corollary and as a result of the above finding, that the habitation upon the farmstead is used in the corporation's business as a residence for its on-site manager-operator. The corporation is, therefore, entitled to deduct the depreciation and utility expense deductions disallowed by the Commissioner. Secs. 162 and 167.

Charley v. Commissioner

91 F.3d 72 (9th Cir. 1996)

O'SCANNLAIN, CIRCUIT JUDGE.

Do travel credits converted to cash in a personal travel account established by an employer constitute gross income to the employee for federal income tax purposes?

I

Dr. Philip Charley and his wife Katherine Charley appeal the tax court's determination of an income tax deficiency for tax year 1988 in the amount of $882 and an addition to tax of $44 pursuant to Internal Revenue Code ("IRC") §6653. We affirm on the merits and reverse the penalty.

During 1988, Truesdail Laboratories ("Truesdail") engaged in the testing business, including testing urine for horse racing activities and investigating the causes of industrial accidents. Philip was the President of Truesdail and, together with Katherine, owned 50.255% of its shares. Philip performed various services for Truesdail including inspecting mechanical devices suspected of failure.

Philip, in his capacity as an employee of Truesdail, traveled to various accident sites to inspect machinery. Truesdail had an "unwritten policy" that the frequent flyer miles that were earned during an employee's travel for Truesdail became the sole property of the employee.

During the year at issue, the following procedures were followed by Truesdail with respect to Philip's travel:

(1) A client would engage the services of Truesdail and would direct that Philip travel to a particular accident site;

(2) If Philip chose to travel to the site by air, Truesdail would bill the client for round-trip, first class air travel;

(3) Philip would instruct a travel agent, Archer Travel Services ("Archer"), to arrange for coach service to and from the site, but to charge Truesdail for first class travel;

(4) Philip then would use his frequent flyer miles (largely earned in connection with his business travel for Truesdail) to upgrade the coach ticket to first class; and

(5) Philip would instruct Archer to transfer funds to his personal travel account amounting to the difference in price between the first class ticket for which Truesdail was charged and the coach ticket, albeit upgraded, which Philip actually used.

Over the course of 1988, Archer maintained separate travel accounts for Philip and Truesdail. Philip took four business trips that year, and using the procedures outlined above, received $3,149.93 in his personal travel account from his "sale" of the frequent flyer miles.

The parties stipulated that Philip and Katherine did not know that the receipt of the travel credits was taxable income, and that they did not intend to conceal the process utilized to obtain the travel credits.

The tax court held that the travel credits constituted taxable income. The tax court also upheld imposition of [a penalty] ... which provided for an addition to tax if any part of an underpayment resulted from negligence or intentional disregard of rules and regulations.

The petitioners appeal both the tax court's determination of an income tax deficiency and its imposition of the addition to tax (penalty).

II

The statute at issue, IRC § 61, provides that gross income "means all income from whatever source derived." Gross income has been defined as an "undeniable accession[] to wealth, clearly realized, and over which the taxpayer[] [has] complete dominion." Commissioner v. Glenshaw Glass, 348 U.S. 426, 431 (1955). The tax court noted that there was no indication Philip could not use the travel credits for personal travel or redeem them for cash. Consequently, the tax court upheld the IRS' determination of deficiency on the ground that:

Whether we regard this fact situation as a straight "rip-off" by petitioner of his employer or a highly technical "sale" of his frequent flyer miles (which have zero basis) for the credits, the fact remains that petitioner was wealthier after the transaction than before. In such circumstances, the accretion of wealth is the receipt of income.

The Charleys do not dispute the tax court's finding that travel credits were Philip's to use for personal travel. Nor do they dispute the tax court's conclusion that Philip had sole control over the credits in his account. Rather, the Charleys argue that no taxable event occurred. We find this argument unpersuasive.

The Charleys argue that this case raises the question of whether, in the abstract, frequent flyer miles constitute gross income. We disagree and do not reach that issue.

As the tax court noted, the case can be analyzed in one of two ways. First, the travel credits which were converted to cash can be characterized as additional compensation. On this view, Philip received property from his employer in the form of an account upon which he could draw up to $3,149.93, which he did. This is so because Truesdail paid for first-class airfare and allowed Archer to credit Philip's account with the difference between the first-class price and the coach price. The funds constituting the difference came from Truesdail; Philip consequently received compensation in the amount of $3,149.93 from his employer. The fact that the travel credits were exchanged for frequent flyer miles simply is not relevant to the analysis.

In the alternative, if it is assumed that the frequent flyer miles were not given to Philip by Truesdail, but belonged to him all along, then the transaction can be viewed as a disposition of his own property. Gross income includes "[g]ains derived from dealings in property." IRC § 61(a)(3). A gain from the disposition of property is equal to the "amount realized" from the disposition minus the property's adjusted basis. IRC § 1001(a). The amount realized from a disposition of property is the sum of any money received plus the fair market value of the property (other than money) received. IRC § 1001(b). The adjusted basis is generally determined by reference to cost. IRC § 1012.

Because Philip received the frequent flyer miles at no cost, he had a basis of zero. He then exchanged his frequent flyer miles for cash, resulting in a gain of $3,149.93 (the fair market value of the property received minus the adjusted basis of zero).

Thus, the funds credited to Philip's account are taxable, whether they are characterized as a gain from the disposition of property or as additional compensation, unless he can show that they qualify for an exclusion. Philip cannot maintain that the funds constituted a non-taxable gift because IRC § 102(c), concerning exclusions for gifts, provides that "[s]ubsection (a) shall not exclude from gross income any amount transferred by or for an employer to, or for the benefit of, an employee."

Philip argues the credits should be construed as a "no-additional-cost service," which is excludable pursuant to IRC § 132(a). However, in order to qualify for this exclusion, the service in question must, among other things, be "offered for sale to customers in the ordinary course of the line of business of the employer in which the employee is performing services." IRC § 132(b). Truesdail obviously did not offer frequent flyer miles to customers in the ordinary course of its business; thus, the travel credits at issue here cannot be deemed an excludable no-additional-cost service.

In sum, we hold that the tax court was correct in concluding that the travel credits under the facts of this case constituted taxable income.

III

The IRS imposed an addition to tax in the amount of $44 pursuant to the former version of IRC § 6653 [now § 6662], which provided for an addition to tax if any part of an underpayment is due to negligence or intentional disregard of rules or regulations.

Philip has the burden of proving that the underpayment was not due to negligence. *Allen v. Commissioner*, 925 F.2d 348, 353 (9th Cir.1991). Former section 6653(a)(3) defined "negligence" as including "any failure to make a reasonable attempt to comply with the provisions of this title." Similarly, caselaw has defined "negligence" as the "lack of due care or the failure to do what a reasonable and prudent person would do under similar circumstances." *Allen*, 925 F.2d at 353.

We are persuaded that the tax court erred in sustaining the penalty. There is nothing in the record which would cause a reasonable person to conclude that the travel credit conversion would constitute taxable income. As the government conceded in its brief, "the tax treatment of frequent flyer bonus programs is still under consideration." There is no showing that the conventional personal use of frequent flyer miles in the late 1980s gave rise to taxable income under then-current IRS policy. Therefore, the penalty for negligent or intentional disregard of IRS rules was not warranted.

The decision of the tax court is AFFIRMED in part and REVERSED in part.

V. Related Matters

As mentioned earlier there are many other exclusions for employer provided fringe benefits.

- **Section 132.** Additional exclusions addressed by section 132 include:
  - Qualified transportation fringe (§ 132(a)(5)) (note, however, the $20 per month exclusion for reimbursement of bicycle commuting expenses is eliminated for tax years 2018 through 2025 per § 132(f)(8));
  - Qualified moving expense reimbursement (§ 132(a)(6)) (note, however, that the exclusion is suspended for years 2018 through 2025, except for members of the U.S. Armed Forces on active duty who move pursuant to military order, per § 132(g));
  - Qualified retirement planning services (§ 132(a)(7));
  - On premises athletic facilities (§ 132(j)(4)).

- **Other Code Provisions.** Fringe benefit exclusions and deductions provided for elsewhere include:
  - Housing for ministers of religion (§ 107);
  - Education subsidies (§§ 117, 127);
  - Combat pay (§ 112);
  - Term life insurance (§ 79);
  - Dependent care assistance (§ 129);
  - Adoption assistance (§ 137);
  - Disaster relief payments (§ 139);
  - Health savings accounts (§ 223).

All of these provisions are subject to various requirements and restrictions and must be examined carefully in any given case.

Chapter 7

Business and Investment Expense Deductions

I. Assignment

Read: Internal Revenue Code: §§ 161; 162(a); 212; 274(a), (n)(1), (o).
Skim §§ 163(d), (j); 195(a)–(c); 199A; 262(a); 274(n)(2); 280A(a), 280E.

Treasury Regulations: §§ 1.162-1(a), -2(e), -3(a) & (b), -4, -5, -17(b);
1.212-1(a)–(h), -1(l); 1.263(a)-1(e)(1).

Text: Overview
Welch v. Helvering
Jenkins v. Commissioner
Henderson v. Commissioner
Related Matters

Complete the problems.

II. Problems

1. Yao Ming is a licensed acupuncturist and medicinal herbalist. Not only does he perform acupuncture on his clients, but he also prescribes and sells herbal remedies that he imports from China.

   (a) Which of the following expenditures may Yao deduct under section 162?

      (1) Office rent for a plush office in a downtown building. ✓

      (2) Office electricity. ✓

      (3) Disposable acupuncture needles. ✓

      (4) Office linen services. ✓

      (5) Subscription to *Time* magazine for the waiting room. ✓

      (6) Subscription to *Acupuncture* magazine for continuing education. ✓

      (7) Home subscriptions to *The New Yorker* magazine and to *Entertainment Weekly*. Does it matter if after he has read them Yao puts them in his waiting room. ✓

      (8) Childcare payments for his four-year-old daughter for while he is working. ✓

    (9) Payments routinely made to homeless persons living in the area to induce them to stay out of his office doorway.

    (10) White shirts, white jackets, black pants, and cotton twill slippers he wears as his office uniform.

    (11) Payments to his eleven-year-old son to clean the office on Saturdays.

    (12) Payments to his accountant to keep his books.

(b) When Yao first prescribes an herbal remedy to one of his clients he often gives the client a free sample of the remedy. May he deduct the cost of that free sample?

(c) What if Yao does not have to buy the free samples because his supplier gives them to him?

2. Elizabeth Blackwell is a general practitioner doctor who works out of offices located in two small towns, Moscow and Warsaw, ten miles apart. She works three days a week in Moscow and two days a week in Warsaw. By having offices in both towns she is able to attract patients from both towns. Most of her staff is located in her Moscow office. Seventy percent of her revenue is generated out of her Moscow office. Elizabeth maintains her personal residence with her husband and children in Moscow. Consider the deductibility of her expenses in the following circumstances.

(a) Elizabeth drives directly from her home to whichever office she is working in that day. She has lunch brought in and does paperwork while eating. She drives directly home from whichever office she is working in that day. Can she deduct her transportation expense or the cost of her meals? Her office rent at both locations?

(b) Elizabeth sometimes drives between the two offices during the day in order to see patients at both locations and in order to meet with her staff. She also meets with her accountant occasionally over lunch, her only free time during the day. At these lunches she pays for only her meal. Are her transportation expenses between offices deductible? The costs of her luncheon meetings with her accountant?

(c) The facts are the same as in the original scenario except that Moscow and Warsaw are 100 miles apart and Elizabeth spends two nights a week in Warsaw in a small apartment she rents for the sole purpose of having a place to stay when she is working in Warsaw. May she deduct the costs of traveling to Warsaw and living there two days a week?

(d) Same as (c) except that Elizabeth's personal residence where her husband and children reside is in Warsaw. She rents an apartment in Moscow and lives there three days a week. May she deduct the cost of one of her dwellings? If so, which one?

3. Martha Stewart owns a modest stock portfolio which she manages with the aid of an online broker. When she buys stock her broker charges her $25 per trans-

action. When she sells stock her broker charges her $25 per transaction. She keeps her stock certificates, along with her jewelry, in a bank safe deposit box for which she pays $25 per year. Near the end of each year she consults with her tax adviser about the advisability of selling a portion of her stock portfolio in light of her income, gains, and losses for the year. Her tax advisor charges her $150 per hour for the advisor's services. At the beginning of each year the tax advisor prepares Ms. Stewart's tax returns and charges the same hourly rate. Which, if any, of these fees are deductible by Ms. Stewart?

III. Overview

A. The Main Provisions

It is a truism of business that you have to spend money to make money. The income tax is ostensibly a tax on net income. That is, it only attempts to tax the net increase in wealth generated by money making activities. This implies that we should be entitled to deduct the money we spend from the money we make before we apply the tax rates to the remainder. In general this is what the tax rules try to do. Thus, for example, a business that is conducted through the activities of its employees is entitled to deduct the reasonable salaries of those employees from its gross income in determining its taxable income. IRC § 162(a)(1). For the most part, the rules for deducting expenses arising from money making efforts are straightforward. But there are some interesting complexities in reaching a fair result with respect to business deductions. In this chapter we will examine the general deduction rules and some of the difficulties associated with applying them. Keep in mind that the factual variations that pervade the realm of deductions are infinite. The arguments that can be constructed for the deductibility of this huge array of potential expenditures is limited only by human imagination.

The rich complexity of this area is inherent in its nature, but the key rules addressing deductions are short and, seemingly, simple. The two primary Code provisions in question are sections 162 and 212. Section 162 addresses trade or business deductions. Section 212 addresses expenses related to investment activities and expenses related to obtaining tax advice. The need for a separate provision addressing investment activities arose from an early Supreme Court decision in which the Court ruled that buying and selling stocks and other investment activities did not constitute a trade or business and, thus, what is now section 162 did not apply to the expenses arising from those activities. Higgins v. Commissioner, 312 U.S. 212 (1941). Congress responded by enacting what is now section 212 in order to allow for the deduction of those expenses.

B. Some Limitations

Section 262 stands in contradistinction to sections 162 and 212. It generally prohibits deductions for "personal, living, or family expenses." This is straightforward enough. However, as was discussed in our earlier chapter on fringe benefit exclusions, many expenditures connected to money making activities can provide personal non-business benefits. There is an area of gray between purely business and purely personal expenses. The potential for abuse in this area has led Congress to enact various provisions that attempt to narrow the ability of taxpayers to manipulate their business affairs so as to make personal expenses deductible. The more prominent of these provisions are sections 274 and 280A. Both of these provisions are long and detailed and we will not seek to fully address them here.

Section 274 limits or prohibits the deductibility of meal and entertainment expenses. Perhaps its single rule of most pervasive importance is the 50% limit on the deductibility of business meals contained in section 274(n)(1). There are a number of narrowly crafted exceptions to the 50% limit. *See* IRC § 274(n)(2). The most significant exception for the average employee is the rule that allows the employee to deduct one hundred percent of the cost of the meal if the expense is reimbursed by the employer. This rule works in combination with other rules considered later that permit an employee whose deductible expenses are reimbursed by the employer to simply disregard those reimbursements and expenses for tax reporting purposes. Other limitations imposed by section 274 are highlighted near the end of this chapter.

Section 280A limits the deductibility of expenses related to home offices and related to vacation homes used as rental property and will receive more attention in a later chapter dealing with real estate taxation.

C. Section 162(a) — General Principles

Section 162(a) authorizes the deduction of "ordinary and necessary expenses" arising from the "carrying on [of] any trade or business."

1. Ordinary and Necessary

An area of continuing development and uncertainty is the meaning and application of the phrase "ordinary and necessary" as used in the statute. A case included in the materials, *Welch v. Helvering*, is the seminal case interpreting that phrase. As illustrated in the *Jenkins v. Commissioner* case, also included in the materials, *Welch* leaves a lot of room for maneuvering.

The items of expense that may be considered ordinary and necessary are nearly infinite. Deductible expenses can include supplies, employee uniforms, utility bills, business lunches (subject to the 50% limit of section 274(n)(1)), consultants' fees, contractors' fees (such as the charges for janitorial services), professional dues, journal subscriptions, and so on. *See* Treas. Reg. § 1.162-1(a). The deductibility of expenditures for business attire has been the subject of a number of cases. The settled rule is that such expenses are deductible only if the clothing is of a type specifically required as a condition of employment and is not suitable for general usage as ordinary clothing. *See, e.g.,* Pevsner v. Commissioner, 628 F.2d 467 (5th Cir. 1980). What would you say should be the treatment of the costs of stage clothing for the typical rock star?

2. What Is an "Expense"?

A point of importance is understanding how "expenses" differ from capital expenditures. Capital expenditures will be taken up in the next chapter. In general, an expense is an expenditure that benefits the current year only. A capital expenditure is an expenditure that benefits more than the current year. Thus, for example, when a law firm buys a building in which to conduct its business the cost of the building is a capital expenditure and cannot be deducted currently because the building will help produce income over many years. As we will see, the law firm will recover its costs for the building over time through depreciation. (Depreciation is addressed in Chapter 9.) On the other hand, if the firm chose to rent office space from a third party the rent can be deducted immediately since it only helps produce income in the current year. IRC § 162(a)(3). This simplistic treatment of a complex area will be fleshed out later in various contexts. The point to take from the present discussion is that even an expenditure that is clearly for the purpose of making money may not be currently deductible if the expenditure will help produce income over a longer period of time than the current year. The focus of the present chapter is that category of business and investment expenditures that benefit only the current period and, thus, are currently deductible.

3. Carrying On

The deduction under section 162 is available for ordinary and necessary expenses paid or incurred by the taxpayer "in carrying on" a trade or business. The purpose of the "in carrying on" requirement is to differentiate between expenses that are associated with the operation of an actual, existing business and those expenses associated with the development of a new business. The result is that section 162 permits current deductions only for those costs paid or incurred in connection with an active, ongoing business and denies current deductibility for start-up or pre-opening costs incurred prior to the beginning of actual business operations. Whether a venture has crossed the line from start-up to active trade or business depends generally on whether the business has begun to function as a going concern and is engaged in those activities for which it was organized. This determination is a question of fact that depends on the circumstances of each case. For the leading case on the "carrying on" requirement, see Frank v. Commissioner, 20 T.C. 511 (1953) (holding that travel expenses and legal fees spent in searching for a newspaper business with a view to purchasing the same could not be deducted under section 162 since the taxpayer was not engaged in any trade or business at the time the expenses were incurred).

It should be noted that section 195 provides some relief for start-up expenditures. Under section 195, a taxpayer may elect to deduct up to $5,000 of start-up expenditures in the tax year in which an active trade or business begins, with the remainder deducted ratably over fifteen years. IRC § 195(b). A start-up expenditure is an amount paid in connection with investigating the creation or acquisition of a business and other expenses incurred preliminarily to actively engaging in the business. The expenditure involved must be one that would otherwise be allowable as a deduction (e.g., under section 162) if it were paid or incurred in connection with an existing trade or business. IRC § 195(c)(1).

4. Trade or Business

Neither the Code nor the Treasury Regulations define the term "trade or business." Courts considering the meaning of the term have generally concluded that to be engaged in a trade or business, (1) "the taxpayer must be involved in the activity with continuity and regularity," and (2) "the taxpayer's primary purpose for engaging in the activity must be for income or profit." Commissioner v. Groetzinger, 480 U.S. 23 (1987). In *Groetzinger*, the Supreme Court held that an individual's gambling activities constituted a trade or business because they were pursued full time, in good faith, and with regularity, for the production of income as a livelihood. The Court refused to adopt the position of Justice Frankfurter in his concurring opinion in Deputy v. du Pont, 308 U.S. 488 (1940), that a trade or business "involves holding one's self out to others as engaged in the selling of goods or services." The Court noted that although "one who clearly satisfies the Frankfurter adumbration usually is in a trade or business," it does not follow that "one who does not satisfy the Frankfurter adumbration is not in a trade or business." Whether a taxpayer has engaged in the requisite scope of activities and has demonstrated the requisite profit motive are questions to be determined by an examination of all the facts in each case. Higgins v. Commissioner, 312 U.S. 212, 217 (1941).

An activity will not qualify as a trade or business under section 162 if it is "[a] sporadic activity, a hobby, or an amusement diversion." *Groetzinger*, 480 U.S. at 35. Although expenses incurred in a hobby activity are not deductible under section 162, they are allowed under section 183 to the extent the hobby activity generates income. We will consider in more detail section 183 and hobby expenses in Chapter 23.

D. Substantiation

Substantiation is an obstacle to deduction that can arise. It is the taxpayer's obligation to prove that the deductible expense was actually incurred. *See, e.g.,* IRC § 274(d) (requiring substantiation of meals and entertainment expenses). Usually this means a receipt or record of payment must be provided. Every tax lawyer, however, should know the rule arising from the case of *Cohan v. Commissioner*, 39 F.2d 540 (2d Cir. 1930) (involving the Broadway impressario George M. Cohan) which allows the approximation of deductible expenses by the trial court when it is established that some such expense was incurred. The continued vitality of the *Cohan* rule, especially with respect to expenses addressed by section 274(d), is subject to question. *See* Treas. Reg. § 1.274-5T(c)(1). Nonetheless it remains the taxpayer position of last resort on proving expenses.

E. Section 162(a)(1) — Reasonable Salaries

Section 162(a)(1) authorizes the deduction of "reasonable salaries or other compensation." This provision is subject to the "ordinary and necessary" requirement of the opening sentence of section 162. But historically the pressure point in the statute is the word "reasonable." One might assume that no business would ever pay more than it has to in order to obtain competent employees. However, there are circumstances in which a business might be inclined to overpay some or all of its employees. The classic case involves the employee who also owns stock in a closely held corporation. When a corporation pays its individual shareholder a cash dividend on its stock, the recipient has taxable income but the corporation gets no deduction. On the other hand when the corporation pays its employee a reasonable salary it gets a section 162 deduction which, in turn, reduces the corporation's income tax liability. Thus, when an employee such as the president of the corporation is also a substantial or even sole shareholder there is a temptation to pay out dividends in the form of salary. Since the payee may control the corporation, the method of payment is easily manipulated. The courts have often been called upon to police such situations by determining whether the employee's salary is "reasonable" within the meaning of section 162(a)(1). *See, e.g.*, Elliotts, Inc. v. Commissioner, 716 F.2d 1241 (9th Cir. 1983) (evaluating reasonableness of salary from the perspective of a hypothetical independent investor—"whether an inactive, independent investor would be willing to compensate the employee as he was compensated"); Exacto Spring Corp. v. Commissioner, 196 F.3d 833 (7th Cir. 1999) (adopting the independent investor test, stating "[t]he higher the rate of return (adjusted for risk) that a manager can generate, the greater the salary he can command"). *But see* Eberl's Claim Service, Inc. v. Commissioner, 249 F.3d 994 (10th Cir. 2001) (applying a multi-factor, fact-intensive test); Owensby & Kritikos, Inc. v. Commissioner, 819 F.2d 1315 (5th Cir. 1987) (same).

To some degree the pressure in this area of tax law has declined because of the rise of the limited partnership, the limited liability company (LLC) (taxed as a partnership), and the S Corporation as the vehicles of choice for closely held businesses. These "pass through" entities are not taxed on their income. IRC §§ 701, 1363. Instead they are conduits. Each partner, member, or shareholder is taxed on her share of the entity's income. IRC §§ 702, 1366. Thus, the deductibility of payments from the entity to the owner/employee is largely irrelevant for income tax purposes. However, there are still enough closely held regular corporations remaining in existence to be aware of the issue.

F. Section 162(a)(2) — Travel Expenses

Section 162(a)(2) authorizes the deduction of "traveling expenses ... while away from home in the pursuit of a trade or business." This provision has engendered substantial litigation over a wide range of circumstances.

1. Where Is Home?

A central problem that has emerged is determining the location of the taxpayer's home for purposes of this statute when the taxpayer works or lives in more than one place during the year. The Service takes the position that the taxpayer's home is where the taxpayer's principal place of employment is located. Rev. Rul. 75-432, 1975-2 C.B. 60. Some courts have accepted this view. *See, e.g.,* Markey v. Commissioner, 490 F.2d 1249 (6th Cir 1974). Some courts argue for a functional test that focuses on whether duplicate living expenses arise from business necessity. *See, e.g.,* Andrews v. Commissioner, 931 F.2d 132 (1st Cir. 1991). If such duplicate expenses do occur, the court may then look to a variety of factors such as length of residence and amount earned in the location to determine which location should be deemed the taxpayer's home. Some courts take the common sense view that the taxpayer's home is determined by principal place of residence. The dissenting opinion in the *Henderson* case in the materials presents this perspective. An odd twist is that some unfortunate taxpayers who travel for business reasons have been found to have no entitlement to the deduction. The paradigm case is the traveling salesman who has no permanent residence. This person either has no home to be away from or she is like the turtle who carries her home on her back. In either event she is never away from home and thus can never incur "traveling expenses ... while away from home." The *Henderson* case also elucidates this perspective. *See also* Rosenspan v. United States, 438 F.2d 905, *cert. denied,* 404 U.S. 864 (2d Cir. 1971). The logic supporting this outcome is that such a person has no duplicate living expenses. However, the statute does not expressly require that the business traveler must have duplicate living expenses.

2. Commuting Expenses

An early Supreme Court case determined that commuting expenses are not deductible under the statute. Commissioner v. Flowers, 326 U.S. 465 (1946). *Flowers* involved a lawyer who commuted by train between his residence in Jackson, Mississippi and his principal place of business in Mobile, Alabama. He actually spent more of his time working at his home in Jackson. In denying any deduction for his travel expenses relating to living in Jackson and working in Mobile, the Court reasoned that a person's decision to locate at some distance from work was personal in nature and thus the costs incurred in commuting did not arise from business necessity. Simply put, such expenses were not incurred "in pursuit of business." In *Flowers,* the Court could have resolved the controversy over the meaning of home under the statute but it chose not to do so. Focusing instead on the personal nature of commuting expenses, it avoided the question. Recently the Seventh Circuit Court of Appeals relied on *Flowers* to deny travel expense deductions to a laid-off airline mechanic who took temporary jobs at various locales around the country while maintaining a residence in Minneapolis. *See* Wilbert v. Commissioner, 553 F.3d 544 (7th Cir. 2009).

3. The Sleep or Rest Rule

Another Supreme Court decision of importance to the travel expense deduction is United States v. Correll, 389 U.S. 299 (1967). In *Correll,* the Supreme Court upheld the Service's administrative interpretation that the only meal expenses covered by section 162(a)(2) were those involving a lengthy period of rest or an overnight stay away from home. This is called the "sleep or rest rule" and it derives from three points.

It rests first on the language of the statute requiring that the business travel must take the taxpayer "away from home." Arguably a taxpayer who completes his work and returns home within the confines of a single day has not left home in a meaningful sense. The second point is administrative convenience. The sleep or rest rule provides a bright line test. The third is that the deductibility of meals is inherently doubtful from a policy perspective and thus a narrow construction of the statute on this point is justified.

Take note that the sleep or rest rule has no application to transportation expenses associated with business such as plane fares and automobile mileage. The main rule of section 162 still applies. Thus, for example, the accountant who flies on business from San Francisco to Los Angeles and back to San Francisco all in the same day may deduct her plane fare under the statute even though the sleep or rest rule denies a deduction for her meals. It is also important to remember that an expense for a meal at which business is conducted may be separately deductible under the main rule of section 162(a) as an ordinary and necessary business expense. Normally, such business meals must involve clients or customers and not merely one's work colleagues. Moss v. Commissioner, 758 F.2d 211 (7th Cir. 1985). Under this logic a meal taken at the office while working alone is not deductible.

4. Temporary Reassignments

A final area of importance to the travel expense deduction concerns taxpayers who are temporarily assigned by their employers to work at a different location from their usual employment base. By and large the employee's expenses are deductible under section 162(a)(2) while living in the temporary location. Peurifoy v. Commissioner, 358 U.S. 59 (1958). However, the flush language of section 162(a) cuts back on this rule by setting a one year limit on how long an assignment can be considered temporary. The Service has embellished on this principle in a revenue ruling. *See* Rev. Rul. 93-86, 1993-2 C.B. 71.

G. Section 163(j) — Business Interest

Interest paid or incurred on debt allocable to a trade or business is generally deductible from gross income. IRC § 163(a), (h)(2)(A). There are many limitations and exceptions to this general rule. Section 163(j), for example, limits the deduction of business interest for any taxable year to the sum of: (1) the taxpayer's business interest income for the year; (2) 30 percent of the taxpayer's adjusted taxable income for the year; and (3) where applicable, the taxpayer's floor financing interest for the year (a specialized category for car dealers). IRC § 163(j)(1). The practical effect of the rule is to limit the deduction of net business interest expenses to 30 percent of the taxpayer's adjusted taxable income. An exception to the limitation is provided for small businesses (those with average gross receipts of $25 million or less). IRC § 163(j)(3). For other exceptions, see IRC § 163(j)(7) (providing exceptions, at the taxpayers' election, for real property businesses and farming businesses). Any interest not deductible may be carried forward indefinitely to succeeding years. IRC § 163(j)(2).

H. Section 280E — The Curious Case of Legalized Marijuana

Even illegal income must be reported under the income tax laws. As a result, a line of cases has arisen applying section 162 to illegal businesses. In response to those cases Congress enacted section 280E which denies business expense deductions for drug traffickers. Over the past few years a number of states have legalized sales of marijuana for recreational or medical use. But marijuana remains a Schedule 1 controlled substance under federal law, and, thus, marijuana businesses that operate legally in their respective states are still unable to take advantage of section 162. If the legalized marijuana industry continues to grow, we expect that the pressure to repeal or amend section 280E will grow also. Interestingly, section 280E has been interpreted to not apply to the drug traffickers' inventory costs (also known as cost of goods sold). *See, e.g.*, Olive v. Commissioner, 139 T.C. 19 (2012). For helpful articles on section 280E and the marijuana industry, *see* Kimberly A. Houser, Jeffrey Gramlich & Debra Sanders, *How Current Tax Policy Affects the Marijuana Industry*, 150 Tax Notes 899 (Feb. 22, 2016); Edward J. Roche, Jr., *Federal Income Taxation of Medical Marijuana Businesses*, 66 Tax Law. 429 (2013).

I. Entertainment, Meal and Transportation Expenses

Expenses for *entertainment*, or a facility used in connection with entertainment, are generally not deductible even if related to or associated with a taxpayer's business. IRC § 274(a)(1). *But see* IRC 274(e) (providing some exceptions). In addition, expenses for any *qualified transportation fringe and for any employee commuting* are not deductible by an employer, except if necessary for employee safety. IRC § 274(a)(4). *Employer-provided meals* are subject to some transition rules. Currently, the deduction an employer can take for meals is 50% of the costs of such meals. IRC § 274(n)(1). After 2025, however, no deduction will be allowed for employer-provided meals that are excluded from an employee's income under section 119 or section 132(e). IRC § 274(o).

J. Section 199A — Deduction for Qualified Business Income

Most deduction provisions in the Code require some outlay or expenditure by the taxpayer. Occasionally, however, Congress will create a tax deduction just for having a certain type of income. For example, section 199A provides for a deduction equal to 20% of a taxpayer's "qualified business income." The deduction, which is temporary for tax years 2018 through 2025, applies to certain sole proprietors engaged in eligible trades or businesses. Because it is immensely complicated, and because it also applies to owners in many pass-through businesses (e.g., partnerships, LLCs, or S corporations), we defer treatment of the provision to Chapter 37, which deals specifically with entity taxation. For present purposes, the effect of this deduction is to reduce the effective tax rate on business income of sole proprietorships and pass-through entities in order to level the playing field with C corporations, which are subject to a low 21% tax rate.

K. Section 212 — Investment Expenses

Section 212 allows deduction of ordinary and necessary expenses incurred or paid for the production or collection of income, for the management of income producing property, or in connection with the determination, collection, or refund of taxes. Typical items covered by section 212 include office rent, custodial services, investment counsel fees, and tax return preparation fees. Treas. Reg. § 1.212-1(g) & (l). (Note that "investment interest" is subject to its own set of limitations provided under section 163(d).) Like section 162, section 212 does not cover commuting or other personal expenses. Treas. Reg. § 1.212-1(f). The costs of repairs and maintenance of investment real property, such as a home rented to third parties, are deductible under section 212. However, despite the fact that most people consider their homes a form of investment, the costs of maintaining the taxpayer's own residence are considered personal in nature and are not deductible. Treas. Reg. § 1.212-1(h). The vacation home, the personal residence converted to rental property, and the mixed use home raise special issues that are addressed in later chapters.

It is important to remember that capital expenditures may not be deducted under section 212 just as they cannot be deducted under section 162. The most obvious place where this comes into play is with respect to broker's fees. When a fee is paid upon acquisition of stock it is added to the cost basis in the stock. Spreckels v. Helvering, 315 U.S. 626 (1942). Thus, the fee will reduce any gain realized or increase any loss realized when the stock is sold. A broker's fee paid upon sale of stock will reduce the amount realized. Treas. Reg. § 1.263(a)-1(e)(1).

IV. Materials

Welch v. Helvering

290 U.S. 111 (1933)

Mr. Justice Cardozo delivered the opinion of the Court.

The question to be determined is whether payments by a taxpayer, who is in business as a commission agent, are allowable deductions in the computation of his income if made to the creditors of a bankrupt corporation in an endeavor to strengthen his own standing and credit.

In 1922 petitioner was the secretary of the E. L. Welch Company, a Minnesota corporation, engaged in the grain business. The company was adjudged an involuntary bankrupt, and had a discharge from its debts. Thereafter the petitioner made a contract with the Kellogg Company to purchase grain for it on a commission. In order to re-establish his relations with customers whom he had known when acting for the Welch Company and to solidify his credit and standing, he decided to pay the debts of the Welch business so far as he was able. In fulfillment of that resolve, he made payments of substantial amounts during five successive years. The Commissioner ruled that these payments were not deductible from income as ordinary and necessary expenses, but were rather in the nature of capital expenditures, an outlay for the development of reputation and good will. The Board of Tax Appeals sustained the action of the Commissioner, and the Court of Appeals for the Eighth Circuit affirmed. The case is here on certiorari.

"In computing net income there shall be allowed as deductions … all the ordinary and necessary expenses paid or incurred during the taxable year in carrying on any trade or business." [Citations omitted. The statute quoted was the predecessor of current section 162(a). Ed.]

We may assume that the payments to creditors of the Welch Company were necessary for the development of the petitioner's business, at least in the sense that they were appropriate and helpful. McCulloch v. Maryland, 4 Wheat. 316, 4 L.Ed. 579. He certainly thought they were, and we should be slow to override his judgment. But the problem is not solved when the payments are characterized as necessary. Many necessary payments are charges upon capital. There is need to determine whether they are both necessary and ordinary. Now, what is ordinary, though there must always be a strain of constancy within it, is none the less a variable affected by time and place and circumstance. Ordinary in this context does not mean that the payments must be habitual or normal in the sense that the same taxpayer will have to make them often. A lawsuit affecting the safety of a business may happen once in a lifetime. The counsel fees may be so heavy that repetition is unlikely. None the less, the expense is an ordinary one because we know from experience that payments for such a purpose, whether the amount is large or small, are the common and accepted means of defense against attack. The situation is unique in the life of the individual affected, but not in the life of the group, the community, of which he is a part. At such times there are norms of conduct that help to stabilize our judgment, and make it certain and objective. The instance is not erratic, but is brought within a known type.

The line of demarcation is now visible between the case that is here and the one supposed for illustration. We try to classify this act as ordinary or the opposite, and the norms of conduct fail us. No longer can we have recourse to any fund of business experience, to any known business practice. Men do at times pay the debts of others without legal obligation or the lighter obligation imposed by the usages of trade or by neighborly amenities, but they do not do so ordinarily, not even though the result might be to heighten their reputation for generosity and opulence. Indeed, if language is to be read in its natural and common meaning we should have to say that payment in such circumstances, instead of being ordinary is in a high degree extraordinary. There is nothing ordinary in the stimulus evoking it, and none in the response.

Here, indeed, as so often in other branches of the law, the decisive distinctions are those of degree and not of kind. One struggles in vain for any verbal formula that will supply a ready touchstone. The standard set up by the statute is not a rule of law; it is rather a way of life. Life in all its fullness must supply the answer to the riddle.

The Commissioner of Internal Revenue resorted to that standard in assessing the petitioner's income, and found that the payments in controversy came closer to capital outlays than to ordinary and necessary expenses in the operation of a business. His ruling has the support of a presumption of correctness, and the petitioner has the burden of proving it to be wrong. Unless we can say from facts within our knowledge that these are ordinary and necessary expenses according to the ways of conduct and the forms of speech prevailing in the business world, the tax must be confirmed. But nothing told us by this record or within the sphere of our judicial notice permits us to give that extension to what is ordinary and necessary. Indeed, to do so would open the door to many bizarre analogies. One man has a family name that is clouded by thefts committed by an ancestor. To add to his own standing he repays the stolen money, wiping off, it may be, his income for the year. The payments figure in his tax return as ordinary expenses. Another man conceives the notion that he will be able to practice his vocation with greater ease and profit if he has an opportunity to enrich his culture. Forthwith the price of his education becomes an expense of the business, reducing the income subject to taxation. There is little difference between these expenses and those in controversy here. Reputation and learning are akin to capital assets, like the good will of an old partnership. For many, they are the only tools with which to hew a pathway to success. The money spent in acquiring them is well and wisely spent. It is not an ordinary expense of the operation of a business.

Many cases in the federal courts deal with phases of the problem presented in the case at bar. To attempt to harmonize them would be a futile task. They involve the appreciation of particular situations, at times with border-line conclusions.

The decree should be Affirmed.

Jenkins v. Commissioner

T.C. Memo 1983-667

IRWIN, JUDGE:

The sole issue presented for our decision is whether payments made by petitioner to investors in a failed corporation known as Twitty Burger, Inc., are deductible as ordinary and necessary business expenses of petitioner's business as a country music performer.

The relevant facts are as follows: Petitioner Conway Twitty is a well-known country music entertainer. Most of his income is derived from his performances, songwriting, and record royalties. In 1968, Conway and several of his friends decided to form a chain of fast food restaurants and incorporated Twitty Burger under the laws of Oklahoma. During 1968 and 1969, approximately 75 of petitioner's friends and business associates invested money in Twitty Burger. Subsequently it was determined that it would be some time before the requirements of the Security and Exchange Commission could be met and a public offering of stock made. It was determined, therefore, that debentures should be issued to those persons who had invested money in the undertaking as interim evidence of their investments.

By late 1970, Twitty Burger was experiencing financial difficulties and it was determined by Twitty Burger's attorney that further attempts to obtain registration of the corporate stock would be futile. Shortly thereafter it was decided that Twitty Burger should be shut down. Except for one independently-owned franchise operating in Texas, the last Twitty Burger restaurant was closed in May 1971. Subsequently, Conway Twitty decided that the investors should be repaid the amount of their investments in the failed corporation. As Twitty Burger had no assets with which to satisfy the debentures, Conway Twitty decided he would repay the investors from his future earnings. During the years in issue, 1973 and 1974, Conway Twitty made payments to the investors of $92,892.46 and $3,600, respectively.

Respondent argues that the payments Conway Twitty made to the investors in Twitty Burger are not deductible by him as ordinary and necessary business expenses under section 162 because there was no business purpose for the payments and, additionally, there was no relationship between his involvement in Twitty Burger and his business of being a country music entertainer. Respondent argues that the payments in question here were made by Conway Twitty gratuitously in that petitioner had no personal liability to the holders of the debentures and made the payments merely out of a sense of moral obligation. Relying on *Welch v. Helvering*, and certain of its progeny, respondent concludes that while it was "very nice" of petitioner to reimburse the investors in Twitty Burger, the required nexus between the expenditures and Conway Twitty's career as a country music entertainer does not exist and therefore the payments were not "ordinary and necessary" within the meaning of section 162.

Petitioner argues that the rule of *Welch v. Helvering* is not applicable to the case at bar because petitioner made the payments in question to protect his reputation and earning capacity in his ongoing business of being a country music entertainer whereas in *Welch* the Supreme Court held that the payments made there were capital expenditures of the taxpayer's new business. Petitioner maintains that the expenditures in issue here are deductible under section 162 if the payments were made primarily with a business motive and if there is a sufficient connection between the payments and the taxpayer's trade or business.

The question presented for our resolution is purely one of fact. While previously decided cases dealing with this issue are somewhat helpful there is, quite understandably, no case directly on point with the facts before us. As the Supreme Court recognized in *Welch v. Helvering*,

Many cases in the federal courts deal with phases of the problem presented in the case at bar. To attempt to harmonize them would be a futile task. They involve the appreciation of particular situations, at times with border-line conclusions.

There is no suggestion in the record that any of the payments were made in order to protect petitioner's investment in Twitty Burger or to revitalize the corporation. It is petitioner's contention that Conway Twitty repaid the investors in Twitty Burger from his personal funds in order to protect his personal business reputation. While it is clear from the facts that Conway was under no legal obligation to make such payments (at least in the sense that the corporate debentures were not personally guaranteed by him), the law is clear that the absence of such an obligation is not in itself a bar to the deduction of such expenditures under section 162. In addition, the fact that the petitioner also felt a moral obligation to the people who had entrusted him with their funds does not preclude the deductibility of the payments so long as the satisfaction of the moral obligation was not the primary motivation for the expenditure.

After a thorough consideration of the record we are convinced that petitioner Conway Twitty repaid the investors in Twitty Burger with the primary motive of protecting his personal business reputation. There was the obvious similarity of the name of the corporation and petitioner's stage name. There is no doubt that the corporation's name was chosen with the idea of capitalizing on Conway Twitty's fame as a country music performer. Additionally, many of the investors were connected with the country music industry. While there is no doubt that part of petitioner's motivation for making the payments involved his personal sense of morality, we do not believe that this ethical consideration was paramount.

Petitioner testified as follows concerning his motivations for repaying the Twitty Burger investors:

I'm 99 percent entertainer. That's just about all I know. The name Conway Twitty, and the image that I work so hard for since 1955 and 1956 is the foundation that I, my family, and the 30 some odd people that work for me stand on. They depend on it, and they can depend on it. I handled it that way because of the image. And second, I handled it that way because I think it is morally right, and if you owe a man something, you pay him. When we got the letter from Walter Beach and from [Merle] Haggard's lawyer and from a couple other places, my people said, hey, you know, we've got some letters from people saying they are going to sue you, and that you might have done something wrong as far as securities and all that stuff goes. It just scares you to death. A law suit like that with — say if Merle Haggard sued Conway Twitty or if Walter Beach sued Conway Twitty and you're in court, and they are saying it's fraud and something to do with the securities thing, and, you know, all the years I've worked for are gone. If my fans didn't give up on me, it would warp me psychologically. I couldn't function anymore because I'm the type of person I am.

Petitioner presented the expert testimony of William Ivey, the Director of Country Music Foundation in Nashville, Tennessee. In his report which was introduced into evidence in lieu of direct testimony he stated as follows:

> Had, in the matter before this court, Conway Twitty allowed investors to be left dangling with heavy losses following the collapse of the Twitty Burger chain, the multiple lawsuits, unfavorable news stories and disgruntled investors would have all damaged that very reputation which was a key element in Conway's image as an artist. Though he would have continued to perform and record, there exists serious doubt that he would have achieved the unparalleled success he enjoyed during the 1970's had his reputation been so injured.

We conclude that there was a proximate relationship between the payments made to the holders of Twitty Burger debentures and petitioner's trade or business as a country music entertainer so as to render those payments an ordinary and necessary expense of that business. Although, as respondent argues, the chances of a successful lawsuit against Conway Twitty by any of the investors or the Securities and Exchange Commission was remote we agree with petitioner that the possibility of extensive adverse publicity concerning petitioner's involvement with the defunct corporation and the consequent loss of the investors' funds was very real. We do not believe it is necessary for us to find that adverse publicity emanating from Conway Twitty's failure to repay the investors in Twitty Burger would have ruined his career as a country music singer. Rather, we need only find that a proximate relationship existed between the payments and petitioner's business. We find that such relationship exists. It is not necessary that the taxpayer's trade or business be of the same type as that engaged in by the person on whose behalf the payments are made.

In making these payments petitioner was furthering his business as a country music artist and protecting his business reputation for integrity. The mere fact that they were voluntary does not deprive them of their character as ordinary and necessary business expenses. Under the unique circumstances presented in this case, we hold that the payments in issue are deductible as business expenses under section 162.[13]

---

13. We close with the following "Ode to Conway Twitty":
    Twitty Burger went belly up
    But Conway remained true
    He repaid his investors, one and all
    It was the moral thing to do.
    His fans would not have liked it
    It could have hurt his fame
    Had any investors sued him
    Like Merle Haggard or Sonny James.
    When it was time to file taxes
    Conway thought what he would do
    Was deduct those payments as a business expense
    Under section one-sixty-two.
    In order to allow these deductions

Henderson v. Commissioner

143 F.3d 497 (9th Cir. 1998)

WIGGINS, CIRCUIT JUDGE:

We must decide whether a taxpayer may claim Boise, Idaho as his "tax home" for the 1990 tax year even though virtually all of his work that year was for a traveling ice show. James Henderson claimed deductions under Internal Revenue Code § 162(a)(2) for living expenses incurred "away from home" while on the tours. The Commissioner disallowed the deductions, concluding that Henderson had no legal tax home for purposes of § 162(a)(2) because he lacked the requisite business reasons for living in Boise between ice show tours. As a result of the disallowance, Henderson had a deficiency in his 1990 federal income tax of $1,791. The Tax Court upheld the Commissioner's decision. We have jurisdiction under 26 U.S.C. § 7482(a), and we affirm.

Henderson's parents lived in Boise, where they had reared him. Even after graduating from the University of Idaho in 1989, he maintained many personal contacts with Boise. For instance, he received mail at his parents' residence, lived there between work assignments, and kept many belongings and his dog there. He also was registered to vote in Idaho, paid Idaho state income tax, maintained an Idaho driver's license, and maintained his bank account in Idaho. During 1990, he spent about two to three months in Boise, staying at his parents' residence. While he was there, he performed a few minor jobs to maintain or improve the family residence.

In 1990, Henderson worked as a stage hand for Walt Disney's World of Ice, a traveling show. His employers' corporate offices were in Vienna, Virginia. Henderson was employed on a tour by tour basis. He testified that at the end of one tour, he would be contacted about participating in the next one. Following the completion of a tour, he returned to his parents' home in Boise. He worked on three different Disney tours that year. The first lasted from January 1 to May 13, the second from July to November, and the third from December 5 to December 31. He traveled on tour to thirteen states and Japan. The tours stopped in each city for a few days or weeks. While traveling, he received $30 per day to cover expenses.

Henderson claims that he looked periodically for employment in Boise between the tours, but the evidence showed that he worked as a stage hand only for a single ZZ Top concert. The Tax Court found that while he returned to Boise in his "idle time," his source of employment during the tax year had no connection to Boise. On appeal, Henderson contends that his 1990 tax home was Boise, primarily based on his extensive personal contacts there.

Goes the argument of the Commissioner
The payments must be ordinary and necessary
To a business of the petitioner.
Had Conway not repaid the investors
His career would have been under cloud,
Under the unique facts of this case
Held: The deductions are allowed.

Internal Revenue Code § 162(a)(2) allows a deduction for all ordinary and necessary "traveling expenses ... while away from home in the pursuit of a trade or business." 26 U.S.C. § 162(a)(2). This section embodies "a fundamental principle of taxation"— that the cost of producing income is deductible from a person's taxable income. Hantzis v. Commissioner, 638 F.2d 248, 249 (1st Cir.1981). To qualify for the "away from home" deduction, the Supreme Court has held that the taxpayer's expenses must (1) be reasonable and necessary expenses, (2) be incurred while away from home, and (3) be incurred while in the pursuit of a trade or business. Commissioner v. Flowers, 326 U.S. 465, 470 (1946).

The first and third criteria are not at issue. The subject of this appeal is whether the expenses Henderson claims as deductions were incurred while "away from home." If Henderson establishes that his home was Boise, his reasonable traveling expenses on the Disney tours are deductible. The Tax Court concluded that Boise was not Henderson's tax home because his choice to live there had nothing to do with the needs of his work; thus, the Tax Court held that Henderson could not claim the deduction for traveling expenses incurred while away from Boise. It held that Henderson had no tax home because he continuously traveled for work. We agree.

Henderson builds a strong case that he treated Boise as his home in the usual sense of the word, but "for purposes of [section] 162, 'home' does not have its usual and ordinary meaning." Putnam v. United States, 32 F.3d 911, 917 (5th Cir.1994) ("In fact, 'home'— in the usual case—means 'work.'"). We have held that the term "home" means "the taxpayer's abode at his or her principal place of employment." Folkman v. United States, 615 F.2d 493, 495 (9th Cir.1980); see also Coombs v. Commissioner, 608 F.2d 1269, 1275 (9th Cir.1979) (stating that "tax home" is generally, but not always, exact locale of principal place of employment). If a taxpayer has no regular or principal place of business, he may be able to claim his place of abode as his tax home. See Holdreith v. Commissioner, 57 T.C.M. (CCH) 1383.

A taxpayer may have no tax home, however, if he continuously travels and thus does not duplicate substantial, continuous living expenses for a permanent home maintained for some business reason. James v. United States, 308 F.2d 204, 207 (9th Cir.1962). Clearly, if a taxpayer has no "home" for tax purposes, then he cannot deduct under § 162(a)(2) for expenses incurred "away from home." This is for good reason. In *James*, we examined the statutory precursor to the present version of § 162(a) and explained that the deduction was designed to mitigate the burden on taxpayers who travel on business. 308 F.2d at 207. The burden exists "only when the taxpayer has a 'home,' the maintenance of which involves substantial continuing expenses which will be duplicated by the expenditures which the taxpayer must make when required to travel elsewhere for business purposes." *Id.*; see also Andrews, 931 F.2d at 135 (emphasizing that the deduction's purpose was to mitigate duplicative expenses); *Hantzis*, 638 F.2d at 253. Thus, a taxpayer only has a tax home—and can claim a deduction for being away from that home—when it appears that he or she incurs substantial, continuous living expenses at a permanent place of residence. *James*, 308 F.2d at 207–08.

Revenue Ruling 73-539, 1973-2 C.B. 37, outlines three factors to consider in determining whether a taxpayer has a tax home or is an itinerant. Essentially, they are (i) the business connection to the locale of the claimed home; (ii) the duplicative nature of the taxpayer's living expenses while traveling and at the claimed home; and (iii) personal attachments to the claimed home. While subjective intent can be considered in determining whether he has a tax home, objective financial criteria are usually more significant.

The location of Henderson's tax home is a determination of fact reviewed for clear error. Frank v. United States, 577 F.2d 93, 97 (9th Cir.1978). Similarly, we believe the determination of whether a taxpayer has a tax home or is an itinerant depends on the facts of each case and should be reviewed for clear error. Considering these factors, the Tax Court did not clearly err when it concluded that Henderson is an itinerant taxpayer.

First, Henderson had virtually no business reason for his tax home to be in any location—he constantly traveled in 1990 as part of his work with the World on Ice tours. His personal choice to return to Boise was not dictated by business reasons. Except for brief intervals, he was employed for the tours. He worked only one night in Boise. While he testified he looked for other work in Boise between tours, he also testified that at the end of each tour he would have a contract talk with the company manager about the next tour. The Tax Court determined that Henderson merely returned to Boise during his "idle time" between tours. While his reasons for returning may be entirely understandable, we cannot say the Tax Court clearly erred in concluding they were personal, not business, reasons. His minimal employment efforts in Boise do not change this analysis.

The importance of the business reason for residing in a certain place is illustrated in *Hantzis*. In that case, the First Circuit disallowed the "away from home" deduction for a law student from Boston who took a summer job in New York. The court held that she did not have a tax home in Boston, even though her husband lived in Boston and she lived there during the school year, because she had no business reason to maintain a home in Boston during the summer while she worked in New York. The court explained why the deduction did not apply in those circumstances:

> Only a taxpayer who lives one place, works another and has business ties to both is in the ambiguous situation that the temporary employment doctrine is designed to resolve.... [A] taxpayer who pursues temporary employment away from the location of his usual residence, but has no business connection with that location, is not "away from home" for purposes of section 162(a)(2).

Hantzis, 638 F.2d at 255.

Second, Henderson did not have substantial, continuing living expenses in Boise that were duplicated by his expenses on the road. The evidence showed that he lived with his parents when he stayed in Boise. The Tax Court found that he paid no rent and had no ownership interest in his parents' home. His financial contributions in Boise were limited. He contributed some labor to maintenance and improvement of the home while he was there, and he paid about $500 for supplies. While his parents may have expended money that benefitted Henderson as well—i.e., maintaining a mortgage, paying utilities, and so forth—this is not a substantial living expense incurred by Henderson. Further, any minor expense he may have incurred while living with his parents was not continuing during the periods while he traveled on tour. That is, there is no evidence he had any expenses in Boise while he traveled on the Disney tours.

The fact that Henderson may have incurred higher expenses while traveling with Disney than he would have if he had obtained a full-time job in Boise is not dispositive. The issue presented is whether his claimed expenses were incurred while he was away from his tax home. To assume that Henderson is entitled to the deduction simply because Henderson incurred higher expenses than he would have had he worked in Boise ignores the important question of whether Boise was his tax home at all. Only if Boise is his tax home can Henderson claim deductions for expenses incurred while away from Boise.

Because these two factors weigh against finding that he had a tax home in Boise, the Tax Court did not clearly err when it discounted his evidence on the third factor: personal attachment to Boise. Henderson cites cases, e.g. Horton v. Commissioner, 86 T.C. 589, 593 (1986), which hold that a taxpayer may treat a personal residence as his tax home even if it is not the same as the place of his temporary employment with a certain employer. This principle does not help Henderson, however, because he cannot establish any (non-de minimis) business connection to Boise to justify the position that it was his permanent tax home. *See Hantzis*, 638 F.2d at 254–55. Thus, travel away from Boise while on tour with Disney was not travel "away from home" as that term is understood for income tax purposes.

Affirmed.

KOZINKSKI, Circuit Judge, dissenting.

The Tax Code provides that travel expenses are fully deductible, so long as they are incurred while "away from home" in the pursuit of business. IRC § 162(a)(2). Henderson fits comfortably within this language. He lived with his parents in Boise, which made their home his home under any reasonable definition of the term. And he incurred travel expenses in pursuing a job that moved from town to town. Given the itinerant nature of his employment, Henderson could not have avoided these travel expenses by moving his home closer to work. He is thus easily distinguished from the taxpayer in Hantzis v. Commissioner, 638 F.2d 248 (1st Cir.1981), who could have avoided the travel expenses altogether by moving closer to her work. *Hantzis*'s extra-statutory requirement that a home is not a "tax home" unless dictated by business necessity has no application when the job itself has no fixed location.

The other reasons offered by the IRS for denying Henderson his traveling expense deduction are not supported by the Code or the regulations, nor do they make any sense. That Henderson's parents did not charge him room and board is of no consequence. Neither the Code nor common experience requires that a taxpayer pay for his home, else all minors and many in-laws would be deemed homeless. "Home" is not a term of art; it is a common English word meaning a permanent place where a person lives, keeps his belongings, receives his mail, houses his dog—just as Henderson did. Indeed, a grown son living in his parents' house is said to be living "at home." Whether he compensates his parents in cash, by doing chores or through filial affection is none of the Commissioner's business. What matters is that, by going on the road in pursuit of his job, Henderson had to pay for food and lodging that he would not have had to buy had he stayed home.

James v. United States, 308 F.2d 204 (9th Cir.1962), cuts against the government. Despite some imprecise language in the opinion, the facts there were very different. George James was on the road 365 days a year and had no permanent home; he spent his entire life traveling from hotel to motel. Wherever a weekend or holiday found him, he would stay there until it came time to go to his next location. James thus was, indeed, a tax turtle—someone with no fixed residence. Henderson is very different: He had a home in Boise, a place where he returned when he wasn't working. He was no more a tax turtle than anyone else who travels a lot for business. That his home happens to be owned by his parents makes it no less his home.[1]

Fast planes and automobiles have turned us into a nation of itinerants. The tradition of families living together in one city, even under one roof, is sadly disappearing. Yet there is virtue in keeping families together, in parents who welcome their adult children under their roof. Leave it to the IRS to turn a family reunion into a taxable event. Henderson is being hit with extra taxes because his lifestyle doesn't conform to the IRS's idea of normalcy. But why should the government get extra money because the Hendersons chose to let their son live at home? Had they given him $600 a month to rent an apartment next door, Henderson surely would have gotten the travel deduction. I see no reason why the Henderson family ought to be penalized because the parents gave their son a gift of housing rather than cash—or why the Commissioner should be the beneficiary of this parental generosity. If Congress had said it must be so, I would bow to its wisdom. But Congress said no such thing and I do not feel bound to give the same deference to the Commissioner's litigating position.[2] Given the dearth of authority or common sense supporting the Commissioner's view,

---

1. *James*'s emphasis on duplication of expenses is unnecessary to the holding, and mistaken to boot. Duplication is one possible method of sifting out business expenses from personal ones, but not the method chosen by Congress. Section 162(a)(2) requires only that the taxpayer be away from home in pursuit of business; meals, for example, are fully deductible even though the expense is not duplicated back at home.

2. Revenue Ruling 73-529 is entitled to some deference—exactly how much is unclear—but certainly far less than the statutesque deference we give regulations. *See* Estate of McLendon v. Commissioner, 135 F.3d 1017, 1023–24 (5th Cir.1998); First Chicago NBD Corp. v. Commissioner, 135 F.3d 457, 459–60 (7th Cir.1998). Because the Service cannot easily recant a position after a ruling is published, it has reason to be overly stingy in drafting. Institutional pressures may also drive the Service to stretch the language of the Code; it's easier for the Executive Branch to have the Service milk more revenue out of the existing Code than to persuade Congress to amend it. Moreover, unlike most regulations, Revenue Rulings are not subject to the notice-and-comment procedures of the Administrative Procedure Act. Ruling 73-529 sweeps too broadly to be persuasive here: Under the Ruling, Henderson would get no deduction even if he spent ten months a year at home instead of ten weeks, simply because he paid no rent.

we are free to encourage happy family arrangements like those between Henderson and his mom and dad. In the name of family values, I respectfully dissent.

V. Related Matters

- **Other Provisions.** As mentioned earlier there are a vast array of expenses that are potentially deductible under section 162. Subparts of section 162 (not considered above), and the regulations and cases interpreting section 162, have addressed many of these expenses. The Code and regulations address such topics as expenditures for:
  - employee benefits (Treas. Reg. §§ 1.162-9, -10, -10T);
  - farm expenses (Treas. Reg. § 1.162-12);
  - membership dues (Treas. Reg. § 1.162-15);
  - illegal bribes (IRC § 162(c); Treas. Reg. § 1.162-18);
  - lobbying expenditures (IRC § 162(e); Treas. Reg. § 1.162-20); and
  - fines and penalties (IRC § 162(f); Treas. Reg. §§ 1.162-21 & -29).
- **Case law.** Case law has addressed such disparate issues as expenditures for:
  - spiritual advice (Trebilcock v. Commissioner, 64 T.C. 852 (1975));
  - designer clothes (Pevsner v. Commissioner, 628 F.2d 467 (5th Cir. 1980), discussed in the overview); and
  - obtaining a divorce (United States v. Gilmore, 372 U.S. 39 (1963), discussed in Chapter 35).
- **Education Costs.** The cost of education is sometimes deductible under section 162. *See* Treas. Reg. § 1.162-5. See also Chapter 33 where the tax treatment of education benefits and costs is addressed.
- **Materials and Supplies.** Regulations attempt to clarify the tax treatment of expenditures for materials and supplies. Generally, such expenditures are deductible in the year in which the materials and supplies are used or consumed in the taxpayer's business operations. Treas. Reg. § 1.162-3(a)(1). In cases where the materials and supplies are carried on hand without being inventoried the deduction is permitted at the time of purchase. Treas. Reg. § 1.162-3(a)(2). These rules do not overrule the capitalization requirement for materials and supplies that are incorporated into the production of some other asset the cost of which must be capitalized. Treas. Reg. § 1.162-3(b). Capitalization is addressed in Chapter 8.
- **Excessive Employee Remuneration.** A publicly held corporation may not deduct compensation in excess of $1 million paid to any covered employee for a tax year. IRC § 162(m).
- **Confidential Sexual Harassment Settlements.** In the wake of a series of high profile scandals involving allegations of sexual harassment and the rise of the #metoo movement, Congress enacted section 162(q) denying deductions for payments to

settle sexual harassment or abuse cases where the settlement agreement is made confidential. The attorney's fees in such cases are also non-deductible. The apparent intent of this provision is to encourage making such settlements public, perhaps to protect victims from serial harassers. A number of the more sensational cases involved allegations of repeated sexual harassment or abuse followed by repeated payments to keep the alleged victims silent. It seems that the limitation on the deduction of attorney's fees applies to the payee as well as the payor of the settlement. Chapter 35 considers the deductibility of attorney's fees.

Chapter 8

Capital Expenditures

I. Assignment

Read: Internal Revenue Code: §§ 161; 263(a); 263A(a), (b), (g), (h), (i). Skim § 195.

Treasury Regulations: §§ 1.162-3, -4, -6; 1.263(a)-1, -2(d)(1), -2(f), -3(d), -3(j)–(l), -4(a)–(b)(3), -(c)(1), -4(d)(1), -4(d)(3),-4(d)(5), -4(d)(6), -4(e)(1)(i), -4(e)(4)(i), -4(f)(1), -5(d)(1), (3).

Text: Overview
Midland Empire Packing Co. v. Commissioner
Mt. Morris Drive-In Theatre Co. v. Commissioner
Related Materials

Complete the problems.

II. Problems

1. Xochipilli, Inc., a perfume manufacturing and marketing company, made the following expenditures. Discuss whether each is currently deductible as an expense under section 162 or constitutes a nondeductible capital expenditure.

    (a) $1 million to buy land and an old warehouse building; $250,000 to construct a new parking garage next to the building; $5,000 to pave a few ground parking spaces; $500 for new signs on the buildings.

    (b) $70,000 for work on the warehouse ($4,000 to fix a leak in the roof; $6,000 to repaint the exterior; and $60,000 to replace cornices and parapets to bring the building in compliance with a new city ordinance setting higher earthquake safety standards).

    (c) $300,000 in salary to the company's president. The president spent 2/3 of his time running the day-to-day affairs of the business, and 1/3 of his time negotiating the acquisition of a parcel of land.

    (d) $50,000 in severance payments to ex-employees in connection with business down-sizing, and $50,000 in special training of existing employees.

    (e) $18,000 for a new machine; $2,000 to install the machine; and $3,000 for a 12-month maintenance contract on the machine for the period from October 1 of this year to September 30 of next year.

(f) $2,000 for the annual premium for general liability insurance covering from February 1 of next year to January 31 the year after.

(g) $40,000 to develop a package design for its newest perfume product, and a $5,000 fee paid to a government agency to obtain trademark and copyright protection on certain elements of the package design.

(h) $15,000 on print advertising ($5,000 for newspaper advertising; $10,000 to develop an advertising catalog, to be in circulation for two years, featuring all of the company's perfume products).

(i) $1,000 to remove and discard an old advertising billboard on a local highway and $3,000 to install a new one.

2. Isha Sharvani is a full-time editor for a local publishing company. For the past three years, Isha has also been a choreographer for a dance company that has performed in a number of places and has received local and national media attention. She travels with the dance group on weekends, keeps detailed records of her traveling expenses, and consults with experts in the dance industry to further her choreography. This year, Isha spent $300 to create a dance score and $1,500 to create and produce an instructional video tape of her choreography. Are these amounts currently deductible?

III. Overview

We learned in the previous chapter that ordinary and necessary business and investment expenses are immediately deductible. IRC §§ 162, 212. Therefore, if a taxpayer purchases a legal pad to use in her ongoing business, the cost of that pad should be deductible in the year paid or incurred. What if the taxpayer purchases a computer to use in her business? Isn't it fair to say that a computer, like a legal pad, is an ordinary and necessary component of one's business?

There are a number of *overriding* Code provisions that prevent the current deductibility of otherwise allowable items. *See* IRC § 261 (warning that no deduction shall be allowed "in any case" with respect to certain items specified in Part IX of the Code). Thus, what may seem to be a deductible expense under one provision (e.g., § 162) may be classified as non-deductible under a separate overriding provision. Two important overriding provisions are section 263(a) and section 263A(a). These two overriding Code provisions are the subject of this chapter.

We will learn in Chapter 9 that there are some important exceptions to the general rules addressed in this chapter. In other words, Congress sometimes permits a current deduction for certain expenditures that would otherwise be classified as non-deductible under section 263(a) or section 263A(a). These exceptions, which permit full or partial expensing of otherwise non-deductible expenditures, are generally designed to spur increased business investment in certain property in order to grow the economy.

A. Section 263(a)

1. In General

Section 263(a) disallows the immediate deduction of "capital expenditures." This provision is less than clear in its full impact and depends on the regulations, administrative rulings, and case law for much amplification and clarification. Capital expenditures are generally those amounts paid to create, acquire, or improve long-lived assets. The reason such costs are not currently deductible is that the property produced, acquired, or improved is not consumed or used up within the year, but rather it continues to contribute to income over a period of years. If the costs incurred in the creation, acquisition, or improvement of such property were deductible in full in the current year, there would be a mismatching of income and expenses that produced that income; income would be understated in the year of acquisition and overstated in later years. By prohibiting the immediate deduction of capital expenditures this problem is avoided.

If expenditures are not deductible when paid or incurred, they are *capitalized*, that is, they are added to the taxpayer's basis in the property to which the expenditures relate. Although they are not immediately deductible, these capitalized costs may be eligible to be deducted over time through an appropriate depreciation or amortization allowance under a separate Code provision. As explained in the next chapter, tax depreciation is an accounting device that allocates the capitalized cost of an asset to the various periods during which the asset is used. In other words, tax depreciation allows a taxpayer to recover (deduct) the capitalized cost of an asset over a certain period of time (the period of time that usually correlates to the asset's production of income). As also explained in the next chapter, there are certain "bonus" tax depreciation rules that allow a taxpayer to deduct 100% of the capitalized cost of certain property in the year of purchase. Bonus depreciation violates the matching principle discussed above, but is often used by the government as a tool to spur economic growth.

2. Distinguishing Deductible Expenses from Nondeductible Capital Expenditures

a. Case Law

Distinguishing deductible expenses from nondeductible capital expenditures is often difficult. In Commissioner v. Lincoln Savings & Loan Ass'n, 403 U.S. 345 (1971), the Supreme Court concluded that an expenditure that serves to create or enhance a separate and distinct asset must be capitalized. The Supreme Court noted: "[T]he presence of an ensuing benefit that may have some future aspect is not controlling; many expenses concededly deductible have prospective effect beyond the tax year. What is important and controlling, we feel, is that the ... payment serves to create or enhance for Lincoln what is essentially a separate and distinct additional asset and that, as an inevitable consequence, the payment is capital in nature and not an expense." *Id.* at 354.

In 1992, in INDOPCO, Inc. v. Commissioner, 503 U.S. 79 (1992), the Supreme Court minimized the importance of the separate-and-distinct asset test of *Lincoln Savings* and in turn expanded the test for capitalization. In *INDOPCO,* the Supreme Court held that, although the separate-and-distinct asset standard is a sufficient condition for capitalization, it is not a necessary condition. If an expenditure gives rise to future benefits, even if it does not give rise to a separate and distinct asset, capitalization may be required. The Supreme Court noted: "Although the mere presence of an incidental future benefit ... may not warrant capitalization, a taxpayer's realization of benefits beyond the year in which the expenditure is incurred is undeniably important in determining whether the appropriate tax treatment is immediate deduction or capitalization."

b. Administrative Rulings

The "future benefits" standard adopted in *INDOPCO* has created much controversy and confusion because it seems to require the capitalization of many costs that were previously thought to be currently deductible even though they produce benefits in current and future years. In the wake of *INDOPCO,* the government issued numerous administrative pronouncements on how *INDOPCO* affects the treatment of different types of expenditures that give rise to long-term benefits.

In Revenue Ruling 92-80, 1992-2 C.B. 57, for example, the Service ruled that *INDOPCO* "[would] not affect the treatment of advertising costs as business expenses which are generally deductible under section 162(a) of the Code." Thus, ordinary business advertising expenditures will remain currently deductible notwithstanding the fact that they often produce benefits (such as distinctive intangible assets including trade dress, trademarks, trade names, and copyrights) that continue well beyond the current taxable year. *See* Nabisco, Inc. v. Commissioner, 76 T.C.M. (CCH) at 71 (holding that both advertising campaign and advertising execution expenditures were deductible). The Service notes in Revenue Ruling 92-80 that only in unusual circumstances where advertising is directed toward obtaining future benefits significantly beyond those traditionally associated with ordinary product, institutional, or goodwill advertising must the costs be capitalized. The Service also notes that expenditures for billboards, signs, and other tangible assets associated with advertising remain subject to the usual rules with respect to capitalization. *See* Best Lock Corp v. Commissioner, 31 T.C. 1217, 1235 (1959) ("[A]mounts paid ... to produce [a sale catalog] were capital items contributing to earning income for several years in the future and not ordinary and necessary expenses of doing business.").

For other examples of IRS rulings issued in the aftermath of *INDOPCO,* see Rev. Rul. 94-77, 1994-2 C.B. 19 (ruling that severance payments made by a taxpayer to its employees in connection with a business down-sizing were deductible, even though such payments may produce some future benefits, such as reducing operating costs and increasing operating efficiencies); Rev. Rul. 96-62, 1996-2 C.B. 9 (ruling that employee training costs will generally be deductible despite the fact that employee training produces future benefits).

c. Treasury Regulations

Although regulations under section 263 existed for some time, they were long considered vague, subjective, and the source of much litigation. As a result, the Treasury in recent years has replaced these regulations with sets of new regulations expanding and clarifying the rules surrounding capital expenditures. In 2004, the Treasury issued final regulations on the capitalization of costs related to *intangible* property. Treas. Reg. § 1.263(a)-4. More recently, in 2013, the Treasury issued final regulations on the capitalization of costs related to *tangible* property. Treas. Reg. § 1.263(a)-1 (providing general rules for capital expenditures), -2 (providing rules for amounts paid for the acquisition or production of tangible property), -3 (providing rules for amounts paid for the improvement of tangible property). *See also* Treas. Reg. § 1.162-3 (providing rules for materials and supplies), -4 (addressing repairs and maintenance). The following material addresses selected categories of capital expenditures for both tangible and intangible property. All references to regulations are to final regulations currently in effect.

3. Capitalization Rules Governing Tangible Property

a. Amounts Paid to Acquire Tangible Property

Regulations under section 263 require capitalization of amounts paid to acquire "a unit of real or personal property" (other than "materials or supplies"). Treas. Reg. § 1.263(a)-2(d)(1). *But see* Treas. Reg. 1.263(a)-1(f) (allowing certain taxpayers to currently deduct de minimis costs).

The regulations provide guidance for determining the appropriate *unit of property*. *See generally* Treas. Reg. § 1.263(a)-3(e). The definition of a unit of property has multiple sub definitions in various contexts. For example, in the real property context a building is usually a unit of property but in the condominium context a single apartment within a larger building may be a unit of property if the taxpayer only owns one apartment. Treas. Reg. § 1.263(a)-3(e)(2). For personal property the general rule is that "all the components that are functionally interdependent comprise a single unit of property." Treas. Reg. § 1.263(a)-3(e)(3)(i). Two components are functionally interdependent if placing one component in service is dependent on placing the other component in service. *Id.* Thus, for example, though a train locomotive may have many component parts it is regarded as a single unit of property because all parts are needed to make it work. Treas. Reg. § 1.263(a)-3(e)(6), ex 8.

The regulations also provide guidance on the treatment of *materials and supplies*, which are deductible under section 162. *See* Treas. Reg. § 1.162-3. Materials and supplies are defined as tangible property used or consumed in the taxpayer's operations that has an economic useful life of 12 months or less or cost $200 or less. Treas. Reg. § 1.162-3(a)(2), (c)(1)(iii), (iv). Amounts paid for materials and supplies are deductible in the year in which the supplies are used or consumed in the taxpayer's operations. Treas. Reg. § 1.162-3(a)(1). If no record of consumption is kept, the amounts are deductible in the year in which they are paid. Treas. Reg. § 1.162-3(a)(2).

It should be noted that capitalized acquisition costs include not only the purchase price of an asset, but also related transaction costs such as appraisal fees, commissions, and accounting and legal fees. *See* Treas. Reg. § 1.263(a)-2(f)(1) (requiring capitalization of amounts paid to facilitate the acquisition of real or personal property). For an early case illustrating this principle, see Woodward v. Commissioner, 397 U.S. 572 (1970). For example, assume a taxpayer purchases a building for $100,000 and in connection with the purchase incurs $5,000 in appraisal fees and closing costs. The taxpayer must capitalize all acquisition costs and so his basis in the building becomes $105,000. When the taxpayer will recover the capitalized acquisition costs depends on the applicable rules governing tax depreciation of buildings. The regulations provide a list of inherently facilitative costs that generally must be capitalized as transaction costs. Treas. Reg. § 1.263(a)-2(f)(2)(ii). But the regulations also provide an exception for certain costs incurred in investigating real property purchases (e.g., costs connected with deciding whether to purchase real property), which are currently deductible as expansion costs. Treas. Reg. § 1.263(a)-2(f)(4), ex. 8.

b. Amounts Paid to Construct Tangible Property

As with acquisition costs, the costs of producing a unit of real or personal property must be capitalized. Treas. Reg. § 1.263(a)-2(d)(1). To provide parity with a purchaser of property, all costs allocable to the construction must be capitalized and included in the constructed asset's basis. This includes costs that otherwise would be immediately deductible expenses, for example, wages paid to construction workers, rent paid for construction tools, interest paid on construction loans, etc. Although section 263(a)(1) is the authority for this rule, the provision does not clearly specify all the construction costs that should be capitalized.

In Commissioner v. Idaho Power, 418 U.S. 1 (1974), the Supreme Court held that equipment depreciation allocable to the taxpayer's construction of capital facilities must be capitalized under section 263(a)(1). The facts were as follows: The taxpayer, a public utility company, used its own transportation equipment (e.g., trucks) to construct capital facilities having a useful life of more than one year. The taxpayer claimed depreciation deductions on the equipment used in constructing its capital facilities; the deductions were computed based on the 10-year life of the equipment. According to the Court, requiring the capitalization of construction-related equipment depreciation by the taxpayer that does its own construction work maintains tax parity with the taxpayer that has such work done independently. Therefore, the public utility company had to add the equipment depreciation to the adjusted basis of the capital facility and depreciate over the 30-year useful life of that property. The principles of *Idaho Power* have been codified in section 263A, discussed more fully below.

It should be noted that, like facilitative transaction costs in purchases, amounts paid to facilitate the production of real or personal property must be capitalized. Treas. Reg. § 1.263(a)2(f).

c. Amounts Paid to Sell Tangible Property

The costs of selling or otherwise disposing of tangible property, such as sales commissions and fix-up costs, are not deductible when paid or incurred; rather they must be capitalized. Treas. Reg. § 1.263(a)-1(e)(1). Disposition costs are subtracted from the amount realized upon disposition. *Id.*

In contrast, removal costs (i.e., costs of retiring, removing, or discarding property) are generally deductible in the year the asset is retired and the costs are incurred. *See* Rev. Rul. 2000-7, 2000-1 C.B. 712 (ruling that costs of removing telephone poles were deductible even though new poles were installed); Rev. Rul. 94-12, 1994-1 C.B. 36 (ruling costs of removing and disposing of underground storage tanks were deductible). *But see* IRC § 280B (requiring capitalization of demolition costs). The final regulations generally do not affect the holding of these previous rulings. *See* Treas. Reg. § 1.263(a)-3(g)(2) (clarifying the treatment of removal costs in certain contexts).

d. Amounts Paid to Defend or Perfect Title to Tangible Property

The costs incurred in defending or perfecting title to real or personal property are considered to be a part of the cost of the property and they must be capitalized. Treas. Reg. § 1.263(a)-2(e). This rule is functionally equivalent to the general rule requiring acquisition costs to be capitalized. As one would expect, the tax treatment of litigation costs varies depending on the nature of the litigation. To be immediately deductible, litigation must not relate to the title of property, but rather to income from it. To determine the "origin of the claim," a fact specific inquiry articulated by the Supreme Court in United States v. Gilmore, 372 U.S. 39 (1963), consideration must be given to the issues involved, the nature and objectives of the suit in which the expenditures were made, the defenses asserted, the purpose for which the claimed deductions were expended, the background of the litigation, and all facts pertaining to the entire controversy. To illustrate, "[a]ttorneys' fees paid in a suit to quiet title to lands are not deductible; but if the suit is also to collect accrued rents thereon, that portion of such fees is deductible which is properly allocable to the services rendered in collecting such rents." Treas. Reg. § 1.212-1(k). The deductibility of attorney's fees is explored more fully in Chapter 35.

e. Amounts Paid to Improve Tangible Property

It has long been the rule that costs for replacements or improvements (e.g., the cost of replacing an entire roof) must be capitalized, while costs for repairs and maintenance (e.g., the cost of replacing a few shingles on a roof) may be deducted currently. But distinguishing between nondeductible improvements and deductible repairs often is difficult. Read *Midland Empire Packing Co. v. Commissioner* and *Mt. Morris Drive-*

In Theatre Co. v. Commissioner, included in the materials below, for an illustration of how courts historically addressed the repair versus improvement distinction. Can you reconcile the two decisions?

Treasury regulations that became effective in 2013 attempt to provide better guidance for distinguishing deductible repairs from capital improvements. In fact, the regulations are often referred to as the IRS's "repair" regulations. Generally, amounts paid for repairs and maintenance to tangible property are deductible unless they are required to be capitalized. Treas. Reg. § 1.162-4(a). A taxpayer must generally capitalize expenditures that result in an "improvement" to a "unit of property."

In order to determine whether an amount improves an asset, the relevant unit of property must first be determined. For example, maintenance on an aircraft engine might be deemed a deductible repair if the unit of property was the entire plane but a nondeductible improvement if the unit of property was just the engine. As noted above, the regulations provide rules for determining the appropriate unit of property. For personal property the general rule is that all the components that are functionally interdependent comprise a single unit of property. Treas. Reg. § 1.263(a)-3(e)(3)(i). Special rules are provided for real property.

Once the appropriate unit of property is ascertained, the question then turns to whether that unit of property was improved. The final regulations provide that a unit of property is deemed to be improved in three situations — (1) betterments, (2) restorations, and (3) adaptations to new or different uses. Treas. Reg. § 1.263(a)-3(d). (Note that under a regulatory safe harbor, certain routine maintenance procedures performed on a unit of property, including certain buildings, are deemed not to improve property. Treas. Reg. § 1.263(a)-3(i).)

First, expenditures for *betterments* to a unit of property must be capitalized. "Betterments" are changes to the property that (1) ameliorate a material condition or defect in the property, or (2) are a material addition to the property, or (3) are reasonably expected to materially increase the productivity, efficiency, strength, quality, or output of the unit of property. Treas. Reg. § 1.263(a)-3(j)(1)(i)–(iii). Whether a change is a betterment is determined under a facts and circumstances test that is illustrated in the regulations by numerous examples. Treas. Reg. § 1.263(a)-3(j)(3).

Second, expenditures for *restorations*, like expenditures for betterments, must be capitalized. A restoration occurs in a variety of situations but typically involves a major renovation or refurbishing of an asset. *See* Treas. Reg. § 1.263(a)-3(k)(1). Thus, for example, expenditures to restore the functionality of a farm outbuilding that has reached a state of disrepair so great that it is no longer usable would be restoration expenditures and must be capitalized. *See* Treas. Reg. § 1.263(a)-3(k)(7), ex. 6.

Third, expenditures that *adapt a unit of property to a new or different use* (if the adaptation is not consistent with the taxpayer's ordinary use at the time originally placed in service by the taxpayer) must also be capitalized. Treas. Reg. § 1.263(a)-3(l)(1). For example, the conversion of a manufacturing building into a showroom for the manufacturer's products would constitute such an adaptation. *See* Treas. Reg. § 1.263(a)-3(l)(3), ex. 1.

Reconsider *Midland Empire Packing Co. v. Commissioner* and *Mt. Morris Drive-In Theatre Co. v. Commissioner*, included in the materials below. Would these cases be decided the same way under the new final regulations? Hint: *See* Treas. Reg. § 1.263(a)-3(j)(3), ex. 12.

Under the regulations an improvement to a unit of property generally becomes part of that unit of property rather than a separate unit of property. Treas. Reg. § 1.263(a)-3(e)(4). Thus, a new roof is simply part of the building rather than a separate unit. The significance of this fact is limited, however, by the separate requirement that the new roof must be depreciated over the life of a new building rather than over the remaining useful life of the improved building. *See* IRC § 168(i)(6). Tax depreciation is the subject of the next chapter.

4. Capitalization Rules Governing Intangible Assets

As noted at the outset of this chapter, the IRS has issued regulations under section 263(a) that provide comprehensive rules for capitalization of amounts paid to acquire or create intangibles.

a. Amounts Paid to Acquire Intangible Property

Under the regulations, a taxpayer is required to capitalize amounts paid to *acquire* an intangible. Treas. Reg. § 1.263(a)-4(b)(1)(i). Examples of acquired intangibles include, but are not limited to, ownership interests in corporations, partnerships, and other entities; debt instruments; options to provide or acquire property; leases; intellectual property, such as patents, copyrights, trademarks, trade names, and computer software; and franchises. Treas. Reg. § 1.263(a)-4(c).

b. Amounts Paid to Create Intangible Property

Subject to an important exception discussed below, the "12-month rule," the regulations require a taxpayer to capitalize amounts paid to *create* an intangible. Treas. Reg. § 1.263(a)-4(b)(1)(ii). Created intangibles specifically include: financial interests (e.g., ownership interests in corporations, partnerships, and other entities; debt instruments, and options to provide or acquire property); prepaid expenses; and certain memberships and privileges. Treas. Reg. § 1.263(a)-4(d)(1)–(4). Also specifically included are certain rights obtained from a governmental agency. For example, a taxpayer must capitalize amounts paid to a governmental agency to obtain or renew a trademark, trade name, copyright, license, permit, franchise, or other similar right granted by that governmental agency. Treas. Reg. § 1.263(a)-4(d)(5). This rule does not affect the treatment of expenditures that are specifically dealt with under other provisions of the Code.

The regulations under section 263 also require capitalization of amounts paid to create or enhance a *separate and distinct intangible asset*. Treas. Reg. § 1.263(a)-4(b)(1)(iii). A separate and distinct intangible asset means (1) a property interest of ascertainable and measurable value in money's worth (2) that is subject to protection under applicable state, federal, or foreign law, and (3) the possession and control of which is intrinsically capable of being sold, transferred, or pledged (ignoring any restrictions imposed on assignability). Treas. Reg. § 1.263(a)-4(b)(3). It should be noted that amounts paid to create computer software or package designs are *not* treated as amounts that create separate and distinct intangible assets. Treas. Reg. § 1.263(a)-4(b)(3)(iv)–(v). As discussed in Chapter 28, such amounts are generally deductible.

The regulations under section 263 adopt an exception, termed the *12-month rule*, applicable to most created intangibles. Under the 12-month rule, a taxpayer is not required to capitalize amounts that provide benefits only for a relatively brief duration. Specifically, the regulations provide that a taxpayer is not required to capitalize amounts paid to create or enhance an intangible asset if the amounts do not create or enhance any right or benefit for the taxpayer that extends beyond the earlier of 12 months after the first date on which the taxpayer realizes the right or benefit, or the end of the taxable year following the taxable year in which the payment is made. Treas. Reg. § 1.263(a)-4(f)(1). Renewal periods are to be taken into account if, based on all of the facts and circumstances in existence during the taxable year in which the right is created, the facts indicate a reasonable expectancy of renewal. The 12-month rule is illustrated in following examples.

Example 1: 12-Month Rule Does not Apply. On December 1, Year 1, Taxpayer pays a $10,000 insurance premium to obtain an insurance policy with a one-year term that begins on February 1, Year 2. Because the right or benefit attributable to the $10,000 payment extends beyond the end of the taxable year following the taxable year in which the payment is made, the 12-month rule does not apply and Taxpayer must capitalize the payment. *See* Treas. Reg. § 1.263(a)-4(f)(8), ex 1.

Example 2: 12-Month Rule Applies. Same facts as in Example 1, except that the policy has a term beginning on December 15, Year 1. The 12-month rule applies because the right or benefit attributable to the $10,000 payment neither extends more than 12 months beyond December 15, Year 1 (the first date the benefit is realized by Taxpayer) nor beyond the end of the taxable year following the taxable year in which the payment is made. Accordingly, Taxpayer is not required to capitalize the payment. *See* Treas. Reg.§ 1.263(a)-4(f)(8), ex 2.

c. Transaction Costs

The regulations under section 263 require the capitalization of an amount paid to *facilitate* the acquisition or creation of an intangible if the amount is paid in the process of investigating or otherwise pursuing the asset. Treas. Reg. § 1.263(a)-4(b)(1)(v), -4(e)(1)(i). Whether an amount is paid to facilitate a transaction depends on all the facts and circumstances. Treas. Reg. § 1.263(a)-4(e)(1)(i). One fact that is relevant, but not determinative, is whether the amount would or would not have been paid but for the transaction. *Id.* The regulations adopt two simplifying conventions applicable to transaction costs (i.e., rules of administrative convenience). First, a taxpayer is not required to capitalize employee compensation and overhead costs related to the acquisition or creation of an intangible. Second, de minimis transaction costs (costs that do not exceed $5,000, as determined on a transaction-by-transaction basis) do not have to be capitalized.

B. Section 263A

In 1986, Congress codified the principles of *Idaho Power* in section 263A. Section 263A requires the capitalization of all direct and indirect costs allocable to construction or production of real property or tangible personal property. It also applies to taxpayers who acquire or hold inventory property for resale. *See* IRC § 263A(a), (b), (f), (g). *Direct costs* include the costs of materials that become an integral part of the asset produced and those materials that are consumed in the production process, as well as compensation paid for full-time, part-time, and contract labor. Treas. Reg. § 1.263A-1(e)(2). *Indirect costs* include, for example, purchasing costs, storage costs, depreciation, rent, taxes, insurance, utilities, maintenance, and interest on debt. Treas. Reg. § 1.263A-1(e)(3). Certain costs do not need to be capitalized. Selling and distribution costs such as marketing, selling, and advertising costs do not fall within the ambit of section 263A. Treas. Reg. § 1.263A-1(e)(3)(iii)(A). Moreover, costs incurred in the rendition of services are not within the uniform capitalization rules of section 263A even if the rendition of services results in the production of tangible personal property. Treas. Reg. § 1.263A-1(e)(2)(B)(2). For example, costs incurred by a photographer who takes pictures at a wedding do not fall within section 263A because production of property is incidental to the services rendered.

There are a number of exceptions from the uniform capitalization requirements of section 263A. In 1988, for example, Congress added section 263A(h), an exemption for certain freelance writers, photographers, and artists. Section 263A(h) provides that *qualified creative expenses* are not required to be capitalized. A qualified creative expense is defined as any expense paid or incurred by an individual in the trade or business of being a writer, photographer, or artist, which, except for the uniform capitalization rules of section 263A, would otherwise be deductible for the taxable year. IRC § 263A(h)(2). The purpose of the exemption was to relieve free-lance individuals from the burden of the uniform capitalization rules, especially when their activities may not generate income for years. Note that even if an individual is engaged in the trade or business of being a writer, photographer, or artist, not all expenses are deemed to be qualified creative expenses. The Code specifically provides that a qualified creative expense does not include "any expense related to printing, photographic plates, motion picture films, video tapes, or similar items." IRC § 263A(h)(2), flush language.

Prior to 2018, businesses could qualify for an exception to the uniform capitalization rules for personal property *purchased for resale* if the business had average annual *gross receipts of $10 million or less* for the preceding three tax years. IRC § 263A(b)(2). The Tax Cuts and Jobs Act expanded the gross receipts test to $25 million. In addition, it expanded the exception to apply, not only to taxpayers that purchase personal property for resale, but also to any *producer* or *reseller* that meets the $25 million gross receipts test. IRC § 263A(i).

IV. Materials

Midland Empire Packing Co. v. Commissioner

14 T.C. 635 (1950)

ARUNDELL, JUDGE:

The issue in this case is whether an expenditure for a concrete lining in petitioner's basement to oilproof it against an oil nuisance created by a neighboring refinery is deductible as an ordinary and necessary expense under section [162] of the Internal Revenue Code on the theory it was an expenditure for a repair.

The respondent has contended, in part, that the expenditure is for a capital improvement and should be recovered through depreciation charges and is, therefore, not deductible as an ordinary and necessary business expense.

It is none too easy to determine on which side of the line certain expenditures fall so that they may be accorded their proper treatment for tax purposes. In Illinois Merchants Trust Co., Executor, 4 B.T.A. 103, at page 106, we discussed this subject in some detail and in our opinion said:

> In determining whether an expenditure is a capital one or is chargeable against operating income, it is necessary to bear in mind the purpose for which the expenditure was made. To repair is to restore to a sound state or to mend, while a replacement connotes a substitution. A repair is an expenditure for the purpose of keeping the property in an ordinarily efficient operating condition. It does not add to the value of the property, nor does it appreciably prolong its life. It merely keeps the property in an operating condition over its probable useful life for the uses for which it was acquired. Expenditures for that purpose are distinguishable from those for replacements, alterations, improvements, or additions which prolong the life of the property, increase its value, or make it adaptable to a different use. The one is a maintenance charge, while the others are additions to capital investment which should not be applied against current earnings.

It will be seen from our findings of fact that for some 25 years prior to the taxable year petitioner had used the basement rooms of its plant as a place for the curing of hams and bacon and for the storage of meat and hides. The basement had been entirely satisfactory for this purpose over the entire period in spite of the fact that there was some seepage of water into the rooms from time to time. In the taxable year it was found that not only water, but oil, was seeping through the concrete walls of the basement of the packing plant and, while the water would soon drain out, the oil would not, and there was left on the basement floor a thick scum of oil which gave off a strong odor that permeated the air of the entire plant, and the fumes from the oil created a fire hazard. It appears that the oil which came from a nearby refinery had also gotten into the water wells which served to furnish water for petitioner's plant, and as a result of this whole condition the Federal meat inspectors advised petitioner that it must discontinue the use of the water from the wells and oilproof the basement, or else shut down its plant.

To meet this situation, petitioner during the taxable year undertook steps to oilproof the basement by adding a concrete lining to the walls from the floor to a height of about four feet and also added concrete to the floor of the basement. It is the cost of this work which it seeks to deduct as a repair. The basement was not enlarged by this work, nor did the oilproofing serve to make it more desirable for the purpose for which it had been used through the years prior to the time that the oil nuisance had occurred. The evidence is that the expenditure did not add to the value or prolong the expected life of the property over what they were before the event occurred which made the repairs necessary. It is true that after the work was done the seepage of water, as well as oil, was stopped, but, as already stated, the presence of the water had never been found objectionable. The repairs merely served to keep the property in an operating condition over its probable useful life for the purpose for which it was used.

While it is conceded on brief that the expenditure was "necessary," respondent contends that the encroachment of the oil nuisance on petitioner's property was not an "ordinary" expense in petitioner's particular business. But the fact that petitioner had not theretofore been called upon to make a similar expenditure to prevent damage and disaster to its property does not remove that expense from the classification of "ordinary" for, as stated in Welch v. Helvering, 290 U.S. 111, "ordinary in this context does not mean that the payments must be habitual or normal in the sense that the same taxpayer will have to make them often. * * * [T]he expense is an ordinary one because we know from experience that payments for such a purpose, whether the amount is large or small, are the common and accepted means of defense against attack. The situation is unique in the life of the individual affected, but not in the life of the group, the community, of which he is a part." Steps to protect a business building from the seepage of oil from a nearby refinery, which had been erected long subsequent to the time petitioner started to operate its plant, would seem to us to be a normal thing to do, and in certain sections of the country it must be a common experience to protect one's property from the seepage of oil. Expenditures to accomplish this result are likewise normal.

In American Bemberg Corporation, 10 T.C. 361, we allowed as deductions, on the ground that they were ordinary and necessary expenses, extensive expenditures made to prevent disaster, although the repairs were of a type which had never been needed before and were unlikely to recur. In that case the taxpayer, to stop cave-ins of soil which were threatening destruction of its manufacturing plant, hired an engineering firm which drilled to the bedrock and injected grout to fill the cavities where practicable, and made incidental replacements and repairs, including tightening of the fluid carriers. In two successive years the taxpayer expended $734,316.76 and $199,154.33, respectively, for such drilling and grouting and $153,474.20 and $79,687.29, respectively, for capital replacements. We found that the cost (other than replacement) of this program did not make good the depreciation previously allowed, and stated in our opinion:

> In connection with the purpose of the work, the Proctor program was intended to avert a plant-wide disaster and avoid forced abandonment of the plant. The purpose was not to improve, better, extend, or increase the original plant, nor to prolong its original useful life. Its continued operation was endangered; the purpose of the expenditures was to enable petitioner to continue the plant in operation not on any new or better scale, but on the same scale and, so far as possible, as efficiently as it had operated before. The purpose was not to rebuild or replace the plant in whole or in part, but to keep the same plant as it was and where it was.

The petitioner here made the repairs in question in order that it might continue to operate its plant. Not only was there danger of fire from the oil and fumes, but the presence of the oil led the Federal meat inspectors to declare the basement an unsuitable place for the purpose for which it had been used for a quarter of a century. After the expenditures were made, the plant did not operate on a changed or larger scale, nor was it thereafter suitable for new or additional uses. The expenditure served only to permit petitioner to continue the use of the plant, and particularly the basement for its normal operations.

In our opinion, the expenditure of $4,868.81 for lining the basement walls and floor was essentially a repair and, as such, it is deductible as an ordinary and necessary business expense.

Mt. Morris Drive-In Theatre Co. v. Commissioner
25 T.C. 272 (1955)

KERN, JUDGE:

FINDINGS OF FACT.

In 1947 petitioner purchased 13 acres of farm land located on the outskirts of Flint, Michigan, upon which it proceeded to construct a drive-in or outdoor theatre. Prior to its purchase by the petitioner the land on which the theatre was built was farm land and contained vegetation. The slope of the land was such that the natural drainage of water was from the southerly line to the northerly boundary of the property and thence onto the adjacent land, owned by David and Mary D. Nickola, which was used both for farming and as a trailer park. The petitioner's land sloped sharply from south to north and also sloped from the east downward towards the west so that most of the drainage from the petitioner's property was onto the southwest corner of the Nickolas' land. The topography of the land purchased by petitioner was well known to petitioner at the time it was purchased and developed. The petitioner did not change the general slope of its land in constructing the drive-in theatre, but it removed the covering vegetation from the land, slightly increased the grade, and built aisles or ramps which were covered with gravel and were somewhat raised so that the passengers in the automobiles would be able to view the picture on the large outdoor screen.

As a result of petitioner's construction on and use of this land rain water falling upon it drained with an increased flow into and upon the adjacent property of the Nickolas. This result should reasonably have been anticipated by petitioner at the time when the construction work was done.

The Nickolas complained to the petitioner at various times after petitioner began the construction of the theatre that the work resulted in an acceleration and concentration of the flow of water which drained from the petitioner's property onto the Nickolas' land causing damage to their crops and roadways. On or about October 11, 1948, the Nickolas filed a suit against the petitioner in the Circuit Court for the County of Genesee, State of Michigan, asking for an award for damages done to their property by the accelerated and concentrated drainage of the water and for a permanent injunction restraining the defendant from permitting such drainage to continue. Following the filing of an answer by the petitioner and of a reply thereto by the Nickolas, the suit was settled by an agreement dated June 27, 1950. This agreement provided for the construction by the petitioner of a drainage system to carry water from its northern boundary across the Nickolas' property and thence to a public drain. The cost of maintaining the system was to be shared by the petitioner and the Nickolas, and the latter granted the petitioner and its successors an easement across their land for the purpose of constructing and maintaining the drainage system. The construction of the drain was completed in October 1950 under the supervision of engineers employed by the petitioner and the Nickolas at a cost to the petitioner of $8,224, which amount was paid by it in November 1950. The performance by the petitioner on its part of the agreement to construct the drainage system and to maintain the portion for which it was responsible constituted a full release of the Nickolas' claims against it. The petitioner chose to settle the dispute by constructing the drainage system because it did not wish to risk the possibility that continued litigation might result in a permanent injunction against its use of the drive-in theatre and because it wished to eliminate the cause of the friction between it and the adjacent landowners, who were in a position to seriously interfere with the petitioner's use of its property for outdoor theatre purposes. A settlement based on a monetary payment for past damages, the petitioner believed, would not remove the threat of claims for future damages.

On its 1950 income and excess profits tax return the petitioner claimed a deduction of $822.40 for depreciation of the drainage system for the period July 1, 1950, to December 31, 1950. The Commissioner disallowed without itemization $5,514.60 of a total depreciation expense deduction of $19,326.41 claimed by the petitioner. In its petition the petitioner asserted that the entire amount spent to construct the drainage system was fully deductible in 1950 as an ordinary and necessary business expense incurred in the settlement of a lawsuit, or, in the alternative, as a loss, and claimed a refund of part of the $10,591.56 of income and excess profits tax paid by it for that year.

OPINION.

When petitioner purchased, in 1947, the land which it intended to use for a drive-in theatre, its president was thoroughly familiar with the topography of this land which was such that when the covering vegetation was removed and graveled ramps were constructed and used by its patrons, the flow of natural precipitation on the lands of abutting property owners would be materially accelerated. Some provision should have been made to solve this drainage problem in order to avoid annoyance and harassment to its neighbors. If petitioner had included in its original construction plans an expenditure for a proper drainage system no one could doubt that such an expenditure would have been capital in nature.

Within a year after petitioner had finished its inadequate construction of the drive-in theatre, the need of a proper drainage system was forcibly called to its attention by one of the neighboring property owners, and under the threat of a lawsuit filed approximately a year after the theatre was constructed, the drainage system was built by petitioner who now seeks to deduct its cost as an ordinary and necessary business expense, or as a loss.

We agree with respondent that the cost to petitioner of acquiring and constructing a drainage system in connection with its drive-in theatre was a capital expenditure.

Here was no sudden catastrophic loss caused by a "physical fault" undetected by the taxpayer in spite of due precautions taken by it at the time of its original construction work as in American Bemberg Corporation, 10 T.C. 361; no unforeseeable external factor as in Midland Empire Packing Co., 14 T.C. 635; and no change in the cultivation of farm property caused by improvements in technique and made many years after the property in question was put to productive use as in J. H. Collingwood, 20 T.C. 937. In the instant case it was obvious at the time when the drive-in theatre was constructed, that a drainage system would be required to properly dispose of the natural precipitation normally to be expected, and that until this was accomplished, petitioner's capital investment was incomplete. In addition, it should be emphasized that here there was no mere restoration or rearrangement of the original capital asset, but there was the acquisition and construction of a capital asset which petitioner had not previously had, namely, a new drainage system.

That this drainage system was acquired and constructed and that payments therefor were made in compromise of a lawsuit is not determinative of whether such payments were ordinary and necessary business expenses or capital expenditures. "The decisive test is still the character of the transaction which gives rise to the payment." Hales-Mullaly v. Commissioner, 131 F.2d 509, 511, 512.

In our opinion the character of the transaction in the instant case indicates that the transaction was a capital expenditure.

Decision will be entered for the respondent.

RICE, J., dissenting: It seems to me that J. H. Collingwood, 20 T.C. 937 (1953), Midland Empire Packing Co., 14 T.C. 635 (1950), American Bemberg Corporation, 10 T.C. 361 (1948), *affd.* 177 F.2d 200 (C. A. 1949), and Illinois Merchants Trust

Co., Executor, 4 B.T A. 103 (1926), are ample authority for the conclusion that the expenditure which petitioner made was an ordinary and necessary business expense, which did not improve, better, extend, increase, or prolong the useful life of its property. The expenditure did not cure the original geological defect of the natural drainage onto the Nickolas' land, but only dealt with the intermediate consequence thereof. The majority opinion does not distinguish those cases adequately. And since those cases and the result reached herein do not seem to me to be able to "live together," I cannot agree with the majority that the expenditure here was capital in nature.

V. Related Matters

- **Expanding an Existing Business.** Expenses paid or incurred to expand an existing business are generally deductible. *See, e.g.*, NCNB Corp. v. United States, 684 F.2d 285 (4th Cir. 1982); Colorado Springs National Bank v. United States, 505 F.2d 1185 (10th Cir. 1974); Briarcliff Candy Corp. v. Commissioner, 475 F.2d 775 (2d Cir. 1973); Rev. Rul. 2000-4, 2000-1 C.B. 331.

- **Entering a New Business.** Start-up costs paid or incurred in entering a new business must generally be capitalized. *See, e.g.*, Richmond Television Corp. v. United States, 345 F.2d 901 (4th Cir. 1965) (holding job training expenses incurred before obtaining FCC license were not deductible because the company was not carrying on a trade or business); Frank v. Commissioner, 20 T.C. 511 (1953) (holding expenses incurred in investigating properties for newspaper and radio business were not deductible as such expenses were incurred prior to entering a business) *See also* Treas. Reg. § 1.263(a)-5(a) (requiring amounts paid to facilitate the acquisition of a new business to be capitalized), -5(b)(1) (stating that an amount is paid to facilitate an acquisition "if the amount is paid in the process of investigating or otherwise pursuing the transaction"), -5(d) (providing exceptions for employee compensation and overhead costs, and certain di minimis expenses). Section 195 provides some relief for capitalized start-up expenditures. It allows taxpayers to immediately deduct $5,000 of such costs and amortize the rest over fifteen years. When reading IRC § 195(a)–(c), pay close attention to the type of start-up costs eligible for section 195 treatment.

- **Job-Seeking Expenses.** It is now the position of the Service that expenses incurred in seeking new employment in the same trade or business are deductible under section 162 if directly connected with such trade or business. However, such expenses are not deductible if an individual is seeking employment in a new trade or business even if employment is secured, as such expenses are not incurred "in carrying on a trade or business." Rev. Rul. 75-120, 1975-1 C.B. 55. Query: Does section 195 allow amortization of capitalized job-seeking expenses?

- **Environmental Cleanup.** The Service has ruled that a taxpayer may deduct environmental cleanup costs (e.g., soil remediation expenses) to bring property to its pre-contamination state. *See, e.g.,* Rev. Rul. 94-38, 1994-1 C.B. 35 (permitting deduction where environmental cleanup costs merely restored soil and groundwater to their appropriate condition before they were contaminated by the taxpayer's manufacturing operations). *See also* IRC § 198 (relating to "qualified contamination sites").

Chapter 9

Depreciation and Amortization

I. Assignment

Read: Internal Revenue Code: §§ 167(a)–(c), (i)(2); 168(a)–(e), (k)(1)–(2), (6)(A); 179(a), (b)(1)–(3)(A), (b)(5), (d)(1); 197(a)–(d)(1); 1016(a)(2).

Treasury Regulations: §§ 1.167(a)-3, -14(a); 1.167(b)-1(a), -2(a); 1.167(g)-1.

Text: Overview
Simon v. Commissioner
Revenue Procedure 87-56 (Excerpt)
Revenue Procedure 87-57 (Excerpt)
Related Matters

Complete the problems.

II. Problems

1. During the current year, Sigmund purchased two pieces of equipment for active use in his business. Equipment A, which is new property with an applicable recovery period of 5 years, was purchased for $1,000,000 and placed in service in March. Equipment B, which is used property with an applicable recovery period of 7 years, was purchased for $1,800,000 and placed in service in May. Ignoring inflation adjustments, to what extent can Sigmund elect to expense the cost of these assets under sections 179 and 168(k)? (Assume the section 179 deduction is not limited by Sigmund's income.)

2. On March 1 of 2027, Oriana Fallaci buys new equipment for $300,000 for use in business. The equipment has an 8-year class life and is, thus, 5-year property under section 168(c). Oriana makes no bonus depreciation elections under sections 179 or 168(k). Compute Oriana's depreciation deductions in each year and the adjusted basis of the equipment under the following circumstances.

   (a) Oriana elects to employ the straight line method under section 168(b)(5).

   (b) What if Oriana does not make the election under section 168(b)(5) and instead employs the regular ACRS method?

   (c) Same as (b) except Oriana sells the equipment on November 1, Year 4, for $100,000.

   (d) Same as (c) except that Oriana gives the equipment to Son.

3. The law firm of Muggles, Snitch & Quidditch bought a rare Persian carpet reputed to have magical qualities. The carpet sits before the gas fireplace in Mr. Muggles' corner office where all employees have specific instructions not to tread upon the carpet. Clients, however, do step on the carpet from time to time without remonstrance from Mr. Muggles. The carpet has increased in value every year since it was made over a century ago. May the law firm claim depreciation deductions for the carpet? Why or why not?

4. Your client L.L. Bean acquires, for a lump sum, all the assets of Trout Illustrated, Inc., which publishes a monthly fishing magazine. Part of the purchase price is allocated to Trout Illustrated's customer lists, trademarks, trade names, and goodwill.

   (a) What are the tax consequences to L.L. Bean upon the acquisition of these intangible assets?

   (b) Would L.L. Bean be better off, from a tax standpoint, if it allocates more of the purchase price to Trout Illustrated's tangible assets instead of its intangible assets? Would such allocation necessarily be respected by the Service?

   (c) Would L.L. Bean be better off, from a tax standpoint, if it purchases all the stock of Trout Illustrated, Inc., instead of its assets?

III. Overview

It is necessary to begin this chapter with a warning. Congress made some radical, but temporary, changes in the area of tangible property depreciation in the Tax Cuts and Jobs Act of 2017. That radical approach deserves our special attention. Congress amended section 179 and temporarily reenacted a modified section 168(k) in order to go a long way toward allowing *full current expensing* of capital costs other than purchases of depreciable real estate. Congress left in place the architecture of section 168, which we address in what follows, but made much of it temporarily irrelevant for taxpayers. We will more fully explain sections 179 and 168(k) after addressing the overall structure of section 168.

In an economic sense, depreciation is the decline in value of an asset due to wear and tear and obsolescence. In the tax sense, depreciation is a deduction from gross income to permit the taxpayer to recover the cost of that asset. So, for example, if we have a vehicle used in our business for five years that cost us $20,000, we might take a $4,000 deduction each year on our taxes for five years to reflect the decline in value of that asset and to reflect its contribution to the production of gross income. Depreciation methods are sometimes called cost recovery systems. In our example we don't deduct the entire cost of the vehicle all at once because it helped produce income over five years. If we are going to match our expenses against the revenues they helped produce we must spread out the deduction over the useful life of the vehicle. This is, of course, a basic application of the principle discussed in Chapter 8 that the costs of assets must be capitalized.

A. Depreciation of Tangible Property

The depreciation deduction for tangible property is *authorized* in section 167 and is limited to property used in a trade or business or property held for production of income. IRC § 167(a). Among other things this excludes inventory and personal use property, such as a personal residence. Where property is used partly for personal use and partly for business purposes, the depreciation deduction is prorated on the basis of the relative amount of use for each purpose. *See* Sharp v. United States, 199 F. Supp. 743, aff'd, 303 F.2d 783 (3rd Cir. 1962). We will revisit this in Chapter 22 when we address home office deductions. Moreover, as a general rule, only property that is subject to wear and tear or obsolescence is subject to depreciation. The *Simon* case in the materials sheds some light on this proposition. This means that bare land is not depreciable; however, a building on the land potentially is depreciable. *See* Treas. Reg. § 1.167(a)-2.

Rules for *computing* the depreciation deductions for tangible property, authorized by section 167, are found in section 168. IRC § 167(b). Section 168(a) was enacted in 1981 to simplify depreciation computation rules and stimulate the economy. It provides that depreciation deductions for tangible property shall be determined by using: (1) the applicable depreciation method, (2) the applicable recovery period, and (3) the applicable convention. As will be seen shortly, section 168 applies an arbitrary cost recovery system that generally allows a taxpayer to recover her capitalized cost in tangible property well before it ceases to be useful in her business or income-producing activity. Indeed, the general depreciation system provided in section 168 is called the Accelerated Cost Recovery System ("ACRS").

Before getting into the computational rules, a couple of points are worthy of mention. First, the amount that can be depreciated in the aggregate is limited to our basis in the asset, which is usually our cost. IRC §§ 167(c)(1), 1012. For personal use property converted to business use, the basis for depreciation purposes cannot exceed the fair market value of the property on the date of conversion. Treas. Reg. § 1.167(g)-1. Second, a taxpayer is permitted to recover her full basis in depreciable property even if the property is expected to have some value at the end of the applicable recovery period (this is known as salvage value). Indeed, the ACRS method of depreciation ignores salvage value by presuming it is zero. IRC § 168(b)(4). Finally, basis in depreciable property must be reduced by the greater of the amount allowed (claimed) or allowable (could have been claimed). IRC § 1016(a)(2). This rule prevents taxpayers from deciding when to take depreciation deductions; in other words, if a taxpayer fails to deduct an allowable depreciation amount, basis is reduced nevertheless.

1. Applicable Recovery Period

The "applicable recovery period" is a variation of what we initially think of as useful life. Historically, taxpayers had the burden of establishing what the useful life of an asset was in order to claim depreciation deductions. Section 168 eliminates the need for this determination by prescribing artificial recovery periods for all tangible property. These periods are often shorter for tax purposes than for economic purposes. This means that the taxpayer recovers her costs more quickly than economic reality would dictate.

To find a tangible asset's applicable recovery period, one must generally look to Revenue Procedure 87-56, which is included in the materials, section 168(e), and section 168(c) in that order. Revenue Procedure 87-56 sets forth the class lives of various tangible assets. Section 168(e) then provides the classification of property with reference to the "class life" of property. Finally, section 168(c) provides a table of applicable recovery periods with reference to the classes of property. To illustrate, assume that a taxpayer purchases a large copier to use in her business. According to Revenue Procedure 87-56, the copier has a class life of six years. According to section 168(e), property with a class life of six years is treated as "5-year" property. And, according to section 168(c), five-year property has an applicable recovery period of five years.

It should be noted that section 168(e) provides the classification of certain property, making reference to Revenue Procedure 87-56 unnecessary in many cases. For example, section 168(e) provides five-year property includes any automobiles, light general purpose trucks, and computers. Seven-year property includes any property that does not have a class life.

Generally speaking there are two recovery periods that apply to depreciable real estate. The applicable recovery period for residential rental real estate is 27.5 years. The recovery period for non-residential real estate is 39 years. IRC § 168(c). Section 168(e)(2)(A) defines real estate as residential if 80% of the income it produces comes from *dwelling units*. Dwelling units are living accommodations largely used for long-term occupancy. Thus, hotels and motels are excluded. *See* IRC § 168(e)(2)(A)(ii). Non-residential real estate encompasses a broad array of depreciable real property including office buildings, factories, stores, and, as already noted, hotels and motels. *See* IRC §§ 168(e)(2)(B), 1250(c).

2. Applicable Depreciation Method

The two most important methods of depreciation under section 168 are the straight-line method and the double declining balance method. IRC § 168(b). The straight-line method requires ratable cost recovery over the applicable recovery period of the asset. This can be made into a percentage by dividing 100 by the applicable recovery period. *See* Treas. Reg. § 1.167(b)-1. It can be stated as a simple formula:

Determining the Straight-Line Percentage

$$\frac{100}{\text{Applicable Recovery Period}} = \text{Straight-line Percentage}$$

Thus, if an asset has a 5-year recovery period, the depreciation deduction under the straight-line method would be twenty percent of our original basis each year

(100/5 = 20). The double declining balance method takes the straight-line percentage, doubles it, and applies it to the basis reduced by all prior years' deductions for depreciation. *See* Treas. Reg. § 1.167(b)-2. Therefore, in our example of property with a five-year recovery period the double declining balance percentage is two times twenty or forty. In the end both methods will yield the same total amount of deductions, but the double declining balance method accelerates the largest part of deductions to the earliest years of the asset's applicable recovery period.

As mentioned above, the double declining balance method takes the straight-line percentage, doubles it, and applies that percentage to the asset's adjusted basis each year. Since this method would never allow us to reach a zero basis, the Code specifies that we switch to the straight-line method in the first year it yields a greater deduction. IRC § 168(b)(1)(B). The double declining balance method generally applies if the property is tangible and has a recovery period of less than 15 years. IRC § 168(b)(1). The 150 per cent declining balance method applies to tangible personal property with a recovery period of fifteen or twenty years. IRC § 168(b)(2). The straight-line method applies to depreciable real property. IRC § 168(b)(3). Taxpayers can also elect to apply the straight-line method rather than one of the accelerated recovery methods. IRC § 168(b)(5).

3. Applicable Convention

Taxpayers buy property all during the year and sell property at various times in the year. Thus, the question arises, how do we know how much depreciation to take in the year of purchase and in the year of sale? Though we could do an exact proration, the Code specifies that we employ an arbitrary rule called the "applicable convention." IRC § 168(d). For depreciable tangible personal property most of the time the applicable convention is the half year convention. This convention treats all the depreciable property acquired or disposed of by the taxpayer during the year as acquired or disposed of half way through the year. IRC §§ 168(d)(1), (4)(A). However, for most depreciable real property we apply the mid-month convention. IRC §§ 168(d)(2), (d)(4)(B). A special convention (the mid-quarter convention) potentially applies when substantial property is placed in service during the last quarter of the year.

4. Example of ACRS Depreciation

On January 15 of Year 1, Taxpayer buys a computer for $10,000 for use in business. Taxpayer, who purchased no other depreciable property during the year, expects the computer to be useful in his business for seven years. Taxpayer makes no bonus depreciation elections under section 179 or 168(k), discussed below. To prepare a depreciation schedule for the computer, we must ascertain the applicable convention, the applicable recovery period, and the applicable depreciation method. IRC § 168(a)(1)–(3).

The *applicable convention* is the half-year convention, which means Taxpayer is treated as having acquired the computer on July 1st of Year 1. IRC § 168(d)(1), (4)(A). Therefore, Taxpayer will be entitled to a half-year's worth of depreciation for the first year even though he purchased the computer on January 15th. [Note: The mid-month convention in section 168(d)(2) does not apply because the computer is not depreciable real property, and the mid-quarter convention in section 168(d)(3) does not apply because Taxpayer did not acquire a substantial portion of total depreciable assets during the last quarter of the year.]

Revenue Procedure 87-56, included in the materials, tells us that the computer has a class life of six years. Section 168(e) tells us that property with a class life of six years is treated as "5-year property." Section 168(c) tells us that "5-year property" has an *applicable recovery period* of five years. In short, the cost of the computer will be recovered over a five-year recovery period even though Taxpayer projects that the computer might last seven years. Actually, to make up for the half-year convention, we must extend the depreciation schedule into Year 6. Nothing in the Code tells us to do this, but one-half a year's depreciation will have to be allowed in Year 6 since only one half is allowed in Year 1.

The default *applicable depreciation method* for the computer is the 200% declining balance method, which gives Taxpayer larger depreciation deductions in the earlier years of the computer's recovery period and smaller amounts in later years. IRC § 168(b)(1)(A). The 200% declining balance method refers to 200% of the straight line rate. The straight line rate is 20% (i.e., 100 divided by the applicable recovery period of five years). Hence, the double declining balance rate is 40%.

To determine the depreciation allowance for Year 1, we multiply Taxpayer's basis in the computer of $10,000 by our rate of 40% and then multiply that amount by .5 (because, remember, only one-half is allowed in the first year). This yields a depreciation allowance for Year 1 of $2,000. The basis in the computer would be reduced by $2,000 allowed in Year 1 per section 1016(a)(2). To determine the depreciation allowance for Year 2, we multiply Taxpayer's downward-adjusted basis of $8,000 (notice we are not using the original $10,000 basis, but we're using a declining balance basis which reflects prior years' depreciation allowances) by 40%. This yields a depreciation allowance of $3,200 in Year 2. Continuing this method yields a depreciation allowance of $1,920 in Year 3 and $1,152 in Year 4. So far, the schedule looks like this:

Year	HYC	×	%	×	Base	=	Dep. Ded.
1	1/2	×	40	×	$10,000	=	$2,000
2	1	×	40	×	8,000	=	3,200
3	1	×	40	×	4,800	=	1,920
4	1	×	40	×	2,880	=	1,152
5	1						
6	1/2						

Note that when using the double declining balance method (applying a percentage to a declining amount), we will never get to $0. At some point down the line, we will have to make some adjustment. Read section 168(b)(1)(A) carefully. We are told that we will use the same double declining balance method (the 40% rate) until the first taxable year where the straight line method would yield a larger depreciation allowance. After Year 4, the straight rate would be 66 2/3% (that is, 100 divided by 1.5 years remaining in the original recovery period). Because the straight line rate at the end of Year 4 of 66 2/3% is greater than our declining balance rate we have been using of 40%, we will switch to the straight line method in Year 5. Under the straight line method, we take a flat rate (66 2/3%) and multiply it by the same base ($1,728 adjusted basis at the beginning of Year 5). The depreciation allowance in Year 5 is $1,152 ($1,728 × .666). The depreciation allowance in Year 6 is $576 ($1,728 × .666 × .5). The complete depreciation schedule for the computer looks like this:

Year	HYC	×	%	×	Base	=	Dep. Ded.
1	1/2	×	40	×	$10,000	=	$2,000
2	1	×	40	×	8,000	=	3,200
3	1	×	40	×	4,800	=	1,920
4	1	×	40	×	2,880	=	1,152
5	1	×	66 2/3	×	1,728	=	1,152
6	1/2	×	66 2/3	×	1,728	=	576

At the end of Year 6, Taxpayer will have fully recovered the cost of the computer as all yearly depreciation allowances add up to $10,000. His adjusted basis in the computer at the end of Year 6 will be $0 per section 1016(a)(2). The basis of property must be reduced to account for amounts "allowed" (were actually taken) or "allowable" (which could have been taken) for depreciation deductions, whichever is greater. Read section 1016 carefully. If no deduction is taken, basis must nevertheless be reduced by the amount that could have been taken under the straight line method. The effect of this is to force taxpayers to take depreciation.

The Service has issued Revenue Procedure 87-57, which is excerpted in part below, to help compute the proper depreciation allowances. It sets forth tables that incorporate the various recovery periods, depreciation methods, and conventions discussed above. Your professor may permit you to use them in answering Problem 1 in lieu of creating your own depreciation schedule. We said "may"!

B. Bonus Depreciation

1. Section 179

As mentioned already, there is a significant bonus depreciation rule, section 179. Its purpose is to encourage investment in productive property and to encourage economic activity by granting additional depreciation deductions in the year of acquisition. It allows one to elect to write off the cost of acquisition of section 179 property as an expense "not chargeable to a capital account." IRC § 179(a). Section 179 property is tangible property or off-the-shelf computer software which is section 1245 property and which is purchased for the active conduct of a trade or business. IRC § 179(d)(1). Section 1245 property is generally depreciable personal property (as opposed to depreciable real property). Skim IRC § 1245(a)(3); *but see* IRC § 179(d)(1)(B)(ii), (f) (including within section 179 "qualified real property," which mainly includes improvements to the interior of any nonresidential real property, as well as roofs, heating, ventilation, and air-conditioning property, fire protection and alarm systems, and security systems installed on such property). Section 179 property can be new or used property.

There are limits on the amount that can be expensed in any given year. The maximum allowable deduction for all qualifying property placed in service during any year is $1,000,000, adjusted for inflation after 2018. IRC § 179(b)(1), (b)(6)(A). The maximum amount is reduced dollar-for-dollar (but not below zero) by the amount by which the cost of qualifying property placed in service during the tax year exceeds $2,500,000, also adjusted for inflation. IRC § 179(b)(2), (b)(6)(A).

Note the amount eligible to be expensed cannot exceed the taxable income derived by the taxpayer from the active conduct of any trade or business, with any disallowed deductions due to this limitation permitted to be carried forward. IRC § 179(b)(3). Note also that the section 179 deduction applies ahead of the deductions authorized under section 168 and, as a result of the "not chargeable to a capital account" language, reduces basis just as they do.

Example. In 2018, Taxpayer purchases section 179 property (depreciable tangible personal property for active use in business) costing $2,600,000. Taxpayer may elect to expense up to $1,000,000 of the cost of the property, subject to the limitations imposed under section 179(b). Under section 179(b)(2), the $1,000,000 amount is reduced dollar-for-dollar by the amount by which the cost of the property exceeds $2,500,000 (here $100,000). Thus, the amount eligible to be expensed is only $900,000. [This amount cannot exceed taxable income. IRC § 179(b)(3).] Basis is reduced by the expensed amount of $900,000, before applying regular depreciation rules (i.e., section 168(k), if applicable, and the double declining balance method under section 168(a)) to the $1,700,000 remaining basis. If Taxpayer buys $3,500,000 of section 179 property in 2018, he would get no section 179 deduction because of the dollar and investment limitations. Remember, the section 179 dollar amounts adjust for inflation after 2018.

Planning Pointer

Section 179 is elective, thus presenting some planning opportunities. If a taxpayer has purchased section 179 properties during the year, each with a different applicable recovery period for depreciation purposes, the taxpayer may have to pick and choose which assets it wants subject to section 179 and the amount. IRC § 179(c). If the taxpayer is running up against the dollar limit, it would be best to allocate the section 179 deduction to section 179 property with longer depreciable lives rather than to section 179 property with shorter depreciable recovery periods. Of course, this is less of an issue if bonus depreciation under section 168(k) is available.

2. Section 168(k)

To further stimulate the economy, Congress has occasionally enacted a temporary provision that provides an extra, up-front depreciation deduction for qualified property (i.e., depreciable tangible personal property as well as certain interior improvements to nonresidential real property). Through 2022, section 168(k) authorizes a taxpayer to deduct 100 percent of the cost of qualified property as depreciation in the year of acquisition. This deduction is computed after applying section 179 (if it was elected) and before the regular depreciation deduction is calculated for the year. Thus, the adjusted basis used for section 168(k) purposes is the cost basis minus the section 179 deduction. The basis reduction resulting from the section 168(k) deduction from 2018 through 2022 then further reduces the amount of basis available for the regular section 168(a) deduction to zero. The extra depreciation deduction is scheduled to gradually phase out for purchases beginning in 2023 and completely sunset in 2027. The provision has been reenacted several times in more modest forms, and some version of it may be extended.

Example. In 2019, Taxpayer purchased new depreciable personal property for $1,600,000, which qualified for both section 179 and section 168(k) bonus depreciation. In the year of purchase, Taxpayer elected to expense up to $1,000,000 of the cost of the property under section 179, reducing adjusted basis to $600,000. Also in the year of purchase, Taxpayer took an additional depreciation deduction of $600,000 allowed under temporary section 168(k) (i.e., 100% of the downward-adjusted basis of $600,000), reducing adjusted basis to zero. In sum, Taxpayer was able to deduct all $1,600,000 of the $1,600,000 cost in the year of purchase ($1,000,000 per section 179 + $600,000 per section 168(k)).

From a practical perspective, section 168(k) in its 2018 form, swallows both section 179 and the rest of section 168 by allowing full expensing of the capital expenditures to which it applies. Presumably, this was done to inspire capital investment. But it does so at the cost of a mismatch between revenues and the expenditures to produce those revenues. Section 168(k)'s short-term benefits may have long-term adverse consequences. Or it may just lead to a lull in purchases at some later date. Notice that a taxpayer who churns assets in order to generate deductions would have income from the sale of old assets because of their zero bases. Thus, taxpayers may be inspired to buy and hold until the asset has largely depreciated just as they would have under the regular system. If that is the case, what has been gained by the economy as a whole? Perhaps the best case would be continuous spending on capital investment and corresponding continuous growth. Is that possible?

C. Amortization of Intangible Property

Section 197, enacted in 1993, dramatically changed the tax treatment of intangible assets, including goodwill. Prior to 1993, the capitalized costs of acquiring an intangible asset could be depreciated (or "amortized") only if the intangible asset had a useful life that could be determined with reasonable accuracy. This seemingly simple rule for recovering the capitalized costs of intangibles created several problems.

One problem with the historical tax regime for intangibles was that it caused much litigation concerning the identification of intangible assets and their useful lives. No deduction for depreciation was allowable with respect to goodwill, so taxpayers tried to distinguish intangible assets from goodwill, and the IRS often challenged those determinations. Of course, taxpayers who had the resources to litigate over the identification, valuation, and establishment of limited useful lives of intangibles were better off than those taxpayers who lacked resources.

Another problem stemmed from the fact that the rule for recovering costs of acquired intangible assets differed dramatically from the corresponding set of rules for recovering the costs of acquired tangible assets. As discussed above, the Code provides arbitrary conventions and methods for recovering costs of tangible assets and, more importantly, provides artificially low recovery periods (3, 5, and 7 year recovery periods) for many tangible assets that arguably have longer useful lives. This disparate treatment between intangible and tangible assets created distortions that were unfair to taxpayers.

Section 197, which was enacted to address these and other problems, created an arbitrary fifteen-year recovery period for many types of intangible property. IRC § 197(a). It generally only applies to purchased rather than self-generated section 197 intangibles. IRC § 197(c)(2). Section 197 intangible property includes goodwill, going concern value, customer lists, patents, copyrights, licenses, covenants not to compete, franchises, trademarks, trade names, and a few other intangibles. *See* IRC § 197(d)(1). NOTE: If section 197 does not apply to an intangible asset (i.e., the asset is not listed as a section 197 intangible or is specifically excluded from the definition), amortization continues to be governed by pre-section 197 law. Treas. Reg. § 1.167(a)-14.

More detailed treatment of section 197 is given in Chapter 28 in connection with intellectual property acquisitions.

Example. Taxpayer purchases a section 197 intangible asset for $180,000 on March 10, Year 1, and immediately begins using the asset in its trade or business. Taxpayer must amortize ratably the $180,000 purchase cost over 180 months (15 years × 12 months), or at $1,000 per month. Thus Taxpayer's amortization deduction in Year 1 is $10,000 (10 months @ $1,000 per month). Taxpayer's amortization deduction in Years 2–15 will be $12,000 (12 months @ $1,000 per month). Taxpayer's amortization deduction in Year 16 will be $2,000 in order that the entire purchase price is recovered.

IV. Materials

Simon v. Commissioner

68 F.3d 41 (2d Cir. 1995), *Non-Acq.* 1996-2 C.B. 2.

WINTER, Circuit Judge:

This appeal from the Tax Court raises the question whether professional musicians may take a depreciation deduction for wear and tear on antique violin bows under the Accelerated Cost Recovery System ("ACRS") although the taxpayers cannot demonstrate that the bows have a "determinable useful life."

The parties agree that under the pre-ERTA Internal Revenue Code of 1954 and the Treasury Department regulations interpreting that Code, the bows would be considered depreciable property only if the taxpayers could demonstrate a determinable useful life. The issue here is to what extent, if any, the ACRS modified the determinable useful life requirement.

BACKGROUND

The facts are essentially undisputed. Richard and Fiona Simon are highly skilled professional violinists. Richard Simon began to play and study the violin at the age of 7. He received a bachelor of music degree from the Manhattan School of Music in 1956 and subsequently pursued his master's degree in music at the Manhattan School of Music and Columbia University. In 1965, Mr. Simon joined the New York Philharmonic Orchestra ("Philharmonic") as a member of its first violin section. Since then, he has also been a soloist, chamber music player, and teacher. Mr. Simon was a full-time performer with the Philharmonic throughout the relevant tax year.

Fiona Simon has played and studied the violin since the age of 4. She studied at the Purcell School in London from 1963 to 1971 and at the Guildhall School of Music from 1971 to 1973. Ms. Simon joined the first violin section of the Philharmonic in 1985. She, too, has been a soloist, chamber music player, teacher, and free-lance performer. Ms. Simon was a full-time performer with the Philharmonic throughout the pertinent tax year.

The business property at issue consists of two violin bows ("the Tourte bows") made in the nineteenth century by Francois Tourte, a bowmaker renowned for technical improvements in bow design. These bows were purchased by the Simons in 1985 and were in a largely unused condition at the time. The Tax Court found that "old violins played with old bows produce exceptional sounds that are superior to sounds produced by newer violins played with newer bows." The Tax Court also found that violin bows suffer wear and tear when used regularly by performing musicians. With use, a violin bow will eventually become "played out," producing an inferior sound. However, a "played out" Tourte bow retains value as a collector's item notwithstanding its diminished utility. The Simons' Tourte bows, for example, were appraised in 1990 at $45,000 and $35,000, even though they had physically deteriorated since their purchase by the Simons in 1985 for $30,000 and $21,500, respectively.

The Simons use the Tourte bows regularly in their trade. In 1989, the tax year in question, the Simons performed in four concerts per week as well as numerous rehearsals with the Philharmonic. Their use of the Tourte bows during the tax year at issue subjected the bows to substantial wear and tear. Believing that they were entitled to depreciate the bows under the ACRS, the Simons claimed depreciation deductions for the two bows on their 1989 Form 1040 in the amount of $6,300 and $4,515. The parties stipulated that these amounts represent the appropriate ACRS deductions if deductions are allowable.

The Tax Court agreed with the Simons and allowed the depreciation deductions. The Commissioner brought the present appeal.

DISCUSSION

This appeal turns on the interpretation of the ACRS provisions of I.R.C. § 168, which provide a depreciation deduction for "recovery property" placed into service after 1980. Recovery property is defined by that section as "tangible property of a character subject to the allowance for depreciation" when "used in a trade or business, or ... held for the production of income." I.R.C. § 168(c)(1). The record establishes that the Simons' Tourte bows were tangible property placed in service after 1980 and used in the taxpayers' trade or business. The Commissioner contends, however, that the bows are not "property of a character subject to the allowance for depreciation."

The parties agree that Section 168's phrase "of a character subject to depreciation" must be interpreted in light of the I.R.C. § 167(a) allowances for "exhaustion, wear and tear, and ... obsolescence." The Simons and the Tax Court maintain that, when read in conjunction with the plain language of Section 167, Section 168 requires only that the Tourte bows suffer wear and tear in the Simons' trade to qualify as "recovery property." The Commissioner, on the other hand, argues that because all property used in a trade or business is necessarily subject to wear and tear, the Simons' construction of Section 168 would effectively render Section 168's phrase "of a character subject to the allowance for depreciation" superfluous, a result that Congress presumably could not have intended. *See* United States v. Nordic Village, Inc., 503 U.S. 30, 35, (1992) (It is a "settled rule that a statute must, if possible, be construed in such a fashion that every word has some operative effect."). Therefore, Section 168's requirement that the property be "of a character subject to the allowance for depreciation" must include an element beyond wear and tear, namely the "determinable useful life" requirement embodied in 26 C.F.R. § 1.167(a)-1, a Treasury regulation of pre-ERTA vintage.

We do not agree with the Commissioner's premise because some tangible assets used in business are not exhausted, do not suffer wear and tear, or become obsolete. For example, paintings that hang on the wall of a law firm merely to be looked at— to please connoisseur clients or to give the appearance of dignity to combative professionals do not generally suffer wear or tear. More to the point, the Simons' Tourte bows were playable for a time precisely because they had been kept in a private collection and were relatively unused since their manufacture. Indeed, it appears that one had never been played at all. Had that collection been displayed at a for-profit museum, the museum could not have depreciated the bows under ERTA because, although the bows were being used in a trade or business, they were not subject to wear and tear. The Tourte bows are not unlike numerous kinds of museum pieces or collectors' items. The Commissioner's textual argument thus fails because there are tangible items not subject to wear and tear.

The Commissioner next argues that Congressional intent and the notion of depreciation itself require that Section 168's statutory language be supplemented by reading into the word "character" a requirement that tangible property have a demonstrable useful life. To address that issue, we must briefly examine the history of the depreciation allowance.

The tax laws have long permitted deductions for depreciation on certain income-producing assets used in a trade or business. The original rationale for the depreciation deduction was to allow taxpayers to match accurately, for tax accounting purposes, the cost of an asset to the income stream that the asset produced. *See* Massey Motors, Inc. v. United States, 364 U.S. 92, 104 (1960) ("it is the primary purpose of depreciation accounting to further the integrity of periodic income statements by making a meaningful allocation of the cost entailed in the use ... of the asset to the periods to which it contributes"). In its traditional incarnation, therefore, the pace of depreciation deductions was determined by the period of time that the asset would produce income in the taxpayer's business. As the Supreme Court noted in *Massey*, "Congress intended by the depreciation allowance not to make taxpayers a profit thereby, but merely to protect them from a loss.... Accuracy in accounting requires that correct tabulations, not artificial ones, be used."

To implement this accurate tax accounting, the concept of a determinable useful life was necessary because, without such a determination, one could not calculate the proper annual allowance—"the sum which should be set aside for the taxable year, in order that, at the end of the useful life of the plant in the business, the aggregate of the sums set aside will (with the salvage value) suffice to provide an amount equal to the original cost." The regulation that the Commissioner now relies upon was promulgated under the 1954 Internal Revenue Code and reflects the rationale underlying the accounting scheme in effect just prior to ERTA. *See* Treas. Reg. § 1.167(a)-1 (1972).

ERTA, however, altered the depreciation scheme for two reasons other than sound accounting practice that are not consistent with the Commissioner's argument. First, the ACRS introduced accelerated depreciation periods as a stimulus for economic growth. Under ACRS, the cost of an asset is recovered over a predetermined period unrelated to—and usually shorter than—the useful life of the asset. Moreover, the depreciation deductions do not assume consistent use throughout the asset's life, instead assigning inflated deductions to the earlier years of use. *See* I.R.C. § 168(b). Therefore, the purpose served by the determinable useful life requirement of the pre-ERTA scheme—allowing taxpayers to depreciate property over its actual use in the business—no longer exists under the ACRS. *See generally Massey*, 364 U.S. 92. Because the ACRS is different by design, there is no logic in the Commissioner's suggestion that depreciation practice under the old Section 167 calls for the imposition of a determinable useful life requirement after ERTA.

A second congressional purpose embodied in ERTA also militates against reading a determinable useful life prerequisite into Section 168. In addition to stimulating investment, Congress sought to simplify the depreciation rules by eliminating the need to adjudicate matters such as useful life and salvage value, which are inherently uncertain and result in unproductive disagreements between taxpayers and the Internal Revenue Service. Indeed, the legislation specifically sought to "de-emphasize" the concept of useful life. On this point, we agree with the Tax Court that:

[The Commissioner's] argument that a taxpayer must first prove the useful life of personal property before he or she may depreciate it over the 3-year or 5-year period would bring the Court back to pre-ERTA law and reintroduce the disagreements that the Congress intended to eliminate by its enactment of ERTA.

We also cannot accept the Commissioner's suggestion that her proposed interpretation de-emphasizes useful life by requiring establishment of a demonstrable useful life for only a "narrow category" of property. Insofar as the Commissioner seeks to do this by singling out usable antiques and other business property likely to appreciate in real economic value, she relies on a concept that has nothing whatsoever to do with the useful life of the asset in the business. As the Supreme Court noted in *Massey*, "useful life is measured by the use in a taxpayer's business, not by the full abstract economic life of the asset in any business." *Massey*, 364 U.S. at 97. Nor, a fortiori, does the concept of useful life bear on the asset's eligibility under the ACRS. Indeed, the Commissioner's position that deductions for depreciation may not be taken for property that retains value after use in a business seems designed to avoid the consequences of ERTA's explicit rejection of "salvage value."[5]

The Commissioner's strongest support for her claim that Congress intended to maintain Section 1.167(a)-1's determinable useful life requirement comes from the House Conference Report, which noted that

Under present law, assets used in a trade or business or for the production of income are depreciable if they are subject to wear and tear, decay or decline from natural causes or obsolescence. Assets that do not decline in value on a predictable basis or that do not have a determinable useful life, such as land, goodwill, and stock, are not depreciable.

The Simons unsuccessfully attempt to recharacterize this statement as an inartful catalogue of assets that are not subject to exhaustion, wear and tear, or obsolescence. The House report means what it says but gives us slight pause. In light of the overriding legislative intent to abandon the unnecessarily complicated rules on useful life, we cannot employ two sentences in a legislative report to trump statutory language

---

5. We accept the Tax Court's finding that the bows have no "determinable useful life." That finding is based on the assumption that there is no distinction between the value of the bows to professional violinists and their value as antiques after they are no longer functional.

ERTA's abandonment of the concept of salvage value may be the rub that causes the Commissioner to take the position that the Tourte bows have no determinable useful life and are not depreciable. If salvage value could be used to offset depreciation, the Commissioner could, without loss to the Treasury, concede that the bows could be used to play the violin for only so long and simply offset the depreciation deduction by their continued value as antiques. The bows had been sparingly used, or not used at all, before they were purchased by the Simons and, having been used extensively, now have much less value as business property while retaining substantial value as antiques. The Commissioner may thus lean upon the thin reed of a supposed continuing determinable useful life requirement because Congress's intent to do away with the concept of salvage value is indisputable. In doing so, however, she fails to distinguish between a useful life as property used in a particular business—playing the violin as a professional—and value as non-functioning antiques.

and a clearly stated legislative purpose. Continued reliance on 26 C.F.R. § 1.167(a)-1 is in sharp conflict with the overall legislative history of ERTA, which definitively repudiates the scheme of complex depreciation rules, including "current regulations." We are thus not persuaded by the Commissioner's call for us to interpret a statute that abrogates a current regulatory regime as in fact incorporating the details of that scheme. In particular, we reject the argument that we should retain regulatory provisions now divorced from their functional purpose.

When a coherent regulatory system has been repudiated by statute—as this one has—it is inappropriate to use a judicial shoehorn to retain an isolated element of the now-dismembered regulation. We thus hold that, for the purposes of the "recovery property" provisions of Section 168, "property subject to the allowance for depreciation" means property that is subject to exhaustion, wear and tear, or obsolescence.

We acknowledge that the result of our holding may give favorable treatment to past investment decisions that some regard as wasteful, such as a law firm's purchase of expensive antique desks, the cost of which could have been quickly depreciated under our current ruling. However, Congress wanted to stimulate investment in business property generally, and it is not our function to draw subjective lines between the wasteful and the productive. Moreover, courts should take care that the Commissioner's role as revenue maximizer does not vitiate Congress's intent to sacrifice revenue to generate economic activity. If taxpayers cannot trust that such tax measures will be fully honored, some or all of the hoped-for activity will not occur.

One should not exaggerate the extent to which our holding is a license to hoard and depreciate valuable property that a taxpayer expects to appreciate in real economic value. The test is whether property will suffer exhaustion, wear and tear, or obsolescence in its use by a business. Even without a determinable useful life requirement, a business that displayed antique automobiles, for example, and kept them under near-ideal, humidity-controlled conditions, would still have difficulty demonstrating the requisite exhaustion, wear and tear, or obsolescence necessary to depreciate the automobiles as recovery property. Nor is valuable artwork purchased as office ornamentation apt to suffer anything more damaging than occasional criticism from the tutored or untutored and it too would probably fail to qualify as recovery property. Indeed, even a noted artwork that serves as a day-to-day model for another artist's work cannot be depreciated as recovery property if it does not face exhaustion, wear and tear, or obsolescence in the pertinent business.

For the foregoing reasons, we affirm.

DISSENT: Oakes, Senior Circuit Judge, dissenting:

I cannot believe that Congress, in changing the depreciation deduction from the Asset Depreciation Range System ("ADRS") for recovery of assets placed in service after December 31, 1980, to the Accelerated Cost Recovery System ("ACRS") whereby the cost of an asset is recovered over a predetermined period shorter than the useful life of the asset or the period the asset is used to produce income, intended to abandon the concept underlying depreciation, namely, that to permit the deduction the property must have a useful life capable of being estimated. I find no indication in either the changes of statutory language or the well-documented legislative history that Congress intended such a radical change as the majority of this panel, the Tax Court majority, and the Third Circuit in Liddle v. C.I.R., 65 F.3d 329 (3d Cir. 1995), have held it did. Indeed, it seems to me that the statutory language and the legislative history—consistent with the dual congressional purpose of simplification and stimulating economic growth by permitting accelerated depreciation periods—retained the fundamental principle that, in order to depreciate, the asset involved must have a determinable useful life.

First, with respect to the statutory language, the question before us is whether antique violin bows constitute depreciable "recovery property" under section 168(c)(1) of the Internal Revenue Code effective during 1989, the year in issue. I.R.C. § 168(c)(1) defined "recovery property" by saying:

> except as provided in subsection (e) the term "recovery property" means tangible property of a character subject to the allowance for depreciation—(A) used in a trade or business, or (B) held for the production of income.

Moreover, section 168(c)(2) assigned "recovery property" into four classes or tiers, and defined "recovery property" (other than real property) as "section 1245 property." Section 1245(a)(3) defined "section 1245 property" as "any property which is or has been property of a character subject to the allowance for depreciation provided in section 167...." How section 168(c)(2), section 1245(a)(3), and section 167 could all be read out of the statute as they have been by the majority of this panel, the Tax Court majority, and the Third Circuit, seems to me incomprehensible. Needless to say, the cases are legion that under section 167, taxpayers must establish that the property being depreciated has a determinable useful life.

Under the majority's interpretation, however, the only criterion necessary to obtain a deduction under section 168(c) is that the property be subject to wear and tear. Thus, a car buff in the trade or business of buying, collecting, and selling antique automobiles, who drives his autos to auto shows may obtain a depreciation deduction, or the law office that buys fine Sheraton or Chippendale desks or chairs for office use can take a deduction, though in each case the auto or furniture is actually appreciating in value and has no determinable useful life.

As for legislative history, the majority candidly admits that House Conference Report 97-215, which states that "assets that do not decline in value on a predictable basis or that do not have a determinable useful life, such as land, goodwill, and stock, are not depreciable," "means what it says." The majority then adds that the Report "gives us slight pause."

Since, concededly, taxpayers Richard and Fiona Simon have not established that the bows in question have determinable useful lives, the bows do not qualify for the depreciation deduction. It is a long way from the dual purpose of section 168 (to shorten the depreciation periods for property that would have been depreciable under section 167 in order to stimulate investment and to simplify the complex series of rules and regulations pertaining to useful lives by substituting a four-tier system of three-year, five-year, ten-year, and fifteen-year property), to abandonment of the underlying concept of depreciable property altogether. In my view, the decision of the Tax Court should be reversed and accordingly I hereby dissent.

Revenue Procedure 87-56 (Excerpt)

1987-2 C.B. 674

[The purpose of this revenue procedure is to set forth the class lives of property that are necessary to compute the depreciation allowances available under section 168. Rev. Proc. 87-57, excerpted below, provides tables that may be used in computing depreciation allowances under section 168. Eds.]

| | | | Recovery Periods (in years) | |
| | | | General Depre- ciation System | Alternative Depre- ciation System |
Asset class	Description of assets included	Class Life (in years)		
	SPECIFIC DEPRECIABLE ASSETS USED IN ALL BUSINESS ACTIVITIES, EXCEPT AS NOTED:			
00.11	**Office Furniture, Fixtures, and Equipment:** Includes furniture and fixtures that are not a structural component of a building. Includes such assets as desks, files, safes, and communications equipment. Does not include communications equipment that is included in other classes	10	7	10
00.12	**Information Systems:** Includes computers and their peripheral equipment used in administering normal business transactions and the maintenance of business records, their retrieval and analysis. Information systems are defined as:			
	1) Computers: A computer is a programmable electronically activated device capable of accepting information, applying prescribed processes to the information, and supplying the results of these processes with or without human intervention. It usually consists of a central processing unit containing extensive storage, logic, arithmetic, and control capabilities. Excluded from this category are adding machines, electronic desk calculators, etc., and other equipment described in class 00.13.			
	2) Peripheral equipment consists of the auxiliary machines which are designed to be placed under control of the central processing unit. Nonlimiting examples are: Card readers, card punches, magnetic tape feeds, high speed printers, optical character readers, tape cassettes, mass storage units, paper tape equipment, keypunches, data entry devices, teleprinters, terminals, tape drives, disc drives, disc files, disc packs, visual image projector tubes, card sorters, plotters, and collators. Peripheral equipment may be used on-line or off-line.			
	Does not include equipment that is an integral part of other capital equipment that is included in other classes of economic activity, i.e., computers used primarily for process or production control, switching, channeling, and automating distributive trades and services such as point of sale (POS) computer systems. Also, does not include equipment of a kind used primarily for amusement or entertainment of the user	6	5*	5*
00.13	**Data Handling Equipment, except Computers:** Includes only typewriters, calculators, adding and accounting machines, copiers, and duplicating equipment.	6	5	6
00.21	**Airplanes (airframes and engines), except those used in commercial or contract carrying of passengers or freight, and all helicopters (airframes and engines)**	6	5	6
00.22	**Automobiles, Taxis**	3	5	5
00.23	**Buses**	9	5	9
00.241	**Light General Purpose Trucks:** Includes trucks for use over the road (actual unloaded weight less than 13,000 pounds)	4	5	5
00.242	**Heavy General Purpose Trucks:** Includes heavy general purpose trucks, concrete ready mix-truckers, and ore trucks, for use over the road (actual unloaded weight 13,000 pounds or more).	6	5	6
00.25	**Railroad Cars and Locomotives, except those owned by railroad transportation companies.**	15	7	15
00.26	**Tractor Units For Use Over-The-Road**	4	3	4
00.27	**Trailers and Trailer-Mounted Containers**	6	5	6
00.28	**Vessels, Barges, Tugs, and Similar Water Transportation Equipment, except those used in marine construction.**	18	10	18
00.3	**Land Improvements:** Includes improvements directly to or added to land, whether such improvements are section 1245 property or section 1250 property, provided such improvements are depreciable. Examples of such assets might include sidewalks, roads, canals, waterways, drainage facilities, sewers (not including municipal sewers in Class 51), wharves and docks, bridges, fences, landscaping, shubbery, or radio and television transmitting towers. Does not include land improvements that are explicitly included in any other class, and buildings and structural components as defined in section 1.48-1(e) of the regulations. Excludes public utility initial clearing and grading land improvements as specified in Rev. Rul. 72-403, 1972-2 C.B. 102.	20	15	20

Revenue Procedure 87-57 (Excerpt)

1987-2 C.B. 687

Table 1.   General Depreciation System
Applicable Depreciation Method: 200 or 150 Percent
Declining Balance Switching to Straight Line
Applicable Recovery Periods: 3, 5, 7, 10, 15, 20 years
Applicable Convention: Half-year

If the Recovery Year is:	3-year	and the Recovery Period is:				
		5-year	7-year	10-year	15-year	20-year
		the Depreciation Rate is:				
1	33.33	20.00	14.29	10.00	5.00	3.750
2	44.45	32.00	24.49	18.00	9.50	7.219
3	14.81	19.20	17.49	14.40	8.55	6.677
4	7.41	11.52	12.49	11.52	7.70	6.177
5		11.52	8.93	9.22	6.93	5.713
6		5.76	8.92	7.37	6.23	5.285
7			8.93	6.55	5.90	4.888
8			4.46	6.55	5.90	4.522
9				6.56	5.91	4.462
10				6.55	5.90	4.461
11				3.28	5.91	4.462
12					5.90	4.461
13					5.91	4.462
14					5.90	4.461
15					5.91	4.462
16					2.95	4.461
17						4.462
18						4.461
19						4.462
20						4.461
21						2.231

Table 6.   General Depreciation System
Applicable Depreciation Method: Straight Line
Applicable Recovery Period: 27.5 years
Applicable Convention: Mid-month

If the Recovery Year is:	And the Month in the First Recovery Year the Property is Placed in Service is: the Depreciation Rate is:											
	1	2	3	4	5	6	7	8	9	10	11	12
1	3.485	3.182	2.879	2.576	2.273	1.970	1.667	1.364	1.061	0.758	0.455	0.152
2	3.636	3.636	3.636	3.636	3.636	3.636	3.636	3.636	3.636	3.636	3.636	3.636
3	3.636	3.636	3.636	3.636	3.636	3.636	3.636	3.636	3.636	3.636	3.636	3.636
4	3.636	3.636	3.636	3.636	3.636	3.636	3.636	3.636	3.636	3.636	3.636	3.636
5	3.636	3.636	3.636	3.636	3.636	3.636	3.636	3.636	3.636	3.636	3.636	3.636
6	3.636	3.636	3.636	3.636	3.636	3.636	3.636	3.636	3.636	3.636	3.636	3.636
7	3.636	3.636	3.636	3.636	3.636	3.636	3.636	3.636	3.636	3.636	3.636	3.636
8	3.636	3.636	3.637	3.637	3.637	3.637	3.636	3.636	3.636	3.636	3.636	3.636
9	3.636	3.636	3.636	3.636	3.636	3.636	3.637	3.637	3.637	3.637	3.637	3.637
10	3.637	3.637	3.637	3.637	3.637	3.637	3.636	3.636	3.636	3.636	3.636	3.636
11	3.636	3.636	3.636	3.636	3.636	3.636	3.637	3.637	3.637	3.637	3.637	3.637
12	3.637	3.637	3.637	3.637	3.637	3.637	3.636	3.636	3.636	3.636	3.636	3.636
13	3.636	3.636	3.636	3.636	3.636	3.636	3.637	3.637	3.637	3.637	3.637	3.637
14	3.637	3.637	3.637	3.637	3.637	3.637	3.636	3.636	3.636	3.636	3.636	3.636
15	3.636	3.636	3.636	3.636	3.636	3.636	3.637	3.637	3.637	3.637	3.637	3.637
16	3.637	3.637	3.637	3.637	3.637	3.637	3.636	3.636	3.636	3.636	3.636	3.636
17	3.636	3.637	3.636	3.636	3.636	3.636	3.637	3.637	3.637	3.637	3.637	3.637
18	3.637	3.636	3.637	3.637	3.637	3.637	3.636	3.636	3.636	3.636	3.636	3.636
19	3.636	3.636	3.636	3.636	3.636	3.636	3.637	3.637	3.637	3.637	3.637	3.637
20	3.637	3.636	3.637	3.637	3.637	3.637	3.636	3.636	3.636	3.636	3.636	3.636
21	3.636	3.636	3.636	3.636	3.636	3.636	3.637	3.637	3.637	3.637	3.637	3.637
22	3.637	3.637	3.637	3.637	3.637	3.637	3.636	3.636	3.636	3.636	3.636	3.636
23	3.636	3.636	3.636	3.636	3.636	3.636	3.637	3.637	3.637	3.637	3.637	3.637
24	3.637	3.637	3.637	3.637	3.637	3.637	3.636	3.636	3.636	3.636	3.636	3.636
25	3.636	3.636	3.636	3.636	3.636	3.636	3.637	3.637	3.637	3.637	3.637	3.637
26	3.637	3.637	3.637	3.637	3.637	3.637	3.636	3.636	3.636	3.636	3.636	3.636
27	3.636	3.636	3.636	3.636	3.636	3.636	3.637	3.637	3.637	3.637	3.637	3.637
28	1.970	2.273	2.576	2.879	3.182	3.485	3.636	3.636	3.636	3.636	3.636	3.636
29	0.000	0.000	0.000	0.000	0.000	0.000	0.152	0.455	0.758	1.061	1.364	1.667

V. Related Matters

- **Nuances.** There are many nuances to tax depreciation not touched upon above. Mainly these rules relate to alternative methods of depreciation (*see, e.g.,* IRC § 168(g)) and to various loophole closing provisions. The latter category includes rules limiting:

    - The amount of deductions available on luxury automobiles and mixed use personal property (IRC § 280F).

    - Deductions arising from sales of depreciable property between related individuals and entities (IRC § 168(f)(5)).

    - Rules concerning depreciation and other expenses arising from personal residences that are partly used for business purposes addressed in Chapter 22 (IRC § 280A).

Chapter 10

Deductible Personal Expenses: Casualty and Theft Losses

I. Assignment

Read: Internal Revenue Code: §§ 165(a), (b), (c), (h).

Treasury Regulations: §§ 1.165-1(c)(4), -1(d)(1)–(2)(i), -7(b)(1), -7(b)(2)(ii), -9(b)(2).

Text: Overview
Chamales v. Commissioner
Blackman v. Commissioner
Related Matters

Complete the problems.

II. Problems

In all of the following problems, you may assume the President of the United States lawfully declared a "major disaster."

1. Judy Garland's adjusted gross income in the current year is $50,000. What is the amount of her casualty loss deduction, if any, arising from the various events described below?

   (a) Her uninsured personal use car was destroyed by a tornado at a time when it was worth $12,100 and her basis was $18,000.

   (b) Assume that instead of her car it is Judy's detached garage that was damaged by the tornado. She had the garage constructed after she bought her home. Her basis in the garage was $30,000 and its fair market value before the tornado was $60,000. The decline in value of the garage was $40,000. Her aggregate basis in her home (including the garage) was $180,000. The fair market value of her home (including the garage) before the tornado was $240,000. The fair market value of her home after the tornado was $200,000.

   (c) Same as (b) except that Judy's insurance company reimbursed her for $20,000 of her loss.

   (d) Assume that under the combined facts of (b) and (c), Judy spends $25,000 to restore her garage to its original condition. What is her ending integrated basis in her home and garage?

2. Paul von Hindenburg was fond of barbecues and often hosted large ones at his home. Normally he used a state-of-the-art gas grill to do his cooking. Recently Paul upped the ante by roasting a whole pig over a newly dug fire pit in his backyard. More than 100 guests attended, and the last guest didn't depart until after 1:00 AM. Paul immediately went to bed. Around 3:00 AM a sudden strong wind sprang up and carried some fiery ashes from the pit onto Paul's cedar shingle roof. The home was quickly engulfed in flames and burnt to the ground along with much of the surrounding town. Paul and his family barely escaped with their lives. Fortunately, none of his neighbors died either. Assuming that his loss is uncompensated and that the ten percent threshold is exceeded, consider whether Paul has a deductible loss in the following circumstances.

    (a) Before going to bed, Paul poured two large buckets of water into the fire pit. The fire appeared completely out.

    (b) Alternatively, Paul did not put any water on the fire and there were some low flames still burning in the pit when Paul went to bed. Moreover, the weather forecast was for high winds before dawn.

    (c) Same as (a) except that the fire pit barbecue was in violation of a local law which forbid open burning and made such conduct a criminal misdemeanor. Paul was charged with violating the law, pled *nolo contendre*, and paid a substantial fine.

3. Alfred Kinsey owns a once valuable home in a nice suburban neighborhood. Recently a fire swept through his neighborhood but missed his home. However, two local Realtors tell Alfred that his property is now worth $500,000 less than it was before the fire because of the overall degradation the fire caused to his neighborhood. The Realtors also noted that some scientists have been quoted in the local paper as saying the fire may be part of a continuing effect of global climate change and that it is capable of repetition. Assuming the ten percent threshold is not at issue, is Alfred's loss deductible under the following circumstances?

    (a) The neighborhood is expected to be rebuilt with homes of equal quality to those that were destroyed and with some of the area turned into a public golf course.

    (b) A national real estate developer is buying up the burned out lots and plans to build low income housing in the area surrounding Alfred's home.

III. Overview

A. A Look at the Tax Treatment of Business, Investment, and Personal Losses

This chapter is about losses. Specifically, we will focus on a narrow category of personal losses known as personal casualty losses. When we speak of a loss we are usually referring to property dispositions. Section 1001 tells us that a loss is realized when the adjusted basis of the property disposed of exceeds the amount realized on the disposition. Of course, the amount of the loss is the difference between the adjusted basis and the amount realized.

The deductibility of uncompensated losses is governed, in major part, by section 165. This provision authorizes deductions for losses arising from business and investment activities. IRC § 165(c)(1) & (2). This is the main import of section 165. Thus, if a sole proprietor sells business property for less than he paid for it, or if an investor sells stock for less than she paid for it, the loss sustained is generally deductible. Likewise, if business or investment property is destroyed in a casualty (e.g., a storm), any uncompensated loss is generally deductible.

Generally speaking, taxpayers are <u>not</u> allowed to deduct losses or expenses that arise from personal concerns. Thus, if your car breaks down your loss is non-deductible, and your costs to repair it are also non-deductible. *See* IRC §§ 165(a), (c), & 262. (As we saw earlier, you also get no depreciation deduction for its gradual decline in value.) The rationale for disallowing all but a few personal losses is that those losses are deemed to arise from personal consumption. As we have already seen from our study of section 162, personal expenditures are non-deductible. A potential point of ambiguity inherent to this area is distinguishing between investment property and personal use property. For example, most people might contend that their purchase of a home had a substantial investment component. It is well settled, however, that personal residences are not treated as investment property for tax loss purposes. Gevirtz v. Commissioner, 123 F.2d 707 (2d Cir. 1941). A personal residence may be converted to investment property by renting it out. But in such cases any loss recognition will be limited to losses that arose after the residence was converted. Treas. Reg. § 1.165-9(b)(2).

B. The Personal Casualty Loss Deduction

The law provides limited relief for a category of personal losses known as casualty losses. We will consider this deduction in some detail in this chapter. In the next chapter we will look at a variety of other personal expenses that are also deductible but in a more summary fashion. As you consider the material in this chapter and the next keep in mind that every aspect of the income tax contains more levels of detail below the level at which we treat it here. If we conceive that there are ten levels of detail in total (ten being deepest), this chapter is about level four. The next chapter will address its topics at about level two. Our goal is not to utterly master the narrow areas of law addressed here but rather to grasp the general shape of the law and position ourselves to confidently delve deeper if the need arises.

1. Temporary Definition

Section 165(c)(3) authorizes the deduction of personal losses "if such losses arise from fire, storm, shipwreck, or other *casualty*, or from theft." However, effective for the years 2018 through 2025, Congress has further narrowed the deduction to apply only to losses from a "federally declared disaster." IRC § 165(h)(5). A federally declared disaster is an event that has been declared a "major disaster" by the President pursuant to 42 U.S.C. § 5170. The term major disaster is defined in 42 U.S.C. § 5122(2) as:

> "... [A]ny natural catastrophe (including any hurricane, tornado, storm, high water, winddriven water, tidal wave, tsunami, earthquake, volcanic eruption, landslide, mudslide, snowstorm, or drought), or, regardless of cause, any fire, flood, or explosion, in any part of the United States, which in the determination of the President causes damage of sufficient severity and magnitude to warrant major disaster assistance...."

2. The Traditional Definition

Under the traditional understanding (which is scheduled to return in 2026), casualty losses arise when there is damage or destruction of property by sudden, unexpected, or unusual events. Ruecker v. Commissioner, 41 T.C.M. 1587, 1588 (1981). This requirement of suddenness arises from the doctrine of *ejusdem generis*. Under this doctrine the word "casualty" is to be interpreted in a manner consistent with the other words with which it is associated. Thus, the words "fire, storm, shipwreck" in section 165(c)(3) imply a narrowing of the meaning ascribed to "casualty" to include only sudden events. "However, the term 'sudden' is comparative and each case must turn on its own facts." *Id.* Losses from natural disasters such as floods, hurricanes, earthquakes, and tornados have been acknowledged as casualties by the Internal Revenue Service. Other recognized casualty-causing events include volcanic eruptions, mine cave-ins, sonic booms, vandalism, and car accidents.

A theft loss deduction is separately authorized by section 165(c)(3). In order to obtain the benefit of that deduction the taxpayer "must suffer a criminal taking of his property as defined by the law of the jurisdiction." Riederich v. Commissioner, 985 F.2d 574 (9th Cir. 1993) (holding that investment in a tax shelter was not deductible as a theft loss). As indicated above, personal theft losses are currently disallowed along with other casualty losses that do not arise from presidentially declared major disasters.

C. Rationale for the Deduction

The rationale for the existence of a personal casualty loss deduction probably rests in the realm of compassion rather than in the realm of tax theory. One can argue that the suddenness and unexpectedness of such losses are likely to create liquidity problems for taxpayers that deserve some countenance in the tax law. But the lack of a strong tax theory justification of the personal casualty loss deduction probably explains in part why Congress has set up the temporary restrictions on its availability that are discussed earlier and the long standing restrictions that are discussed later. Do you see any logic in treating losses from presidentially declared disasters differently from smaller scale disasters? Business and investment property losses due to casualties are not subject to either the temporary or the permanent limitations.

D. Proof of Causation

To state the obvious, in order to be entitled to a casualty loss deduction, under current law, the taxpayer must show that the damage or destruction was caused by a presidentially declared disaster. Generally, this is not a problem, but some interesting issues can arise. The *Chamales* and *Blackman* cases in the materials illustrate some of the niceties. Difficulties may arise when the damages are the *indirect* result of the casualty or when the loss may be temporary. For example, one might question whether a flood that damages the road to a taxpayer's home and also damages surrounding houses and thereby renders the taxpayer's home less valuable gives rise to a deductible casualty loss. If the likelihood is that, in time, the neighborhood will be repaired, it seems certain that no loss deduction is available. But if the taxpayer demonstrates that the quality of the neighborhood is *permanently* degraded, it is possible that a court would find a deductible loss. *See, e.g.,* Finkbohner v. Commissioner, 788 F.2d 723 (11th Cir. 1986). However, temporary declines in market value due to a disaster do not qualify as casualty losses. Moreover, it is doubtful that a taxpayer can prevail in indirect damages cases without strong expert evidence. *Id.*

E. Measuring the Loss

Non-property losses are not deductible under section 165. Thus, an individual's loss of future earning capacity due to physical injury is not deductible. But note that compensation for such injuries may be excluded from gross income. *See* IRC § 104(a)(2), discussed in Chapter 34. Deductible losses are limited to losses with respect to property. Assuming she receives no compensation, the amount of the taxpayer's personal casualty loss is determined by reference to either the property's adjusted basis or to the property's decline in fair market value, *whichever is less.* IRC § 165(b); Treas. Reg. § 1.165-7(b)(1). This means that for *appreciated* property rendered totally worthless by a casualty the maximum amount of loss the taxpayer can claim is limited to her adjusted basis. The maximum casualty loss for personal use property with a basis greater than its fair market value is its fair market value. This disallowance of losses in excess of fair market value (when basis exceeds value) seems to contradict the language of Code section 165(b). However, it has been judicially upheld and it comports with the disallowance of a depreciation deduction for personal use property. *See* Helvering v. Owens, 305 U.S. 468 (1939). Where property is only damaged but not rendered worthless, the difference between its fair market value before the disaster and its fair market value after the disaster is the appropriate measure of the loss unless that amount exceeds the taxpayer's basis in the property. Improvements to non-business real property such as ornamental trees are regarded as integral components of the real property and have no separate basis for purposes of computing the loss. Treas. Reg. § 1.165-7(b)(2)(ii).

1. Effect of Reimbursements

The amount of the taxpayer's loss is reduced by any reimbursements received on account of the loss. Treas. Reg. § 1.165-1(c)(4). Thus, for example, a taxpayer whose home (with a $100,000 basis) is totally destroyed by a flood, and who receives $80,000 in insurance proceeds has only a $20,000 casualty loss. Similarly, the amount of the loss is reduced by any claim for reimbursement for which there is a reasonable prospect of recovery. Treas. Reg. § 1.165-1(d)(2)(i). Other forms of reimbursement that may also reduce the amount of the loss include: condemnation awards, disaster relief grants, and cancellation of disaster relief loans. However, money received to help a taxpayer recover from a casualty that is not specifically earmarked for repair or replacement of damaged property is not considered a reimbursement for tax loss purposes. Rev. Rul. 76-144, 1976-1 C.B. 17. Thus, for example, insurance payments and disaster relief grants for out-of-pocket expenses caused by a casualty are not considered property loss reimbursements and will not reduce the amount of the tax loss. Spak v. Commissioner, 76 T.C. 464 (1981).

2. Examples (You may assume the President declared the event a major disaster)

Example 1. Amy's personal use automobile is completely destroyed by a hurricane. Her cost basis in the automobile is $15,000. Just prior to the hurricane it was worth $10,000. Amy's insurance does not cover her loss. Since the fair market value of the automobile was less than its basis, the amount of her loss for tax purposes is $10,000, the fair market value of the property.

Example 2. Ralph's personal residence is damaged by a tornado. Several trees that Ralph had planted after buying the home were destroyed. Ralph's original cost basis in his home was $80,000. Ralph's cost basis in the trees was $500. Thus, his total basis in his home at the time of the tornado was $80,500. The decline in the fair market value of his property as a result of the loss of the trees was $2,000. Since he is entitled to use a single aggregate basis for measuring any loss to his home, his loss is $2,000 (the decline in the fair market value of the residence).

F. Restrictions on the Deduction

Losses from casualties to personal use property are subject to two main limitations: a $100 threshold, and a ten percent of adjusted gross income threshold.

1. The $100 Threshold

A casualty loss with respect to personal use property is subject to a $100 threshold before it can be considered for tax deduction purposes. IRC § 165(h)(1). For example, if a taxpayer sustains an $800 *actual* personal casualty loss, only $700 of that loss is potentially tax deductible. The $100 threshold applies separately to each casualty. Treas. Reg. § 1.165-7(b)(4)(ii). However, if a single casualty damages several properties, the deductible applies only once. Thus, for example, if a hurricane damages a taxpayer's house and car, only one $100 deductible must be met with respect to the total damages. Whether damages to two different pieces of property arise out of a single casualty is a question of fact. The Service says that events closely related in origin are considered a single casualty. *Id.* Thus, a hailstorm that damages two widely separated properties owned by the same taxpayer is a single casualty. *Id.* Similarly, damages from wind and damages from flooding may be a single casualty if the wind and flood were part of the same storm. When the damages from a single casualty extend over two tax years, only one $100 threshold need be satisfied. *Id.*

The deductible applies separately to each owner of property. This means that when a single piece of property damaged by a casualty is held by multiple owners, each owner is subject to a separate $100 deductible. Treas. Reg. § 1.165-7(b)(4)(iii). An exception to this rule is provided for married couples who file a joint return. In such cases the spouses are treated like a single individual and only one $100 deductible applies. *See* IRC § 165(h)(4)(B).

2. The Ten Percent of Adjusted Gross Income Threshold

After the $100 threshold has been met, the taxpayer must net together all of her personal casualty losses and personal casualty gains for the taxable year. If the losses exceed the gains, the taxpayer has a "net casualty loss" which is then only deductible to the extent it exceeds ten percent of her adjusted gross income (AGI). IRC § 165(h)(2)(A). Adjusted gross income for this purpose is arrived at by treating personal casualty gains and losses as though they were equal in amount and equally deductible. IRC § 165(h)(4)(A). But for this purpose "personal casualty loss" refers to the taxpayer's loss after application of the $100 per casualty threshold. *See* IRC § 165(h)(3)(B). In effect, adjusted gross income is computed as though there were no personal casualty gains or losses for the year. The combined operation of the $100 threshold and the ten percent threshold may be illustrated as follows:

Example. Joan's home declined in value by $8,000 as a result of a major flood. Her insurance company reimbursed her in the amount of $3,000. Thus, Joan has an actual personal casualty loss of $5,000. In addition, her Persian rug worth $5,000 was destroyed. Her basis in the rug was $3,500. Her insurance company reimbursed her for the full $5,000 value of the destroyed rug. Thus, Joan has a $1,500 personal casualty gain on the rug. Casualty gains and losses aside, Joan's adjusted gross income for the year is $18,000. Her personal casualty loss for federal income tax purposes is $4,900. (Her $5,000 actual loss reduced by the $100 threshold). Her net personal casualty loss is $3,400. (Her personal casualty loss of $4,900 reduced by her $1,500 personal casualty gain). Her deductible loss is $1,600. (Her $3,400 net personal casualty loss reduced by $1,800, ten percent of her AGI).

G. Adjustments to Basis for Casualty Loss Deduction and Reimbursements

A reimbursement for damage to a piece of property reduces one's basis in the asset to the extent of the reimbursement. Thus, a taxpayer who is reimbursed for $1,000 of damages to her home will have her basis in her home reduced by $1,000. IRC § 1016(a). Of course, if the taxpayer spends $1,000 restoring her home, she may be entitled to a

$1,000 basis increase. *Id.; see* Treas. Reg. § 1.263(a)-3. Thus, the reimbursement and the repair expenditure may be a wash leaving her with the same basis with which she began. Just as reimbursements will decrease basis so too will losses that are allowed as deductions on the taxpayer's income tax return. Only the amount of the "deductible loss" reduces basis. Thus, the part of the loss that is disallowed by the $100 threshold and the ten percent of adjusted gross income threshold will not reduce basis. Once again it is worth noting that expenditures to repair the damage caused by the casualty can increase basis.

IV. Materials

Chamales v. Commissioner

T.C. Memo 2000-33

NIMS, JUDGE: Respondent determined a Federal income tax deficiency for petitioners' 1994 taxable year in the amount of $291,931. Respondent also determined an accuracy-related penalty of $58,386 for 1994, pursuant to section 6662(a).

The issue ... for decision [is] as follows: Whether petitioners are entitled to deduct a net casualty loss of $751,427 for the taxable year 1994....

FINDINGS OF FACT

Gerald and Kathleen Chamales (petitioners) are married and resided in Los Angeles, California, at the time of filing their petition in this case. In the spring of 1994, petitioners became interested in purchasing a residence in Brentwood Park, an exclusive Los Angeles neighborhood. They were attracted to the beautiful, parklike setting and the quiet peacefulness of the area. Subsequently, on June 2, 1994, petitioners opened escrow on property located in Brentwood Park, at 359 North Bristol Avenue. They were represented in this transaction by Jay Solton (Solton), a real estate agent with more than 20 years of experience. Solton's work focused on sales of properties in the Westwood, Brentwood, Palisades, and Santa Monica areas of Los Angeles.

At the time petitioners opened escrow, O.J. Simpson (Simpson) owned and resided at the property located directly west of and adjacent to that being purchased by petitioners. Simpson's address was 360 North Rockingham Avenue. Both parcels were corner lots, bounded on the north by Ashford Street. The rear or westerly side of petitioners' land abutted the rear or easterly side of the Simpson property.

During the escrow period, on June 12, 1994, Nicole Brown Simpson and Ronald Goldman were murdered at Ms. Brown Simpson's condominium in West Los Angeles. Simpson was arrested for these murders shortly thereafter. Following the homicides and arrest, the Brentwood Park neighborhood surrounding the Simpson property became inundated with media personnel and equipment and with individuals drawn by the area's connection to the horrific events. The media and looky-loos[1] blocked

---

1. As explained by petitioners' counsel, "looky-loo" is a term developed in Hollywood to describe individuals who gather at places and events in hopes of glimpsing celebrities. The phrase is apparently used in California to denote those who frequent a location not because of its status as a conventional

streets, trespassed on neighboring residential property, and flew overhead in helicopters in their attempts to get close to the Simpson home. Police were summoned to the area for purposes of controlling the crowds, and barricades were installed at various Brentwood Park intersections to restrict traffic. This police presence, however, had little practical effect. Significant media and public attention continued throughout 1994 and 1995. Although Simpson was acquitted on October 4, 1995, civil proceedings in 1996 reignited public interest.

Petitioners closed escrow on June 29, 1994, purchasing the residence on North Bristol Avenue for $2,849,000. Petitioners had considered canceling the escrow and had discussed this possibility with their attorney, but upon being advised that liability would result from a cancellation, they decided to go through with the transaction. Later that summer, as the crowds and disruption persisted, Gerald Chamales (petitioner) inquired of his broker Solton whether the value of his property had declined. Solton indicated that she estimated a decrease in value of 20 to 30 percent.

Petitioners' 1994 tax return was prepared by Ruben Kitay (Kitay), a certified public accountant. In the course of preparing this return, Kitay and petitioner discussed the possibility of claiming a deduction for casualty loss. After preliminary research in the regulations addressing casualty loss, Kitay spoke with two area real estate agents regarding the amount by which petitioners' property had decreased in value. The agents estimated the decline at 30 to 40 percent. Kitay and petitioner decided to use the more conservative 30 percent figure in calculating the deduction to be taken on petitioners' return. An expert appraisal was not obtained at this time, as Kitay felt that a typical appraisal based on values throughout the Brentwood Park area would be inconclusive as to the loss suffered by the few properties closest to the Simpson home.

Kitay and petitioner also recognized and discussed the fact that there existed a substantial likelihood of an audit focusing on petitioners' 1994 return. Hence, to clarify the position being taken and the reasons underlying petitioners' deduction, an explanatory supplemental statement labeled "Casualty Loss" was attached to the return. After indicating the location of petitioners' property in relation to that of Simpson, it stated that the casualty loss was premised on "the calamity of the murder & trial, which was sudden & unavoidable & which resulted in a permanent loss to value of property." A table enumerating instances of minor physical damage to petitioners' property, such as damage to lawn and sprinklers, was also attached to the return, but no valuation was placed upon the harm caused thereby.

At the time petitioners purchased their property, they were aware that the existing home required remodeling and repair. In the fall of 1994, petitioners demolished most of the house. Then, in March of 1995, they began a reconstruction project costing approximately $2 million. This reconstruction was completed in December of 1996, and petitioners moved into the residence. Petitioners continued to reside at 359 North Bristol Avenue up to and through the date of trial.

---

tourist sight but because of its association with a famous or notorious person. We adopt the terminology and spelling as used in petitioners' briefs and by the witnesses at trial.

Other residents of Brentwood Park have undertaken similar reconstruction projects in recent years. The Nebekers, who own the property across Ashford Street from the former Simpson residence, are proceeding with a $1 million remodeling of their home. Likewise, the property owned by Simpson was sold after he moved out in 1998, the existing house was demolished, and a new residence is currently being constructed.

As of early 1999, the area surrounding the former Simpson home was no longer inundated with media personnel or equipment. The police barricades restricting traffic in the immediate vicinity of petitioners' property had been removed. Looky-loos, however, continued to frequent the neighborhood, often advised of the location of Simpson's former residence by its inclusion on "star maps" published for the Los Angeles area. Anniversaries of the murders were also typically accompanied by periods of increased media and public attention.

OPINION

We must decide whether petitioners are entitled to a casualty loss deduction based upon a postulated decline in the value of their residential property and, if not, whether they are liable for the section 6662(a) accuracy-related penalty.

Petitioners contend that the media and onlooker attention following the murders and focusing on Simpson's home has decreased the value of their adjacent property. They argue that because the homicides were a sudden, unexpected, and unusual event, and because aspects of the public interest precipitated thereby continued at least to the time of trial in this case, they have suffered a permanent casualty loss. Petitioners further allege that the proximity of their residence to that of Simpson has stigmatized their property and rendered it subject to permanent buyer resistance.

Conversely, respondent asserts that public attention over the course of a lengthy murder trial is not the type of sudden and unexpected event that will qualify as a casualty within the meaning of the Code. Respondent additionally contends that the Court of Appeals for the Ninth Circuit, to which appeal in this case would normally lie, has limited the amount that may be claimed as a casualty loss deduction to the loss suffered as a result of physical damage to property. According to respondent, since petitioners have failed to substantiate any such damage, they are entitled to no deduction. In respondent's view, any decline in market value represents merely a temporary fluctuation and not a permanent, cognizable loss.

We agree with respondent that petitioners have not established their entitlement to a casualty loss deduction. The difficulties suffered by petitioners as a consequence of their proximity to the Simpson residence do not constitute the type of damage contemplated by section 165(c)(3). However, because we find that petitioners acted reasonably and in good faith in the preparation of their tax return, no additional liability for the section 6662(a) accuracy-related penalty will be imposed.

Section 165 governs the tax treatment of losses and reads in relevant part as follows:

(a) General Rule. — There shall be allowed as a deduction any loss sustained during the taxable year and not compensated for by insurance or otherwise.

* * *

(c) Limitation on Losses of Individuals.—In the case of an individual, the deduction under subsection (a) shall be limited to—

* * *

(3) except as provided in subsection (h), losses of property not connected with a trade or business or a transaction entered into for profit, if such losses arise from fire, storm, shipwreck, or other casualty, or from theft.

Subsection (h) of section 165 further limits the allowable deduction to the amount by which the casualty loss exceeds (1) $100 and (2) the sum of personal casualty gains plus 10 percent of the adjusted gross income of the individual.

Regulations promulgated under section 165 additionally provide that, to be allowable as a deduction, a loss must be both "evidenced by closed and completed transactions" and "fixed by identifiable events." Sec. 1.165-1(b), Income Tax Regs.

As interpreted by case law, a casualty loss within the meaning of section 165(c)(3) arises when two circumstances are present. First, the nature of the occurrence precipitating the damage to property must qualify as a casualty. Second, the nature of the damage sustained must be such that it is deductible for purposes of section 165. At issue here then are whether the events surrounding the alleged Simpson murders and affecting petitioners' property can properly be termed a casualty and whether the type of loss suffered by petitioners as a consequence of these events is recognized as deductible. We conclude that both inquiries must be answered in the negative.

A. NATURE OF OCCURRENCE CONSTITUTING A CASUALTY

The word "casualty" as used in section 165(c)(3) has been defined, through application of the principle of ejusdem generis, by analyzing the shared characteristics of the specifically enumerated casualties of fire, storm, and shipwreck. As explained by this Court:

> wherever unexpected, accidental force is exerted on property and the taxpayer is powerless to prevent application of the force because of the suddenness thereof or some disability, the resulting direct and proximate damage causes a loss which is like or similar to losses arising from the causes specifically enumerated in section 165(c)(3). [Citation omitted.]

Hence, casualty for purposes of the Code denotes "'an undesigned, sudden and unexpected event,'" or "'an event due to some sudden, unexpected or unusual cause.'" Conversely, the term "'excludes the progressive deterioration of property through a steadily operating cause.'" The sudden and unexpected occurrence, however, is not limited to those events flowing from forces of nature and may be a product of human agency. [Citations omitted.]

Here, we cannot conclude that the asserted devaluation of petitioners' property was the direct and proximate result of the type of casualty contemplated by section 165(c)(3). While the stabbing of Nicole Brown Simpson and Ronald Goldman was a sudden and unexpected exertion of force, this force was not exerted upon and did not damage petitioners' property. Similarly, the initial influx of onlookers, although perhaps sudden, was not a force exerted on petitioners' property and was not, in and of itself, the source of the asserted decrease in the home's market value. Rather, petitioners base their claim of loss on months, or even years, of ongoing public attention. If neither media personnel nor looky-loos had chosen to frequent the Brentwood Park area after the murders, or if the period of interest and visitation had been brief, petitioners would have lacked grounds for alleging a permanent and devaluing change in the character of their neighborhood. Hence, the source of their difficulties would appear to be more akin to a steadily operating cause than to a casualty. Press and media attention extending for months bears little similarity to a fire, storm, or shipwreck and is not properly classified therewith as an "other casualty."

B. NATURE OF DAMAGE RECOGNIZED AS DEDUCTIBLE

With respect to the requisite nature of the damage itself, this Court has traditionally held that only physical damage to or permanent abandonment of property will be recognized as deductible under section 165. [Citations omitted.] In contrast, the Court has refused to permit deductions based upon a temporary decline in market value.

For example, in *Citizens Bank v. Commissioner* the Court stated that "physical damage or destruction of property is an inherent prerequisite in showing a casualty loss." When again faced with taxpayers seeking a deduction premised upon a decrease in market value, the Court further explained in *Pulvers v. Commissioner*, "The scheme of our tax laws does not, however, contemplate such a series of adjustments to reflect the vicissitudes of the market, or the wavering values occasioned by a succession of adverse or favorable developments." Such a decline was termed "a hypothetical loss or a mere fluctuation in value." The Court likewise emphasized in *Squirt Co. v. Commissioner*, that "Not all reductions in market value resulting from casualty-type occurrences are deductible under section 165; only those losses are deductible which are the result of actual physical damage to the property." This rule was reiterated yet again in *Kamanski v. Commissioner*, when the Court observed:

> In the instant case there was likewise relatively small physical damage to petitioner's property and the primary drop in value was due to buyer resistance to purchasing property in an area which had suffered a landslide. If there had been no physical damage to the property, petitioner would be entitled to no casualty loss deduction because of the decrease in market value resulting from the slide ... [T]he only loss which petitioner is entitled to deduct is for the physical damage to his property.

Moreover, the Court of Appeals for the Ninth Circuit, to which appeal in the present case would normally lie, has adopted this rule requiring physical damage. *See, e.g.*, Kamanski v. Commissioner, 477 F.2d at 452; Pulvers v. Commissioner, 407 F.2d 838, 839 (9th Cir. 1969), affg. 48 T.C. 245 (1967). In *Pulvers v. Commissioner*, the Court of Appeals reviewed the specific casualties enumerated in section 165(c)(3) and concluded: "Each of those surely involves physical damage or loss of the physical property. Thus, we read 'or other casualty,' in para materia, meaning 'something like those specifically mentioned.'" Even more explicitly, the Court of Appeals based affirmance in *Kamanski v. Commissioner*, on the following grounds:

> The Tax Court ruled that the loss sustained was a nondeductible personal loss in disposition of residential property and not a casualty loss; that the drop in market value was not due to physical damage caused by the [earth]slide, but to "buyer resistance"; that casualty loss is limited to damage directly caused by the casualty. We agree.

We conclude that petitioners here have failed to establish that their claimed casualty loss is of a type recognized as deductible for purposes of section 165(c)(3). They have not proven the extent to which their property suffered physical damage, and their attempt to base a deduction on market devaluation is contrary to existing law.

With respect to physical damage and assuming arguendo that petitioners' loss stemmed from an occurrence that could properly be deemed a casualty, they would be entitled to a deduction for physical harm to their property. Nonetheless, although petitioners attached to their return a list of minor instances of physical damage and mentioned several other items at trial, they have neither offered evidence of the monetary value of nor provided any substantiation for such losses. We therefore have no basis for determining what, if any, portion of the claimed deduction might be allowable, and we cannot sustain a $751,427 deduction on the grounds of damage to a lawn or a sprinkler system.

As regards decrease in property value, petitioners' efforts to circumvent the established precedent repeatedly rejecting deductions premised on market fluctuation, through reliance on Finkbohner v. United States, 788 F.2d 723 (11th Cir. 1986), are misplaced. In *Finkbohner v. United States*, the Court of Appeals for the Eleventh Circuit permitted a deduction based on permanent buyer resistance in absence of physical damage. The Finkbohners lived on a cul-de-sac with 12 homes, and after flooding damaged several of the houses, municipal authorities ordered 7 of the residences demolished and the lots maintained as permanent open space. Such irreversible changes in the character of the neighborhood were found to effect a permanent devaluation and to constitute a casualty within the meaning of section 165(c)(3).

However, as explicated above, this Court has long consistently held that an essential element of a deductible casualty loss is physical damage or, in some cases, physically necessitated abandonment. Furthermore, under the rule set forth in Golsen v. Commissioner, 54 T.C. 742, 756–757 (1970), affd. 445 F.2d 985 (10th Cir. 1971), we are in any event constrained to apply the law of the court in which an appeal would normally lie. Since the Court of Appeals for the Ninth Circuit has adopted and has not diverged from a requirement of physical damage for a section 165(c)(3) deduction, to hold otherwise would contravene *Golsen*.

Moreover, we further note that petitioners' circumstances do not reflect the type of permanent devaluation or buyer resistance which would be analogous to that held deductible in *Finkbohner v. United States*. The evidence in the instant case reveals that media and onlooker attention has in fact lessened significantly over the years following the murders. Access to petitioners' property is no longer restricted by media equipment or police barricades. Residents of Brentwood Park have continued to invest substantial funds in remodeling and upgrading their homes. Hence, petitioners' difficulties are more akin to a temporary fluctuation in value, which no court has found to support a deduction under section 165(c)(3). We therefore hold that petitioners have failed to establish their entitlement to a casualty loss deduction. Respondent's determination of a deficiency is sustained.

To reflect the foregoing,

An appropriate order will be issued, and decision will be entered for respondent with respect to the deficiency.

———————

Blackman v. Commissioner

88 T.C. 677 (1987)

The Commissioner determined a deficiency of $22,737.38 in the petitioner's Federal income tax for 1980. After concessions, the issue ... remaining for decision [is] [w]hether the petitioner is entitled to a deduction for the loss of his residence by fire when that fire was started by him.

FINDINGS OF FACT

At the time of the filing of the petition in this case, the petitioner, Biltmore Blackman, resided in Billerica, Massachusetts. He and his wife filed their joint Federal income tax return for 1980 on April 28, 1981, with the Internal Revenue Service Center, Atlanta, Georgia.

The petitioner's employer transferred him from Baltimore, Maryland, to South Carolina. The petitioner relocated his wife and children to South Carolina. Mrs. Blackman was dissatisfied with South Carolina and returned, with the couple's five children, to Baltimore. During the 1980 Labor Day weekend, the petitioner returned to Baltimore, hoping to persuade his wife to give South Carolina another chance. When he arrived at his Baltimore home, he discovered that another man was living there with his wife. The neighbors told the petitioner that such man had been there on other occasions when the petitioner had been out of town on business.

On September 1, 1980, the petitioner returned to his former home to speak to his wife. However, Mrs. Blackman was having a party; her guests refused to leave despite the petitioner's request that they do so. He returned to the house several times, repeating his request, and emphasizing it by breaking windows. Mrs. Blackman's guests did not leave the house until about 3 a.m., September 2, 1980.

Later, on September 2, 1980, the petitioner again went to his former home. He wanted to ask his wife whether she wanted a divorce. They quarreled, and Mrs. Blackman left the house. After she left, the petitioner gathered some of Mrs. Blackman's clothes, put them on the stove, and set them on fire. The petitioner claims that he then "took pots of water to dowse the fire, put the fire totally out" and left the house. The fire spread, and the fire department was called. When the firefighters arrived, they found some of the clothing still on the stove. The house and its contents were destroyed.

The petitioner was arrested later that day and charged with one count of Setting Fire while Perpetrating a Crime, a violation of Md. Ann. Code art. 27, sec. 11 (Repl. vol. 1982), and one count of Destruction of Property (Malicious Mischief), a violation of Md. Ann. Code art. 27, sec. 111 (Repl. vol. 1982). The arson charge was based on the allegation that the petitioner "had set fire to and burned ... [the house] while perpetrating the crime of Destruction of Property" and the malicious destruction charge was based on the allegation that he "did willfully and maliciously destroy, injure, deface and molest clothing, the property of" Mrs. Blackman. The petitioner pleaded not guilty to both charges. On November 5, 1980, by order of the District Court of Baltimore County, the arson charge was placed on the "stet" docket. The petitioner was ordered to serve 24 months unsupervised probation without verdict on the malicious destruction charge.

The petitioner filed a claim for the fire damage with his insurer, State Farm Fire & Casualty Co. of Baltimore, Maryland. The company refused to honor the claim due to the cause of the fire.

On his 1980 Federal income tax return, the petitioner deducted as a casualty loss $97,853 attributable to the destruction of his residence and its contents. In his notice of deficiency, the Commissioner disallowed the deduction and made other adjustments. He now concedes those other adjustments and does not dispute the amount of the casualty loss, if the loss is allowable.

OPINION

The primary issue for our decision is whether the petitioner is allowed to deduct the loss resulting from the fire started by him. Section 165(a) allows a deduction for "any loss sustained during the taxable year and not compensated for by insurance or otherwise." Section 165(c)(3) provides, in pertinent part, that in the case of an individual, the deduction allowed in subsection (a) is to be limited to "losses of property not connected with a trade or business, if such losses arise from fire, storm, shipwreck, or other casualty, or from theft." The Commissioner concedes that the petitioner sustained a loss through fire. However, the Commissioner argues that the petitioner intentionally set the fire which destroyed his home in violation of Maryland's public policy, that allowing the deduction would frustrate that public policy, and that, therefore, under the doctrine of Commissioner v. Heininger, 320 U.S. 467 (1943), and subsequent cases, the petitioner is not entitled to a deduction for the damage caused by his fire.

Courts have traditionally disallowed business expense and casualty loss deductions under section 162 or 165 where national or State public policies would be frustrated by the consequences of allowing the deduction. *Commissioner v. Heininger, supra.* "[The] test of non-deductibility always is the severity and immediacy of the frustration resulting from allowance of the deduction." Tank Truck Rentals v. Commissioner, 356 U.S. 30, 35 (1958). "From the cases, it is clear that the question of illegality to frustrate public policy is, in the last analysis, *one of degree, to be determined from the peculiar facts of each case.*" Fuller v. Commissioner, 213 F.2d 102, 106 (10th Cir. 1954), affg. 20 T.C. 308 (1953); emphasis supplied. In examining the facts of each case, courts have examined both the taxpayer's conduct and the policy his conduct is said to frustrate. *See, e.g., Commissioner v. Heininger, supra; Tank Truck Rentals v. Commissioner, supra;* Holt v. Commissioner, 69 T.C. 75 (1977), affd. per curiam 611 F.2d 1160 (5th Cir. 1980); Mazzei v. Commissioner, 61 T.C. 497 (1974); Richey v. Commissioner, 33 T.C. 272 (1959).

Conviction of a crime is not essential to a showing that the allowance of a deduction would frustrate public policy. In *Richey v. Commissioner, supra,* and *Mazzei v. Commissioner, supra,* we denied theft loss deductions to two different taxpayers who were swindled by their coconspirators in counterfeiting schemes. In *Richey*, we said the acts of the taxpayer constituted "an attempt to counterfeit, an actual start in the counterfeiting activity, and overt acts looking to consummation of the counterfeiting scheme." 33 T.C. at 276. In *Mazzei*, we said "The petitioner conspired with his covictim to commit a criminal act, namely, the counterfeiting of United States currency." 61 T.C. at 502. Neither of the taxpayers in *Richey* or *Mazzei* was charged with a crime. In Wagner v. Commissioner, 30 B.T.A. 1099 (1934), the Commissioner disallowed the taxpayer's deduction of losses which resulted from confiscation of the taxpayer's business. The taxpayer was alleged to have violated State usury statutes, but he was not arrested, nor were any charges filed against him. We upheld the disallowance of the loss deduction on the grounds that the taxpayer's business practices violated the policy expressed by the State lending and usury laws. 30 B.T.A. at 1105–1107. Similarly, in Davis v. Commissioner, 17 T.C. 549 (1951), the taxpayer was accused, by the SEC, of a violation of section 16(b) of the Securities Exchange Act of 1934. The SEC ordered the taxpayer to pay a corporation, of which the taxpayer was general counsel, the profits taxpayer had received from sales of the corporation's stock. The taxpayer was not formally charged with any crime. We upheld the Commissioner's disallowance of a deduction of the payment as a loss on the ground that allowing the deduction would frustrate the public policy expressed in section 16(b). 17 T.C. at 556.

Moreover, it is well settled that the negligence of the taxpayer is not a bar to the allowance of the casualty loss deduction. Anderson v. Commissioner, 81 F.2d 457, 460 (10th Cir. 1936); Shearer v. Anderson, 16 F.2d 995, 997 (2d Cir. 1927). On the other hand, gross negligence on the part of the taxpayer will bar a casualty loss deduction. Heyn v. Commissioner, 46 T.C. 302, 308 (1966). "Needless to say, the taxpayer may not knowingly or willfully sit back and allow himself to be damaged in his property or willfully damage the property himself." White v. Commissioner, 48 T.C. 430, 435 (1967).

In our judgment, the petitioner's conduct was grossly negligent, or worse. He admitted that he started the fire. He claims that he attempted to extinguish it by putting water on it. Yet, the firemen found clothing still on the stove, and there is no evidence to corroborate the petitioner's claim that he attempted to dowse the flame. The fact is that the fire spread to the entire house, and we have only vague and not very persuasive evidence concerning the petitioner's attempt to extinguish the fire. Once a person starts a fire, he has an obligation to make extraordinary efforts to be sure that the fire is safely extinguished. This petitioner has failed to demonstrate that he made such extraordinary efforts. The house fire was a foreseeable consequence of the setting of the clothes fire, and a consequence made more likely if the petitioner failed to take adequate precautions to prevent it. We hold that the petitioner's conduct was grossly negligent and that his grossly negligent conduct bars him from deducting the loss claimed by him under section 165(a) and (c)(3).

In addition, allowing the petitioner a deduction would severely and immediately frustrate the articulated public policy of Maryland against arson and burning. Maryland's policy is clearly expressed. Article 27, section 11, of the Maryland Annotated Code (Repl. vol. 1982), makes it a felony to burn a residence while perpetrating a crime. The petitioner admits that he set fire to his wife's clothes, and he has not denied that the residence burned as a result of the fire started by him. The petitioner was charged with violating that section, but that charge was placed on the "stet" docket. As we understand Maryland practice, such action merely postponed any action on the charge. *See* Maryland Rule 4-248(a); Fuller v. State, 64 Md. App. 339, 495 A.2d 366 (1985); State v. Weaver, 52 Md. App. 728, 451 A.2d 1259 (1982). However, the mere fact that the petitioner was never brought to trial for burning the house does not foreclose a finding by this Court that the petitioner acted in violation of that policy. *See Richey v. Commissioner, supra; Mazzei v. Commissioner, supra; Wagner v. Commissioner, supra; Davis v. Commissioner, supra.* We are mindful, also, that Maryland has an articulated public policy against domestic violence. We refuse to encourage couples to settle their disputes with fire. We hold that allowing a loss deduction, in this factual setting, would severely and immediately frustrate the articulated public policies of Maryland against arson and burning, and against domestic violence.

V. Related Matters

- **Additional Points About Presidentially Declared Major Disasters**
  - When the President declares a major disaster, the Federal Emergency Management Agency (FEMA) is authorized to take a wide variety of steps to provide relief to the affected areas.
  - In addition, the President's declaration activates certain provisions of the Internal Revenue Code. One of these, section 165(i), provides greater flexibility to the taxpayer concerning the year in which disaster losses may be deducted from the taxpayer's income.
  - Section 165(k) relates to residences located in disaster areas that are required to be demolished by order of a state government or one of its political subdivisions.

- Periodically the Service publishes lists of recently declared major disaster areas in the Internal Revenue Bulletin.
- **Bad Debts**
  - Section 166 authorizes deduction of bad debts.
  - Business bad debts are deductible as ordinary losses. Business bad debts are those debts related to the taxpayer's trade or business.
  - Non-business bad debts are deductible as short term capital losses. Capital gains and losses are addressed in Chapter 17.
  - Business bad debts are deductible when they become partially or totally worthless.
  - Non-business bad debts are deductible only when they become totally worthless.

Chapter 11

Other Deductible Personal Expenses: Interest, Taxes, Charitable Gifts, and Medical Expenses

I. Assignment

Read: Internal Revenue Code: §§ 163(a), (h); 164(a), (b)(5)–(6), (d)(1); 170(a)(1), (b)(1)(A)–(B), (G)–(H), (d)(1)(A); 213(a), (d)(1), (9), (f); 280A(d)(1)(A); 461(g). Skim § 163(d).

Treasury Regulations: § 1.213-1(e)(1)(iii).

Text: Overview
Revenue Ruling 87-106
Revenue Ruling 2003-57
Related Matters

Complete the problems.

II. Problems

1. Maggie May and Rod Stewart, a married couple, purchase a home in Year 1 and use it as a principal residence. In the problems below, unless otherwise advised, assume that the loans involved are secured by the real property described. Consider the deductibility of the loan interest in the various circumstances described.

   (a) The home cost $400,000 and they borrow $300,000 from a bank to help pay for the home and pay market rate interest along with 2 points. The points are paid from their personal savings.

   (b) Same as (a) except that by Year 5 they have paid down the mortgage to $250,000 and the house is now worth $500,000. They take out a second mortgage for $200,000 and use half the proceeds to build an addition to their home and the other half to finance the college education of their daughter, Martha May-Stewart.

   (c) Same as (a) except that in Year 10 the mortgage is paid down to $100,000 and the house is worth $500,000. In year 10, they borrow $300,000 secured by the home. They use the funds to pay off the mortgage, buy themselves new cars, make a large graduation gift to Martha, and take an around-the-world cruise.

(d) Same as (a) except that they also buy five acres of lakefront land in Montana not far from a ski resort and build a cabin on it. The total cost of acquisition and construction is $1,000,000 and they finance $800,000 of the cost. They live in the cabin for three weeks in the summer and three weeks during the ski season and elect to treat it as a qualified residence. They make the cabin available for renting when they are not in residence and rent it for 200 days of the year.

2. Ty Cobb, a single individual, paid the following state and local taxes during the year: local real property tax of $8,000 with respect to his personal residence; local real property tax of $6,000 in connection with investment rental property; state income tax of $12,000 with respect to his salary income; and state sales tax of $7,000 on personal goods purchased. What is the total deduction he can claim for these tax payments? Would your answer change if Ty were married and filed a joint return with his spouse?

3. Cole Porter was injured in a car accident and is now permanently confined to a wheelchair. In the current year, Cole expended $20,000 to modify his home to accommodate his disability. These modifications included entrance ramps, wider doorways, lower kitchen cabinets, and bathroom rails. In addition, Cole installed an elevator in his home at a cost of $15,000. The elevator enhanced the value of the home by $5,000. Other un-reimbursed expenses incurred in the current year included $500 for a wheelchair, $200 for prescription medicines, and $300 for doctors' bills. Cole also paid $2,000 for health insurance. If Cole's adjusted gross income is $100,000 what is his medical expense deduction?

4. Baron Vladimir Harkonnen suffered from morbid obesity, a serious medical disorder, and underwent gastric bypass surgery to relieve this medical condition. Later, Baron underwent liposuction to remove excess abdominal fat in order to improve his appearance. Which, if any, of these costs are deductible under section 213?

III. Overview

As discussed in the last chapter, section 262 prohibits the deduction of personal, living or family expenses from income. As we have just seen, personal casualty losses are an exception to that general rule. In this chapter we will engage in a less detailed discussion of several other personal expenses that can be deducted from income. These deductible personal expenses include home mortgage interest, state and local taxes, charitable gifts, and medical expenses. Most of these deductions are *itemized deductions*. This means that their deductibility is limited in the manner described in the next chapter. Despite the limitations, they are important tools used by many Americans to minimize their federal income tax liability.

It is important to recall that businesses can also deduct expenses such as interest and taxes. Indeed, just as in the case of losses, business deductions for these items are granted more freely than personal ones. *See, e.g.,* IRC §§ 163(a), (h)(1), (h)(2)(A);

164(a). However, there are special rules for the deduction of investment interest. Basically investment interest may only be deducted to the extent of "net investment income." IRC § 163(d)(1). The excess investment interest expense carries over to later years. IRC § 163(d)(2). The definition of investment income excludes net capital gains from the disposition of investment property and qualified dividend income unless the taxpayer agrees to have them taxed at ordinary income rates. IRC §§ 1(h)(3); 163(d)(4).

The purpose of the section 163(d) limitation is to prevent timing and character distortions that would arise from allowing a current ordinary deduction for expenditures that will generate income in the future that will ultimately be taxed at the lower rates reserved for capital gains. A related problem, *tax arbitraging*, is addressed by a variety of other Code sections. Tax arbitraging occurs when a tax favored item is acquired with debt, the interest on which is deductible. To illustrate, suppose that a taxpayer with a 30% marginal income tax rate bought a tax exempt bond paying 3% interest with $1,000,000 of funds borrowed from a bank. Suppose further that the interest rate on the borrowed funds was 4%. The $30,000 of annual interest income on the bond is exempt from tax. IRC § 103. A $40,000 deduction of the interest paid on the bank debt would save the taxpayer $12,000 in taxes. Thus the taxpayer nets a $2,000 gain ($30,000 bond income + $12,000 tax savings − $40,000 loan interest expense = $2,000) from a transaction involving none of her own money. To prevent this sort of arbitraging, the Code denies a deduction for the interest. *See* IRC § 265(a)(2).

But not all arbitraging is prevented by the Code. The deduction for home mortgage interest is, arguably, a form of officially approved tax arbitraging.

A. Qualified Residence Interest

Section 163(a) authorizes the deduction of "all interest paid or accrued within the taxable year on indebtedness." The remainder of this long Code section details the many limitations and exceptions to this general rule, some of which were just discussed. Section 163(h)(1) establishes the non-deductibility of "personal interest." Section 163(h)(2) then defines personal interest. Section 163(h)(2)(D) provides that *qualified residence interest* is excluded from the definition of personal interest thereby allowing a deduction for home mortgage interest. For many Americans this is their single largest income tax deduction. This deduction is an indirect subsidy of housing costs that rises with income and mortgage size. Thus, poor people receive little or no benefit from the subsidy and the well heeled are likely to receive the largest benefit. Is this justified? If we want to subsidize housing is there a better way?

Qualified residence interest is currently limited to interest with respect to so-called *acquisition indebtedness*. IRC § 163(h)(3)(A). Temporarily, at least, qualified residence interest does not include interest with respect to home equity indebtedness. IRC § 163(h)(3)(F)(i)(I). Acquisition indebtedness is debt which is incurred to acquire, construct, or substantially improve a *qualified residence* which is secured by the residence. IRC § 163(h)(3)(B)(i). Acquisition indebtedness includes indebtedness arising from the refinancing of acquisition indebtedness, subject to some limitations. *See* IRC § 163(h)(3)(B)(i), flush language. There is currently a $750,000 limit on acquisition indebtedness ($375,000 for a married individual filing separately). IRC § 163(h)(3)(B)(ii), (F)(i)(II). The original limit of $1 million, however, still applies to debt incurred on or before December 15, 2017. IRC § 163(h)(3)(F)(i)(III). The original $1 million limit also continues to apply to any debt incurred after December 15, 2017, to refinance existing acquisition indebtedness on the taxpayer's qualified residence to the extent the new debt does not exceed the amount of the refinanced debt. IRC § 163(h)((3)(F)(i)(iii).

An interesting question is whether the section 163(h) limitation on the deductibility of mortgage interest ($750,000 of acquisition indebtedness) is applied on a *per-residence* basis (for a total of $750,000 of debt) or on a *per-taxpayer* basis (for a total of $1.5 million of debt for two unmarried co-owners). The statute makes clear that a married couple is treated as one taxpayer. *See* IRC § 163(h)(4)(A)(ii). The Ninth Circuit recently reversed the Tax Court and held, contrary to the Service's position, that the limitation is applied on a per-taxpayer basis. Voss v. Commissioner, 796 F.3d 1051 (9th Cir. 2015). The IRS has acquiesced to the *Voss* decision. 2016-31 I.R.B. 193. Do you think the decision, which allows unmarried taxpayers who buy an expensive residence together to deduct twice the amount of interest spouses would be allowed to deduct, comports with the language of the statute?

The term qualified residence, as used above, refers to the taxpayer's principal residence (as defined in section 121) and one other residence selected by the taxpayer. IRC § 163(h)(4)(A). Note the reference in section 163(h)(4)(A) to section 280A. Section 280A(d)(1) requires that the second residence be used by the taxpayer for the greater of fourteen days or ten percent of the number of the days the home is rented out. In sum, a taxpayer can deduct the interest on two homes, one of which is the taxpayer's place of regular abode. The other might be a summer home or vacation property, for example. This can include trailers and boats. Treas. Reg. § 1.163-10T(p)(3)(ii). If a taxpayer owns more than two residences, he or she must select only one second home each year for purposes of the interest deduction.

When a person borrows from a bank or other professional lender, she often must pay one or more points at the time of borrowing. One point is equal to one percent of the amount borrowed. Points are sometimes described as a form of pre-paid interest, and the tax law generally requires that such interest be capitalized and deducted over the life of the debt. IRC § 461(g)(1). However, the Code allows points paid on home acquisition indebtedness to be currently deducted. IRC § 461(g)(2). The IRS has taken the position that this rule does not extend to points paid to refinance an existing home mortgage. Rev. Proc. 94-27, 1994-1 C.B. 613. It is worth noting that in order to be currently deductible the points must be paid from the taxpayer's separate funds rather than merely withheld from the loan. Cathcart v. Commissioner, 36 T.C.M. 1321 (1977).

B. State and Local Taxes

Section 164(a) authorizes a deduction of up to $10,000 ($5,000 for a married tax-payer filing a separate return) for a combination of the following of taxes: (1) state and local real property taxes; (2) state and local personal property taxes; and (3) state and local income taxes (or state and local sales taxes in lieu of state and local income taxes). This is popularly known as the SALT deduction. IRC § 164(a), (b)(5)–(6). (Foreign income taxes are also included in the SALT cap; however, no deduction is allowed for foreign real property taxes. IRC § 164(b)(6)(A).) It should be noted that the $10,000 limit applies to state and local taxes unrelated to the taxpayer's trade or business or other profit-seeking activity. A deduction is allowed with no limit if taxes are paid or incurred in carrying on a business, or on property held for the production of income. But it is in the context of persons in their non-business roles that we are presently concerned with the deduction.

Property taxes are normally assessed on an annual basis against the owner of the property. Where the property is transferred from one person to another during the year, the tax deduction is allocated between the owners in proportion to their respective periods of ownership. IRC § 164(d)(1).

The primary policy justification for the deduction of state and local taxes by individuals is that it serves as an indirect transfer of funds from the federal government to state and local governmental entities. In other words the deduction may be seen as a form of revenue sharing. To understand this it is useful to consider the effect of there being no such deduction. The absence of the deduction would cause the federal government to receive a greater amount of revenue without any change in its present tax rate structure. This, presumably, would make taxpayers less amenable to paying the present rates of state and local taxes. In other words, the deduction at the federal level makes the taxes more palatable at the state and local level. This justification, it may be noted, has nothing to do with the most theoretically sound structure of an income tax. Like the rationale for many other tax provisions, the justification has a significant political aspect. The $10,000 cap on the SALT deduction disfavors taxpayers in higher tax states. It was enacted in 2017 as a temporary provision slated to sunset in 2026 and we can expect continued discussion in Congress and among the states of its appropriateness.

C. Charitable Contributions

Section 170(a)(1) authorizes a deduction for *charitable contributions* to certain charities. This provision is among the more complex and difficult sections of the Code and will be considered more fully in Chapter 20. At present we will touch upon it lightly, without seeking to penetrate its depths, by only noting the general rules for deducting cash gifts.

A charitable contribution is a gift of cash or other property to an organization described in section 170(c). These organizations include governmental entities and non-profit organizations operating exclusively for religious, charitable, scientific, literary, or educational purposes. There is a substantial overlap between these organizations and tax exempt organizations recognized in section 501(c)(3).

The charitable deduction in any single year for gifts of *cash* to *public charities* may not exceed 60% of the taxpayer's "contribution base" for the year. For *non-cash gifts* to *public charities*, the limit on the charitable deduction is 50% of the taxpayer's "contribution base" for the year. IRC § 170(b)(1)(A), (G)(i). (Cash contributions that qualify for the 60% limit are not taken into account in determining contributions allowed under the 50% limit. IRC § 170(b)(1)(G)(iii)(I).) Public charities are the entities described above except for certain private foundations. The contribution base is the taxpayer's adjusted gross income with some modifications not relevant here. IRC § 170(b)(1)(H). We will discuss adjusted gross income in some detail in the next chapter but will treat it as a given for present purposes. For the average taxpayer, the contribution base limit is rarely a problem. If the contribution base limit is exceeded, however, the excess deduction is not lost. Instead it carries over for deduction within the next five years. IRC § 170(b)(1)(G)(ii), (d)(1)(A).

For gifts to certain private foundations, the limit on the charitable deduction is the *lesser* of 30% of the taxpayer's contribution base or the excess of 60% (or 50% as the case may be) of the contribution base over the amount given to public charities. IRC § 170(b)(1)(B), (G)(iii)(II). This is an indicator that if the taxpayer has made gifts to both public charities and these less favored private foundations, the deduction applies first to the gifts to public charities.

There is no single theoretical justification for the charitable contribution deduction that is fully satisfying. Perhaps the main justification for the existence of the charitable deduction rests on the idea that charities help government fulfill its service obligations to the public. However, some charities fulfill purposes that, though laudable, do not substitute for any government service. Churches are an example of this category of charity. To the extent that the charitable deduction operates as an indirect subsidy of a broad array of useful organizations by encouraging contributions, perhaps one can say that it promotes overall general welfare and that this is justification enough.

D. Medical Expenses

Section 213(a) permits the deduction of unreimbursed medical care expenses of the taxpayer, the taxpayer's spouse, and dependents. For 2017 and 2018, the deduction is limited to that part of the otherwise deductible medical expenses that exceeds 7.5% of one's adjusted gross income regardless of the taxpayer's age. IRC § 213(f). (The income threshold increases to 10% after 2018.) Thus, in most cases taxpayers are not entitled to the deduction. Potentially deductible expenses include the costs of prescription medications as well as costs for doctors, insurance, laboratory tests, and hospitalization. IRC § 213(b), (d)(1). Even some medical related travel expenses may be deductible. *See* IRC § 213(d)(2). Treas. Reg. § 1.213-1(e)(1). However, most elective cosmetic surgery costs are not deductible. IRC § 213(d)(9). Revenue Ruling 2003-57 included in the materials bears on this issue. The Tax Court has ruled that the medical expense deduction is applicable to some costs arising from sex reassignment surgery. *See* O'Donnabhain v. Commissioner, 134 T.C. 34 (2010), *acq.*, A.O.D. 2011-03, I.R.B. 2011-47.

As discussed in Revenue Ruling 87-106 included in the materials, some capital expenditures qualify for the medical expense deduction. In general such expenditures include those which relate only to the sick person and which do not constitute an improvement to property. Examples of deductible capital expenditures include eyeglasses, seeing eye dogs, prosthetic limbs, and wheelchairs. Treas. Reg. § 1.213-1(e)(1)(iii). Under the regulations and case law, even some medically necessary improvements to property, such as air conditioning, may qualify for the deduction to the extent that the expenditure does not enhance the value of the property. *See* Gerard v. Commissioner, 37 T.C. 826 (1962).

IV. Materials

Revenue Ruling 87-106

1987-2 C.B. 67

ISSUE

What capital expenditures incurred to accommodate a residence to a handicapped condition of the taxpayer, the taxpayer's spouse, or one of the taxpayer's dependents are deductible in full under section 213 of the Internal Revenue Code?

LAW AND ANALYSIS

Section 213(a) of the Code allows a deduction in computing taxable income for expenses paid during the taxable year, not compensated for by insurance or otherwise, for medical care of the taxpayer, the taxpayer's spouse, or a dependent (as defined in section 152) to the extent that the expenses exceed 7.5 percent of the taxpayer's adjusted gross income [10 percent under current law].

Section 213(d)(1) of the Code defines the term "medical care" to include amounts paid for the diagnosis, cure, mitigation, treatment, or prevention of disease, or for the purpose of affecting any structure or function of the body.

Section 1.213-1(e)(1)(ii) of the regulations provides, in part, that deductions for expenditures for medical care allowable under section 213 of the Code will be confined strictly to expenses incurred primarily for the prevention or alleviation of a physical or mental defect or illness. An expenditure that is merely beneficial to the general health of an individual is not an expenditure for medical care.

Section 1.213-1(e)(1)(iii) of the regulations provides, in part:

Capital expenditures are generally not deductible for Federal income tax purposes. See section 263 and the regulations thereunder. However, an expenditure which otherwise qualifies as a medical expense under section 213 shall not be disqualified merely because it is a capital expenditure. For purposes of section 213 and this paragraph, a capital expenditure made by the taxpayer may qualify as a medical expense, if it has as its primary purpose the medical care (as defined in subdivisions (i) and (ii) of this subparagraph) of the taxpayer, his spouse, or his dependent. Thus, a capital expenditure which is related only to the sick person and is not related to permanent improvement or betterment of property, if it otherwise qualifies as an expenditure for medical care, shall be deductible; for example, an expenditure for eye glasses, a seeing eye dog, artificial teeth and limbs, a wheel chair, crutches, an inclinator or an air conditioner which is detachable from the property and purchased only for the use of a sick person, etc. Moreover, a capital expenditure for permanent improvement or betterment of property which would not ordinarily be for the purpose of medical care (within the meaning of this paragraph) may, nevertheless, qualify as a medical expense to the extent that the expenditure exceeds the increase in the value of the related property, if the particular expenditure is related directly to medical care. Such a situation could arise, for example, where a taxpayer is advised by a physician to install an elevator in his residence so that the taxpayer's wife who is afflicted with heart disease will not be required to climb stairs. If the cost of installing the elevator is $1,000 and the increase in the value of the residence is determined to be only $700, the difference of $300, which is the amount in excess of the value enhancement, is deductible as a medical expense. If, however, by reason of this expenditure, it is determined that the value of the residence has not been increased, the entire cost of installing the elevator would qualify as a medical expense.

In making a capital expenditure that would otherwise qualify as being for medical care, any additional expenditure that is attributable to personal motivation does not have medical care as its primary purpose and is not related directly to medical care for purposes of section 213 of the Code. Such personal motivations include, for instance, architectural or aesthetic compatibility with the related property. Consequently, such additional expenditures are not deductible under section 213. Ferris v. Commissioner, 582 F.2d 1112 (7th Cir. 1978), rev'g and rem'g T.C.M. 1977-186. In *Ferris,* the taxpayer had incurred additional costs for architectural and aesthetic reasons in building an enclosed pool that otherwise qualified as an expenditure for medical care. A deduction for the additional costs was denied.

In Jacobs v. Commissioner, 62 T.C. 813 (1974), the Tax Court held that for an expense to be deductible under section 213 of the Code it both must be an essential element of treatment and must not have otherwise been incurred for nonmedical reasons. An expenditure failing either test would be a nondeductible personal, living, or family expense under section 262. *See* Rev. Rul. 76-80, 1976-1 C.B. 71.

In S. Rep. No. 99-313, 99th Cong., 2d Sess. 59 (1986), 1986-3 (Vol. 3) C.B. 59, and 2 H.R. Rep. No. 99-841 (Conf. Rep.), 99th Cong., 2d Sess. II-22 (1986), 1986-3

(Vol. 4) C.B. 22, Congress expressed a desire to clarify that certain capital expenditures generally do not increase the value of a personal residence and thus generally are deductible in full as medical expenses. These expenditures are those made for removing structural barriers in a personal residence for the purpose of accommodating it to the handicapped condition of the taxpayer or the taxpayer's spouse or dependents who reside there.

The Internal Revenue Service has determined that expenditures for the following purposes generally do not increase the fair market value of a personal residence and thus generally are eligible in full for the medical expense deduction when made for the primary purpose of accommodating a personal residence to the handicapped condition of the taxpayer, the taxpayer's spouse, or dependents who reside there:

1. constructing entrance or exit ramps to the residence;

2. widening doorways at entrances or exits to the residence;

3. widening or otherwise modifying hallways and interior doorways;

4. installing railing, support bars, or other modifications to bathrooms;

5. lowering of or making other modifications to kitchen cabinets and equipment;

6. altering the location of or otherwise modifying electrical outlets and fixtures;

7. installing porch lifts and other forms of lifts (generally, this does not include elevators, as they may add to the fair market value of the residence and any deduction would have to be decreased to that extent. See section 1.213-1(e)(1)(iii) of the regulations.);

8. modifying fire alarms, smoke detectors, and other warning systems;

9. modifying stairs;

10. adding handrails or grab bars whether or not in bathrooms;

11. modifying hardware on doors;

12. modifying areas in front of entrance and exit doorways; and

13. grading of ground to provide access to the residence.

The above list of expenditures is not exhaustive. If substantially similar expenditures are incurred to accommodate a personal residence to the handicapped condition of the taxpayer or the taxpayer's spouse or dependents who reside there, those expenditures may be eligible in full for the medical deduction, provided they do not increase the fair market value of the personal residence. Moreover, only reasonable costs incurred to accommodate a personal residence to the handicapped condition are considered to be incurred for the purpose of medical care or are directly related to medical care for purposes of section 213 of the Code. Additional costs attributable to personal motivations are not deductible under section 213.

HOLDING

Subject to the percentage limitation of section 213(a) of the Code, the above capital expenditures incurred to accommodate a residence to the handicapped condition of the taxpayer, the taxpayer's spouse, or one of the taxpayer's dependents generally are deductible in full under section 213 provided that the residence is the personal residence of the handicapped individual.

Revenue Ruling 2003-57

2003-1 C.B. 959

ISSUE

Are amounts paid by individuals for breast reconstruction surgery, vision correction surgery, and teeth whitening medical care expenses within the meaning of §213(d) and deductible under §213 of the Internal Revenue Code?

FACTS

Taxpayer *A* undergoes mastectomy surgery that removes a breast as part of treatment for cancer and pays a surgeon to reconstruct the breast. Taxpayer *B* wears glasses to correct myopia and pays a doctor to perform laser eye surgery to correct the myopia. Taxpayer *C*'s teeth are discolored as a result of age. *C* pays a dentist to perform a teeth-whitening procedure. *A*, *B*, and *C* are not compensated for their expenses by insurance or otherwise.

LAW AND ANALYSIS

Section 213(a) allows a deduction for expenses paid during the taxable year, not compensated for by insurance or otherwise, for medical care of the taxpayer, spouse, or dependent, to the extent the expenses exceed 7.5 percent of adjusted gross income [10 percent under current law]. Under §213(d)(1)(A), medical care includes amounts paid for the diagnosis, cure, mitigation, treatment, or prevention of disease, or for the purpose of affecting any structure or function of the body.

Medical care does not include cosmetic surgery or other similar procedures, unless the surgery or procedure is necessary to ameliorate a deformity arising from, or directly related to, a congenital abnormality, a personal injury resulting from an accident or trauma, or a disfiguring disease. Section 213(d)(9)(A). Cosmetic surgery means any procedure that is directed at improving the patient's appearance and does not meaningfully promote the proper function of the body or prevent or treat illness or disease. Section 213(d)(9)(B).

A's cancer is a disfiguring disease because the treatment results in the loss of *A*'s breast. Accordingly, the breast reconstruction surgery ameliorates a deformity directly related to a disease and the cost is an expense for medical care within the meaning of §213(d) that *A* may deduct under §213 (subject to the limitations of that section).

The cost of *B*'s laser eye surgery is allowed under §213(d)(9) because the surgery is a procedure that meaningfully promotes the proper function of the body. Vision correction with eyeglasses or contact lenses qualifies as medical care. *See* Rev. Rul. 74-429, 1974-2 C.B. 83. Eye surgery to correct defective vision, including laser procedures such as LASIK and radial keratotomy, corrects a dysfunction of the body. Accordingly, the cost of the laser eye surgery is an expense for medical care within the meaning of § 213(d) that B may deduct under § 213 (subject to the limitations of that section).

In contrast, the teeth-whitening procedure does not treat a physical or mental disease or promote the proper function of the body, but is directed at improving C's appearance. The discoloration is not a deformity and is not caused by a disfiguring disease or treatment. Accordingly, C may not deduct the cost of whitening teeth as an expense for medical care.

HOLDING

Amounts paid by individuals for breast reconstruction surgery following a mastectomy for cancer and for vision correction surgery are medical care expenses under § 213(d) and are deductible under § 213 (subject to the limitations of that section). Amounts paid by individuals to whiten teeth discolored as a result of age are not medical care expenses under § 213(d) and are not deductible.

V. Related Matters

- **Education**. Education is often treated as a personal matter within the meaning of section 262 even though much of education may be devoted to preparing to enter a job or profession. Nevertheless, Congress has enacted several provisions that allow either a deduction or a credit for personal educational expenses. *See, e.g.,* IRC §§ 25A, 221, 222. These deductions and credits, as well as varying exclusion provisions relating to scholarships and grants, employer-provided educational assistance, and educational savings, are covered in Chapter 33.

- **Moving Expenses**. Code section 217 authorized deduction of some moving expenses. However, the provision was temporarily suspended by the TCJA. Currently, employees and self-employed individuals may no longer claim a deduction for moving expenses (e.g., costs of moving household goods and of moving oneself and one's family to change a job). An exception exists for members of the U.S. Armed Forces on active duty if the move is pursuant to a military order and incident to a permanent change of station. IRC § 217(g), (k). If an employee receives reimbursement from her employer for moving expenses, the employee must include the reimbursement in gross income. IRC § 132(g) (again with an exception for active duty armed forces members).

- **Qualified Tuition Programs**. Sections 529 authorizes saving after-tax dollars for education expenses in an account or trust which is then permitted to grow tax free until disbursement. If the funds are used for "qualified higher education expenses," there are no income tax consequences upon withdrawal. Interestingly, the term qualified higher education expenses includes tuition expenses at "an elementary or secondary public, private, or religious school." IRC § 529(c)(7), (e)(3). Distributions for elementary or secondary tuition, however, are limited to no more than $10,000 per student. If the funds are not used for qualifying expenses, the earnings are taxable and a penalty will apply.

- **Health Savings Accounts.** Section 223 allows an above the line deduction (IRC §62(a)(19)) for certain amounts contributed by or on behalf of a taxpayer to a health savings account when the taxpayer has a high deductible health insurance policy. IRC §223(a). The funds in the account are permitted to grow tax free. IRC §223(e). Expenditures from the account to pay qualified medical expenses are excluded from the income of the taxpayer. IRC §223(f)(1). Thus, the funds and the investment growth on those funds that are used for health care costs are never taxed to the taxpayer. At death unexpended funds in the account can be left to one's spouse as a health savings account. IRC §223(f)(8)(A). Other beneficiaries receive the account as gross income. IRC §223(f)(8)(B).

- **Nonbusiness Bad Debts.** When a debtor defaults on a nonbusiness debt and the debt becomes totally worthless, the person owed on the debt is permitted to take a bad debt deduction in the form of a short-term capital loss. IRC §166(d). The loss is measured by the lender's adjusted basis in the debt. IRC §166(b).

Chapter 12

The Deduction Hierarchy: Adjusted Gross Income, the Standard Deduction, and the Dependency Rules

I. Assignment

Read: Internal Revenue Code: §§ 62; 63; 67(a)–(b), (g); 151; 152. Skim § 68.

Treasury Regulations: §§ 1.62-2(c)(4); 1.152-4(b).

Text: Overview
IRS Form 1040, U.S. Individual Income Tax Return
IRS Form 8332, Release of Claim to Exemption for Child of Divorced or Separated Parents
Related Matters

Complete the problems.

II. Problems

1. Are the following expenses deductible? If so, are they deductible above the line or below the line? If they are deductible below the line, are they itemized deductions or miscellaneous itemized deductions?

   (a) A homeowner's payment to Roto Rooter to clean out a root infested sewer line at her personal residence.

   (b) An apartment building owner's payment to Roto Rooter to clean out a root infested sewer line at one of her rental properties.

   (c) A homeowner's payment of mortgage interest and property taxes relating to her personal residence.

   (d) An apartment building owner's payments of mortgage interest and property taxes with respect to one of her rental properties. Assume that section 163(d) has no application.

   (e) A tax law professor's un-reimbursed purchase of a copy of the federal income tax regulations.

(f) What if the tax professor in (e) is reimbursed by her employer and reports the reimbursement as income?

(g) An associate in a law firm pays $1,500 of interest on student loans incurred while a law student. *See* IRC § 221.

(h) Taxpayer pays an accountant to do her personal tax return.

(i) Taxpayer pays an accountant to do her business tax return.

2. For purposes of considering whether Jed would be able to claim a child tax credit under section 24 for the individuals below, determine whether each is a "dependent" under section 152 — i.e., either a *qualifying child* or a *qualifying relative*. Assume, unless stated otherwise, that Jed provided over one half of the support for the particular person involved. Assume further that the potential dependent did not earn more than the exemption amount and that no one else is entitled to claim the person as a dependent. [Do not concern yourself with the workings of section 24, which will be covered in a later chapter; merely determine whether each of the following is a dependent under section 152.]

(a) The potential dependent, who is away at school, is Ellie May, Jed's 21-year-old niece. Ellie May lives with Jed when she is not in school.

(b) Same as (a) except Ellie May was adopted by Jed's sister.

(c) The potential dependent is Granny, Jed's mother, who lives next door. Granny has no gross income.

(d) Same as (c) except that Granny is Jed's mother's aunt.

(e) Same as (d) except that Granny lives with Jed.

(f) The potential dependent is Ellie May again, but who now is Jed's minor daughter residing with Jed's former spouse, Maggie May. Maggie May has custody of Ellie May.

3. Hillary and Bill, married taxpayers in their thirties with one infant child, file a joint return in the current year. They have the following items of income and expense: combined salaries of $60,000, $7,000 of rental income on a home rented out to tenants, $3,000 of depreciation expense on the rental property, $4,000 in property taxes on the rental property, $9,000 of interest paid on their personal residence mortgage, $8,000 property taxes on their personal residence, $5,000 in state income taxes, $1,000 of un-reimbursed employee travel expenses, and a $4,000 charitable expense.

(a) Ignoring any of the statutorily authorized inflation adjustments, what are Hillary and Bill's adjusted gross income and taxable income? Will they elect to itemize?

(b) Same as (a) except that Hilary is over age 65 but Bill is not.

III. Overview

We began our study of the income tax by considering what constitutes gross income under section 61. More recently we have considered various deductions to arrive at taxable income. Now we will look at the hierarchy established in the Code for the various deductions. This hierarchy primarily arises from the operation of sections 62 and 63.

Section 62 authorizes certain deductions to be subtracted from gross income to arrive at "adjusted gross income." These are often referred to as "above the line" deductions. Looking at the list in section 62, you will see that above the line deductions are generally deductions otherwise allowed under the Code for expenditures incurred to produce income. Perhaps the largest category includes expenses attributable to a trade or business. IRC § 62(a)(1). (Note the exception for unreimbursed employee business expenses in section 62(a)(1), but some limited exceptions to that exception in section 62(a)(2).) Other above the line deductions include business and investment losses from the sale of property (§ 62(a)(3)), expenses and depreciation attributable to rental property (§ 62(a)(4)), and a few other expenses beyond the scope of our study. *See* IRC § 62(a).

Section 63 authorizes other deductions to be taken from adjusted gross income to arrive at taxable income. These are referred to as "below the line" deductions. Below the line deductions are also known as "itemized" deductions. IRC § 63(b) & (d). It is easy to identify itemized deductions. If they are not listed in section 62 as above the line deductions, then they automatically fall into the category of itemized deductions (with the exception of the section 199A deduction). Itemized deductions include, for example, home mortgage interest (§ 163), state and local taxes (§ 164), charitable contributions (§ 170), and medical expenses (§ 213). As discussed below, some itemized deductions are labeled as "miscellaneous itemized" deductions, which means they cannot be claimed by an individual for tax years 2018 through 2025.

It is important to understand at the outset that section 62 does not create any tax deductions. Instead it merely establishes the point in the tax calculation process at which deductions authorized by other Code sections may be taken. Section 63 has a similar traffic cop function, but it also authorizes a deduction, the standard deduction discussed below.

A. Itemized Deductions versus the Standard Deduction

Adjusted gross income (or AGI for short) is often a reference point for limitations on deductions. For example, in the previous chapter we saw that the medical care expense deduction under section 213(a) is limited to those otherwise deductible medical expenses that exceed 7.5% of AGI (10% of AGI after 2018). We saw a similar limitation on charitable deductions (e.g., cash gifts to public charities are limited to 60% of AGI). But there is another critical reason for the distinction between above the line deductions and itemized deductions; itemized deductions must be taken in lieu of what is known as "the standard deduction." *See* IRC § 63(b) & (d). This is a distinct disadvantage if the taxpayer would otherwise have taken the standard deduction.

The standard deduction was enacted in 1944 to simplify compliance and enforcement. Congress assumes that all of us incur a certain amount of personal deductible expenses, such as mortgage interest, state and local property taxes, and charitable gifts. In lieu of listing all of these deductions (and other "below the line" or "itemized" deductions), the Code permits a taxpayer to take a deduction in the amount of the standard deduction. By doing so, the taxpayer does not need to substantiate various below the line deductions and the Service does not need to scrutinize the tax return as much.

The amount of the standard deduction is determined by reference to the taxpayer's filing status, and it is adjusted annually for inflation. In 2018, the standard deduction was $24,000 for married couples filing jointly (including surviving spouses) and $12,000 for single individuals and married individuals filing separately. IRC § 63(c)(7). It is available to every taxpayer without having to prove any deductible expenses. Since a taxpayer must choose between itemizing and taking the standard deduction, this means that a married couple's itemized deductions in 2018 must exceed $24,000 before the couple will receive any tax benefit from those deductions. Persons over age 64 and blind persons are entitled to an extra standard deduction of $600 (indexed for inflation; it was $1,600 in 2018). IRC § 63(f)(1); Rev. Proc. 2017-58.

The standard deduction for 2018 is significantly higher than it was in prior years. That is because the Tax Cuts and Jobs Act (TCJA) materially increased it (indeed, nearly doubled it) for tax years 2018 through 2025. Recall from the previous chapter that the TCJA also restricted the amount of the mortgage interest deduction (by lowering the mortgage limit from $1,000,000 to $750,000) and the state and local tax deduction (by capping it at $10,000 per year). These changes mean that many fewer taxpayers will itemize than in the past. Some commentators fear that with fewer taxpayers itemizing, charitable donations will decline. Others counter that people donate primarily out of generosity and only secondarily out of a desire to save taxes. The next few years may show which view is the better one.

B. Miscellaneous Itemized Deductions

Some itemized deductions are known as the "miscellaneous itemized deductions." This is not a good thing from the standpoint of their deductibility.

Prior to 2018, miscellaneous itemized deductions were deductible only to the extent that they exceeded 2% of the taxpayer's adjusted gross income. IRC § 67(a). In 2017, for example, if a taxpayer, whose adjusted gross income was $100,000, incurred $3,000 in miscellaneous itemized deductions, the first $2,000 was not deductible, but the remaining $1,000 was.

For tax years 2018 through 2025, however, no deduction is allowed for miscellaneous itemized deductions. IRC § 67(g) (added by the TCJA). The suspension of miscellaneous itemized deductions is temporary as with most individual tax changes made by TCJA.

So, what types of itemized deductions fall within the category of non-deductible miscellaneous itemized deductions? The answer can be found in section 67(b). Note the term is defined negatively, so only those deductions not listed in section 62 (above the line) and not listed in section 67(b) are miscellaneous itemized deductions. The most prominent miscellaneous itemized deduction is the deduction under section 162 for un-reimbursed employee business expenses. *See* IRC §§ 62(a)(1) &(2)(A); 67(b). Another prominent category is the deduction under section 212 for expenses related to the production of income as well as for tax return preparation and advice. The hobby loss deductions under section 183 are also miscellaneous itemized deductions. Again, none of these type expenses, once subject to the two-percent-of-AGI limit, may be claimed by an individual for tax years 2018 through 2025. Even under prior law, the fairness of the limitation on miscellaneous itemized deductions was subject to question. The complete elimination of their deductibility is likely to come as a surprise to many taxpayers. Why should one person's legitimate business expense be deductible and another person's not?

As noted, structurally, the Code arrives at taxable income by two similar but slightly different routes. Below is a simple flow chart depicting the routes followed. Note: The Code provisions which serve as our guideposts for the computation of taxable income are sections 61, 62, and 63. The key provisions for understanding the divergence between the two routes are subsections 63(a) and (b).

Getting to Taxable Income

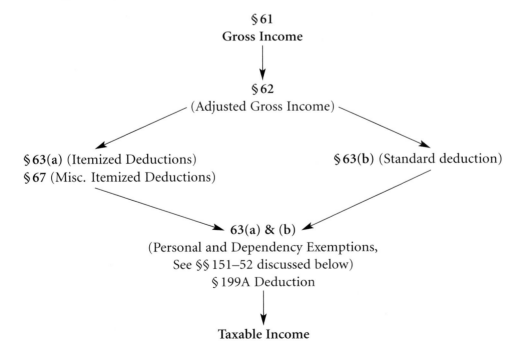

§ 61
Gross Income

§ 62
(Adjusted Gross Income)

§ 63(a) (Itemized Deductions)   § 63(b) (Standard deduction)
§ 67 (Misc. Itemized Deductions)

63(a) & (b)
(Personal and Dependency Exemptions,
See §§ 151–52 discussed below)
§ 199A Deduction

Taxable Income

C. Personal and Dependency Exemptions

In the chart above, you'll see that we added a special deduction in the formula in reaching taxable income — the deduction for so-called personal exemptions. Historically, the personal exemption was an automatic deduction to which most individual taxpayers were entitled. IRC § 151(a). Prior to 2018, the statutorily set amount for each personal exemption was $2,000, annually adjusted for inflation. IRC §§ 151(d)(1) & (4). In 2017, for example, it was $4,050. A taxpayer could also claim a personal exemption for each individual who was a *dependent* of the taxpayer. IRC § 151(c). A dependent could be either a *qualifying child* or a *qualifying relative*. IRC § 152(a). A person claimed as a dependent by another taxpayer was not entitled to a personal exemption on his or her own return. IRC § 151(d)(2). Nor could such person claim anyone else as a dependent. IRC § 152(b)(1).

The TCJA temporarily reduced the deduction for personal and dependency exemptions to zero for tax years 2018 through 2025 while leaving the rest of section 151 in place. IRC § 151(d)(5). At first, the loss of this deduction may seem quite harsh, especially for larger families. For example, in 2017, a married couple with three children could potentially claim five exemptions on the joint tax return, for a deduction of $20,250 (5 exemptions × $4,050 each). In 2018, that same couple could claim $0. But it is worth pointing out that the TCJA significantly expanded the child tax credit, and such credit enhancements should help offset the loss of the exemption deductions. We explore the child tax credit in Chapter 15. As we will learn, a $2,000 credit is generally available for each *qualifying child* of the taxpayer. IRC § 24(h)(2). In addition, a $500 credit is potentially available for each *qualifying relative* who is not a qualifying child. IRC § 24(h)(4). As you can see, although the deduction for personal and dependency exemptions has effectively been temporarily repealed by the TCJA, the definition of a dependent is still directly determinative of who may claim the child tax credit and the qualifying relative tax credit. For this reason, we address the definitions of qualifying child and qualifying relative in some detail below.

1. Qualifying Child

A qualifying child can include not only the taxpayer's biological children but also adopted children, stepchildren, and the descendants of these persons. IRC §§ 152(c)(1), (c)(2), & (f)(1)(B). Moreover, siblings and the descendants of siblings can also be qualifying children of the taxpayer. IRC §§ 152(c)(1), (c)(2), & (f)(1)(B). In addition to bearing the proper relationship to the taxpayer, a qualifying child must also share the same residence with the taxpayer for more than half of the year, meet certain age requirements, and not have provided more than one-half of his or her own support for the year. IRC § 152(c)(1). A qualifying child can be no older than age 18 or, in the case of students, no older than age 23. IRC § 152(c)(3).

Under earlier versions of the dependency rules, a child who was away on a temporary basis retained the parent's home as his or her residence. *See* Treas. Reg. § 1.152-1(b). Thus, typically, the fact that a child was away at college or boarding school would not prevent the parent from claiming a dependency exemption for that child (or from claiming the child tax credit, assuming other requirements were met).

a. Tie Breakers

When two or more persons are entitled to claim a person as a qualifying child there are various tie breaking rules that come into play to prevent more than one person from claiming the child as a dependent. The first tie breaker is parentage. IRC § 152(c)(4)(A)(i). If neither person is the parent, the one with the higher adjusted gross income gets the exemption. IRC § 152(c)(4)(A)(ii). If both claimants are parents, the one with whom the child resided for the longer period of time during the year gets the exemption. IRC § 152(c)(4)(B)(i). If the period of residence with each parent was equal, the parent with the higher adjusted gross income gets the exemption. IRC § 152(c)(4)(B)(ii).

b. Children of Divorced Parents

Notwithstanding the tie breakers just described, there are additional special rules for allocating the dependency exemption (and, therefore, the child tax credit) for children of divorced parents. Essentially, these rules permit the *custodial parent* to transfer the exemption (and the child tax credit) to the other parent by way of written release. IRC § 152(e)(2). See IRS Form 8332, included in the materials, which can be used for the release of all child-related tax benefits for a child, including the dependency exemption (repealed through 2025) and the child tax credit. For this purpose the custodial parent is the parent who has custody of the child for the greater portion of the year. IRC § 152(e)(4)(A). There is a similar special rule for allocating the exemption for a child who is the subject of a multiple support agreement. IRC § 152(d)(3). Query: in the divorce context, when would the custodial parent decide to release the dependency exemption (and, therefore, the child tax credit) to the non-custodial spouse?

2. Qualifying Relative

A qualifying relative can include persons who stand in any one of eight different relations to the taxpayer. IRC §§ 152(d)(1)(A), (2). These relationships are:

1. A child or descendant of a child,

2. A sibling (including step siblings),

3. A parent or ancestor of a parent,

4. A step parent,

5. A niece or nephew,

6. An aunt or uncle,

7. Most in-laws (i.e., son, daughter, father, mother, brother, or sister in-law), and

8. A person who has shared the taxpayer's home for the year and is a member of the taxpayer's household.

But more is required than just the proper relationship. The potential dependent must also have less gross income than the exemption amount (determined under prior law) and must receive more than half of his or her support from the taxpayer. IRC §§ 152(d)(1)(B) & (C). A potential dependent who is a qualifying child of the taxpayer or of any other taxpayer is excluded from being a qualifying relative. IRC § 152(d)(1)(D).

3. Phase Out Rules

As discussed above, the TCJA suspended the deduction for personal and dependency exemptions for tax years 2018 through 2025, by reducing the exemption amount for those years to zero. For higher-income earners, however, this change will generally have no significant effect for a couple reasons. First, there were rules for phasing out the exemptions for higher-income individuals. *See* IRC § 151(d)(3). Under pre-TCJA law, the total amount of exemptions that could be claimed was reduced by two percent for each $2,500 ($1,250 for married couples filing separately) by which adjusted gross income exceeded the following income thresholds: $300,000 for married couples filing jointly and surviving spouses; $275,000 for heads of households; $250,000 for unmarried taxpayers; and $150,000 for married taxpayers filing separately. (These amounts were adjusted for inflation.) Second, some or all of the benefit of the exemptions were eliminated for higher-income taxpayers subject to the alternative minimum tax, which is discussed in Chapter 14.

D. Section 199A Deduction for Qualified Business Income

As introduced in Chapter 7 and explored more fully in later chapters, section 199A allows owners of certain sole proprietorships and other pass-through entities to take a deduction equal to 20% of their "qualified business income." Because the deduction is business related, one might conclude that it is probably an above the line deduction. Interestingly, this deduction is neither an above the line deduction, nor an itemized deduction. *See* IRC § 62, flush language. It is, however, an extra deduction taken below the line in arriving at taxable income. IRC § 63(b)(3). This means that it does not reduce AGI, which can impact the extent to which some other deductions, such as medical expenses and losses from Presidentially declared disasters, can be deducted. And it means that it can be taken even if the taxpayer takes the standard deduction.

IV. Materials

Form 8332

Release of Claim to Exemption for Child of Divorced or
Separated Parents (Rev. January 2010)

Form **8332** (Rev. January 2010) Department of the Treasury Internal Revenue Service	**Release/Revocation of Release of Claim to Exemption for Child by Custodial Parent** ▶ Attach a separate form for each child.	OMB No. 1545-0074 Attachment Sequence No. **115**

Name of noncustodial parent	Noncustodial parent's social security number (SSN) ▶

Part I Release of Claim to Exemption for Current Year

I agree not to claim an exemption for _____
_____ Name of child

for the tax year 20 ____ .

_____   _____   _____
Signature of custodial parent releasing claim to exemption   Custodial parent's SSN   Date

Note. If you choose not to claim an exemption for this child for future tax years, also complete Part II.

Part II Release of Claim to Exemption for Future Years (If completed, see **Noncustodial Parent** on page 2.)

I agree not to claim an exemption for _____
_____ Name of child

for the tax year(s) _____ .
                         (Specify. See instructions.)

_____   _____   _____
Signature of custodial parent releasing claim to exemption   Custodial parent's SSN   Date

Part III Revocation of Release of Claim to Exemption for Future Year(s)

I revoke the release of claim to an exemption for _____
_____ Name of child

for the tax year(s) _____ .
                         (Specify. See instructions.)

_____   _____   _____
Signature of custodial parent revoking the release of claim to exemption   Custodial parent's SSN   Date

General Instructions

What's New

Post-2008 decree or agreement. If the divorce decree or separation agreement went into effect after 2008, the noncustodial parent cannot attach certain pages from the decree or agreement instead of Form 8332. See *Release of claim to exemption* below.

Definition of custodial parent. New rules apply to determine who is the custodial parent and the noncustodial parent. See *Custodial Parent and Noncustodial Parent* on this page.

Purpose of Form

If you are the custodial parent, you can use this form to do the following.

● Release a claim to exemption for your child so that the noncustodial parent can claim an exemption for the child.

● Revoke a previous release of claim to exemption for your child.

Release of claim to exemption. This release of the exemption will also allow the noncustodial parent to claim the child tax credit and the additional child tax credit (if either applies). Complete this form (or sign a similar statement containing the same

information required by this form) and give it to the noncustodial parent. The noncustodial parent must attach this form or similar statement to his or her tax return each year the exemption is claimed. Use Part I to release a claim to the exemption for the current year. Use Part II if you choose to release a claim to exemption for any future year(s).

Note. If the decree or agreement went into effect after 1984 and before 2009, you can attach certain pages from the decree or agreement instead of Form 8332, provided that these pages are substantially similar to Form 8332. See *Post-1984 and pre-2009 decree or agreement* on page 2.

Revocation of release of claim to exemption. Use Part III to revoke a previous release of claim to an exemption. The revocation will be effective no earlier than the tax year following the year in which you provide the noncustodial parent with a copy of the revocation or make a reasonable effort to provide the noncustodial parent with a copy of the revocation. Therefore, if you revoked a release on Form 8332 and provided a copy of the form to the noncustodial parent in 2010, the earliest tax year the revocation can be effective is 2011. You must attach a copy of the revocation to your tax return each year the exemption is claimed as a result of the revocation. You must also keep for your records a copy of the revocation and evidence

of delivery of the notice to the noncustodial parent, or of reasonable efforts to provide actual notice.

Custodial Parent and Noncustodial Parent

The custodial parent is generally the parent with whom the child lived for the greater number of nights during the year. The noncustodial parent is the other parent. If the child was with each parent for an equal number of nights, the custodial parent is the parent with the higher adjusted gross income. For details and an exception for a parent who works at night, see Pub. 501.

Exemption for a Dependent Child

A dependent is either a qualifying child or a qualifying relative. See your tax return instruction booklet for the definition of these terms. Generally, a child of divorced or separated parents will be a qualifying child of the custodial parent. However, if the special rule on page 2 applies, then the child will be treated as the qualifying child or qualifying relative of the noncustodial parent for purposes of the dependency exemption, the child tax credit, and the additional child tax credit.

For Paperwork Reduction Act Notice, see back of form.   Cat. No. 13910F   Form **8332** (Rev. 1-2010)

Special Rule for Children of Divorced or Separated Parents

A child is treated as a qualifying child or a qualifying relative of the noncustodial parent if all of the following apply.

1. The child received over half of his or her support for the year from one or both of the parents (see the *Exception* below). Public assistance payments, such as Temporary Assistance for Needy Families (TANF), are not support provided by the parents.

2. The child was in the custody of one or both of the parents for more than half of the year.

3. Either of the following applies.

a. The custodial parent agrees not to claim an exemption for the child by signing this form or a similar statement. If the decree or agreement went into effect after 1984 and before 2009, see *Post-1984 and pre-2009 decree or agreement* below.

b. A pre-1985 decree of divorce or separate maintenance or written separation agreement states that the noncustodial parent can claim the child as a dependent. But the noncustodial parent must provide at least $600 for the child's support during the year. This rule does not apply if the decree or agreement was changed after 1984 to say that the noncustodial parent cannot claim the child as a dependent.

For this rule to apply, the parents must be one of the following.

● Divorced or legally separated under a decree of divorce or separate maintenance.

● Separated under a written separation agreement.

● Living apart at all times during the last 6 months of the year.

If this rule applies, and the other dependency tests in your tax return instruction booklet are also met, the noncustodial parent can claim an exemption for the child.

Exception. If the support of the child is determined under a multiple support agreement, this special rule does not apply, and this form should not be used.

Post-1984 and pre-2009 decree or agreement. If the divorce decree or separation agreement went into effect after 1984 and before 2009, the noncustodial parent can attach certain pages from the decree or agreement instead of Form 8332, provided that these pages are substantially similar to Form 8332. To be able to do this, the decree or agreement must state all three of the following.

1. The noncustodial parent can claim the child as a dependent without regard to any condition (such as payment of support).

2. The other parent will not claim the child as a dependent.

3. The years for which the claim is released.

The noncustodial parent must attach all of the following pages from the decree or agreement.

● Cover page (include the other parent's SSN on that page).

● The pages that include all of the information identified in (1) through (3) above.

● Signature page with the other parent's signature and date of agreement.

 The noncustodial parent must attach the required information even if it was filed with a return in an earlier year.

The noncustodial parent can no longer attach certain pages from a divorce decree or separation agreement instead of Form 8332 if the decree or agreement was executed after 2008.

Specific Instructions

Custodial Parent

Part I. Complete Part I to release a claim to exemption for your child for the current tax year.

Part II. Complete Part II to release a claim to exemption for your child for one or more future years. Write the specific future year(s) or "all future years" in the space provided in Part II.

 To help ensure future support, you may not want to release your claim to the exemption for the child for future years.

Part III. Complete Part III if you are revoking a previous release of claim to exemption for your child. Write the specific future year(s) or "all future years" in the space provided in Part III.

The revocation will be effective no earlier than the tax year following the year you provide the noncustodial parent with a copy of the revocation or make a reasonable effort to provide the noncustodial parent with a copy of the revocation. Also, you must attach a copy of the revocation to your tax return for each year you are claiming the exemption as a result of the revocation. You must also keep for your records a copy of the revocation and evidence of delivery of the notice to the noncustodial parent, or of reasonable efforts to provide actual notice.

Example. In 2007, you released a claim to exemption for your child on Form 8332 for the years 2008 through 2012. In 2010, you decided to revoke the previous release of exemption. If you completed Part III of Form 8332 and provided a copy of the form to the noncustodial parent in 2010, the revocation will be effective for 2011 and 2012. You must attach a copy of the revocation to your 2011 and 2012 tax returns and keep certain records as stated earlier.

Noncustodial Parent

Attach this form or similar statement to your tax return for each year you claim the exemption for your child. You can claim the exemption only if the other dependency tests in your tax return instruction booklet are met.

 If the custodial parent released his or her claim to the exemption for the child for any future year, you must attach a copy of this form or similar statement to your tax return for each future year that you claim the exemption. Keep a copy for your records.

Note. If you are filing your return electronically, you must file Form 8332 with Form 8453, U.S. Individual Income Tax Transmittal for an IRS *e-file* Return. See Form 8453 and its instructions for more details.

Paperwork Reduction Act Notice. We ask for the information on this form to carry out the Internal Revenue laws of the United States. You are required to give us the information. We need it to ensure that you are complying with these laws and to allow us to figure and collect the right amount of tax.

You are not required to provide the information requested on a form that is subject to the Paperwork Reduction Act unless the form displays a valid OMB control number. Books or records relating to a form or its instructions must be retained as long as their contents may become material in the administration of any Internal Revenue law. Generally, tax returns and return information are confidential, as required by Internal Revenue Code section 6103.

The average time and expenses required to complete and file this form will vary depending on individual circumstances. For the estimated averages, see the instructions for your income tax return.

If you have suggestions for making this form simpler, we would be happy to hear from you. See the instructions for your income tax return.

V. Related Matters

- **Citizen/Residency Requirement.** Dependents must be citizens of the U.S. or residents of the U.S. or countries contiguous to the U.S. IRC § 152(b)(3).

- **Married Persons.** Married persons who file joint returns cannot be claimed as the dependent of another. IRC § 152(b)(2).

- **Scholarships.** Scholarships are disregarded for purposes of the support element of the dependency test as applied to children of the taxpayer. IRC § 152(f)(5).

- **Disabled Persons.** The age requirements for otherwise qualifying children are waived for dependency purposes in the case of persons who are permanently and totally disabled. IRC § 152(c)(3)(B).

- **Missing Children.** Missing children can still be claimed as their parents' dependents under certain circumstances. IRC § 152(f)(6).

- **Handicapped Persons.** There are special rules that disregard for purposes of the support element certain income of handicapped dependents. IRC § 152(d)(4).

- **The 3% Rule.** Prior to 2018, there was an additional limitation on itemized deductions that applied to higher-income taxpayers. *See* IRC § 68. Essentially section 68 reduced a taxpayer's allowable itemized deductions by 3% of the amount by which the taxpayer's adjusted gross income exceeded an applicable threshold: $300,000 for married couples filing jointly and surviving spouses; $275,000 for heads of households; $250,000 for unmarried taxpayers; and $150,000 for married taxpayers filing separately. (These dollar amounts were adjusted for inflation for tax years after 2013.) Itemized deductions, however, could not be reduced by more than 80%, and certain items, such as medical expenses and casualty losses, were excluded. For tax years 2018 through 2025, this phase-out or overall limitation on itemized deductions is repealed. IRC § 68(f).

- **Social Security Benefits.** In some cases a taxpayer may claim a family member as a dependent even if they receive social security benefits provided the taxpayer provides more than half of the family member's support. This is because some portion of a person's social security benefits is not included in gross income. *See* IRC § 86(a). Thus, the recipient of social security benefits may not have gross income in excess of the exemption amount. *See* IRC § 152(d)(1)(B).

- **Exemptions for estates and trusts.** Although the TCJA temporarily reduced the personal and dependency exemption amount to zero for individuals, it retained the current exemptions for estates ($600) and trusts ($100 or $300 depending on the type of trust). It also retained the regular personal exemption for so-called "qualified disability trusts" at $4,150, indexed for inflation after 2018. IRC § 642(b)(2)(C).

Chapter 13

Timing Rules and Related Principles

I. Assignment

Read: Internal Revenue Code: §§ 446; 451(a)–(c), (h)(1)–(2); 461(a), (g), (h)(1)–(2); 471(c). Skim §§ 111; 1341.

Treasury Regulations: §§ 1.170A-1(b); 1.446-1(a)(4)(i), -1(c)(1)(i) & (ii)(A), -1(c)(2)(i); 1.451-1(a), -2(a); 1.461-1(a)(1)–(2)(i).

Text: Overview
Ames v. Commissioner
Schlude v. Commissioner
Related Matters

Complete the problems.

II. Problems

1. Slim Aarons is a freelance paparazzo who earns his living by selling candid photos of celebrities to tabloid magazines. On December 15, Year 1, Slim photographs Fred Jolly, a movie star, walking hand in hand on a Cancun beach with Angie Patt, also a movie star. Fred's wife, Jennifer Anderson, is nowhere in the picture. Slim sells the non-exclusive right to publish the picture one time for $100,000 to the National Investigator, a.k.a., "The Gator." Assuming Slim is a cash method taxpayer and The Gator is an accrual method taxpayer, when does Slim have income and when does The Gator have a deduction under the following circumstances? [Assume that The Gator does not have an applicable financial statement or other financial statement specified by the IRS.]

(a) Slim delivers the picture to The Gator on December 27th. The Gator cuts a check on December 28th and mails it to Slim's home. Slim receives the check on December 31st and cashes the check on January 2nd of Year 2.

(b) Same as (a) except Slim is out of town on December 31st.

(c) Same as (a) except that the check arrives at Slim's home on January 2nd of Year 2.

(d) Same as (a) except that Slim delivers the picture to The Gator on January 2nd of Year 2.

(e) Same as (a) except that Fred and Angie sue Slim on December 30th of Year 1 claiming that he violated their rights of privacy and that, consequently, he must pay them the proceeds from his sale of the picture to The Gator. Slim denies their claim.

(f) Same as (a) except that The Gator pays Slim with Google stock worth $100,000 in which The Gator had a basis of $60,000.

(g) How would your answers in (a) through (e), above, change if Slim was an accrual method taxpayer. [Assume that Slim does not have an applicable financial statement or other financial statement specified by the IRS.]

2. Mad Max is an accrual method taxpayer who sells marijuana for medicinal uses throughout the State of California. He is duly licensed by the state to engage in this business. He uses the first in-first out (FIFO) method of inventory accounting. In the current year, Max's beginning inventory was 400 ounces of marijuana which cost him $60 per ounce. In May, Max purchased 200 additional ounces for $70 per ounce. In October, he purchased 300 ounces for $80 per ounce. During the year, Max sold 700 ounces of marijuana for gross revenues of $100,000.

(a) What was Max's cost of goods sold and gross profit for the year?

(b) Would Max be obliged to report his income if he conducted his business in violation of Federal criminal law and, thus, was not entitled to keep any of the proceeds of his selling activities? *See* James v. United States, 366 U.S. 213 (1961). *See also* IRC §280E.

3. Dr. Rustom Jamshed Maneksha is a high-living plastic surgeon with offices in Miami and Hollywood. He is an accrual method taxpayer. Much of his work is elective surgery that is not covered by insurance and many of Rustom's clients are slow to pay. As a consequence, Rustom eases his cash flow problems by selling his accounts receivable to a Miami bank at a 5% discount from face value. In Year 1, Rustom generated $1,000,000 of accounts receivable which he sold in Year 2 for $950,000. What was Rustom's basis in those accounts receivable and what is the tax consequence of the sale of the receivables? What difference would it make if Rustom were a cash method taxpayer?

4. Bilbo Baggins, a cash method taxpayer, won the lottery in Year 1 and was given two choices for the payout. He could elect to take $100,000,000 in a lump sum, or he could take installments of $10,000,000 per year for 20 years. Bilbo elected the installment payout. Assuming that the present value of the total payout is $100,000,000, how much income for tax purposes does Bilbo have in Year 1?

III. Overview

A. Introduction

The income tax is imposed on an annual basis, the tax year. Thus, it is necessary to establish rules concerning *when* an item of income is included and *when* an item of expense is deducted. That is this chapter's topic. As one considers the topic of timing of income and deductions it is important to keep in mind where the "pressure" is. Taxpayers will nearly always be economically advantaged by the deferral of taxable income. Also, there is often advantage in the acceleration of tax deductions. Both of these advantages will reduce the taxpayer's current tax liability thereby leaving him with the use of his money for a while longer. Since money makes money, the use of money has value. We call this "the time value of money." The government has an interest in the acceleration of income reporting and deferral of deduction reporting since that will increase the government's current tax revenues. An evenhanded set of rules should impartially navigate between these competing interests of taxpayer and government.

The primary determinant of the timing of income and deductions is the taxpayer's accounting method. There are two main methods: the cash method and the accrual method. IRC § 446(c). Both methods employ some version of the "matching" principle. This means they seek to match expenses to the income they produce so that we get a fair and accurate picture of net income. As we will see, the cash method is less effective at matching. But it is also more simple and intuitive. It is the method that most individuals employ.

An individual taxpayer can generally choose his tax accounting method; however, big businesses are obliged to use the accrual method. *See* IRC § 448. The accrual method is in accordance with "Generally Accepted Accounting Principles" or GAAP. These are the principles that have been adopted by the Financial Accounting Standards Board. The cash method is not always in accordance with GAAP. Furthermore, the GAAP rules were developed for financial accounting rather than tax accounting purposes. As will be discussed, tax accounting under the accrual method is not identical to financial accounting under the accrual method.

One must recognize that the timing rules do not establish that an item is income or that one has the right to deduct an expenditure. The timing rules just tell us *when* to report or to deduct it. We still need to refer to the various applicable sections of the Code such as section 61 or section 162 to see if an item is includable or deductible.

B. The Cash Method

1. Income under the Cash Method

The basic principle of the cash method is that income is reported when it is actually or constructively received. *See* Treas. Reg. § 1.451-1(a). Though it is called the cash method, the medium of payment under this method is not limited to cash payments. Thus, the cash method applies to receipts in the form of property or services. Treas. Reg. § 1.446-1(c)(1)(i). In a world in which every transaction occurs in person and with cash, the cash method is quite clear and simple. But, of course, in the real world transactions often occur by mail, over the phone, or on the Internet. And, often, payment is not in the form of cash. Thus, of necessity, various rules have arisen to explain the application of the cash method to these different circumstances.

a. The Doctrine of Cash Equivalence and the Related Principle of Economic Benefit

An obvious concern under the cash method is the treatment of checks. Are they income when received or after they are cashed? In response to this question and related ones the courts have fashioned the doctrine of cash equivalence. Under this doctrine the receipt of an instrument such as a check that is readily negotiable at or near its face value is treated the same as the receipt of cash. In other words, it is income immediately upon receipt. *See, e.g.,* Kahler v. Commissioner, 18 T.C. 31 (1952). This is true even if the check is received after the banks have closed for the day. Thus, technically a check received the evening of December 31st of Year 1 is income in Year 1 even though it could not possibly have been cashed until some time in January of Year 2. *Id.*

Drawing the line between an item that is a cash equivalent and one that is a mere evidence of obligation to make a future payment can be difficult. If an evidence of indebtedness that has little or no negotiability is transferred to the taxpayer in order to secure the taxpayer's right to a future payment, it is doubtful whether payment has occurred under the cash method of accounting because no significant economic benefit has yet been conferred. For example, suppose an individual with a weak credit history gave her lawyer a non-interest bearing IOU for $1,000 payable in six months' time. Would receipt of the note be current income under the cash method? The answer according to the case law is generally no. This is because there is a substantial risk of non-payment and no third party is likely to be willing to buy the IOU for anything approaching its face value. *See, e.g.,* Williams v. Commissioner, 28 T.C. 1000 (1957). The answer can grow murkier if the maker of the note is a good credit risk and if the note bears market rate interest. As the obligation to pay becomes more like a cash equivalent the issue tends to shift from whether it is current income (it is) to what is the amount of current income represented by the indebtedness. *See* Cowden v. Commissioner, 20 T.C.M. 1134 (1961). This latter question is best understood as a present value problem, and is resolved by reference to what a willing buyer would pay a willing seller for the debt instrument. This point of analysis is consistent with what was said earlier about the receipt of property and services as also constituting income at the time of receipt. In other words, payments with something marketable other than cash tend to raise valuation issues not timing issues. Those valuation issues are resolved by determining the cash value of whatever is received. *See* Treas. Reg. § 1.446-1(a)(3).

b. The Doctrine of Constructive Receipt

As noted earlier, the cash method causes a person to have income at the time the compensation is actually or *constructively* received. An item is constructively received when it is credited to the taxpayer's account or set aside for him and there are no substantial restrictions on his control. Treas. Reg. § 1.451-2(a). For example, suppose that an employee declines to accept her paycheck on a payday which happens to coincide with December 31st of Year 1. Instead the employee asks that the paycheck be given to her on January 2nd of Year 2. Her purpose in making this request is to defer the tax on that paycheck until Year 2. The doctrine of constructive receipt will cause her to have the income in Year 1 even if the employer agrees to hold off on delivery of the check until Year 2. The same would be true even if the employee was merely at home sick on December 31st. Should it also apply if she were on an airplane half way around the world? Probably, since the employee had advance notice of the payment and could have arranged for someone to pick up her check for her. From these examples one may infer the reason for the doctrine. It serves to limit the taxpayer's ability to defer income for tax purposes when in substance the taxpayer has notice and control of the income.

In the day and age of direct deposit, constructive receipt has little relevance to regular compensation. But its application can arise in a number of contexts. A particularly famous case involved Paul Hornung, a professional football player who played for the Green Bay Packers. He was awarded a Corvette Stingray for being the outstanding player in the National Football League championship game in 1961. The award was made on December 31, 1961 (a Sunday) after the championship game played in Green Bay, Wisconsin. The car was in New York. On Wednesday, January 3, 1962 a luncheon was held in New York to honor the winner and the car was presented. The car was worth $3,331. Mr. Hornung sold it for that amount in 1962. He reported the car on his 1962 tax return as a gift and paid no taxes on it. The IRS said it was not a gift and that the value received was taxable. At trial Mr. Hornung argued that if receipt of the car was income it was constructively received in 1961 and thus was income in that year and not in 1962. Presumably he made this argument because the statute of limitations had run for the year 1961. The Tax Court ruled that the doctrine did not apply in Mr. Hornung's case because he did not have the ability to control the car in 1961. The dealer was closed on Sunday, December 31st, and was located hundreds of miles away. Moreover, Mr. Hornung did not have advance notice of the award. Therefore, he could not have arranged to get possession on December 31st. *See* Hornung v. Commissioner, 47 T.C. 428 (1967).

A more contemporary case in the materials involving the doctrine of constructive receipt is that of Aldrich Ames, a CIA agent turned Soviet spy.

Interesting issues concerning the doctrine of constructive receipt are raised by lottery winnings paid out in installments. One can reasonably argue that the present value of all future payments should be treated as current income under constructive receipt and economic benefit principles. This is particularly true if the taxpayer had the option of taking a lump sum payment up front but elected to receive installments instead. However, Congress addressed the matter in section 451(h) by establishing that if the payout is over a period of ten years or more the option to take a lump sum payout is to be disregarded. Moreover, even without section 451(h) the courts have declined to apply the doctrine of constructive receipt to these situations. *See, e.g.,* Jombo v. Commissioner, 398 F.3d 661 (D.C. Cir. 2005).

2. Deductions under the Cash Method

The cash method of accounting operates with respect to deductions in much the same way as it does for income. Thus, the central principle is that the deduction is taken when the expense is paid. Treas. Reg. § 1.446-1(c)(1)(i). The mailing of a check is effective to set the year of a deduction as long as the check is honored and paid and there are no restrictions as to the time and manner of payment. Rev. Rul. 54-465, 1954-2 C.B. 93. *See also* Treas. Reg. § 1.170-1(b). However, the payment of a debt with one's own note does not entitle one to a deduction since one has not yet parted with anything of value. *See, e.g.,* Vander Poel v. Commissioner, 8 T.C. 407 (1947). *Vander Poel* stands for the related proposition that there is no doctrine of constructive payment under the cash method. However, a credit card payment is immediately deductible under the cash method. Rev. Rul. 78-38, 1978-1 C.B. 67. This is partly an administrative convenience. But it is analogous to paying a bill with borrowed funds. So perhaps it is justified on theoretical grounds as well.

a. Prepayment of Expenses

As noted, the cash method is not necessarily in accordance with GAAP because it is subject to some degree of manipulation. One way in which taxpayers have sought to manipulate the cash method is by prepaying otherwise deductible expenses in a year earlier than the year to which the expenses relate. For example, a cash method business might prepay its rent for the next tax year in order to accelerate the tax deduction authorized for rent under section 162. The main limitation on this strategy arises from the principle of capitalization, i.e., an expenditure that benefits more than one accounting period must be capitalized and recovered over the life of the asset acquired through the expenditure. Treas. Reg. § 1.461-1(a). In other words, a prepayment of future expenses creates an asset the cost of which is recovered through depreciation or amortization. *See* Commissioner v. Boylston Market Association, 131 F.2d 966 (1st Cir. 1942). Still, in practice there is considerable flexibility in the timing of deductions under the cash method. Case law established a rule that allows deduction of prepayments of expenses that relate to more than one tax year if the prepayment itself covers no more than 12 months. *See* Zaninovich v. Commissioner, 616 F.2d 429 (9th Cir. 1980).

Regulations under section 263 now deal specifically with prepayment of expenses. As discussed more fully in Chapter 8, a taxpayer must generally capitalize prepaid expenses (Treas. Reg. § 1.263(a)-4(d)(3)) and amounts paid for certain contract rights (Treas. Reg. § 1.263(a)-4(d)(6)). Under an important exception, termed the 12-month rule, a taxpayer is not required to capitalize amounts if the amounts do not create any right or benefit for the taxpayer that extends beyond the earlier of (1) 12 months after the first date on which the taxpayer realizes the right or benefit, or (2) the end of the taxable year following the taxable year in which the payment is made. Treas. Reg. § 1.263(a)-4(f)(1).

b. The Special Rule for Interest Expenses

A cash method taxpayer who borrows money cannot prepay the interest on that debt to increase her current interest deduction. Instead, section 461(g)(1) requires that she take the deduction as the interest accrues, that is, as the obligation to pay interest grows with the passage of time. There is an exception for payments of points on a mortgage for one's home, as was discussed in Chapter 11. IRC § 461(g)(2).

C. The Accrual Method

1. Income under the Accrual Method

Under the accrual method of accounting, income is generally included in the taxable year in which all events have occurred fixing the right to the income and in which the amount of the income can be determined with reasonable accuracy. Treas. Reg. § 1.446-1(c)(1)(ii)(A). This is known as the "all events" test. Under this approach an accrual method taxpayer who provides goods or services to a customer in Year 1 will have income in Year 1 even though payment is not received until Year 2. In short, for accrual taxpayers, income is reportable when it is earned.

a. Inclusion Based on Financial Accounting Treatment

The Tax Cuts and Jobs Act (TCJA) modified the income recognition rule for accrual method taxpayers for tax years beginning in 2018. Under the TCJA, the "all events" test is satisfied no later than the year in which income is recognized for financial accounting purposes (recognized on an "applicable financial statement"). *See* IRC § 451(b) & (b)(3) (definition of applicable financial statement). Under this provision, an accrual method taxpayer will include an item in income upon the *earlier of* (1) when the all events test is met or (2) when the taxpayer includes such item in revenue in an applicable financial statement. This new book conformity requirement may cause acceleration in the recognition of income for taxpayers. Accrual method taxpayers without an applicable or other specified financial statement will continue to determine income inclusion under the all events test discussed above. There are some other exceptions to the new book conformity requirement such as an exception for installment sales agreements under section 453.

b. Prepayments

As noted earlier, the accrual method is consistent with Generally Accepted Accounting Principles (GAAP). The GAAP rules were developed for financial accounting rather than tax accounting purposes. The application of the all events test in the tax context has an important caveat. The IRS, with substantial judicial support, usually takes the position that even under the accrual method a taxpayer will have income when a cash payment is received despite the fact that the all events test has not been satisfied. *See, e.g.*, Schlude v. Commissioner, 372 U.S. 128 (1963), included in the materials. Thus, an accrual method service provider, for example, will have income upon receipt of an advance payment even though the money has not yet been earned and must be refunded if the provider fails to perform. On occasion taxpayers have prevailed in contesting this position. The most notable example is the case of Artnell Co. v. Commissioner, 400 F.2d 981 (7th Cir. 1968). *Artnell* concerned advance payments made for Chicago White Sox baseball team season tickets and for media coverage of the games. In that case the taxpayer was ultimately permitted to accrue the income as the games were played since this approach clearly reflected its income.

Some relief for prepayments is provided in section 451(c), which was added by the TCJA. For tax years beginning in 2018, an accrual method taxpayer who receives an advance payment can make an election to defer the inclusion of the advance payment in gross income to the end of the year following the year of receipt if such income is deferred for financial statement purposes. IRC § 451(c) (codifying IRS guidance in Rev. Proc. 2004-34 on deferral of advance payments). The deferral option does not apply to advance receipt of rents and other specified items. IRC § 451(c)(4)(B).

2. Deductions under the Accrual Method

Under the accrual method, deductions are taken in the year in which all events have occurred establishing the fact of liability and the amount of liability and in which economic performance has occurred with respect to the liability. Treas. Reg. § 1.461-1(a)(2)(i). Economic performance occurs when the person to whom the liability is owed performs his end of the bargain. *See* IRC § 461(h)(1) & (2). Thus, for example, if an accrual method taxpayer hired an accountant in Year 1 to prepare her tax return for Year 1 and the return was duly prepared and filed in Year 2, the taxpayer would take her deduction for the accountant's fee in Year 2. *See* IRC § 212(3). This would be true whether the taxpayer actually paid the accountant in Years 1, 2, or 3. In short, it is economic performance that controls the timing of the deduction, and the time of payment is irrelevant from the deduction perspective.

a. Inventory Accounting

Taxpayers who have inventory are generally required to use the accrual method. Treas. Reg. §§ 1.446-1(a)(4)(i), -1(c)(2)(i). Inventory is the stock of goods held for sale to customers. Accounting for inventory is subject to a number of complexities beyond the scope of this course. However, it is useful to know the rudiments of inventory accounting so as to be able to understand the jargon of business folks and their accountants.

Under the accrual method, both income and deductions arising from the sale of inventory are taken into account for tax purposes when the goods change hands since that is when the all events test is satisfied. But this does not answer all the questions about inventory accounting. Each sale of an inventory item may be seen as a disposition of property subject to the rules of section 1001. Thus, each sale is likely to result in either a realized gain or loss. The central question is what is the seller's basis? It is possible that each individual item sold has a clearly identifiable basis. This is particularly true if each item is listed in a computer data base and has been bar coded. In such cases the amount of the seller's cumulative costs for inventory for the year, known as "cost of goods sold," is readily determinable. But what if the seller's inventory is not identified to a specific purchase by the seller? Suppose, for example, that a seller of widgets has made bulk purchases of widgets on three different occasions and paid a different price per widget each time. Suppose further that all of the widgets are stored together without any differentiation. At the end of the year, the seller will know how many widgets were sold and the gross revenues from those sales, but the seller will not know the aggregate bases of those widgets sold. In short, the seller will not know her "cost of goods sold" for the year. To overcome this obstacle, accountants use one of two conventions known as FIFO and LIFO. FIFO (first in-first out) assumes that the first widgets purchased are the first ones sold. LIFO (last in-first out) assumes that the most recently purchased widgets are the first ones sold. Consider the following example.

Example. In Year 1 Retailer buys 100 widgets on February 1st for $400 ($4 each), 100 widgets on July 1st for $500 ($5 each), and 100 widgets on September 1st for $600 ($6 each). During the year Retailer sold 210 widgets for a total amount of $1,470.

Under FIFO, Retailer's cost of goods sold would be $960 (the sum of the February 1st costs ($400), the July 1st costs ($500), and the cost of 10 widgets from September 1st ($60)).

Under LIFO, Retailer's cost of goods sold would be $1,140 (the sum of the September 1st costs ($600), the July 1st costs ($500), and the cost of 10 widgets from February 1st ($40)).

Therefore, under FIFO, Retailer will have a gross profit from widget sales of $510 for Year 1.

Gross Sales	$1,470
Cost of Goods sold	− $960
Gross Profit (FIFO)	**$510**

Under LIFO, Retailer will have a gross profit from widget sales of $330 for Year 1.

Gross Sales	$1,470
Cost of Goods sold	− $1,140
Gross Profit (LIFO)	**$330**

As can readily be seen, the choice of inventory accounting methods will affect the amount of gross profit in any given year. In our example, Retailer's gross profit from widget sales is $180 greater under FIFO than under LIFO ($510 − $330 = $180). However, over time these differences will even out as the inventory items with different bases are sold. One way to see this is to consider Retailer's basis in his inventory at the end of the year.

Example Continued: Ending Inventory and Beginning Inventory. In the example above, Retailer will have 90 widgets left in inventory at the end of the year. This is his Year 1 ending inventory. It is also his Year 2 beginning inventory. Under FIFO, his aggregate basis in his Year 2 beginning inventory is $540 (90 × $6). Under LIFO, his aggregate basis in his Year 2 beginning inventory is $360 (90 × $4). The difference between the two aggregate bases is $180 ($540 − $360 = $180), the same as the difference in our gross profits in Year 1. If in Year 2 Retailer sold the remaining widgets and did not buy any new ones, he would have $180 more gross profit under LIFO than under FIFO. Thus, over the course of the two years his gross profit under the two methods is identical. The key is that either method must be applied consistently from year to year.

b. Exception for Small Businesses with Inventory

Although businesses that have inventory must generally use the accrual method of accounting for tax purposes, the TCJA expanded an important exception. Under the TCJA, businesses with average annual gross receipts of $25 million or less (based on the prior three years) are permitted to use the cash method of accounting even if the business has inventories. IRC § 471(c) (adjusted for inflation). With the gross receipts threshold so high, many businesses qualify to use the cash method. Businesses that qualify for the exception may (1) account for inventory as non-incidental materials and supplies (e.g., deductible in the year used or paid, whichever is later) or (2) use a method that conforms to the business's financial accounting treatment of inventories. IRC § 471(c)(1)(B); Treas. Reg. § 1.162-3.

D. Principles Applicable to Both the Cash Method and the Accrual Method

1. The Claim of Right Doctrine

Earnings held under an unrestricted claim of right must be reported as income when received even if another person is asserting a claim to those same funds. *See North American Oil Consolidated v. Burnet*, 286 U.S. 417 (1932). For example, a building contractor may receive a $100,000 payment for the completion of a home, but the homeowner may dispute whether the home was properly built and demand a refund of $20,000. Does the builder have $80,000 or $100,000 of gross income? Under the claim of right doctrine, the builder has $100,000 of income. What happens if, in a later year, the builder is obliged to refund $20,000 to the homeowner? The Supreme Court in *North American Oil Consolidated* suggested in dictum that a deduction would be allowable in the year of repayment. In some cases, a deduction in year of repayment would not be as beneficial as a tax refund from an earlier year. In other words, it might be better to file an amended return for the earlier year of inclusion and get a refund from the government than to take a deduction on the tax return for the year of repayment (for example, if the taxpayer's marginal tax rate was higher in the earlier year of inclusion than the later year of repayment). Fortunately, section 1341 allows qualified taxpayers to get the better of both alternatives. For qualified taxpayers, the tax liability for the year of repayment is the lesser of: (1) tax computed after deducting the repayment or (2) a hypothetical tax for the repayment year without deducting the repayment minus the savings in tax for the earlier year that would have resulted if the repaid amount had been excluded from that year's gross income. It should be noted that the computation in section 1341 is for the repayment year. It does not allow taxpayers to amend their earlier year's return.

For reasons of policy, the claim of right doctrine has been extended to ill-gotten gains. Thus, for example, an embezzler is obliged to report wrongfully obtained funds as income on her tax return. James v. United States, 366 U.S. 213 (1961). If she later makes restitution she will be entitled to a deduction. *See, e.g.*, Rev. Rul. 82-74, 1982-1 C.B. 110 (holding that refund of insurance proceeds when arson is discovered is deductible under section 165); Rev. Rul. 65-254, 1965-2 C.B. 50 (holding repayment of embezzled funds is a loss deductible under section 165). The use of tax laws to punish criminals has some history. Notable cases involved Al Capone, a notorious gangster of the 1930's, and Spiro Agnew, Vice President of the United States during the Nixon administration.

2. The Tax Benefit Rule

If a taxpayer properly takes a deduction in one year and in a later year recovers the amount deducted then usually the taxpayer must take the amount of the recovery into income. Bliss Dairy, Inc. v. United States, 460 U.S. 370 (1983). This is known as the tax benefit rule. A classic example of the rule's application arises when a taxpayer properly takes a bad debt deduction under section 166 and, in a later year, the debtor, to the lender's surprise, pays the debt. Normally, a repayment of a debt would not create income for the lender (except for any interest paid). However, it is fair in this case to require the lender to report the collection as income in order to offset the tax benefit it received from the deduction which, in retrospect, we can see was unwarranted. There is a significant statutory qualification to what has just been said. Section 111 provides that gross income does not include income from the recovery of a prior year's deduction to the extent that the prior year's deduction did not reduce the taxpayer's tax liability. Thus, the recovery of a deduction will not create income for a taxpayer unless there was a "tax benefit" in taking the deduction in the first place.

One might wonder why in the foregoing circumstance the taxpayer would not be obliged to file an amended return to correct the erroneous deduction rather than apply the tax benefit rule to the current year's recovery. First, a taxpayer has no obligation to file an amended return if the original return was filed in good faith. Second, the return was correct when filed. In this limited sense the taxable year stands alone and hindsight is irrelevant. Finally, the statute of limitations may have run on the original return. Thus, if the government could not oblige the taxpayer to report the current year recovery in income, it would have no redress.

3. The Ancillary Effects of Paying Expenses with Services or
Appreciated Property

When a taxpayer pays for an item by providing services, the taxpayer not only may have a deduction, he also will likely have income. For example a lawyer who pays her landlord $10,000 in office rent by performing legal services worth $10,000 has both a deduction and income of $10,000. This gets us to the same place as if both the rent and the services had been paid for with cash. Similarly, if the lawyer had paid her rent by giving the landlord a piece of land worth $10,000 in which the lawyer had a basis of $4,000, the lawyer will have $6,000 of taxable gain on the disposition of the land. IRC § 1001. *See, e.g.*, International Freighting Corp., Inc. v. Commissioner, 135 F.2d 310 (2d Cir. 1943). Of course, in both cases the landlord will also have $10,000 of rental income. The landlord may or may not have a deduction for the legal services depending on the nature of the matter being addressed by the lawyer on the landlord's behalf. See Chapter 35 for the treatment of legal fees. In the case of the land, what will be the amount of the landlord's adjusted basis? *See* IRC § 1012.

IV. Materials

Ames v. Commissioner

112 T.C. 304 (1999)

GERBER, JUDGE: Respondent determined deficiencies in petitioner's Federal income tax and section 6662(a) penalties as follows:

Year	Deficiency	Sec. 6662(a) Penalty
1989	$214,303.51	$42,860.70
1990	19,970.77	3,994.15
1991	27,367.39	5,473.48
1992	58,684.57	11,736.91

The issues for our consideration are: (1) Whether petitioner constructively received income from illegal espionage activities during 1985, when it was allegedly promised and/or set aside for him, or when it was received and/or deposited in his bank accounts during the taxable years 1989, 1990, 1991, and 1992 in the amounts of $745,000, $65,000, $91,000, and $187,000, respectively. [The other issues are omitted. Eds.]

FINDINGS OF FACT

Petitioner is incarcerated in a Federal penitentiary for turning over state secrets to a foreign government at a time when he held a position with the Central Intelligence Agency (CIA) of the United States. He had his legal residence in Allenwood, Pennsylvania, at the time the petition in this case was filed. Petitioner's employment with the CIA spanned the years 1962 to 1994, during which he was assigned to progressively more responsible positions involving the Union of Soviet Socialist Republics (Soviet Union) and Soviet Bloc Eastern European countries. Throughout that time, petitioner held a Top Secret security clearance, and he had access to information and documents classified Secret and Top Secret.

Petitioner timely filed joint Federal income tax returns with his wife, Rosario C. Ames, for the taxable years 1989, 1990, 1991, and 1992. Petitioner's returns were filed on the cash basis for reporting income and deductions. The returns primarily reflected income from petitioner's CIA employment in the amounts of $70,337, $60,340, $62,514, and $67,578 for 1989, 1990, 1991, and 1992, respectively.

In 1984, as part of his duties as a CIA Operations officer, petitioner began meeting with officials of the Soviet Union's Embassy in Washington, D.C. These meetings were authorized by the CIA and the Federal Bureau of Investigation (FBI) and were designed to allow petitioner access to Soviet officials as possible sources for intelligence information and recruitment.

Sometime during April 1985, petitioner entered into a relationship with Soviet officials under which he betrayed his country and sold classified CIA information and information sourced in other branches of the U.S. Government to the KGB (the Soviet intelligence directorate) in return for large amounts of remuneration. Petitioner provided the KGB with classified Top Secret information relating to the penetration of the Soviet military and intelligence services by the CIA, including the identities of Soviet military and intelligence officers who were cooperating with the CIA and foreign intelligence services of governments friendly to the United States. Because of petitioner's disclosures, a number of these individuals were arrested and executed by the KGB.

In the fall of 1985, petitioner received a communication from a Soviet agent that $2 million had been set aside for him in an account that he would be able to draw upon. Petitioner was told that the money was being held by the Soviet Union, rather than in an independent or third-party bank or institution, on petitioner's behalf. Petitioner received $50,000 in cash for his initial disclosure to the KGB and additional cash payments, the specific dates of which have not been detailed in the record of this case.

Petitioner met with Soviet officials in Washington, D.C., and in 1989 he met with them in Rome. In the spring of 1989, as petitioner was preparing to return to CIA headquarters in Langley, Virginia, the KGB provided him with two written documents. The first was a financial accounting that indicated that as of May 1, 1989, approximately $1.8 million had been set aside for petitioner and that some $900,000 more had been designated for him. The second document was a nine-page letter containing a list of the types of classified U.S. Government information sought by the KGB. The second document also contained a discussion of arrangements for cash dropoff payments to petitioner upon his return to the United States, a warning to petitioner to avoid traps set by the CIA, and a detailed plan governing future communications between petitioner and the KGB.

After his return to Washington, D.C., in 1989, petitioner communicated with the Soviets primarily through a complex arrangement of signal sites (a prearranged location where an individual leaves an impersonal mark or item to convey a prearranged message) and dead drops (locations for secretly leaving packages for anonymous pickup). Petitioner personally met with the Soviets only about once a year. Throughout this period, it was typical for petitioner to make a delivery of information and receive cash by means of signal sites and dead drops. Petitioner continued his unlawful espionage activities until his arrest in 1994.

During the years 1989, 1990, 1991, and 1992, petitioner and his wife made deposits of cash received in connection with petitioner's unlawful espionage activities in the amounts of $745,000, $65,000, $91,000, and $187,000, respectively. These deposits did not represent transfers of funds from other accounts or redeposits of currency previously withdrawn from other accounts. Petitioner did not report on his income tax returns for taxable years 1989, 1990, 1991, and 1992 any of the amounts received from the KGB in connection with his illegal espionage activities. Petitioner did not report on a Federal income tax return (including his 1985 return) any amount of unlawful income he received or that had been set aside for him.

On April 26, 1994, petitioner was indicted in the U.S. District Court for the Eastern District of Virginia on charges of conspiracy to commit espionage, under 18 U.S.C. sec. 794(c), and conspiracy to defraud the U.S. Internal Revenue Service, under 18 U.S.C. sec. 371. On April 28, 1994, petitioner pled guilty to both counts of the indictment. The indictment contained a criminal forfeiture count pursuant to 18 U.S.C. sec. 794(d). Petitioner was sentenced to life imprisonment on the espionage charge and to 27 months' imprisonment on the tax charge, the two sentences to run concurrently. In addition, the plea agreement provided for the criminal forfeiture of whatever interest petitioner had in espionage-related assets. At the time of trial, petitioner was serving a life sentence in a Federal penitentiary.

OPINION

* * *

II. WHEN SHOULD PETITIONER HAVE REPORTED THE INCOME FROM HIS ILLEGAL ESPIONAGE ACTIVITIES?

Petitioner contends that he constructively received most[6] of the unlawful espionage income in 1985, and, accordingly, he was not required to report the income received and deposited during the taxable years 1989, 1990, 1991, and 1992. Respondent contends that the income was reportable in 1989 through 1992, the years petitioner actually received and deposited cash in his bank accounts. Petitioner concedes that the

---

6. Petitioner contends that he constructively received almost $2 million in 1985 and, in addition, that he received $10,000 per month or $120,000 per year during each of the years at issue. Other than his constructive receipt contention, petitioner does not contend that we should modify respondent's determination. Respondent determined, on the basis of petitioner's bank deposits, that he underreported his income by $745,000, $65,000, $91,000, and $187,000 for the taxable years 1989, 1990, 1991, and 1992, respectively. Petitioner, however, does not argue that we should increase respondent's determinations for the 1990 and 1991 years, which are less than the amounts petitioner has contended that he received. Likewise, respondent did not assert an increased deficiency for the 1990 or 1991 tax years.

funds deposited during the years in issue represent cash received from the Soviet Union during the years of the deposits. Petitioner argues, however, that most of the amounts he received during the taxable years under consideration were constructively received in 1985.[7]

A taxpayer reporting income on the cash method of accounting, such as petitioner, must include an item in income for the taxable year in which the item is actually or constructively received. *See* sec. 451(a). The concept of constructive receipt is well established in tax law. The courts have regularly looked to section 1.451-2(a), Income Tax Regs., for the following definition of the term "constructive receipt":

> (a) GENERAL RULE. Income although not actually reduced to a taxpayer's possession is constructively received by him in the taxable year during which it is credited to his account, set apart for him, or otherwise made available so that he may draw upon it at any time, or so that he could have drawn upon it during the taxable year if notice of intention to withdraw had been given. However, income is not constructively received if the taxpayer's control of its receipt is subject to substantial limitations or restrictions.

Following the regulatory definition, courts have held that income is recognized when a taxpayer has an unqualified, vested right to receive immediate payment. Normally, the constructive receipt doctrine precludes the taxpayer from deliberately turning his back on income otherwise available. Here, however, petitioner relies on constructive receipt as a foil to respondent's determination that the unlawful income was reportable during the years before the Court. In any event, the essence of constructive receipt is the unfettered control over the date of actual receipt. *See* Hornung v. Commissioner, 47 T.C. 428, 434 (1967).

The determination of whether a taxpayer has constructively received income is to be made largely on a factual basis. Resolution of the controversy in petitioner's favor depends on whether he can show that he constructively received about $2 million in 1985, the year he was informed that an amount had been set aside for him. Under the circumstances here, petitioner did not possess "unfettered control" over the $2 million in 1985.

Assuming arguendo that some type of account was created and funds were segregated for petitioner, he did not have ready access to it, and certain conditions had to be met or had to occur before he could gain physical access to any funds. Petitioner had to contact the Soviets, using a complex arrangement of signal sites, to determine whether a "withdrawal" could be made. Next, the Soviets had to arrange to have the cash transferred into the United States and have it secretly left in a prearranged location

---

7. At trial, petitioner testified that he constructively received but fraudulently failed to report the illicit income for 1985. He explained that if he had reported the income on his Federal income tax return, his illicit and secret relationship with the Soviet Union would have been revealed. We note that petitioner's concession may have placed him at a disadvantage irrespective of our holding here. For example, if petitioner fraudulently failed to report income for 1985, the period for assessment would not have expired for 1985. *See* sec. 6501(c)(1).

for petitioner. There was no certainty that these conditions and steps could be accomplished under the existing circumstances, and the conditions represented substantial risks, limitations, and restrictions on petitioner's control of the funds, assuming they were even in existence and segregated for his exclusive benefit. *See Paul v. Commissioner*, T.C. Memo 1992-582 (no constructive receipt where taxpayer would have had to travel 68 miles in order to turn in winning lottery ticket). There is no constructive receipt of income where delivery of the cash is not dependent solely upon the volition of the taxpayer. *See Hornung v. Commissioner*, supra at 435.

So long as the Soviets retained control over any funds or promised set-asides, there was no practical or legal way in which petitioner could compel payment. Constructive receipt of income has been found where a corporation offers payment or pays by check in one year, but the recipient refuses delivery or fails to cash the check until the following year. *See, e.g.*, Frank v. Commissioner, 22 T.C. 945 (1954), affd. per curiam 226 F.2d 600 (6th Cir. 1955); Southeastern Mail Transp., Inc. v. Commissioner, T.C. Memo 1987-104. Here, no such proffer was made, and petitioner did not have a legally enforceable claim. If the KGB had questioned petitioner's loyalty at any time before payment, there is no assurance that petitioner would have continued to receive cash deliveries or payments. So long as the Soviet Union retained the ability to withhold or control the funds, there was no constructive receipt. Petitioner did not constructively receive the income before it was made physically and/or practically available to him. Accordingly, we hold that petitioner received and failed to report income in the amounts of $745,000, $65,000, $91,000, and $187,000 for the years 1989, 1990, 1991, and 1992, respectively.

Decision will be entered for respondent.

Schlude v. Commissioner
372 U.S. 128 (1963)

MR. JUSTICE WHITE delivered the opinion of the Court.

This is still another chapter in the protracted problem of the time certain items are to be recognized as income for the purposes of the federal income tax. The Commissioner of Internal Revenue increased the 1952, 1953 and 1954 ordinary income of the taxpayers by including in gross income for those years amounts received or receivable under contracts executed during those years despite the fact that the contracts obligated taxpayers to render performance in subsequent periods.

Taxpayers, husband and wife, formed a partnership to operate ballroom dancing studios (collectively referred to as "studio") pursuant to Arthur Murray, Inc., franchise agreements. Dancing lessons were offered under either of two basic contracts. The cash plan contract required the student to pay the entire down payment in cash at the time the contract was executed with the balance due in installments thereafter. The deferred payment contract required only a portion of the down payment to be paid in cash. The remainder of the down payment was due in stated installments and the balance of the contract price was to be paid as designated in a negotiable note signed at the time the contract was executed.

Both types of contracts provided that (1) the student should pay tuition for lessons in a certain amount, (2) the student should not be relieved of his obligation to pay the tuition, (3) no refunds would be made, and (4) the contract was noncancelable.[2] The contracts prescribed a specific number of lesson hours ranging from five to 1,200 hours and some contracts provided lifetime courses entitling the student additionally to two hours of lessons per month plus two parties a year for life. Although the contracts designated the period during which the lessons had to be taken, there was no schedule of specific dates, which were arranged from time to time as lessons were given.

Cash payments received directly from students and amounts received when the negotiable notes were discounted at the bank or fully paid[3] were deposited in the studio's general bank account without segregation from its other funds. The franchise agreements required the studio to pay to Arthur Murray, Inc., on a weekly basis, 10% of these cash receipts as royalty and 5% of the receipts in escrow, the latter to continue until a $20,000 indemnity fund was accumulated. Similarly, sales commissions for lessons sold were paid at the time the sales receipts were deposited in the studio's general bank account.

The studio, since its inception in 1946, has kept its books and reported income for tax purposes on an accrual system of accounting. In addition to the books, individual student record cards were maintained showing the number of hours taught and the number still remaining under the contract. The system, in substance, operated as follows. When a contract was entered into, a "deferred income" account was credited for the total contract price. At the close of each fiscal period, the student record cards were analyzed and the total number of taught hours was multiplied by the designated rate per hour of each contract. The resulting sum was deducted from the deferred income account and reported as earned income on the financial statements and the income tax return. In addition, if there had been no activity in a contract for over a year, or if a course were reduced in amount, an entry would be made canceling the untaught portion of the contract, removing that amount from the deferred income account, and recognizing gain to the extent that the deferred income exceeded the balance due on the contract, *i.e.*, the amounts received in advance. The amounts representing lessons taught and the gains from cancellations constituted the chief sources of the partnership's gross income. The balance of the deferred income account would

---

2. Although the contracts stated they were noncancelable, the studio frequently rewrote contracts reducing the number of lessons for a smaller sum of money. Also, despite the fact that the contracts provided that no refunds would be made, and despite the fact that the studio discouraged refunds, occasionally a refund would be made on a canceled contract.

3. Notes taken from the students were ordinarily transferred, with full recourse, to a local bank which would deduct the interest charges and credit the studio with approximately 50% of the face amount. The remaining 50% was held in a reserve account, unavailable to the studio, until the note was fully paid, at which time the reserved amount was transferred to the studio's general bank account.

be carried forward into the next fiscal year to be increased or decreased in accordance with the number of new contracts, lessons taught and cancellations recognized.

Deductions were also reported on the accrual basis except that the royalty payments and the sales commissions were deducted when paid irrespective of the period in which the related receipts were taken into income. Three certified public accountants testified that in their opinion the accounting system employed truly reflected net income in accordance with commercial accrual accounting standards.

The Commissioner included in gross income for the years in question not only advance payments received in cash but the full face amounts of notes and contracts executed during the respective years. The Tax Court and the Court of Appeals upheld the Commissioner, but the United States in this Court has retreated somewhat and does not now claim the includibility in gross income of future payments which were not evidenced by a note and which were neither due by the terms of the contract nor matured by performance of the related services. The question remaining for decision, then, is this: Was it proper for the Commissioner, exercising his discretion under § 446(b), to reject the studio's accounting system as not clearly reflecting income and to include as income in a particular year advance payments by way of cash, negotiable notes and contract installments falling due but remaining unpaid during that year? We hold that it was since we believe the problem is squarely controlled by *American Automobile Association*, 367 U.S. 687.

The Court there had occasion to consider the entire legislative background of the treatment of prepaid income. The retroactive repeal of § 452 of the 1954 Code, "the only law incontestably permitting the practice upon which [the taxpayer] depends," was regarded as reinstating long-standing administrative and lower court rulings that accounting systems deferring prepaid income could be rejected by the Commissioner.

"The fact is that § 452 for the first time specifically declared petitioner's system of accounting to be acceptable for income tax purposes, and overruled the long-standing position of the Commissioner and courts to the contrary. And the repeal of the section the following year, upon insistence by the Treasury that the proposed endorsement of such tax accounting would have a disastrous impact on the Government's revenue, was just as clearly a mandate from the Congress that petitioner's system was not acceptable for tax purposes." 367 U.S., at 695.

Confirming that view was the step-by-step approach of Congress in granting the deferral privilege to only limited groups of taxpayers while exploring more deeply the ramifications of the entire problem.

Plainly, the considerations expressed in *American Automobile Association* are apposite here. We need only add here that since the *American Automobile Association* decision, a specific provision extending the deferral practice to certain membership corporations was enacted, § 456, 1954 Code, added by § 1, Act of July 26, 1961, 75 Stat. 222, continuing, at least so far, the congressional policy of treating this problem by precise provisions of narrow applicability. Consequently, as in the *American Automobile Association* case, we invoke the "long-established policy of the Court in deferring, where possible, to congressional procedures in the tax field," and, as in that case, we cannot say that the Commissioner's rejection of the studio's deferral system was unsound.

The *American Automobile Association* case rested upon an additional ground which is also controlling here. Relying upon Automobile Club of Michigan v. Commissioner, 353 U.S. 180, the Court rejected the taxpayer's system as artificial since the advance payments related to services which were to be performed only upon customers' demands without relation to fixed dates in the future. The system employed here suffers from that very same vice, for the studio sought to defer its cash receipts on the basis of contracts which did not provide for lessons on fixed dates after the taxable year, but left such dates to be arranged from time to time by the instructor and his student. Under the contracts, the student could arrange for some or all of the additional lessons or could simply allow their rights under the contracts to lapse. But even though the student did not demand the remaining lessons, the contracts permitted the studio to insist upon payment in accordance with the obligations undertaken and to retain whatever prepayments were made without restriction as to use and without obligation of refund. At the end of each period, while the number of lessons taught had been meticulously reflected, the studio was uncertain whether none, some or all of the remaining lessons would be rendered. Clearly, services were rendered solely on demand in the fashion of the *American Automobile Association* and *Automobile Club of Michigan* cases.

Moreover, percentage royalties and sales commissions for lessons sold, which were paid as cash was received from students or from its note transactions with the bank, were deducted in the year paid even though the related items of income had been deferred, at least in part, to later periods. In view of all these circumstances, we hold the studio's accrual system vulnerable under § 446(b) with respect to its deferral of prepaid income. Consequently, the Commissioner was fully justified in including payments in cash or by negotiable note[10] in gross income for the year in which such payments were received.

DISSENT:

Mr. Justice Stewart, with whom Mr. Justice Douglas, Mr. Justice Harlan, and Mr. Justice Goldberg join, dissenting.

As the Court notes, this case is but the most recent episode in a protracted dispute concerning the proper income tax treatment of amounts received as advances for services to be performed in a subsequent year by a taxpayer who is on an accrual rather than a cash basis. The Government has consistently argued that such amounts are taxable in the year of receipt, relying upon two alternative arguments: It has claimed that deferral of such payments would violate the "annual accounting" principle which requires that income not be postponed from one year to the next to reflect the long-term economic result of a transaction. Alternatively, the Government has argued

---

10. Negotiable notes are regarded as the equivalent of cash receipts, to the extent of their fair market value, for the purposes of recognition of income.

that advance payments must be reported as income in the year of receipt under the "claim-of-right doctrine," which requires otherwise reportable income, held under a claim of right without restriction as to use, to be reported when received despite the fact that the taxpayer's claim to the funds may be disputed.

As I have elsewhere pointed out, neither of these doctrines has any relevance to the question whether any reportable income at all has been derived when payments are received in advance of performance by an accrual-basis taxpayer.[2] The most elementary principles of accrual accounting require that advances be considered reportable income only in the year they are earned by the taxpayer's rendition of the services for which the payments were made. The Government's theories would force upon an accrual-basis taxpayer a cash basis for advance payments in disregard of the federal statute which explicitly authorizes income tax returns to be based upon sound accrual accounting methods. [The remainder of the dissent is omitted. Eds.]

V. Related Matters

- **Section 453.** Section 453 provides a major exception to the accounting methods just described. It is addressed in Chapter 26.

- **Gross Receipts Test.** As a general rule, certain taxpayers, such as C corporations and partnerships that have a C corporation as a partner, cannot use the cash method of accounting and must adopt the accrual method. IRC § 448(a). However, despite the general rule, these taxpayers can use the cash method if they meet a $25 million gross receipts test. IRC § 448(b)(3). Specifically, a C corporation or partnership with a C corporation partner meets the gross receipts test if its average annual gross receipts for the prior three years do not exceed $25 million. IRC § 448(c)(1). Other businesses (e.g., qualified personal service corporations, S corporations and other pass-through entities), can use the cash method regardless of whether they meet the $25 million gross receipts test if the cash method clearly reflects income. The $25 million amount is adjusted for inflation. IRC § 448(c)(4).

- **Gift Cards.** Accrual method taxpayers who issue gift cards redeemable for goods or services may defer accruing the income until the year after issuance. *See* Rev. Proc. 2004-34, 2004-1 C.B. 991; Rev. Proc. 2011-18, 2011-5 I.R.B. 443.

---

2. *See* American Automobile Assn. v. United States, 367 U.S. 687, at 699–702 (dissenting opinion).

Chapter 14

Ordinary Tax Rates and Taxpayer Classification

I. Assignment

Read: Internal Revenue Code: §§ 1(j)(1)–(3); 2. Skim §§ 55(b)(2); 56; 57; 58; 6013(a); 7703(a).

Treasury Regulations: None.

Text: Overview
Section 1(j) 2018 Tax Rate Schedules for Individuals
Related Matters

Complete the problems.

II. Problems

1. Laurence Olivier is a calendar year taxpayer. In each subpart below, compute Laurence's tax liability for Year 1 before credits. Assume, unless otherwise directed, that he and anyone else filing with him have $500,000 of taxable earned income. Use the rate tables in the text excerpted from section 1.

   (a) On December 31, Year 1, Laurence is unmarried and has no children or dependents.

   (b) On March 1, Year 1, Laurence marries Vivien Leigh but they divorce on November 1, Year 1.

   (c) Same as (b) except that Laurence and Vivien remain married through the remainder of Year 1 and file jointly.

   (d) Same as (c) except that Laurence and Vivien file separately and reside in a non-community property state. Laurence's taxable income is $500,000.

   (e) Same as (d) except that Laurence and Vivien live in a community property state. Their total taxable income of $500,000 is all earned income. Laurence earned $200,000 and Vivien earned $300,000.

   (f) Same as (c) except that Vivien died on October 1, Year 1.

(g) What if Laurence and Vivien had married the year prior to Year 1, had a child in that year, and Vivien died in that year?

(h) Same as (g) except that all events occurred three years prior to Year 1.

III. Overview

A. Introduction

In this chapter, we will fill in some of the final details leading to a comprehensive view of the architecture of the income tax. Specifically, we will look at the ordinary income tax rate structure. This, in conjunction with the material in the preceding chapters and in conjunction with the next chapter's consideration of tax credits, will bring us to the point where we can take a typical taxpayer's income and expenses for the year and compute a final tax liability.

The completion of an income tax return can be analogized to a complex word game such as the *New York Times* Sunday crossword puzzle. Many people enjoy such games. Many do not. Those who do not may take comfort in knowing that much of the computational work of tax return preparation has become automated. There are now a wide array of computer software programs that perform the routine aspects of tax return preparation. Moreover, lawyers do not often do tax returns for pay. Return preparation is largely the province of accountants. Still it is helpful to understand something about the mechanics of getting from gross income to a tax liability. This understanding is the spring board for the tax related work of everyday lawyers and accountants, that is *basic tax planning*. Lawyers and accountants learn the tax rules in order to plan transactions and to manage other tax events in a fashion to achieve the client's aims with a minimum of tax liability. Whether the client is selling a home, making a gift, starting a business, or dissolving a marriage, there is a good way to do the deal and there is a bad way. Much of the rest of this book will examine how to do common transactions to the best tax advantage.

We arrive at a taxpayer's federal income tax liability through a series of related steps. First, we derive what might be called *pre-exclusion gross income*. We reduce this amount by any applicable exclusions (such as the exclusion under section 102 for gifts and bequests) to arrive at *gross income*. Next, we reduce this amount by *above the line deductions* under section 62. We further reduce the resulting *adjusted gross income* by either the *standard deduction* or the *itemized deductions*. Then we subtract the *personal exemptions* ($0 through 2025) and the deduction provided in *section 199A* (20% of qualified business income) to arrive at *taxable income*. At this point we apply the *tax rates* to establish a *pre-credits tax liability*. Finally, we reduce this amount by any applicable *tax credits* to reach a *final tax liability*. This process is summarized in the table that follows. It is worth mentioning that for some taxpayers there is a further step not described here. That step is the application of what is known as the *Alternative Minimum Tax*. This special tax is addressed briefly at the end of this chapter.

Computing a Final Tax Liability

```
        Pre-Exclusions Gross Income
     −  Exclusions
        Gross Income
     −  Above the Line Deductions
        Adjusted Gross Income
     −  Standard Deduction or Itemized Deductions
     −  Personal and Dependency Exemptions
     −  Section 199A Deduction
        Taxable Income
     ×  Tax Rates
        Pre-Credits Tax Liability
     −  Tax Credits
        Final Tax Liability
```

B. The Rate Structure for Ordinary Income

There are two rate structures specified in section 1 of the Code: the ordinary income rate structure and the capital gains rate structure. In this chapter we are only concerned with the ordinary income rate structure. Capital gains, the gains that arise from the sale or exchange of capital assets, will be addressed in a later chapter. The ordinary rate structure described below was created by the Tax Cuts and Jobs Act (TCJA) of 2017 and is scheduled to sunset in 2026.

1. The Basic Rates

At present, the basic tax rates for individuals are set out in subsection 1(j). This subsection establishes seven tax rates: 10%, 12%, 22%, 24%, 32%, 35%, and 37%. Each rate applies to a different segment of income known as a tax bracket. It is the combined effect of the tax rates and the tax brackets that creates the rate structure. The rates rise with the tax brackets. Thus, the 10% rate applies to the lowest tax bracket and the 37% rate applies to the highest tax bracket. The percentage of one's total income that one pays in taxes is termed the person's *effective tax rate*. The highest rate at which a taxpayer pays taxes is his or her *marginal tax rate*. The tax brackets change slightly every year due to the fact that they have been indexed for inflation. *See* IRC §§ 1(f)(1)–(2), (j)(3). The IRS publishes new brackets each year in a revenue procedure. There are various other complexities in the rate structure due to transition rules and sunset clauses. If all this seems unduly complicated, it is good to remember that in practice, computer software does the calculations painlessly. Even tax returns done by hand are relatively easy since the IRS publishes tax tables that specify how much tax is owed at any particular level of taxable income for any particular class of person.

2. The Principle of Progressivity

As we have seen, the rate and bracket structure for the federal income tax is progressive, that is, the rate rises with income. One might posit that it is fairer to impose a flat rate of tax on all income. Today some do question the validity of the principle of progressivity. This is indicated by the fact that the present rate structure is considerably less progressive than in earlier times when the top marginal rates exceeded 70%. One of the basic justifications for an income tax is that it is thought to more fairly correlate to ability to pay than other forms of taxation. The principle of progressivity is a logical extension of this idea. In short, as income rises so does the ability to pay. Further support for progressive taxation derives from the theory that as income rises each marginal dollar is less useful to its owner than the dollar that preceded it. For example, it is more important to put food on the table than to buy a new Maserati sports car. Perhaps the main counter argument is that progressivity may tend to discourage increases in productivity and efficiency. The student who is interested in developing a deeper understanding of the issues surrounding progressivity should begin by reading WALTER BLUM & HARRY KALVEN, THE UNEASY CASE FOR PROGRESSIVE TAXATION (1953) and CHARLES GALVIN & BORIS I. BITTKER, THE INCOME TAX: HOW PROGRESSIVE SHOULD IT BE? (1969).

Two additional points about the present rate of progressivity are worth noting. First, over the past forty years or so, payroll taxes (e.g., Social Security and Medicaid) have risen significantly, especially for the lower and middle classes. These regressive taxes have rendered the overall federal tax structure even less progressive than appears to be the case when only the income tax rate structure is considered. Second, as we will discuss later, the tax rates on capital gains and dividends are generally lower than the tax rates on ordinary income. Most capital gains and dividends are realized by wealthier individuals. These two facts taken together tend to further reduce the overall progressivity of the federal tax system.

C. Taxpayer Classifications

One of the basic questions that flows from adopting a progressive tax structure is how to tax the family. Under a progressive rate system, if family income is aggregated before it is taxed the resulting total tax liability may be higher than if each member of the family is taxed separately. This is because if the members are taxed separately each family member can take advantage of the lower tax brackets. To illustrate, suppose we have only two tax brackets, a 10% bracket for the first $10,000 of income and a 20% bracket for all income above $10,000. Assume that W and H, wife and husband, each have $30,000 of taxable income. If H and W each file separately, each will owe $5,000 of tax for an aggregate tax liability of $10,000.

$$10\% \times \$10,000 = \$1,000$$
$$20\% \times \$20,000 = \underline{\$4,000}$$
$$\$5,000$$
$$\underline{\times\ 2}$$
$$\mathbf{\$10,000}$$

On the other hand, if W and H file a return that combines their income their combined tax liability will be $11,000.

$$10\% \times \$10{,}000 = \$1{,}000$$
$$20\% \times \$50{,}000 = \underline{\$10{,}000}$$
$$\textbf{\$11{,}000}$$

The additional $1,000 of tax liability derives from the fact that in the second scenario W and H got to use the 10% bracket only once.

The solution to this apparent inequity, one could argue, is to have everyone report his or her own income separately. There are a number of practical objections to this approach. We will note only two. First, individual income reporting tends to favor two-earner families over equal-income one-earner families. Second, it tends to create disparities in tax treatment between married couples living in community property states and married couples residing elsewhere. This is because in community property states each spouse is deemed to own half of the earned income of the couple no matter who earned it. This led the Supreme Court to conclude in 1930 that in community property states each spouse should be taxed on half of their aggregate earned income. *Poe v. Seaborn*, 282 U.S. 101 (1930). This means that even one-earner couples who reside in community property states get to use the lower income tax brackets twice if they file separately. Obviously this is a decided advantage for those couples as compared with equal-income one-earner couples in non-community property states. The decision in *Poe v. Seaborn* contributed heavily to our present arrangement in which married couples may file joint returns and, if they do, are treated as if each earned half of their aggregate income. The foregoing is a simplified treatment of an issue that is complex and controversial. A place to begin for the reader who wants to delve more deeply into this area is Boris I. Bittker's seminal article appropriately titled *Federal Income Taxation and the Family*, 27 STANFORD LAW REVIEW 1389 (1975). The basic point made by Professor Bittker is that it is not possible to have a progressive income tax that is neutral in its treatment of equal-income married persons and unmarried persons and at the same time is neutral in its treatment of equal-income one-earner and two-earner couples. This forces society to make value choices in the income tax structure.

Today we have four classes of individuals for rate structure purposes: married persons filing jointly (including surviving spouses), heads of households, unmarried persons, and married persons filing separately. The tax rates are the same for all four classes but the brackets are different. The higher tax brackets take effect sooner for the various categories of taxpayers in the following order: married persons filing separately, unmarried persons, heads of household, and married persons filing jointly. Thus, married persons will almost always find it advantageous to file jointly rather than separately. Marital status is determined in part by federal tax law rather than simply by reference to state law. Moreover, the terms *surviving spouse* and *head of household* have specific tax meanings that are delineated by statute.

1. Marital Status

Normally marital status for tax purposes is determined at year's end. *See* IRC §7703(a)(1). *See also* IRC §6013. Marriage is a legal union recognized by state law. Under federal tax law, however, a person who is legally separated from her spouse under a decree of divorce or separate maintenance is not considered married for federal tax purposes. IRC § 2(b)(2)(A). Nor is a person considered married for tax purposes if the person's spouse is a nonresident alien. IRC § 2(b)(2)(B). In addition, sometimes if a married couple lives apart for an extended period, they are treated as unmarried for tax purposes. IRC § 7703(b). On the other hand, a person whose spouse died during the tax year is treated as married for tax purposes for that tax year. IRC § 2(b)(2)(C). Thus, if one's spouse dies during the tax year, it is permissible for such person to file a joint return with the decedent spouse in the year of death. IRC § 7703(a)(1).

Same Sex Couples and Domestic Partners: Until recently, same sex couples who were legally married under state law could not file joint federal income tax returns. This was because of a federal law known as the Defense of Marriage Act (DOMA). 1 U.S.C. § 67; 28 U.S.C. § 1738C. Section 3 of DOMA provided, "In determining the meaning of any act of Congress, or of any ruling, regulation or interpretation of the various administrative bureaus and agencies of the United States, the word 'marriage' means only a legal union between one man and one woman, and the word 'spouse' refers only to a person of the opposite sex who is a husband or a wife."

However, in 2013 in the case of *United States v. Windsor* the U.S. Supreme Court declared DOMA's denial of the estate tax marital deduction to a lawfully married same sex couple unconstitutional under the equal protection clause of the 14th Amendment as applied to the federal government under the 5th Amendment. *See* United States v. Windsor, 570 U.S. ___, 133 S. Ct. 2675 (2013), *aff'g* 699 F.3d 199 (2nd Cir. 2012). Following *Windsor*, the IRS issued a series of rulings and notices delineating its impact on other taxes, including the income tax. Its first pronouncement was Revenue Ruling 2013-17, 2013-38 IRB 1. This ruling accepted that under *Windsor* all legally married same sex couples will be treated as married for all federal tax purposes. It adopted what is known as the "state of celebration" rule. Under the state of celebration rule, a same sex couple that was lawfully married in a state recognizing same sex marriage is treated as married for federal tax purposes even if they reside in a state that does not recognize same sex marriage. Another issue addressed in Revenue Ruling 2013-17 was the treatment of "registered domestic partners." A number of states have adopted domestic partnership statutes creating a status for same sex couples that is like marriage but not called marriage. The revenue ruling concludes that domestic partners will not be treated as married for federal tax purposes.

Post *Windsor*, the battleground on same sex marriage shifted to the states, many of which had their own DOMAs. Based on *Windsor*, many of those statutes were held unconstitutional by lower courts. The U.S. Supreme Court ruled on that question in 2015, in Obergefell v. Hodges, 576 U.S. ___, 135 S. Ct. 2584 (2015). In the 5–4 decision, the Supreme Court held that state same-sex marriage bans violate both the 14th Amendment's Due Process Clause and Equal Protection Clause. The decision requires all states to grant same-sex marriages and recognize same-sex marriages granted in other states. In 2016, the IRS issued final regulations under section 7701 reflecting the holdings of *Windsor* and *Obergefell* and defining terms in the

Code describing the marital status of taxpayers. The regulations provide that the term "husband and wife" mean two individuals lawfully married to each other. The regulations also provide that a marriage of two individuals is recognized for federal tax purposes if the marriage is recognized by the state, possession, or territory of the United States in which the marriage is entered into, regardless of where the couple is living.

A further point to consider is how to treat income earned by registered domestic partners residing in community property states. One could argue that *Poe v. Seaborn* requires income splitting by means of separate returns in such cases. *See* Patricia A. Cain, 111 TAX NOTES 561 (May 1, 2006). Subsequent to a change in California community property law that clarified the community status of income of registered domestic partners, the IRS has agreed that *Poe v. Seaborn* does apply and requires that each partner must report one half of their combined incomes on his or her federal return. Priv. Ltr. Rul. 201021048 (May 5, 2010). For some analysis, *see* Patricia A. Cain, *Taxation of Domestic Partner Benefits: The Hidden Costs*, 45 UNIVERSITY OF SAN FRANCISCO LAW REVIEW 481 (2010). *See also* Patricia A. Cain, *Planning for Same-Sex Couples in 2011*, ALI-ABA Estate Planning Course Materials Journal, Vol. 17, p. 5, June 2011 (available on SSRN).

2. Surviving Spouse

For a limited time after a spouse's death the survivor may qualify as a surviving spouse and thus get the benefit of the rate structure applicable to married couples filing jointly. There are several requirements that must be met in order to qualify as a surviving spouse. First, the taxpayer's spouse must have died in one of the two immediately preceding years. IRC § 2(a)(1)(A). Second, the taxpayer must maintain a household and provide over half the cost of such maintenance. IRC § 2(a)(1) last sentence. Third, the taxpayer's household must constitute the principal place of abode for one or more children of the taxpayer. Fourth, the children must be qualified dependants of the taxpayer under section 152(a)(1) for whom the taxpayer can claim deductions under section 151(c)(1). IRC § 2(a)(1)(B)(i) & (ii). Finally, the taxpayer cannot have remarried before or during the taxable year in question. IRC § 2(a)(2)(A).

3. Head of Household

As noted earlier, a taxpayer who qualifies as a head of household gets the benefit of a rate structure that while not as advantageous as the rate structure for married couples who file jointly is still more advantageous than the rate structures applicable to single persons or to married persons who file separately. In general, a head of household is an unmarried person who is not a surviving spouse and who has a child or other dependent at home. IRC § 2(b). There are a number of nuances to the definition that we will not detail here. Some married persons who would otherwise likely file as married filing separately can qualify as heads of household. *See* IRC § 2(c).

D. Alternative Minimum Tax

So far we have been concerned with determining a taxpayer's *regular tax.* Since 1969, a parallel tax system (the *alternative minimum tax,* or AMT) has been in place. The AMT was originally designed to prevent taxpayers with high incomes from paying little to no tax by taking advantage of various deductions and preferences in the Code. The AMT is really a separate tax system. It has its own set of rates (26% on the first $175,000 and 28% on the excess), *with brackets that are adjusted for inflation.* It has its own exemption amounts that, beginning in 2012, are *adjusted for inflation.* For 2018, the exemptions amounts were $70,300 for unmarried individuals, $109,400 for married taxpayers filing jointly and surviving spouses, and $54,700 for married taxpayers filing separately.

The temporary changes to the individual income tax made by the TCJA in 2017 have reduced the significance of the AMT. This is because among those changes was the suspension of the personal exemptions, the suspension of the miscellaneous itemized deductions, and the addition of a cap on the amount of the state and local tax deduction. All of those changes were already part of the AMT regime. Specifically, personal exemptions, miscellaneous itemized deductions, and state and local taxes are not allowed for AMT purposes. In effect the TCJA made the regular tax function more like the AMT. *Skim* IRC §§ 55(b)(2), 56, 57, 58.

The AMT is structurally an addition to regular income taxes (the amount by which AMT liability exceeds regular tax liability), although taxpayers effectively calculate their tax liabilities under the two systems and pay the higher amount. Consider the following example based on 2018 tax parameters:

Example: AMT Calculation. In 2018, a married couple with three children had wage income of $190,000. The couple pays $25,000 in mortgage interest and $35,000 in state and local taxes. Under the regular tax, the couple can deduct $10,000 of their state and local taxes. Under the alternative minimum tax, however, they cannot deduct any of these taxes. They are allowed the AMT exemption of $109,400. Under the regular tax, their tax is determined using the graduated regular tax rates of 10%, 12%, 22% and 24%. Under the AMT, their tax is 26% of AMT taxable income:

2018 Regular Tax		2018 Alternative Minimum Tax	
Income	$190,000	Income	$190,000
Minus mortgage interest	– 25,000	Minus mortgage interest	– 25,000
Minus state & local taxes	– 10,000	Minus AMT exemption	– 109,400
Taxable Income	$155,000	AMT Taxable Income	$55,600
Regular Tax	**$25,979**	AMT (26%)	$14,456
		Minus Regular Tax	– 25,979
		AMT Tax Liability	**$0**

In the 2018 example above, the AMT did not affect the taxpayers. Indeed, very few taxpayers will be subject to the AMT, because the TCJA temporarily eliminated many of the same deductions that the AMT has long disallowed. (This is also due, in part, to the fact that since 2012, the AMT exemptions are adjusted annually for inflation. In addition, the law allows the use of nonrefundable personal credits against the taxpayer's AMT liability.) Prior to 2018, the taxpayers in the example above may have been subject to the AMT. For *regular* tax purposes they would have been allowed five personal and dependency exemptions totaling more than $20,000, and they would have been entitled to deduct the full $35,000 in state and local taxes. For *AMT* purposes, however, none of these deductions would have been allowed.

As a final point, the AMT for *corporations* was permanently repealed by the TCJA.

IV. Materials

Section 1(j)(2) 2018 Tax Rate Schedules for Individuals

"(A) MARRIED INDIVIDUALS FILING JOINT RETURNS AND SURVIVING SPOUSES. — The following table shall be applied in lieu of the table contained in subsection (a):

"If taxable income is:	The tax is:
Not over $19,050	10% of taxable income.
Over $19,050 but not over $77,400	$1,905, plus 12% of the excess over $19,050.
Over $77,400 but not over $165,000	$8,907, plus 22% of the excess over $77,400.
Over $165,000 but not over $315,000	$28,179, plus 24% of the excess over $165,000.
Over $315,000 but not over $400,000	$64,179, plus 32% of the excess over $315,000.
Over $400,000 but not over $600,000	$91,379, plus 35% of the excess over $400,000.
Over $600,000	$161,379, plus 37% of the excess over $600,000.

"(B) HEADS OF HOUSEHOLDS. — The following table shall be applied in lieu of the table contained in subsection (b):

"If taxable income is:	The tax is:
Not over $13,600	10% of taxable income.
Over $13,600 but not over $51,800	$1,360, plus 12% of the excess over $13,600.
Over $51,800 but not over $82,500	$5,944, plus 22% of the excess over $51,800.
Over $82,500 but not over $157,500	$12,698, plus 24% of the excess over $82,500.
Over $157,500 but not over $200,000	$30,698, plus 32% of the excess over $157,500.
Over $200,000 but not over $500,000	$44,298, plus 35% of the excess over $200,000.

Over $500,000 . . . . $149,298, plus 37% of the excess over $500,000.

"(C) UNMARRIED INDIVIDUALS OTHER THAN SURVIVING SPOUSES AND HEADS OF HOUSEHOLDS. — The following table shall be applied in lieu of the table contained in subsection (c):

"If taxable income is:	The tax is:
Not over $9,525	10% of taxable income.
Over $9,525 but not over $38,700	$952.50, plus 12% of the excess over $9,525.
Over $38,700 but not over $82,500	$4,453.50, plus 22% of the excess over $38,700.
Over $82,500 but not over $157,500	$14,089.50, plus 24% of the excess over $82,500.
Over $157,500 but not over $200,000	$32,089.50, plus 32% of the excess over $157,500.
Over $200,000 but not over $500,000	$45,689.50, plus 35% of the excess over $200,000.
Over $500,000	$150,689.50, plus 37% of the excess over $500,000.

"(D) MARRIED INDIVIDUALS FILING SEPARATE RETURNS. — The following table shall be applied in lieu of the table contained in subsection (d):

"If taxable income is:	The tax is:
Not over $9,525	10% of taxable income.
Over $9,525 but not over $38,700	$952.50, plus 12% of the excess over $9,525.
Over $38,700 but not over $82,500	$4,453.50, plus 22% of the excess over $38,700.
Over $82,500 but not over $157,500	$14,089.50, plus 24% of the excess over $82,500.
Over $157,500 but not over $200,000	$32,089.50, plus 32% of the excess over $157,500.
Over $200,000 but not over $300,000	$45,689.50, plus 35% of the excess over $200,000.
Over $300,000	$80,689.50, plus 37% of the excess over $300,000.

V. Related Matters

- **Innocent Spouses.** When spouses file a joint return they are jointly and severally liable for the resulting tax liability. IRC § 6013(d)(3). Sometimes this may lead to an inequitable result, such as when one spouse prepares a fraudulent return understating income and induces the other spouse to sign the return without knowledge of the fraud. Section 6015 provides relief for innocent spouses in a variety of circumstances including the one just described. We will not seek to detail the mechanics of section 6015 here. But it is one of those provisions every general practitioner should know of and be prepared to study closely in the appropriate case. A federal circuit court opinion interpreting the statute is Cheshire v. Commissioner, 282 F.3d 326 (5th Cir. 2002). The IRS has also issued interpretational guidance for the statute in Rev. Proc. 2003-61, 2003-2 C.B. 296. The innocent spouse rules also serve as a reminder to the attorney who represents both spouses in a tax related matter to be alert to conflicts of interest between the spouses that might render such joint representation inappropriate. *See, e.g.,* Devore v. Commissioner, 963 F.2d 280 (9th Cir. 1992).

- **Community Property**. There is another spousal relief provision that applies only to married persons living in community property states. In certain cases, section 66 countermands the principles enunciated in *Poe v. Seaborn* discussed earlier. In essence, instead of treating the earned income of the spouses as being taxable half and half, the statute treats earned income as taxable to the earner spouse alone. A typical example of its application is when the spouses live apart for most of the year and do not share their income.

- **The Kiddie Tax**. Because of the progressive rate structure of the income tax it can be advantageous for parents to shift income to their children in order to use the lower tax brackets more than once. For example, if Parent's marginal tax rate is 35% and Child's marginal tax rate is 10%, a shift of $10,000 of income from Parent to Child will save $2,500 of tax. Such a shift might be accomplished by transferring title to income producing property to Child. If Child is a minor, Parent can still control the property and the income. Add to this the fact that Parent is likely to have spent the money on Child anyway and the income shift seems like good financial planning. Congress judged that shifts of income from parents (and other family members) to young children should not result in such substantial tax savings and enacted section 1(g) to prevent those savings. Known as the *Kiddie Tax*, section 1(g) generally subjects unearned income of children under the age of 18 to the child's parents' marginal tax rate no matter what the source of the income. This rule was temporarily modified by the TCJA to, in effect, apply the tax rates for trusts and estates to the child's unearned income. *See* § 1(j)(4). Those rates are less graduated than the individual tax rates.

Chapter 15

Tax Credits

I. Assignment

Read: Internal Revenue Code: §§ 21(a)–(c), (d)(1); 24(a)–(c), (h); 25A(a)–(g)(2), (i); 31; 32(a)–(b).

Treasury Regulations: None.

Text: Overview
Related Matters

Complete the problems.

II. Problems

1. Gustave Flaubert is a full-time student with a double major in economics and acrobatics at Cirque De Soleil University, an eligible education institution within the meaning of section 25A(f)(2). Gustave is married to Nurse Betty who works in the operating room at nearby Hospital of the Setting Sun. Betty supports Gustave on her salary. Consider how section 25A applies to them if they file a joint return. In doing so, ignore the inflation adjustments called for by section 25A(h).

   (a) Their modified adjusted gross income is $45,000, and Gustave pays $20,000 of tuition to Cirque U as a first-year student.

   (b) Same as (a) except that Gustave was convicted of a felony drug offense during the year.

   (c) Same as (a) except that Gustave is in his third year.

   (d) Same as (c) except that the tuition is paid from a student loan.

   (e) Same as (c) except that Gustave gets a $16,000 student scholarship which is excluded from income by section 117.

   (f) Same as (c) except that Nurse Betty is also a half time student working on an advanced degree in nursing. She pays $5,000 tuition.

   (g) Same as (c) except that they have modified adjusted gross income of $90,000.

2. Jean Valjean is unmarried and has one young daughter, Cosette. Jean qualifies as a head of household for tax purposes. Cosette is his dependent. Jean has $22,000 of earned income and has no other income. Income tax of $500 was withheld from his wages by his employer. Assuming no inflation adjustments, what are Jean's tax consequences for the current year? In making this calculation,

assume that Jean does not itemize deductions and that no tax credits apply other than the credits under sections 24, 31, and 32. To calculate his initial tax liability, use the tables from section 1(j) excerpted in Chapter 14.

III. Overview

The technical difference between a deduction and a credit rests upon their different places in the calculation of final tax liability. A deduction reduces income before the tax rate is applied to arrive at a tax liability. A credit reduces tax liability dollar for dollar.

Computing a Final Tax Liability

Pre-Exclusions Gross Income
– Exclusions
Gross Income
– Above the Line Deductions
Adjusted Gross Income
– Standard Deduction or Itemized Deductions
– Personal and Dependency Exemptions
– Section 199A Deduction
Taxable Income
× Tax Rates
Pre-Credits Tax Liability
– Tax Credits
Final Tax Liability

That being so, would you rather have a deduction or a credit of the same amount? The answer should be obvious that the credit is worth more since the deduction only reduces tax liability in proportion to the taxpayer's top marginal tax rate. Thus, while a $100 credit saves $100 in taxes, a $100 deduction for a taxpayer in the 35% bracket saves only $35 in taxes. This points the way to another notable difference between credits and deductions. While deductions are more valuable as one's marginal tax rate rises, credits are equally valuable to everyone who is able to utilize them. In our example above, if the taxpayer's marginal rate was 24%, the $100 deduction would only save $24 of taxes. The equality aspect of the credit makes it particularly appropriate for use in providing tax subsidies and incentives.

As a very general proposition, we may say that deductions were justified historically as a means to tax only net income. Clearly the main business and investment deductions under section 162 and section 212 serve that purpose. Credits, on the other hand, often derived from political judgments to subsidize or encourage certain conditions or activities. Thus we have credits to encourage construction of low income housing (IRC § 42), credits to encourage the use of renewable energy resources (IRC § 48), and credits to encourage the creation of access for disabled persons (IRC § 44) to name but a few. However, today it is difficult to see any clear distinction between those areas where the tax law employs deductions and those where it employs credits.

In this chapter, we will consider only a few of the many available credits found in the Code. Our purpose here is to acquaint the reader with some of the more commonly encountered credits and to complete the tax liability calculation picture in preparation for a major review of the previous chapters. The credits we will focus upon are the dependent care tax credit, the child tax credit, the two higher education credits, the withholding tax credit, and the earned income credit. The first four are non-refundable credits and the last two are refundable. A non-refundable credit can reduce one's tax liability no lower than zero. A refundable credit can trigger a payment from the government to the taxpayer if the credit exceeds her tax liability.

A. Non-Refundable Credits

There are several provisions intended to recognize that persons who have children or other dependents experience an increase in living expenses and a corresponding reduction in their ability to pay taxes. The temporarily zeroed personal and dependency exemptions authorized under sections 151 and 152 are among those provisions. The dependent care credit and the child tax credit are others. The two higher education credits are designed to encourage people to attend college and in some cases may be available to the student's parents.

1. The Dependent Care Credit

Section 21 provides a credit equal to the *applicable percentage* of a taxpayer's employment related dependent care expenses. The applicable percentage begins at 35% and phases down to 20% as adjusted gross income rises above $15,000. IRC § 21(a)(2). In any event, the expenses subject to the applicable percentage cannot exceed $3,000 for one *qualifying individual* and $6,000 for two or more qualifying individuals. IRC § 21(c). Thus, the amount of the credit can range from a low of $600 (.2 × $3,000) to a high of $2,100 (.35 × $6,000). There are two categories of qualifying individuals. The main category includes dependents of the taxpayer who are under the age of 13. The second category includes the spouse or a dependent of the taxpayer who is mentally or physically disabled. IRC § 21(b)(1).

2. The Child Tax Credit and the Partial Credit for Other Dependents

Section 24 establishes a tax credit for each *qualifying* child of the taxpayer. Currently the credit is $2,000, without inflation adjustments. *See* IRC § 24(h)(2). The credit phases out for higher income individuals. *See* IRC § 24(b)(1)–(2), (h)(3). A qualifying child is a section 152 dependent under the age of 17 who is closely related to the taxpayer. IRC § 24(c). *See also* IRC § 32(c)(2)(B). Though discussed here as a non-refundable credit, it is worth noting that it can be partially refundable in a limited number of cases. *See* IRC § 24(d)(1). The maximum portion of the credit that can be refundable is $1,400 (indexed for inflation) per qualifying child. IRC § 24(h)(5). In cases of divorce, the credit goes to the parent who is entitled to the dependency exemption for that child. *See* IRC § 24(a). This makes the dependency rules important even though the exemption amount is currently zero.

The Tax Cut and Jobs Act of 2017 temporarily expanded the child tax credit to cover dependents under section 152 other than qualifying children. IRC § 24(h)(4). Section 152 refers to those dependents as "qualifying relatives." *See* IRC § 152(a)(2) & (d). This new partial credit is limited to $500. The partial credit is scheduled to sunset at the end of 2025. At that time, the child tax credit will fall to $1,000 and the personal and dependency exemptions set out in section 151 will return to their previous amounts. Sections 151 and 152 are both addressed in Chapter 12. The TCJA added a requirement that in order to obtain the credit for a qualifying child, the child's social security number must be on the return. IRC § 24(h)(7). An otherwise qualifying child with no social security number still qualifies for the $500 partial credit. IRC § 24(h)(4)(C).

3. The Hope Scholarship Credit and the Lifetime Learning Credit

These credits are for qualified tuition and related fees (IRC § 25A(f)(1)) at an eligible institution of higher education for a taxpayer who is the student, the student's spouse, or if the student is the taxpayer's dependent. IRC § 25A(f)(1)(A). Except as noted below, costs of books and housing are not included. IRC § 25A(f)(1)(C); Treas. Reg. § 1.25A-2(d)(2)(ii), (3).

The *Hope Scholarship Credit* has been modified permanently by the *American Opportunity Tax Credit*. IRC § 25A(i). Although the Hope Scholarship Credit was only available for the first two years of college, the modified credit applies to the first four years of post-secondary education. The amount of the credit was increased to 100% of the first $2,000 of qualified tuition and related expenses (including course materials) and 25% of the next $2,000. In addition to raising the maximum credit and extending it over four years of post-secondary education, the modified credit expanded the income phase-outs and made 40% of the credit refundable. These modifications were made permanent by Congress in 2015.

The *Lifetime Learning Credit* is a credit for the qualified tuition and related expenses paid by the taxpayer with respect to one or more students. It is limited to 20% of up to $10,000 of qualified expenses, that is $2,000. IRC § 25A(c)(1). The Lifetime Learning Credit is available for an unlimited number of years, and it is available for both undergraduate and graduate or professional degree expenses.

Both credits are subject to phase out as the taxpayer's *modified* adjusted gross income rises above certain limits. IRC § 25A(d), (i)(4). The phase out limits are adjusted for inflation. IRC § 25A(h)(2).

There are several coordination rules:

a. Any expenses satisfied by funds excluded from income under section 117 (certain scholarships) cannot be credited or deducted. IRC §§ 25A(g)(2)(C), 222(d)(1).

b. The Lifetime Learning Credit is a *per taxpayer* credit. In contrast, the Hope Scholarship Credit (now American Opportunity Tax Credit) is a *per student* credit, so it can be claimed with respect to each qualifying student of the taxpayer. IRC § 25A(b)(1). But no student can qualify for both the Hope Scholarship Credit and the Lifetime Learning Credit in the same year. In case of overlap, the Hope Scholarship Credit will apply. IRC § 25A(c)(2)(A).

c. A taxpayer can claim both the Hope Scholarship Credit and the Lifetime Learning Credit in the same year for different students. *Cf.* IRC § 25A(c)(2)(A).

d. A taxpayer can claim only one Lifetime Learning Credit in any year even if more than one student (e.g. children of the taxpayer or husband and wife) otherwise qualifies. IRC § 25A(c)(1). However, the qualifying expenditures of the qualifying students may be aggregated to obtain the maximum credit. IRC § 25A(f)(1).

B. Refundable Credits

As mentioned earlier a refundable credit can trigger a payment from the government to the taxpayer if the credit exceeds her tax liability. As the term implies, a refundable credit may simply serve to return to a taxpayer monies paid in excess of what was owed. However, as we will see, the earned income credit is actually a positive transfer of funds from the government to certain taxpayers.

1. The Credit for Withholding on Wages

One of the central enforcement mechanisms of the federal income tax is the requirement that employers withhold taxes from their employees' wages and remit them to the Treasury. Thus, as far as wages are concerned, the federal income tax is a pay as you go system. But withholding on income is necessarily an approximation since there are many variables that may affect a final tax liability. By the end of the tax year, most wage earners will have been under withheld or over withheld. When they file their income tax returns, those taxpayers will either need to write the IRS a check or they will be entitled to a refund. In the latter case, the legal chain that creates that entitlement is section 31 by way of sections 6401(b) and 6402(a). Section 31 is the classic refundable credit. It entitles the taxpayer to a credit for taxes withheld from his paycheck. Section 6401(b) provides that any tax paid in excess of the amount actually owed is an "overpayment." Section 6402(a) says that overpayments, with a few exceptions, shall be refunded.

Taxpayers have some degree of control over the level of their employers' withholding on their wages. This control is principally exercised by advising their employers in advance about their marital status and the number of dependents they intend to claim when they file their returns.

2. The Earned Income Credit

The section 32 earned income credit is intended to encourage people earning at or near the poverty level to continue to work rather than go on welfare. Thus, a taxpayer must have earned income in order to qualify for the credit. At first the credit increases by the "credit percentage" of earned income as the "earned income amount" increases. But after the earned income amount reaches specified levels the credit plateaus and begins to phase out by the "phaseout percentage" of earned income in excess of the "phaseout amount." *See* IRC § 32(a) & (b). The credit is adjusted for inflation. See IRC § 32(j). To describe the earned income credit as refundable is not entirely accurate since it normally causes the eligible taxpayer to receive a payment from the federal government in excess of the income taxes withheld. For this reason, it is sometimes called a negative income tax. The assigned problem obliges the student to wrestle with some of the workings of section 32.

It is worth noting that the earned income credit percentage increases with the number of qualifying children of the taxpayer to a maximum of 45% for taxpayers with three or more qualifying children. IRC § 32(b)(1). The earned income amount also increases slightly for taxpayers with two or more children. IRC § 32(b)(2)(A). In addition, the phase-out amount for the credit increases by $5,000 for joint filers (subject to inflation adjustment), regardless of the number of qualifying children. IRC § 32(b)(2)(B). The overall effect of these adjustments is allow some accommodations for family size. The complexity of the EITC is a problem from the standpoints of fairness and of enforceability.

C. Ordering Rules

The order in which credits are consumed can be very important. Obviously, it would be better from the taxpayer's perspective if she could take non-refundable credits before refundable credits to maximize the amount of tax refund. So, what is the proper pecking order for credits? Form 1040, produced by the I.R.S., calls for deduction of non-refundable credits ahead of refundable credits. Since this is a taxpayer favorable result, no one seems likely to question it.

IV. Related Matters

- **§ 23 Credit for Qualified Adoption Expenses.** The process of adopting a child can be quite expensive. It is not uncommon for a foreign adoption, for instance, to cost in excess of $20,000. Section 23 authorizes a tax credit for certain adoption expenses. Like most credits, it has a number of complexities such as expense caps and income phase outs.

- **§ 27 Foreign Tax Credit.** As explained in Chapter 40, the United States taxes the world wide income of its citizens and resident aliens. Income earned abroad may also be subject to taxation in the country where it is earned. To ameliorate this problem of double taxation, section 27 creates a credit for foreign taxes. Section 901 controls the parameters of this credit, and is considered in greater detail in Chapter 40.

- **Health Coverage Tax Credit.** Section 36B, enacted as part of health care reform in March 2010, created a Health Coverage Tax Credit (HCTC). The HCTC is a refundable credit equal to 80% of the costs of certain health care insurance of qualified low income individuals. The provision is effective for tax years after December 31, 2013.

Chapter 16

First Review Problem

The following problem is designed to review what has been addressed in the preceding chapters and to help integrate what has been learned. The problem simulates many aspects of a typical middle to upper-middle class married couple's tax return. In doing this problem, assume that Taxpayers file a joint return for the year. To calculate their tax liability please use the rate structure set out in IRC § 1(j)(2), which is excerpted in Chapter 14. You may assume the standard deduction for a married couple filing jointly is $24,000.

Taxpayers, William T. Sherman and Scarlett O'Hara, a married couple, have two children, Karl Rove and Valerie Plame, ages 4 and 7. In January of the year in question Scarlett's mother, Maureen O'Hara, moves in with William and Scarlett. They provide over half of her support for the entire year. Maureen's gross income for the year is $1,200. Prior to living with William and Scarlett, Maureen lived on her own and supported herself with personal savings. William and Scarlett are cash method taxpayers. William is an architect who generated $150,000 of cash receipts in the current year as a sole proprietor. He has various expenses relating to his business considered below. Scarlett is a hospital operating room nurse who has a $60,000 annual salary.

Part I: Gross Income. Determine Taxpayers' gross income, if, in addition to the amounts above, the following amounts are received during the year:

(a) William provides architectural services to his lawyer in exchange for the lawyer's drafting of wills for William and Scarlett. The services were worth $4,000.

(b) William and Scarlett recover $12,000 from their insurance company when their car, used solely for personal purposes, is totaled by a falling tree during a hurricane (which the President of the United States lawfully declared a "major disaster"). They paid $18,000 for the car two years ago. Before the storm its fair market value was $14,100.

(c) Scarlett finds fifteen Canadian Maple Leaf gold coins in an old trunk. The coins are worth $5,000.

(d) Scarlett receives a $700,000 cash inheritance from her father's estate.

(e) Scarlett invested the inheritance in certificates of deposit at a local bank and earns $15,000 of interest.

(f) William performs services for various clients during the year for which he has not yet been paid. At year's end these accounts receivable amount to $40,000.

(g) In order to improve his cash flow situation, William sells $11,000 of his accounts receivable to his bank for $10,000.

(h) Scarlett is paid $10,000 by her father's estate as compensation for serving as the executor of the estate.

(i) In recognition of his outstanding service to the profession, William is awarded an all-expenses paid vacation to Hawaii worth $5,000. *See* IRC § 74.

(j) Scarlett has knee surgery at the hospital where she works. The hospital discounts her bill by $2,000. This is 20% of the amount of the hospital's usual charge for the surgery. *See* IRC § 132(a) & (c).

Part II: Adjusted Gross Income (AGI). Determine Taxpayers' AGI assuming they make the expenditures listed below. (Though more than one approach is rational, we recommend that you first determine which expenditures are potentially deductible and then segregate deductible items into above the line (IRC § 62) and below the line (IRC § 63) deductions.)

(a) William incurs the following expenses in his architectural business: (1) $20,000 cost of supplies; (2) $27,000 of rent; (3) $2,000 of utilities; and (4) $39,000 of salaries.

(b) William purchases new equipment at a cost of $40,000. The equipment has a 7-year class life; however, William properly elects to expense the entire amount under section 179.

(c) Scarlett incurs $2,400 of out-of-pocket expenses to attend a seminar related to her employment. $600 are for meals and $1,800 are for plane fare and lodging. Her employer separately paid the seminar tuition of $1,000.

(d) Scarlett spends $200 for New Balance shoes that she only wears at work. The shoes have a special design for arch support and are quite fashionable in appearance.

(e) Scarlett pays $300 in dues to the Association of Operating Room Nurses.

(f) William pays $1,000 in dues to the Association of Professional Architects.

(g) Taxpayers pay $9,000 of interest on the mortgage of their residence, $1,000 of interest on their personal credit cards, and $5,000 of property taxes.

(h) Taxpayers give $8,000 of cash to various public charities.

(i) Taxpayers pay $7,000 in state income taxes and $3,000 in state sales taxes.

(j) Taxpayers incur $4,000 in medical expenses.

(k) Taxpayers spend $25,000 to remodel the kitchen of their residence.

Part III: Taxable Income. Determine Taxpayers' taxable income. As a sole proprietor, William is entitled to a deduction under section 199A equal to 20% of the net operating income from his business. We explore the 20% deduction more fully in Chapter 37. For purposes of this review problem, assume that William's qualified business income is $35,000, and that his deduction is therefore $7,000 ($35,000 × .20). This is an extra deduction that is taken below the line in arriving at taxable in-

come. It is not, however, an itemized deduction, meaning Taxpayers can take it on their joint return even if they choose to take the standard deduction.

Part IV: Pre-Credit Tax Liability. Determine Taxpayers' pre-credit tax liability under section 1(a), which applies to taxpayers who file a joint return. To calculate their tax liability please use the rate structure set out in section 1(j)(2), which is excerpted in Chapter 14.

Part V: Final Tax Liability. Determine Taxpayers' post-credit tax liability and the amount of any further payment they must make or refund they will receive if Scarlett's employer withheld $6,000 in federal income taxes and William paid $10,000 in estimated taxes. *See* IRC §§ 24 and 31.

Chapter 17

Capital Gains and Losses

I. Assignment

Read: Internal Revenue Code: §§ 1211(a)–(b); 1212(a)–(b); 1221; 1222; 1223(1)–(2), (10). Skim §§ 1(h), (j)(5); 165(c), (f), (g)(1)–(2); 408(m); 1060, 1202(a)–(e); 1411; 1235; 1236; 1237; 1241; 1271.

Treasury Regulations: §§ 1.1221-1(a)–(d). Skim § 1.1060-1(c).

Text: Overview
Bynum v. Commissioner
Williams v. McGowan
Related Matters

Complete the problems.

II. Problems

1. Jean Jolly will sell an existing dry cleaning business that Jean has operated as a sole proprietor for the last ten years. Comet Cleaners, Inc. agrees to pay Jean $1 million for the following tangible and intangible assets:

   • supply of 10,000 hangers

   • machine used in pressing shirts

   • building and land Jean uses in the business

   • valuable antique rug on the floor in the lobby

   • self-painted portrait of Jean, which is hanging on the wall

   • purchased portrait of the inventor of the steam iron, which is hanging on the wall

   • accounts receivable

   • trademark ("Where Buttons Don't Dissolve")

   (a) Which of the above are capital assets?

   (b) In general, how will the tax consequences of the sale be determined? *See Williams v. McGowan*, in the materials below. *See also* IRC § 1060; Treas. Reg. § 1.1060-1(c).

   (c) Assume that Jean did not operate the dry cleaning business as a sole proprietorship, but instead was the sole shareholder and president of Jolly

251

Cleaners, Inc. which owned and operated the business. Assuming he has an adjusted basis in his stock of $500,000, what are the tax consequences to Jean if he sells all of his stock in Jolly Cleaners to Comet Cleaners for $1 million?

2. In Year 1, William Bonney moved to New Mexico to engage in the cattle business. He bought 160 acres of land one-half mile from a city with a population of 5,000. At that time, the land was particularly suitable for cattle feeding, but not suitable for residential development. Shortly after the purchase, however, William decided not to go into the cattle business because of drought, crop failures, and a decline in the cattle business which continued several years. In Year 3, William tried to sell the property for less than he paid for it, but was unsuccessful, partly because a highway had been surveyed across the land, splitting it into two tracts rendering it less suitable for cattle feeding. A real estate agent advised him that he would have a better chance of selling the land if he divided it into small tracts and blocks. So he did. He subdivided the land into 29 tracts, and some of the tracts into lots, and then devoted most of his time to the sale of lots (listing them with agents and otherwise promoting sales). Between Years 3–10, William sold enough lots to get completely out of debt, thanks to the land being included in the city limits. Thereafter, he did nothing to promote sales, and devoted his full time to the lumber business. During Years 11–15, William had no real estate office, did not advertise the lots, and had no fixed price for the lots. Because it was a "sellers'" market, however, he did sell numerous lots through unsolicited offers when the price was right. In fact, he sold more lots in Year 15, when it was a sellers' market, than he did in Year 10, when it was a "buyers'" market. What is the character of the gain recognized on the sale of the lots in Year 15?

3   During the current year, Mary Bethune had salary income of $300,000 and engaged in only two property transactions: On December 30th, she sold stock held for investment for $4,000, which she bought eight months before for $6,000. On December 31st, she sold different stock held for investment for $4,000, which she bought eight years before for $11,000. To what extent are the losses from the property transactions deductible in the current year, and what is the amount and character of the "net capital loss?"

4. During the current year, Abigail Adams, a single taxpayer, had salary income of $300,000 and incurred the following transactions:

    • Abigail sold stock in ABC, Inc. for $15,000. Abigail bought the stock three years before for $5,000.

    • Abigail sold stock in XYZ, Inc. for $6,000. Abigail bought the stock seven months before for $2,000.

    • Abigail sold an antique desk for $10,000. Abigail bought the desk four years before for $4,000.

    (a) What is Abigail's net capital gain?

(b) Same as (a) except that Abigail also sold a parcel of land for $150,000. Abigail purchased the land eight months ago for $158,000 and held it for investment.

(c) Same as (b) except that Abigail purchased the land eighteen months ago.

III. Overview

In earlier chapters, we studied gains and losses from property transactions. Now that we have considered ordinary tax rates, it is appropriate to revisit gains and losses. After determining whether a gain is included in gross income or whether a loss is deductible from gross income, the "character" of the gain or loss must be determined. A recognized gain or deductible loss is characterized either as *capital* or *ordinary* depending on a number of factors, including the nature of the property, the taxpayer's holding period of the property, and whether the taxpayer disposed of the property in a sale or exchange transaction.

Individual taxpayers generally prefer gains to be classified as capital gains rather than ordinary income because certain capital gains are afforded preferential tax treatment. Presently, the maximum rate at which most *long-term capital gains* are taxed is 15% (20% for high income earners), whereas the highest rate at which other types of income (*ordinary income* and *short-term capital gains*) are taxed is 37%—a significant rate differential for high earners. Several policy reasons are offered for the tax rate preference accorded to capital gains. First, it is argued that it would be inequitable to tax capital gains at high rates in the year of disposition when those gains may have accrued over several years. Second, it is contended that a high tax on capital gains may effectively lock some taxpayers into their existing investments and impair the mobility of capital, whereas a tax preference encourages the free flow of capital into new enterprises and productive investments, increases economic activity and growth, and ultimately creates more tax revenue for the government. Third, it is argued that it would be inequitable to tax capital gains at high rates as the gains may be illusory gains attributable to the effects of inflation and not to true economic appreciation. One response to these arguments is to suggest that a dollar of income is a dollar of income. Why should a capitalist's income be taxed at a lower rate than a working person's if they both have the same amount of income? Doesn't this violate the principle of horizontal equity? For a detailed treatment of the policy arguments for a capital gains preference, see Noel B. Cunningham & Deborah H. Schenk, *The Case for a Capital Gains Preference*, 48 TAX LAW REV. 319 (1993).

In contrast to gains, taxpayers tend to prefer that their losses be characterized as ordinary losses because of a statutory limitation on capital loss deductions. In the case of individuals, capital losses can only be used to offset capital gains plus $3,000 of ordinary income. IRC § 1211(b). Unused capital losses are carried forward and can be deducted in future years subject to the same limitation on deductibility. IRC

§ 1212(b). The main reason for the limitation on capital losses is to prevent taxpayers from using capital losses from property transactions to wipe out or to shelter ordinary income from other sources.

A. The Mechanics of Capital Gains

The capital gain preference comes into play only if a taxpayer has a "net capital gain" for the year. IRC § 1(h). The term "net capital gain" is defined via a statutory netting mechanism in section 1222(11). This special statutory structure requires a taxpayer to aggregate all of the capital asset transactions that occur during a taxable year (first netting "long-term capital losses" against "long-term capital gains" and netting "short-term capital losses" against "short-term capital gains" and, second, netting the "net short-term capital loss" against the "net long-term capital gain"). If all of the transactions, taken together, result in a "net capital gain" for the year, then the special capital gains preference comes into play.

Net Capital Gain

NCG	=	NLTCG	–	NSTCL
§ 1222(11)		§ 1222(7)		§ 1222(6)

Net Long Term Capital Gain

NLTCG	=	LTCG	–	LTCL
1222(7)		§ 1222(3)		§ 1222(4)

Net Short Term Capital Loss

NSTCL	=	STCL	–	STCG
§ 1222(6)		§ 1222(2)		§ 1222(1)

To illustrate, consider the following example. In Year 1, Taxpayer recognized $10,000 in long-term capital gains and $5,000 in short-term capital gains. Taxpayer has no other capital gains or losses. Although Taxpayer has recognized $15,000 of capital gains, Taxpayer has a "net capital gain" of only $10,000 (the amount by which the "net long-term capital gain" ($10,000) exceeds the "net short-term capital loss" ($0)). Only the $10,000 of "net capital gain" will be taxed at a preferential rate under section 1(h). The $5,000 of "short-term capital gain" is not eligible for preferential tax treatment and will be taxed as ordinary income.

As you can see, the capital gains preference applies only if a taxpayer has a "net long-term capital gain" for the year, which is possible only if the taxpayer has a "long-term capital gain" for the year. A long-term capital gain is defined in section 1222 as gain (1) from the sale or exchange, (2) of a capital asset, (3) held for more than one year. IRC § 1222(3). The presence of each of these three factors is necessary before a recognized gain can receive preferential tax treatment. We will consider each in turn.

1. The Sale or Exchange Requirement

A taxpayer's interest in property must be terminated in a special way—a sale or exchange—in order to qualify for capital gain treatment. Like the phrase "sale or other disposition" in section 1001, the phrase sale or exchange in section 1222 has broad meaning. For example, in Helvering v. Hammel, 311 U.S. 504 (1941), the Supreme Court held that a foreclosure sale of property was a sale or exchange even though the sale did not result from the taxpayer's voluntary action. In Freeland v. Commissioner, 74 T.C. 970 (1980), the Tax Court held that the voluntary reconveyance of encumbered property to the vendor-mortgagee by a quit claim deed was a sale or exchange even though the mortgagor received no monetary consideration and was not personally liable for the non-recourse mortgage debt.

Although Congress intended the phrase "sale or exchange" to have broad meaning, it is not as broad as the meaning of "sale or other disposition" in section 1001. For example, in Helvering v. William Flaccus Oak Leather Co., 313 U.S. 247 (1941), a taxpayer's business plant was destroyed by fire and the taxpayer was compensated for the loss by insurance. The Court held that although the conversion of the plant into cash was an "other disposition" within the meaning of section 1001, it did not constitute a "sale or exchange" within the meaning of section 1222. Therefore, if property is stolen or destroyed in a casualty transaction and the taxpayer is reimbursed by insurance or otherwise, the involuntary conversion is not a sale or exchange and so it produces ordinary gain or loss unless another Code provision adds to the characterization issue.

2. The Capital Asset Requirement

A transaction must involve a "capital asset" in order to qualify for capital gain treatment. Section 1221(a) defines the term capital asset as all property held by the taxpayer (whether or not connected with a trade or business), subject to certain exceptions noted below. In short a capital asset is everything except for what it is not. As you will see, the exceptions cover many kinds of property. Thus, the definition is not as all encompassing as it first seems.

a. Inventory and Inventory-Like Property—Section 1221(a)(1)

Section 1221(a)(1) lists three categories of property specifically excluded from the definition of capital asset: (1) stock-in-trade, (2) inventory, and (3) property held by the taxpayer primarily for sale to customers in the ordinary course of a trade or business. Notice there is considerable overlap among these items—they are all inventory-type property. The purpose for excluding each is the same. Profits arising from everyday business operations should be taxed at ordinary income rates, just as wages are taxed. In contrast, profits arising from the realization of appreciation from property transactions that are not a part of the taxpayer's business operations should be taxed at lower capital gains rates for the policy reasons described in the introduction to this chapter. Malat v. Riddell, 383 U.S. 569 (1966); Corn Products Refining Co. v. Commissioner, 350 U.S. 46, 52 (1955).

Although "stock-in-trade" and "inventory" are easily identified, the catch-all phrase "property held by the taxpayer primarily for sale to customers in the ordinary course of a trade or business" is not as straightforward and has been the subject of much litigation. In *Malat v. Riddell*, the Supreme Court addressed the meaning of "primarily for sale" and held that "primarily" should be interpreted "literally" to mean "of first importance" or "principally." It is often difficult to ascertain whether a taxpayer has held property primarily for sale (not a capital asset) or primarily for investment (a capital asset). Consider a dealer in securities who recognizes gain on the sale of stock. Did the taxpayer hold the stock in his capacity as a dealer or did he hold the stock as an investor? Consider also a landowner who subdivides real property and then recognizes gain on the sale of one of the subdivided tracts. Did the seller hold the tract as a dealer or as an investor? For an example of how courts have determined the character of gains from the sale of subdivided land, read *Bynum v. Commissioner*, which is excerpted below.

b. Trade or Business Property — Section 1221(a)(2)

The second type of property excluded from the definition of capital asset is depreciable or real property used in the taxpayer's trade or business. IRC § 1221(a)(2). This exclusion is quite broad and includes land, buildings, and depreciable equipment used in a taxpayer's business. It also includes many forms of intangible property used in business, such as patents and copyrights. Section 197 intangibles used in business, although amortizable over a statutorily prescribed 15-year period, are nevertheless treated as property subject to the allowance for depreciation under section 167 and, thus, fall within the capital asset exclusion. IRC § 197(f)(7).

The capital asset exclusion for trade or business property seems overly broad until section 1231 is considered. As noted in the next chapter, section 1231 is a special characterization provision that may qualify property used in a trade or business for preferential capital gain treatment. More specifically, although depreciable and real property used in a trade or business are not capital assets under section 1221, such property may nevertheless qualify for capital gain treatment under section 1231.

c. Self-Created Property — Section 1221(a)(3)

The definition of capital asset also excludes a patent, invention, model or design, a secret formula or process, a copyright, a literary, musical, or artistic composition, and similar property held by the creator (taxpayer whose personal efforts created the property) or a taxpayer with a basis carried over from the creator. IRC § 1221(a)(3); Treas. Reg. 1.1221-1(c)(1). The purpose of treating self-created property as non-capital in the hands of its creator is consistent with taxing wages and salaries as ordinary income. Gains from personal efforts should be taxed as ordinary income just as wages and salaries are taxed as ordinary income. One should note that although patents are excluded from the definition of capital asset, a qualified holder's gain on the disposition of a patent to an unrelated person may still be eligible for capital gains treatment under section 1235, a special characterization rule discussed in Chapter 29.

Musical Compositions. It should be noted that the inventory exclusion and the self-created property exclusion do not apply to musical compositions or copyrights in musical works. *See* IRC § 1221(b)(3). As a result, songwriters get to pay capital gains tax rates, rather than higher personal income tax rates, on sales of their songs. Capital gains treatment is not available to other artists, such as novelists, painters, sculptors, and designers. Does this violate the principle of horizontal equity discussed in Chapter 1?

d. Accounts Receivable for Service or Inventory— Section 1221(a)(4)

Excluded from the capital asset definition are accounts receivable (money owed to the taxpayer for services rendered or inventory-like property sold). IRC § 1221(a)(4). Assume a cash-method taxpayer renders services worth $100 and receives a note or an account receivable instead of cash. When the cash-method taxpayer receives the note or receivable (merely a piece of paper or a journal entry on his books), the taxpayer is not required to report any income. If the taxpayer later receives a $100 payment on the note or receivable, the taxpayer must report $100 of *ordinary income* at that time. What if, instead of receiving $100 on the note and reporting ordinary income, the taxpayer sells the note for $100 to a third party. Would gain from the sale of the note be treated as capital gain? Absolutely not. Section 1221(a)(4) prevents the conversion of ordinary income into capital gain by clarifying that notes and accounts receivable for services rendered or for inventory sold are non-capital assets.

e. Federal Publications — Section 1221(a)(5)

Section 1221(a)(5) excludes from capital assets U.S. government publications received by a taxpayer without charge or at a reduced price. As noted in Chapter 20, this effectively precludes a charitable tax deduction if such items are donated to libraries or other charitable organizations. *See* IRC § 170(e) (reducing the amount of a charitable deduction by the amount of ordinary income lurking in donated property).

f. Hedging Transactions — Section 1221(a)(7)

Section 1221(a)(7) excludes from capital asset treatment certain hedging transactions (i.e., those clearly identified as such before the close of the day on which they were acquired or entered into). A hedging transaction is a transaction entered into by a taxpayer in the normal course of the taxpayer's business primarily to manage risk of price changes or currency fluctuations with respect to ordinary property held or to be held by the taxpayer or to manage the risk of interest rate or price changes or currency fluctuations with respect to loans or ordinary business obligations. IRC § 1221(b)(2).

g. Supplies Used in a Trade or Business — Section 1221(a)(8)

Supplies regularly used or consumed by the taxpayer in the taxpayer's trade or business are not capital assets. IRC § 1221(a)(8).

3. The Holding Period Requirement

The tax treatment of a capital gain depends on the property's holding period. As discussed above, only long-term capital gains are accorded preferential tax treatment. A "long-term capital gain" requires a holding period of more than one year. IRC § 1222(3). In computing the holding period, the taxpayer must disregard the day of acquisition, but may include the day of sale. Rev. Rul. 66-7, 1966-1 C.B. 188.

In certain circumstances, a taxpayer can tack on to his or her actual holding period (1) the period during which another taxpayer held the same property, or (2) the period during which he or she held other similar property. IRC § 1223(1)–(2). For example, in the case of property received by gift, the donor's previous holding period of the gifted property is tacked on to the taxpayer's actual holding period of the same property. IRC § 1223(2).

4. Special Characterization Provisions

Long-term capital gain treatment requires a sale or exchange of a capital asset held for longer than a year. If a transaction is missing one or more of these requirements, it gives rise to ordinary income unless a special characterization provision applies. There are several special characterization provisions that supply one or more of the three requirements to a transaction. For example, under section 1231 considered in the next chapter, property excluded from the definition of capital asset (trade or business property) may nevertheless be accorded capital asset status, and involuntary conversions which are not considered sales or exchanges may be accorded sale or exchange status. Under section 1235, all three requirements for long-term capital gain treatment (sale or exchange, capital asset, and requisite holding period) are supplied for transactions involving certain dispositions of patent rights. For other special characterization provisions supplying one of the three requirements, see IRC § 1223 (providing artificial holding periods for certain property); § 1241 (providing that a lessee's relinquishment of his lease may be considered an "exchange" of the lease); § 1271 (providing that retirement of a bond may be considered an "exchange" of the bond).

Congress has enacted other special characterization provisions in an attempt to clarify the character of certain assets or transactions as capital or not. Section 1236, for example, clarifies the character of stock held by a securities dealer as a capital asset or not when its actual classification may not be clear. If a dealer in securities wants securities to be characterized as capital assets, she must clearly indicate on her records on the day the securities are acquired that the securities are held for investment purposes. Section 1237 clarifies the character of land when a landowner subdivides real property and sells it. If a developer is in the business of buying land, making improvements to it, subdividing it, and selling it, he is a dealer in land. The land is inventory-like and the gain from the sale should be ordinary income. However, section

1237, when applicable, assures a taxpayer who holds property for many years and makes minimal subdivision improvements before selling it will not fall under the "dealer" category so that he can sell a certain number of lots and enjoy capital gains treatment. Note that section 1237 is of limited application and is not exclusive. Treas. Reg. § 1.1237-1(a)(4). If a taxpayer does not qualify for its benefits, he can still argue that he is an "investor" rather than a "dealer" to receive capital gain treatment.

Not all special characterization provisions are pro-taxpayer such as those described above. Several overriding characterization provisions require a transferor to recognize ordinary income even if all the elements for capital gain treatment are otherwise satisfied. For example, section 1239 mandates ordinary income treatment for any gain recognized on the sale or exchange of depreciable property to a related person. Section 1245 mandates that gain on the disposition of certain property be treated as ordinary income to the extent of the depreciation or amortization deductions taken with respect to the property. Section 1253 imposes ordinary income treatment on certain transfers of trademarks and trade names. These three special characterization rules are discussed more fully in later chapters.

5. Determining the Appropriate Capital Gains Rate on "Net Capital Gain"

If a taxpayer has a "net capital gain" in the current year, it is necessary to determine the special rate(s) at which that net capital gain is taxed. Current income tax rates on ordinary income are 10%, 12%, 22%, 24%, 32%, 35%, and 37%. By contrast, the rates on "net capital gain" are much lower—0%, 15%, or 20% in most cases (25% or 28% in special cases). The applicable rate depends on several factors, including the nature of the asset producing long-term capital gain, and the amount of the taxpayer's taxable income. There are three components to "net capital gain." Each has its own special rate.

28 Percent Rate Gain. First, part of net capital gain may be made up of "28-percent rate gain" which is taxed at a maximum rate of 28%. IRC § 1(h)(4). Twenty-eight percent rate gain includes gain from the sale of "collectibles" (e.g., artworks, rugs, antiques, metals, gems, stamps, coins, alcoholic beverages and other collectibles as defined by section 408(m)). Note that the 28% rate applies only if the taxpayer is in an ordinary bracket higher than 28% (e.g., 32%, 35%, or 37%). If a taxpayer is in a bracket lower than 28%, any 28-percent rate gain would be taxed at that lower rate just as would the taxpayer's ordinary income.

Unrecaptured Section 1250 Gain. Second, part of net capital gain may be made up of "unrecaptured section 1250 gain" which is taxed at a maximum tax rate of 25%. IRC § 1(h)(1)(D). Unrecaptured section 1250 gain is long-term capital gain attributable to depreciation allowed with respect to depreciable real estate held for more than one year. IRC § 1(h)(6). Unrecaptured section 1250 gain is taxed at 25% only if the taxpayer is in a bracket higher than 25%. If a taxpayer is in a bracket lower than 25%, any unrecaptured section 1250 gain would be taxed at that lower rate just as would the taxpayer's ordinary income.

Adjusted Net Capital Gain. Finally, any capital gain that does not fall under one of the two categories above is considered "adjusted net capital gain." IRC § 1(h)(3). Most capital gains fall within this third category. Adjusted net capital gain is taxed at a rate of 0%, 15%, or 20%, depending on the taxpayer's income level. The taxable income breakpoint between the 0% and 15% rates is $38,600 for unmarried individuals ($77,200 for joint filers). The breakpoint between the 15% and 20% rates is $425,800 for unmarried individuals ($479,000 for joint filers). IRC § 1(j)(5)(B). These breakpoints are indexed for inflation after 2018. IRC § 1(j)(5)(C). Therefore, in the case of a single taxpayer with adjusted net capital gain in 2018, to the extent the gain would not result in taxable income exceeding $38,600, such gain is taxed at 0%. To the extent the gain would result in taxable income exceeding $38,600 but not exceeding $425,800, the gain is taxed at 15%. To the extent the gain would result in taxable income exceeding $425,800, the gain is taxed at 20%.

To illustrate the mechanics of the capital gains tax rates, consider the following examples (assume Taxpayer is single and has no deductions):

Example 1. In 2018, Taxpayer has ordinary taxable income of $100,000 and a "net capital gain" of $10,000 from the sale of non-section 1202 stock. Taxpayer's "net capital gain" is not made up of "28 percent rate gain" or "unrecaptured section 1250 gain" and, therefore, is considered "adjusted net capital gain." Taxpayer's ordinary income of $100,000 is already between the 15% breakpoint of $38,600 and the 20% breakpoint of $425,800. Because the $10,000 of capital gain would not cause total taxable income to exceed $425,800, it is taxed at 15%.

Example 2. In 2018, Taxpayer has ordinary taxable income of $20,000 and a "net capital gain" of $10,000 from the sale of non-section 1202 stock. Taxpayer's ordinary income of $20,000 is below the 15% breakpoint of $38,600. Because the $10,000 of capital gain would not cause total taxable income to exceed $38,600, it is taxed at 0%.

Example 3. In 2018, Taxpayer has ordinary taxable income of $300,000 and a "net capital gain" of $20,000, made up of $10,000 gain from the sale of non-section 1202 stock and $10,000 gain from the sale of an antique. Now Taxpayer's "net capital gain" is made up of both "28 percent rate gain" and "adjusted net capital gain." With respect to the 28 percent rate gain, Taxpayer's ordinary income of $300,000 puts him in the 35% rate bracket (the ceiling of the 35% bracket is $500,000). Therefore, the 28% rate gain would be taxed at only 28%. With respect to the adjusted net capital gain, Taxpayer's ordinary income of $300,000 is between the 15% breakpoint of $38,600 and the 20% breakpoint of $425,800. Because the adjusted net capital gain would not cause taxable income to exceed $425,800, it is taxed at 15%.

B. The Mechanics of Capital Losses

You may recall that losses, both ordinary and capital, are deductible under section 165(a) if they satisfy the requirements imposed by section 165(b) and section 165(c). After determining whether a loss is deductible, one must determine the extent to which the loss may be deducted in the current year. Section 165(f) provides that the deduction of capital losses is restricted by sections 1211 and 1212. Section 1211(b) provides that capital losses (whether long-term or short-term) may be deducted to the extent of capital gains (whether long-term or short-term). To the extent capital losses exceed capital gains in a given tax year, up to $3,000 of the excess can be used to offset ordinary income in that year. Consider the following three examples:

Example 1.	Capital Losses	$5,000
	Capital Gains	$6,000
	Capital Losses Allowed	$5,000
Example 2.	Capital Losses	$5,000
	Capital Gains	$1,000
	Capital Losses Allowed	$4,000
Example 3.	Capital Losses	$5,000
	Capital Gains	$0
	Capital Losses Allowed	$3,000

Capital losses not allowed because of the section 1211(b) limitation may be carried over into subsequent tax years. IRC § 1212(b)(1). These carryover losses are treated as though they arose in the carryover year and are treated as long-term or short-term capital losses depending on their original character. If both net short-term and net long-term capital losses are not fully allowed in the current year, the Code has a cryptic device to determine which type of loss is deductible from ordinary income in the current year and which type of loss remains to be carried over. IRC § 1212(b)(2). The effect of this provision is to cause net short-term losses to be used first to offset the $3,000 of ordinary income permitted by section 1211.

Because capital losses offset capital gains and because long-term capital gains are taxed at varying special rates depending on the nature of the asset sold (e.g., 0%, 15%, or 20% for adjusted net capital gain, a maximum 25% for unrecaptured section 1250 gain, and a maximum 28% for 28-percent rate gain), it is necessary to determine which capital losses offset which long-term capital gains. Fortunately, the Code has taken a pro-taxpayer approach.

Short-term capital losses are applied to reduce short-term capital gains. Any excess (i.e., net short-term capital loss) is first applied to reduce gain taxed at 28% (i.e., 28-percent rate gain), is then applied to reduce gain taxed at 25% (i.e., unrecaptured section 1250 gain), and is finally applied to reduce gain taxed at 0%, 15% or 20% (i.e., adjusted net capital gain). IRC § 1(h)(4). As you can see, this approach maximizes the amount of net capital gain taxed at the lower capital gains rates.

In contrast to the allocation of short-term capital losses, long-term capital losses are generally allocated to their related category of long-term capital gain. Long-term capital losses from the sale of collectibles are applied to reduce any 28-percent rate gain (gain from the sale of collectibles). IRC § 1(h)(4). Long-term capital losses not resulting from the sale of collectibles will not be applied against 28-percent rate gain, but instead will be applied against adjusted net capital gain taxed at either 0%, 15%, or 20% (depending on the taxpayer's ordinary bracket).

To illustrate the mechanics of capital losses, consider the following examples:

Example 1: Allocation of Short-Term Capital Loss. In 2018, Taxpayer has ordinary income of $300,000 and a net capital gain of $11,000 as a result of three property transactions: $10,000 long-term capital gain from the sale of non-section 1202 stock; $7,000 long-term capital gain from the sale of a work of art; and $6,000 short-term capital loss from the sale of stock. The net capital gain (made up of both 28 percent rate gain and adjusted net capital gain) will receive preferential rate treatment. To determine the applicable rate(s), we must look to the character of the capital loss. The short-term capital loss ($6,000) is first applied to reduce any short-term capital gains ($0). The net-short term capital loss ($6,000) is then applied to reduce the long-term capital gains, in a particular order—first to reduce 28 percent rate gain ($7,000), then unrecaptured section 1250 gain ($0), and then adjusted net capital gain ($10,000). As a result, $1,000 of the net capital gain (28 percent rate gain) will be taxed at 28%, and $10,000 of the net capital gain (adjusted net capital gain) will be taxed at 15%.

Example 2: Allocation of Long-Term Capital Loss. Same as Example 1, above, except that instead of having a $6,000 short-term capital loss from the sale of stock, Taxpayer had a $6,000 long-term capital loss from the sale of stock. Taxpayer's net capital gain is still $11,000. To determine the applicable rates, we must look to the character of the capital loss. Long-term capital losses, in contrast to net short-term capital losses, are not automatically applied to reduce 28 percent rate gain first. Instead, long-term capital losses are allocated to long-term capital gains in the same category. As a result, the $6,000 long-term capital loss offsets $6,000 of the $10,000 of long-term capital gain from the sale of stock (and not any of the 28 percent rate gain from the sale of the collectible). In sum, $7,000 of the net capital gain (28 percent rate gain) will be taxed at 28%, and $4,000 of the net capital gain (adjusted net capital gain) will be taxed at 15%.

IV. Materials

Bynum v. Commissioner

46 T.C. 295 (1966)

FORRESTER, Judge:

Respondent has determined deficiencies in petitioners' income taxes for the calendar years 1960 and 1961 in the amounts of $4,512.68 and $3,220.02. The only issue now remaining for our decision is whether admitted gains from sales of real estate during the years in issue are taxable as ordinary income or as long-term capital gain.

FINDINGS OF FACT

Petitioners S. O. Bynum and Fannie R. Bynum are husband and wife residing in Tuscaloosa, Ala., and for the years in issue they filed their joint Federal income tax returns with the district director of internal revenue, Birmingham, Ala. In said return for 1960 they showed the sales of 12 subdivided lots in Morayshire Estates to 9 separate vendees for a total sales price of $40,075 (resulting in total gain of $28,749.78) and in their 1961 return they showed the sales of 8 similar lots to 7 separate vendees for a total sales price of $31,035 (resulting in total gain of $21,020.45). The amounts shown as the total gains in each year are not contested by respondent.

The subdivided lots sold in 1960 and 1961 were originally a part of the farm of about 113 acres which petitioners first leased in 1936. It is located on the Greensboro Road at the edge of the city of Tuscaloosa, Ala., and is approximately 3 1/2 miles from downtown Tuscaloosa. Petitioners have continuously used a portion of the tract for growing trees, plants, and shrubbery in connection with a nursery and landscaping business owned and operated by them and known as Southern Tree & Landscaping Co. Petitioners have also lived on this farm since about 1941 and have maintained an office separate from their residence on the farm since 1940 or 1941. From this office they have conducted all activities related to their nursery and landscaping business such as keeping records, preparing landscaping proposals, drawings, bids, etc.

Petitioners purchased this farm in January 1942, and although the record is not clear as to the price they paid, it indicates an allocated cost of $250 to each of the lots sold during the years in issue, and we so find.

Petitioners have had varying acreages of the farm under cultivation in connection with the nursery and landscape business; the maximum so employed being about 50 acres and the amount so employed during the years in issue being about 35 acres. Apparently none of this acreage was subdivided or sold. Also in connection with such business they maintained and used a small barn for the storage of equipment, etc., and a lattice shed of approximately 13,000 square feet for the growing of tender plants and shrubs.

Through the years and during the years in issue petitioners regularly employed 8 to 12 workmen in the nursery and landscaping business and petitioner husband personally supervised and participated in all phases of the planning and work for subject business, acting as his own foreman and superintendent and even working on Sundays a good portion of the time.

Petitioner wife apparently spent little or no time in connection with selling the subdivided lots during the years in issue and respondent does not contend otherwise. Petitioner husband spent 90 or 95 percent of his time during the years in issue in connection with the nursery and landscaping business and spent the other 5 or 10 percent in spasmodic intervals of subdividing and selling activities.

During 1960 sales of the shrubbery and landscaping business amounted to $27,435.43, which resulted in net income of $606.55. During 1961 such sales were $24,250.29, resulting in a loss of $4,321.74.

At some time prior to 1958 petitioners suffered losses in their landscaping and nursery business and began borrowing money from the City National Bank of Tuscaloosa, Ala. The record does not show how these loans were originally secured but by October 1958 they totaled $70,000 and had been questioned and partially charged off by national bank examiners. At about this same time such bank was acquired by new owners or acquired new management and the loans were combined and secured by a mortgage on the subject 113-acre farm. At the same time the bank put and continued heavy pressure upon petitioners to pay off or at least reduce such loan.

During 1959 the bank suggested that petitioners should sell the farm in order to pay off their loan and sent a prospective purchaser to talk with them. Such prospect made an offer of about $40,000 for the farm "as is" and petitioners discussed the matter with several realtors and concluded that they could not realize more than this without subdividing and improving. During the years in issue, absent petitioners' subdividing and improving activities, the farm would have had a fair market value of $450 per acre.

Late in 1959 petitioners finally decided to improve and subdivide a portion of their farm. In this connection they worked out an arrangement with the bank for partial releases from the mortgage on payments of about $2,750 for each lot sold, the average selling price of the lots, which were about six-tenths of an acre each in size, being a little under $4,000 each.

By September 1960, 38 lots had been subdivided and improved as follows:

Item	Amount
Streets	$6,117.60
Water	4,278.13
Sewerage	5,449.10
Curb, gutter, drainage	3,708.98
Other	5,210.16
Total	24,763.97

This amounted to about $650 for each of the 38 lots and to almost $1,100 per acre.

There was no further improvement or subdivision until 1962 when an additional 17 lots were similarly created at a development cost of $22,543.97, or about $1,300 for each of the 17 lots. The initial subdivision of 38 lots consumed between 20 and 25 acres of the 113-acre farm. Petitioners have purchased no additional land.

Petitioners had the formal opening of their subdivision which they called Morayshire Estates, on Sunday, September 11, 1960. It was announced by a full-page advertisement in the Graphic, a magazine-type newspaper circulated in Tuscaloosa, on September 8, 1960, and also by a full-page ad in the Sunday, Tuscaloosa News newspaper on September 11, 1960. Both of these ads advised the public to contact S. O. Bynum "or your favorite realtor." Petitioners also inserted a 2- by 5-inch advertisement regarding the subdivision in the yellow pages of the 1961 Tuscaloosa telephone directory. In the newspaper and Graphic ads both daytime and nighttime telephone numbers were given for S. O. Bynum, and the newspaper ad purported to offer 73 lots (although only 38 had then been subdivided) and announced "160 Lots to Be Developed Later."

Petitioners listed their subdivided lots with all of the reputable realtors in and around Tuscaloosa, Ala., and neither of them sought or obtained a realtor's license;

we conclude however, that all of the sales of lots during the years in issue were made by petitioner husband since no real estate commissions were paid.

OPINION

We are here concerned with the proper application of the language of two sections of the Code to the facts in this case. The sections are 1221(1) and 1231(b)(1)(B). The statutory language in the two Code sections is identical. It is, "property held by the taxpayer primarily for sale to customers in the ordinary course of his trade or business." Section 1221 is the section which defines capital assets and the above-quoted language is an exclusion from the defined class. Section 1231 sets out special rules applicable to sales of property used in taxpayers' trade or business and again the above-quoted language is an exclusion from such special rules.

Petitioners in the instant case seek long-term capital gain treatment for the profits on the sales of lots subdivided out of their farm. The question or issue for our determination under each of the above-noted sections of the Code is singular; it is whether the taxpayers during the years in issue were in the real estate business and selling property held by them primarily for sale to customers in the ordinary course of such trade or business. The burden of proof, to establish the negative of this proposition, is on petitioners, and we recognize, as we must, that the capital gain provisions, being an exception to the normal-tax rates, are to be construed narrowly. Corn Products Co. v. Commissioner, 350 U.S. 46, 52 (1955).

The Supreme Court in the recent case of Malat v. Riddell, 383 U.S. 569 (1966), vacating and remanding 347 F.2d 23 (C.A. 9, 1965), has held that where the acquisition and holding of property was for a dual purpose (either to develop for rental, or to sell) that a "substantial" purpose is not necessarily the "primary" purpose, but that the statutory word "primarily" means "of first importance" or "principally" and that "The purpose of the statutory provision with which we deal is to differentiate between the 'profits and losses arising from the everyday operation of a business' on the one hand (Corn Products Co. v. Commissioner, 350 U.S. 46, 52) and 'the realization of appreciation in value accrued over a substantial period of time' on the other. (Commissioner v. Gillette Motor Co., 364 U.S. 130, 134.)" Our considerations of the facts in the instant case have all been in the light of such teaching; however, we note at the outset that we are not dealing with such a dual purpose as concerned the Supreme Court in *Malat*, but with a change in purpose between the time the petitioners purchased this farm in 1942 and the sales at issue which occurred in 1960 and 1961.

The respondent contends only that the property here involved was being "held" by petitioners primarily for sale in the ordinary course of business at the times the sales occurred. The statutory word is "held" and the law is now well settled that no more is required. The taxpayers' purpose at the time of acquisition was evidentiary weight, but the end question is the purpose of the "holding" at the time of the sale or sales. As stated in Mauldin v. Commissioner, 195 F.2d 714, 717 (C.A. 10, 1952):

> While the purpose for which the property was acquired is of some weight,
> the ultimate question is the purpose for which it was held.... Admittedly,

Mauldin originally purchased the property for purposes other than for sale in the ordinary course of trade or business. When, however, he subdivided and offered it for sale, he was undoubtedly engaged in the vocation of selling lots from this tract of land.

See also Pool v. Commissioner, 251 F.2d 233 (C.A. 9, 1957); Kelley v. Commissioner, 281 F.2d 527 (C.A. 9, 1960).

Without any notable exceptions the many, many cases in this particular field have noted that each individual case must be considered and evaluated on its peculiar and particular facts, e.g., Kelley v. Commissioner, supra; Pool v. Commissioner, supra; Lazarus v. United States, 172 F.Supp. 421 (Ct. Cl. 1959). As stated in *Lazarus*, "Perhaps the only guiding principle of general application that can be gleaned from the judicial decisions dealing with the problem … is that every case of the type mentioned must be decided on the basis of its own facts, there being no single test that can be applied to all such cases with decisive results." For this reason we have endeavored to make our findings of fact in the instant case full and comprehensive.

Petitioners' position, of course, is that they were simply passive investors engaged in liquidating a portion of their farm to their best advantage in order to satisfy their mortgage, after having ascertained that on a single sale of the entire property they would have realized less than the existing mortgage. We cannot agree with petitioners' position since we believe it is not supported by the facts.

In 1959 petitioners were under pressure from the bank to pay off, or substantially reduce their $70,000 mortgage. They examined into their situation and concluded that an outright sale of the farm "as is" would still leave them in debt and that they would realize very much more if they improved and subdivided before selling.

To this end they spent over $1,000 per acre on the 20 or 25 acres which comprised the first subdivision of 38 lots. This amount was more than double either the allocated fair market value of such acreage or petitioners' original cost, and must be considered substantial. Cf. Wellesley A. Ayling, 32 T.C. 704.

Petitioners' position that they were trying to do just enough to get out of debt is not supported by the facts. Under their arrangement with the bank, $2,750 was paid on the mortgage for every lot sold, consequently the proceeds from 26 lots would have more than amortized the mortgage. But petitioners' efforts went far beyond this. Their initial subdivision was 38 lots, their advertising indicated that a total of 233 lots would eventually be offered, and 17 additional lots were in fact subdivided in 1962. This is not the posture of a passive investor who improved his property simply to make it more readily acceptable. W. T. Thrift, Sr., 15 T.C. 366; Wellesley A. Ayling, supra.

Nor are petitioners in the same position as the taxpayer in such cases as Fahs v. Crawford, 161 F.2d 315 (C.A. 5, 1947), and Smith v. Dunn, 224 F.2d 353 (C.A. 5, 1955), where the improving and selling activities as to the property were completely turned over to a third party under contractual arrangements which left taxpayer free of details. Petitioners here personally conducted all phases of the considerable improving, subdividing, and promotional activities, and the record indicates that petitioner husband personally made each of the sales we are considering during the 2 years before us. The fact that the subdivided lots were "listed for sale" with various local realtors is of little moment when considered against this background. Petitioners urge that petitioner husband continued to spend 90 to 95 percent of this time on the nursery and landscaping business, only devoting the remaining 5 to 10 percent to all the above activities. We do not doubt that petitioner husband remained in the nursery and landscaping business during 1960 and 1961, but we are convinced, from all the facts of record, that during these years he had entered into, and was actively engaged in, a second business—that of selling the subdivided lots from petitioners' farm— and that such property was then held by petitioners primarily and principally for sale to customers in the ordinary course of that business, and that this purpose was of first importance to petitioners. See Morris W. Zack, 25 T.C. 676, 680–681, affd. 245 F.2d 235 (C.A. 6, 1957).

> The purchase and sale of the hoists was not a part of any other business reg-ularly carried on by Zack, but it has long been recognized that a taxpayer may be engaged in several businesses. The question is whether Zack and his associates were selling the bomb hoists in the ordinary course of a business carried on by them. The only purpose in buying the bomb hoists was to resell them at a higher price. There was no "investment" such as might be made in other types of property, but on the contrary there was a general public offering and sales in such a manner that the exclusion of the statute cannot be denied. The activities amounted to the carrying on of a business of selling the bomb hoists and the sales were to customers in the ordinary course of that business.

See also Oliver v. Commissioner, 138 F.2d 910 (C.A. 4, 1943).

That this purpose had become of first importance to petitioners is confirmed by the more extensive (as to each individual lot) improvement activities engaged in in 1962 when the expenditures as to each of the 17 lots then subdivided amounted to $1,300 as against the $650 spent on each of the first 38 lots. In our view, petitioners were engaging in the business of adding extensive improvements to real estate, and then selling those improvements at a profit. Cf. Morris W. Zack, supra.

The record facts indicate that the value of the raw land of petitioners' farm had appreciated very little since 1942, such appreciation amounting to about $35 per acre, yet the gain on the approximately 13 acres sold during the years at issue amounted to almost $4,000 per acre. We cannot believe that gain of this character was contemplated by the Supreme Court in Commissioner v. Gillette Motor Co., 364 U.S. 130 (1960), when it said at page 134:

> This Court has long held that the term "capital asset" is to be construed narrowly in accordance with the purpose of Congress to afford capital-gains treatment only in situations typically involving the realization of appreciation in value accrued over a substantial period of time, and thus to ameliorate the hardship of taxation of the entire gain in one year. Burnet v. Harmel, 287 U.S. 103, 106.

We do believe that the gain here was generated by petitioners' actions and activities with regard to this property, and as such, it is taxable as ordinary income.

Reviewed by the Court.

Decision will be entered for the respondent.

Williams v. McGowan

152 F.2d 570 (2d Cir. 1945)

L. Hand, Circuit Judge.

This is an appeal from a judgment dismissing the complaint in an action by a taxpayer to recover income taxes paid for the year 1940.

Williams, the taxpayer, and one, Reynolds, had for many years been engaged in the hardware business in the City of Corning, New York. On the 20th of January, 1926, they formed a partnership, of which Williams was entitled to two-thirds of the profits, and Reynolds, one-third. They agreed that on February 1, 1925, the capital invested in the business had been $118,082.05, of which Reynolds had a credit of $29,029.03, and Williams, the balance—$89,053.02. At the end of every business year, on February 1st, Reynolds was to pay to Williams, interest upon the amount of the difference between his share of the capital and one-third of the total as shown by the inventory; and upon withdrawal of one party the other was to have the privilege of buying the other's interest as it appeared on the books. The business was carried on through the firm's fiscal year, ending January 31, 1940, in accordance with this agreement, and thereafter until Reynolds' death on July 18th of that year. Williams settled with Reynolds' executrix on September 6th in an agreement by which he promised to pay her $12,187.90, and to assume all liabilities of the business; and he did pay her $2,187.98 in cash at once, and $10,000 on the 10th of the following October. On September 17th of the same year, Williams sold the business as a whole to the Corning Building Company for $63,926.28—its agreed value as of February 1, 1940—"plus an amount to be computed by multiplying the gross sales of the business from the first day of February, 1940 to the 28th day of September, 1940," by an agreed fraction. This value was made up of cash of about $8,100, receivables of about $7,000, fixtures of about $800, and a merchandise inventory of about $49,000, less some $1,000 for bills payable. To this was added about $6,000 credited to Williams for profits under the language just quoted, making a total of nearly $70,000. Upon this sale Williams suffered a loss upon his original two-thirds of the business but he made a small gain upon the one-third which he had bought from Reynolds' executrix; and in his income tax return he entered both as items of "ordinary income," and not as transactions in "capital assets." This the Commissioner disallowed and recomputed the tax accordingly; Williams paid the deficiency and sued to recover it in this action. The only question is whether the business was "capital assets" under section 117(a)(1) of the Internal Revenue Code [the predecessor of section 1221].

It has been held that a partner's interest in a going firm is for tax purposes to be regarded as a "capital asset." Stilgenbaur v. United States, 9 Cir., 115 F.2d 283; Commissioner v. Shapiro, 6 Cir., 125 F.2d 532. We too accepted the doctrine in McClellan v. Commissioner, 2 Cir., 117 F.2d 988, although we had held the opposite in Helvering v. Smith, 2 Cir., 90 F.2d 590, 591, where the partnership articles had provided that a retiring partner should receive as his share only his percentage of the sums "actually collected" and "of all earnings for services performed." Such a payment, we thought, was income; and we expressly repudiated the notion that the Uniform Partnership Act had, generally speaking, changed the firm into a juristic entity. See also Doyle v. Commissioner, 4 Cir., 102 F.2d 86. If a partner's interest in a going firm is "capital assets" perhaps a dead partner's interest is the same. New York Partnership Law §§ 61, 62(4), Consol. Laws N.Y. c. 39. We need not say. When Williams bought out Reynolds' interest, he became the sole owner of the business, the firm had ended upon any theory, and the situation for tax purposes was no other than if Reynolds had never been a partner at all, except that to the extent of one-third of the "amount realized" on Williams' sale to the Corning Company, his "basis" was different. The judge thought that, because upon that sale both parties fixed the price at the liquidation value of the business while Reynolds was alive, "plus" its estimated earnings thereafter, it was as though Williams had sold his interest in the firm during its existence. But the method by which the parties agreed upon the price was irrelevant to the computation of Williams' income. The Treasury, if that served its interest, need not heed any fiction which the parties found it convenient to adopt; nor need Williams do the same in his dealings with the Treasury. We have to decide only whether upon the sale of a going business it is to be comminuted into its fragments, and these are to be separately matched against the definition in § 117(a)(1), or whether the whole business is to be treated as if it were a single piece of property.

Our law has been sparing in the creation of juristic entities; it has never, for example, taken over the Roman "universitas facti"; and indeed for many years it fumbled uncertainly with the concept of a corporation. One might have supposed that partnership would have been an especially promising field in which to raise up an entity, particularly since merchants have always kept their accounts upon that basis. Yet there too our law resisted at the price of great continuing confusion; and, even when it might be thought that a statute admitted, if it did not demand, recognition of the firm as an entity, the old concepts prevailed. Francis v. McNeal, 228 U.S. 695. And so, even though we might agree that under the influence of the Uniform Partnership Act a partner's interest in the firm should be treated as indivisible, and for that reason a "capital asset" within § 117(a)(1), we should be chary about extending further so exotic a jural concept. Be that as it may, in this instance the section itself furnishes the answer. It starts in the broadest way by declaring that all "property" is "capital assets," and then makes three exceptions. The first is "stock in trade ... or other property of a kind which would properly be included in the inventory"; next comes "property held ... primarily for sale to customers"; and finally, property "used in the trade or business of a character which is subject to ... allowance for depreciation." In the face of this language, although it may be true that a "stock in trade," taken by itself, should be treated as a "universitas facti," by no possibility can a whole business be so treated; and the same is true as to any property within the other exceptions. Congress plainly did mean to comminute the elements of a business; plainly it did not regard the whole as "capital assets."

As has already appeared, Williams transferred to the Corning Company "cash," "receivables," "fixtures" and a "merchandise inventory." "Fixtures" are not capital because they are subject to a depreciation allowance; the inventory, as we have just seen, is expressly excluded. So far as appears, no allowance was made for "goodwill"; but, even if there had been, we held in Haberle Crystal Springs Brewing Company v. Clarke, Collector, 2 Cir., 30 F.2d 219, that "good-will" was a depreciable intangible. It is true that the Supreme Court reversed that judgment — 280 U.S. 384 — but it based its decision only upon the fact that there could be no allowance for the depreciation of "good-will" in a brewery, a business condemned by the Eighteenth Amendment. There can of course be no gain or loss in the transfer of cash; and, although Williams does appear to have made a gain of $1,072.71 upon the "receivables," the point has not been argued that they are not subject to a depreciation allowance. That we leave open for decision by the district court, if the parties cannot agree. The gain or loss upon every other item should be computed as an item in ordinary income.

Judgment REVERSED.

V. Related Matters

- **Qualified Dividends.** Prior to 2003, dividends were taxed at ordinary rates. Since 2003, qualified dividends have been taxed at capital gains rates. Thus, qualified dividends are taxed at either 0%, 15%, or 20% depending on the taxpayer's income level. IRC § 1(j)(5). To receive this special treatment, the dividends received must be with respect to stock held for at least 61 days during a prescribed period. IRC § 1(h)(11)(A)–(B). It should be noted that although qualified dividends are taxed at capital gains rates, they are not characterized as capital gains. Therefore, dividends cannot be used to offset capital losses.

- **Characterization Dependent on Prior Tax Treatment.** The character of a gain or loss may be dictated by the taxpayer's prior treatment of a related gain or loss. In Arrowsmith v. Commissioner, 344 U.S. 6 (1952), the taxpayer properly reported *capital gain* upon liquidation of a corporation. Four years later, the taxpayer paid a judgment against the company and claimed an *ordinary loss* deduction since payment of the debt did not constitute a "sale or exchange." The Supreme Court held that the loss was capital subject to capital loss limitation rules. If payment of the judgment had been made at liquidation, the losses would have been capital. The losses could not be characterized as ordinary merely because the transaction covered more than one year. This is known as the *Arrowsmith* doctrine.

- **Virtual Currency and Characterization**. Virtual currency is a recently invented digital medium of exchange. "Bitcoin is one example of a convertible virtual currency. Bitcoin can be digitally traded between users and can be purchased for, or exchanged into, U.S. dollars, Euros, and other real or virtual currencies." Notice 2014-21, 2014-16 IRB 938. One issue concerning this currency is whether it is property for purposes of gain and loss recognition under the Code. The IRS has answered that question in the affirmative. *See id.* at Q&A 6. This means, for example, that a person who buys a Bitcoin when it was worth $100 and spends it when it is worth $150 would have $50 of gross income when he or she spends the Bitcoin. The character of that gain or loss is determined under the same rules as for any other property. Thus, an investor in Bitcoins could have a capital gain or loss while a dealer in Bitcoins could have an ordinary gain or loss. *Id.* at Q&A 7.

- **Net Investment Income Tax**. Section 1411 imposes a "net investment income tax" at a rate of 3.8% on certain net investment income of individuals, estates and trusts that have income above applicable threshold amounts. In general investment income includes interest, dividends, rents, royalties, and capital gains (not otherwise offset by capital losses). Individuals will owe the tax if they have modified adjusted gross income over the following thresholds: $250,000 for married filing jointly and for qualifying widow(er)s with dependent child; $125,000 for married filing separately; and $200,000 for single taxpayers and heads of households. These amounts are not indexed for inflation.

Chapter 18

Quasi-Capital Assets

I. Assignment

Read: Internal Revenue Code: § 1231. Skim §§ 1(h); 165(a)–(c); 1211(b); 1221(a)(2); 1222.

Treasury Regulations: § 1.1231-1(d).

Text: Overview
Wasnok v. Commissioner
Related Matters

Complete the problems.

II. Problems

1. Poseidon is in the business of catching and selling lobster on the Maine coast. In the current year, Poseidon sold a parcel of land used in his business for $115,000; he paid $100,000 for the land four years ago. Poseidon also sustained an uninsured loss as a result of the theft of his lobster boat that he used in his business for three years; at the time of theft, the boat had an adjusted basis of $10,000 and a value of $15,000.

   (a) What are the tax consequences of the land sale and boat loss?

   (b) Same as (a) except that, in addition to the land sale and boat loss, Poseidon had a $20,000 gain as a result of collecting insurance proceeds when his building, used for several years to store lobster traps, was destroyed in a fire.

   (c) Same as (a) except that, in addition to the land sale and boat loss, Poseidon had a $20,000 loss as a result of the condemnation of his building, used for several years to store lobster traps.

   (d) Same as (a) except that one year before the current tax year, Poseidon had a $5,000 "net section 1231 loss."

2. Nathaniel Hawthorne, who was employed as a salesman, inherited a one-family house from his mother fourteen years ago. At the time of her death, the house had been rented to the same tenant for some years, who thereafter continued to occupy the house and pay rent to Nathaniel. Nathaniel provided, either by himself or through an agent, necessary upkeep and repair for the maintenance of the house (e.g., several years ago, Nathaniel installed a furnace on which he took depreciation). In the current year, Nathaniel realized a $10,000 loss on the sale of

the house. This was the only real estate sale he was ever involved in. Nathaniel had no other capital gains or losses during the year. What are the tax consequences of the sale?

III. Overview

Under general tax principles, capital gain and loss treatment requires a sale or exchange of a capital asset. If a transaction does not constitute a sale or exchange or if a transaction does not involve a capital asset, the transaction will give rise to ordinary income or loss unless a special characterization provision applies to supply the missing requirement. Section 1231, the subject of this chapter, is a prime example of such a special characterization provision. Section 1231 operates on certain transactions that are not already characterized under general tax principles covered in the previous chapter. In general, property excluded from the definition of capital asset (i.e., trade or business property) may be accorded capital asset status. Likewise, transactions that do not rise to the level of a "sale or exchange" (i.e., thefts and casualties of property) may be accorded sale or exchange status.

A. Transactions to Which Section 1231 Applies

Section 1231 applies to only two types of transactions. The first transaction to which section 1231 applies is the *sale or exchange* of "property used in the trade or business." IRC § 1231(a)(3)(A)(i). The phrase "property used in the trade or business" includes depreciable business property held for more than one year or real property used in business that has been held more than one year. IRC § 1231(b)(1). The phrase specifically excludes (1) inventory, (2) property held by the taxpayer primarily for sale to customers in the ordinary course of his trade or business, and (3) copyrights, literary, musical, or artistic compositions, or similar property if held by the creator or a taxpayer with a basis carried over from the creator. IRC § 1231(b)(1)(A)–(C). The property types covered by section 1231 are commonly referred to as "quasi-capital assets." It should be noted that in referring to property subject to the allowance for depreciation, section 1231 embraces property that is not considered a capital asset under section 1221(a)(2). Intangibles amortizable under section 197 are also eligible for section 1231 treatment because such assets are treated as property subject to the allowance for depreciation under section 167. IRC § 197(f)(7). Read *Wasnok v. Commissioner*, included below, which dealt with whether property was a capital asset under section 1221 (used for the production of income) or a quasi-capital asset under section 1231 (used in the taxpayer's trade or business). Do you agree with the court?

The second transaction to which section 1231 applies is the *involuntary or compulsory conversion* of (1) property used in the trade or business held for more than one year or (2) capital assets held for more than one year in connection with a trade or business or a transaction entered into for profit. IRC § 1231(a)(3)(A)(ii). Involuntary conversions include loss or destruction of property from casualties and thefts.

Compulsory conversions arise primarily through governmental processes such as condemnation or eminent domain.

B. The Mechanics of Section 1231

The operation of section 1231 requires a taxpayer to place in an imaginary basket (commonly known as the "principal hotchpot") all "section 1231 gains" and "section 1231 losses" that occur during the year and to net those gains and losses to determine their overall character. If the taxpayer's section 1231 gains exceed section 1231 losses, all gains and losses are treated as long-term capital gains and losses. IRC § 1231(a)(1). On the other hand, if the taxpayer's section 1231 losses equal or exceed section 1231 gains, then all such gains and losses are ordinary. IRC § 1231(a)(2). This treatment gives the taxpayer the best of both worlds. Gains may be characterized as capital gains and losses may be characterized as ordinary losses.

It should be noted that a special rule provides that gains and losses from involuntary conversions (e.g., fire or storm losses) are not subject to section 1231 if the total involuntary losses exceed the involuntary gains. IRC § 1231(a)(4)(C). To apply the rule, those section 1231 gains and section 1231 losses arising from involuntary conversions (as opposed to compulsory conversions, such as condemnations) must first be placed in a preliminary basket (commonly known as the preliminary hotchpot or "fire" pot). If the involuntary losses for the year exceed the involuntary gains for the year, then the losses and gains are treated as ordinary. If, however, the involuntary gains equal or exceed the involuntary losses, then the involuntary gains and losses drop down into the principal hotchpot for netting with all other section 1231 gains and section 1231 losses. This too is a pro-taxpayer rule, permitting casualty losses to remain characterized as ordinary losses while permitting section 1231 gains in the same year to be characterized as capital gains.

To illustrate the pro-taxpayer nature of section 1231, consider the following examples:

Example 1. Eight years ago, Jane purchased Blackacre for $100,000 to use in her trade or business. This year, Jane sells Blackacre for $115,000. Jane clearly has $15,000 of gain realized and recognized, but what is the character of this gain? Jane hopes for long-term capital gain treatment since such gains are taxed at lower rates. To receive long-term capital gain treatment, the gain must be from: (1) the sale or exchange, (2) of a capital asset, (3) held for more than one year. IRC § 1222(3). Although there has been a sale of real property held for more than one year, the property is excluded from the definition of "capital asset" by section 1221(a)(2). Therefore, it seems that the $15,000 gain will be treated as ordinary income taxed at high rates. But wait! Section 1231 may add to the characterization issue. Do we have a "section 1231 gain"? Yes. We have gain from the sale or exchange of real property used in Jane's business that has been held for more than one year. IRC §§ 1231(a)(3)(A)(i), (b). Does that mean that the $15,000 gain is automatically treated as long-term capital gain? Not yet. Since the section 1231 gain was not from an involuntary conversion, we must place the $15,000 section 1231 gain in the principal hotchpot to be netted with other section 1231 gains and losses that may have occurred during the year. Assuming that this was Jane's only section 1231 transaction that occurred during the year, the character would be long-term capital gain because the section 1231 gains for the year ($15,000) exceed the section 1231 losses ($0) for the year. IRC §1231(a)(1). Assuming no other capital gain or loss transactions during the year, Jane would have a net capital gain of $15,000 taxed at preferential rates. IRC §1(h). Section 1231 worked its magic!

Example 2. Assume the same facts as above except that Jane sells Blackacre this year for $85,000 instead of $115,000. Jane has realized a loss of $15,000. The next issue is whether the loss is deductible (who cares about the character of a loss if it is not even deductible). The loss would be deductible under section 165(a) because it was incurred in a trade or business. IRC §165(c). Now that we know it's deductible, the next issue is whether it is an ordinary loss or capital loss. Jane would prefer ordinary loss treatment due to the capital loss limitation rule in section 1211(b). It looks like the loss is ordinary because Blackacre is not a capital asset as defined in section 1221. But wait! The loss is a section 1231 loss as defined in section 1231(a)(3)(B). So to determine its ultimate character, we must toss the section 1231 loss into the principal hotchpot to net with other section 1231 gains and losses that may have occurred during the year (we do not place the loss in the fire pot for preliminary netting since the loss did not result from an involuntary conversion). Assuming the sale of Blackacre was the only section 1231 transaction for the tax year, the $15,000 loss would come out of the basket as an ordinary loss (section 1231 gains ($0) did not exceed section 1231 losses ($15,000)). IRC §1231(a)(2). Section 1231 again worked its magic!

Example 3. Assume the facts as in Example 1 (i.e., Jane has a $15,000 section 1231 gain in the current year). Assume also that in the current year Jane realized an uninsured $10,000 loss from a storm that damaged property she used in her trade or business for over a year. What is the character of the $10,000 loss? The loss would appear to be an ordinary loss since two elements for capital loss treatment (sale or exchange and capital asset) are not met. IRC §1222 (4)(defining long-term capital loss). But wait! The loss is clearly a section 1231 loss as defined in section 1231(a)(3)(B). Because the section 1231 loss resulted from a storm, we must place it in the preliminary hotchpot. Assuming no other property transactions during the year, we must net the preliminary hotchpot first. Because involuntary losses ($10,000) exceed involuntary gains ($0) for the year, the involuntary loss is not subject to section 1231 (does not drop into the principal hotchpot for netting with the $15,000 section 1231 gain) and is characterized as ordinary loss under general tax principles. We can then net the principal hotchpot to determine the character of the $15,000 section 1231 gain that resulted from the sale of real property. Because the section 1231 gains ($15,000) exceed the section 1231 losses ($0) for the year, the section 1231 gain will be characterized as long-term capital gain. Jane got what she wanted. Under section 1231, the $10,000 loss is treated as ordinary and is deductible in full, and the $15,000 gain is treated as long-term capital gain and is taxed at low rates.

To recap, these three examples illustrate the pro-taxpayer nature of section 1231. In Example 1, gain on the disposition of Blackacre would, but for section 1231, be ordinary gain. Under section 1231, however, gain on the sale of Blackacre was characterized as long-term capital gain. In Example 2, loss on the disposition of Blackacre would, but for section 1231, be ordinary loss. Under section 1231, the loss remained ordinary. In Example 3, but for section 1231, the gain and loss would both be ordinary. Under section 1231, only the loss remained ordinary but the gain became long-term capital gain.

You're probably wondering why section 1231 was structured to provide taxpayers with the best of both worlds. Section 1231 was enacted as a relief provision in 1942 during World War II. Following the depression in the late 1930s, Congress enacted section 1221(a)(2), which excluded trade or business property from the definition of capital asset, to give taxpayers ordinary loss treatment on the sale of trade or business property that had declined in value. The enactment of section 1221(a)(2), however, simultaneously eliminated capital gain treatment for business property that had increased in value. As a result, during World War II, when tax rates were quite high, taxpayers in the shipping industry realized substantial gains when the government requisitioned vessels for use in battle or when ships were destroyed in battle. Viewing it as inappropriate to tax such war-related gains as ordinary income, Congress enacted section 1231 to provide relief. Do you believe justification still exists for section 1231?

C. Recapture of "Net Ordinary Loss"

Suppose a taxpayer wants to sell two assets he has owned and used in his trade or business for over a year, Blackacre (with a lurking loss of $5,000) and Whiteacre (with a lurking gain of $20,000). If the taxpayer were to sell both assets in the same year, he would recognize a $5,000 section 1231 loss and a $20,000 section 1231 gain. After applying section 1231(a)(1), the $5,000 loss would be characterized as long-term capital loss and the $20,000 gain would be characterized as long-term capital gain, for a net long-term capital gain of $15,000. If, however, the taxpayer were to sell Blackacre this year and Whiteacre next year, the tax results would be more favorable. He would have a $5,000 ordinary loss this year (because section 1231 losses would exceed section 1231 gains) and he would have a $20,000 long-term capital gain next year (because section 1231 gains would exceed section 1231 losses). Does it seem fair that a taxpayer can play this game? Congress doesn't think so, and enacted section 1231(c) as a response.

Under section 1231(c), if a taxpayer's section 1231 gains exceed his section 1231 losses for a year, the excess (referred to "net section 1231 gain") must be recaptured and treated as ordinary income to the extent of any "net section 1231 losses" from the preceding five years which have not previously been recaptured. Going back to the example above, if the taxpayer were to sell Blackacre in Year 1 and Whiteacre in Year 2, he would have a net section 1231 loss of $5,000 in Year 1 and a net section 1231 gain of $20,000 in Year 2. Under section 1231(c), the net section 1231 gain of $20,000 for Year 2 would be treated as ordinary income to the extent of the $5,000 nonrecaptured net section 1231 loss in Year 1 (let's assume there were no other net ordinary losses in prior years). The remaining $15,000 of gain in Year 2 would be treated as long-term capital gain. The effect of this recapture is to limit the taxpayer's long-term capital gain in Year 2 to $15,000, which would have been the net long-term capital gain if he sold both Blackacre and Whiteacre in the same year. Query: Could the taxpayer still play the game by selling Whiteacre in Year 1 and Blackacre in Year 2?

D. Summary

There are four steps potentially involved in the application of section 1231 summarized in the chart below:

Section 1231 Checklist

1. Determine if there is a section 1231 transaction:

    i.   A sale or exchange of property used in the trade or business, or

    ii. An involuntary or compulsory conversion of property used in the trade or business or of a capital asset held for more than 1 year in connection with a trade or business or a transaction entered into for profit.

2. Apply the section 1231(a)(4)(C) fire pot rules to gains and losses from involuntary conversions.

3. Apply the principal hotchpot rules of section 1231(a)(1)–(2).

4. Apply the recapture rules of section 1231(c).

IV. Materials

Wasnok v. Commissioner

30 T.C.M. (CCH) 39 (1971)

SACKS, COMMISSIONER: Respondent determined deficiencies in the income tax of petitioners for the taxable years and in the amounts set forth below:

Petitioner	Taxable Year	Amount
Stephen P. Wasnok	1967	$195.70
Mary Alice Wasnok	1967	158.66
Stephen P. and Mary Alice Wasnok	1968	54.46

The sole issue for decision is whether petitioners' disposition of certain real property at a loss constitutes an ordinary loss fully deductible in 1965, the year in which the loss was sustained, or a capital loss, deductible as a loss carryover in 1967 and 1968.

FINDINGS OF FACTS

Stephen P. and Mary Alice Wasnok, sometimes hereinafter referred to as petitioners or as Stephen and Mary, are husband and wife who resided in Fullerton, California at the time of the filing of their petition herein. Their separate income tax returns for the taxable year 1967 and their joint income tax return for the taxable year 1968 were filed with the district director of internal revenue, Los Angeles, California.

In 1960 petitioners were residing in Cincinnati, Ohio. Sometime during that year they purchased a home there located at 5654 Sagecrest Drive, hereinafter referred to as the Sagecrest property. A substantial portion of the purchase price of this property was borrowed on a promissory note secured by a first mortgage on the property from Spring Grove Avenue Loan and Deposit Company (hereinafter referred to as Spring Grove Loan Co.).

Early in 1961 petitioners decided to move to California. They listed the Sagecrest property with its builder for sale, but without result since the market at the time was extremely poor. Finally, on June 15, 1961 petitioners leased the property for a monthly rental of $225.00 and thereafter departed for California.

Between June 15, 1961 and May 7, 1965 petitioners leased the Sagecrest property to various tenants at an average rental of $200.00 per month. Such tenants were located by advertising the property for rent in Cincinnati newspapers and by referrals from former neighbors. During this period petitioners on two occasions listed the property for sale with brokers, in each case, however, for only a ninety day period of time. Neither listing generated an offer for more than the amount due on the mortgage.

By 1965 petitioners found themselves unable to continue payments due on their note on the Sagecrest property to Spring Grove Loan Co. Spring Grove thereafter notified petitioners that they would either have to deed the property back or the company would have to institute foreclosure proceedings. On May 7, 1965 petitioners executed a deed conveying their interest in the Sagecrest property to Spring Grove Loan Co. in satisfaction of the then balance due on their note in the amount of $24,421.04.

For the taxable years 1961 through 1964 petitioners filed federal income tax returns reporting thereon rental income and claiming various expenses, including depreciation, on the Sagecrest property. Their return for 1961 was examined by the Internal Revenue Service and the cost basis of the land and improvements was agreed upon in the amount of $32,729.70. Total depreciation on the improvements claimed and allowed for the taxable years 1961 through 1964 was $4,697.42.

Petitioners did not file federal income tax returns for the taxable years 1965 and 1966 on the premise that no returns were required because no tax appeared to be due. For 1965, however, petitioners had gross income in the amount of $5,603.21 and for 1966, in the amount of $3,180.00.

On their separate returns for the taxable year 1967, petitioners for the first time each claimed a capital loss carry-forward deduction in the amount of $1,000.00 which was predicated upon their disposition in 1965 of the Sagecrest property to Spring Grove Loan Co. Thereafter, on their joint return for 1968, petitioners claimed a further capital loss carry-forward deduction of $389.00, computed as follows:

Cost of Sagecrest property	$32,729.70
Less: depreciation taken	4,697.42
Adjusted basis	$28,032.28
Sale on May 7, 1965	24,421.04
Capital loss	$3,611.24
Claimed in 1967 (separate return)	2,000.00
Sub-total	$1,611.24
Claimed in 1968	389.00
Balance to carry-over	**$1,222.24**

In his notices of deficiency, respondent disallowed to petitioners the claimed capital loss carry-over deductions for the taxable years 1967 and 1968 on the ground that the loss involved was an ordinary loss deductible in the year sustained (1965) rather than a capital loss subject to the carry-over provisions of the Internal Revenue Code of 1954.

Petitioners' disposition of the Sagecrest property at a loss constitutes an ordinary loss fully deductible in 1965, the year in which the loss was sustained and not a capital loss.

OPINION

It is petitioners' position herein that the Sagecrest property was a capital asset in their hands, and that its disposition at a loss resulted in a capital loss which they properly deferred deducting on their returns until 1967 and 1968 when they had sufficient income to file returns.

Respondent contends that the property in question was not a capital asset in petitioners' hands, but an asset of the type described in section 1231 of the Code losses upon the disposition of which are ordinary in nature and required to be deducted, to the extent that there is gross income, in the year in which sustained. Since petitioners' gross income in 1965 was more than sufficient to absorb the loss in that year, no deduction of any kind is allowable in the years here at issue.

Section 1221 of the Code defines the term "capital asset" as any property held by the taxpayer, *excluding however*, "property used in his trade or business, of a character which is subject to the allowance for depreciation ... or real property used in his trade or business." With respect to "property used in the trade or business" of a taxpayer, section 1231 provides that while net gains on sales or exchanges of such property shall be treated as capital gains, net losses are not to be treated as capital losses, but as ordinary losses.

The evidence presented to the Court is not complex. Simply stated, it shows that when petitioners moved from Ohio to California in 1961 they could not sell their residence in Ohio and therefore rented it to various tenants until May, 1965, when it was deeded back to the mortgagee because petitioners could no longer make the mortgage payments and did not desire the mortgagee to foreclose. It further shows that during the period 1961 through 1964 petitioners received rents of about two hundred dollars per month except for brief periods when the property was vacant.

Their return for 1961 was examined by respondent and the tax basis for the property agreed upon. Depreciation was claimed on the improvements during the period 1961 to 1964 and, after reducing basis by the amount of depreciation claimed, the difference between the adjusted basis and mortgage balance produced a loss of $3,611.24.

In our view petitioners' activity in renting out the Sagecrest property for a fairly continuous period of four years between 1961 and 1965, at a substantial rental, together with the concurrent claiming on their income tax returns for these years of the expenses incurred in such rental activity, including depreciation, establishes the use of such property in a "trade or business." Leland Hazard, 7 T.C. 372 (1946).

We therefore find that the property in question was not a capital asset in petitioners' hands at the time of its disposition, but an asset of the kind described in section 1231. The loss sustained on the disposition of such an asset is an ordinary loss. Since such loss was sustained in 1965, when petitioners had gross income sufficient to entirely absorb it, no loss is allowable to petitioners in either 1967 or 1968.

Reviewed and adopted as the report of the Small Tax Case Division.

Decision will be entered for respondent.

V. Related Matters

- **Other Special Characterization Rules.** Like section 1231, there are other special characterization provisions in the Code that clarify the classification of certain gains and losses. *See, e.g.*, IRC § 1234 (determining the character of an option to buy property by reference to the character of the property subject to the option); § 1235 (supplying all three requirements for long-term capital gain treatment — sale or exchange, capital asset, and requisite holding period — for transactions involving certain dispositions of patent rights); § 1236 (clarifying the status of a security as a capital asset or not); § 1237 (providing limited capital gain assurance to land developers provided they make minimal subdivision improvements); § 1241 (providing that a lessee's relinquishment of his lease may be considered an "exchange" of the lease); § 1253 (providing that a transfer of a franchise, trademark, or trade name shall not be considered a "sale or exchange" if the transferor retains any significant power, right, or continuing interest in the property); § 1271 (providing that retirement of a bond may be considered an "exchange" of the bond).

- **Above the Line.** Section 62(a)(1) allows an above the line deduction for losses attributable to property held in connection with a trade or business. Section 62(a)(3) allows an above the line deduction for losses from the sale or exchange of property. And section 62(a)(4) allows an above the line deduction for losses attributable to property held for the production of rent. Don't forget, however, the capital loss limitation of section 1211, discussed in the previous chapter.

Chapter 19

Recapture of Depreciation

I. Assignment

Read: Internal Revenue Code: §§ 64; 179(d)(10); 1239(a), (b)(1), (c); 1245(a)(1)–(3), (b)(1)–(2), (c), (d); Skim §§ 1(h)(1), (3), (6); 267(b)–(c); 1250(a)(1)(A), (a)(1)(B)(v), (b)(1), (b)(3), (b)(5), (c); (d)(1)–(2), (g), (h).

Treasury Regulations: §§ 1.179-1(e); 1.1245-1(a)(1), (b), (c)(1), (d), -2(a)(1), (3), (6), (7).

Text: Overview
Revenue Ruling 69-487
Related Matters

Complete the problems.

II. Problems

1. Charlie Allnut, a calendar-year taxpayer, owns a piece of equipment that he uses solely in his business. Charlie paid $100,000 for the equipment, and has fully depreciated it under section 168.

    (a) What result to Charlie if he later sells the equipment to Buyer for $110,000?

    (b) Same as (a) except that Charlie gives the equipment to his daughter, and she immediately sells the equipment for $110,000.

    (c) Same as (a) except that Charlie takes the equipment home and converts it from business use to personal use.

    (d) Same as (a) except that Charlie sells the equipment to his spouse, Rosie.

2. In Year 1, Richmond Lamb purchased a parcel of commercial property at a cost of $1,500,000, of which $1,000,000 was properly allocated to the building and $500,000 was properly allocated to the land. In Year 3, Richmond sold the property for $2,000,000, of which $1,300,000 was properly allocated to the building and $700,000 was properly allocated to the land. During Years 1–3, Richmond properly claimed $75,000 of depreciation with respect to the building. What are the tax consequences to Richmond on the sale of the property?

III. Overview

In the last chapter, we studied our first recapture provision, section 1231(c), which transforms certain long-term capital gains into ordinary income. This chapter considers depreciation recapture provisions—principally section 1245 pertaining to depreciable personal property and section 1250 pertaining to depreciable real property.

A. Recapture under Section 1245 for Certain Depreciable Property

1. An Overview

The general concept of depreciation recapture is simple. Gain recognized on the disposition of depreciable property should be recaptured and characterized as ordinary income to the extent the gain is attributable to depreciation deductions previously taken with respect to the property. Indeed, this is the result achieved by section 1245, which overrides the characterization rules addressed in the last two chapters. IRC § 1245(d). Section 1245 is necessary to prevent taxpayers from receiving a windfall with respect to depreciable property—that is, taking ordinary depreciation deductions in early years (in most cases accelerated deductions producing large tax benefits for the taxpayer), and then claiming preferential capital gains treatment on later sale of the property.

Example. In Year 1, Taxpayer acquired a machine, to be used solely in his business, for $10,000. Taxpayer claimed a total of $4,000 in depreciation allowances in Years 1, 2, and 3, and reduced the adjusted basis in the machine accordingly to $6,000. In Year 3, Taxpayer sells the machine for $15,000, which results in a realized gain of $9,000 ($15,000 amount realized minus $6,000 adjusted basis). Although the machine increased in value by only $5,000, Taxpayer realized $9,000 of gain. This was due to the fact that the Taxpayer took ordinary depreciation deductions with respect to the property even though the property was increasing in value. Under section 1245, $4,000 of the $9,000 gain will have to be recaptured as ordinary income while the remaining $5,000 of the gain may be entitled to capital gains treatment under section 1231.

2. The Statutory Mechanics

a. Amount Recaptured as Ordinary Income

Section 1245 recapture comes into play whenever "section 1245 property" is "disposed of." IRC § 1245(a)(1). These terms will be discussed in detail below. The amount treated as ordinary income under section 1245 is generally the lower of: (1) "recomputed basis" minus adjusted basis; or (2) amount realized minus adjusted basis. The second figure is easy to calculate, since it is merely the gain realized on the transaction. The first figure seems more difficult since it requires figuring the "recomputed basis"; however, recomputed basis is simply the property's adjusted basis recomputed by adding back all the depreciation or amortization adjustments reflected in the adjusted basis. IRC § 1245(a)(1)(A). In most cases, recomputed basis is simply the property's original cost basis. Note that in determining recomputed basis, a taxpayer must add back not only depreciation deductions under section 167 and amortization deductions under section 197, but also amounts expensed under section 179. IRC § 1245(a)(2)(C). Let's revisit the sale of Taxpayer's machine in the example above now that we understand the statutory mechanics of section 1245 recapture.

Example Revisited. Recomputed basis of $10,000 (that is, adjusted basis of $6,000 plus depreciation deductions of $4,000) exceeds adjusted basis of $6,000 by $4,000 (the amount of depreciation deductions claimed). Amount realized of $15,000 exceeds adjusted basis of $6,000 by $9,000 (the amount of gain realized). The lower of the two figures ($4,000) is the amount to be recaptured as ordinary income (the amount attributable to previous depreciation deductions). The balance of the gain ($5,000) may be entitled to capital gains treatment under section 1231 (the amount attributable to economic appreciation in value).

b. Meaning of "Section 1245 Property"

Section 1245 property is defined generally as depreciable personal property. It includes both tangible and intangible personal property. IRC § 1245(a)(3); Treas. Reg. § 1.1245-3(b). Note that section 1245 property includes intangible property that is subject to the allowance for depreciation under section 167 (e.g., separately acquired patents and copyrights), as well as intangible property that is subject to fifteen-year amortization under section 197 (e.g., acquired trademarks and trade names)—since section 197 intangibles are treated as property subject to the allowance for depreciation under section 167. IRC § 197(f)(7).

c. Meaning of "Disposed Of"

Section 1245 comes into play only when section 1245 property is "disposed of," a broad term that encompasses many transactions. However, certain transactions are excluded. For example, section 1245 does not apply to dispositions by gift. *See* IRC § 1245(b) (providing several exceptions). If Taxpayer, in the example above, did not sell the machine, but instead gave it to Sister, section 1245 would not apply to Taxpayer. However, if Sister later sells the machine, she will be required to recapture as ordinary income any gain attributable to the depreciation deductions claimed by Taxpayer. This is because "recomputed basis" is adjusted basis plus "*all* adjustments reflected in such adjusted basis on account of deductions," including adjustments made by others. IRC § 1245(a)(2)(A).

Section 1245 also does not apply to conversions of depreciable property from business to personal use, as indicated by the Service in Revenue Ruling 69-487, included below. Accordingly, if Taxpayer, in the example above, did not sell the business machine, but instead took it home and converted it to personal use, section 1245 would not apply. However, the recapture potential is still lurking in the machine. If Taxpayer later sells the machine, gain from the sale will be characterized as ordinary income to the extent of previous depreciation deductions taken. [NOTE: Although a conversion from business use to personal use will not trigger section 1245 recapture, it may trigger section 179(d)(10) recapture if a section 179 deduction was taken with respect to the property. IRC § 179(d)(10); Treas. Reg. § 1.179-1(e). The amount included in ordinary income is the benefit derived from electing section 179 treatment (i.e., the deductions taken under sections 179 and 168 minus the deductions that could have been taken under section 168 if a section 179 election had not been made). Treas. Reg. § 1.179-1(e)(1). This amount is added to the basis of the property at the time of conversion.]

B. Recapture under Section 1250 for Certain Depreciable Realty

While section 1245 generally applies to depreciable personal property, section 1250 generally applies to depreciable real property, such as residential rental property (apartment buildings) and non-residential real property (office buildings and warehouses). IRC § 1250(c). The amount treated as ordinary income under section 1250 is the "applicable percentage" (typically 100%) of the lower of: (1) "additional depreciation" or (2) the excess of amount realized on the sale over adjusted basis. IRC § 1250(a). "Additional depreciation," in the case of property held for more than one year, is defined as depreciation adjustments in excess of what would be allowed under the straight line method. IRC § 1250(b)(1). Now recall from Chapter 9, that for depreciable real property acquired after 1986, the straight line method must be used. Hence, for real property acquired after 1986, there will be no "additional depreciation" and hence, no amount recaptured as ordinary income. Before you conclude that section 1250 is statutory surplus, however, keep in mind that the disposition of section 1250 property may trigger ordinary income if the property was held for less than a year or was acquired before 1986 and depreciated under pre-1986 law.

In contrast to section 1245, section 1250 seems to give taxpayers the best of both words—they can claim ordinary depreciation deductions in early years (albeit using the slow straight line method), and then enjoy preferential capital gains treatment on a later sale of the property. Recall from Chapter 17, however, that "unrecaptured section 1250 gains" are taxed at a maximum rate of 25%; although it is lower than the 28% maximum rate applicable to collectible gains, it is higher than the 15% (or 20% for high-bracket taxpayers) maximum rate applicable to most other long-term capital gains. The term "unrecaptured section 1250 gain" means long-term capital gain from the sale of depreciable real property attributable to depreciation deductions taken that are not recaptured as ordinary income. IRC § 1(h)(6). Thus, gain attributable to depreciation, while not taxed at ordinary income rates, is taxed at a higher capital gains rate. Consider the following example.

Example. In Year 1, high-bracket Taxpayer purchased a large apartment building to use in his rental trade or business at a cost of $1,500,000, of which $1,000,000 was allocated to the building. In Year, 3, Taxpayer sold the property for $2,300,000, of which $1,500,000 was properly allocated to the building. During Years 1–3, Taxpayer properly claimed $100,000 of depreciation with respect to the building (using the straight line method of depreciation, a 27.5-year recovery period, and a mid-month convention). For now, let's focus only on the sale of the building. Taxpayer's gain on the sale of the building is $600,000 ($1,500,000 AR minus $900,000 AB). What is the character of this gain? The building is section 1250 property. The amount recaptured as ordinary income is the applicable percentage (assume 100%) of the lower of additional depreciation or gain realized. Additional depreciation is zero since Taxpayer did not take depreciation adjustments in excess of straight line. Applying the "lower of" rule, the amount recaptured is 100% of $0 or $0. Assuming no other section 1231 transactions, the entire $600,000 gain comes out of the section 1231 hotchpot as long-term capital gain. However, $100,000 of the gain is "unrecaptured section 1250 gain" (i.e., gain attributable to depreciation deductions not recaptured as ordinary income) and is taxed at a maximum rate of 25%. The remaining $500,000 of the gain is long-term capital gain taxed at a maximum rate of 20%.

C. Characterization under Section 1239

Under section 1239, any gain recognized on the direct or indirect sale or exchange of property between related parties will be treated as ordinary income if such property is, in the hands of the transferee, subject to the allowance for depreciation provided in section 167. IRC § 1239(a). Section 1239 is an overriding characterization rule requiring all such gain to be reported as ordinary income; therefore, no part of the gain may be characterized as capital gain under any other general or special characterization provision. *See* IRC 1239(d); Treas. Reg. 1.1239-1(b); Rev. Rul. 59-210, 1959-1 C.B. 217. The purpose behind section 1239 is to prevent taxpayers from selling low-basis, high-value depreciable property to a related party in order to step up the property's basis in the hands of the related transferee (for depreciation purposes) at the low cost of a capital gains tax to the transferor.

For purposes of section 1239, "related persons" include an individual and a corporation if the individual owns 50 percent or more in value of the outstanding stock of the corporation. IRC § 1239(b), (c); Treas. Reg. § 1.1239-1(b). In determining whether a transferor and transferee are related parties, the constructive stock ownership rules of section 267(c) should be applied. Under the constructive ownership rules, for example, a taxpayer constructively owns stock that is owned or deemed to be owned by his or her children. IRC § 267(c)(2), (4).

Section 1239 comes into play only when the property sold is, in the hands of the transferee, subject to the allowance for depreciation provided in section 167. Review Chapter 9 for the types of property that are and are not depreciable under section 167. It should be noted that although patent applications are not depreciable, section 1239 specifically provides that patent applications are treated as depreciable for section 1239 purposes. IRC § 1239(e). Additionally, "section 197 intangibles" are treated as depreciable property under section 167 and thus fall within section 1239. IRC § 197(f)(7). Review Chapter 9 for assets that are considered "section 197 intangibles."

IV. Materials

Revenue Ruling 69-487

1969-2 C.B. 165

An individual taxpayer operating a business as a sole proprietorship converted to personal use an automobile that had been used solely for business purposes. At that time, the fair market value of the automobile was substantially higher than its adjusted basis.

Held, for the purposes of section 1245 of the Internal Revenue Code of 1954, the conversion to personal use is not a "disposition" of the automobile. Accordingly, there is no gain to be recognized by the taxpayer upon the conversion to personal use. However, the provisions of section 1245 of the Code would apply to any disposition of the automobile by the taxpayer at a later date.

V. Related Matters

- **Recognition Too**. Sections 1245 and 1250 are not merely "characterization" provisions. On occasion they are "recognition" provisions as well. For example, the installment method of reporting gains under section 453 does not apply to the extent of any section 1245 or section 1250 recapture gain. This means that the amount of gain recognized in an installment sale could exceed the actual installment payment. *See* IRC §453(i). The installment method of reporting gain from an installment sale is discussed more fully in Chapter 26.

- **Section 174 Research and Development Costs**. Research and experimental expenditures expensed under section 174 need not be recaptured as ordinary income on later sale. *See* Rev. Rul. 85-186, 1985-2 C.B. 84.

- **Section 181 TV and Film Production Costs**. An interesting issue is whether television and film production costs that were immediately expensed under section 181, a temporary provision added to the Code by the American Jobs Creation Act of 2004, have to be recaptured at ordinary income rates under section 1245. While there was initial uncertainty concerning whether recapture applied, Congress clarified that it does. Qualified film and television production costs expensed under section 181 are treated as deductions allowable for amortization. IRC §1245(a)(2)(C).

- **Section 707(b) Ordinary Income**. Although section 707(b) does not target depreciable property, it is similar to section 1239 in that it targets related-party transactions. It requires that gain realized and recognized on the sale or exchange of property to a controlled partnership or between controlled partnerships be treated as ordinary income. Specifically, section 707(b) requires ordinary income treatment on the sale or exchange of property between a person and a partnership in which the person owns a 50% capital or profits interest. Moreover, section 707(b) requires ordinary income treatment on the sale or exchange of property between two partnerships, if a person owns a 50% capital or profits interest in both. IRC § 707(b)(2). In determining a taxpayer's ownership interest, the Code imposes certain attribution rules for constructive ownership of partnership interests. IRC § 707(b)(3). Accordingly, a taxpayer may be considered to own, in addition to his direct interest, the partnership interest owned by members of his family or other entities in which he has an interest.

Chapter 20

The Charitable Contribution Deduction

I. Assignment

Read: Internal Revenue Code: §§ 170(a), (b)(1), (c), (d)(1)(A), (e)(1), (f)(8)(A)–(B); 1011(b). Skim §§ 170(f)(11), (m); 501(a)–(c); 511(a)(1).

Treasury Regulations: Skim §§ 1.170A-1(c)(1), -1(c)(5), -1(g), -13.
Text: Overview
   Sklar v. Commissioner
   Related Matters

Complete the problems.

II. Problems

1. BoBo Brazil, who is in the construction business, has a contribution base of $250,000. What is his current charitable deduction and carryover, if any, in the situations below?

    (a) Bobo gave $500,000 cash to Memorial Hospital, a public charity.

    (b) Instead of cash Bobo gave Memorial a generator used in his business worth $500,000 to be used by the hospital as a back up power source. Bobo's basis in the generator is $300,000. The generator has $100,000 of section 1245 depreciation recapture inherent in it.

    (c) Same as (b) except that the generator is given to Metro Museum which, in turn, sells it to Memorial Hospital for $500,000.

    (d) Same as (b) except that all of the gain is section 1245 gain and Memorial takes the generator subject to a non-recourse mortgage of $200,000.

    (e) Bobo makes a $100,000 cash gift to Memorial Hospital and a $75,000 cash gift to the Bronco Burnett Family Foundation, a DPF.

    (f) Same as (e) except that Bobo gives $25,000 cash to Memorial and $150,000 cash to the Bronco Foundation.

2. John Marquand owns the copyright of a novel entitled *From Here to Maternity* and has held it for more than a year. It is worth $100,000. John's contribution

base is $200,000. What are the charitable deduction consequences to John under the following circumstances?

(a) John wrote the book and his basis in it is zero. John gives the copyright to his church.

(b) Same as (a) except that John bought the copyright from James Joyce for $50,000 as an investment.

(c) Same as (b) except that John is a publisher and the copyright is part of his inventory.

3. Carlos Castaneda and Evita Peron, a married couple, send their two children, Matthew and Penelope, to the Church of Now Day School. In the morning of each school day the children do conventional school work. In the afternoon of each school day the children study principles of Nowology. These principles are a blend of philosophical and ethical principles derived from Buddhism, Taoism, and Christianity. The church charges $10,000 a year to attend the morning sessions and $10,000 a year to attend the afternoon sessions. Students can attend either or both sessions. Matthew and Penelope attend both sessions. Carlos and Evita want to deduct the costs of their children's attendance at the afternoon sessions as charitable deductions. What are the arguments for and against deduction? Would it change anything if the church gave Carlos and Evita a statement that the value of child care services it provides in the afternoons is $5,000 per year per child?

4. Hugo Black has a very high contribution base and has three assets of equal value he is considering giving away to a DPF. The first is highly appreciated publicly traded stock. The second is highly appreciated closely held stock. The third is publicly traded stock in which his basis substantially exceeds its value. Which asset should he use for the gift?

III. Overview

A. Introduction

We have reserved study of the charitable deduction until now because its application depends on a good understanding of characterization issues. Under section 170 gifts of capital gain property are treated differently than gifts of cash or of ordinary income property. This is one of several aspects of this provision that make it particularly challenging. Section 170 is like a vertical maze with various sluices and gates through which a charitable donation must pass on its way to partial or full deductibility. First one provision wrings out the ordinary gain, then another may wring out the capital gain. Then another places a percentage limit on the deduction. Still another lifts that limit if the taxpayer elects to have some of his gain chipped away. And so on. By the end of the process the deduction has been whittled down to an acceptable level. It is no exaggeration to say that this provision is among the most complex that still belongs in a course on the fundamentals of federal taxation. But do not fear. With some textual help you will find that the provision is not as impenetrable as it may seem upon initial consideration. Now is the time for you to remind yourself of the intelligence and self discipline that has brought you to this present pass. You can do it!

The primary difficulty lies in determining the order in which to apply the various provisions and then, in some cases, understanding those provisions. Below you will see a chart that helps you find your way along the path.

But let's begin at the beginning. Section 170(a) authorizes a deduction for a "charitable contribution." A charitable contribution is a gift to or for the use of an organization described in section 170(c). This includes governmental entities and various private non-profit entities that are deemed to do public good. While this requires some fleshing out, the essential point to observe at the outset is that not every gift from charitable impulses is entitled to a deduction. A gift to a homeless person or to a friend in need is not a charitable contribution for tax purposes. It must be a gift to a recognized charitable entity. For the most part those entities are "[c]orporations, and any community chest, fund, or foundation, organized and operated exclusively for religious, charitable, scientific, testing for public safety, literary, or educational purposes." IRC § 501(c)(3). The entities that are customarily thought of as charities typically qualify for tax exempt status under section 501. Thus, a gift to a charitable entity entitles the donor to a tax deduction but does not create taxable income for the donee.

Another fundamental point is that there can be no required consideration passing from the charity to the donor for the deductible part of a contribution. Treas. Reg. § 1.170A-1(c)(5). Thus, if a charity stages a play and charges standard market prices for tickets, the buyers are not entitled to a charitable deduction even if they choose not to attend the play. If the charity charges an amount above the market value of the admission price, it should designate what amount is considered a charitable contribution and only that amount can be deducted. Rev. Rul. 67-246, 1967-2 C.B. 104. An interesting case with respect to the Church of Scientology held that contributions by members in exchange for "auditing" and "training" were not deductible because they were part of a *quid pro quo* exchange. *See* Hernandez v. Commissioner, 490 U.S. 680 (1989). Curiously enough, the Service later ruled that it will grant deductions for such contributions. *See* Rev. Rul. 93-73, 1993-2 C.B. 75. We mention these matters in passing here to remind the reader that black letter law should not be applied mechanically. Individual cases require individual analysis. The *Sklar* case in the materials more fully illustrates this point.

One other preliminary point is that there is no charitable deduction for the contribution of services to a charity. Treas. Reg. § 1.170A-1(g). The logic supporting this result is that the taxpayer has no tax basis in services she performs. Thus, allowing a deduction for services would amount to allowing a deduction with dollars that have never been, and never will be, taxed. This leads naturally to a second point. Out of pocket expenses related to contributions of charitable services are deductible. For example, suppose that twenty years from now, when you are a leading citizen, you agree to serve on the advisory board of your college. Doubtless you will serve without any compensation, and you will likely pay your own travel costs to attend meetings.

Though you cannot deduct an hourly rate for your time expended, you can take a charitable contribution deduction for your travel expenses (assuming your school qualifies as a charity as most do).

B. The Structure of the Code: Sluices and Gates

1. Defining Terms

Our analysis of section 170 employs four terms with special meanings. It is useful to have these meanings already in mind as you work through the structure of this provision.

Public charity (PC). A public charity for purposes of our analysis is any charity described in section 170(b)(1)(A). This includes most charities other than certain private foundations which we will call *disfavored private foundations* (DPFs). *Compare* IRC §§ 170(b)(1)(A) & (B). DPFs tend to rely on a very limited number of donors for their funding and tend to simply pass money on to more active charities.

Contribution base (CB). An individual taxpayer's contribution base generally is the same as adjusted gross income. IRC § 170(b)(1)(H).

Long-term capital gain. In addition to what is normally called long-term capital gain, in the context of section 170 the phrase should be understood to refer to section 1231 gains. *See* IRC §§ 170(e)(1) flush language, (b)(1)(C)(iv).

Like many provisions section 170 is not applied in the sequence in which it appears in the Code. Instead it should be applied in the sequence used below and detailed in the chart that follows.

2. Section 170(e)

The *beginning* amount for purposes of determining the deduction is the amount of cash and the fair market value of property contributed. Treas. Reg. § 1.170A-1(c)(1). One might inquire, why begin with value rather than basis? After all any unrealized gain has never been taxed to the donor just as in the case of contributed services. A partial response is to look to the benefit being conferred upon the charity. In addition, as we will see, often the unrealized gain is made non-deductible by other provisions. Indeed, the message of section 170(e)(1)(A) is that any gain other than long-term capital gain is wrung out. Thus, for example, any gain that is characterized as ordinary by operation of sections 64, 1221, or 1245 is excluded from the deduction. *See* IRC § 170(e)(1) (flush language).

If the contribution is a gift to a public charity of tangible personal property unrelated to its charitable purpose, the long-term capital gain in the property is also excluded. IRC § 170(e)(1)(B)(i)(I). Thus, for example, a gift of an appreciated work of art to a hospital for sale by it will trigger the wring out rule just described. However, a gift of that same piece of art to a museum that plans to put it on display will not.

Even if tangible personal property is related to the public charity's purpose, the long-term capital gain in the property is excluded if the property is sold by the charity in the year in which the contribution is made. IRC § 170(e)(1)(B)(i)(II). If such property is sold by the charity within three years, the donor must include in income (in the year of disposition) an amount equal to the excess of the donor's deduction over the donor's basis in the property at the time of contribution. IRC § 170(e)(7).

Under section 170(e)(1)(B)(ii), the long-term capital gain is removed from contributions to DPFs. In this case there is an exception for gifts of publicly traded stock. IRC § 170(e)(5).

Another gain wring out rule in section 170(e) excludes the long-term capital gain inherent in most donated intellectual property. IRC § 170(e)(1)(B)(iii). This gain wring out rule was intended to curb improper deductions resulting from overvaluation of donated intellectual property. A final gain wring out rule excludes any long-term capital gain inherent in certain donated "taxidermy property." IRC § 170(e)(1)(B)(iv). Apparently, this gain wring out rule was to prevent trophy hunters from effectively writing off the costs of their hunting trips by donating their mounted prizes.

3. Sections 170(b)(1)(A) & (B)

Section 170(b)(1)(A) provides that in any single year, a taxpayer's charitable deduction for gifts to public charities may not exceed 50% of the taxpayer's contribution base. IRC § 170(b)(1)(A). The Tax Cuts and Jobs Act of 2017 (TCJA) increased the percentage limitation to 60%, but only for *cash* donations to public charities in 2018 through 2025. IRC § 170(b)(1)(G)(i). The 60% limit for cash gifts to public charities was apparently intended "to encourage taxpayers to provide essential monetary support to front-line charities," because "a robust charitable sector is vital to our economy." *See* Report of the House Ways and Means Committee on H.R. 1, Tax Cuts and Jobs Act, H. Rept. 115-409, 177. Do you agree? Recall that the TCJA also scaled back many itemized deductions (e.g., capped SALT deductions at $10,000) and increased the standard deduction, changes that many fear will actually reduce tax incentives to donate. (Note that cash contributions that qualify for the 60% limit are not taken into account in determining non-cash contributions allowed under the 50% limit. IRC § 170(b)(1)(G)(iii)(I).)

A taxpayer's charitable deduction for gifts to DPFs is limited to the *lesser* of 30% of the taxpayer's contribution base or the excess of 60% (or 50% as the case may be) of the contribution base over the amount given to PCs. IRC § 170(b)(1)(B), (G)(iii)(II). This rule implies that when a taxpayer has made gifts to both PCs and to DPFs, the gifts to PCs are deducted first.

If any of the above limits apply, the excess deduction carries over for up to five years. IRC § 170(d)(1)(A), (b)(1)(G)(ii) (gifts to public charities); IRC § 170(b)(1)(B), flush language (gifts to DPFs).

4. Section 170(b)(1)(C)

Section 170(b)(1)(C)(i) limits the deduction to 30% of the taxpayer's contribution base if the gift is capital gain property given to a PC to which subsection (e)(1)(B) did not apply (i.e., the long-term capital gain was not wrung out). Again the excess carries over for five years. IRC § 170(b)(1)(C)(ii). Notice that the final sentence of section 170(b)(1)(C)(i) says to apply this rule next to last. This is an indicator that if the taxpayer has made gifts of cash and of other property to a PC, *deduct the cash gift first*. This same rule applies for gifts to DPFs. *See* IRC § 170(b)(1)(D) (flush language).

There is an election under section 170(b)(1)(C)(iii) allowing the taxpayer to avoid the 30% limit in exchange for having the long-term capital gain wrung out as though section 170(e)(1)(B) had applied.

Note that in applying section 170(b)(1)(B), section 170(b)(1)(C) has no significance. *See* IRC § 170(b)(1)(B)(ii) (parenthetical language).

5. Section 170(b)(1)(D)

This provision states that deductions for gifts of capital gain property to DPFs are limited to the *lesser of* 20% of the taxpayer's contribution base or the excess of 30% of the contribution base over the section 170(b)(1)(C) amount. In this context capital gain property includes property which has had the gain wrung out under section 170(e)(1)(B)(ii). Gifts of capital gain property to DPFs are taken into account after all other charitable contributions. IRC § 170(b)(1)(D)(i) (flush language).

As you have just seen, section 170 is a daunting provision. In recognition of this, we offer the following summary of the way in which the charitable deduction may be computed. Preliminary to the computation one must first have determined that a gift has been made and that the donee is an entity for which contributions qualify for deduction (i.e., it is an organization described in section 170(c)). There are some complexities which are not fully resolved by the analysis below, but this is the basic pattern.

The Charitable Deduction Summarized

1. Start with the FMV of donated property. Treas. Reg. § 1.170A-1(c)(1).

2. Exclude non-long-term capital gains. (This includes both short-term capital gains and ordinary income.) IRC § 170(e)(1)(A).

3. If the gift is of tangible personal property to a public charity and the property donated is unrelated to its charitable function, exclude long-term capital gains. IRC § 170(e)(1)(B)(i).

4. If the gift is to a DPF (i.e., a private foundation other than a foundation described in § 170(b)(1)(E)), exclude long-term capital gains. IRC § 170(e)(1)(B)(ii) (but note section 170(e)(5) exception).

5. If the gift consists of intellectual property other than self-created copyrights, exclude long-term capital gains. IRC § 170(e)(1)(B)(iii). Section 170(m) may apply.

6. If the gift consists of taxidermy property, exclude long term capital gains. IRC § 170(e)(1)(B)(iv).

7. If the gift is to a public charity, limit the deduction to 50% (60% in the cash of cash gifts in 2018 through 2025) of the donor's contribution base. *See* IRC § 170(b)(1)(H). Carry over the remainder. IRC § 170(b)(1)(A).

8. If the gift is to a DPF, limit the deduction to 30% of the contribution base (but this must be coordinated with step 7 when there are gifts to both PCs and DPFs). Carry over the remainder. IRC § 170(b)(1)(B).

9. If the gift is capital gain property given to a PC (to which step 3 or 5 or 6 did not apply), limit the deduction to 30% of the contribution base. Do not change step 8. If an election under section 170 (b)(1)(C)(iii) is made, exclude long-term capital gains but do not apply the 30% limit to the remainder. Carry over any excess. (See below for further discussion.) IRC § 170(b)(1)(C).

10. If the gift is capital gain property given to a DPF, limit the deduction to the lesser of 20% of the contribution base or 30% of the contribution base reduced by the section 170(b)(1)(C) amount. Carry over the remainder. IRC § 170(b)(1)(D).

With respect to step 9, if no section 170(b)(1)(C)(iii) election is made, follow these steps in this order. A step 9 limitation does not affect the step 8 computation. *See* IRC § 170(b)(1)(B)(ii) (parenthetical language). However, if a section 170(b)(1)(C) election is made, the step 7 and step 8 computations must be reworked. The regulations permit this result despite the apparent conflict with the parenthetical language of section 170(b)(1)(B)(ii). *See* Treas. Reg. § 1.170A-8(f), Ex. 15(a).

C. Gifts of Intellectual Property: Section 170(m)

Two of the gain wring out rules discussed above can apply to gifts of intellectual property such as patents and copyrights. The first of these, section 170(e)(1)(A), will wring out the gain from self-created patents and copyrights since self-created patents and copyrights are not capital assets. *See* IRC § 1221(a)(3). (This first wring out rule would not apply to self-developed patents eligible for long-term capital gain treatment under the special rule of section 1235, considered in Chapter 29.) The second applicable wring out rule, section 170(e)(1)(B)(iii), more broadly denies a deduction for the long-term capital gain inherent in other forms of self-generated or purchased intellectual property (which can be a capital asset). The result of these two wring out rules is that there is now very little *immediate* economic incentive for charitable giving of any type of intellectual property. But that is not the end of the story. To encourage charitable giving of intellectual property, Congress deemed it appropriate to grant donors of intellectual property future charitable deductions based on the income received by the donee charity. This provision, section 170(m), allows the donor a deduction for up to ten years for gifts of royalty producing intellectual property to public charities. It does not apply to gifts to DPFs. The amount of the charitable deduction is a percentage of the royalty income earned by the donee. The percentage declines over time. *See* IRC § 170(m)(1) & (7). The deduction under section 170(m) is subject to the percentage limits in section 170(b)(1)(A) and is reduced by the amount of the deduction allowed in the year of the gift. *See* IRC §§ 170(m)(2), (m)(10)(A).

D. Bargain Sales to Charities

A sale of property to a charity at less than its fair market value is called a bargain sale. A bargain sale is really two transactions, a sale and a gift. The taxpayer has made a charitable contribution to the extent value exceeds selling price. But as we have just seen, if there is any gain inherent in the property, the charitable deduction may be reduced by the amount of the gain. In order to know how to properly treat a bargain sale to a charity, it is necessary to know how much of the taxpayer's basis to allocate to the sale and how much to allocate to the gift. That issue is addressed by section 1011(b). It provides that the basis shall be allocated to the sale in the same ratio as amount realized bears to fair market value.

Stated formulaically, section 1011(b) provides:

$$\frac{\text{Amount Realized}}{\text{Fair Market Value}} \times \text{Adjusted Basis} = \text{Basis Allocated to Sale}$$

The rest of the taxpayer's basis in the property is allocated to the charitable gift. After allocating the taxpayer's basis, the tax effects of the sale and of the charitable contribution can be determined separately. The sale will be treated under section 1001 and the characterization rules, and the gift will be treated under the rules of section 170.

Notice how this approach differs from the treatment of bargain sales between family members studied earlier in Chapter 4.

It is also useful to keep in mind that if property is transferred subject to a mortgage, the debt relief is an amount realized to the transferor. Treas. Reg. § 1.1011-2(a)(3). For an illustration, see Rev. Rul. 81-163, 1981-1 C.B. 433.

Example: Bargain Sale. Ava's only charitable gift for the year is a piece of land worth $100,000 transferred to a public charity. She has held it for investment for several years. Her basis is $50,000. The land is subject to a mortgage of $30,000 which the charity assumes. This is a bargain sale since Ava has an amount realized of $30,000 (the mortgage). The portion of her basis allocated to the sale is $15,000 ($30,000 AR / $100,000 FMV × $50,000 AB = $15,000). Thus, she has a long-term capital gain on the sale portion of the transaction of $15,000 ($30,000 AR − $15,000 AB allocated to the sale under § 1011(b) = $15,000 GR). Ava also has a charitable contribution of $70,000 under section 170 ($100,000 FMV − $30,000 AR = $70,000). Assuming her contribution base is large enough, she can deduct the entire $70,000 currently since section 170(e) does not apply.

E. Substantiation

There are a number of provisions in section 170 and in the regulations designed to require the taxpayer to prove entitlement to the deduction. For donations of $250 or more in value, the donor must obtain a contemporaneous written acknowledgment of the gift from the donee. IRC § 170(f)(8); Treas. Reg. § 1.170A-13(f). For gifts in excess of $500 in value, other than gifts of readily valued property, the donor must provide a description of the property with her return. For gifts of more than $5,000 in value, the donor must obtain a professional appraisal of the property. *See* Treas. Reg. § 1.170A-13(f). For gifts of more than $500,000 in value, the appraisal must be filed with the return. *See* IRC § 170(f)(11). There are special substantiation rules and limits for gifts of used vehicles, boats and planes. *See* IRC § 170(f)(12). For limits on contributions of clothing and household items, see IRC § 170(f)(16). For record keeping requirements for contributions of cash, checks or other monetary gifts, see IRC § 170(f)(17).

Valuation of gifts of property other than cash or marketable securities is often problematic. A particularly interesting example of this challenge is Rolfs v. Commissioner, 668 F.3d 888 (7th Cir. 2012). *Rolfs* involved a donation of a home to a local fire department. The donation was conditioned on the burning of the home in a training exercise. The taxpayers sought to determine the value of the donation by a before-and-after-value comparison. The Seventh Circuit denied any deduction on the grounds that the home had no value for moving or salvage and that this was the appropriate comparison to its value for demolition. *See also* Patel v. Commissioner, 138 T.C. No. 23 (2012), where a deeply divided tax court denied the deduction on the grounds that it did not satisfy the requirements for the deduction of a gift of a "partial interest" in real estate under section 170(f).

F. Tax Policy and the Charitable Deduction

The central justification for the charitable deduction is that it promotes support for organizations that do public good. Some of these organizations carry out functions that might otherwise be carried out by the federal government. Thus, some charitable contributions may serve to reduce the need for taxes. But this benefit is hard to quantify and far from a direct correlation. Moreover, the effect of the charitable deduction on charitable giving is debatable. It is reasonably clear however, that the deduction costs the government tens of billions of dollars in foregone tax revenues each year. Assuming the government's revenue needs are relatively inflexible, this means that tax rates are higher than they need be in the absence of the deduction.

Many charitable organizations hold views that conflict with one another. They may take differing stances on such issues as gun control, abortion, sexual orientation discrimination, environmental protection, military interventions abroad, proper religious practice and so forth. Is it rational for government to subsidize, albeit indirectly, all of these divergent organizations? Perhaps in a free and open society it is. But, remember, not only is the charity indirectly subsidized by deduction, it is also free from direct taxation most of the time under section 501.

As with any deduction, the dollar benefit of the charitable deduction correlates with the taxpayer's top marginal bracket. Thus, higher income taxpayers benefit more from the charitable deduction than lower income taxpayers even if they each contribute the same amount. Indeed, since the deduction is an itemized deduction, non-itemizers get no benefit at all. A tax credit could avoid both these impacts.

As we have seen, in many cases the charitable deduction applies to untaxed appreciation. This feature of the deduction tends to favor wealthier persons who have held stock and real estate for long periods as compared with the average working stiff who, lacking any other property, makes his charitable gifts in post-tax cash. Is that fair?

G. Tax Planning and the Charitable Deduction

There are many tax planning aspects to using the charitable deduction. This is a natural outgrowth of its complexity. The percentage limitations and five year carry over rules under section 170(b), for example, mean that a taxpayer may need to spread charitable giving over time in order to reap maximum benefit. Larger deductions can be had currently for gifts to public charities than for gifts of the same amount to DPFs; and, in years 2018 through 2025, larger deductions can be had for cash gifts to public charities than non-cash gifts of the same amount to public charities. When the gain wring out rules apply it is best to give property that has little appreciation in it. Since fair market value is the beginning point of the deduction it is best to sell loss property and donate the cash so that the loss is recognized. Appreciated tangible personal property should be given to charities that can make direct use of the property. Gifts of appreciated real estate and stock tend to make the most advantageous gifts, but they must have been held for at least a year. Royalty-producing intellectual property given to commercially-driven charities (i.e., those organizations endowed with the facilities, financial resources, and personnel capability to exploit the intellectual property) will yield larger deductions in future years per section 170(m).

There are planning opportunities with trusts that involve the charitable deduction. Properly tailored term interests and remainders can have distinct estate planning advantages the discussion of which is beyond the scope of this book. But the reader should know that the rules in this area are quite technical and should be employed with care. *See, e.g.,* IRC §§ 170(f)(2), 664.

IV. Materials

Sklar v. Commissioner

282 F.3d 610 (9th Cir. 2002)

REINHARDT, Circuit Judge:

The taxpayer-petitioners in this action, Michael and Marla Sklar, challenge the Internal Revenue Service's ("IRS") disallowance of their deductions, as charitable contributions, of part of the tuition payments made to their children's religious schools. In the notice of deficiency sent to the Sklars, the IRS explained that "since these costs are personal tuition expenses, they are not deductible." Specifically, the Sklars sought to deduct 55% of the tuition, on the basis that this represented the proportion of the school day allocated to religious education. The Sklars contend that these costs are deductible under section 170 of the Internal Revenue Code, as payments for which they have received "solely intangible religious benefits." They also argue that they should receive this deduction because the IRS permits similar deductions to the Church of Scientology, and it is a violation of administrative consistency and of the Establishment Clause to deny them, as Orthodox Jews, the same deduction. The Tax Court found that under De Jong v. Commissioner, 309 F.2d 373, 376 (9th Cir. 1962), tuition paid for the education of a taxpayer's children is a personal expense which is non-deductible under § 170. The Tax Court also rejected the administrative inconsistency argument and the Establishment Clause claim, and ruled inadmissible several documents supporting the Sklars' contentions with respect to the Church of Scientology on the ground that the Sklars are not similarly situated to the members of the Church of Scientology. The Sklars filed this timely appeal.

We review the Tax Court's conclusions of law and its construction of the tax code de novo, and no deference is owed that court on its application of the law.

I. The Provisions of the Tax Code Governing Charitable Contribution Deductions Do Not Appear to Permit the Deduction Claimed by the Sklars

The Sklars assert that the deduction they claimed is allowable under section 170 of the Internal Revenue Code which permits taxpayers to deduct, as a charitable contribution, a "contribution or gift" to certain tax-exempt organizations. Not only has the Supreme Court held that, generally, a payment for which one receives consideration does not constitute a "contribution or gift" for purposes of § 170, see United States v. American Bar Endowment, 477 U.S. 105, 118 (1986) (stressing that "the sine qua non of a charitable contribution is a transfer of money or property without adequate consideration"), but it has explicitly rejected the contention made here by the Sklars: that there is an exception in the Code for payments for which one receives only religious benefits in return. Hernandez v. Commissioner, 490 U.S. 680 (1989). The taxpayers in *Hernandez*, members of the Church of Scientology, sought to deduct, as charitable contributions under § 170(c), payments made by them to the Church of Scientology in exchange for the religious exercises of "auditing" and "training."[1] The Court affirmed the Tax Court's reading of the statute disallowing the deductions on the following three grounds: (1) Congress had shown no preference in the Internal Revenue Code for payments made in exchange for religious benefits as opposed to other benefits; (2) to permit the deductions the taxpayers demanded would begin a slippery slope of expansion of the charitable

---

1. The Supreme Court, in *Hernandez*, described "auditing" as the process by which, through a one-to-one encounter with a Church of Scientology official, one becomes aware of his spiritual dimension. 490 U.S. at 684–85. The Court describes "training" as one of several "doctrinal courses" in which members study the tenets of the faith and train to become the leaders of auditing sessions. 490 U.S. at 685.

contribution deduction beyond what Congress intended; and (3) to permit these deductions could entangle the IRS and the government in the affairs and beliefs of various religious faiths and organizations in violation of the constitutional principle of the separation of church and state. Specifically, the Supreme Court stated that to permit these deductions might force the IRS to engage in a searching inquiry of whether a particular benefit received was "religious" or "secular" in order to determine its deductibility, a process which, the Court said, might violate the Establishment Clause.

Despite the clear statutory holding of *Hernandez*, the Sklars contend that recent changes to the Internal Revenue Code have clarified Congressional intent with respect to the deductibility of these payments. We seriously doubt the validity of this argument. The amendments to the Code appear not to have changed the substantive definition of a deductible charitable contribution, but only to have enacted additional documentation requirements for claimed deductions. Omnibus Budget Reconciliation Act of 1993 ("OBRA '93"), P.L. No. 103-66, 107 Stat. 312 (codified as amended in scattered sections of 26 U.S.C.). Section 170(f) of the Code adds a new requirement that taxpayers claiming a charitable contribution deduction obtain from the donee an estimate of the value of any goods and services received in return for the donation, and exempts from that new estimate requirement contributions for which solely intangible religious benefits are received. I.R.C. § 170(f)(8)(A) & (B)(ii). Similarly, § 6115 requires that tax-exempt organizations inform taxpayer-donors that they will receive a tax deduction only for the amount of their donation above the value of any goods or services received in return for the donation and requires donee organizations to give donors an estimate of this value, exempting from this estimate requirement contributions for which solely intangible religious benefits are received.

Given the clear holding of *Hernandez* and the absence of any direct evidence of Congressional intent to overrule the Supreme Court on this issue, we would be extremely reluctant to read an additional and significant substantive deduction into the statute based on what are clearly procedural provisions regarding the documentation of tax return information, particularly where the deduction would be of doubtful constitutional validity. Hernandez, 490 U.S. at 694; see Lemon v. Kurtzman, 403 U.S. 602, 612–13 (1971) (holding that a statute is unconstitutional under the Establishment Clause if it fosters "an excessive government entanglement with religion"). We need not, however, decide this issue definitively in this case.[3]

---

3. Our concurring colleague may well be correct that *Hernandez* is still controlling of this case and that § 170 has not been amended to permit deductions of contributions for which the consideration consists of "intangible religious benefits." As we have stated in the text, we are strongly inclined to that view ourselves. However, we need not issue a definitive holding on the effect of the statutory amendments here, because we can reject the Sklars' claim on the ground that they have failed to satisfy the requirements for the partial deductibility of dual payments set out in United States v. American Bar Endowment, 477 U.S. 105 (1986). Anderson v. United States, 417 U.S. 211, 218 (finding it "inadvisable ... reach out ... to pass on important questions of statutory construction when simpler, and more settled, grounds are available for deciding the case at hand"). See Section IV, infra (rejecting the Sklars' claim on the "dual payment" ground).

II. The IRS Policy Regarding the Church of Scientology May Not Be Withheld from Public Scrutiny and Appears to Violate the Establishment Clause; Further, It Appears That the Sklars Have Not Made Out a Claim of Administrative Inconsistency

Additionally, the Sklars claim that the IRS engages in a "policy" of permitting members of the Church of Scientology to deduct as charitable contributions, payments made for "auditing," "training," and other qualified religious services, and that the agency's refusal to grant similar religious deductions to members of other faiths violates the Establishment Clause and is administratively inconsistent. They assert that the "policy" is contained in a "closing agreement"[4] that the IRS signed with the Church of Scientology in 1993, shortly after the *Hernandez* decision and the 1993 changes to §170 of the Internal Revenue Code.[5] Because the IRS erroneously asserted that it is prohibited from disclosing all or any part of the closing agreement, we assume, for purposes of resolving this case, the truthfulness of the Sklars' allegations regarding the terms of that agreement. However, rather than concluding that the IRS's pro-Scientology policy would require it to adopt similar provisions for all other religions, we would likely conclude, were we to reach the issue, that the policy must be invalidated on the ground that it violates either the Internal Revenue Code or the Establishment Clause. See *Hernandez*, 490 U.S. at 694; *Lemon v. Kurtzman*, 403 U.S. at 612–13.

A. The IRS's Refusal to Disclose the Terms of Its Closing Agreement with the Church of Scientology

We are required, for purposes of our analysis, to assume the contents of the IRS's policy towards the Church of Scientology, because of the IRS's refusal to reveal to the Sklars, to this court, or even to the Department of Justice,[6] the contents of its closing agreement, although that agreement has apparently been reprinted in the Wall Street Journal. See *Scientologists and IRS Settle for $12.5 Million*, WALL ST. J., DEC. 30, 1997, at A12; agreement reprinted in Wall St. J. Interactive Edition (www.wsj.com). The IRS insists that the closing agreement in this case cannot be disclosed as it contains return information which the IRS is required to keep confidential under I.R.C. §6103. Under §6103, the IRS is prohibited from disclosing "return information," which is defined to include closing agreements. I.R.C. §6103(b)(2).[7] The pro-

---

4. Closing agreements are governed by I.R.C. §7121, which permits the IRS to enter into "an agreement in writing with any person relating to the liability of such person (or of the person or estate for whom he acts) in respect of any internal revenue tax for any taxable period." I.R.C. §7121(a); 26 C.F.R. §301.7121-1.

5. The year 1993 also saw the issuance by the IRS of Revenue Ruling 93-73, which declared "obsolete" Revenue Ruling 78-189, which had explicitly prohibited the deduction of the costs of auditing, training and other courses in the Church of Scientology as charitable contribution deductions under §170.

6. At oral argument the Justice Department lawyer specifically represented to the court that the Department of Justice has not been informed of the contents of the agreement, even for purposes of this appeal, because the IRS deems it to be confidential.

7. In our original opinion we stated that "§6103 does not discuss closing agreements, nor does it explicitly prohibit their disclosure." Slip Op. at 1379–1380. Shortly after the issuance of the opinion, however, the IRS brought to the court's attention that subsequent to briefing in this case, Congress

hibitions of § 6103 are subject to § 6104, where that provision applies, and § 6104 mandates public disclosure by each tax-exempt entity of its application for tax exemption (which itself contains detailed financial information about the entity, including revenues and expenses) as well as all documentation in support of that application. § 6104(a)(1)(A). The legislative history of the amendment to § 6103 which added closing agreements to the definition of "return information," makes it clear that

> the [new] provision [§ 6103(b)(2)(D)] is not intended to foreclose the disclosure of tax-exempt organization closing agreements to the extent that such disclosure is authorized under section 6104. Since section 6103 permits the disclosure of return information as authorized by Title 26, a disclosure authorized by section 6104 is permissible, notwithstanding the fact that a closing agreement is return information.

H.R. Conf. Rep. No. 106-1033, 2000 WL 1868642 at *1010 (footnote omitted).

In Tax Analysts v. IRS, 214 F.3d 179 (D.C. Cir. 2000), the only circuit court case on this issue, the D.C. Circuit rejected the IRS's argument, and held that disclosure of closing agreements is not categorically prohibited by § 6103, but may be required under § 6104. The legislative history of the § 6103 amendment, in addition to stating that § 6104 may still require disclosure of tax-exempt organization closing agreements, also specifically cites to *Tax Analysts*, stating that the new provision does not overrule its reasoning or its result. The *Tax Analysts* court concluded that the IRS's reading of § 6103 was directly at odds with the broad language of § 6104, the statutory provision requiring public disclosure by each tax-exempt entity of its application for tax exemption as well as all documentation in support of that application. § 6104(a)(1)(A). In that case, Tax Analysts sought disclosure of a closing agreement between the IRS and the Christian Broadcasting Network ("CBN"), a tax-exempt entity. The IRS had audited CBN and examined its eligibility for tax-exempt status after the network allegedly engaged in impermissible political activities. Tax Analysts argued that because CBN was able to retain its tax-exempt status only after signing the closing agreement, the agreement constituted documentation in support of the exemption application that must be publicly disclosed pursuant to § 6104(a)(1)(A). Rejecting the IRS's argument that disclosure of closing agreements is categorically prohibited by § 6103, the D.C. Circuit held that judicial examination of such closing agreements is necessary to determine whether or not they might indeed constitute

---

had amended § 6103 to prohibit the disclosure of closing agreements. I.R.C. § 6103(b)(2)(D). Despite this statutory change, our conclusion that § 6103 does not categorically prohibit the disclosure of closing agreements remains the same. As the IRS concedes, some "return information" prohibited from disclosure under § 6103 may nevertheless be required to be disclosed by tax-exempt entities under § 6104, because the disclosure prohibitions of § 6103 are subject to the mandatory disclosure requirements of § 6104. Therefore the critical question is not whether closing agreements constitute "return information" under § 6103, but whether they constitute information required to be disclosed by tax-exempt entities under § 6104. We conclude that these agreements constitute, at least in part, information required to be disclosed under § 6104.

information in support of an application for tax exemption required to be disclosed under §6104. 214 F.3d at 184. As the court stated with respect to the closing agreements at issue in that case:

> Precluding disclosure of a closing agreement, without regard to its content or circumstances, merely because it carries that particular label is … inconsistent with the statutory inclusion [in the disclosure requirements for tax-exempt organizations] of "any papers submitted" and "any letter or document issued" [in connection with an application for tax exemption]. Particularly in this case, where [the evidence] suggests that the closing agreement and application for exempt status were part of a single, overall negotiation between the IRS and [the Christian Broadcasting Network], the IRS's rigid reliance on the type of documents at issue rather than their content is questionable.

214 F.3d at 184.

We agree with the D.C. Circuit. Disclosure of closing agreements is not categorically prohibited by §6103, which is subject to §6104; in appropriate circumstances, disclosure may be required under §6104 or otherwise. Similarly, we reject the notion that §6103 prohibits the disclosure of the entire closing agreement whenever part of the agreement contains return information. We also conclude that there are several reasons why the closing agreement in the case before us likely is subject to disclosure, at least in substantial part. First, just as in the *Tax Analysts* case the settling of the Church of Scientology's tax liability through the closing agreement was required in order for the organization to regain the tax-exempt status it had previously lost. Therefore the closing agreement would appear to constitute documentation in support of the exemption application which must be publicly disclosed pursuant to §6104(a)(1)(A). See Alison H. Eaton, *Can the IRS Overrule the Supreme Court?* 45 EMORY L.J. 987, 987–89 (1996) (discussing the fact that, as part of the closing agreement, the main Church of Scientology regained the tax-exempt status it had lost in the 1960s). This is fully consistent with the already extensive disclosure generally required of tax-exempt organizations under §6104: in this case, the publication of the Church of Scientology's application for tax-exempt status, which contains detailed financial information about the organization, including its revenues and expenses. I.R.C. §6104(a)(1)(A); 26 U.S.C. 6104(d)-1; IRS Form 1023.

Second, public disclosure of agreements that affect not just one taxpayer or a discrete group of taxpayers, but a broad and indeterminate class of taxpayers with a large and constantly changing membership, is also necessary as a practical matter. In the case of the Church of Scientology agreement, there are potentially tens, if not hundreds, of thousands of taxpayers who were not parties to the agreement and must be informed of the nature of the tax deductions available to them. Indeed, the IRS, likely in recognition of that fact, has itself already disclosed some of the terms of this agreement, further confirming its adoption of the position that policymaking closing agreements can and must be disclosed. See Letter from Derome O. Bratvold, Chief, Adjustments Branch, IRS, to petitioners Michael and Marla Sklar (Feb. 4, 1994) ER 32 ("The settlement agreement between the Internal Revenue Service and the Church of Scientology allows individuals to claim, as charitable contributions, 80 percent of the cast [sic] of qualified religious services.").[10]

Third, where a closing agreement sets out a new policy and contains rules of general applicability to a class of taxpayers, disclosure of at least the relevant part of that agreement is required in the interest of public policy. That this is the IRS's understanding as well is demonstrated by the fact that public disclosure has been a requirement contained in at least two such policymaking closing agreements. The IRS required publication of its closing agreement with Hermann Hospital of Houston, Texas, a tax-exempt entity, concluded following the hospital's disclosure to the IRS of certain physician recruitment practices which might have constituted prohibited transactions for a tax-exempt entity. John W. Leggett, *Physician Recruitment and Retention by Tax-Exempt Hospitals: The Hermann Hospital Physician Recruitment Guidelines*, 8 HEALTH LAW. 1, 6 (Spring 1995). Under the closing agreement, the hospital was required to engage only in permissible physician recruitment activities, as detailed extensively in an attached set of "Guidelines." Public disclosure of the closing agreement put other non-profit hospitals on notice of the IRS's definition of permissible physician recruitment activities. That such was the purpose of requiring publication is clear from the fact that the agreement included provisions that did not apply to Hermann Hospital, but that might in the future be applicable to other tax-exempt hospitals. Similarly, publication on the Internet was required of the IRS's closing agreement with the Kamehameha Schools Bishop Estate, a tax-exempt educational trust in Hawaii. The agreement was concluded after the IRS threatened to revoke the trust's tax-exempt status because the trustees had engaged in serious financial misconduct and self-dealing. Evelyn Brody, *A Taxing Time for the Bishop Estate: What is the I.R.S. Role in Charity Governance?*, 21 U. HAW. L. REV. 537, 539–540 (1999). It required that the incumbent trustees be removed, that the estate pay a penalty of nine million dollars, and that future governance of the estate conform to the agreement's provisions, including restrictions on who could become trustees and a requirement that the estate make its financial records publicly available. Because the IRS had not traditionally intervened to this extent in matters of estate governance, the publication of the closing agreement served to put the members of other trusts on notice that the failure to administer trusts along the lines that the IRS required of the Bishop Estate might lead

---

10. In 1993, the Sklars filed an amendment to their 1991 tax return in which they claimed as a charitable contribution deduction the tuition paid for their children's religious education and requested an appropriate refund. Michael Sklar stated, "Pursuant to Revenue Ruling 93-73, Revenue Ruling 78-189 disallowing charitable contribution deductions for 'auditing' payments to the Church of Scientology, has been obsoleted. As it now appears that the I.R.S. is now allowing a charitable deduction for payments to qualified organizations which provide religious education, I have added payments to religious school to charitable contributions." ER 33–34. The IRS responded with the 1994 letter, cited above, explaining the nature of the deduction permitted to members of the Church of Scientology pursuant to the closing agreement, and disallowing the refund to the Sklars as they had "provided no verification to show that nay [sic] of the amount claimed was for specified services." ER 32. For some reason, the IRS was apparently under the impression that the Sklars were Scientologists rather than Orthodox Jews.

to loss of tax-exempt status.[12] Here, there is a strong public interest in the disclosure of the contents of the IRS's agreement with the Church of Scientology, especially as the agreement establishes a new policy governing charitable contributions to a particular religious organization which, while the pertinent statute may be unclear, clearly contravenes a prior Supreme Court holding.

Therefore, we reject the argument that the closing agreement made with the Church of Scientology, or at least the portion establishing rules or policies that are applicable to Scientology members generally, is not subject to public disclosure. The IRS is simply not free to enter into closing agreements with religious or other tax-exempt organizations governing the deductions that will be available to their members and to keep such provisions secret from the courts, the Congress, and the public.[13]

B. The Constitutionality of the IRS's Agreement with the Church of Scientology

The Supreme Court has developed a framework for determining whether a statute grants an unconstitutional denominational preference. Under that test, articulated in Larson v. Valente, 456 U.S. 228, 246–47 (1982), the first inquiry is whether or not the law facially discriminates amongst religions. The second inquiry, should it be found that the law does so discriminate, is whether or not, applying strict scrutiny, that discrimination is justified by a compelling governmental interest. *Id.* Applying this test to the policy of the IRS towards the Church of Scientology, the initial inquiry must be whether the policy facially discriminates amongst religions. Clearly it does, as this tax deduction is available only to members of the Church of Scientology.

The second *Larson* inquiry is whether or not the facially discriminatory policy is justified by a compelling governmental interest. 456 U.S. at 246–47. Although the IRS does not concede that it is engaging in a denominational preference, it asserts in its brief that the terms of the settlement agreement cannot be used as a basis to find an Establishment Clause violation because "in order to settle a case, both parties are required to make compromises with respect to points on which they believe they are legally correct." This is the only interest that the IRS proffers for the alleged policy. Although it appears to be true that the IRS has engaged in this particular preference in the interest of settling a long and litigious tax dispute with the Church of Scientology,[14] and as compelling as this interest might otherwise be, it does not rise to the

---

12. Evelyn Brody, *The Limits of Charity Fiduciary Law*, 57 MD. L. REV. 1400, 1410–1411 & n. 49 (1998) ("Lately, perhaps responding to criticism that closing agreements create a secret body of law, some [IRS] regulators have conditioned settlement on the charity's assenting to public disclosure of the agreement.").

13. We believe that the Tax Court's ruling that the closing agreement is not relevant is in all likelihood correct. The Tax Court concluded that the Sklars were not similarly situated to the members of the Church of Scientology who benefitted from the closing agreement. While we have no doubt that certain taxpayers who belong to religions other than the Church of Scientology would be similarly situated to such members, we think it unlikely that the Sklars are. Religious education for elementary or secondary school children does not appear to be similar to the "auditing" and "training" conducted by the Church of Scientology. See note 1, supra. Again, however, we need not resolve that issue here.

14. *See* Alison H. Eaton, *Can the IRS Overrule the Supreme Court?* 45 EMORY L.J. 987, 987–89 (1996) ("Since its inception the Church [of Scientology] has been embroiled in an endless stream of

level that would pass strict scrutiny. The benefits of settling a controversy with one religious organization can hardly outweigh the costs of engaging in a religious preference. Even aside from the constitutional considerations, a contrary rule would create a procedure by which any denomination seeking a denominational preference could bypass Congressional lawmaking and IRS rulemaking by engaging in voluminous tax litigation. Such a procedure would likely encourage the proliferation of such litigation, not reduce it. *Larson*, 456 U.S. at 248 (holding that even assuming arguendo that the government has a compelling governmental interest for a denominational preference, it must show that the rule is "closely fitted to further the interest that it assertedly serves"). Because the facial preference for the Church of Scientology embodied in the IRS's policy regarding its members cannot be justified by a compelling governmental interest, we would, if required to decide the case on the ground urged by the Sklars, first determine that the IRS policy constitutes an unconstitutional denominational preference under *Larson*. 456 U.S. at 230.

The Sklars contend that because "the IRS has admitted that it permits members of the Church of Scientology to deduct their payments for religious instruction ... in order to avoid violating the First Amendment, [the] IRS must permit adherents of other faiths to deduct their payments for religious instruction." To the extent that the Sklars claim that the Establishment Clause requires that we extend the Scientology deduction to all religious organizations, they are in error for three reasons: First, we would be reluctant ever to presume that Congress or any agency of the government would intend that a general religious preference be adopted, by extension or otherwise, as such preferences raise the highly sensitive issue of state sponsorship of religion. In the absence of a clear expression of such intent, we would be unlikely to consider extending a policy favoring one religion where the effect of our action would be to create a policy favoring all. Second, the Supreme Court has previously stated that a policy such as the Sklars wish us to create would be of questionable constitutional validity under *Lemon*, because the administration of the policy could require excessive government entanglement with religion. *Hernandez*, 490 U.S. at 694; see *Lemon*, 403 U.S. at 612–13. Third, the policy the Sklars seek would appear to violate section § 170. See *Hernandez*, 490 U.S. at 692–93. To the extent that the Sklars are also making an administrative inconsistency claim, we reject that claim on two grounds. First, in order to make an administrative inconsistency claim, a party must show that it is similarly situated to the group being treated differently by the agency. United States v. Kaiser, 363 U.S. 299, 308 (Frankfurter, J., concurring) ("The Commissioner [of the IRS] cannot tax one and not tax another without some rational basis for the difference. And so, ... it can be an independent ground of decision that the Commissioner has been inconsistent...."). We seriously doubt that the Sklars are similarly situated to the persons who benefit from the Scientology closing agreement because the religious education of the Sklars' children does not appear to be similar to the "auditing", "training" or other "qualified religious services" conducted by the Church

---

litigation with the Internal Revenue Service ... however, in late 1993, a truce was called [by way of the Closing Agreement].").

of Scientology. Second, even if they were so situated, because the treatment they seek is of questionable statutory and constitutional validity under § 170 of the IRC, under *Lemon*, and under *Hernandez*, we would not hold that the unlawful policy set forth in the closing agreement must be extended to all religious organizations. In the end, however, we need not decide the Establishment Clause claim or the administrative inconsistency claim as the Sklars have failed to show that their tuition payments constitute a partially deductible "dual payment" under the Tax Code.

III. The Sklars' Tuition Payments Do Not Constitute Partially Deductible "Dual Payments" Under the Tax Code

A "dual payment" (or "quid pro quo payment") under the Tax Code is a payment made in part in consideration for goods and services, and in part as a charitable contribution. I.R.C. § 6115. For example, the purchase, for seventy-five dollars, of an item worth five dollars at a charity auction would constitute a dual payment: five dollars in consideration for goods, and seventy dollars as a charitable contribution. The IRS permits a deduction under § 170 for the portion of a dual payment that consists of a charitable contribution, but not for the portion for which the taxpayer receives a benefit in return. Although the Sklars concede that they received a benefit for their tuition payments, in that their children received a secular education, they claim that part of the payment — the part attributable to their children's religious education — should be regarded as a charitable contribution because they received only an "intangible religious benefit" in return. Leaving aside both the issue, discussed in section I, of whether the Tax Code does indeed treat payments for which a taxpayer receives an "intangible religious benefit" as a charitable contribution, as well as any constitutional considerations, we are left with the Sklars' contention that their tuition payment was a dual one: in part in consideration for secular education, and in part as a charitable contribution. The Sklars assert that because 45% of their children's school day was spent on secular education, and 55% on religious education, they should receive a deduction for 55% of their tuition payments.

On the record before this court, the Sklars failed to satisfy the requirements for deducting part of a "dual payment" under the Tax Code. The Supreme Court discussed the deductibility of such payments in United States v. American Bar Endowment, 477 U.S. 105 and held that the taxpayer must establish that the dual payment exceeds the market value of the goods received in return. The facts of that case were as follows: The American Bar Endowment ("ABE"), a tax-exempt corporation organized for charitable purposes and associated with the American Bar Association ("ABA"), raised money for its charitable work by providing group insurance policies to its members, all of whom were also members of the ABA. ABE negotiated premium rates with insurers, collected premiums from its members and passed those premiums on to the insurers. Because the group policies purchased by ABE were "experience rated," the group members were entitled to receive, each year, a refund of the portion of their premiums paid above the actual cost to the insurer of providing insurance to the group. Although normally these refunds, called "dividends," would be distributed to individual policyholders, ABE required its members to agree to turn the dividends over to ABE for use in its charitable work. ABE members sought to deduct the dividends as charitable contributions to ABE, claiming that the premiums paid constituted partially deductible "dual payments." The Supreme Court held that the ABE members could not deduct the dividends as charitable contributions because they had not shown that the premiums they paid to ABE exceeded the market value of the insurance they purchased, or that the "excess payment," if any, was made with the intention of making a gift. Because the ABE insurance was no more costly to its members than other policies that were available to them, the taxpayers could not prove that they "purposely contributed money or property in excess of the value of any benefit [they] received in return."

Similarly, the Sklars have not shown that any dual tuition payments they may have made exceeded the market value of the secular education their children received. They urge that the market value of the secular portion of their children's education is the cost of a public school education. That cost, of course, is nothing. The Sklars are in error. The market value is the cost of a comparable secular education offered by private schools. The Sklars do not present any evidence even suggesting that their total payments exceeded that cost. There is no evidence in the record of the tuition private schools charge for a comparable secular education, and thus no evidence showing that the Sklars made an "excess payment" that might qualify for a tax deduction. This appears to be not simply an inadvertent evidentiary omission, but rather a reflection of the practical realities of the high costs of private education. The Sklars also failed to show that they intended to make a gift by contributing any such "excess payment." Therefore, under the clear holding of American Bar Endowment, the Sklars cannot prevail on this appeal.[15]

IV. Conclusion

We hold that because the Sklars have not shown that their "dual payment" tuition payments are partially deductible under the Tax Code, and, specifically, that the total payments they made for both the secular and religious private school education their children received exceeded the market value of other secular private school education available to those children, the IRS did not err in disallowing their deductions, and the Tax Court did not err in affirming the IRS's decision. We affirm the decision of the Tax Court on that ground.

AFFIRMED.

---

15. Moreover, as the IRS argues in its brief, the Sklars' deduction was properly denied on the alternative ground that they failed to meet the contemporaneous substantiation requirement of § 170(f)(8)(A), (B) & (C). The Sklars did not present, prior to filing their tax return, a letter from the schools acknowledging their "contribution" and estimating the value of the benefit they received, as is required under the statute. As noted earlier, certain reporting requirements are not applicable where intangible religious benefits are received in exchange, but such exemptions apply only where the consideration consists solely of such benefits. See the discussion of § 170(f)(8) supra.

SILVERMAN, Circuit Judge, concurring:

Why is Scientology training different from all other religious training? We should decline the invitation to answer that question. The sole issue before us is whether the Sklars' claimed deduction is valid, not whether members of the Church of Scientology have become the IRS's chosen people.

The majority states that the Church of Scientology's closing agreement is not relevant because "the Sklars are not similarly situated to the members of the Church of Scientology...." That may or may not be true, but it has no bearing on whether the tax code permits the Sklars to deduct the costs of their children's religious education as a charitable contribution. Whether the Sklars are entitled to the deduction they claim is governed by 26 U.S.C. § 170, Hernandez v. Commissioner, 490 U.S. 680 (1989), and United States v. American Bar Endowment, 477 U.S. 105 (1986), not by the Church of Scientology closing agreement.

> Section 170 states that quid pro quo donations, for which a taxpayer receives something in return, are not deductible.
>
> *Hernandez* holds that § 170 applies to religious quid pro quo donations.
>
> *American Bar Endowment* holds that charitable donations are deductible only to the extent that they exceed the fair market value of what is received in exchange.

The Sklars receive something in return for their tuition payments — the education of their children. Thus, they are not entitled to a charitable deduction under § 170, as Judge Reinhardt carefully shows. *Hernandez* clearly forecloses the argument that § 170 should not apply because the tuition payments are for religious education. Finally, the Sklars have not demonstrated that what they pay for their children's education exceeds the fair market value of what they receive in return; therefore, they have not shown that they are entitled to a deduction under *American Bar Endowment*. It is as simple as that.

Accordingly, under both the tax code and Supreme Court precedent, the Sklars are not entitled to the charitable deduction they claimed. The Church of Scientology's closing agreement is irrelevant, not because the Sklars are not "similarly situated" to Scientologists, but because the closing agreement does not enter into the equation by which the deductibility of the Sklars' payments is determined. An IRS closing agreement cannot overrule Congress and the Supreme Court.

If the IRS does, in fact, give preferential treatment to members of the Church of Scientology — allowing them a special right to claim deductions that are contrary to law and rightly disallowed to everybody else — then the proper course of action is a lawsuit to stop to that policy. The remedy is not to require the IRS to let others claim the improper deduction, too.

[Authors' Note: The Sklars have continued to litigate with the IRS over their right to deduct part of the cost of their children's religious education. Recently, they lost for a second time in the Ninth Circuit. *See* Sklar v. Commissioner, 549 F.3d 1252 (9th Cir. 2009).]

V. Related Matters

- **Gifts to Trusts.** This chapter has assumed gifts made directly "to" qualified charities. A charitable deduction is also available for gifts made "for the use of" qualified organizations. Read carefully IRC § 170(c). A gift is "for the use of" a qualified organization when it is held in a legally enforceable trust for the qualified organization or in a similar legal arrangement. *See* Davis v. United States, 495 U.S. 472 (1990) (holding that funds parents transferred to their two sons while they served as full-time, unpaid missionaries for the Church of Jesus Christ of Latter-day Saints were not deductible as charitable contributions "to or for the use of" the church). Gifts "for the use of" public charities or DPFs are subject to the 30% limitation and not the 50% (or 60%) limitation. Read carefully IRC § 170(b).

- **Business Deductions.** Sometimes a transfer without any express quid pro quo to a charity may qualify as a deductible business expense under section 162. *See, e.g.,* Marquis v. Commissioner, 49 T.C. 695 (1968). Even transfers with a quid pro quo may qualify under section 162. *See* Treas. Reg. § 1.170A-1(c)(5).

- **Stadium Tickets.** Prior to 2018, up to 80% of an amount paid to a university for the right to buy stadium tickets was deductible. IRC § 170(l). The TCJA effectively repealed the charitable deduction for amounts paid for college athletic seating rights. *Id.* This change is consistent with the disallowance of entertainment expenses as business expenses. *See* IRC § 274, mentioned in Chapter 7.

- **Conservation Easements.** There are specialized deductible charitable gifts involving conservation easements. IRC § 170(h).

- **Wealth Transfer Taxes.** The estate and gift taxes have charitable deduction provisions as well. IRC §§ 2055 & 2522.

- **UBIT.** Charities are subject to taxation on their business income that is unrelated to their charitable functions. IRC § 511 et seq.

- **Risk of Losing Exempt Status.** Charities can lose their tax exemption if they engage in too much activity designed to influence legislation. IRC § 501(h).

- **Excise Tax on Investment Income of Private Colleges and Universities.** Private colleges and universities are generally considered 501(c)(3) education organizations and, thus, public charities not subject to private foundation excise taxes on net investment income. Beginning in 2018, however, the TCJA added a new Code section that imposes a 1.4% excise tax on the net investment income of certain private colleges and universities, as well as their supporting organizations, similar to private foundations. IRC § 4968. This was apparently in response to a number of private universities accumulating significant assets inside of endowment funds rather than reducing student costs. Part of Congress' motivation may simply have been to raise revenue to offset the revenue losses from the corporate tax rate reduction in the TCJA.

Chapter 21

Second Set of Review Problems

The following problems are designed to review what has been addressed in the preceding four chapters on characterization of gains and losses, and to help integrate what has been learned.

1. Ernest Flagg, who is single and has no dependents, has a calendar taxable year and reports on the cash receipts and disbursements method. For several years, Ernest has operated as a sole proprietor a "parking lot" business. Specifically, Ernest owns some unimproved land (1/2 of an acre) in downtown ("Cityland"), and, for a fee each day, he allows customers to park on Cityland. Ernest uses only two assets in running his business: (1) Cityland, and (2) a sophisticated computer, which is used to keep track of parking decals, license plate and vehicle identification numbers, money received, etc.

During the current year (Year 1), Ernest had $10,000 of *ordinary* taxable income (before the property transactions below). In addition, two unfortunate events occurred that forced Ernest out of business:

(a) On November 1, Year 1, Ernest's computer was stolen from the lot while Ernest was attending to a customer. Ernest paid $10,000 for the computer two years ago and elected to fully utilize the IRC § 179 deduction and expense the entire cost of the computer in the year of purchase. In December, Year 1, Ernest received $20,000 in insurance proceeds as the sophisticated computer was fully insured against theft. Ernest does not intend to use the cash received to purchase any other property.

(b) On November 10, Year 1, the government condemned Cityland, the real estate Ernest used in his trade or business. In December Year 1, the government paid a condemnation award in the amount of $65,000. Ernest does not intend to use the cash received to purchase any other property. Ernest paid $70,000 for Cityland two years ago.

Part I. Determine Ernest's income tax liability for Year 1, using the rate structure set out in section 1(j) (which is provided in Chapter 14). In completing this part, please: (1) fully analyze the two property transactions and their impact on taxable income; (2) compute Ernest's net capital gain for the year; and (3) explain the maximum rate(s) that will apply to the net capital gain. You may assume that no credits are available to Ernest.

Part II. Same as Part I, above, except that Ernest had $160,000 of ordinary taxable income in addition to the two property transactions described above.

Part III. Same as Part I, above. In addition to the two property transactions described above, Ernest is considering selling some stock in ABC Company before the close of Year 1. He acquired the stock eighteen months ago for $7,000. Its current value is $4,000. He can wait until January, Year 2 to sell, however, and he asks your tax advice whether he should. What advice do you give and why?

Part IV. Same as Part II, above. In addition to the two property transactions described above, Ernest is considering selling some stock in ABC Company before the close of Year 1. He acquired the stock eighteen months ago for $7,000. Its current value is $4,000. He can wait until January, Year 2 to sell, however, and he asks your tax advice whether he should. What advice do you give and why?

2. Van Rjin is a painter who has a contribution base of $50,000. What are the tax consequences of the following transactions:

(a) Van makes a gift to an art museum (a public charity) of a work of art that he created that is worth $5,000. The museum will include the painting as part of its permanent display. You may assume the painting has a zero basis in his hands.

(b) Same as (a) except the painting was by Van's friend, Titian. Van bought it twelve years ago for $300.

(c) Same as (b) except the painting is given to the United Way to auction off.

(d) Same as (a) except that Van sells the painting to the art museum for $5,000.

(e) Same as (b) except that Van sells the Titian painting to the art museum for $5,000.

(f) Van donates his studio to the city of Leiden (where he lives and works) to establish a museum. Van bought the studio for $40,000. The studio is worth $100,000. It has been depreciated under the straight-line method, and Van's basis is $20,000.

(g) Same as (f) except that Van sells the studio to the city for $100,000. What is the character of any recognized gain and what tax rate applies to it?

(h) Same as (g) except that Van sells the studio for $50,000 even though it is worth $100,000.

Chapter 22

Residential Real Estate

I. Assignment

Read: Internal Revenue Code: §§ 121; 280A(a)–(c)(1), (3), (5), (d)(1), (e), (f)(1), (g). Skim §§ 163(a), (h)(1)–(4); 164(a)–(d)(2)(A).

Treasury Regulations: §§ 1.121-1(a), -1(b)(1)–(4), -1(c)(1)–(2), (4), -2, -3, -4(a)–(b), (g); Prop. Treas. Reg. § 1.280A-2(i)(5), -3(d)(3).

Text: Overview
Popov v. Commissioner
Guinan v. United States
Related Matters

Complete the problems.

II. Problems

1. Astrud Gilberto is a self-employed, professional cabaret singer who performs several nights per week at various hotels. Although one of the hotels provides her with a small room where she could develop and practice her songs, she rarely uses it. Instead, she uses a 300 square foot room in her 3,000 square foot home that she has converted to an office. She spends four to five hours per day practicing in the home office. She also uses the office to contact hotels and musicians regarding scheduling, prepare for performances, and maintain billing records.

   (a) Does Astrud's home office qualify as her principal place of business for deducting expenses for its use? Why?

   (b) Assume Astrud's home office qualifies as her principal place of business, and that the gross income from her singing activity was $60,000. To what extent may Astrud deduct the following expenses: home mortgage interest — $20,000; real estate taxes — $10,000; business expenses not related to the use of her home, such as advertising, office telephone, supplies — $17,000; fire and casualty insurance — $1,000; utility charges (other than home telephone) — $3,000. If the home were fully depreciable, the depreciation allowance would have been $8,000.

   (c) How would your answer to (b) change if the gross income from Astrud's singing activity was only $21,000 (and she had $50,000 of interest income)?

2. Larry Crabbe, a stockbroker, owns a beach house on the Florida coast not far from several major golf courses. In the current year he spends 30 days vacationing at the house and rents it to unrelated third persons for another 60 days. Gross rental income from renting the house is $18,000. Expenses relating to the house are as follows:

Property Taxes	$6,000
Mortgage Interest	$9,000
Insurance	$1,200
Utilities	$4,500
Maintenance	$6,000
Depreciation	$18,000
Total	**$44,700**

(a) Applying the allocation method supported by Prop. Treas. Reg. § 1.280A-3, what amount of the expenses are deductible for the rental activity? What is the amount of Larry's carry-over deduction, if any?

(b) Applying the allocation method supported by the case law, what amount of the expenses are deductible for the rental activity? What is the amount of Larry's carry-over deduction, if any?

3. On January 1, Year 1, Rebecca Sharpe, who is single and unemployed, purchased a principal residence in Fort Worth, Texas, for $300,000. Determine the amount of gain that must be reported in the following situations:

(a) Three years after the purchase, Rebecca sold the Fort Worth residence for $600,000.

(b) Twelve months after the purchase, Rebecca sold the Fort Worth residence for $600,000 because she obtained a job in Houston, Texas (255 miles from her Fort Worth residence).

(c) What result in (b) if Rebecca sold the Fort Worth residence for $600,000 because she obtained a job in Dallas, Texas (30 miles from her Fort Worth residence)?

(d) Six months after the purchase, Rebecca married Rawdon Crawley who, at that time, moved into the Fort Worth residence. Title remained in Rebecca's name alone. Eighteen months after the marriage, Rebecca sold the Fort Worth residence for $600,000, and filed a joint return with Rawdon.

(e) What result in (d) if Rawdon had been living in the Fort Worth residence since January 1, Year 1?

(f) Six months after the purchase, Rebecca married Rawdon who, at that time, moved in to the Fort Worth residence. Twelve months later, Rebecca died and bequeathed title to the residence to Rawdon who continued to use it as his principal residence. Six months after Rawdon inherited the house, Rawdon sold it for $600,000.

(g) What result in (f) if Rawdon did not inherit the residence twelve months after marriage, but instead received title under the terms of a divorce settlement twelve months after marriage and then six months later Rawdon sold the home for $600,000?

III. Overview

Congress believes that widespread home ownership is an important policy goal, and it uses the tax law to achieve it. The goal is achieved in part by exempting from taxation the imputed rental value of owner-occupied housing. That goal is also achieved in part by providing taxpayers itemized deductions for real property taxes and mortgage interest on personal residences. These matters were addressed in Chapter 11. For many persons, one of the most important tax benefits of home ownership is the substantial exclusion of gain from the sale of a principal residence provided by section 121. That provision is considered in this chapter. This gain exclusion provision in conjunction with the deductions for mortgage interest and property taxes constitutes a massive tax subsidy for housing. As you consider the tax benefits of home ownership, ask yourself the following questions: Is the subsidy for home ownership distributed fairly among homeowners? Is there a rational reason for favoring home owners over renters? [Note: Congress has not been so generous when it comes to losses realized on the sale of a home. Loss on the sale of a personal residence, although capital, is non-deductible because the residence is personal-use property. IRC §§ 262, 165(c).]

The tax benefits of home ownership provided some planning opportunities that were greater than Congress intended. These opportunities involved the delicate mixing of personal and profit-oriented activities. The response was section 280A. This provision is confusingly drawn because it seeks to address two distinctly different matters without clearly delineating when it is addressing one and when it is addressing the other. The two matters in question are (1) the use of some portion of one's residence for business purposes and (2) the use of one's vacation home as a rental property for some portion of the year. We will consider those two matters in the order just stated before turning to the section 121 gain exclusion rules.

A. Home Office Deductions

As a general rule, expenses associated with maintaining a household (e.g., water, utilities, cleaning services, insurance, and depreciation) are non-deductible personal expenses under section 262. But what if a taxpayer uses part of his home as an office to conduct business? Many Americans have done this, and many more are likely to do so in the future because advances in technology make telecommuting easy and practical. Should a portion of the household expenses attributable to maintaining a home office be deductible as a trade or business expense under section 162? Before answering, consider that if such expenses were freely deductible there would be considerable opportunity for "jobbing" the system. For example, a lawyer, accountant, or other professional who has an office downtown might designate a substantial section of her home as an office and proceed to deduct a large portion of her living expenses despite making little business use of the designated area. On the other hand, one can readily imagine circumstances in which a home office is a thoroughly ordinary and necessary business activity. Section 280A attempts to fairly delineate when the expenses of a home office are deductible and when they are not.

The general rule of section 280A disallows deductions for a *dwelling unit* used by the taxpayer as a residence. IRC § 280A(a). However, later subsections create important exceptions. The first exception is for expenses such as property taxes and mortgage interest that would be deductible without regard to personal or business use. IRC § 280A(b). But it is the second exception that is our greater immediate concern. To deduct expenses for conducting business activities from a home, a taxpayer must use part of the home *exclusively* and *regularly* as:

(1) the taxpayer's *principal place of business* for conducting any trade or business, or

(2) a place where the taxpayer meets or deals with patients, clients, or customers in the normal course of the taxpayer's trade or business. IRC § 280A(c)(1)(A)–(B).

In both cases, if the taxpayer is an employee, the home office expenses must also be incurred for the convenience of the employer — a difficult test to satisfy. IRC § 280A(c)(1)(C). This provision will eliminate deductions for many of the professionals' home offices mentioned above.

Whether a home office constitutes the taxpayer's *principal* place of business has been the subject of much litigation. In 1993, the Supreme Court considered conflicting lower court standards and developed a facts and circumstances test, stressing two primary considerations: "the relative importance of the activities performed at each business location and the time spent at each place." Commissioner v. Soliman, 506 U.S. 168, 174–75 (1993), discussed in *Popov v. Comissioner* below. In *Soliman*, the taxpayer, a self-employed anesthesiologist, did not have an office at the hospitals where he worked thirty plus hours per week, but he did have a home office that he used exclusively to perform essential administrative activities related to his practice (contact patients and doctors, maintain billing records and patient logs, prepare for treatments, etc.). The Supreme Court denied the taxpayer a home office deduction because his hospital work was more important than the office work he performed at home, and he spent more time at the hospitals than at the home office. The *Soliman* decision was a blow to taxpayers who used a home office for administrative and management activities of a trade or business and who had no other fixed office. In 1997, in response to *Soliman*, Congress amended section 280A(c)(1) to add the following: "[T]he term 'principal place of business' includes a place of business which is used by the taxpayer for the administrative or management activities of any trade or business of the taxpayer if there is no other fixed location of such trade or business where the taxpayer conducts substantial administrative or management activities of such trade or business." IRC § 280A(c)(1) (last sentence). This 1997 amendment, potentially applicable when a taxpayer has no other fixed office, reversed the principal-place-of-business test applied in *Soliman*. When inapplicable, courts continue to apply the *Soliman* test.

If a home office qualifies as a taxpayer's principal place of business, the deductions allowed must be determined. Certain expenses, such as real estate taxes and home mortgage interest, are fully deductible without regard to the use of a home as a trade or business. Other expenses for keeping up and running the home (e.g., property insurance, utilities, general repairs and maintenance, depreciation) are partially deductible. The deductions are limited based on the percentage of the home used for business. A common method to determine the percentage of a home used for business is to divide the square footage of the home office by the square footage of the total home. For example, if in a 1,200 square foot home, a 240 square foot spare bedroom is used as an office, the percent used for business is 20% (240/1,200), and so 20% of these household expenses would be deductible.

It should be noted that section 280A(c)(5) limits the deduction of otherwise deductible expenses, such as insurance, utilities, and depreciation (with depreciation taken last), that are allocable to the home office. The total amount of these deductions may not exceed the gross income from the business, reduced by both the business portion of expenses deductible without regard to business use of a home (e.g., real estate taxes and home mortgage interest allocable to the office), and the business expenses that relate to the business activity of the home (e.g., supplies, separate telephone line for the business and other expenses not allocable to use of the office). Any deductions disallowed may be carried over to the succeeding tax year. IRC § 280A(c)(5). The operation of section 280A(c)(5) is explored more fully in the next section in the context of vacation homes.

Example. Taxpayer uses a room in his home exclusively and regularly as his principal place of business. In Year 1, Taxpayer earns $6,000 and incurs the following expenses with respect to the home: $2,000 business telephone line and supplies; $15,000 real estate taxes and mortgage interest; and $4,000 insurance and utilities. Depreciation on the property would have been $8,000 if used entirely for business. Taxpayer can deduct the $2,000 of business expenses not related to the use of his home. Additionally, Taxpayer can deduct the $15,000 of property taxes and home mortgage interest, allowable under section 280A(b) without regard to business use of the home. Deductibility of the remaining $12,000 of expenses (for insurance, utilities, and depreciation) depends on the percentage of the home used for business. Assuming the square footage of the office is 20% of the total square footage of the home, Taxpayer could deduct $800 for insurance and utilities (20% × $4,000) and $1,600 for depreciation (20% × $8,000), subject to the overall limitation under section 280A(c)(5). The deduction is limited under section 280A(c)(5) to only $1,000 (i.e., income from the business ($6,000), minus business expenses not related to the office ($2,000) and the portion of the taxes and interest allocable to the office ($3,000)). In determining which of these expense deductions are allowed in Year 1, ordering rules require depreciation to be taken last. Prop. Treas. Reg. § 1.280A-2(i)(5). Accordingly, all $800 for insurance and utilities is currently deductible; but only $200 of the $1,600 in depreciation is currently deductible, with the remaining $1,400 carried over to Year 2.

B. Vacation Home Deductions

Many Americans own second homes used for vacations. Typically these homes are located near beaches, lakes, rivers, mountains, or other desirable areas that make them attractive short-term rental properties. As discussed in Chapter 7, expenses relating to rental properties are generally deductible under sections 162 or 212. Moreover such properties may be depreciated under sections 167 and 168. Can you see the economic and tax planning opportunity here? Why not acquire property that can provide personal enjoyment while also serving as an investment and an income-producing tax shelter? The problem that arises in the tax context, thus, is separating the non-deductible personal expenses from the deductible profit-seeking expenses of such a residence. As in the case of home offices, section 280A attempts to solve this problem by drawing lines and making allocations.

1. Use as a Residence

The beginning of our analysis is the same as for home offices. The general rule of section 280A disallows deductions for a dwelling unit used by the taxpayer as a residence. IRC § 280A(a). From this we can see that if the taxpayer does not use the property as a residence, section 280A does not apply. (However, in that case the limitations of section 183, the subject of our next chapter, will apply.) The first question, then, is what constitutes use as a residence? The statute adopts an arbitrary bright-line test. The taxpayer uses the dwelling unit as a residence "if he uses such unit ... for personal purposes for a number of days which exceeds the greater of—

(A) 14 days, or

(B) 10 percent of the number of days during such year for which such unit is rented at a fair rental." IRC § 280A(d)(1).

2. Deductible Expenses and Their Limits

Assuming that the taxpayer uses the vacation home as a residence, we are then obliged to consider which expenses are deductible and in what amount under the further provisions of section 280A. Just as with home offices, subsection (b) creates an exception for expenses such as property taxes and mortgage interest to the extent that they would be deductible without regard to personal or business use. IRC § 280A(b). The otherwise deductible expenses that are attributable to the use as a rental property are also not subject to general rule of section 280A. IRC § 280A(c)(3). However various other limitations come into play with respect to the deductible expenses attributable to the rental use.

In essence the proposed regulation sets up three prioritized categories of rental activity deductions and subjects them to an overall cap equal to the gross rental income from the activity. *See* IRC § 280A(c)(5); Prop. Treas. Reg. § 1.280A-3(c)(3).

Gross rental income is defined as the gross receipts from the rental minus expenditures to obtain tenants such as advertising and management fees. Prop. Treas. Reg. § 1.280A-3(c)(2). The three prioritized categories of rental activity deductions are:

Category 1: The expenses that would be deductible in any event (e.g., property taxes and interest) that are properly allocable to the days when the unit is rented.

Category 2: The expenses attributable to the rental activity that do not affect the taxpayer's basis in the property.

Category 3: The expenses attributable to the rental activity that do affect the taxpayer's basis in the property, i.e., depreciation. Prop. Treas. Reg. § 1.280A-3(d)(3).

The expenses are deducted in the order set out above, subject to the overall cap. The deductions disallowed by the gross rental income limit will carry over to the next year.

For the second and third category of expenses, the statute specifies an allocation method for determining the amount of the expenses that are potentially deductible. The allocation is made based on the ratio that the number of days that the property was rented bears to the total number of days the property was used during the year. IRC § 280A(e)(1). So, for example, if the property was rented for 75 days and used by the owner for 25 days of vacation time, then 75/100 or 3/4 of the Category 2 and 3 expenses are potentially deductible.

For the first category of expenses, the statute does not specify an allocation method and litigation has ensued. There is a proposed regulation of long standing that asserts that Category 1 expenses should be allocated using the same ratio as the other two categories (i.e., days of rental divided by days of use). *See* Prop. Treas. Reg. §§ 1.280A-3(d)(1) & (3). Taxpayers have taken the position that the allocation should be based on the ratio that days of rental bears to the total number of days in the year. The taxpayer position has met with success in the courts. *See, e.g.,* Bolton v. Commissioner, 694 F.2d 556 (9th Cir. 1982); McKinney v. Commissioner, 732 F.2d 414 (10th Cir. 1983). The reason that the allocation method is important is because of the gross income cap on the rental activity deductions. The smaller the Category 1 deductions (which get deducted anyway under the exception rule of section 280A(b)) the more room that is left under the cap to deduct the Category 2 and 3 deductions.

Understanding the operation of section 280A with respect to vacation homes is aided by examples. Consider this one:

Example. Taxpayer, a stockbroker, owns a spacious lakeside cabin in upstate New York not far from a ski resort. In the current year she spends 40 days vacationing at the cabin and rents it to unrelated third persons for another 120 days. Gross rental income from renting the cabin is $20,000. Expenses relating to the cabin are as follows:

Category 1	Property Taxes	$6,000
	Mortgage Interest	$10,000
Category 2	Utilities	$5,000
	Maintenance	$4,000
Category 3	Depreciation	$18,000
Total		**$43,000**

If we use the allocation method supported by the proposed regulation, we would allocate $12,000 of the Category 1 expenses to the rental activity (120/160 × 16,000 = $12,000). This would leave only another $8,000 of deductions from Categories 2 and 3 before encountering the income cap. We would then deduct those expenses as follows:

Utilities	$5,000	× 3/4 =	$3,750
Maintenance	$4,000	× 3/4 =	$3,000
Depreciation	$18,000	× 3/4 =	$1,250 (+ $12,250 disallowed)
Total	**$27,000**		**$8,000**

If we use the allocation method supported by the case law, we would allocate about $5,260 of the Category 1 expenses to the rental activity (120/365 × 16,000 = $5,260). This would leave another $14,740 of deductions from Categories 2 and 3 before encountering the income cap. We would then deduct those expenses as follows:

Utilities	$5,000	× 3/4 =	$3,750
Maintenance	$4,000	× 3/4 =	$3,000
Depreciation	$18,000	× 3/4 =	$7,990 (+ $5,510 disallowed)
Total	**$27,000**		**$14,740**

Remember that any of the Category 1 expenses that are disallowed under section 280A(c)(5) remain deductible under the regular deduction rules for property taxes and mortgage interest. *See* IRC §§ 62, 163, 164, 280A(b). The disallowed depreciation deductions carry over to the next year.

C. Exclusion of Gain on Sale of Residence

Many taxpayers buy and sell a number of homes over the course of a lifetime. Prior to 1997, two statutory rules governed the sale of a principal residence. Under the *gain rollover rule*, no gain was recognized on the sale of a principal residence if a taxpayer bought a new residence (two years before or after the sale of the old residence) at least equal in cost to the sales price of the old residence and used the new residence as his or her principal residence within a specified period of time. The gain not recognized was rolled over into the new residence by making its basis equal to cost less gain not recognized on the sale of the old residence. Under the *one-time exclusion rule*, a taxpayer could exclude from gross income up to $125,000 of gain from the sale of a principal residence if the taxpayer had attained age 55 and had owned and used the property as a principal residence for three or more of the five years preceding the sale.

There were inherent problems with the rollover provision and the $125,000 one-time exclusion. The gain rollover rule promoted inefficient use of taxpayers' financial resources by requiring taxpayers to purchase larger and more expensive houses than they otherwise would in order to avoid tax liability. The one-time exclusion discouraged many elderly taxpayers from selling their homes if they would realize gain in excess of $125,000 or if they had previously used the one-time exclusion. Both required taxpayers to keep detailed records of transactions affecting basis (such as improvements and untaxed gains from previous residential transactions) for decades, making it difficult to calculate gain on the sale of a residence.

In 1997, Congress repealed the gain rollover rule and amended the exclusion rule. Under current section 121, a taxpayer may exclude from gross income up to $250,000 ($500,000 with respect to certain married couples filing jointly) of gain realized on the sale or exchange of a principal residence. To be eligible for the exclusion: (1) the taxpayer must have *owned* the residence and *used* it as a *principal residence* for at least two of the five years before the sale or exchange, and (2) the taxpayer must not have claimed the exclusion for another sale within the immediately preceding two year period. These two requirements will be discussed in greater detail.

1. Ownership and Use Requirements

To exclude gain under section 121, a taxpayer must have owned and used the property as the taxpayer's principal residence for an aggregate of at least two years of the five years before the sale or exchange. The regulations under section 121 clarify that the required two years of ownership and use do not have to be continuous, and that short temporary absences for vacations are counted as periods of use. *See* Treas. Reg. § 1.121-1(c)(1), (2), (4) Examples 3–5.

Section 121(d) provides several special rules related to the ownership and use requirements that apply to deceased and divorced spouses. First, a taxpayer who receives property from a deceased spouse is treated as owning and using the property for the period the deceased spouse owned and used the property before death. IRC § 121(d)(2). Second, a taxpayer who obtains property from a spouse or former spouse in a transaction described in section 1041(a) is treated as owning the property for the period the transferor spouse owned the property. IRC § 121(d)(3)(A). Third, a taxpayer, whose spouse or former spouse is granted use of property under a divorce or separation instrument, is treated as using the property as the taxpayer's principal residence, provided the taxpayer has an ownership interest in the property and the spouse or former spouse uses the property as his or her principal residence. IRC § 121(d)(3)(B).

2. One Sale Every Two Years Limitation

The section 121 exclusion is allowed each time a taxpayer selling or exchanging a principal residence meets the eligibility requirements, but generally it is not allowed more than once every two years. IRC § 121(b)(3).

Example. Taxpayer owns two residences: Home A (that she uses as her principal residence for Years 1 and 2) and Home B (that she uses as her principal residence for Years 3 and 4). Taxpayer sells Home A in Year 5 and excludes gain realized on its sale under section 121; Taxpayer then sells Home B in Year 6. Although Home B meets the two-year ownership and use requirements of section 121, Taxpayer is not eligible to exclude gain from the sale of Home B because Taxpayer excluded gain within the last two years under section 121 from the sale of Home A.

Note that a taxpayer may elect not to have the section 121 exclusion apply. IRC § 121(f). In the example above, if the taxpayer anticipated selling both homes within two years, and knew the sale of Home A would generate a smaller gain than the sale of Home B, it would have been beneficial for Taxpayer to elect out of the exclusion for the sale of Home A and preserve the benefits of the exclusion for the sale of Home B.

3. Amount of Exclusion

A taxpayer may exclude from gross income up to $250,000 of gain under section 121. A married couple may exclude up to $500,000 of gain if: (1) the spouses file a joint return for the year of sale; (2) either spouse meets the two-year ownership requirement with respect to the property; (3) both spouses meet the use requirement with respect to the property; and (4) neither spouse used the exclusion within the last two years. IRC § 121(b)(2)(A). There is a special rule for certain sales by surviving spouses. *See* IRC § 121(b)(4) (providing a $500,000 maximum exclusion amount in the case of a sale or exchange of property by an unmarried individual whose spouse is deceased on the date of such sale provided certain requirements are met).

All may not be lost if the requirements for a maximum exclusion of $500,000 are not met, as the exclusion is determined on an individual basis. Thus, a husband and wife who do not share a principal residence but file joint returns may exclude up to $250,000 of gain from the sale of each spouse's principal residence provided that each would be entitled to exclude up to $250,000 if they filed separate returns. Similarly, if a single taxpayer who is otherwise eligible for the exclusion marries someone who has used the exclusion within the two years before the marriage, the newly married taxpayer would be entitled to a maximum exclusion of $250,000. In other words, nothing prevents a taxpayer from claiming the exclusion he or she would otherwise be entitled to. IRC § 121(b)(2)(B).

Section 121(c) provides a reduced maximum exclusion for taxpayers who sell a principal residence, but who fail to satisfy the ownership and use requirements or the one-sale-every-two-years rule. In order to claim a reduced exclusion, the sale must be because of a change in place of employment, health, or unforeseen circumstances. The regulations provide guidance, including several safe harbor provisions, for determining when a sale or exchange is by reason of a change in employment, health, or unforeseen circumstances. *See* Treas. Reg. § 1.121-3. The amount of the reduced maximum exclusion is a portion of the general $250,000 or $500,000 exclusion amount that would otherwise apply if the taxpayer(s) satisfied the ownership and use requirements and the one-sale-every-two years rule. The portion is determined by the following formula:

Formula

$$\begin{matrix} \text{Reduced} \\ \text{Maximum} \\ \text{Exclusion} \end{matrix} = \begin{matrix} \text{Normal} \\ \text{Exclusion} \\ \text{Amount} \end{matrix} \times \frac{\begin{matrix}\text{Shorter of (1) period owned and}\\ \text{used as principal residence or}\\ \text{(2) period between prior sale for}\\ \text{which gain was excluded and}\\ \text{current sale}\end{matrix}}{\text{24 Months or 730 Days}}$$

The following examples illustrate the computation of the reduced exclusion:

Example 1. Taxpayer purchases a house that she uses as her principal residence. Twelve months after purchase, Taxpayer sells the house due to a change in place of her employment. Taxpayer has not excluded gain under section 121 on a prior sale or exchange of property within the last two years. If Taxpayer had owned and used her residence for two years, then she could have excluded up to $250,000 of gain. Since Taxpayer failed to meet the two-year ownership and use requirements for the exclusion by reason of a change in place of employment, she is eligible to exclude up to $125,000 of gain ($250,000 × 12/24).

Example 2. Same facts as Example 1 above, except suppose that Taxpayer had excluded gain under section 121 on a prior sale of property within the last six months. Taxpayer is eligible to exclude up to $62,500 of gain ($250,000 × 6/24). Note that the numerator is six months—the shorter of (1) the period Taxpayer owned and used the house as a principal residence (12 months) or (2) the period of time between the prior sale of property for which she excluded gain under section 121 and the date of the current sale (6 months).

4. Principal Residence

The section 121 exclusion is available only with respect to a sale or exchange of a taxpayer's *principal* residence. Some taxpayers own more than one residence, alternating between them during the year. Consider, for example, a Congressman who owns residences in both Washington, D.C. and his congressional district. Or, a professor who has a joint faculty appointment at two universities in different cities and who owns residences in both cities. If a taxpayer owns more than one residence, only one can qualify as the taxpayer's principal residence for purposes of section 121. Which is considered the taxpayer's principal residence is a factual issue. The regulations provide that the property that the taxpayer uses a majority of the time during the year ordinarily will be considered the taxpayer's principal residence. In addition to use, other factors relevant to identifying the taxpayer's principal residence include: (1) the taxpayer's place of employment; (2) the principal place of abode of the taxpayer's family; (3) the address listed on the taxpayer's tax returns, driver's license, automobile registration, and voter registration card; (4) the taxpayer's mailing address for bills and correspondence; (5) the location of the taxpayer's banks; and (6) the location of the taxpayer's churches and recreational clubs. Treas. Reg. § 1.121-1(b)(2). For a district court case applying these factors, read *Guinan v. United States*, included below.

An owner of vacation or rental property might attempt to qualify the property for the section 121 exclusion by moving into it for two years before sale. To thwart this tactic, section 121(b)(5) provides that gain on the sale of a residence is not excluded from gross income to the extent the gain is allocated to periods of "nonqualified use" of the residence (i.e., periods in which the property is not used as the principal residence of the taxpayer, the taxpayer's spouse, or former spouse). If there is a nonqualified use, the amount of the gain not excluded is determined by multiplying the total gain by a fraction, the numerator of which is the aggregate periods of nonqualified use and the denominator of which is the total time the taxpayer owned the property. There are some important exceptions. *See* IRC § 121(b)(5)(C)(ii).

Note that a taxpayer's principal residence does not have to be a traditional house; it may be a house trailer, a house boat, stock in a cooperative housing unit, or any other dwelling place. Treas. Reg. § 1.121-1(b)(1). A principal residence may also include, in some circumstances, vacant land that is adjacent to the taxpayer's principal residence. Treas. Reg. § 1.121-1(b)(3).

5. Tax Planning

The maximum exclusion under section 121 is sufficiently large to prevent most homeowners from paying any capital gains tax when selling their homes. To that end, is there any need for taxpayers to keep detailed records of capital improvements that increase basis of their homes? Records of improvements and basis should be kept if there is a possibility that gain might be recognized on a later sale (i.e., the gain might exceed the maximum exclusion amount of $250,000 or $500,000 in the case of certain joint returns). This could happen, for example, if the taxpayer lives in the home for a long period of time, or if the home rapidly appreciates, or if the taxpayer does not own or use the home long enough to qualify for the exclusion.

IV. Materials

Popov v. Commissioner

246 F.3d 1190 (9th Cir. 2001)

HAWKINS, CIRCUIT JUDGE:

This case concerns the continuing problem of the home office deduction. We conclude, on the facts of this case, that a professional musician is entitled to deduct the expenses from the portion of her home used exclusively for musical practice.

FACTS AND PROCEDURAL BACKGROUND

Katia Popov is a professional violinist who performs regularly with the Los Angeles Chamber Orchestra and the Long Beach Symphony. She also contracts with various studios to record music for the motion picture industry. In 1993, she worked for twenty-four such contractors and recorded in thirty-eight different locations. These recording sessions required that Popov be able to read scores quickly. The musicians did not receive the sheet music in advance of the recording sessions; instead, they were presented with their parts when they arrived at the studio, and recording would begin shortly thereafter. None of Popov's twenty-six employers provided her with a place to practice.

Popov lived with her husband Peter, an attorney, and their four-year-old daughter Irina, in a one-bedroom apartment in Los Angeles, California. The apartment's living room served as Popov's home office. The only furniture in the living room consisted of shelves with recording equipment, a small table, a bureau for storing sheet music, and a chair. Popov used this area to practice the violin and to make recordings, which she used for practice purposes and as demonstration tapes for orchestras. No one slept in the living room, and the Popovs' daughter was not allowed to play there. Popov spent four to five hours a day practicing in the living room.

In their 1993 tax returns, the Popovs claimed a home office deduction for the living room and deducted forty percent of their annual rent and twenty percent of their annual electricity bill. The Internal Revenue Service ("the Service") disallowed these deductions, and the Popovs filed a petition for redetermination in the Tax Court.

The Tax Court concluded that the Popovs were not entitled to a home office deduction. Although "practicing at home was a very important component to [Popov's] success as a musician," the court found that her living room was not her "principal place of business." In the court's view, her principal places of business were the studios and concert halls where she recorded and performed, because it was her performances in these places that earned her income.

ANALYSIS

The Internal Revenue Code allows a deduction for a home office that is exclusively used as "the principal place of business for any trade or business of the taxpayer." 26 U.S.C. § 280A(c)(1)(A). The Code does not define the phrase "principal place of business."

A. The *Soliman* Tests

Our inquiry is governed by Commissioner v. Soliman, 506 U.S. 168 (1993), the Supreme Court's most recent treatment of the home office deduction. In *Soliman,* the taxpayer was an anesthesiologist who spent thirty to thirty-five hours per week with patients at three different hospitals. None of the hospitals provided Soliman with an office, so he used a spare bedroom for contacting patients and surgeons, maintaining billing records and patient logs, preparing for treatments, and reading medical journals.

The Supreme Court denied Soliman a deduction for his home office, holding that the "statute does not allow for a deduction whenever a home office may be characterized as legitimate." *Id.* at 174. Instead, courts must determine whether the home office is the taxpayer's principal place of business. Although the Court could not "develop an objective formula that yields a clear answer in every case," the Court stressed two primary considerations: "the relative importance of the activities performed at each business location and the time spent at each place." *Id.* at 174–75. We address each in turn.

1. Relative Importance

The importance of daily practice to Popov's profession cannot be denied. Regular practice is essential to playing a musical instrument at a high level of ability, and it is this level of commitment that distinguishes the professional from the amateur. Without daily practice, Popov would be unable to perform in professional orchestras. She would also be unequipped for the peculiar demands of studio recording: The ability to read and perform scores on sight requires an acute musical intelligence that must be constantly developed and honed. In short, Popov's four to five hours of daily practice lay at the very heart of her career as a professional violinist.

Of course, the concert halls and recording studios are also important to Popov's profession. Without them, she would have no place in which to perform. Audiences and motion picture companies are unlikely to flock to her one-bedroom apartment. In *Soliman,* the Supreme Court stated that, although "no one test is determinative in every case," "the point where goods and services are delivered must be given great weight in determining the place where the most important functions are performed." *Id.* at 175. The Service places great weight on this statement, contending that Popov's performances should be analogized to the "service" of delivering anesthesia that was at issue in *Soliman;* these "services" are delivered in concert halls and studios, not in her apartment.

We agree with Popov that musical performance is not so easily captured under a "goods and services" rubric. The German poet Heinrich Heine observed that music stands "halfway between thought and phenomenon, between spirit and matter, a sort of nebulous mediator, like and unlike each of the things it mediates — spirit that requires manifestation in time, and matter that can do without space." Heinrich Heine, Letters on the French Stage (1837), quoted in Words about Music: A Treasury of Writings 2 (John Amis & Michael Rose eds., 1989). Or as Harry Ellis Dickson of the Boston Symphony Orchestra explained more concretely:

> A musician's life is different from that of most people. We don't go to an office every day, or to a factory, or to a bank. We go to an empty hall. We don't deal in anything tangible, nor do we produce anything except sounds. We saw away, or blow, or pound for a few hours and then we go home. It is a strange way to make a living!

Harry Ellis Dickson, Gentlemen, More Dolce Please (1969), quoted in *Drucker v. Comm'r,* 715 F.2d 67, 68–69 (2d Cir.1983).

It is possible, of course, to wrench musical performance into a "delivery of services" framework, but we see little value in such a wooden and unblinking application of the tax laws. *Soliman* itself recognized that in this area of law "variations are inevitable in case-by-case determinations." 506 U.S. at 175. We believe this to be such a case. We simply do not find the "delivery of services" framework to be helpful in analyzing this particular problem. Taken to extremes, the Service's argument would seem to generate odd results in a variety of other areas as well. We doubt, for example, that an appellate advocate's primary place of business is the podium from which he delivers his oral argument, or that a professor's primary place of business is the classroom, rather than the office in which he prepares his lectures.

We therefore conclude that the "relative importance" test yields no definitive answer in this case, and we accordingly turn to the second prong of the *Soliman* inquiry.

2. Amount of Time

Under *Soliman*, "the decisionmaker should ... compare the amount of time spent at home with the time spent at other places where business activities occur." *Id.* at 177. "This factor assumes particular significance when," as in this case, "comparison of the importance of the functions performed at various places yields no definitive answer to the principal place of business inquiry." *Id.* In *Soliman*, the taxpayer spent significantly more time in the hospitals than he did in his home office. In this case, Popov spent significantly more time practicing the violin at home than she did performing or recording.

This second factor tips the balance in the Popovs' favor. They are accordingly entitled to a home office deduction for Katia Popov's practice space, because it was exclusively used as her principal place of business.

Guinan v. United States

2003-1 U.S.T.C. (CCH) ¶ 50,475 (D. Arizona 2003)

ROSENBLATT, J.

This is an action by the plaintiffs seeking a refund of $45,009.00 for income taxes they paid in the 1998 tax year on the gain realized from the sale of their residence in Wisconsin. The plaintiffs filed an amended income tax return in January 2001 in which they excluded that gain pursuant to 26 U.S.C. § 121; the Internal Revenue Service disallowed the requested refund in December 2001. The issue before the Court is whether the plaintiffs' Wisconsin residence was their principal residence for purposes of 26 U.S.C. § 121(a), which, as amended by the Taxpayer Relief Act of 1997, provides in relevant part that "[g]ross income shall not include gain from the sale ... of property if, during the 5-year period ending on the date of sale..., such property has been owned and used by the taxpayer as the taxpayer's principal residence for periods aggregating 2 years or more."

The plaintiffs purchased their Wisconsin residence in March 1993 and sold it on September 15, 1998. During the five-year period prior to the sale of the Wisconsin residence the plaintiffs, who are retired, also owned homes in Georgia and Arizona. Their Georgia residence, which they owned when they purchased the Wisconsin residence, was sold in 1996, at which time they purchased a home in Arizona. The plaintiffs generally resided at their Wisconsin home during the warmer months and at their Georgia or Arizona homes during the rest of the year. According to the plaintiffs' affidavit, which the United States does not dispute, during the five-year period from September 15, 1993 through September 15, 1998 the plaintiffs occupied their Wisconsin residence for 847 days, their Georgia residence for 563 days, and their Arizona residence for 375 days.

The plaintiffs, as the taxpayers claiming a refund due to an exclusion from income, bear the burden of proving that their Wisconsin residence was their principal residence during the relevant time period. The Court concludes as a matter of law that they have not met that burden.

The United States concedes that the plaintiffs owned and used their Wisconsin residence for the duration required by § 121(a) during the relevant five year period. *See* Treasury Regulation § 1.121-1(c). Since what remains disputed is whether the plaintiffs used the Wisconsin residence as their principal residence during that time period, the Court looks to Treasury Regulation § 1.121-1(b)(2) for guidance. That regulation states:

> (2) Principal residence. In the case of a taxpayer using more than one property as a residence, whether property is used by the taxpayer as the taxpayer's principal residence depends upon all of the facts and circumstances. If a taxpayer alternates between 2 properties, using each as a residence for successive periods of time, the property that the taxpayer uses a majority of the time during the year ordinarily will be considered the taxpayer's principal residence. In addition to the taxpayer's use of the property, relevant factors in determining a taxpayer's principal residence include, but are not limited to —
>
> (i) The taxpayer's place of employment;
>
> (ii) The principal place of abode of the taxpayer's family members;
>
> (iii) The address listed on the taxpayer's federal and state tax returns, driver's license, automobile registration, and voter registration card;
>
> (iv) The taxpayer's mailing address for bills and correspondence;
>
> (v) The location of the taxpayer's banks; and
>
> (vi) The location of religious organizations and recreational clubs with which the taxpayer is affiliated.

The Court concurs with the United States that the fact that the plaintiffs utilized the Wisconsin residence on more days in total during the relevant five year period than either the Georgia residence or the Arizona residence is not determinative for purposes of § 121(a) since the governing regulation refers to the time spent in a residence during a single tax year. *See* § 1.121-1(b)(2) ("[T]he property that the taxpayer uses a majority of the time *during the year* ordinarily will be considered the taxpayer's principal residence." (Emphasis added). The plaintiffs' own undisputed figures fail to establish that the Wisconsin house was their principal residence inasmuch as they show that the plaintiffs spent more time in the Wisconsin house only during the first year of the five-year period (1993–1994), and that for each of the other four years they spent the majority of each year either at the Georgia house (1994–1995 and 1995–1996), or the Arizona house (1996–1997 and 1997–1998); their figures also show that for the entirety of the five-year period they spent more time in the Georgia and Arizona houses combined than they did in the Wisconsin house (52.5% versus 47.5%, respectively).

The Court also concurs with the United States that while time spent in a residence is a major factor, if not the most important factor, in determining whether it is the principal residence, other factors are also relevant, *see* § 1.121-1(b)(2), and in this case those other factors, taken as a whole, do not establish that the Wisconsin house was the plaintiffs' principal residence during the relevant time period.

First, a majority of the relevant factors do not actually favor any one of the residences as being the principal residence: the location of the plaintiffs' recreational and other activities do not favor Wisconsin since the evidence reflects activities in both Wisconsin and Georgia, *e.g.,* while Mr. Guinan served on the board of their Wisconsin homeowners' association and the plaintiffs returned to Wisconsin during the winter months for major holidays and to attend Green Bay Packers games, both of the plaintiffs were actively involved in tennis activities in Georgia and Mr. Guinan lectured at local Georgia colleges; the location of the principal abodes of the plaintiffs' children do not favor any of the residences since none of the children then lived in Wisconsin, Georgia, or Arizona; the location where the plaintiffs received their mail and did their banking does not favor Wisconsin since the plaintiffs received mail and had bank accounts at each residence; and the location where the plaintiffs registered their vehicles does not favor Wisconsin since while the plaintiffs kept one car and two boats in Wisconsin, they kept two cars at their Georgia house and then at their Arizona house.

Second, other important factors, however, definitely point to the Wisconsin residence as not being the plaintiffs' principal residence in that, during the relevant time period, neither plaintiff filed any Wisconsin state tax return but did file Georgia and/or Arizona state returns, neither plaintiff was registered to vote in Wisconsin but both were registered in Georgia and then in Arizona, neither plaintiff had a Wisconsin driver's license but both had a Georgia license and then an Arizona license, and the plaintiffs treated their Arizona house as their principal residence for the 1999 tax year for purposes of the now-repealed 26 U.S.C. § 1034(a).

Third, the one relevant factor decidedly favoring Wisconsin as the principal residence, *i.e.,* the imposing size of the Wisconsin house, is insufficient as a matter of law to overcome the facts and circumstances establishing that Wisconsin was not the plaintiffs' principal residence for purposes of § 121(a).

V. Related Matters

- **Use by Family and Friends.** Use of a personal residence by family and friends without paying fair rental value is deemed personal use of the residence by the owner for purposes of section 280A. IRC § 280(d)(2).

- **Home Swaps.** Reciprocal exchanges of vacation homes are deemed the equivalent of personal use by the owner for section 280A purposes. IRC § 280A(d)(2)(B).

- **Exclusive Use of Home Offices.** A big road block to qualifying for the home office deduction is that a taxpayer must use a portion of the home *exclusively* for his or her business. De minimis personal use, a question of fact, does not disqualify the home office. *See, e.g.*, Culp v. Commissioner, T.C. Memo 1993-270; Lind v. Commissioner, T.C. Memo 1985-490. However, use of a home office in connection with the taxpayer's employment is treated as a personal use violating the exclusivity requirement. *See* Hamacher v. Commissioner, 94 T.C. 348 (1990) (denying a home office deduction for an actor who regularly used his home office in connection with two separate independent business activities — one activity concerned that of an employee who was already provided with an office, and the other activity concerned independent contractor status where a large percentage of the activity took place at the home office).

- **Vacation Home Not Used as Residence.** If a vacation home is not a taxpayer's residence for purposes of section 280A, section 183 will apply. This is the subject of the next chapter. If the vacation home rental is considered an activity engaged in for profit, allocable expenses are deductible in full. If the rental is considered an activity not engaged in for profit, then allocable expenses are deductible only to the extent of rental income from the vacation home. Note that even if section 183 applies, expenses will still have to be allocated between personal and rental use. IRC § 280A(e)(1) (parenthetical language).

- **Don't Ask, Don't Tell — Section 280A(g):** There is a special rule for property rented less than 15 days during the year. Under this provision no deductions (except for interest, taxes, etc.) are allowed, but the rental income is excluded from gross income. IRC § 280A(g). Taxpayers who live in places where homes can be rented for large sums for short periods can take good advantage of this rule. Note that it has been suggested that recipients of home renovations, such as through the TV show *Extreme Makeover — Home Edition*, may exclude from income the value of home improvements under section 280A(g). Apparently, the TV show leases the homes it makes over and then argues that the improvements it makes equate to "rent" it pays. The Service's view is that to the extent the improvements constitute prizes or awards, they cannot also be considered rent for purposes of the section 280A(g) exclusion. Letter from Robert M. Brown, Associate Chief Counsel, to Honorable Marsha Blackburn, U.S. House of Representatives (Sept. 14, 2005).

- **Section 121 and Involuntary and Compulsory Conversions.** The destruction, theft, seizure, requisition or condemnation of property is treated as the sale of property for purposes of section 121. IRC § 121(d)(5).

- **Section 121 and Like Kind Exchanges.** Property acquired in a like kind exchange and subsequently converted to the taxpayer's principal residence does not qualify for the section 121 exclusion upon sale or exchange unless the sale or exchange occurs more than five years after its acquisition. IRC § 121(d)(10). Like kind exchanges are addressed in Chapter 24. For the tax treatment of a principal residence that is converted to business use and then is the subject of a like kind exchange, see Revenue Procedure 2005-14, 2005-1 C.B. 528.

- **Section 121 and Depreciation Recapture.** If a taxpayer uses part of his principal residence as a place of business (home office), the taxpayer is entitled to depreciate the business portion of the residence. If the taxpayer later sells the principal residence, however, gain attributable to depreciation is not excludable under section 121. IRC § 121(d)(6). Note that gain does not have to be apportioned between the portion used for business and the portion used as a principal residence.

- **Home Office Deduction Safeharbor.** Starting with the 2013 tax year, qualified taxpayers have a new, simpler option for figuring their home office tax deduction. In short, they can deduct annually $5 per square foot of home office space up to 300 square feet, for up to $1,500 in deductions, in lieu of calculating, allocating, and substantiating actual expenses. Restrictions on claiming the home office deduction discussed earlier (e.g., office must be used regularly and exclusively for business) continue to apply. Rev. Proc. 2013-13, 2013-6 I.R.B. 478.

Chapter 23

Hobby Losses

I. Assignment

Read: Internal Revenue Code: §§ 183(a)–(d). Skim §§ 280A(f)(3), (e)(1).

       Treasury Regulations: §§ 1.67-1T(a)(1)(iv); 1.183-1(a), (b)(1)–(2), (c)(1), (d)(1)–(2), (e); 1.183-2.

    Text: Overview
          Nickerson v. Commissioner
          Related Matters

Complete the problems.

II. Problems

1.   Ida Gray Nelson operated a dental practice that was the sole source of income for her family. A friend who had been in the horse-breeding business for years convinced Ida that there was great potential for profit in breeding and selling Arabian horses. In Year 1, Ida purchased a 34-acre farm located six miles from her family's residence, and purchased two broodmares that were in foal, and a syndicate share of a stallion. Ida, who had no knowledge of breeding Arabian horses, consulted with other horse breeders and read journal articles about horse breeding; she also attended horse shows and seminars and purchased video tapes on breeding Arabian horses. Ida did not create a written business plan, and did not prepare any written profit or loss statements or balance sheets for the horse-breeding activity. But she did establish a separate bank account, obtain business cards, create promotional materials, and maintain extensive books and records on the horse-breeding activity. Ida personally handled many horse-breeding activity duties (such as fencing the farm, repairing equipment, cleaning the barn, and bathing and feeding the horses), and often arrived after dark, very tired, in a bad mood, and dirty with a certain aroma from her work on the farm. During fall, winter, and spring, Ida spent 40 hours a week at her dental practice and 10 to 20 hours on the horse-breeding activity; during summer, she worked 40 hours on the farm and 32 hours at her dental practice. The first seven years were particularly difficult. In Year 2, the horse market began to decline, and Ida was unable to sell her foals. Indeed, between Years 1–7, Ida sold a total of five horses, receiving at most $5,000 plus another horse in return. In response to the market decline, Ida expanded the horse-breeding activity to include dealing in horse ges-

tation monitoring equipment. She also sold several colts to reduce her expenses, and she leased another farm to board other people's horses. In Year 7, two of the horses died in a sinkhole accident, and one died in a collision with a car. Ida sustained net losses from the horse-breeding activity during Years 1–11 (during Years 1–7, net losses averaged $45,000; during Years 8–11, net losses averaged $11,500). Year 12 was the first year she made a profit from the horse-breeding activity. Are Ida's farm losses during Years 1–11 subject to the limitations of section 183?

2. Assume Ida's farm activity in part 1, above, is subject to section 183. In Year 11, Ida had $10,000 of gross income from operating the farm. To what extent are the following expenses deductible in Year 11?

Interest on the farm mortgage	$5,000
Property taxes on the farm	$2,000
Horse feed and other supplies	$1,000
Advertising	$200
Repairs	$800
Depreciation on buildings	$1,600

III. Overview

As we have studied, expenses and losses incurred in carrying on a trade or business or profit-seeking activity are generally deductible. Consider the owner of a farm who devotes all of his time to breeding and selling horses. Clearly, he should be able to deduct the ordinary and necessary expenses of maintaining the horse farm, as well as losses realized from the sale of horses since it is his business. He should also be able to take depreciation deductions for the cost of farm buildings and capital improvements, such as fencing and feed bins. Review IRC §§ 162(a), 165(c)(1)–(2), 167, 212.

Consider now the wealthy dentist who owns a farm outside of town and who spends occasional weekends on the farm clearing brush and raising a pony for future sale. The dentist should be entitled to deductions that are allowable without regard to whether an activity is business or profit related, such as certain taxes and casualty losses. Review IRC §§ 164, 165(c)(3). But should he be entitled to deduct other expenses and losses with respect to the farm, such as medical expenses with respect to the pony and depreciation with respect to buildings and improvements? Would it make a difference if the dentist received some income from the farm, such as rent from leasing some of the land?

Section 183, enacted in 1969, deals specifically with hobby activities and denies business deductions for what amounts to personal consumption expenditures. Section 183 comes up many times in the context of activities involving real property (e.g., ski lodges, cattle ranches, horse-breeding farms), and thus, is considered here in the unit on real estate taxation. But it comes up in other situations as well (e.g., boat chartering, air craft leasing, and fiction writing activities).

Section 183(a) generally prohibits any deductions attributable to a hobby—an *activity not engaged in for profit.* Yet, section 183(b) goes on to permit deductions attributable to a hobby, but only to the extent of income attributable to the hobby. The approach taken by section 183 should not come as a surprise. Expenses and losses from personal hobby activities should not be allowed to shelter income from other sources. However, if a personal hobby activity produces reportable income, then expenses and losses incurred to produce that income should be allowed to offset that income. This is a theme seen throughout the Code. For example, investment interest is deductible only to the extent of net investment income (IRC § 163(d)), gambling losses are deductible only to the extent of gambling winnings (IRC § 165(d)), and losses from passive activities are deductible only to the extent of the taxpayer's income from passive activities (IRC § 469(a)).

So, back to considering the dentist and his pony. If the dentist's farm activity is deemed to be engaged in for profit, he will be entitled to deduct all of his expenses and potentially wipe out some of his income from other sources. If his farm activity is deemed to be not engaged in for profit, it is considered a hobby and he will be entitled to deduct expenses only to the limited extent specified by section 183(b).

There is a major gotcha in all this that must be noted. Hobby expenses are classified as miscellaneous itemized deductions. Treas. Reg. § 1.67-1T(a)(1)(iv). Prior to 2018 that meant they were deductible only if, and to the extent, they exceeded 2% of the taxpayer's adjusted gross income (AGI). IRC § 67(b). Recall from Chapter 12, however, that starting in 2018 and continuing through 2025, the Tax Cuts and Jobs Act (TCJA) completely eliminated miscellaneous itemized deductions. IRC § 67(g). This means that, at least temporarily, taxpayers will not be able to deduct expenses from their hobbies but will still have to report any income they earn from their hobbies. While this may seem unfair, keep in mind that taxpayers still get to deduct expenses that would be allowable whether or not an activity is engaged in for profit (e.g., state and local property taxes, which are itemized deductions and not miscellaneous itemized deductions). Clearly, the TCJA raised the stakes for would-be business owners by making the basic question of whether an activity is a business or a hobby crucial to getting nearly any deduction.

A. Distinguishing Hobbies from Business or Profit-Seeking Activities

Section 183(c) defines an *activity not engaged in for profit* by incorporating the standards applied by sections 162 and 212, which we looked at in Chapter 7. (Recall that to be engaged in a trade or business under section 162, according to *Groetzinger v. Commissioner*, a taxpayer must be involved in an activity with continuity and regularity, and the taxpayer's primary purpose for engaging in the activity must be for profit.) Fortunately, the regulations under section 183 provide an independent set of principles to help determine whether an activity is or is not engaged in for profit.

The regulations under section 183 provide nine relevant factors that should be taken into account in determining whether or not an activity is engaged in for profit:

(1) The manner in which the taxpayer carries on the activity;

(2) The expertise of the taxpayer or his or her advisors;

(3) The time and effort expended by the taxpayer in carrying on the activity;

(4) The expectation that assets used in the activity may appreciate in value;

(5) The success of the taxpayer in carrying on other similar or dissimilar activities;

(6) The taxpayer's history of income or losses with respect to the activity;

(7) The amount of occasional profits, if any, which are earned;

(8) The financial status of the taxpayer; and

(9) Elements of personal pleasure or recreation.

Treas. Reg. § 1.183-2(b). Although the regulations set out and illustrate nine relevant factors that should normally be taken into account, no one factor, nor even a majority of them, is controlling and other factors may be relevant. "[A]ll facts and circumstances with respect to an activity are to be taken into account" with "greater weight given to objective facts [rather] than to the taxpayer's mere statement of his intent." *Id.* The Code creates a rebuttable presumption that an activity is engaged in for profit if the activity was profitable (e.g., gross income exceeded deductions) for three or more years in the five-year period ending with the year in question. IRC § 183(d) (also providing a different rule for horse breeding activities). However, no inference is to be drawn from a failure to establish the presumption. Treas. Reg. § 1.183-1(c)(1).

Read *Nickerson v. Commissioner*, included below, a case that applied these factors to a farming activity. The Seventh Circuit reversed the Tax Court's finding that the taxpayers were not engaged in the activity for profit. Do you agree with the Tax Court or the Seventh Circuit?

In some cases, a taxpayer may wish to amalgamate two or more undertakings into a single activity if doing so shows a profit (to avoid one of the activities from being treated as an activity not engaged in for profit). In ascertaining whether two or more activities of the taxpayer may be treated as one activity, all the facts and circumstances should be considered, including the degree of organizational and economic interrelationship, the business purpose served by the undertakings, and the similarity of the undertakings. Treas. Reg. § 1.183-1(d).

B. Allowable Deductions

If an activity is not engaged in for profit, deductions attributable to the activity are deductible only to the extent permitted by section 183(b). Although section 183(b) establishes two tiers of permitted deductions, the regulations under section 183 split the second tier into two parts, effectively creating the following three tiers of permitted deductions:

Tier 1: Deductions that would be allowable whether or not an activity is engaged in for profit (e.g., state and local property taxes under section 164). Treas. Reg. § 1.183-1(b)(1).

Tier 2: Deductions that would be allowable if the activity in question had been conducted for profit but that do not result in adjustments to basis of property (e.g., business expenses under section 162). Treas. Reg. § 1.183-1(b)(2).

Tier 3: Deductions that would be allowable if the activity had been conducted for profit but, unlike Tier 2 deductions, result in basis adjustments (e.g., depreciation). Treas. Reg. § 1.183-1(b)(3).

Deductions attributable to a hobby activity are marshaled into one of these three tiers for the following reasons. Tier 1 deductions are allowed in full subject, of course, to any limitations to which they would otherwise be subject (e.g., $100 floor for casualty losses). Tier 2 deductions are allowed only to the extent that gross income from the activity exceeds the total Tier 1 deductions. Tier 3 deductions are allowed only to the extent that gross income from the activity exceeds the sum of Tier 1 and Tier 2 deductions. As noted at the outset, however, the TCJA indirectly suspended the Tier 2 and Tier 3 deductions by eliminating miscellaneous itemized deductions for years 2018 through 2025. These principles can be illustrated with the following simple example.

Example. Taxpayer owns 20 acres on the side of a mountain. Each weekend in the winter, he allows his friends to snow tube on his property. This year, Taxpayer receives $10,000 from his friends to help out with expenses. Taxpayer incurs the following expenses: $5,000 for real estate taxes; $4,000 for wages paid to a neighbor to groom the snow; and $3,000 of depreciation attributable to a snow blowing machine. Assuming the activity is not engaged in for profit, Taxpayer is entitled to deductions to the extent of income from the activity, $10,000. Thus, the $5,000 in property taxes (Tier 1) are deductible in full. Gross income exceeds Tier 1 deductions by $5,000. Thus, the $4,000 in wages is considered a Tier 2 deduction and only $1,000 of depreciation is considered a Tier 3 deduction. Prior to 2018, these Tier 2 and Tier 3 deductions would have been deductible as miscellaneous itemized deductions subject to the 2% of AGI floor. For years 2018 through 2025, however, these amounts are not deductible.

Section 183 applies to individuals, S corporations, estates, and trusts. Treas. Reg. § 1.183-1(a). Some courts have applied section 183 to partnerships as well. *See* Brannen v. Commissioner, 78 T.C. 471 (1982), aff'd, 722 F.2d 695 (11th Cir. 1984).

Section 183 Checklist

Step 1: Define the "activity" of the taxpayer. Note that two or more undertakings may be treated as one activity for purposes of section 183. *See* Treas. Reg. § 1.183-1(d).

Step 2: Is the activity engaged in for profit? Consider the IRC § 183(d) presumption. Consider the nine factors in Treas. Reg. § 1.183-2(b).

Step 3: If the activity is not engaged in for profit, deductions are allowed to the extent of hobby income. Apply IRC § 183(b); Treas. Reg. § 1.183-1(b).

For years 2018 through 2025, Tier 1 deductions are allowed (as itemized deductions), but Tier 2 and Tier 3 deductions are not allowed (as miscellaneous itemized deductions). IRC § 67(g).

Step 4: If the activity is engaged in for profit, determine whether the activity is a "trade or business" activity or an "investment" activity. Apply *Groetzinger v. Commissioner*, discussed in Chapter 7.

Step 5: If the activity is a trade or business, see IRC §§ 162 (expenses), 165(c)(1) (losses), 167(a)(1) (depreciation).

Step 6: If the activity is an investment, see IRC §§ 212 (expenses), 165(c)(2) (losses), 167(a)(2) (depreciation).

IV. Materials

Nickerson v. Commissioner

700 F.2d 402 (7th Cir. 1983)

PELL, CIRCUIT JUDGE.

Petitioners appeal the judgment of the United States Tax Court finding that profit was not their primary goal in owning a dairy farm. Based on this finding the tax court disallowed deductions for losses incurred in renovating the farm. The sole issue presented for our review is whether the tax court's finding regarding petitioners' motivation was clearly erroneous.

FACTS

Melvin Nickerson (hereinafter referred to as petitioner) was born in 1932 in a farming community in Florida. He worked evenings and weekends on his father's farm until he was 17. Petitioner entered the field of advertising after attending college and serving in the United States Army. During the years relevant to this case he was self-employed in Chicago, serving industrial and agricultural clients. His wife, Naomi W. Nickerson, was a full-time employee of the Chicago Board of Education. While petitioners were not wealthy, they did earn a comfortable living.

At the age of forty, petitioner decided that his career in the "youth oriented" field of advertising would not last much longer, and he began to look for an alternative source of income for the future. Petitioners decided that dairy farming was the most desirable means of generating income and examined a number of farms in Michigan and Wisconsin. After several years of searching, petitioners bought an 80-acre farm in Door County, Wisconsin for $40,000. One year later they purchased an additional 40 acres adjoining the farm for $10,000.

The farm, which had not been run as a dairy for eight years, was in a run-down condition. What little equipment was left was either in need of repair or obsolete. The tillable land, about 60 acres, was planted with alfalfa, which was at the end of its productive cycle. In an effort to improve this state of affairs petitioners leased the land to a tenant-farmer for $20 an acre and an agreement that the farmer would convert an additional ten acres a year to the cultivation of a more profitable crop. At the time of trial approximately 80 acres were tillable. The rent received from the farmer was the only income derived from the farm.

Petitioner visited the farm on most weekends during the growing season and twice a month the rest of the year. Mrs. Nickerson and the children visited less frequently. The trip to the farm requires five hours of driving from petitioners' home in Chicago. During these visits petitioner and his family either worked on their land or assisted neighboring farmers. When working on his own farm petitioner concentrated his efforts on renovating an abandoned orchard and remodeling the farm house. In addition to learning about farming through this experience petitioner read a number of trade journals and spoke with the area agricultural extension agent.

Petitioners did not expect to make a profit from the farm for approximately 10 years. True to their expectations, petitioners lost $8,668 in 1976 and $9,872.95 in 1977. Although they did not keep formal books of account petitioners did retain receipts and cancelled checks relating to farm expenditures. At the time of trial, petitioners had not yet acquired any livestock or farm machinery. The farm was similarly devoid of recreational equipment and had never been used to entertain guests.

The tax court decided that these facts did not support petitioners' claim that the primary goal in operating the farm was to make a profit. We will examine the tax court's reasoning in more detail after setting out the relevant legal considerations.

THE STATUTORY SCHEME

Section 162(a) of the Internal Revenue Code of 1954 allows deduction of "all the ordinary and necessary expenses paid or incurred during the taxable year in carrying on any trade or business." Section 183, however, limits the availability of these deductions if the activity "is not engaged in for profit" to deductions that are allowed regardless of the existence of a profit motive and deductions for ordinary and necessary expenses "only to the extent that the gross income derived from such activity for the taxable year exceeds [otherwise allowable deductions]." I.R.C. § 183(b)(2). The deductions claimed by petitioners are only allowable if their motivation in investing in the farm was to make a profit.

Petitioners bear the burden of proving that their primary purpose in renovating the farm was to make a profit. In meeting this burden, however, "it is sufficient if the taxpayer has a bona fide expectation of realizing a profit, regardless of the reasonableness of such expectation." Although petitioners need only prove their sincerity rather than their realism the factors considered in judging their motivation are primarily objective. In addition to the taxpayer's statements of intent, which are given little weight for obvious reasons, the tax court must consider "all facts and circumstances with respect to the activity," including the following:

(1) *Manner in which the taxpayer carries on the activity.* The fact that the taxpayer carries on the activity in a businesslike manner and maintains complete

and accurate books and records may indicate that the activity is engaged in for profit....

(2) *The expertise of the taxpayer or his advisors.* Preparation for the activity by extensive study of its accepted business, economic, and scientific practices, or consultation with those who are expert therein, may indicate that the taxpayer has a profit motive where the taxpayer carries on the activity in accordance with such practices....

(3) *The time and effort expended by the taxpayer in carrying on the activity.* The fact that the taxpayer devotes much of his personal time and effort to carrying on the activity, particularly if the activity does not have substantial personal or recreational aspects, may indicate an intention to derive a profit.... The fact that the taxpayer devotes a limited amount of time to an activity does not necessarily indicate a lack of profit motive where the taxpayer employs competent and qualified persons to carry on such activity.

(4) *Expectation that assets used in activity may appreciate in value....*

(5) *The success of the taxpayer in carrying on other similar or dissimilar activities....*

(6) *The taxpayer's history of income or losses with respect to the activity....*

(7) *The amount of occasional profits, if any, which are earned....*

(8) *The financial status of the taxpayer....*

(9) *Elements of personal pleasure or recreation.* The presence of personal motives in carrying on of an activity may indicate that the activity is not engaged in for profit, especially where there are recreational or personal elements involved. On the other hand, a profit motivation may be indicated where an activity lacks any appeal other than profit. It is not, however, necessary that an activity be engaged in with the exclusive intention of deriving a profit or with the intention of maximizing profits....

Treas.Reg. § 1.183-2(b)(1)–(9). None of these factors is determinative, nor is the decision to be made by comparing the number of factors that weigh in the taxpayer's favor with the number that support the Commissioner. *Id.* There is no set formula for divining a taxpayer's true motive, rather "[o]ne struggles in vain for any verbal formula that will supply a ready touchstone. The standard set by the statute is not a rule of law; it is rather a way of life. Life in all its fullness must supply the answer to the riddle." Welch v. Helvering, 290 U.S. 111, 115 (1933). Nonetheless, we are given some guidance by the enumerated factors and by the Congressional purpose in enacting section 183.

> The legislative history surrounding section 183 indicates that one of the prime motivating factors behind its passage was Congress' desire to create an objective standard to determine whether a taxpayer was carrying on a business for the purpose of realizing a profit or was instead merely attempting to create and utilize losses to offset other income.

Jasionowski v. Commissioner, 66 T.C. 312, 321 (1976).

Congressional concern stemmed from a recognition that "[w]ealthy individuals have invested in certain aspects of farm operations solely to obtain 'tax losses' — largely bookkeeping losses — for use to reduce their tax on other income.... One of the remarkable aspects of the problem is pointed up by the fact that persons with large nonfarm income have a remarkable propensity to lose money in the farm business." S.Rep. No. 91-552, 91st Cong., 1st Sess., *reprinted in* 1969 U.S.Code Cong. & Ad.News 2027, 2376. With this concern in mind we will now examine the decision of the tax court.

DECISION OF THE TAX COURT

The tax court analyzed the relevant factors and determined that making a profit was not petitioners' primary goal in engaging in farming. The court based its decision on a number of factors that weighed against petitioners. The court found that they did not operate the farm in a businesslike manner and did not appear to have a concrete plan for improving the profitability of the farm. The court believed that these difficulties were attributable to petitioners' lack of experience, but did not discuss the steps actually taken by Melvin Nickerson to gain experience in farming.

The court found it difficult to believe that petitioners actually believed that the limited amount of time they were spending at the farm would produce a profit given the dilapidated condition of the farm. Furthermore, the court found that petitioners' emphasis on making the farm house habitable rather than on acquiring or repairing farm equipment was inconsistent with a profit motive. These factors, combined with the consistent history of losses borne by petitioners, convinced the court that "petitioner at best entertains the hope that when he retires from the advertising business and can devote his complete attention to the farming operation, he may at that time expect to produce a profit." The court did not think that this hope rose to the level of a bona fide expectation of profit.

REVIEW OF THE TAX COURT'S FINDINGS

Whether petitioners intended to run the dairy farm for a profit is a question of fact, and as such our review is limited to a determination of whether the tax court was "clearly erroneous" in determining that petitioners lacked the requisite profit motive. This standard of review applies although the only dispute is over the proper interpretation of uncontested facts. It is not enough, then, that we would have reached a different conclusion had the decision been ours to make. Rather, "[a] finding is 'clearly erroneous' when although there is evidence to support it, the reviewing court on the entire evidence is left with the definite and firm conviction that a mistake has been committed." This is one of those rare cases in which we are convinced that a mistake has been made.

Our basic disagreement with the tax court stems from our belief that the court improperly evaluated petitioners' actions from the perspective of whether they sincerely believed that they could make a profit from their current level of activity at the farm. On the contrary, petitioners need only prove that their current actions were motivated by the expectation that they would later reap a profit, in this case when they finished renovating the farm and began full-time operations. It is well established that a taxpayer need not expect an immediate profit; the existence of "start up" losses does not preclude a bona fide profit motive.

> The presence of losses in the formative years of a business ... is not inconsistent with an intention to achieve a later profitable level of operation, bearing in mind, however, that the goal must be to realize a profit on the entire operation, which presupposes not only future net earnings but also sufficient net earnings to recoup the losses which have meanwhile been sustained in the intervening years.

Bessenyey v. Commissioner, 45 T.C. 261, 274 (1965), aff'd, 379 F.2d 252 (2nd Cir.1967), cert. denied 389 U.S. 931. The tax court was apparently of the view that petitioners' decision to spread these start-up losses over a period of years before starting full-time operation of the farm was inconsistent with a bona fide intention to make a profit. It is uncontested, however, that substantial time, effort, and money were needed to return the farm to a profitable operation, petitioners' only choice being when they would make this investment. We see no basis for distinguishing petitioners' actions from a situation in which one absorbs larger losses over a shorter period of time by beginning full-time operations immediately. In either situation the taxpayer stands an equal chance of recouping start-up losses. In fact, it seems to us a reasonable decision by petitioners to prepare the farm before becoming dependent upon it for sustenance. Keeping in mind that petitioners were not seeking to supplement their existing incomes with their current work on the farm, but rather were laying the ground work for a contemplated career switch, we will examine the factors relied upon by the tax court.

The tax court found that the amount of time petitioners devoted to the farm was inadequate. In reaching this conclusion the court ignored petitioners' agreement with the tenant-farmer under which he would convert 10 acres a year to profitable crops in exchange for the right to farm the land. In this situation the limited amount of time spent by petitioners, who were fully employed in Chicago, is not inconsistent with an expectation of profit. "The fact that the taxpayer devotes a limited amount of time to an activity does not necessarily indicate a lack of profit motive where the taxpayer employs competent and qualified persons to carry on such activity." Treas.Reg. § 1.183-2(b)(3). There is no indication in the record that the tenant-farmer was not qualified to convert the land, or that 10 acres a year was an unreasonable amount. In these circumstances the tax court erred in inferring a lack of profit motive from the amount of time personally spent by petitioners on renovating the farm.

The court also rested its decision on the lack of a concrete plan to put the farm in operable condition. Once again, this ignores petitioners' agreement with the tenant-farmer concerning reclamation of the land. Under this agreement the majority of the land would be tillable by the time petitioners were prepared to begin full-time farming. The tax court also believed that petitioners' decision to renovate the farm house and orchard prior to obtaining farm equipment evidenced a lack of profit motive. As petitioners planned to live on the farm when they switched careers refurbishing the house would seem to be a necessary first step. The court also failed to consider the uncontradicted testimony regarding repairs made to the hay barn and equipment shed, which supported petitioners' contention that they were interested in operating a farm rather than just living on the land. Additionally, we fail to understand how renovating the orchard, a potential source of food and income, is inconsistent with an expectation of profit.

The tax court took into account the history of losses in considering petitioners' intentions. While a history of losses is relevant, in this case little weight should be accorded this factor. Petitioners did not expect to make a profit for a number of years, and it was clear from the condition of the farm that a financial investment would be required before the farm could be profitable. Accordingly, that petitioners lost money, as they expected, does not cast doubt upon the sincerity of their motivation. In this regard, the tax court should have also considered the fact that petitioners were reaping what profit they could through leasing the land to a local farmer.

The court believed that most of petitioners' problems were attributable to their lack of expertise. While lack of expertise is relevant, efforts at gaining experience and a willingness to follow expert advice should also be considered. Treas.Reg. § 1.183-2(b)(2). The court here failed to consider the uncontradicted evidence that Melvin Nickerson read trade journals and Government-sponsored agricultural newsletters, sought advice from a state horticultural agent regarding renovation of the orchard and gained experience by working on neighboring farms. In addition, petitioners' agreement with the tenant-farmer was entered into on the advice of the area agricultural extension agent. To weigh petitioners' lack of expertise against them without giving consideration to these efforts effectively precludes a bona fide attempt to change careers. We are unwilling to restrict petitioners in this manner and believe that a proper interpretation of these facts supports petitioners' claims.

The tax court recognized that the farm was not used for entertainment and lacked any recreational facilities, and that petitioners' efforts at the farm were "prodigious," but felt that this was of little importance. While the Commissioner need not prove that petitioners were motivated by goals other than making a profit, we think that more weight should be given to the absence of any alternative explanation for petitioners' actions. As we previously noted the standard set out by the statute is to be applied with the insight gained from a lifetime of experience as well as an understanding of the statutory scheme. Common sense indicates to us that rational people do not perform hard manual labor for no reason, and if the possibility that petitioners performed these labors for pleasure is eliminated the only remaining motivation is profit. The Commissioner has argued that petitioner was motivated by a love of farming that stems from his childhood. We find it difficult to believe that he drove five hours in order to spend his weekends working on a dilapidated farm solely for fun, or that his family derived much pleasure from the experience. Furthermore, there is no support for this contention in the record. At any rate, that petitioner may have chosen farming over some other career because of fond memories of his youth does not preclude a bona fide profit motive. Treas.Reg. § 1.183-2(b)(9). We believe that the absence of any recreational purpose strongly counsels in favor of finding that petitioners' prodigious efforts were directed at making a profit. *See* Allen v. Commissioner, 72 T.C. 28, 36 (1979); Gregory v. United States, 76-1 U.S. Tax Cas. (CCH) & 9220 (W.D.La. 1976).

Based upon these facts we conclude that the tax court erred in finding that petitioners had failed to prove a bona fide expectation of profit. We recognize that the scope of our review in this case is limited. In a similar situation the Supreme Court observed that:

> Decision of the issue presented in these cases must be based ultimately on the application of the factfinding tribunal's experience with the mainsprings of human conduct to the totality of the facts of each case. The nontechnical nature of the statutory standard, the close relationship of it to the data of practical human experience, and the multiplicity of relevant factual elements, with their various combinations, creating the necessity of ascribing the proper force to each, confirms us in our conclusion that primary weight in this area must be given to the conclusions of the trier of fact.

Commissioner v. Duberstein, 363 U.S. at 289. Nonetheless, when the basic facts are not disputed and the inference drawn from them by the trier of fact is the result of an overly restrictive view of what a party must prove in order to prevail we will not hesitate to exercise our power to reverse. In this case the court erroneously concluded that petitioners were required to prove a bona fide expectation of profit from their current efforts at the farm. We think that it is sufficient that petitioners had a bona fide expectation that their current work would allow them to commence profitable farming in the future, and that the uncontested facts establish that they had this expectation.

If this were a case in which wealthy taxpayers were seeking to obtain tax benefits through the creation of paper losses we would hesitate to reverse. Before us today, however, is a family of modest means attempting to prepare for a stable financial future. The amount of time and hard work invested by petitioners belies any claim that allowing these deductions would thwart Congress's primary purpose, that of excluding "hobby" losses from permissible deductions. Accordingly, we hold that the tax court's finding was clearly erroneous and reverse.

V. Related Matters

- **Vacation Home Deductions.** If section 280A applies, section 183 will not determine deductibility of expenses. Review Chapter 22 for section 280A treatment. However, the year counts for purposes of the section 183(d) presumption. IRC § 280A(f)(3). If section 280A does not apply, section 183 will determine deductibility.

- **Vacation Home Not Used as Residence.** If the vacation home is not a taxpayer's residence for purposes of section 280A, section 183 will apply. If the vacation home rental is considered an activity engaged in for profit, allocable expenses are deductible in full. If the rental is considered an activity not engaged in for profit, then allocable expenses are deductible only to the extent of rental income from the vacation home. Whether section 280A or section 183 applies, expenses still have to be allocated between personal and rental use. IRC § 280A(e)(1) (parenthetical language).

Chapter 24

Like Kind Exchanges

I. Assignment

Read: Internal Revenue Code: §§ 1001(c); 1031(a)–(d).

Treasury Regulations: §§ 1.1031(a)-1(a)(1) 1st par., -1(b), -1(c), -2(a); 1.1031(b)-1(c); 1.1031(d)-2 ex. 2.

Text: Overview
Revenue Ruling 77-297
Revenue Procedure 2008-16
Related Matters

Complete the problems.

II. Problems

1. Ernest Hemingway has 1,000 acres of unimproved timber land held for investment in Idaho with a cost basis of $1,000,000. Ernest trades with Barbara Kingsolver for an office building in Arizona held for rental income worth $2,000,000 in which Barbara has a basis of $1,200,000. Ernest also gives $10,000 cash and a logging truck worth $40,000 with an adjusted basis of $60,000. None of the properties are mortgaged and there is no depreciation recapture inherent in the gain in the office building. What are the tax consequences of this exchange for Ernest and for Barbara?

2. Jack Johnson owns an undeveloped tract of land called Fairhaven used exclusively in his business which cost $2,500,000 when it was purchased ten years ago. Half of the purchase price ($1,250,000) of Fairhaven was financed with a bank loan. The loan was secured by a lien on Fairhaven. In the current year Jack exchanged Fairhaven for another similar piece of land called Montblanc (also to be used in his business) worth $4,000,000. Jack transferred Fairhaven subject to the mortgage which the buyer assumed and which now has a balance of $500,000. His basis in Fairhaven in the current year remains $2,500,000.

    (a) What are Jack's tax consequences from the exchange?

    (b) What if the facts were the same as (a) except that the mortgage assumed by Jack's buyer stood at $1,000,000, and the buyer transferred Montblanc subject to a $500,000 mortgage which Jack assumed?

(c) Same as (b) except that Jack takes Montblanc subject to a $1,500,000 mortgage.

(d) Same as (c) except that Jack's buyer also paid Jack $100,000 in cash.

3. Anna Karenina is tired of life in the city and wants to acquire fifty acres of Leo Tolstoy's vineyard land in order to develop her own winery. Leo wants to diversify his investments by acquiring an apartment building in the city. Leo has a low basis in his extensive vineyard property which he inherited more than forty years ago. Because of his low basis he prefers to engage in a tax free exchange. Discuss the results to Leo in the following circumstances:

(a) Leo agrees to transfer the land to Anna in exchange for replacement property that Leo will designate later. As part of the agreement Anna puts cash equal to the value of the vineyard land into an escrow account. The escrow agreement provides that Anna will use the money to acquire the replacement property designated by Leo and then exchange the replacement property for Leo's vineyard property. If Leo fails to designate replacement property within 6 months the deal falls through and the money goes back to Anna. Five months after the escrow is set up Leo designates the replacement property, a twenty unit apartment building, and one month later Anna directs the escrow agent to purchase the apartment building. One month later the building is transferred to Leo in exchange for the land which is transferred on the same day.

(b) What difference in results if Leo purchases the apartment building directly for cash and then transfers the building to Anna for cash before engaging in the exchange of the land for the building? Assume the contract of sale for the building between Leo and Anna specifies that Anna will later transfer the building in exchange for the vineyard land. The contract further specifies that Leo will pay all operating expenses relating to the building and receive all rents from the building during Anna's period of ownership.

4. Stephen King has owned a waterfront cabin near Acadia National Park for ten years. Each year he spends 20 days at the cabin and rents it to others at fair value for 250 days. In the current year, Stephen exchanges the cabin for a condominium in downtown Portland worth $700,000. He rents the condominium to a year-round tenant for fair value under a two-year lease.

(a) If Stephen's basis in the cabin is $100,000, what are the tax consequences of the exchange?

(b) Suppose that two years after the exchange in (a) Stephen ceases to lease out the condominium and instead makes it his principal residence for the next two years. What are the tax consequences to Stephen if, four years after the exchange when his basis in the condominium is $90,000, he sells the condominium for $800,000 in cash? *See* IRC § 121(d)(10).

III. Overview

A. Introduction

Ordinarily a sale or exchange of property will trigger the recognition of gain or loss on the transaction by operation of section 1001(c). However, there are a number of provisions that overrule section 1001. These are known collectively as *non-recognition provisions*. One of the most prominent of these is section 1031 which addresses what are known as like kind exchanges. The like kind exchange is a widely employed tax avoidance technique, especially in the area of commercial real estate transactions. It will grant complete non-recognition when a taxpayer swaps real property for other real property of equal value. It may grant partial non-recognition in other cases. We will get to the details shortly.

The basic rationale for most non-recognition provisions is that the taxpayer has not changed her overall economic position. The investment vehicle may have changed but the substance of the investment remains. Put another way, one might say that the taxpayer has not cashed in her chips. Sometimes non-recognition, especially loss non-recognition, is to the taxpayer's disadvantage. The law seeks to prevent taxpayer manipulation of losses to shelter income. But non-recognition of gains is usually to the taxpayer's advantage. Thus, provisions such as section 1031 are generally considered taxpayer friendly. However, there is a catch. Non-recognition usually means deferral not exemption from gain recognition. This results because basis of property received is not stepped-up. We have already seen an example of this in the operation of section 1041, which applies to transfers between spouses and former spouses incident to divorce. The transferee takes the transferor's basis and, thus, any unrecognized gain in the asset is still lurking in the transferee's basis. Section 1031 represents a similar but more complex variation on this pattern.

B. Determining Like Kindness

The fundamental thrust of section 1031 is to grant non-recognition of gain or loss on the exchange of business or investment real property for like kind business or investment real property. IRC § 1031(a)(1). The general rule for determining like kindness is that the properties exchanged must be similar in "*nature or character.*" Treas. Reg. § 1.1031(a)-1(b). In this context any sort of fee interest in real estate is similar in nature or character to any other form of fee interest in real estate. Thus, for example, an exchange of farm land for an apartment building can qualify as a like kind exchange. *See* Treas. Reg. §§ 1.1031(a)-1(b) & (c); 1.1031(b)-1(b), ex. 1. *See also* Commissioner v. Crichton, 122 F.2d 181 (5th Cir. 1941). Implicit in this example is the further point that a taxpayer is within section 1031 if she exchanges real property held for investment for real property to be used in a trade or business or vice versa. Treas. Reg. § 1.1031(a)-1(a).

C. Planning the Exchange

Often the taxpayer who wants to do a like kind exchange will have difficulty finding a buyer who holds just the sort of like kind property that is being sought. This lack of fit does not pose an insuperable barrier, however, because of the possibility of a *three cornered exchange*. This typically involves the buyer first purchasing the desired exchange property from a third party and then engaging in the exchange with the seller who is seeking non-recognition. Thus, although it may take two to tango, it often takes three to do a like kind exchange. *See* Revenue Ruling 77-297, included in the materials below.

The three cornered exchange has several tricky aspects. As an initial matter there is the enforceability of the arrangement between the seller and the buyer. The seller wants to be certain that the buyer will obtain the right exchange property. The buyer wants to be certain that the seller will not back out of the deal after the buyer has bound himself to purchase that exchange property. These objectives are typically accomplished through the use of a contract that includes an escrow arrangement. The buyer will deposit some funds with an escrow agent. Those funds may be forfeitable by the buyer if he fails to perform. A concern for the seller is whether the doctrine of constructive receipt could cause the money placed in escrow to be treated as boot, or, even worse, as an outright cash sale. The regulations provide that cash held in escrow is not constructively received by the seller as long as the seller's right to control receipt is subject to substantial restrictions. *See* Treas. Reg. § 1.1031(k)-1(f)(2). Thus, for example, constructive receipt will not apply where the seller has no right to the funds as long as the buyer performs under the agreement. *See* Treas. Reg. § 1.1031(k)-1(f)(3), ex. (iii). But if the seller has right to take the cash at any time prior to replacement property being found, the doctrine of constructive receipt will apply and may cause the whole transaction to be treated as a sale outside of section 1031 even if like kind property is ultimately received. *See* Treas. Reg. § 1.1031(k)-1(f)(3), ex. (i) & (ii).

Deferred Exchanges. Since it is often difficult to arrange the timing of the title transfers to meet the requirements of section 1031(a)(3), the parties may need to "park" one of the exchange properties with an intermediary who can hold title to the property until the parties are ready for the exchange to proceed. The government has been fairly accommodating in allowing intermediaries to hold property without attributing ownership from the intermediary to one of the parties. *See* Treas. Reg. § 1.1031(k)-1(g) (establishing a safe harbor for deferred exchanges involving the use of *qualified escrow accounts* and *qualified intermediaries*). The Service has issued a revenue procedure establishing a safe harbor for exchanges involving deferred relinquishments. *See* Rev. Proc. 2000-37, 2000-2 C.B. 308. These are sometimes referred to as reverse deferred exchanges. In essence, if the transactions are structured properly, the person seeking to engage in a like kind exchange can acquire the replacement property through an intermediary before finding a buyer for the property he intends to relinquish.

D. The Mechanics of Section 1031

1. Exceptions and Timing

Section 1031 is *not* elective. When it applies, it applies mandatorily. But in most cases it is easily avoided. One way to fail to come within section 1031 is to fail to comply with its timing rules. Those rules require that the taxpayer must *identify* the replacement property within 45 days after the transfer of the property given up. IRC § 1031(a)(3)(A). In addition the replacement property must be *received* within 180 days after the taxpayer transfers the property given up. IRC § 1031(a)(3)(B). The regulations allow identification of multiple properties in some cases. Treas. Reg. § 1.1031(k)-1(c)(4).

2. Boot and Recognition of Gains and Losses

As one might imagine, it is often difficult to find like kind properties that are precisely equal in value. Often one party may have to pay some cash or transfer some non-like kind property to equalize the deal. This equalizing payment is called *boot*. Since boot is by definition not like kind, the Code provides that the recipient of the boot must recognize gain to the extent of the *lesser* of gain realized or the value of the boot received. IRC § 1031(b). However, the recipient of boot is not allowed to recognize a loss on the like kind property given up. IRC § 1031(c). The student should note that this non-recognition of loss rule does not prevent loss recognition on losses resulting from *giving* boot. That is, if a taxpayer gives up non-like kind loss property, the loss on that property is recognized.

Where more than one property is transferred and only one property is received, each asset surrendered is allocated an amount realized equal to its fair market value. Thus, for example, suppose Taxpayer gives up Land A worth $80,000 and a tractor worth $20,000 for Land B (like kind to Land A). Land B is worth $100,000. Taxpayer is deemed to have an amount realized of $80,000 with respect to Land A (four-fifths of Land B) and an amount realized of $20,000 with respect to the tractor (one-fifth of Land B). No gain or loss will be recognized on the exchange of Land A for four-fifths of Land B but gain or loss will be recognized with respect to the exchange of the tractor for one-fifth of Land B. Thus, if Taxpayer has a $15,000 adjusted basis in the tractor, she will have a $5,000 recognized gain with respect to its transfer. If Taxpayer has a $23,000 adjusted basis in the tractor, she will have a $3,000 recognized loss on its transfer.

3. Basis in New Property and in Boot Received

As noted above, section 1031 grants deferral of gain recognition rather than complete forgiveness. This deferral derives from the basis rules. The taxpayer's basis in the newly acquired property is governed by section 1031(d) as embellished upon in the regulations. Essentially, section 1031(d) provides that the taxpayer's basis in the property received is her basis in the property given up minus any money received, plus any gain recognized, and minus any loss recognized. The beginning basis number is the aggregate of the bases in all property given up and includes the amount of any cash given as well. Treas. Reg. § 1.1031(d)-1(a).

Aggregate Basis under § 1031(d)

> **Aggregate Bases of Property Given (Including Cash)**
> **− Money Received**
> **+ Gain Recognized**
> **− <u>Loss Recognized</u>**
> **Aggregate Bases in Property Received**

If more than one property is received, the basis of the property given must be allocated among the property received. This is accomplished by first allocating a fair market value basis to any non-cash boot received. *See* IRC § 1031(d) (next to last sentence). The like kind property received will be allocated any of the aggregate basis that remains after the boot has been given a fair market value basis.

Basis of Like Kind Property Received

> **Aggregate Bases in Property Received**
> **− <u>FMV Basis for Boot Received</u>**
> **Basis of Like Kind Property Received**

If more than one like kind property is received, the basis is allocated among the like kind properties in proportion to their fair market values. Rev. Rul. 68-36, 1968-1 C.B. 357. *See also* Treas. Reg. § 1.1031(j)-1(c).

4. Holding Period

If the property given up is either a capital asset or trade or business property described in section 1231, the taxpayer will tack her holding period for the property given up to the holding period of the property received. IRC § 1223(1).

E. Assumptions of Liability

Section 1031 treats assumptions of liability as the equivalent of cash payments for most purposes. *See* IRC § 1031(d) (last sentence). This is consistent with our understanding gained from the *Crane* case that relief from a liability as part of a sale or exchange is included in a seller's amount realized. This has significance for both gain recognition under subsection 1031(b) and for the basis calculation under subsection 1031(d). Sometimes liabilities may pass in both directions, as when each property is subject to a mortgage. In these situations, the assumptions of liability are netted for boot purposes. Treas. Reg. § 1.1031(d)-2, ex. 2(c). Thus, only the transferor of the property subject to the greater liability is deemed to have boot for gain recognition purposes. However, an assumption of liability cannot offset cash received for boot purposes. *Id.* But cash paid can offset an assumption of liability for boot purposes. *Id.*

F. Illustrations

The principles described above are best understood by working through some examples.

Example 1. Alberto Gonzales has land worth $100,000 in which he has a basis of $25,000. Assume that Alberto engages in a like kind exchange in which he receives land worth $75,000 and $25,000 of cash.

Step 1: Determine *realized* gain or loss.

Here we have a realized gain of $75,000 determined as follows:

$75,000	FMV of property received
+ 25,000	Cash
100,000	Amount realized
− 25,000	Basis
$75,000	Gain realized (IRC § 1001)

Step 2: Determine *recognized* gain.

His recognized gain is $25,000, the lesser of FMV of boot received or gain realized. IRC § 1031(b).

Step 3: Determine his basis and holding period in the new property.

Alberto's new basis is $25,000 determined as follows:

$25,000	Old basis
− 25,000	Cash received
+ 25,000	Gain recognized
$25,000	New basis (IRC § 1031(d))

Alberto's holding period for the new property includes his holding period in the land exchanged, assuming it was a capital asset or section 1231 property. IRC § 1223(1).

Example 2. William Rehnquist has real property with a $40,000 basis subject to a $75,000 mortgage. William exchanges that property for real property with a $100,000 fair market value subject to a $50,000 mortgage. The mortgages pass with the properties.

Step 1: Determine *realized* gain or loss.

Here we have a realized gain of $85,000 determined as follows:

$100,000	FMV of property received
+ 75,000	Mortgage transferred (*Crane*)
175,000	Total consideration received
− 50,000	Mortgage assumed (reverse *Crane* notions)
125,000	Amount realized
− 40,000	Basis
$85,000	Gain realized (IRC § 1001(a))

Step 2: Determine *recognized* gain.

William's recognized gain is $25,000, which represents the net liability relief on the exchange of mortgages ($75,000 – $50,000 = $25,000). *See* Treas. Reg. § 1.1031(d)-2, ex. 2(c). Remember, gain recognized is the lesser of the FMV of boot received or gain realized. IRC § 1031(b).

Step 3: Determine his basis and holding period in the new property.

William's new basis is $40,000 determined as follows:

$40,000	Old basis
– 25,000	Money received (net liability relief on mortgages)
+ 25,000	Gain recognized
$40,000	New basis (Treas. Reg. § 1.1031(d)-2, ex. 2(c))

William's holding period for the new property includes the holding period of his old property, assuming it was a capital asset or section 1231 property in William's hands. IRC § 1223(1).

Example 3. Ruth Bader Ginsburg has real property with a $40,000 basis subject to a $50,000 mortgage. Ruth exchanges it for like kind property worth $100,000 subject to a $75,000 mortgage. Ruth also receives $20,000 of cash.

Step 1: Determine her *realized* gain or loss.

Ruth has a realized gain of $55,000 determined as follows:

$100,000	FMV of property received
+ 20,000	Cash received
+ 50,000	Mortgage transferred (*Crane*)
170,000	Total consideration received
– 75,000	Mortgage assumed (reverse *Crane* notions)
95,000	Amount realized
– 40,000	Basis
$55,000	Gain realized (IRC § 1001)

Step 2: Determine *recognized* gain.

Ruth's recognized gain is $20,000. This is so despite the fact that she received $5,000 less boot then she paid. (She received $70,000 of boot and paid $75,000 of boot.) This result arises from the rule that receipt of cash cannot be offset by the assumption of a liability. *See* Treas. Reg. § 1.1031(d)-2, ex. 2(c).

Step 3: Determine Ruth's basis and holding period in the new property.

Her new basis is $65,000 determined as follows:

$40,000	Old basis
– 20,000	Cash received
+ 75,000	Mortgage assumed (treated as cash paid)
– 50,000	Mortgage transferred (treated as cash received)
+ 20,000	Gain recognized
$65,000	New basis (IRC § 1031(d))

Ruth's holding period in the old property tacks onto the new property provided the old property was a capital asset or section 1231 property. IRC § 1223(1).

G. Mixed-Use Property

Often property can have both business or investment uses and personal uses. In Chapter 22 we looked at some of those mixed-use assets, including vacation rental properties and home offices. In Chapter 22 we also looked at the section 121 exclusion for gains on the sale of a taxpayer's principal residence. As noted previously, section 1031 only defers gain and loss recognition with respect to exchanges of like kind business and investment property. How then, for example, should section 1031 apply to the exchange of a principal residence with a home office for another residence with a home office? The answer, in general, is that section 1031 can apply to the home office portion of the exchange and section 121 may apply to the personal residence portion of the exchange. *See* Revenue Procedure 2005-14, 2005-1 C.B. 528. Sometimes the mixed uses may be simultaneous as in the case of a home office just described. Sometimes the mixed use may be sequential as when a principal residence is converted to rental property. Both section 121 and section 1031 can also apply to a principal residence that is converted to a business use and then is later the subject of a like kind exchange. *Id*. One restriction on the use of section 121 in combination with section 1031 is set out in section 121(d)(10). This provision requires that property which is acquired in a like kind exchange and then converted into a principal residence must be held for five years before it can qualify for the section 121 exclusion.

In the materials below we have set out Revenue Procedure 2008-16 that establishes a safe harbor for applying section 1031 to mixed-use rental property.

IV. Materials

Revenue Ruling 77-297
1977-2 C.B. 304

Advice is requested whether the transaction described below is an exchange of property in which no gain or loss is recognized pursuant to section 1031(a) of the Internal Revenue Code of 1954.

A entered into a written agreement with *B* to sell *B* for 1,000*x* dollars a ranch (the "first ranch") consisting of land and certain buildings used by *A* in the business of raising livestock. Pursuant to the agreement, *B* placed 100*x* dollars into escrow and agreed to pay at closing an additional 200*x* dollars in cash, to assume a 160*x* dollar liability of *A*, and to execute a note for 540*x* dollars. The agreement also provided that *B* would cooperate with *A* to effectuate an exchange of properties should *A* locate suitable property. No personal property was involved in the transaction. *A* and *B* are not dealers in real estate.

A located another ranch (the "second ranch") consisting of land and certain buildings suitable for raising livestock. The second ranch was owned by *C*. *B* entered into an agreement with *C* to purchase the second ranch for 2,000x dollars. Pursuant to this agreement, *B* placed 40x dollars into escrow, agreed to pay at closing an additional 800x dollars, assume 400x dollars liability of *C*, and execute a note for 760x dollars. No personal property was involved in the transaction. *C* could not look to *A* for specific performance on the contract, thus, *B* was not acting as *A*'s agent in the purchase of the second parcel of property.

At closing, *B* purchased the second ranch as agreed. After the purchase, *B* exchanged the second ranch with *A* for the first ranch and assumed *A*'s liability of 160x dollars. With *C*'s concurrence, *A* assumed *C*'s 400x dollar liability and *B*'s note for 760x dollars. *C* released *B* from liability on the note. The escrow agent returned the 100x dollars to *B* that *B* had initially placed in escrow. This sum had never been available to *A*, since the conditions of the escrow were never satisfied.

Section 1031(a) of the Code provides that no gain or loss shall be recognized if property held for productive use in trade or business or for investment (not including stock in trade or other property held primarily for sale, nor stocks, bonds, notes, choses in action, certificates of trust or beneficial interest, or other securities or evidence of indebtedness or interest) is exchanged solely for property of a like kind to be held either for productive use in trade or business or for investment.

Section 1031(b) of the Code states that if an exchange would be within the provisions of subsection (a) if it were not for the fact that the property received in exchange consists not only of property permitted by such provisions to be received without the recognition of gain, but also of other property or money, then the gain, if any, to the recipient shall be recognized, but in an amount not in excess of the sum of such money and the fair market value of such other property.

Section 1.1031(b)-1(c) of the Income Tax Regulations states that consideration received in the form of an assumption of liabilities is to be treated as "other property or money" for the purpose of section 1031(b) of the Code. However, if, on an exchange described in section 1031(b), each party to the exchange assumes a liability of the other party, then, in determining the amount of "other property or money" for purposes of section 1031(b), consideration given in the form of an assumption of liabilities shall be offset against consideration received in the form of an assumption of liabilities.

Ordinarily, to constitute an exchange, the transaction must be a reciprocal transfer of property, as distinguished from a transfer of property for a money consideration only.

In the instant case *A* and *B* entered into a sales agreement with an exchange option if suitable property were found. Before the sale was consummated, the parties effectuated an exchange. Thus, for purposes of section 1031 of the Code, the parties entered into an exchange of property. *See* Alderson v. Commissioner, 317 F.2d 790 (9th Cir. 1963), in which a similar transaction was treated as a like-kind exchange of property even though the original agreement called for a sale of the property. In addition, *A*'s 160*x* dollar liability assumed by *B* was offset by *B*'s liabilities assumed by *A,* pursuant to section 1.1031(b)-1(c) of the regulations.

Accordingly, as to *A,* the exchange of ranches qualifies for nonrecognition of gain or loss under section 1031 of the Code. As to *B,* the exchange of ranches does not qualify for nonrecognition of gain or loss under section 1031 because *B* did not hold the second ranch for productive use in a trade or business or for investment. *See* Rev. Rul. 75-291, 1975-2 C.B. 332, in which it is held that the nonrecognition provisions of section 1031 do not apply to a taxpayer who acquired property solely for the purpose of exchanging it for like-kind property.

However, in the instant case, *B* did not realize gain or loss as a result of the exchange since the total consideration received by *B* of 2,160*x* dollars (fair market value of first ranch of 1,000*x* dollars plus *B*'s liabilities assumed by *A* of 1,160*x* dollars) is equal to *B*'s basis in the property given up of 2,000*x* dollars plus *A*'s liability assumed by *B* of 160*x* dollars. See section 1001 of the Code and the applicable regulations thereunder.

Revenue Procedure 2008-16

2008-1 C.B. 547

SECTION 1. PURPOSE

This revenue procedure provides a safe harbor under which the Internal Revenue Service (the "Service") will not challenge whether a dwelling unit qualifies as property held for productive use in a trade or business or for investment for purposes of § 1031 of the Internal Revenue Code.

SECTION 2. BACKGROUND

.01 Section 1031 (a) provides that no gain or loss is recognized on the exchange of property held for productive use in a trade or business or for investment (relinquished property) if the property is exchanged solely for property of like kind that is to be held either for productive use in a trade or business or for investment (replacement property). Under § 1.1031(a)-(1)(a)(1) of the Income Tax Regulations, property held for productive use in a trade or business may be exchanged for property held for investment, and property held for investment may be exchanged for property held for productive use in a trade or business.

.02 Rev. Rul. 59-229, 1959-2 C.B. 180, concludes that gain or loss from an exchange of personal residences may not be deferred under § 1031 because the residences are not property held for productive use in a trade or business or for investment.

.03 Section 2.05 of Rev. Proc. 2005-14, 2005-1 C.B. 528, states that § 1031 does not apply to property that is used solely as a personal residence.

.04 In Moore v. Comm'r, T.C. Memo. 2007-134, the taxpayers exchanged one lakeside vacation home for another. Neither home was ever rented. Both were used by the taxpayers only for personal purposes. The taxpayers claimed that the exchange of the homes was a like-kind exchange under § 1031 because the properties were expected to appreciate in value and thus were held for investment. The Tax Court held, however, that the properties were held for personal use and that the "mere hope or expectation that property may be sold at a gain cannot establish an investment intent if the taxpayer uses the property as a residence."

.05 In Starker v. United States, 602 F.2d 1341, 1350 (9th Cir. 1979), the Ninth Circuit held that a personal residence of a taxpayer was not eligible for exchange under § 1031, explaining that "[it] has long been the rule that use of property solely as a personal residence is antithetical to its being held for investment."

.06 The Service recognizes that many taxpayers hold dwelling units primarily for the production of current rental income, but also use the properties occasionally for personal purposes. In the interest of sound tax administration, this revenue procedure provides taxpayers with a safe harbor under which a dwelling unit will qualify as property held for productive use in a trade or business or for investment under § 1031 even though a taxpayer occasionally uses the dwelling unit for personal purposes.

SECTION 3. SCOPE

.01 In general. This revenue procedure applies to a dwelling unit, as defined in section 3.02 of this revenue procedure, that meets the qualifying use standards in section 4.02 of this revenue procedure.

.02 Dwelling unit. For purposes of this revenue procedure, a dwelling unit is real property improved with a house, apartment, condominium, or similar improvement that provides basic living accommodations including sleeping space, bathroom and cooking facilities.

SECTION 4. APPLICATION

.01 In general. The Service will not challenge whether a dwelling unit as defined in section 3.02 of this revenue procedure qualifies under § 1031 as property held for productive use in a trade or business or for investment if the qualifying use standards in section 4.02 of this revenue procedure are met for the dwelling unit.

.02 Qualifying use standards.

(1) Relinquished property. A dwelling unit that a taxpayer intends to be relinquished property in a § 1031 exchange qualifies as property held for productive use in a trade or business or for investment if:

(a) The dwelling unit is owned by the taxpayer for at least 24 months immediately before the exchange (the "qualifying use period"); and

(b) Within the qualifying use period, in each of the two 12-month periods immediately preceding the exchange,

(i) The taxpayer rents the dwelling unit to another person or persons at a fair rental for 14 days or more, and

(ii) The period of the taxpayer's personal use of the dwelling unit does not exceed the greater of 14 days or 10 percent of the number of days during the 12-month period that the dwelling unit is rented at a fair rental.

For this purpose, the first 12-month period immediately preceding the exchange ends on the day before the exchange takes place (and begins 12 months prior to that day) and the second 12-month period ends on the day before the first 12-month period begins (and begins 12 months prior to that day).

(2) Replacement property. A dwelling unit that a taxpayer intends to be replacement property in a § 1031 exchange qualifies as property held for productive use in a trade or business or for investment if:

(a) The dwelling unit is owned by the taxpayer for at least 24 months immediately after the exchange (the "qualifying use period"); and

(b) Within the qualifying use period, in each of the two 12-month periods immediately after the exchange,

(i) The taxpayer rents the dwelling unit to another person or persons at a fair rental for 14 days or more, and

(ii) The period of the taxpayer's personal use of the dwelling unit does not exceed the greater of 14 days or 10 percent of the number of days during the 12-month period that the dwelling unit is rented at a fair rental.

For this purpose, the first 12-month period immediately after the exchange begins on the day after the exchange takes place and the second 12-month period begins on the day after the first 12-month period ends.

.03 Personal use. For purposes of this revenue procedure, personal use of a dwelling unit occurs on any day on which a taxpayer is deemed to have used the dwelling unit for personal purposes under § 280A(d)(2) (taking into account § 280A(d)(3) but not § 280A(d)(4)).

.04 Fair rental. For purposes of this revenue procedure, whether a dwelling unit is rented at a fair rental is determined based on all of the facts and circumstances that exist when the rental agreement is entered into. All rights and obligations of the parties to the rental agreement are taken into account.

.05 Special rule for replacement property. If a taxpayer files a federal income tax return and reports a transaction as an exchange under § 1031, based on the expectation that a dwelling unit will meet the qualifying use standards in section 4.02 (2) of this revenue procedure for replacement property, and subsequently determines that the dwelling unit does not meet the qualifying use standards, the taxpayer, if necessary, should file an amended return and not report the transaction as an exchange under § 1031.

.06 Limited application of safe harbor. The safe harbor provided in this revenue procedure applies only to the determination of whether a dwelling unit qualifies as property held for productive use in a trade or business or for investment under § 1031. A taxpayer utilizing the safe harbor in this revenue procedure also must satisfy all other requirements for a like-kind exchange under § 1031 and the regulations thereunder.

V. Related Matters

- **More on Like Kindness.** In Peabody Natural Res. Co. v. Commissioner, 126 T.C. No. 14 (2006), the Tax Court held that an exchange of a gold mine for a coal mine subject to coal supply contracts qualified as a like kind exchange. Moreover, the supply contracts were not treated as boot. This illustrates the breadth of the real property for real property like kindness principle.

- **Another Non-Recognition Rule — Section 267.** Section 267 disallows recognition of a taxpayer's loss on the sale of property to a *related person*. The rationale for disallowing this loss is the belief that the taxpayer's actual economic circumstances have not been sufficiently changed. The property is still within his deemed control. In essence the related parties are viewed as a single economic unit. Generally speaking related persons are family members of the taxpayer or business entities controlled directly or *indirectly* by the taxpayer. Attribution rules apply.

- **And one more — Wash Sales.** Section 1091 denies losses on sales of stock when substantially identical stock is acquired by the taxpayer within 30 days before or after the sale. The effect of non-recognition is ameliorated by a provision that has the effect of increasing the cost basis of the new shares by the amount of the disallowed loss. The purpose of section 1091, like section 267, is to prevent loss recognition when the taxpayer has not changed her economic circumstance, i.e., has not cashed in her investment.

Chapter 25

Involuntary Conversions

I. Assignment

Read: Internal Revenue Code: §§ 1001(c); 1033(a)(1)–(2), (b)(1)–(2), (g)(1)–(2), (4), (h)(2). Skim §§ 1245(b)(4); 1250(d)(4).

Treasury Regulations: § 1.1033(b)-1(b).

Text: Overview
Clifton Inv. Co. v. Commissioner
Revenue Ruling 64-237
Related Matters

Complete the Problems.

II. Problems

1. Sinclair Lewis, owner-lessor of an office and warehouse building, received $1 million in insurance proceeds when the building was totally destroyed by fire. Which of the following transactions qualify for nonrecognition of gain under section 1033?

    (a) Sinclair used all of the proceeds to purchase a residential apartment building that Sinclair leased to tenants.

    (b) Sinclair used all of the proceeds to construct a gas station that Sinclair leased to tenants.

    (c) Sinclair used all of the proceeds to construct a gas station that Sinclair operated as a business.

    (d) Sinclair used all of the proceeds to purchase unimproved farm land that Sinclair leased to farmers.

    (e) Would your answers above change if the original building was condemned?

2. Calendar-year taxpayer, Alaa Al Aswany, owned and leased a residential apartment building with an adjusted basis of $120,000. On January 13, Year 1, the government condemned the building. On July 10, Year 1, Alaa received $180,000 in condemnation proceeds, and estimated that the entire $180,000 would be used to replace the original apartment building with a new apartment building.

    (a) What is Alaa's gain realized on the condemnation?

    (b) What is the latest date Alaa has to purchase qualified replacement property to not recognize the gain?

(c) Are there any restrictions on the type of property Alaa may purchase?

(d) Assuming Alaa paid $200,000 for qualified replacement property within the prescribed time limit, what is Alaa's basis in the new property?

(e) Assuming Alaa paid only $175,000 for qualified replacement property within the prescribed time limit, what is the amount of gain recognized on the condemnation proceeds (to be reflected on an amended return), and what is Alaa's basis in the new property?

III. Overview

In the last chapter, we looked at section 1031—a special non-recognition provision that applies to certain *voluntary* exchanges of property. In this chapter, we consider section 1033—another significant non-recognition provision that potentially applies when property is *involuntarily* converted into other property. The policy behind both provisions is similar: non-recognition is warranted if a taxpayer's investment is continued and the taxpayer has not really changed his or her economic position.

In contrast to section 1031, section 1033 applies only to gains (and not losses) realized from involuntary conversions. Under section 1033(a)(1), if property is involuntarily converted directly into similar-use property, the gain realized, if any, will not be recognized. Under section 1033(a)(2), if property is involuntarily converted into money (e.g., condemnation award or fire insurance proceeds), the gain realized, if any, will be recognized unless the taxpayer elects non-recognition treatment by purchasing similar-use property within a prescribed time period. However, gain is recognized to the extent that the conversion proceeds exceed the cost of the replacement property.

A. Involuntary Conversions

Section 1033 applies only if property is *compulsorily or involuntarily converted*. Not all involuntary conversions fall within the scope of section 1033; to qualify, a conversion must result from one of four identified events: (1) destruction in whole or in part, (2) theft, (3) seizure, or (4) requisition or condemnation (or threat or imminence thereof).

The phrase *destruction in whole or in part* encompasses unusual and unexpected events constituting casualties within the meaning of section 165(c)(3) (e.g., the destruction of a house by tornado, the destruction of livestock by lightning, or the destruction of a wheat crop by hail). Review Chapter 10. The phrase does not, however, incorporate the element of suddenness, which is a prerequisite to a casualty loss deduction under section 165(c)(3). *See* Rev. Rul. 59-102, 1959-1 C.B. 200. For example, the gradual deterioration of property attributable to termites or drought could qualify as section 1033 destruction so long as it is unusual and unexpected. *See* Rev. Rul. 63-232, 1963-2 C.B. 97. *See also* Rev. Rul. 89-2, 1989-1 C.B. 753 (holding that property rendered unsafe by chemical contamination was *destroyed* for purposes of section 1033).

Partial destruction of property may qualify for section 1033 treatment. A taxpayer might realize gain if he receives damages, insurance, or other reimbursements for the partial destruction of property. Or, a taxpayer might realize gain if he sells partially destroyed property. Whether a post-casualty sale is treated as an involuntary conversion depends on whether the taxpayer had a choice to either keep or sell the partially damaged property; the choice turns, in part, on whether the taxpayer could restore or repair the property. If the taxpayer had a choice, section 1033 does not apply to the post-casualty sale. *See* C.G. Willis, Inc. v. Commissioner, 41 T.C. 468 (1964) (denying section 1033 treatment to sale of ship damaged in a collision because the ship could have been repaired). *But see* Rev. Rul. 96-32, 1996-1 C.B. 177 (holding that, where the dwelling portion of a taxpayer's principal residence was destroyed by tornado, and subsequently the remaining land was sold, the sale was treated as an involuntary conversion).

The term *seizure* is different from the term *requisition or condemnation*. A *seizure* encompasses the confiscation of property by a governmental entity without compensation (e.g., confiscation of a boat used in illegal drug trafficking activity). Few section 1033 cases apply to seizures due to the nonpayment of compensation.

A *requisition* or *condemnation* typically encompasses the compensable taking of property by a governmental entity or quasi-governmental entity for a public use (e.g., exercise of eminent domain by the government). A considerable number of cases and rulings apply section 1033 to requisitions and condemnations. Indeed, from a practitioner's point of view, the core of section 1033 is the non-recognition of gain when property is converted as a result of a condemnation. Section 1033 applies not only when there is an actual requisition or condemnation, but also when there is a sale made under *threat or imminence* of requisition or condemnation. This is designed to encourage sales to condemning authorities in advance of formal takings of property.

B. Similar or Related in Service or Use

If an involuntary conversion has occurred, non-recognition of gain is available only if a taxpayer acquires qualified replacement property; that is, *property similar or related in service or use* to the converted property (or a controlling stock interest in a company owning such property). Neither the Code nor the regulations define the phrase similar or related in service or use. As a result, the phrase has been the subject of much litigation. Several courts have focused on the uses to which the converted and replaced properties were put by the taxpayer. According to the Tax Court in Maloof v. Commissioner, 65 T.C. 263 (1975), it is not necessary for a taxpayer to acquire property that is the exact duplicate of the converted property; however, a taxpayer cannot change the character of his or her investment.

Read *Clifton Investment Co. v. Commissioner*, and Revenue Ruling 64-237, included in the materials below. Revenue Ruling 64-237 has been cited in a number of other revenue rulings that provide good examples of replacement property that is and is not similar or related in service or use. In Revenue Ruling 71-41, 1971-1 C.B. 223, a state condemned a taxpayer's warehouse, which he rented to third parties, and the land upon which it was located. The taxpayer used the condemnation proceeds to erect a gas station, on other land already owned by the taxpayer, which he rented to an oil company. Citing Revenue Ruling 64-237, the Service held that the gas station was property similar or related in service or use to the converted warehouse. Compare this ruling with Revenue Ruling 76-319, 1976-2 C.B. 242, wherein the taxpayer operated a recreational bowling center, which consisted of bowling alleys, a lounge area, and a bar. The bowling center was completely destroyed by fire and the taxpayer received ample insurance proceeds. The taxpayer invested the insurance proceeds in a new recreational billiard center, which consisted of billiard tables, a lounge area, and a bar. Citing Revenue Ruling 64-237, the Service held that the billiard center did not qualify as replacement property for purposes of section 1033 since bowling alleys and bowling equipment are not similar to billiard tables and billiard equipment.

As you can probably surmise, the similar or related in service or use standard of section 1033 is more stringent than the like-kind standard of section 1031. For example, improved real estate and unimproved real estate are considered like-kind for purposes of section 1031, but not similar or related in service or use for purposes of section 1033. Along the same lines, property used in the operation of a trade or business and rented property are considered like-kind, but not similar or related in service or use. In 1958, to achieve a better parity between the replacement requirements in sections 1031 and 1033, Congress enacted section 1033(g), which allows certain converted real property to be replaced by like-kind property. This special rule only applies to real property held for business use or investment (and not to property held for personal use such as a residence), and only applies if the property is converted by reason of seizure, requisition or condemnation, or threat or imminence thereof (and not by reason of fire, flood, or other catastrophe). Query whether these limitations are sound given that the rationale underlying both section 1031 and section 1033 is that the taxpayer's investment is continued.

C. When Replacement Must Occur

Non-recognition of gain upon the involuntary conversion of property hinges on whether the taxpayer acquires similar use property within the time period prescribed by section 1033. As a general rule, the replacement period begins on the date of involuntary conversion and ends two years after the close of the taxable year in which gain is first realized (i.e., when proceeds in excess of basis become available to the taxpayer). IRC § 1033(a)(2)(B). A three-year replacement period applies to condemnations of business or investment real property described in section 1033(g); and, a four-year replacement period applies to involuntary conversions of principal residences as a result of Presidentially declared disasters. IRC § 1033(h).

D. Basis and Holding Period of Replacement Property

Section 1033 does not permanently exclude gain, instead, it defers gain until disposition of the replacement property. As with section 1031, deferral of gain is achieved through the mechanism of basis. If property is involuntarily converted into similar-use property and gain is not recognized pursuant to section 1033(a)(1), then the basis of the replacement property is the same as the taxpayer's basis in the converted property. IRC § 1033(b)(1). If property is involuntarily converted into money and the taxpayer elects not to recognize gain pursuant to section 1033(a)(2), then the basis of the replacement property is the cost of the replacement property minus the amount of unrecognized gain on the conversion. IRC § 1033(b)(2).

The holding period of the replacement property includes the holding period of the converted property if the latter was a capital asset or section 1231 property at the time of conversion. Rev. Rul. 72-451, 1972-2 C.B. 480.

IV. Materials

Clifton Inv. Co. v. Commissioner

312 F.2d 719 (6th Cir. 1963)

Boyd, District Judge.

Petitioner is a real estate investment corporation organized and existing under the laws of the State of Ohio, with head-quarters in Cincinnati. In 1956 the petitioner sold to the City of Cincinnati under its threat of exercising its power of eminent domain a six-story office building, known as the United Bank Building, located in the downtown section of that city, which building was held by petitioner for production of rental income from commercial tenants. The funds realized from the sale of this property to the city were used by the petitioner to purchase eighty percent of the outstanding stock of The Times Square Hotel of New York, Inc., also an Ohio corporation, which had as its sole asset a contract to buy the Times Square Hotel of New York City. The purchase of the hotel was effected by the corporation. The taxpayer-petitioner contends herein that the purchase of the controlling stock in the hotel corporation was an investment in property "similar or related in service or use" to the office building it had been forced to sell, thus deserving of the non-recognition of gain provisions of Section 1033(a)(3)(A), Internal Revenue Code of 1954. More specifically, the taxpayer contends that since both the properties herein were productive of rental income, the similarity contemplated by the statute aforesaid exists. The Commissioner ruled to the contrary, holding that any gain from the sale of the office building was recognizable and a deficiency was assessed against the taxpayer for the year 1956 in the amount of $19,057.09. The Tax Court agreed with the Commissioner, finding that the properties themselves were not "similar or related in service or use" as required by the statute. From the decision of the Tax Court this appeal was perfected.

In order to determine whether the requisite similarity existed under the statute between the properties herein, the Tax Court applied the so-called "functional test" or "end-use test." This it seems has been the Tax Court's traditional line of inquiry, when similar cases under the within statute have been considered by it. This approach takes into account only the actual physical end use to which the properties involved are put, whether that use be by the owner-taxpayer or by his tenant; that is, whether the taxpayer-owner is the actual user of the property or merely holds it for investment purposes, as in the case of a lessor. We reject the functional test as applied to the holder of investment property, who replaces such property with other investment property, as in the case at bar.

The Tax Court in this case relied in part on its earlier decision in Liant Record, Inc. v. Commissioner, 36 T.C. 224 and chiefly on the decision of the Court of Appeals for the Third Circuit in McCaffrey v. Commissioner, 275 F.2d 27, 1960, cert. denied 363 U.S. 828, the latter case approving and applying the aforesaid functional test in such a case as here presented. However, the Court of Appeals for the Second Circuit has since reversed the Tax Court's decision in *Liant*, 303 F.2d 326, 1962, and in so doing advanced what we consider to be the soundest approach among the number of decisions on this point. We need not here review all the relevant decisions, since this is done in the recent cases of Loco Realty Company v. Commissioner, 306 F.2d 207 (C.A.8) 1962, and Pohn v. Commissioner, 309 F.2d 427 (C.A.7) 1962, both of which decisions approved the Second Circuit Court's approach in *Liant*, the court in the *Pohn* case relying specifically on the *Liant* decision.

I.

Congress must have intended that in order for the taxpayer to obtain the tax benefits of Section 1033 he must have continuity of interest as to the original property and its replacement in order that the taxpayer not be given a tax-free alteration of his interest. In short, the properties must be reasonably similar in their relation to the taxpayer. This reasonableness, as noted in the *Liant* case, is dependent upon a number of factors, all bearing on whether or not the relation of the taxpayer to the property has been changed. The ultimate use to which the properties are put, then, does not control the inquiry, when the taxpayer is not the user of the properties as in the case under consideration. As exemplary of the factors which are relevant the *Liant* decision mentions the following, after advancement of its "relation of the properties to the taxpayer" test:

> In applying such a test to a lessor, a court must compare, inter alia, the extent and type of the lessor's management activity, the amount and kind of services rendered by him to the tenants, and the nature of his business risks connected with the properties.

Thus, each case is dependent on its peculiar facts and the factors bearing on the service or use of the properties to the taxpayer must be closely examined. The Tax Court employed an erroneous test in this case, but on examination of the record, the correctness of the result is manifest.

II.

The record before us discloses that the United Bank Building and the Times Square Hotel both produced rental income to the taxpayer. However, examination of what the properties required in the way of services to the tenants, management activity, and commercial tenancy considerations reveals an alteration of the taxpayer's interest. The record herein shows that the taxpayer corporation itself managed the United Bank Building, but deemed it necessary to procure professional management for the

Times Square Hotel. There were primarily two employees for the United Bank Building, who afforded elevator and janitorial services to the tenants. In the Times Square Hotel between 130 and 140 employees were necessary to attend the hotel operation and offer services to the commercial tenants and hotel guests. Approximately 96% of the rental income from the hotel was from the guest room facilities and the large number of transients required daily services of varying kinds. Furniture, linens, personal services of every description were furnished the hotel guests, which were not furnished the commercial tenants of the United Bank Building. The hotel guests reside in the hotel rooms and that is obviously the only reason they are tenants. In the office building herein several tenants also used parts of the premises for living quarters, but were clearly not furnished the typical services the hotel guest demands. There was no great limitation placed on the types of commercial tenants to whom space was rented in the United Bank Building, but as the enumeration of commercial tenants of the hotel building reveals, space therein was leased for the most part and primarily with an eye to how such a business operation might fit in with the operation of a hotel, how it relates to the hotel guests. It is common experience that the services offered by a lessee of business premises in a hotel will reflect in the minds of its guests on the service they associate with the hotel itself. If a leased restaurant in a hotel offers good or bad service, there is a tendency to think of the food service at the hotel as good or bad. A number of unique business considerations enter when leasing commercial space in a hotel which do not apply to an office building.

We consider there to be, then, a material variance between the relation of the office building in question and the within hotel operation of the taxpayer, in the light of the relevant inquiry found in the *Liant* case. It is true that what the taxpayer derived from both properties herein was generally the same, rental income. But what the properties demanded of the taxpayer in the way of management, services, and relations to its tenants materially varied. That which the taxpayer receives from his properties and that which such properties demand of the taxpayer must both be considered in determining whether or not the properties are similar or related in service or use to the taxpayer.

The decision of the Tax Court is affirmed.

Revenue Ruling 64-237
1964-2 C.B. 319

The Internal Revenue Service has reconsidered its position with respect to replacement property that is "similar or related in service or use" to involuntarily converted property within the meaning of section 1033(a) of the Internal Revenue Code of 1954 in light of the decision of the United States Court of Appeals for the Second Circuit in the case of Liant Record, Inc. v. Commissioner, 303 Fed.(2d) 326 (1962), and other appellate court decisions.

In previous litigation, the Service has taken the position that the statutory phrase, "similar or related in service or use," means that the property acquired must have a close "functional" similarity to the property converted. Under this test, property was not considered similar or related in service or use to the converted property unless the physical characteristics and end uses of the converted and replacement properties were closely similar. Although this "functional use test" has been upheld in the lower courts, it has not been sustained in the appellate courts with respect to investors in property, such as lessors.

In conformity with the appellate court decisions, in considering whether replacement property acquired by an investor is similar in service or use to the converted property, attention will be directed primarily to the similarity in the relationship of the services or uses which the original and replacement properties have to the taxpayer-owner. In applying this test, a determination will be made as to whether the properties are of a similar service to the taxpayer, the nature of the business risks connected with the properties, and what such properties demand of the taxpayer in the way of management, services and relations to his tenants.

For example, where the taxpayer is a lessor, who rented out the converted property for a light manufacturing plant and then rents out the replacement property for a wholesale grocery warehouse, the nature of the taxpayer-owner's service or use of the properties may be similar although that of the end users change. The two properties will be considered as similar or related in service or use where, for example, both are rented and where there is a similarity in the extent and type of the taxpayer's management activities, the amount and kind of services rendered by him to his tenants, and the nature of his business risks connected with the properties.

In modifying its position with respect to the involuntary conversion of property held for investment, the Service will continue to adhere to the functional test in the case of owner-users of property. Thus, if the taxpayer-owner operates a light manufacturing plant on the converted property and then operates a wholesale grocery warehouse on the replacement property, by changing his end use he has so changed the nature of his relationship to the property as to be outside the nonrecognition of gain provisions.

V. Related Matters

- **Section 1245 Recapture.** Section 1245(a), which overrides all other income tax provisions, requires recognition of ordinary income (recapture of depreciation) upon the disposition of section 1245 property (depreciable tangible personal property). Section 1245(b)(4) provides an exception for involuntary conversions. Specifically, section 1245 will not apply if the requirements of section 1033 are met and if the conversion proceeds attributable to section 1245 property are reinvested entirely in section 1245 property.

- **Section 1250 Recapture.** Section 1250 requires recognition of ordinary income (recapture of depreciation in excess of straight-line depreciation) on certain dispositions of section 1250 property (depreciable real property placed in service before 1987). Section 1250(d)(4) provides an exception for involuntary conversions.

Chapter 26

Installment Sales

I. Assignment

Read: Internal Revenue Code: §§ 453(a)–(d), (e)(1), (4), (f)(3), (i); 453B(a)–(c), (g)(2); 691(a)(4); 1014(c); 1271(a). Skim §§ 1272(a); 1273(a); 1274(a)–(b).

Treasury Regulations: §§ 1.453-4(c); 15A.453-1(b)–(c).

Text: Overview
Revenue Ruling 79-371
Related Matters

Complete the problems.

II. Problems

1. Robert Newhouse, a cash method taxpayer, owns an incorporated newspaper business that has been in his family for generations. His basis in the stock is $400,000. In the current year, Robert sold his stock in the business to his daughter, Christine Hefner, for $2,000,000. Under the terms of the agreement Robert receives $100,000 cash in the current year and nineteen notes of $100,000 each. The notes bear adequate interest at the rate of 5% compounded semi-annually and come due sequentially over the succeeding nineteen years. What are the tax consequences to Robert in the current and succeeding years in the following circumstances?

   (a) Robert does not elect out under section 453(d).

   (b) What if in (a) Robert had borrowed $200,000 using the stock as security and Christine assumed the debt as part of the sale and only 17 notes are given by Christine?

   (c) What results in (b) if the mortgage is $500,000 and Christine gives 14 notes?

   (d) What if in (a) Robert sells the notes for $1,800,000?

   (e) What if in (a) Robert gives the notes (which have a fair market value of $1,800,000) to his grandson, Rupert Murdoch, prior to collecting them?

   (f) What if in (a) Robert dies before collecting on the notes and bequeaths them to Rupert?

2. I.M. Pei is in the construction business as a sole proprietor. He agrees to sell a crane to Harry Houdini, an employee who wants to use the crane in his side business as an escape artist. The terms of sale provide that Harry will pay I.M.

$120,000 in four annual installments of $30,000 each. The first installment is due upon delivery of the crane. The other three are due over the next three years and are evidenced by notes bearing interest at 6%. In addition, Harry takes the crane subject to a mortgage of $30,000. I.M.'s basis in the crane is $90,000. He has taken $30,000 of depreciation on the crane. What are the income tax consequences of the sale to I.M.?

3. Woo Suk Hwang bought a patent for a biological mechanism for healing damaged nerves for $1,000,000 as an investment. Two years later he sold the patent to a major drug company for 5% of the earnings from the patent for 10 years up to a maximum stated sales price of $5,000,000. He received $500,000 a year for ten years.

   (a) What are the income tax consequences of the sale to Hwang?

   (b) What are the tax consequences to Hwang if there is no maximum stated sales price?

III. Overview

A. Introduction

It is not unusual for sellers and buyers of property to agree that payment will be made in installments over time rather than all at once. The tax law fosters these installment sale contracts by permitting the seller to recognize the tax gain on such sales over time as well. This is an excellent gain deferral opportunity. But before considering the tax treatment of installment sales it is helpful to consider their utility in the business and estate planning context. Installment sales allow sellers to sell property to buyers who might have trouble obtaining alternative financing. This can be especially important for hard-to-sell items such as closely held businesses. In effect, the added feature of seller financing helps create a market for what is being sold. Installment sales are also used by sellers to transfer property to family members who could not otherwise afford to purchase the property. In this context the installment sale may function as an annuity for a retiring parent or other family member while keeping the property in the family. In both the business and family context the buyer may be able to use the income from the property or business to help make the installment payments. In addition the interest payments may be tax deductible to the buyer. But there are potential down sides for both the buyer and the seller. The seller runs the risk that the buyer may default on the terms of sale. In this case the property will usually revert back to the seller but it may have declined in value due to the buyer's neglect or other reasons. From the buyer's perspective default may not only lead to forfeiture of the property but also loss of the equity gained from earlier payments. For both the buyer and seller, default can lead to other expenses such as accountant's and attorney's fees. Thus, installment sales are not to be entered into lightly.

As in the case of like kind exchanges it is common for a lawyer to draw up the agreement between the parties. It is important to be alert to the conflict of interest issues that can arise in this context. Usually it is best to represent only one of the parties and to advise the other party of her need for her own counsel. Additionally the lawyer should advise the client to obtain an expert appraisal of the value of the property in question. The fact that the agreement was beautifully drawn is cold comfort to the client who later learns that he sold for too little or paid too much. Even though it is not the lawyer's job to tell the client whether the proposed price is a fair one, the client may tend to blame her lawyer if the deal turns out badly. It is good practice to put in writing your recommendation to the client that an expert appraisal be obtained.

Now to the tax treatment of installment sales. As implied above, the installment method of reporting is favorable to taxpayers because it defers tax liability until the actual payment (as distinguished from the installment note) is received. This is different from the outcome that would normally arise under either the cash method or the accrual method of accounting. Under the cash method, the taxpayer would take the fair market value of the note into income at the time of its receipt. After all, the note is property under section 1001. (The doctrine of cash equivalence might apply.) Under the accrual method, the taxpayer would have income upon execution of the contract and transfer of title. (Remember, the accrual method requires that gain be recorded when *all events* have occurred fixing the right to receive income and the amount is reasonably ascertainable. Treas. Reg. § 1.451-1(a).)

The installment method is an exception to both of these methods. It automatically applies unless the taxpayer elects out under subsection 453(d). The installment method is justified primarily on the basis of taxpayer liquidity.

B. The Mechanics of Section 453 and the Defined Terms

An installment sale is a sale where at least one payment comes after the end of the year in which the disposition occurs. IRC § 453(b)(1). Some sales are excluded from installment sale treatment including dealer dispositions and sales of inventory. IRC § 453(b)(2). Nor does the installment method apply to gains arising from the recapture of depreciation. IRC § 453(i). The key to applying the installment method is found in section 453(c). It provides that the tax gain recognized on each payment is that proportion of the payment "which the gross profit ... bears to the total contract price." This may be stated as a formula applying what is known as the gross profit ratio.

Gross Profit Ratio Formula

$$\frac{\text{Gross Profit}}{\text{Total Contract Price}} \times \text{Payment} = \text{Gain Recognized on Payment}$$

The terms "gross profit" (GP), "total contract price" (TKP), and "payment" all have precise definitions set out in the regulations. Other terms that are crucial to our analysis are also set out in the regulations. It is worth noting that the regulations have specific legislative authority. *See* IRC § 453(j).

Gross profit means "selling price" (SP) minus the seller's adjusted basis. Treas. Reg. § 15A.453-1(b)(2)(v). Selling price means gross selling price but does not include interest. Treas. Reg. § 15A.453-1(b)(2)(ii). *Total contract price* means selling price reduced by "qualifying indebtedness" (QI) not in excess of seller's basis. Treas. Reg. § 15A.453-1(b)(2)(iii). Qualifying indebtedness is the buyer's acquisition indebtedness assumed from the seller. Treas. Reg. § 15A.453-1(b)(2)(iv). *Payment* does not include the evidences of indebtedness that the seller receives from the buyer. Treas. Reg. §§ 1.453-4(c); 15A.453-1(b)(3)(i). Nor does payment include any debt assumption by the buyer to the extent that the debt does not exceed the seller's adjusted basis. *Id.* Nor does the gross profit ratio apply to payments of interest (which are ordinary income to the seller under section 61).

These definitions have great significance when an installment sale involves property transferred subject to a mortgage. In particular, the exclusion of the buyer's assumption of qualifying indebtedness not in excess of basis from treatment as a payment has the effect of allowing the seller to avoid current gain recognition on such assumptions and permits the seller to reduce basis instead. The operation of this rule and others is illustrated in the following examples.

Example 1: Installment Sale with No Recapture and No Debt Assumption. Seller owns a parcel of investment land bought five years ago for $10,000. Seller sells the property to Buyer for $10,000 cash and three installment notes each with a face amount of $10,000. The first note is payable in full next year. The second is payable in full in two years, and the third is payable in three years. Each note bears interest at the rate of 7 percent annually.

The gross profit is $30,000 (the selling price of $40,000 minus the basis of $10,000). The total contract price is $40,000 (the same as selling price since there is no debt assumption). Thus, the gross profit ratio is 3/4, or 75%.

In the current year there is a payment of $10,000 which when multiplied times the gross profit ratio yields a recognized gain of $7,500 and a return of basis of $2,500. Over the course of all four payments Seller will recognize $30,000 of gain (4 × $7,500 = $30,000) and recover $10,000 of basis (4 × $2,500 = $10,000). Just as in any other sales transaction, the gain is characterized by reference to the property sold. The holding period is determined from the date of the sale. Here the gain would be long-term capital gain. The payment of interest is ordinary income separate and apart from the installment sale analysis.

Example 2: Installment Sale with Recapture. Assume the same facts as above except that the property sold is an airplane used in a trade or business which (somewhat unrealistically) has been subject to $6,000 of tax depreciation (assume that current basis is still $10,000). Recognition of the $6,000 of gain arising from the depreciation is not permitted to be deferred under the installment method. It is recognized immediately as ordinary income. IRC §§ 453(i)(1)(A), 1245(a). The remaining gain is accounted for under the installment method. IRC § 453(i)(1)(B). This is accomplished mechanically by increasing the basis of the property by the recapture gain amount ($10,000 + $6,000 = $16,000) before calculating the gross profit. Thus, the gross profit is now $24,000 ($40,000 SP − $16,000 AB = $24,000 GP). The gross profit ratio is 24/40 or 3/5. The portion of each payment that is gain is $6,000 (3/5 × $10,000 = $6,000). Over the course of the four payments there will be $24,000 of gain recognized in addition to the $6,000 of ordinary income recognized immediately. Thus, a total of $30,000 of gain will be recognized from the sale just as in the previous example ($6,000 + $24,000 = $30,000). The $24,000 of gain recognized under the installment method is section 1231 gain. *See* IRC § 1231(b)(1).

Example 3: Installment Sale with Debt Assumption Not in Excess of Seller's Adjusted Basis. Assume the same facts as in Example 1, above, except that the property is transferred to Buyer subject to a $10,000 mortgage and there are only two $10,000 installment notes issued, which keeps selling price at $40,000. The mortgage is qualifying indebtedness and does not exceed Seller's adjusted basis. Thus, its assumption is not treated as a "payment" from Buyer to Seller. Treas. Reg. §§ 1.453-4(c), 15A.453-1(b)(3)(i). Thus, no gain is recognized as a result of the debt assumption. However, the assumption amount is excluded from the selling price to derive total contract price for purposes of determining the gross profit ratio. Treas. Reg. § 15A.453-1(b)(2)(iii). Thus, total contract price is now $30,000 ($40,000 SP − $10,000 QI = $30,000). In turn, the gross profit ratio is now 30/30 or 1/1. This means that $10,000 of each of the three payments is taxable gain (1 × $10,000 = $10,000). In effect the debt assumption is treated as a return of basis.

Example 4: Installment Sale with Debt Assumption in Excess of Seller's Adjusted Basis. Assume the same facts as in Example 1, above, except that the property is transferred to Buyer subject to a $15,000 mortgage and there are only two installment notes issued, one for $10,000 due next year and the second for $5,000 due in two years, which keeps selling price at $40,000. The mortgage is qualifying indebtedness but exceeds Seller's adjusted basis. The $5,000 amount of the assumption in excess of basis is treated as a "payment" from Buyer to Seller. Treas. Reg. §§ 1.453-4(c), 15A.453-1(b)(3)(i). The assumption amount not in excess of Seller's adjusted basis is excluded from selling price to derive the total contract price for purposes of determining the gross profit ratio. Treas. Reg. § 15A.453-1(b)(2)(iii). Thus, the total contract price is now $30,000 ($40,000 SP − $10,000 QI not in excess of basis = $30,000). In turn, the gross profit ratio is now 30/30 or 1/1. This means that the entire amount of each payment, including the $5,000 of debt assumed in excess of basis, is taxable gain. Thus, $15,000 of gain will be recognized in the current year. $10,000 of gain will be recognized next year. And $5,000 of gain will be recognized in the following year. In the aggregate, $30,000 of gain will be recognized just as in the other examples.

From this example one should see that when the buyer assumes a debt in excess of the seller's basis, the gross profit ratio will always be 1/1.

C. Dispositions of Installment Notes: Section 453B

Generally speaking the transfer of an installment obligation, even as a gift, triggers gain or loss recognition. IRC § 453B(a). If the transfer is a sale, gain or loss recognition is determined by reference to the difference between amount realized and adjusted basis. If the transfer is by gift, the fair market value of the obligation is deemed the amount realized. The fair market value of an installment obligation may differ from its face value for a variety of reasons. One of the most significant of these reasons is when it bears a rate of interest different from the current market rate. For example, if a $100,000 obligation payable in one year bears a 5% rate of interest but the current market rate for such loans is 7%, anyone buying the note would not expect to pay more than about $98,000 for it. In this way the buyer would realize slightly more than a 7% (the current market rate) return on the investment ($105,000 − $98,000 = $7,000; $7,000/98,000 = 7.14%). In short, all other things being equal, the fair market value of the 5% note is about $98,000.

The adjusted basis of the obligation is determined by deducting from its face value an amount equal to the gain that would have been realized had the installment obligation been paid in full. IRC § 453B(b).

Two significant exceptions to the recognition rule of section 453B(a) are transfers at death and transfers between spouses or incident to divorce. IRC §§ 453B(c) & (g). In both cases, the transferee takes the transferor's basis. IRC §§ 691(a)(4), 1014(c), 453B(g)(2). Thus, the gain remains lurking in the note to be recognized by the transferee. The treatment of transfers between spouses and former spouses is consistent with the approach of section 1041. However, one might wonder why, in the case of an installment note received by inheritance there is no basis step up to date of death fair market value as there is with most other property under section 1014. In partial answer we might say that the basis step up rule is itself of doubtful propriety from a tax theory standpoint. Thus, the failure to accede to it here may simply function as a partial correction of bad policy. In saying this we remain mindful of the implicit equal treatment issue that is not addressed by such a response. Nonetheless, the gain on the installment note falls into a category known as income in respect of a decedent (IRD) which is governed by section 691. In general the beneficiary of IRD steps into the shoes of the decedent for purposes of gain and income recognition. *See* IRC §§ 691(a)(1), (3), & (4).

As in the previous section, we end this part with some illustrations.

Example 1: Sale of an Installment Obligation. Seller owned a parcel of investment land bought five years ago for $10,000. Seller sold the property to Buyer for $10,000 in cash and three installment notes each with a face amount of $10,000. The first note is payable in full next year. The second is payable in full in two years, and the third is payable in full in three years. Each note bears interest at the rate of 7% annually. The fair market value of each note is $9,000. Prior to receiving any payments on the notes, Seller transfers the notes to a third party for $27,000 in cash.

As in the earlier examples, the gross profit is $30,000 (the selling price of $40,000 minus the basis of $10,000). The total contract price is $40,000 (the same as selling price since there is no debt assumption). Thus, the gross profit ratio is 3/4.

In the current year there is a payment of $10,000 which when multiplied times the gross profit ratio yields a recognized gain of $7,500 and a return of basis of $2,500. Each of the three notes has a basis of $2,500. *See* IRC § 453B(b). The sale of the three notes yields a gain of $19,500 ($27,000 AR − $7,500 AB = $19,500 GR). The gain is long-term capital gain determined by reference to the character of the land in Seller's hands. *See* IRC § 453B(a) (flush language).

Example 2: Gift of an Installment Obligation. Assume the same facts as in Example 1, above, except that Seller gives the notes to Son. The result for Seller will be the same as in Example 1 since he is deemed to have received the fair market value of the notes, $27,000. *See* IRC § 453B(a)(2). Revenue Ruling 79-371, included in the materials, addresses Son's basis in the notes. When the three notes are paid, Son may have gain to recognize. At one time the character of Son's gain would have been ordinary due to the lack of a sale or exchange when he received payment on the notes. But now section 1271(a) provides for sale or exchange treatment upon the retirement of a debt instrument.

Example 3: Bequest of an Installment Obligation. Assume the same facts as in Example 1, above, except that Seller dies and leaves the notes to Son in his will. Section 453B does not apply so no gain is recognized at the time of the bequest. *See* IRC § 453B(c). However, neither does section 1014(a) apply, so there is no date of death basis step up. *See* IRC § 1014(c). Son succeeds to Seller's basis of $7,500 in the three notes and recognizes $22,500 of gain ($30,000 − $7,500 = $22,500) as they are paid just as Seller would have. The character of the gain will also be determined by reference to its character had Seller received the payments. *See* IRC §§ 691(a)(3) & (4). Thus, it will be long-term capital gain.

D. Contingent Payment Sales

Sometimes an installment sale may be structured with uncertainty as to the duration of the contract or as to the total sales price, or as to both. Installment sales involving these uncertainties are referred to as *contingent payment sales.* The regulations specify how these contingencies are addressed. *See* Treas. Reg. § 15A.453-1(c). Typical examples of contingent payment sales include sales of patents in which the sellers receive royalty payments and sales of closely held businesses in which the sellers receive some share of post-sale revenues or profits. We will not seek to detail all the rules for all the variations that are possible. If there is a stated maximum sales price, that amount is treated as the selling price for purposes of computing the gross profit ratio. Treas. Reg. § 15A.453-1(c)(2)(i)(A). Thus, for example, if a seller with a $200,000 basis is entitled to 10% of post sale profits up to $2,000,000, the $2,000,000 figure will be used to compute the gross profit ratio (here 9/10). *See* Treas. Reg. § 15A.453-1(c)(2)(i)(B), ex.1. If there is no stated maximum sales price but the period of payment is of fixed duration, the seller recovers her basis ratably over the fixed period. Treas. Reg. § 15A.453-1(c)(3)(i). Thus, for example, if the seller above is to receive 10% of post sale profits for five years, she will recover 1/5 of her basis ($40,000) each year. Everything else she receives is gain from the sale or interest. *See* Treas. Reg. § 15A.453-1(c)(3)(i), (ii), ex. 1. If there is neither a maximum stated sales price nor a fixed duration, the seller recovers basis ratably over a fifteen year period. Treas. Reg. § 15A.453-1(c)(4).

E. Installment Sales with Unstated or Understated Interest

A fundamental assumption in the discipline of economics is that money has value over time. This is because it can be invested to produce income. Thus, it is assumed that a dollar in the future is always worth less than a dollar in the present. For this reason, a person who makes an interest free loan is foregoing income. (How much income is foregone is a function of the current market interest rates and the length of time before the loan is repaid.) That is why any loan entered into by knowledgeable persons dealing with one another at arms length will normally have a stated interest component. Since an installment sale involves deferred payments, it is by its very nature a loan. In other words, in the context of an installment sale, the seller is also a lender. It follows from this that in an economic sense an installment sale of property should always involve payment of interest by the buyer.

The sale of an appreciated capital asset under the installment method produces capital gain for the seller except that any interest paid on the notes is ordinary income, which is usually taxed at higher rates. A seller who wants to avoid having any ordinary income might suggest to the buyer that the purchase price be increased in exchange for reducing or eliminating the stated interest on the sale. The advantage to the buyer under this approach is a higher basis in the acquired property (though the buyer may be giving up an interest deduction). Under the economic principles discussed above, such an arrangement is disguising the interest payments as payments of principal.

There are various situations, including this one, where the Internal Revenue Code may reduce the purchase price and impute interest in order to treat the transaction in a manner consistent with economic theory despite how the parties have characterized the transaction. The chief applicable provisions are sections 483, 1272–1274, and 7872. We will not address the complexities of these provisions. But where they apply they re-characterize some portion of the payments as interest rather than as principal. This interest component is known as "Original Issue Discount" (OID). *See* IRC § 1273(a). The measuring rod for determining whether an installment sale has understated the interest component of the sale is the "applicable federal rate" (AFR). Depending on the term of the note involved, the AFR is one of three different rates determined by reference to various government bonds. *See* IRC § 1274(d). The AFR changes with the lending market, and the new rates are published monthly by the Internal Revenue Service. If the sale understates interest, the tax rules will derive an "imputed principal amount" by using the AFR to discount the future payments to their present values, i.e., by wringing out the unstated interest. *See* IRC §§ 1274(a) & (b). The amounts paid in excess of the imputed principal amount are OID and must be reported as interest. A simple illustration of these time value of money rules is set out below.

Example: Imputed Interest on an Installment Sale. Seller agrees to sell a copyright to Buyer for $2,000,000. The terms of payment are $200,000 cash upon execution of the agreement and $600,000 per year for each of the next three years (Years 1, 2, and 3). There is no stated interest. If the AFR is 10%, the *discounted* or present values of the three payments are $545,454.55 for the Year 1 payment, $495,867.77 for the Year 2 payment, and $450,788.90 for the Year 3 payment. The excess paid over those amounts is treated as interest (OID) by Seller and by Buyer. The imputed principal amount of the sale is the sum of the present values of the four payments ($1,692,111.20). This serves as Seller's amount realized and as Buyer's cost basis.

The principles just described can apply in a variety of circumstances. They are again explicitly raised in Chapter 30 in the context of interest free loans between family members. One who advises taxpayers on financial matters should be alert to their potential application in any non-simultaneous exchange where the interest component is unstated or understated. Fortunately, there are exceptions for transactions of lesser financial import.

IV. Materials

Revenue Ruling 79-371

1979-2 C.B. 294

ISSUE

What is the basis of an installment note in the hands of a transferee under the circumstances described below?

FACTS

In 1976, all of the common stock of corporation X owned by A, an individual, was redeemed by X for a cash down payment of $20x$ dollars and a negotiable promissory note in the principal amount of $80x$ dollars. A had a basis of $10x$ dollars in the common stock, which A originally purchased in 1970.

The principal on the note was to be paid in eight annual installments of $10x$ dollars each, commencing in 1980. The note was to bear interest at the rate of 10 percent per annum from the date of redemption of the stock through 1979, and thereafter at the rate of seven percent per annum until the outstanding principal balance was paid.

A's initial basis in the note was $8x$ dollars. $18x$ dollars of the $20x$ dollars received by A from X in 1976 was reported as gain.

Under section 302 of the Internal Revenue Code the redemption qualifies for treatment as a distribution in full payment in exchange for *A*'s stock. *A* elected in 1976 to report the gain from the redemption on the installment method of accounting under section 453 (b).

In January 1978, *A* transferred the note by gift to *A*'s child, *B*. The fair market value of the note at the time of transfer was its principal outstanding balance, the face amount of 80*x* dollars. At the time of the transfer all accrued interest had been paid to *A*.

LAW AND ANALYSIS

Section 453 (d) (1) [now 453B(a). Eds.] of the Code provides that if an installment obligation is satisfied at other than its face value or distributed, transmitted, sold or otherwise disposed of, gain or loss results to the extent of the difference between the basis of the obligation and (A) the amount realized, in the case of a satisfaction at other than face value or a sale or exchange, or (B) the fair market value of the obligation at the time of distribution, transmission, or disposition otherwise than by sale or exchange. Any gain or loss so resulting shall be considered as resulting from the sale or exchange of the property in respect of which the installment obligation was received.

Section 453 (d) (2) [now 453B(b) Eds.] of the Code provides that the basis of an installment obligation is the excess of the face value of the obligation over an amount equal to the income that would be returnable were the obligation satisfied in full.

Section 1015 (a) of the Code provides that a transferee's basis for property acquired by gift is the same as it would be in the hands of the transferor.

A's transfer of the note to *B* was a disposition under section 453 (d) (1) (B) [now 453B(a). Eds.] of the Code. Thus, upon such disposition, gain resulted in the amount of 72*x* dollars, the excess of the fair market value of the note at the time of the gift (80*x* dollars) over *A*'s basis in the note determined under section 453 (d) (2) [now 453B(a). Eds.] without regard to the gift (8*x* dollars).

Furthermore, if *A* were considered to hold the note at the time of transfer to *B*, *A*'s basis in the note would be increased to include the gain resulting under section 453 (d) (1) (B) [now 453B(a). Eds.] of the Code. Thus, at the time of the gift, taking into account the gain resulting pursuant to section 453 (d) (1) (B) [now 453B(a). Eds.] of the Code, *A*'s basis in the obligation under section 453 (d) (2) [now 453B(b). Eds.] would be 80*x* dollars, which is the excess of the face value of the obligation (80*x* dollars) over the amount of income that would be reportable were the obligation satisfied in full (zero).

HOLDING

Under section 1015 (a) of the Code, the basis of the obligation in the hands of *B* is the same as it would be in the hands of *A*, or 80*x* dollars.

V. Related Matters

- **IRC § 453A.** This provision does two things to cut back on the planning opportunities posed by the installment method. First, any borrowing against an installment obligation is treated as a payment on the obligation. IRC § 453A(d). Second, on certain larger sales the seller is obliged to pay interest to the government on the deferred tax liability. IRC § 453A(c).

- **IRC § 453(e).** This provision applies to second dispositions of the property by related persons. In essence if a seller sells property on the installment method to a related person (this can include a corporation or partnership) and within two years that person resells the property, the first seller is deemed to have received a payment equal to the amount realized on the second disposition. This is a variation on the assignment of income doctrine, the subject of Chapter 30.

- **IRC § 453(f)(6).** This provision addresses the interaction between installment sales and like kind exchanges involving boot. In essence the non-recognition property is removed from the gain recognition process by being excluded from total contract price and from the meaning of "payment." Thus, boot gain is recognized over time under the installment method.

- **Open Transactions.** As noted earlier, one may elect out of the installment method under section 453(d). What happens when one does this? Most of the time one recognizes gain or loss immediately under section 1001. An exception to this rule is the open transaction doctrine arising from the case of Burnet v. Logan, 283 U.S. 404 (1931). In *Logan* the court held that when the amount realized on a sale is highly uncertain the taxpayer may delay reporting gains or losses until basis has been fully recovered. The IRS contends that such cases are very rare. See also IRC § 453(j) and regulations under it which close some opportunities for open transaction reporting.

Chapter 27

Limitations on Deductions

I. Assignment

Read: Internal Revenue Code: §§ 465(a)(1)–(2), (b)(2), (b)(4), (b)(6)(A)–(B),
(e)(1); 469(a)–(b), (c)(1)–(2), (c)(7), (d)(1), (e)(1)(A), (g), (h)(1)–(2),
(i)(1)–(3)(A), (i)(6), (j)(6). See also §§ 172(a), 461(l).

Treasury Regulations: §§ 1.469-4(c), -5T(a)(1).

Text: Overview
Excerpt from Sen. Rep. 99-313, 99th Cong. 2d Sess. (1986)
Related Matters

Complete the problems.

II. Problems

1. Ivan Basso established a sole proprietorship, BykePro, that manufactures and
    sells high end racing bikes for Tour de France competitors. Ivan contributed
    $50,000 and a piece of land worth $100,000 in which he had a basis of $25,000.
    He also borrowed $300,000 on a non-recourse basis. What are the consequences
    under section 465 in the following circumstances?

    (a) In its first year of operation BykePro lost $125,000.

    (b) Same as (a) except that the lender has recourse against Ivan personally on
         the $300,000 debt.

    (c) Same as (a) except the following year BykePro had net earnings of $100,000.

    (d) Same as (b) except that in the following year BykePro has net earnings of $25,000
         and the bank agrees to convert the debt, still $300,000, to non-recourse.

2. In Year 1, Zinedine Zidane earns $900,000 of taxable income as an orthopedic
    surgeon specializing in knee and hip replacements. He has another $100,000 of
    interest income from an investment in corporate bonds. Zinedine invests
    $1,000,000 as a limited partner in UVguard LP. UVguard holds the patent on a
    device the size of a quarter that, when carried on a person, effectively blocks all
    UV rays by emitting radio signals. This device, known as a UV blocker, is expected
    to be a big seller eventually. Unfortunately, at the moment it produces some ad-
    verse side effects for human beings, including headaches, nausea, and sudden
    uncontrollable rages. It has not gained government approval for sale to the public

but research is continuing. Discuss the consequences under section 469 to Zinedine under the following circumstances:

(a) In Year 1, UVguard loses money. Zinedine's share of those ordinary losses is $100,000. He spends approximately 20 hours, mostly in meetings, managing his interest in UVguard.

(b) In Year 2, Zinedine's earnings from his practice and his bond interest income are the same as in Year 1. Again he has $100,000 of losses from UVguard but he also invests as a limited partner in Titan LP, which produces titanium and aluminum alloy hip joints that are the gold standard in hip replacements. Zinedine has $50,000 of ordinary income from his investment in Titan in Year 2.

(c) In Year 3, Zinedine's earnings from his practice and his bond interest income are the same as in Year 1. This year, UVguard again produces $100,000 of losses for Zinedine, and again he has $50,000 of income from Titan. However, UVguard makes a partial breakthrough in combating the side effects of the UV blocker (milder headaches and fewer sudden rages) and Zinedine is able to sell his entire interest in UVguard to a major medical supplies manufacturer for a $50,000 long-term capital gain.

(d) Same as (c) except that, instead of selling his interest, on December 31st of Year 3, Zinedine gifts his partnership interest to his daughter, Mia Hamm, at a time when it is worth $1,200,000 and his basis stands at $700,000.

(e) Same as (d) except that Zinedine dies on December 31st of Year 3 and leaves his partnership interest to Mia. At the time of Zinedine's death, the partnership interest is worth $775,000 and his basis is $700,000.

3. Ma and Pa Kettle jointly own, in its entirety, a ten unit apartment building which they actively manage and maintain. In the current year, the building generates a $30,000 tax loss because of a glut of rental properties on the market. What are the tax consequences to Ma and Pa in the following circumstances?

(a) The loss from the apartment building aside, Ma and Pa have $90,000 of adjusted gross income and file a joint return.

(b) Same as (a) except that their adjusted gross income is $130,000.

4. Christian Dior is a general partner in two businesses in Seattle. The first is a very profitable high end shop selling women's clothing that Christian manages on a full time basis. The second is a mildly profitable upscale restaurant in which Christian does not materially participate. Christian and his partners plan to open a fashion shop and a restaurant in Portland. Christian will also be a general partner in each new business, but he does not plan to manage either of them on a daily basis. The Portland restaurant is the riskier of the two new enterprises and also involves the larger capital outlay. If it does not reach break even status within two years, the partners plan to close it and liquidate its assets. Assuming all four businesses will have identical ownership arrangements, how should Christian seek to structure his business interests under section 469?

III. Overview

A. Introduction

A favorite activity of some business planners is the creation of *tax shelters*. Broadly speaking, these are business ventures, typically limited partnerships, that are designed to produce tax benefits without significant economic risk. Sometimes there is little potential for economic gain in these enterprises aside from the tax savings they are intended to generate. A tax shelter may, on occasion, involve outright dishonesty or law breaking. But, more often, it is an attempt to use the existing rules to gain a tax advantage not contemplated by the rule makers. After all, the tax law is full of invisible boomerangs. Perhaps the most famous example of this is Crane v. Commissioner, 331 U.S. 1 (1947), considered in Chapter 3. The government won the case, but the result created opportunities for taxpayers to lawfully gain large depreciation tax deductions with minimal economic outlays by including non-recourse borrowing in their basis. In this chapter we are going to look at subsequent Congressional enactments designed to disallow some deductions or to defer them to the point in time when they mirror economic reality. Though there are many restrictions on deductions, we are going to concentrate on two in particular, the at-risk rules and the passive loss rules. Of these two sets of rules, you should regard the passive loss rules as the more important of the two since they sweep more broadly.

The most abusive of the tax shelters that these rules are directed against are devices for generating losses from one activity to shelter income from another activity. In other words, their chief purpose for existing is to generate tax deductions, not true economic income. These tax shelters may depend upon non-recourse borrowing. Consider, for example, a limited partnership that buys an office building using minimal investments from its owners and a substantial non-recourse mortgage from the seller (perhaps at an inflated price). Suppose further that the rent from the building is barely adequate to pay the expenses associated with upkeep and the interest on the debt. On its face, this could be a poor investment unless the building enjoys substantial appreciation in value. Even so, without the rules we are about to consider, the partners might be quite content to take the depreciation and other deductions generated by this unprofitable venture and use them to offset income from other economically lucrative activities such as their day jobs as doctors and lawyers. As a caveat, we should note that there is a significant potential tax disadvantage lurking on the horizon. As the building depreciates, the taxpayer's basis in the building is reduced and a tax gain is growing (because of the unpaid mortgage). But from a time value of money standpoint the taxpayer is ahead since the tax deductions come early while the tax gain comes late. Moreover, the taxpayer may avoid taxation on the gain by holding the property till death or by transferring it to a former spouse as part of a divorce settlement. (It would take a particularly nefarious person to plan on the latter course of action and a poorly advised former spouse to fall for it.) A further tax advantage of this arrangement is that the tax deductions produced by the building will offset ordinary income and the gain, if it is ever recognized, may be capital.

As you consider the rules we are about to study you may find it useful to contemplate the difficulty of drawing lines between lawful tax planning and abusive tax sheltering. The mantra of the tax planner is found in an old opinion of Judge Learned Hand where he wrote:

> [A] transaction, otherwise within an exception of the tax law, does not lose its immunity, because it is actuated by a desire to avoid, or, if one choose, to evade, taxation. Any one may so arrange his affairs that his taxes shall be as low as possible; he is not bound to choose that pattern which will best pay the Treasury; there is not even a patriotic duty to increase one's taxes.

Helvering v. Gregory, 69 F.2d 809, 810 (2d Cir. 1934). The rule maker's typical response to Judge Hand's dictum is to assert that rules must be applied to achieve their intended purposes and that usually Congress did not intend the result the planner is seeking. As you can see, the planner's mantra and the rule maker's response leave the courts to face the question of how narrowly or how broadly to apply the rules in particular cases. No matter how many rules are written there is no escaping this exercise of judgment. All the same, Congress has made a strong effort to curb the use of tax shelters by individuals through legislation.

B. The At Risk Rules

1. The At Risk Limitation

Section 465 applies to most business activities for profit in which one participates as a sole proprietor, partner, or a shareholder of a small corporation. *See* IRC §§ 465(a)(1), (c)(3). Its central message is that an investor is *not* permitted to deduct a loss from such an activity in excess of that investor's amount *at risk* in that activity. IRC §§ 465(a), (d) (defining a "loss" as the excess of deductions allocable to the activity over income derived from the activity). Generally speaking, the investor's at risk amount is his investment. His investment is equal to his cash contributions, the basis of property contributed, and some borrowed or pledged contributions. IRC §§ 465(b)(1) & (2). Borrowed contributions that are not included in the investor's at risk amount include funds borrowed directly or indirectly from co-investors and certain non-recourse borrowings. IRC §§ 465(b)(3) & (4). Any loss that is disallowed in the current year under section 465 carries over to the next year. IRC § 465(a)(2). The carryover is indefinite.

2. The Effect of Losses and Distributions on the At Risk Amount

It is implicit in what we have said so far that losses not in excess of a taxpayer's at risk amount in an activity may be used to offset income from another activity. However, each time such a loss is deducted it reduces the taxpayer's amount at risk in the activity that generated the loss. IRC § 465(b)(5). Similarly, a distribution from the business to the investor reduces the investor's at risk amount. Thus, the taxpayer's at risk amount in a particular activity can change from year to year as losses are deducted and distributions are made.

3. Qualified Non-Recourse Financing Exception

For reasons that may have as much to do with politics as policy, certain non-recourse financing is included in a taxpayer's at risk amount. IRC § 465(b)(6)(A). This *qualified non-recourse financing* is defined to include non-recourse borrowings from banks and government entities secured by real property used in a real estate holding activity. IRC §§ 465(b)(6)(B)–(E). The justification for treating this non-recourse debt as being at risk (to the extent there is one) is that it is assumed that a third party professional lender will not loan on a non-recourse basis unless there is adequate value in the property to cover its debt. Whether one accepts this justification or not, the fact remains that the exception for non-recourse financing of real estate transactions from the at risk rules undermines their effectiveness in attacking tax shelters. This is one of the reasons why the passive loss rules discussed later in this chapter came into being.

4. Recapture of Prior Deductions under Section 465(e)

It is theoretically possible for an investor's amount at risk to decrease below zero as a result of distributions or conversions of debt from recourse to non-recourse (except for conversions to qualified non-recourse debt described above). Rather than permitting a negative amount at risk, the statute requires that the investor take an amount into income sufficient to produce a zero at risk amount. The taxpayer is permitted a corresponding loss carryover equal to the amount of income that is recaptured. IRC § 465(e)(1).

5. Examples

Example 1: The Basics. Taxpayer T buys depreciable machinery to rent to an unrelated business for use in a highway construction project. The purchase price is $500,000 but T uses only $25,000 of his own cash and T borrows $475,000 of the purchase price on a non-recourse basis. He is obliged to pay $50,000 of interest on the loan each year. Assume the machinery rents for $75,000 a year and produces $100,000 in depreciation deductions under section 168.

In Year 1, T has $75,000 of gross rental income, a $50,000 interest expense (assuming the interest is deductible), and a $100,000 depreciation deduction yielding a $75,000 tax loss under section 465(d). From a cash flow perspective, in Year 1, T has nothing out of pocket since the rental income equals the sum of his investment and his interest expense. Pretty nice isn't it? (But note his basis in the machinery has been reduced to $400,000 under section 1016(a)(2). If he walks away from the equipment and the debt, he will have $100,000 of tax gain.)

What does section 465 do to this scenario? It says he can't take a loss in excess of his amount at risk which is $25,000. (The non-recourse borrowing is not included in his at risk amount because it is not *qualified* non-recourse debt.) The $50,000 of disallowed loss carries over as a deduction to next year.

As a result of taking the $25,000 loss permitted in Year 1, T's amount at risk is reduced to zero.

Example 2: Using Carried Losses. Now, assume that in Year 2 the rental of the machinery produces $150,000 of gross income, there is still a $50,000 interest deduction, and there is a $75,000 depreciation deduction. So, aside from his carried over loss, T has taxable income of $25,000 from the activity. Therefore, he can deduct another $25,000 of the Year 1 loss. He will still carry over another $25,000 of loss to Year 3 unless he increases his at risk amount by contribution or otherwise. Thus, there are two ways to free up carried losses: (1) generate income in the activity to absorb the losses, or (2) increase the amount at risk.

Example 3: Recapture of Prior Deductions. Assume the same facts as Example 1 except that the borrowing is recourse and therefore T's at risk amount is $500,000. In Year 1, the entire $75,000 loss is deductible and T's at risk amount is reduced to $425,000. Suppose that in Year 2 T's expenses and income are exactly equal but the debt, still at $475,000, is converted from recourse to non-recourse. T's at risk amount plummets to negative $50,000. Under section 465(e), T must recapture $50,000 of ordinary income to bring his at risk amount to zero. T will now have a $50,000 loss to carry over as a deduction in Year 3. Notice that this puts T in the same position as if the loan had been non-recourse all along.

C. The Passive Loss Rules

1. In General

Section 469, the passive loss provision, was enacted in 1986 as part of the most extensive overhaul of our income tax system of the past half century. The provision's plain purpose was to attack tax shelters. But, the attack was somewhat indirect. It separates out a certain class of business activities, passive activities. Gain and loss from these activities are separately aggregated. A net loss from such activities is not permitted to offset income from non-passive activities. IRC § 469(a)(1). Similar rules apply to tax credits in excess of income from passive activities. We will focus on losses in the reading that follows.

The passive loss rules as articulated by the regulations are exceedingly complex. They are also, arguably, over inclusive. In other words, they have been criticized for disallowing the current deduction of legitimate business losses. Nonetheless, most commentators credit them with having effectively curtailed a once flourishing individual tax shelter industry.

2. The Statutory Framework

A passive activity is a trade or business in which the taxpayer does *not* "materially participate." IRC § 469(c)(1). Material participation is participation in the activity on a "regular," "continuous," and "substantial" basis. IRC § 469(h)(1). The regulations set out detailed criteria for meeting the material participation standard. These include some bright line tests. For example, a person who works in the activity for more than 500 hours in a year is deemed to materially participate and one who works in the activity for less than 100 hours is deemed not to materially participate. *See* Treas. Reg.

§§ 1.469-5T(a)(1),(b)(2)(iii). Because limited partnerships are particularly common tax sheltering mechanisms, a limited partner is automatically deemed *not* a material participant unless the limited partner is also a general partner or meets other requirements. IRC § 469(h)(2); Treas. Reg. §§ 1.469-5T(e)(1), (2), & (3)(ii). The IRS has acquiesced to a Federal Claims Court decision that held that an LLC member materially participated in the business even though he had limited liability. Thompson v. United States, 87 Fed. Cl. 728 (2009), *acq.* AOD 2010-02, 2010 I.R.B. 515. Because rental businesses are common tax shelter devices, a rental activity is automatically deemed passive. IRC §§ 469(c)(2) & (4). There are exceptions to this rule for rental real estate professionals and for those who provide substantial services as part of their rental activity. *See* IRC § 469(c)(7); Treas. Reg. § 1.469-1T(e)(3). An important leniency rule is the provision for attribution of participation between spouses. IRC § 469(h)(5). Thus, if one spouse materially participates, the other is deemed to do so also.

A "passive activity loss" is the net loss from all of a taxpayer's passive activities for the year. IRC § 469(d)(1). Thus, for example, if a taxpayer is a limited partner in two activities and one yields a $10,000 loss and the other gives him $2,500 of income, the taxpayer has a $7,500 passive activity loss. The effect of having a passive activity loss, is that it is disallowed. IRC § 469(a). That is, it cannot be deducted against non-passive income. Instead it carries over as a deduction for the next year where it can be used to offset passive income. IRC §§ 469(b) & (d)(1). It is important to note that portfolio income such as stock dividends, which seems passive, is not deemed passive for purposes of section 469. IRC § 469(e)(1). Thus, passive losses cannot offset portfolio income.

3. Special Exception for Mom and Pop Rental Real Estate Activities

There is a limited exception to the loss disallowance rule for losses from rental real estate activities in which the taxpayer who is at least a 10 percent owner "actively participates." IRC § 469(i). By definition a limited partner cannot actively participate. IRC § 469(i)(6)(C). If the exception applies the losses are treated as non-passive up to $25,000. IRC §§ 469(i)(1) & (2). However, this amount is reduced by one dollar for every two dollars by which the taxpayer's adjusted gross income (determined without regard to passive losses) exceeds $100,000. IRC § 469(i)(3)(A). Thus, a taxpayer with $150,000 of adjusted gross income gets no benefit from the exception.

4. The Effects of Dispositions of Passive Activities

Dispositions of passive activities by sale can serve to release some or all of the previously disallowed losses for deduction against non-passive income. In the case of an outright sale of a passive activity to an unrelated person, the carried losses are first used for offsetting income from the activity in the year of the sale, then against all other passive income for the year, and then are released for use against the gain on the sale or even against non-passive income. IRC § 469(g)(1)(A). In the case of a sale of a passive activity to a related person, the suspended losses are not released until the related person sells the interest. In the meantime they remain with the original owner. IRC § 469(g)(1)(B). A taxable installment sale releases the losses in installments in the same proportion as gain recognized in the current year bears to gross profit on the sale. IRC § 469(g)(3). The legislative history of section 469 indicates that if a taxpayer transfers the activity in a non-recognition transaction such as a like kind exchange, the losses remain suspended until the non-recognition property received in the transaction is sold.

A gift of the activity does not release the carried over losses but the donee's basis in the activity may be stepped up by the amount of the carried over loss (not to exceed the fair market value of the activity for loss purposes). IRC § 469(j)(6). *See* IRC § 1015(a). If the interest passes to another by reason of the death of the owner, any suspended losses are deductible on the decedent's final return to the extent they exceed the section 1014 basis step-up. IRC § 469(g)(2). Thus, for example, if a taxpayer dies owning a passive activity worth $15,000 with a basis of $10,000 and carried over losses of $9,000, only $4,000 of the losses may be deducted on the decedent's final return. This assumes that the beneficiary received a $5,000 basis step up under section 1014(a) to $15,000.

5. The Definition of "Activity"

Defining what constitutes an "activity" under section 469 can be important because how undertakings are combined or segregated may operate in either the taxpayer's or the government's favor depending on the circumstances. For example, a narrow definition means that loss recognition can be more readily triggered by a taxable sale of one part of a taxpayer's passive investments. A broad definition might mean that passive and non-passive undertakings could be combined to allow passive loss recognition. The regulations use a flexible approach that looks for the "appropriate economic unit." *See* Treas. Reg. § 1.469-4(c)(1). Taxpayers have some discretion in how undertakings are grouped or divided, but once a configuration is selected it generally must continue from year to year unless there is a material change in circumstances. Treas. Reg. §§ 1.469-4(c)(3) ex. 1, -4(e)(1).

6. Coordination between Sections 465 and 469

The at risk rules apply ahead of the passive loss rules. Treas. Reg. § 1.469-2T(d)(6)(i). Thus, if an item of deduction is denied under section 465, it is not available for deduction as a passive activity deduction.

D. Why Does the Tax Law Use These "Basket" Approaches?

Both the at risk rules and the passive loss rules are examples of "basket" approaches. That is, they put a taxpayer's losses, with respect to a certain category of activity, in a basket and prevent them from being intermingled with income from another category of activity. This is a time honored rulemaking technique in tax law. For example the loss limitation rule for capital losses in section 1211, which goes back many decades, applies this same principle. In the Related Matters of this chapter you will see listed several other examples of the basket approach. Why do we use this approach to curtail tax system abuse? In general, we may say that we use this approach because it is practical in the context of a complex income tax structure. It is difficult to measure income, especially midstream. The basket approach often takes a wait and see attitude toward deductions by saying, in effect, the deduction will be suspended in the basket until the full nature of a financial venture is revealed. For example, the passive loss rules often suspend the deduction of loss on an investment until the activity is sold. At that point the true economic consequences of the investment are clear. Another practical utility of the basket approach is that it permits the rule maker to define the tax consequences of an elaborate transaction by reference to a single objectively identifiable trait. That trait, be it "at risk," "passivity," or whatever, stands as a surrogate for looking into the hearts and minds of taxpayers for impure motives. The use of surrogates runs the risk of being arbitrary and over inclusive. It may also be under inclusive. Finding the surrogate trait that most accurately reflects the underlying economic meaning of a transaction requires a deep understanding of how business works. On balance, both the at risk rules and the passive loss rules reflect such an understanding. The excerpt below from the Senate Report relating to the enactment of section 469 offers further explanation and justification for the enactment of this complex provision.

E. Limitation on Excess Business Losses

In 2018, Congress enacted section 461(l), which disallows any "excess business loss" of a taxpayer. IRC § 461(l)(1)(B). An excess business loss exists when a taxpayer's aggregate deductions from all trades or businesses exceed the taxpayer's aggregate gross income from such trades or businesses by more than $250,000 ($500,000 in the case of joint returns), adjusted annually for inflation. IRC § 461(l)(3)(A). Any excess business loss that is disallowed is treated as a net operating loss (NOL) carryover to the following tax year under section 172. IRC § 461(l)(2). Although NOLs may be carried forward indefinitely, an NOL may only reduce 80% of taxable income in a carry-forward tax year. IRC § 172(a).

The limit on excess business losses applies to taxpayers other than C corporations. For partnerships and S corporations, the limit is applied at the partner or shareholder level. IRC § 461(l)(4). Each partner or shareholder takes into account her allocable share of income and deductions of the partnership or S corporation, and adds these to any other trade or business income and deductions she might have in determining her excess business loss. IRC § 461(l)(4)(B).

Taxpayers must apply the passive activity loss rules of section 469, discussed above, before applying the rules for excess business losses. IRC § 461(l)(6).

Example. In Year 1, Taxpayer, who is single, has $1,000,000 of gross income and $1,400,000 of deductions from a sole proprietorship business that is not a passive activity (assume that section 469 does not apply to the business). His excess business loss is $150,000 ($1,400,000 − ($1,000,000 + $250,000)). Taxpayer must treat this amount as an NOL carryover to Year 2, subject to the 80% taxable income limit (it may only reduce 80% of taxable income in Year 2).

IV. Materials

Excerpt From Senate Report 99-313

99th Cong. 2d Sess. (1986) 1986-3 C.B. 713 et seq.

A. Limitations on Losses and Credits from Passive Activities

Present Law [Prior to Enacting Section 469. Eds.]

In the absence of more broadly applicable limitations on the use of deductions and credits from one activity to reduce tax liability attributable to other activities, taxpayers with substantial sources of positive income are able to eliminate or sharply reduce tax liability by using deductions and credits from other activities, frequently by investing in tax shelters. Tax shelters commonly offer the opportunity to reduce or avoid tax liability with respect to salary or other positive income, by making available deductions and credits, possibly exceeding real economic costs or losses currently borne by the taxpayer, in excess or in advance of income from the shelters.

Reasons for Change [i.e., reasons for enacting section 469. Eds.]

In recent years, it has become increasingly clear that taxpayers are losing faith in the Federal income tax system. This loss of confidence has resulted in large part from the interaction of two of the system's principal features: its high marginal rates (in 1986, 50 percent for a single individual with taxable income in excess of $88,270), and the opportunities it provides for taxpayers to offset income from one source with tax shelter deductions and credits from another.

Extensive shelter activity contributes to public concerns that the tax system is unfair, and to the belief that tax is paid only by the naive and the unsophisticated. This, in turn, not only undermines compliance, but encourages further expansion of the tax shelter market, in many cases diverting investment capital from productive activities to those principally or exclusively serving tax avoidance goals.

The committee believes that the most important sources of support for the Federal income tax system are the average citizens who simply report their income (typically consisting predominantly of items such as salaries, wages, pensions, interest, and dividends) and pay tax under the general rules. To the extent that these citizens feel that they are bearing a disproportionate burden with regard to the costs of government because of their unwillingness or inability to engage in tax-oriented investment activity, the tax system itself is threatened.

Under these circumstances, the committee believes that decisive action is needed to curb the expansion of tax sheltering and to restore to the tax system the degree of equity that is a necessary precondition to a beneficial and widely desired reduction in rates. So long as tax shelters are permitted to erode the Federal tax base, a low-rate system can provide neither sufficient revenues, nor sufficient progressivity, to satisfy the general public that tax liability bears a fair relationship to the ability to pay. In particular, a provision significantly limiting the use of tax shelter losses is unavoidable if substantial rate reductions are to be provided to high-income taxpayers without disproportionately reducing the share of total liability under the individual income tax that is borne by high-income taxpayers as a group.

The question of how to prevent harmful and excessive tax sheltering is not a simple one. One way to address the problem would be to eliminate substantially all tax preferences in the Internal Revenue Code. For two reasons, however, the committee believes that this course is inappropriate.

First, while the bill reduces or eliminates some tax preference items that the committee believes do not provide social or economic benefits commensurate with their cost, there are many preferences that the committee believes are socially or economically beneficial. This is especially true when such preferences are used primarily to advance the purposes upon which Congress relied in enacting them, rather than to avoid taxation of income from sources unrelated to the preferred activity.

Second, it would be extremely difficult, perhaps impossible, to design a tax system that measures income perfectly. For example, the statutory allowance for depreciation reflects broad industry averages, as opposed to providing precise item-by-item measurements. Accordingly, taxpayers with assets that depreciate less rapidly than the average, or that appreciate over time (as may be the case with certain real estate), may engage in tax sheltering unless Congress directly addresses the tax shelter problem.

Even to the extent that rules for the accurate measurement of income can theoretically be devised, such rules may involve undue complexity from the perspective of taxpayers. For example, a system that required taxpayers to use a theoretically pure accrual method of accounting would create serious difficulties in both compliance and administration.

However, when the tax system, in order to avoid such complexity, permits simpler rules to be applied (e.g., generally not taxing unrealized gain, and allowing depreciation based on broad industry averages), opportunities for manipulation are created. Taxpayers may structure transactions specifically to take advantage of the situations in which the simpler rules lead to undermeasurement or deferral of income.

The question of what constitutes a tax shelter that should be subject to limitations is closely related to the question of who Congress intends to benefit when it enacts tax preferences. For example, in providing preferential depreciation for real estate or favorable accounting rules for farming, it was not Congress's primary intent to permit outside investors to avoid tax liability with respect to their salaries by investing in limited partnership syndications. Rather, Congress intends to benefit and provide incentives to taxpayers active in the businesses to which the preferences were directed.

In some cases, the availability of tax preferences to nonparticipating investors has even harmed the industries that the preferences were intended to benefit. For example, in the case of farming, credits and favorable deductions have often encouraged investments by wealthy individuals whose principal or only interest in farming is to receive an investment return, largely in the form of tax benefits to offset tax on positive sources of income. Since such investors may not need a positive cash return from farming in order to profit from their investments, they have a substantial competitive advantage in relation to active farmers, who commonly are not in a position to use excess tax benefits to shelter unrelated income. This has significantly contributed to the serious economic difficulties presently being experienced by many active farmers.

The availability of tax benefits to shelter positive sources of income also has harmed the economy generally, by providing a non-economic return on capital for certain investments. This has encouraged a flow of capital away from activities that may provide a higher pre-tax economic return, thus retarding the growth of the sectors of the economy with the greatest potential for expansion.

The committee believes that, in order for tax preferences to function as intended, their benefit must be directed primarily to taxpayers with a substantial and *bona fide* involvement in the activities to which the preferences relate. The committee also believes that it is appropriate to encourage nonparticipating investors to invest in particular activities, by permitting the use of preferences to reduce the rate of tax on income from those activities; however, such investors should not be permitted to use tax benefits to shelter unrelated income.

There are several reasons why it is appropriate to examine the materiality of a taxpayer's participation in an activity in determining the extent to which such taxpayer should be permitted to use tax benefits from the activity. A taxpayer who materially participates in an activity is more likely than a passive investor to approach the activity with a significant non-tax economic profit motive, and to form a sound judgment as to whether the activity has genuine economic significance and value.

A material participation standard identifies an important distinction between different, types of taxpayer activities. In general, the more passive investor is seeking a return on capital invested, including returns in the form of reductions in the taxes owed on unrelated income, rather than an ongoing source of livelihood. A material participation standard reduces the importance, for such investors, of the tax-reduction features of an investment, and thus increases the importance of the economic features in an investor's decision about where to invest his funds.

Moreover, the committee believes that restricting the use of losses from business activities in which the taxpayer does not materially participate against other sources of positive income (such as salary and portfolio income) addresses a fundamental aspect of the tax shelter problem. As discussed above, instances in which the tax system applies simple rules at the expense of economic accuracy encourage the structuring of transactions to take advantage of the situations in which such rules give rise to undermeasurement or deferral of income. Such transactions commonly are marketed to investors who do not intend to participate in the transactions, as devices for sheltering unrelated sources of positive income (e.g., salary and portfolio income). Accordingly, by creating a bar against the use of losses from business activities in which the taxpayer does not materially participate to offset positive income sources such as salary and portfolio income, the committee believes that it is possible significantly to reduce the tax shelter problem.

Further, in the case of a nonparticipating investor in a business activity, the committee believes that it is appropriate to treat losses of the activity as not realized by the investor prior to disposition of his interest in the activity. The effort to measure, on an annual basis, real economic losses from passive activities gives rise to distortions, particularly due to the nontaxation of unrealized appreciation and the mismatching of tax deductions and related economic income that may occur, especially where debt financing is used heavily. Only when a taxpayer disposes of his interest in an activity is it possible to determine whether a loss was sustained over the entire time that he held the interest.

The relationship to an activity of an investor who does not materially participate may be little different from the relationship of a shareholder to a corporation. So long as the investor retains an interest in the activity, any reduction in the value of such interest not only may be difficult to measure accurately, but has not been realized by the investor to a greater extent than in the context of a C corporation. In the case of a C corporation, losses and expenses borne by the corporation, and any decline in the value of the corporation's stock, do not give rise to the recognition of any loss on the part of shareholders prior to disposition of their stock.

The distinction that the committee believes should be drawn between activities on the basis of material participation bears no relationship to the question of whether, and to what extent, the taxpayer is at risk with respect to the activities. In general, the fact that a taxpayer has placed a particular amount at risk in an activity does not establish, prior to a disposition of the taxpayer's interest, that the amount invested, or any amount, has as yet been lost. The fact that a taxpayer is potentially liable with respect to future expenses or losses of the activity likewise has no bearing on the question whether any amount has as yet been lost, or otherwise is an appropriate current deduction or credit.

At-risk standards, although important in determining the maximum amount that is subject to being lost, are not a sufficient basis for determining whether or when net losses from an activity should be deductible against other sources of income, or for determining whether an ultimate economic loss has been realized. Congress' goal of making tax preferences available principally to active participants in substantial businesses, rather than to investors seeking to shelter unrelated income, can best be accomplished by examining material participation, as opposed to the financial stake provided by an investor to purchase tax shelter benefits.

V. Related Matters

- **Other Restrictions on Deductions:**
  - **Investment Interest.** The Code restricts the current deductibility of interest paid on funds borrowed for investment purposes to the current income generated

by investments. This prevents some forms of tax arbitraging. The disallowed deduction carries forward to the next year. *See* IRC § 163(d).

- **Gambling Losses.** Gambling losses are deductible only to the extent of gambling winnings. *See* IRC § 165(d).

- **Hobby Losses.** If an activity is not engaged in for profit, the taxpayer cannot deduct her expenses from the activity except to the extent of the income from the activity. *See* IRC § 183, considered in Chapter 23. Recall, however, that hobby expenses are miscellaneous itemized deductions, which are disallowed for years 2018 through 2025.

- **Interest on Annuities.** The interest on debts incurred to purchase annuities is non-deductible. *See* IRC § 264(a)(2)–(4).

- **Expenses for Tax Exempt Income.** No deduction is permitted for expenses incurred to earn most forms of tax exempt income. *See* IRC § 265(a).

- **Losses Between Related Parties.** No deduction is permitted for losses on sales between related parties. *See* IRC § 267(a). The fact that a related-party sale is bona fide and involves fair consideration is irrelevant. *See* McWilliams v. Commissioner, 331 U.S. 695 (1947). If a related-party sale is for less than fair market value, no loss is allowed under the part-sale, part-gift rules. Treas. Reg. § 1.1001-1(e) (providing no loss is sustained if the amount realized is less than adjusted basis).

- **Entertainment Expenses.** Entertainment expenses are generally disallowed. *See* IRC § 274(a), considered in Chapter 7.

- **Home Office Deductions.** Some expenses relating to home offices and other residential property are disallowed. *See* IRC § 280A, considered in Chapter 22.

- **Wash Sales.** Deduction of losses are disallowed on sales of stock where substantially identical stock is acquired within 30 days before or after the sale. These transactions are known as "wash sales" because they result in a wash in an economic sense. *See* IRC § 1091.

Chapter 28

Intellectual Property Development and Acquisitions

I. Assignment

Read: Internal Revenue Code: §§ 167(a), (c), (f)(1), (g); 174; 197(a)–(d), (e)(3)–(4), (f)(4)(C); 263(a); 263A(a), (b)(1), (c)(2), (h); 1253(d). Skim §§ 41(a)(1), (c)(4), (d)(1); 179(d); 181(a), (d).

Treasury Regulations: §§ 1.167(a)-1(b), -3(a), -14(a), (c)(4); 1.167(b)-1(a); 1.174-2(a); 1.197-2(a), -2(b)(1), (5), (10), -2(c)(4)–(5), (7), -2(d)(2)(i), -2(e)(1)–(2), -2(f)(1)–(2), -2(g)(8). Skim § 1.263A-1(e)(2)–(3), -2(a)(2).

Text: Overview
Field Service Advice 200125019
Revenue Procedure 2000-50
Related Matters

Complete the problems.

II. Problems

1. Xochipilli, Inc., a perfume manufacturing company, decides to create a new perfume to sell to teenage girls. Discuss the deductibility of the following expenses incurred by Xochipilli during the current year:

   (a) $100,000 to actually develop the basic scent.

   (b) $25,000 to determine whether the perfume causes an allergic reaction.

   (c) $35,000 to develop alternative perfumes with different scents and colors.

   (d) $35,000 in attorney's fees in the prosecution of a patent application.

   (e) $50,000 to initially market the perfume, including package design costs.

2. Loki, Inc., a calendar-year taxpayer, purchases from its competition a secret technique on how to refine crude oil on March 10, Year 1, and immediately begins applying the technique in its refinery business. Loki agrees to pay its competition an initial payment of $1.8 million on March 10, Year 1 and contingent payments in later years pursuant to an agreed-upon formula. What is the proper tax treatment of the initial $1.8 million payment? What is the proper tax treatment of a

$850,000 contingent payment made on January 1, Year 2? What is the proper tax treatment of a $150,000 contingent payment made on January 1, Year 17?

3. On January 1, Year 1, Inari, Inc., a local pizzeria, purchased from a young inventor a patent for tofu-filled pizza crust for $80,000, and immediately began using the patented technique. Inari estimated that the patented pizza would produce $120,000 of income during its 8-year useful life, after which it would have no salvage value. The patent, which was not acquired as part of the acquisition of a trade or business and which had a remaining legal life of 18 years, actually produced $60,000 of income within the first taxable year, $30,000 of income in the second year, and only $1,200 of income in the third year.

    (a) Is the patent amortizable under section 197?

    (b) If the answer to (a) is no, is the patent depreciable under section 167?

    (c) Assuming section 167 applies, what are the proper deductions for Years 1–3 under the straight-line method and income-forecast method?

4. Stiblitz Corporation purchased a new computer. The installation of the new computer required the development by the corporation of an entirely new set of software for use with it. Software costs in the amount of $50,000 were incurred by the corporation in connection with programming the new computer.

    (a) What is the proper treatment of the in-house software development costs?

    (b) Would it make a difference if Stiblitz paid $50,000 to a third party to develop the software?

    (c) Assume the computer came installed with various software. What is the tax treatment of the software acquisition assuming the cost of the software was separately stated? Not separately stated?

    (d) What if six months later, Stiblitz decided to purchase a new package of software for $1,000 from Microsoft?

III. Overview

Intellectual property has become enormously important in recent years. Increasingly, valuable business assets are found in the form of intangibles such as patents, trade secrets, copyrights, trademarks, trade names, and computer software. Major transactions involving intellectual property have different tax consequences depending on the form of intellectual property involved. Although general tax principles are applicable to most types of intellectual property, there are some special tax rules that exclusively govern certain types of intellectual property. This chapter addresses the tax treatment of intellectual property development and acquisitions. The next chapter addresses the tax treatment of intellectual property sales and licenses.

A. Intellectual Property Development

Federal intellectual property laws are intended to facilitate the progress of science and the creation of useful arts by providing, for example, patent holders and authors of copyrights significant legal protections for their patents and copyrights for a limited time. An interesting issue is whether federal tax laws also promote socially desirable inventive and creative activities. Two Code sections — section 162 and section 174 — potentially provide the basis for current deductibility of costs attributed to the development of many types of intellectual property. Further, section 41 provides a credit for certain research expenditures.

1. Deductibility under Section 162 — Ordinary and Necessary Business Expenses

We start with section 162 since it is the most comprehensive section in the Code concerning business deductions. As we saw in Chapter 7, section 162 establishes several requirements for the deduction of costs associated with a business. A cost must be *ordinary and necessary* and must be paid or incurred *in carrying on a trade or business*. Most importantly, however, a cost must be an *expense* as opposed to a nondeductible capital expenditure. Section 162 is subject to two overriding provisions — sections 263 and 263A — that prevent the current deductibility of many intellectual property development costs. We examined the general application of these provisions in Chapter 8.

a. Section 263 Override

Section 263 disallows the immediate deduction of costs that are considered *capital expenditures*. Regulations under section 263 identify categories of intangibles for which amounts are required to be capitalized. Treas. Reg. § 1.263(a)-4(b)(1)(i)–(iv). A taxpayer must capitalize an amount paid to create an intangible described in Treas. Reg. § 1.263(a)-4(d). Specifically identified are certain rights obtained from a governmental agency. For example, a taxpayer must capitalize amounts paid to a governmental agency to obtain or renew a trademark, trade name, copyright or other similar right granted by that governmental agency. Treas. Reg. §§ 1.263(a)-4(d)(1), -4(d)(5). This rule does not affect the treatment of expenditures dealt with under other provisions of the Code. For example, an amount paid to a governmental agency to obtain a patent from that agency is not required to be capitalized if the amount is deductible under section 174, discussed below.

A taxpayer must also capitalize an amount paid to create a *separate and distinct intangible asset*. The regulations define a separate and distinct intangible asset as "a property interest of ascertainable and measurable value in money's worth that is subject to protection under applicable State, Federal or foreign law and the possession and control of which is intrinsically capable of being sold, transferred or pledged (ignoring any restrictions imposed on assignability) separate and apart from a trade or business." Treas. Reg. § 1.263(a)-4(b)(3). The regulations provide certain exceptions. For example, an amount paid to create computer software is *not* treated as an amount that creates a separate and distinct intangible asset. Treas. Reg. § 1.263(a)-4(b)(3)(iv). The costs of creating computer software have been held to be immediately deductible when paid or incurred. *See* Revenue Procedure 2000-50, included in the materials below. Further, an amount paid to create a package design is *not* treated as an amount that creates a separate and distinct intangible asset. Treas. Reg. § 1.263(a)-4(b)(3)(v). It should be noted that although a taxpayer can deduct the costs of developing a package design, the taxpayer must capitalize the costs of obtaining trademark and copyright protections on elements of the package design, since these are rights granted by a governmental agency.

b. Section 263A Override

Section 263A requires the capitalization of direct and indirect costs attributable to tangible personal property produced by a taxpayer. The phrase *tangible personal property* includes films, sound recordings, video tapes, books, and similar property embodying words, ideas, concepts, images, or sounds by the creator thereof. IRC § 263A(b). The regulations define *similar property* for this purpose as "intellectual or creative property for which, as costs are incurred in producing the property, it is intended (or is reasonably likely) that any tangible medium in which the property is embodied will be mass distributed by the creator or any one or more third parties in a form that is not substantially altered." Treas. Reg. § 1.263A-2(a)(2)(ii). As can be seen, section 263A applies to numerous forms of property for which copyright protection is available.

Section 263A(h), added to the Code in 1988, provides an important exemption from the capitalization requirements of section 263A: *qualified creative expenses* are not required to be capitalized. A qualified creative expense is defined as any expense paid or incurred by an individual in the trade or business of being a writer, photographer, or artist, which, except for the capitalization rules of section 263A, would otherwise be deductible for the taxable year. IRC § 263A(h)(2). The purpose of the exemption was to relieve free-lance individuals from the burden of the uniform capitalization rules, especially when their activities may not generate income for years. Even if an individual is engaged in the trade or business of being a writer, photographer, or artist, not all expenses are deemed to be qualified creative expenses. The Code specifically provides that a qualified creative expense does not include "any expense related to printing, photographic plates, motion picture films, video tapes, or similar items." IRC § 263A(h)(2), flush language. Although section 263A(h) does not apply to expenses related to motion picture films or similar property, section 181, enacted by the American Jobs Creation Act of 2004, provides an important exception to the uniform capitalization rules for certain film and television productions. Under section 181, a taxpayer may elect to immediately deduct the costs of any "qualified" film or television production in lieu of capitalizing such costs. IRC § 181(a)(1), (a)(2), (d).

It should be noted that in 2018, Congress added section 263A(i). Under the new law, producers with average annual gross receipts of $25 million or less (based on the prior three years) are fully exempt from the uniform capitalization rules of section 263A.

2. Deductibility under Section 174—Research and Experimental Expenditures

Section 174(a), enacted in 1954, permits a taxpayer to deduct immediately research and experimental expenditures that would otherwise have to be capitalized under section 263. *See* IRC §§ 263(a)(1)(B), 263A(c)(2) (providing that the capitalization rules under sections 263 and 263A do not apply to research or experimental expenditures deductible under section 174(a)). *See also* IRC § 174(b) (providing a five-year amortization option for research and experimental expenditures).

Departure from the capitalization rules is generally justified as necessary to encourage new research and development activity and to stimulate economic growth and technological development. Another justification for departure is that the capitalization rules are difficult to apply to innovation development costs since research may not result in the development of a patent or other identifiable asset, research often spans several years with varying degrees of success, different and simultaneous research activities may contribute in varying degrees to the development of an asset or more than one asset, and research related to a project may partly fail and partly succeed. An immediate deduction for research and development costs thus serves dual functions by encouraging investment in research and by reducing uncertainties caused by the application of the capitalization rules to research and development—namely uncertainties regarding the timing for claiming research and development deductions. Ironically, the Tax Cuts and Jobs Act (TCJA) repeals section 174(a) (immediate expensing) beginning in 2022. At that point, specified research and experimental expenditures (including software development costs) must generally be amortized ratably over a five-year period. Some commentators believe that the law change is more about meeting revenue goals of the TCJA than expected permanent legislation.

Section 174 applies only to costs qualifying as *research or experimental expenditures* and for costs paid or incurred *in connection with a trade or business*.

a. Research and Experimental Expenditures

Research or experimental expenditures are broadly defined in the regulations as "expenditures incurred in connection with the taxpayer's trade or business which represent research and development costs in the *experimental or laboratory sense*," and generally include "all costs incident to the development or improvement of a product." Treas. Reg. § 1.174-2(a)(1). A product, for purposes of section 174, "includes any pilot, model, process, formula, invention, technique, patent, or similar property" that is either "used by the taxpayer in its trade or business [or] held for sale, lease, or license" by the taxpayer. Treas. Reg. § 1.174-2(a)(3). Expenditures are incurred in the *experimental or laboratory sense* if they are incurred in "activities intended to discover information that would eliminate *uncertainty* concerning the development or improvement of a product." Treas. Reg. § 1.174-2(a)(1). Read Field Service Advice 200125019, included in the materials, which dealt with development expenditures for footwear. Given that section 174 applies only to research and developments costs in the experimental or laboratory sense, are you surprised at the outcome?

The regulations under section 174 specifically provide that the costs of obtaining a patent are research and experimental expenditures. Treas. Reg. § 1.174-2(a)(1). Such costs include not only expenses incurred in creating patentable technology, but also attorney's fees in the prosecution of patent applications. The regulations also specifically *exclude* certain expenditures from the scope of section 174, including: (1) expenditures incurred for ordinary quality control testing or inspection; (2) business management expenses such as efficiency surveys, management surveys, and consumer surveys; (3) advertising and promotion costs; and (4) costs of purchasing a patent, model, production, or process of another; and (5) expenditures for research in connection with literary, historical, or similar projects. Treas. Reg. § 1.174-2(a)(6)(i)–(vii).

The regulatory definition of research and experimentation limits the stages of product development during which costs qualify for section 174 treatment. Costs to develop a basic product concept or idea generally qualify. Likewise, initial research costs to develop an operable model and additional research costs to develop a commercially viable model also generally qualify. However, costs incurred after a commercially viable model exists (e.g., manufacturing and marketing costs) will most likely fail to qualify as expenditures that represent research and experimental costs in the laboratory sense.

b. In Connection with a Trade or Business

An expenditure must not only represent a cost in the experimental or laboratory sense, but must also be incurred *in connection with* the taxpayer's trade or business. Prior to 1974, the Service and the courts took the position that in order to qualify for section 174 treatment, a taxpayer must have already engaged in a trade or business. In Snow v. Commissioner, 416 U.S. 500 (1974), however, the United States Supreme Court rejected this narrow approach and held that pre-operational research or experimental expenditures could qualify for the section 174 deduction. In light of *Snow*, compare the *in connection with* requirement of section 174 with the *in carrying on* requirement under section 162.

Although a taxpayer need not be currently conducting a business in order for research or experimental expenditures to qualify under section 174, it must demonstrate a realistic prospect of entering into a trade or business that will exploit the technology under development. In making this determination, the taxpayer must demonstrate both an objective intent to enter into the trade or business and the capability to do so. *See* Kantor v. Commissioner, 998 F.2d 1514 (9th Cir. 1993); Green v. Commissioner, 83. T.C. 667 (1984).

The trade or business issue often arises in situations where a taxpayer contracts out the performance of research and development and subsequently engages in less than substantial production or marketing activities. *See, e.g.,* Spellman v. Commissioner, 845 F.2d 148 at 150 (7th Cir. 1988) (denying a section 174 deduction where the taxpayer contracted out both the research and development and the production and marketing of penicillins to a third party); Diamond v. Commissioner, 930 F.2d 372 (4th Cir. 1991) (denying a section 174 deduction where the taxpayer granted an option to a research contractor to acquire an exclusive license to the technology at some future time for a relatively nominal amount). *But see* Scoggins v. Commissioner, 46 F.3d 950 (9th Cir. 1955) (allowing a section 174 deduction where the option payment ($500,000) was relatively large and the exclusive rights to the technology could not be obtained without paying a large sum ($5 million)).

3. Section 41 Research Credit for Increasing Research Activities

The research credit, found in section 41 of the Code, was created in 1981 and made permanent in 2015. The general research credit is incremental in that it is equal to 20% of qualified research spending above a base amount, which can be thought of as a firm's normal level of research and development investment. The incremental nature of the credit provides an incentive for increasing research and development expenditures over time. *See* IRC § 41(a)(1). As an alternative to using the regular credit, a taxpayer may elect to use the alternative simplified credit, which is an amount equal to 14% of the amount by which the qualified research expenses exceed 50% of the average qualified research expenses for the three preceding taxable years. IRC § 41(c)(5).

The term *qualified research* is defined in section 41(d) as research (1) with respect to which expenditures may be treated as expenses under section 174, (2) that is undertaken for the purpose of discovering information that is technological in nature, and the application of which is intended to be useful in the development of a new or improved business component of the taxpayer, and (3) substantially all of the activities of which constitute elements of a process of experimentation that relates to a new or improved function, performance, reliability, or quality. *See* IRC § 41(d)(1)(A)–(C). The regulations set out the core elements of a *process of experimentation* for purposes of the research credit, requiring a taxpayer to (1) identify the uncertainty regarding the development or improvement of a business component that is the object of the taxpayer's research activities, (2) identify one or more alternatives intended to eliminate that uncertainty, and (3) identify and conduct a process of evaluating the alternatives (e.g., modeling, simulation, or systematic trial and error). A number of research activities are excluded from the term qualified research. *See* IRC § 41(d)(4).

It might be possible for research expenses to qualify for the credit under section 41 as well as the deduction under section 174. In such a case, to the extent a credit is taken under section 41, deductions under section 174 must be reduced pursuant to section 280C. A taxpayer can elect to claim a reduced research credit under section 41 and thereby avoid a reduction of the section 174 deduction. IRC § 280C(c)(1)–(3).

B. Intellectual Property Acquisitions

Intellectual property may be acquired by purchase or license. Moreover, intellectual property may be acquired in a transaction involving the acquisition of a trade or business or may be acquired separately or together with a group of assets that do not constitute a trade or business. As consideration, transferees may make up-front principal payments, installment payments of a fixed amount, payments contingent on exploitation of the intellectual property, or any combination of these approaches. The deductibility of these acquisition costs varies depending on the specific type of intellectual property involved and the manner in which the intellectual property was acquired.

1. Purchase Costs

Unlike certain development costs, which may be immediately deductible due to special provisions such as sections 174 and 263A(h), the costs of acquiring intellectual property are generally subject to the capitalization rules. More specifically, a taxpayer is required to capitalize amounts paid to another party to acquire an intangible (e.g., a patent or other separate and distinct intangible) from that party through a purchase or similar transaction. Treas. Reg. § 1.263(a)-4(b)(1)(i), -4(c)(1). Although not immediately deductible, the capitalized costs of purchasing intellectual property may be recovered over a certain time period through a depreciation allowance to effectuate an allocation of purchase costs to the period in which the taxpayer realizes income.

Prior to 1993, the tax law governing the depreciation of intangible assets favored certain intellectual property rights (patents and copyrights) over other intellectual property forms (trade secrets, trademarks, and trade names). If an acquired intangible asset could be shown to have a limited useful life, then the capitalized acquisition costs were recoverable over that asset's lifetime. As a corollary, the capitalized cost of an intangible asset that had no definite useful life was not recoverable through depreciation, but could only be recovered upon abandonment or disposition of the asset. Under this legal framework, patents and copyrights were eligible for amortization due to the fact that they have limited useful lives (statutory legal lives of 20 years in the case of patents and 70, 95, or 120 years in the case of certain copyrights). Trade secrets, trademarks, and trade names were treated differently due to the fact that they have no definite useful life. There is no specific term of protection for trade secrets; the protection is available as long as confidential proprietary information is kept secret. Likewise, there is no specific term of protection for trademarks and trade names; the protection is available as long as the trademark or trade name is used in commerce and has not been abandoned. Accordingly, under pre-1993 tax law, all trade secret, trademark, and trade name acquisition costs had to be capitalized and could only be recovered upon abandonment or disposition of those assets.

The Revenue Reconciliation Act of 1993 dramatically changed the cost-recovery rules for intellectual property and other intangible rights by enacting section 197 of the Code.

a. Amortization under Section 197

Section 197 provides an arbitrary fifteen year amortization deduction for the capitalized costs of any section 197 intangible held in connection with the conduct of a trade or business or activity conducted for profit, and prohibits any other depreciation or amortization deduction with respect to that property. IRC § 197(a)–(c)(1). Subject to important exceptions, a *section 197 intangible* generally includes any patent, copyright, formula, process, design, pattern, know-how, format, package design, computer software, or interest in a film, sound recording, video tape, book, or other similar property. Treas. Reg. § 1.197-2(b)(5). A section 197 intangible also includes any trademark or trade name. Treas. Reg. § 1.197-2(b)(10). Although the definition of "section 197 intangible" appears broad enough to encompass most forms of intellectual property, there are several important exceptions.

Several exceptions in section 197 apply to property that is *not* acquired in a transaction (or series of related transactions) involving the acquisition of assets constituting a trade or business or substantial portion thereof. IRC § 197(e). For example, the term section 197 intangible does not include any interest in a patent, patent application, or copyright that is *not* acquired as part of a purchase of a trade or business. IRC § 197(e)(4); Treas. Reg. § 1.197-2(c)(7). Likewise, the term section 197 intangible does not include any interest in computer software that is not acquired as part of a purchase of a trade or business. IRC § 197(e)(3); Treas. Reg. § 1.197-2(c)(4). Trade secrets, know-how, trademarks, and trade names are not included within the exception for separately acquired assets. Thus, these forms of intellectual property are subject to fifteen-year amortization under section 197 regardless of whether they were acquired as part of a purchase of a trade or business or separately.

With respect to computer software, there are additional exceptions in section 197 (in addition to the exception for separately acquired software). First, section 197 does not apply to the cost of an interest in off-the-shelf software (i.e., software that is, or has been, readily available to the general public on similar terms, is subject to a nonexclusive license, and has not been substantially modified). Treas. Reg. § 1.197-2(c)(4). Second, section 197 does not apply to the cost of an interest in computer software if such cost is included, without being separately stated, in the cost of hardware or some other tangible property and is consistently treated as part of the cost of hardware or some other tangible property. Treas. Reg. § 1.197-2(g)(7). Instead, the software is included in the hardware's basis and recovered according to the depreciation rules of section 168, which applies to tangible personal property, such as computers. Rev. Rul. 71-177, 1971-1 C.B. 5.

The amount of the section 197 amortization deduction is determined by amortizing the adjusted basis of the acquired intellectual property ratably over a 15-year period irrespective of the intellectual property's useful life. IRC § 197(a); Treas. Reg. § 1.197-2(a)(1). Estimated salvage value is disregarded, so the entire adjusted basis may be recovered over the fifteen-year amortization period. Treas. Reg. § 1.197-2(f)(1)(ii). The fifteen-year period begins on the first day of the month in which the intellectual property is acquired and held in connection with either a trade or business (within the meaning of section 162) or an activity conducted for profit (within the meaning of section 212). Because section 197 applies only to acquired intellectual property held in connection with a trade or business or activity conducted for profit, the fifteen-year period cannot begin before the first day of the month in which the conduct of the trade or business or investment activity begins. IRC § 197(c)(1); Treas. Reg. § 1.197-2(f)(1)(i). The following example illustrates the fifteen-year amortization rule.

Example. ABC Corporation, a calendar year taxpayer, acquires intellectual property that is a section 197 intangible for $180,000 on March 10, Year 1 and immediately begins using the intellectual property in its trade or business. Because the intellectual property is a section 197 intangible, ABC Corporation must amortize ratably the $180,000 purchase cost over 180 months (15 years × 12 months), or at $1,000 per month. Thus, ABC's amortization deduction in Year 1 will be $10,000 (10 months at $1,000 per month). ABC Corporation's amortization deduction in Years 2–15 will be $12,000 (12 months at $1,000 per month). The corporation's amortization deduction in Year 16 will be $2,000 so that the entire purchase price is recovered.

If the purchase contract calls for fixed installment payments, the entire amount of these payments should be included in the basis at the time of purchase and amortized over fifteen years. However, if the contract calls for contingent payments, the basis is increased only as the contingent amounts are paid. Read Treas. Reg. § 1.197-2(f)(2)(i)–(ii). What if a contingent payment is made during the fifteen-year amortization period? What if a contingent payment is made after the expiration of the fifteen-year period? A special rule applies to certain contingent payments for trademarks and trade names. Under section 1253(d)(1), contingent serial payments made by a transferee of a trademark or trade name are not subject to fifteen-year amortization under section 197, but rather are currently deductible under section 162 if several requirements are satisfied. Read IRC § 1253(d)(1) carefully. Are the requirements easily met in the case of most trademark and trade name purchases?

b. Amortization under Section 167

As discussed above, section 197 does not apply to a number of different types of intellectual property. If section 197 does not apply to acquired intellectual property (e.g., separately acquired patents, copyrights, and computer software), depreciation continues to be governed by pre-section 197 law, and capitalized purchase costs may nevertheless be recovered through depreciation deductions under section 167. *See* Treas. Reg. 1.167(a)-14 (providing rules for the depreciation of intellectual property not covered by section 197). To be eligible for depreciation under section 167, the acquired intellectual property must have a determinable useful life, and the taxpayer must be engaged in either a trade or business or an activity conducted for profit. IRC §§ 167(a), (b).

There are different methods of amortizing the capitalized costs of purchasing eligible intellectual property under section 167. The regulations provide that amortization must be determined in accordance with a "reasonably consistent plan." Common methods are the straight-line method and the income-forecast method, both of which are discussed below. Some methods are generally not available. For example, the sliding scale method, under which amortization is typically computed based on a declining rate of exhaustion over time, is generally unavailable. Likewise, the cost recovery method, under which a taxpayer can recover all costs before reporting any income, is generally unavailable. *See* Rev. Rul. 60-358, 1960-2 C.B. 68, *amplified by* Rev. Rul. 79-285, 1979-2 C.B. 91.

The simplest method is the *straight-line method*, under which capitalized costs of acquiring eligible property (less salvage value) are deducted ratably over the period the taxpayer expects the property to be useful in his or her trade or business. The regulations provide that the useful life of an intangible is not necessarily the statutory legal life of the asset, but rather the period over which the asset may reasonably be expected to be useful to the taxpayer in his trade or business or in the production of income. Treas. Reg. § 1.167(a)-1(b). With respect to computer software, the period over which software may reasonably be expected to be useful to the taxpayer in her trade or business is irrelevant. This is because the cost of software not covered by section 197 is amortized ratably over an arbitrary 36-month recovery period beginning on the first day of the month the computer software is placed in service. IRC § 167(f). [Recall that the cost of bundled software is depreciated over the appropriate recovery period of the related hardware.]

A permitted alternative amortization method for eligible intellectual property acquisition costs is the *income-forecast* method. Under the income-forecast method, costs of acquiring eligible intellectual property are recovered as income is earned from exploitation of the property. More specifically, the depreciation allowance for income-forecast property for a given tax year is computed by multiplying the depreciable basis of the property by a fraction, the numerator of which is current year income (income from the asset for the tax year) and the denominator of which is forecasted total income (estimated total income to be earned in connection with the asset during its useful life). The following simple example illustrates the computation.

Example. In Year 1, Fran purchases and places in service income-forecast property with a depreciable basis of $100, and estimates that forecasted total income from the property will be $200. In Year 1, current year income from the property is $80. The depreciation allowance for Year 1 is $40, computed by multiplying the depreciable basis of the property of $100 by the fraction obtained by dividing current year income of $80 by forecasted total income of $200.

Since amortization flows from income, the income-forecast method (in contrast to the straight-line method) results in a fairer allocation of costs to the period in which the taxpayer realizes income from the intellectual property. The income-forecast method may also allow a taxpayer to recover intellectual property acquisition costs more quickly than the straight-line method would allow; however, the method is not without its drawbacks. For example, it is often difficult to estimate all future income to be generated by the asset. Indeed, regulations provide a revised computation for computing depreciation allowances in years when conditions necessitate using a revised forecasted total income that differs from the forecasted total income used in computing depreciation allowances in previous years. Prop. Treas. Reg. § 1.167(n)-4(b). Moreover, property depreciated under the income-forecast method is subject to a series of complicated look-back rules, under which taxpayers are required to pay, or are entitled to receive, interest when either forecasted total income or revised forecasted total income are overestimated or underestimated. Prop. Treas. Reg. § 1.167(n)-6.

Although the income-forecast method of depreciation has been a permissible method for certain properties since the early 1960s (see Revenue Ruling 60-358), Congress enacted section 167(g) in 1996 to ensure proper allowances for depreciation. In 1997, Congress amended section 167(g) to place limitations on the type of property that could be depreciated using the income-forecast method.

An alternative (and popular) method for depreciating intellectual property that is not subject to section 197 is the *variable contingent payment method*. The variable contingent payment method is perhaps the most important method for amortizing intellectual property that is not subject to section 197 but that is purchased for contingent payments. Under the variable contingent payment method, a taxpayer who purchases intellectual property (that is not subject to section 197) for contingent payments (e.g., payments computed by reference to income from the use of the intellectual property) adds such payments to the basis of the intellectual property in the taxable year paid but then amortizes the full amount paid in that year. In other words, the amortization deduction each year equals the amount of the royalty paid or incurred each year. The Tax Court sanctioned the use of this method in Associated Patentees, Inc. v. Commissioner, 4 T.C. 979 91945), *acq.*, 1959-2 C.B. 3. The IRS and Treasury Department later agreed to follow the *Associated Patentees* decision. *See* Revenue Ruling 67-136, 1967-1 C.B. 58; Treas. Reg. § 1.167(a)-14(c)(4). What is the rationale behind permitting an immediate deduction for each year's payment? Is the treatment of contingent payments for intellectual property that is not subject to section 197 (e.g., separately acquired patents) more generous than the treatment of contingent payments for intellectual property that is subject to section 197 (e.g., patents acquired as part of a trade or business)?

2. Licensing of Intellectual Property

It is common for intellectual property to be licensed rather than purchased. The tax consequences of licensing intellectual property are straight forward. Payments made under a contract for the license of intellectual property generally may be deducted under normal tax principles (section 162) over the license term. It should be noted that a license will be closely scrutinized to determine whether the arrangement is really a license as opposed to a sale under the principles of section 1235, a provision we study in the next chapter. Treas. Reg. § 1.197-2(f)(3)(iii).

IV. Materials

Field Service Advice 200125019

June 22, 2001

ISSUE

Whether expenditures incurred by Taxpayer's design and prototype department relating to the design, development, modification, and improvement of athletic footwear constitute "research and experimental expenditures" under I.R.C. § 174.

CONCLUSION

Expenditures incurred by Taxpayer's design and prototype department relating to the design, development, modification, and improvement of athletic footwear constitute "research and experimental expenditures" under section 174 only if such expenditures are attributable to activities intended to eliminate uncertainty concerning the development or improvement of the footwear products and if such expenditures are not otherwise excludable under section 174.

FACTS

Taxpayer is in the trade or business of designing, developing, selling, and distributing athletic footwear products. Taxpayer's design and prototype department (design department) is engaged in all activities related to the design, development, modification, and improvement of Taxpayer's footwear products.

Taxpayer's product development and/or improvement cycle begins with the design phase during which each member of Taxpayer's design department attempts to conceptualize and design either a new footwear product or an improvement to an existing footwear product. Each design department member produces drawings containing ideas or concepts of what product or improvement might appeal to a particular market segment. Because trends in athletic footwear change frequently, Taxpayer is never certain of what might appeal to the current market.

The design department members then draft and evaluate detailed technical "blue print" design drawings of footwear components, including "cut-away" views illustrating how each of the product's components fit together. The design department will discard the majority of drawings while approximately ten percent of the drawings will be redrafted and reevaluated until certain design concepts are identified as potential designs for the coming year's product line. Design department activities include tasks related to nonfunctional aspects of the product, such as evaluating colors or positioning insignia, or more complex tasks related to functional aspects of the product, such as designing a new footwear component (e.g., a tread pattern or lace hook), or improving the functionality of an existing footwear component (e.g., an improved tread or a more water-resistant boot). Design department activities may also include developing a new footwear product, which would include activities related to both functional and nonfunctional aspects of the product.

As soon as the design department arrives at a tentative agreement on the designs for the coming year's product line, the proposed designs are reviewed and evaluated by Taxpayer's management. For those designs approved by Taxpayer's management, the design department determines the necessary components for manufacturing, as well as the appropriate methods of manufacturing, each product. Upon final approval of the component and/or footwear product design, the design department evaluates the appropriate manufacturing process for that new design. Once these various design elements are finalized and approved, Taxpayer then asks a foreign manufacturer to construct a prototype pairs of the footwear design. Taxpayer does not manufacture either the components used in the construction of the footwear or the footwear itself.

As part of the design process, however, the design department frequently constructs a rough prototype of a proposed product or product component while experimenting with different design features. The rough prototypes are constructed from various scrap materials including discarded prototype models and returned merchandise.

When the a prototype pairs of footwear are constructed by the foreign manufacturer, they are returned to Taxpayer where the design department inspects them for inherent design flaws. Such design flaws may be functional (i.e., generally relating to the product's purpose, action or performance) or non-functional (i.e., generally relating to color or style). Once Taxpayer approves the design, the prototypes are marketed to Taxpayer's customers. When and if the prototypes are successfully marketed, Taxpayer submits an order to its foreign manufacturer for further production of the product.

Taxpayer performs no internal testing to determine how the footwear will hold up to sustained use and instead relies upon the ultimate consumer to test its product. Thus, design flaws that are not identified upon inspection during the design evaluation process become apparent only when the consumer has purchased, used, and returned the product to the store where it was purchased. If a product has a correctable problem, members of the design department evaluate and attempt to eliminate the problem. The design department addresses diverse problems, ranging from the color of the shoe, the placement of the insignia, the overall design of the tread, or the design of the entire footwear product.

Taxpayer has claimed all costs incurred by the design department for the x, y, and z taxable years as research or experimental expenditures under § 174. Taxpayer's accounting for the costs incurred by the design department does not delineate the nature of the costs incurred.

LAW

Prior to 1954, the tax laws authorized no specific treatment for research and experimental expenditures. In order to provide guidance to taxpayers on the proper accounting treatment of research and experimental expenditures, as well as to encourage taxpayers to carry on research and experimentation, Congress enacted section 174, effective for expenses incurred after December 31, 1953.

Section 174 generally provides that research and experimental expenditures paid or incurred during the taxable year in connection with a taxpayer's trade or business may, at the taxpayer's election, be deducted currently rather than capitalized. Section 174(c) generally provides that section 174 will not apply to any expenditure for the acquisition or improvement of land, or for the acquisition or improvement of property to be used in connection with the research or experimentation and of a character which is subject to the allowance for depreciation under section 167.

Treas. Reg. § 1.174-2(a)(1) provides, in relevant part, that the term "research or experimental expenditures" means expenditures incurred in connection with the taxpayer's trade or business which represent research and development costs in the experimental or laboratory sense. The term generally includes all such costs incident to the development or improvement of a product. Further, expenditures represent research and development costs in the experimental or laboratory sense if they are for activities intended to discover information that would eliminate uncertainty concerning the development or improvement of a product. Uncertainty exists if the information available to the taxpayer does not establish the capability or method for developing or improving the product or the appropriate design of the product. Whether expenditures qualify as research or experimental expenditures depends on the nature of the activity to which the expenditures relate, not the nature of the product or improvement being developed or the level of technological advancement the product or improvement represents.

Treas. Reg. § 1.174-2(a)(2) provides that the term "product" includes any pilot model, process, formula, invention, technique, patent, or similar property, and includes products to be used by the taxpayer in its trade or business as well as products to be held for sale, lease, or license.

Treas. Reg. § 1.174-2(a)(3) provides that the term "research or experimental expenditures" does not include expenditures for—

(i) The ordinary testing or inspection of materials or products for quality control (quality control testing);

(ii) Efficiency surveys;

(iii) Management studies;

(iv) Consumer surveys;

(v) Advertising or promotions;

(vi) The acquisition of another's patent, model, production or process; or

(vii) Research in connection with literary, historical, or similar projects.

Treas. Reg. § 1.174-2(a)(4) provides that for purposes of Treas. Reg. § 1.174-2(a)(3)(i), testing or inspection to determine whether particular units of materials or products conform to specified parameters is quality control testing. However, quality control testing does not include testing to determine if the design of the product is appropriate.

Treas. Reg. § 1.174-2(b) contains rules relating to certain expenditures with respect to land and other property. Treas. Reg. § 1.174-2(b)(1) provides that expenditures by the taxpayer for the acquisition or improvement of land, or for the acquisition or improvement of property which is subject to an allowance for depreciation under section 167, are not deductible under section 174, irrespective of the fact that the property or improvements may be used by the taxpayer in connection with research or experimentation. However, allowances for depreciation of property are considered as research or experimental expenditures, for purposes of section 174, to the extent that the property to which the allowances relate is used in connection with research or experimentation. If any part of the cost of acquisition or improvement of depreciable property is attributable to research or experimentation (whether made by the taxpayer or another), see Treas. Reg. § 1.174-2(b)(2), (3), and (4).

Treas. Reg. § 1.174-2(b)(2) provides, in relevant part, that expenditures for research or experimentation which result, as an end product of the research or experimentation, in depreciable property to be used in the taxpayer's trade or business may, subject to the limitations of Treas. Reg. § 1.174-2(b)(4), be allowable as a current expense deduction under section 174(a).

Treas. Reg. § 1.174-2(b)(3) provides, in relevant part, that if expenditures for research or experimentation are incurred in connection with the construction or manufacture of depreciable property by another, they are deductible under section 174(a) only if made upon the taxpayer's order and at his risk. No deduction will be allowed (i) if the taxpayer purchases another's product under a performance guarantee (whether express, implied, or imposed by local law) unless the guarantee is limited, to engineering specifications or otherwise, in such a way that economic utility is not taken into account; or (ii) for any part of the purchase price of a product in regular production. However, see Treas. Reg. § 1.174-2(b)(4).

Treas. Reg. § 1.174-2(b)(4) provides, in relevant part, that the deductions referred to in Treas. Reg. § 1.174-2(b)(2) for expenditures in connection with the acquisition or production of depreciable property to be used in the taxpayer's trade or business are limited to amounts expended for research or experimentation. Thus, amounts expended for research or experimentation do not include the costs of the component materials of the depreciable property, the costs of labor or other elements involved in its construction and installation, or costs attributable to the acquisition or improvement of the property. *See* Ekman v. Commissioner, 184 F.3d 522 (6th Cir. 1999), aff'g T.C. Memo. 1997-318 (holding that the cost incurred for the purchase of a used car engine is not deductible under section 174 because the engine is of a character subject to an allowance for depreciation).

ANALYSIS

The issue in this request for Field Service Advice is whether expenditures attributable to Taxpayer's design, development, sale, and distribution of athletic footwear are research or experimental expenditures under section 174. The materials accompanying the incoming request do not state whether Taxpayer's accounting for the costs incurred by the design department include expenses attributable to property that is subject to an allowance for depreciation. Inasmuch as we have been advised that Taxpayer has classified all costs of the design department as section 174 expenses, we believe we should address this issue briefly.

Treas. Reg. § 1.174-2(b)(1) generally provides that expenditures by the taxpayer for the acquisition or improvement of property which is subject to an allowance for depreciation under section 167, are not deductible under section 174, irrespective of the fact that the property or improvements may be used by the taxpayer in connection with research or experimentation. Treas. Reg. § 1.174-2(b)(2) provides, in relevant part, that expenditures for research or experimentation which result, as an end product of the research or experimentation, in depreciable property to be used in the taxpayer's trade or business may, subject to the limitations of Treas. Reg. § 1.174-2(b)(4), be allowable as a current expense deduction under section 174(a).

These rules describe two types of expenses: (1) expenses incurred for activities intended to discover information that would eliminate uncertainty concerning the development or improvement of a product; and (2) expenses attributable to the component material, labor or other elements involved in the construction and installation of a product. The former type of expense, to the extent it can be traced to activities intended to discover information that would eliminate uncertainty concerning the development or improvement of a product, are deductible for purposes of section 174. The latter type of expense, to the extent it represents costs for the construction of a depreciable asset, is not deductible. *See* Rev. Rul. 73-275, 1973-1 C.B. 134 (holding that costs attributable to the development and design of an automated manufacturing system, as distinguished from costs attributable to the production of the manufacturing system, are deductible under section 174). Therefore, if the facts of this case suggest that the rough prototypes produced by Taxpayer's design department for use in Taxpayer's trade or business are property of a character subject to the allowance for depreciation, then the cost of the component materials to produce these prototypes are not deductible under section 174.

Treas. Reg. § 1.174-2(b)(3) generally provides that if expenditures for research or experimentation are incurred in connection with the construction or manufacture of depreciable property by another, they are deductible under section 174(a) only if made upon the taxpayer's order and at his risk. The materials accompanying the incoming request for Field Service Advice contain no information concerning Taxpayer's contractual arrangement with the foreign manufacturer. If it is determined that the prototypes are depreciable property, however, then the contract(s) should be examined to determine which party bears the risk of loss.

Assuming that some, if not all, of the costs incurred by Taxpayer's design department do not include expenses attributable to property that is subject to an allowance for depreciation, then we must consider other bases for disallowance under section 174. As noted above, neither the Code nor the regulations provide an explicit definition of the term "research or experimental expenditures." Existing case law is likewise unhelpful and generally predates the 1994 amendments to the regulations at Treas. Reg. § 1.174-2. *See, e.g.*, Mayrath v. Commissioner, 41 T.C. 582 (1964), aff'd on other grounds, 357 F.2d 209 (5th Cir. 1966) (holding that the regulatory definition of research or experimental expenditures was reasonable and consistent with Congress' intent to limit deductions to those expenditures of an investigative nature expended in developing the concept of a product); Kollsman Instrument Corp. v. Commissioner, T.C. Memo. 1986-66, aff'd on other grounds, 870 F.2d 89 (2d Cir. 1989) (denying section 174 treatment because the contracts in question did not require the taxpayer to invent, develop the concept of, or design any product); Agro Science Co. v. Commissioner, T.C. Memo. 1989-687, aff'd but opinion withdrawn, 927 F.2d 213 (5th Cir. 1991) (finding that research requires an element of experimentation rather than simply a repetition of what has already been done); Crouch v. Commissioner, T.C. Memo. 1990-309 (finding that the amounts expended by petitioner were paid to research, write, publish and promote an ordinary literary work and thus were not research costs in the experimental or laboratory sense); TSR, Inc. v. Commissioner, 96 T.C. 903 (1991) (examining, for section 44 research credit purposes, such terms as "laboratory" and "experimental" under section 174).

At best, we are able to discern from this line of cases, together with the statute and regulations, that the term "research or experimental" encompasses the notion that scientific research and development includes an attempt to develop or improve a product, or develop or improve upon a technique or procedure. The 1994 amendments support the notion that scientific research is distinguishable from research of other types in that the amendments provide that expenditures represent research and development costs in the experimental or laboratory sense if the expenditures are for activities intended to discover information that would eliminate uncertainty concerning the development or improvement of a pilot model, process, formula, invention, technique, patent, or similar property. *See* Treas. Reg. § 1.174-2(a)(2). *See also* H.R. Rep. No. 83-1337, at 28 (1954); S. Rep. No. 83-1622, at 33 (1954).

In delineating the scope of the term "research or experimental," the 1994 amendments clarify that uncertainty exists if the information available to the taxpayer does not establish the capability or method for developing or improving the product. Treas. Reg. § 1.174-2(a)(1). However, the term "uncertainty" must be limited to technological or scientific uncertainty in that a taxpayer must be uncertain as to whether it will be able to develop or improve its product in the scientific or laboratory sense. Put differently, the taxpayer must be uncertain as to whether it will be able to achieve its product development objective through its research activities. Conversely, uncertainty attributable to business or market concerns is not determinative of the existence of research and experimentation for purposes of section 174.

The section 174 regulations provide several exclusions from the definition of research or experimental expenditures. For example, the term does not include expenditures such as those for the ordinary testing or inspection of materials or products for quality control, or those for efficiency surveys, management studies, consumer surveys, advertising, or promotions. Treas. Reg. § 1.174-2(a)(3). Significantly, these exclusions are related to activities that generally occur after the research is completed in that the purpose of such activities is to evaluate and disseminate the results of the research. For example, once a product, such as a shoe, is developed, the existence of this shoe must be promoted and advertised. Advertising in this respect is the publication or announcement to the public of the availability of a new or improved product. The fact that these excluded activities tend to occur after the research is completed is further supported by the clarification in the 1994 amendments to the exclusion for quality control testing. Treas. Reg. § 1.174-2(a)(4) provides that the exclusion for quality control testing does not apply to testing to determine whether the design of the product is appropriate. If a taxpayer finds that the design of its product is inappropriate, then the research is not completed and the taxpayer must resume its research activities.

In reviewing the materials accompanying the request for Field Service Advice, we note that a distinction appears to be drawn between the functional and nonfunctional aspects of the footwear product. Prior to the finalization of the 1994 amendments to the section 174 regulations, this distinction was relevant. The section 174 regulations proposed in 1989 provided six exclusions in addition to the exclusions contained in the 1957 regulations. In relevant part, the 1989 proposed regulations excluded costs incurred in connection with activities not directed at the functional aspects of a product including expenses relating to style, taste, cosmetic, or seasonal design factors. *See* 1989 Prop. Treas. Reg. § 1.174-2(a)(3)(v). The 1994 amendments, while retaining the exclusions contained in the final 1957 regulations, did not retain the six additional exclusions proposed in 1989. Therefore, expenditures for any of these six activities qualify as research or experimental expenditures if they fall within the general definition of the term "research or experimental expenditure" and are not covered by one of the existing exclusions. *See* Explanation of Provisions to the 1993 proposed regulations, 58 Fed. Reg. 15820.

In this case, the fact that Taxpayer's activities are with respect to the development or improvement of any nonfunctional aspects of the footwear product is, by itself, not a supportable basis for disallowance under section 174. Rather, the costs incurred must represent research and development costs in the experimental or laboratory sense and must be attributable to activities intended to eliminate uncertainty concerning the development of the product.

Revenue Procedure 2000-50

2000-2 C.B. 601

Section 1. Purpose

This revenue procedure provides guidelines on the treatment of the costs of computer software.

Section 2. Definition

For the purpose of this revenue procedure, "computer software" is any program or routine (that is, any sequence of machine-readable code) that is designed to cause a computer to perform a desired function or set of functions, and the documentation required to describe and maintain that program or routine. It includes all forms and media in which the software is contained, whether written, magnetic, or otherwise. Computer programs of all classes, for example, operating systems, executive systems, monitors, compilers and translators, assembly routines, and utility programs as well as application programs, are included. Computer software also includes any incidental and ancillary rights that are necessary to effect the acquisition of the title to, the ownership of, or the right to use the computer software, and that are used only in connection with that specific computer software. Computer software does not include any data or information base described in § 1.197-2(b)(4) of the Income Tax Regulations (for example, data files, customer lists, or client files) unless the data base or item is in the public domain and is incidental to a computer program. Nor does it include any cost of procedures that are external to the computer's operation.

Section 3. Background

.01 In the preamble to the final regulations issued January 25, 2000, under §§ 167(f) and 197 of the Internal Revenue Code (T.D. 8865, 2000-7 I.R.B. 589), the Internal Revenue Service advised taxpayers that they may not rely on the procedures in Rev. Proc. 69-21, 1969-2 C.B. 303, to the extent the procedures are inconsistent with § 167(f) or § 197, or the final regulations thereunder.

.02 Except as otherwise expressly provided, §§ 446(e) and 1.446-1(e) provide that a taxpayer must obtain the consent of the Commissioner of Internal Revenue before changing a method of accounting for federal income tax purposes. Section 1.446-1(e)(3)(ii) authorizes the Commissioner to prescribe administrative procedures setting forth the limitations, terms, and conditions deemed necessary to permit a taxpayer to obtain consent to change a method of accounting.

Section 4. Scope

This revenue procedure applies to all costs of computer software as defined in section 2 of this revenue procedure. This revenue procedure does not apply to any computer software that is subject to amortization as an "amortizable section 197 intangible" as defined in § 197(c) and the regulations thereunder, or to costs that a taxpayer has treated as a research and experimentation expenditure under § 174.

Section 5. Costs of Developing Computer Software

.01 The costs of developing computer software (whether or not the particular software is patented or copyrighted) in many respects so closely resemble the kind of research and experimental expenditures that fall within the purview of § 174 as to warrant similar accounting treatment. Accordingly, the Service will not disturb a taxpayer's treatment of costs paid or incurred in developing software for any particular project, either for the taxpayer's own use or to be held by the taxpayer for sale or lease to others, where:

(1) All of the costs properly attributable to the development of software by the taxpayer are consistently treated as current expenses and deducted in full in accordance with rules similar to those applicable under § 174(a); or

(2) All of the costs properly attributable to the development of software by the taxpayer are consistently treated as capital expenditures that are recoverable through deductions for ratable amortization, in accordance with rules similar to those provided by § 174(b) and the regulations thereunder, over a period of 60 months from the date of completion of the development or, in accordance with rules provided in § 167(f)(1) and the regulations thereunder, over 36 months from the date the software is placed in service.

Section 6. Costs of Acquired Computer Software

.01 With respect to costs of acquired computer software, the Service will not disturb the taxpayer's treatment of:

(1) Costs that are included, without being separately stated, in the cost of the hardware (computer) if the costs are consistently treated as a part of the cost of the hardware that is capitalized and depreciated; or

(2) Costs that are separately stated if the costs are consistently treated as capital expenditures for an intangible asset the cost of which is to be recovered by amortization deductions ratably over a period of 36 months beginning with the month the software is placed in service, in accordance with the rules under § 167(f)(1). *See* § 1.167(a)-14(b)(1).

Section 7. Leased or Licensed Computer Software

Where a taxpayer leases or licenses computer software for the use in the taxpayer's trade or business, the Service will not disturb a deduction properly allowable under the provisions of § 1.162-11 as rental. However, an amount described in § 1.162-11 is not currently deductible if, without regard to § 1.162-11, the amount is properly chargeable to capital account. *See* § 1.197-2(a)(3).

Section 8. Application

.01 A change in a taxpayer's treatment of costs paid or incurred to develop, purchase, lease or license computer software to a method described in section 5, 6 or 7 of this revenue procedure is a change in method of accounting to which §§ 446 and 481 apply. However, a change in useful life under the method described in section 5.01(2) of this revenue procedure is not a change in method of accounting. Section 1.446-1(e)(2)(ii)(b).

.02 A taxpayer that wants to change the taxpayer's method of accounting under this revenue procedure must follow the automatic change in method of accounting provisions in Rev. Proc. 99-49,tic 1999-2 C.B. 725 (or its successor), with the following modifications:

(1) In order to assist the Service in processing changes in method of accounting under this section and to ensure proper handling, section 6.02(3)(a) of Rev. Proc. 99-49 is modified to require that a Form 3115, Application for Change in Accounting Method, filed under this section include the statement: "Automatic Change Filed Under Section 8.01 of Rev. Proc. 2000-50." This statement must be legibly printed or typed at the top of any Form 3115 filed under this revenue procedure.

(2) If a taxpayer is changing to the method described in section 5.01(2) of this revenue procedure, the taxpayer must attach a statement to the Form 3115 stating whether the taxpayer is choosing the 60-month period from the date of completion of the development of the software, or the 36-month period from the placed-in-service date of the software.

.03 For taxable years ending on or after December 1, 2000, the Service will not disturb the taxpayer's treatment of costs of computer software that are handled in accordance with the practices described in this revenue procedure.

V. Related Matters

- **Amortization of Capitalized Creation Costs.** Although many *purchased* intangible assets are considered section 197 intangibles, most *self-created* intangible assets are specifically excluded from the definition of section 197 intangibles—thus implicating the depreciation rules under section 167 for any capitalized creation costs. IRC § 197(c)(2); Treas. Reg. § 1.197-2(d)(2). There is one important exception to the exclusion for self-created intangibles. Section 197 does apply to self-created trademarks and trade names. IRC § 197(d)(1)(F); Treas. Reg. § 1.197-2(b)(10). As a result, taxpayers must amortize over 15 years the capitalized costs incurred in connection with the development or registration of a trademark or trade name.

- **Safe Harbor Amortization.** The regulations under section 167 provide a 15-year safe harbor amortization period for certain created intangibles that do not have readily ascertainable useful lives. Treas. Reg. § 1.167(a)-3(b).

- **Domain Name Acquisitions.** The Service issued Chief Counsel Advice 201543014, which concluded that a generic domain name is a section 197 intangible (customer-based intangible) if (a) the generic domain name is associated with a website that is already constructed and will be maintained by the purchaser, and (b) such taxpayer acquired the domain name for use in its trade or business. This assumes that the taxpayer is acquiring an already existing site. What would happen if the domain name was purchased from someone who simply owned the name but was not using it?

- **Expensing Off-the-Shelf Software.** The cost of purchasing off-the-shelf software can be immediately expensed under section 179 rather than capitalized and amortized. IRC § 179(d)(1)(A)(ii) (made permanent by the Protecting Americans from Tax Hikes (PATH) Act of 2015).

Chapter 29

Intellectual Property Sales and Licenses

I. Assignment

Read: Internal Revenue Code: §§ 61(a)(7); 197(f)(1), (f)(7); 1221(a)(1)–(3); 1235; 1239; 1245(a)(1)–(3)(A); 1253(a)–(c). Skim §§ 453(a)–(d); 483(a)–(c)(1), (d)(4); 1274(a)–(c)(1), (c)(3)(C), (c)(3)(E), (d).

Treasury Regulations: §§ 15A.4531(c)(2)(i), -1(c)(3)(i), -1(c)(4), -1(d)(2)(i), -1(d)(2)(iii); 1.1221-1(c)(1), -1(c)(3); 1.1235-1(b), -1(c)(2), -2(a)–(d); 1.1239-1(b), -1(c)(5); 1.1245-3(b). Skim § 1.483-1(a)(2)(ii).

Text: Overview
Watson v. Commissioner
Stern v. United States
Related Matters

Complete the problems.

II. Problems

1. Charlie Barris submitted to the CBS television network his ideas for a weekly reality television program. In consideration of a payment of $50,000 by CBS, Charlie assigned and conveyed to CBS all of his title and interest in the television program conceived and invented by him. What is the proper tax treatment of the assignment, assuming Charlie was not able to obtain copyright protection for either the name or essential features of the television program?

2. Palioxis, the inventor of an electronic surveillance device, applied for a patent and then granted to General Electric, a publicly traded company, the "sole and exclusive right, privilege and license to use, manufacture, produce and sell the invention covered by the patent application for a period of 20 years."

   (a) What is the proper tax treatment of the assignment assuming Palioxis receives a lump sum payment of $200,000?

   (b) Same as (a) except that instead of receiving a lump sum payment, Palioxis receives a percentage of the gross receipts realized by General Electric from the sale of the product.

    (c) Same as (a) except that Palioxis transfers the patent application to a corporation in which Palioxis owns one-third of the outstanding stock.

    (d) Same as (a) except that Palioxis transfers the patent application to a corporation in which Palioxis owns 80% of the outstanding stock.

3. Tuan Vo-Dinh is a successful inventor who has been issued over 200 patents during his lifetime. His latest patented invention is an indicator light which permits the testing of an internal lighting circuit without the removal of a bulb. Tuan agreed to transfer to Signal, Inc., an unrelated corporation, the exclusive right for the life of the patent to manufacture, use, and sell the indicator lights throughout the United States east of the Mississippi River in exchange for 10% of the gross selling price on sales made by Signal.

    (a) How should Tuan treat payments received by Signal each year?

    (b) Would your answer in (a) change if Tuan reserved (1) the right to act jointly with Signal in resisting infringement of the invention, and (2) the right to terminate the agreement if Signal failed to make and sell 1,000 indicator lights during any 6-month period?

III. Overview

In addressing the tax consequences of an intellectual property assignment, a preliminary issue is whether the intellectual property has been sold or whether the intellectual property has been licensed. The stakes can be great. If an intellectual property transfer is characterized as a sale for tax purposes, then the transferor is permitted to recover basis in the intellectual property transferred and may be eligible for preferential capital gains treatment. If an intellectual property transfer is characterized as a license, however, payments received in full, whether lump sum or contingent, are reported in income with no recovery of basis in the transferred property, and are considered royalties taxed as ordinary income and not as capital gains.

Whether a particular transfer or assignment is a sale or license depends on the facts and circumstances of the whole transaction, and not the particular terminology used in the transfer agreement. Waterman v. Mackenzie, 138 U.S. 252 (1891). As a general rule, a transfer of intellectual property will qualify as a sale, as opposed to a license, if the transferor assigns all substantial rights to the intellectual property. All substantial rights generally include the *exclusive* right to make, use, and sell for life the intellectual property. A transfer with a limited duration (transfer for less than the entire life of the intellectual property) is generally characterized as a license rather than sale.

In Revenue Ruling 60-226, 1960-1 C.B. 26, the Service described when a copyright assignment will be considered a sale. According to the Service, a grant transferring the exclusive right to exploit a copyrighted work in a medium of publication throughout the life of the copyright shall be treated as a sale of property regardless of the form of payment (e.g., the existence of contingent payments). In Revenue Ruling

64-56, 1964-1 C.B. 144, the Service described what needs to be transferred in order for a sale of trade secrets or know how to exist: "The unqualified transfer in perpetuity of the exclusive right to make, use, and sell an unpatented but secret process within all the territory of a country." Rev. Rul. 64-56, 1964-1 C.B. 144, *amplified by* Rev. Rul. 71-564, 1971-2 C.B. 179.

In *Watson v. Commissioner*, included in the materials, the Tenth Circuit addressed whether a patent transfer was a sale or a licence for tax purposes. As shown by *Watson*, certain restrictions or limitations do not necessarily preclude a finding of a sale under general sale or exchange principles. Transfers with geographical limitations or field of use restrictions can nevertheless qualify for sale treatment, as long as the entire bundle of rights and privileges within a geographical area or field of use are transferred. Thus, the grant of an exclusive right to make, use, and sell intellectual property to only a certain geographical area may be considered a sale, even though the transferor retains those rights with respect to all other geographical areas. *See Watson v. Commissioner*, included below. Moreover, the grant of an exclusive right to make, use, and sell intellectual property to only a particular industry could be considered a sale, even though the transferor retained those rights with respect to all other industries. *See* United States v. Carruthers, 219 F.2d 21 (9th Cir. 1955).

Restrictions that serve to protect the transferor will not prevent the transfer from being treated as a sale, especially if the restrictions do not interfere with the full use of the intellectual property by the transferee. Thus, a transfer may be deemed a sale even though the transferor reserves the right to terminate for failure to make payments or in the event of insolvency or bankruptcy of the transferee. *See* Myers v. Commissioner, 6 T.C. 258 (1946), *acq.* 1958-2 C.B. 3. Similarly, a transferor's retention of the right to sue for infringement will not necessarily preclude a finding of sale if the restriction is viewed as a security device (e.g., if the transfer involves contingent payments based on the transferee's use). Review *Watson v. Commissioner* below.

A. Sales and Exclusive Licenses of Intellectual Property

If an intellectual property transfer is considered a sale for tax purposes, the transferor must determine (1) the amount of gain or loss *realized*, (2) whether the realized gain or loss is *recognized*, and (3) the *character* of the gain or loss. Earlier chapters addressed realization, recognition, and general characterization principles. The following material addresses general and specific characterization provisions as applied to intellectual property transfers.

1. General Characterization Provisions

Recall from Chapter 17 that the capital gain preference only comes into play if a taxpayer has a *net capital gain* for the year, which is only possible if the taxpayer has a *net long-term capital gain* during the year. Net short-term capital gains, unlike net long-term capital gains, are not included in the term net capital gain and are taxed as ordinary income. A *long-term capital gain* is defined in section 1222 as gain from

(1) the sale or exchange, (2) of a capital asset, (3) held for more than one year. IRC § 1222(3). The presence of each of these three factors is necessary before a recognized gain can receive preferential tax treatment.

Section 1221 defines the term capital asset as all property held by the taxpayer (whether or not connected with a trade or business), subject to several exceptions. The first type of property specifically excluded from the definition of capital asset is stock-in-trade, inventory, and property held by the taxpayer primarily for sale to customers in the ordinary course of a trade or business. IRC § 1221(a)(1). A professional inventor may run afoul of this exception since a professional inventor may be considered to hold his or her inventions as inventory, or property primarily held for sale to customers in the ordinary course of his or her trade or business. See Lockhart v. Commissioner, 258 F.2d 343 (3d Cir. 1958) (finding that 37 inventions over a 19-year period were held primarily for sale to customers in a trade or business).

The second type of property excluded from the definition of capital asset is depreciable property used in the taxpayer's trade or business. IRC § 1221(a)(2). This exclusion is quite broad for two reasons. First, many forms of intellectual property, such as separately acquired patents and copyrights, are subject to the allowance for depreciation under section 167. Second, many other forms of intellectual property, such as trademarks and trade names, are considered section 197 intangible assets, and, although amortizable over a prescribed 15-year period, are nevertheless treated as property subject to the allowance for depreciation under section 167. IRC § 197(f)(7). However, intellectual property, the creation costs of which were immediately deductible under section 174, does not constitute depreciable property and therefore is not excluded from the definition of capital asset. The capital asset exclusion for depreciable trade or business property seems overly broad. It is limited, however, by section 1231, addressed in Chapter 18. Section 1231 is a pro-taxpayer provision that may qualify depreciable intellectual property used in a trade or business for preferential capital gain treatment.

The definition of capital asset also excludes a patent, invention, model or design, a secret formula or process, a copyright, a literary, musical, or artistic composition, or similar property held by the creator (taxpayer whose personal efforts created the property) or a taxpayer with a basis carried over from the creator. IRC § 1221(a)(3). Traditional copyrighted works are obviously included within the scope of the copyright exclusion. But, what about abstract ideas, such as a cartoon character or formats and ideas for a television or radio show, which are not copyrightable per se? In Stern v. United States, a case included in the materials, the court addressed whether a character ("Francis" the talking mule) was similar property and hence within the scope of section 1221(a)(3). Patents, inventions, models or designs, and secret formulae and processes were added to the exclusion in 2018. Although these are no longer capital assets under section 1221, they may nevertheless be entitled to capital gain treatment under section 1235, a special characterization provision addressed below.

The purpose of treating self-created property as noncapital in the hands of its creator is consistent with taxing wages and salaries as ordinary income. Gains from personal efforts should be taxed as ordinary income just as wages and salaries are taxed as ordinary income. Moreover, the exclusion has the effect of putting nonprofessional inventors, writers, authors, and photographers on parity with professional inventors, writers, authors, and photographers who are subject to the inventory exclusion discussed above.

The inventory exclusion and the self-created property exclusion do not apply to musical compositions or copyrights in musical works, as a result of the Tax Increase Prevention and Reconciliation Act of 2005. *See* IRC § 1221(b)(3). As a result, songwriters get to pay capital gains tax rates, rather than higher personal income tax rates, on sales of their songs. Capital gains treatment is not available to other artists, such as novelists, painters, sculptors, and designers. Query: Is there any theoretical justification for this distinction?

2. Special Characterization Provisions

Long-term capital gain consequences require a sale or exchange of a capital asset held for longer than one year. If a transaction does not constitute a sale or exchange or if a transaction does not involve a capital asset, the transaction will give rise to ordinary income unless a special characterization provision applies. There are special characterization provisions that apply to intellectual property transfers. Section 1235 (which provides long-term capital gains treatment for certain dispositions of patent rights) and section 1253 (which imposes ordinary income treatment on certain transfers of trademarks and trade names) are considered below.

a. Section 1235: Transfers of All Substantial Rights to Patents

Section 1235 is a special characterization rule that provides all three requirements for long-term capital gain treatment (sale or exchange, capital asset, and requisite one-year holding period) in connection with the transfer of all the substantial rights to a patent. Specifically, section 1235 provides that a transfer (other than by gift, inheritance, or devise) of all substantial rights to a patent, or of an undivided interest in all such rights to a patent, by a statutorily defined holder to a person other than a related person constitutes the *sale or exchange of a capital asset held for more than one year.* IRC § 1235(a). As can be seen, the sale of a patent may qualify for long-term capital gains treatment even though the transferor is a professional inventor in the business of selling patents to customers in the ordinary course of business (i.e., section 1235 supplies the capital asset requirement). Likewise, the sale of a patent may qualify for long-term capital gains treatment even if the sale occurs the moment the patent is created or if the patent has been held for less than one year (i.e., section 1235 supplies the requisite holding period). Further, the sale of a patent may receive preferential capital gains treatment even though the sale includes installment or contingent payments. By assuring certain patent holders that these sales will qualify for long-term capital gains treatment, section 1235 has the effect of encouraging research and development that will lead to patentable inventions.

To benefit from section 1235, a transaction must involve the *transfer* by a *holder* of *all substantial rights* to a *patent*. Each of these requirements is discussed below.

Transfer. Section 1235 may not apply to transfers of patents that arise out of an employment relationship. *See* Treas. Reg. § 1.1235-1(c)(2) (providing that "[p]ayments received by an employee as compensation for services rendered as an employee under an employment contract requiring the employee to transfer to the employer the rights to any invention by such employee are not attributable to a transfer to which section 1235 applies"). The reason for this exception is that an employee who is hired by an employer to invent cannot make a *transfer* of patents in which he or she has no rights. An employee paid by an employer to invent receives compensation for services rendered (taxable as ordinary income), and not consideration for the assignment of inventions constituting capital assets (taxable as long-term capital gain under section 1235). Whether payments received by an inventor-employee from his or her employer are treated as compensation for services rendered by the employee or as proceeds derived from the transfer of patent rights is a question of fact.

Holder. Section 1235 applies only if the transferor is a statutorily defined *holder* of the patent. The holder of a patent is defined as (1) any individual whose personal efforts created the patent property or (2) any other individual—other than the employer or relative of the inventor—who acquired his interest in the patent property from the original inventor in exchange for money or money's worth prior to the actual reduction to practice of the invention covered by the patent ("financial backer"). IRC § 1235(b). Although corporations, partnerships, trusts, and estates may not be qualified holders, each member of a partnership who is an individual, however, may qualify as a holder as to his pro-rata share of a patent owned by the partnership. *See* Treas. Reg. § 1.1235-2(d)(2).

All Substantial Rights. Section 1235 only applies to a transfer of all the substantial rights to a patent or an undivided interest therein. The term *all substantial rights* refers to all rights (whether or not then held by the grantor) which are of value at the time the rights to the patent (or an undivided interest in it) are transferred. Treas. Reg. § 1.1235-2(b)(1). Whether or not all substantial rights to a patent are transferred in a transaction depends upon the circumstances surrounding the entire transaction and not the particular terminology used in the transfer instrument. *Id.* Although the facts and circumstances surrounding a transfer are to be considered, regulations list four transfers that, because they are limited in scope, do not result in a transfer of all substantial rights to qualify for capital gains treatment under section 1235. They are: (1) the grant of a patent which is *limited geographically* within the country of issuance; (2) the grant of a patent which is limited in duration by the terms of the agreement to a period less than the remaining life of the patent; (3) the grant of a patent which is *limited to fields of use* within trades or industries, which are less than all the rights covered by the patent, which exist and have value at the time of the grant; and (4) the grant of less than all the claims or inventions covered by the patent which exist and have value at the time of the grant. *Id.* Although a geographic or field of use restriction will prevent a transfer from qualifying under section 1235, will it, taken alone, prevent a transfer from being characterized as a sale under general characterization principles? In E.I. du Pont de Nemours & Co. v. United States, 432 F.2d 1052 (3d Cir. 1970), a non-section 1235 case, the Third Circuit allowed capital gains treatment for a transfer having such limitations under general capital gains provisions. *See also* Allied Chemical Corp. v. United States, 370 F.2d 697 (2d Cir. 1967).

Patent. Section 1235 applies only to patents and not to other forms of intellectual property, such as copyrights and trademarks. Although the Code does not define a *patent* for purposes of section 1235, the regulations provide that the term *patent* means a patent granted under the provisions of Title 35 of the United States Code, as well as any similar foreign patent granting provisions. The regulations also provide that it is not necessary that the patent or patent application for the invention be in existence if the requirements of section 1235 are otherwise met. Treas. Reg. § 1.1235-2(a). This is significant since transferors often assign ownership of perfected but unpatented inventions before the patent or patent application is in existence.

Section 1235 applies only to the transfer of a patent and not the provision of services. In other words, if the transferor receives payment for the patent and for significant or unrelated services, he or she must allocate the total between payment for the patent (accorded long-term capital gain treatment) and payment for the services (taxable as ordinary income). Such allocation is not necessary, however, if the services rendered are ancillary to the patent transfer. *See* Rev. Rul. 54-56, 1964-1 C.B. 133.

Related Person. The capital gains benefits of section 1235 are not available when an individual transfers a patent to a related person. IRC § 1235(d). Who is treated as a related person for purposes of section 1235? Read carefully IRC § 1235(d)(2) and §§ 267(b), 707(b). Are brothers and sisters considered related for purposes of section 1235? What about a holder of a patent and a corporation in which the holder owns 25 percent (in value) of the outstanding stock? Why do you think this limitation was added?

If a transfer does not qualify for capital gains treatment under section 1235, can the transfer still qualify for capital gains treatment under the general characterization rules discussed above? *See* Treas. Reg. § 1.1235-1(b). In Poole v. Commissioner, 46 T.C. 392 (1966), the Tax Court held that section 1235 was the exclusive means by which a "holder" could qualify for capital gains treatment. Therefore, the Tax Court denied capital gains treatment for the transfer by a holder not qualifying under section 1235. Later, in Revenue Ruling 69-482, 1969-2 C.B. 164, the Service stated that it would not follow *Poole.* More recently, the Tax Court applied Revenue Ruling 69-482 in permitting capital gains treatment under general characterization principles despite the inapplicability of section 1235. *See* Cascade Designs, Inc. v. Commissioner, 79 T.C.M. (CCH) 1542 (2000).

b. Section 1253: Transfers of Trademarks and Trade Names

Section 1253 is a special characterization rule that applies to certain transfers of trademarks or trade names. First, section 1253 imposes ordinary income treatment on all payments that are contingent on the productivity, use, or disposition of a trademark or trade name. IRC § 1253(c). Contingent amounts received or accrued for the transfer of a trademark or trade name constitute ordinary income regardless of whether the transfer is in substance a sale or a license. Second, section 1253 imposes ordinary income treatment on noncontingent payments (whether up-front or installment payments) received for the transfer of a trademark or trade name if the transferor retains any significant power, right, or continuing interest with respect to the subject matter of the mark or name. IRC § 1253(a). It should be clear that section 1253 parallels section 1235 by denying sale treatment whenever the transferor retains any significant power, right, or continuing interest.

The Code sets forth six potentially significant powers, any one of which, if retained, would require ordinary income treatment. Read IRC § 1253(b)(2). This list of retained powers is not exhaustive; rather, consideration is given to all the facts and circumstances existing at the time of a transfer to determine whether an unenumerated power constitutes a significant power. For example, the duration of the relevant restriction is important in determining whether the restriction is significant. *See* Stokely USA, Inc. v. Commissioner, 100 T.C. 439 (1993) (finding insignificant a five-year right to disapprove a transfer but finding significant a twenty-year restriction preventing the transferee from using the trademark on certain products).

If a transfer is within the scope of section 1253, (e.g., the transferor retains a proscribed power over the trademark or trade name after its sale) then the transferor will realize ordinary income. A question arises whether all payments received in a *sale* should be treated as ordinary income with no basis recovery or whether the transferor should be permitted to recover his or her basis. In other words, does section 1253 transform a transaction which in form and substance is a sale into a license? *See* Tomerlin Trust v. Commissioner, 87 T.C. 876 (1986) (holding characterization of payments under section 1253 was inconclusive in determining whether payments were royalties for purposes of the personal holding company tax, because section 1253 does not determine whether a sale has occurred).

3. Treatment of Deferred Payment Sales and Contingent Payments

A taxpayer typically reports gain or loss at the time of the sale. However, intellectual property is often sold on a deferred payment basis (e.g., payments are contingent on use, productivity, or disposition of the intellectual property). When intellectual property is sold on a contingent basis, a question arises as to the proper amount and timing of the gain realized and recognized on the sale. For example, should gain be reported in the year of sale or should the gain be spread out over the life of the payments?

Section 453, the subject of Chapter 26, provides that *income* from an *installment sale* is to reported under the *installment method*. IRC § 453(a). An *installment sale* occurs when at least one payment of the total purchase price is to be received after the close of the tax year in which the sale or other disposition occurs. IRC § 453(b)(1). As can be seen, this definition is broad and includes all intellectual property sales made on a contingent basis. If section 453 applies, the transferor's gain is included in income only as payments are received from the transferee regardless of whether the transferor reports on the cash method or accrual method. In other words, the gain is spread over the life of the payments. *But see* IRC § 453(i) (requiring a taxpayer to recognize income in the year of sale equal to the amount recaptured as ordinary income under section 1245). The percentage of each payment that must be reported as income is determined by multiplying the amount of each payment by a fraction. The numerator is the gross profit realized on the sale or to be realized when payment is completed and the denominator is the total contract or aggregate selling price. IRC § 453(c). This ratio of gross profit to total contract price is known as the gross profit ratio.

Determining the gross profit ratio seems impossible in the case of contingent payment sales, since gross profit (numerator) or total contract price (denominator) cannot be readily determined in the year of sale when payments are contingent on use, productivity, or disposition of the intellectual property. Nevertheless, the regulations deal with contingent payment sales, and provide guidance. What if the sale is subject to a "stated maximum selling price"? *See* Treas. Reg. § 15A.453-1(c)(2)(i). What if a maximum selling price is not known, but a maximum period of time over which payments may be received is known? *See* Treas. Reg. § 15A.453-1(c)(3)(i). What if there is no maximum selling price or fixed period over which payments may be received? *See* Treas. Reg. § 15A.453-1(c)(4).

If intellectual property is sold on a deferred payment basis, the parties must provide for adequate interest on the unpaid balance (adequate interest must be stated and paid annually). If adequate interest is not provided, minimum interest will be imputed by the Code, and a portion of the selling price (or portion of each deferred payment) will be recharacterized as interest. With the selling price adjusted accordingly, the seller will have less capital gain and some ordinary interest income; therefore, the purchaser will receive less depreciation and have interest expense.

Minimum interest is required under either section 1274 (called "OID") or section 483 (called "unstated interest"), depending on the size of the contract. IRC §§ 483(c)(1)(A), 1274(c)(1)(B), (c)(3)(C); Treas. Reg. 1.483-1(a)(2)(ii). Contingent payments received in a section 1235 transfer are excluded from the interest imputation rules of section 1274 and section 483. IRC §§ 483(d)(4), 1274(c)(3)(E). The minimum interest necessary to avoid the imputation of interest is determined by monthly tables promulgated by the Service and based upon average yields of outstanding U.S. government obligations. IRC § 1274(d).

B. Nonexclusive Licenses of Intellectual Property

The tax treatment of nonexclusive licenses (which do not constitute sales) is straightforward. Payments received, whether lump sum or contingent, are royalties taxed as ordinary income and not as capital gains. IRC § 61(a)(7). Because a nonexclusive license cannot be treated as a sale, the licensor is not permitted to recover the unamortized basis in the transferred property, and full amounts received must be reported as ordinary income. However, because the licensor is still deemed to own the intellectual property, the licensor may continue to depreciate or amortize the property provided the property qualifies for depreciation or amortization allowances.

IV. Materials

Watson v. Commissioner
222 F.2d 689 (10th Cir. 1955)

The crucial question in this case is whether for income tax purposes a contract constituted an assignment of patent rights and therefore the income which the patentee derived therefrom was long-term capital gain, or whether the contract constituted a license and hence the income derived from it was ordinary income.

Orla E. Watson conceived the idea of a cart that could be telescoped horizontally, one into another. The cart was designed particularly for use in grocery stores. Watson made a pencil drawing of the cart, finished two experimental models, tested them successfully, and demonstrated them to others. Watson and Fred E. Taylor entered into a partnership agreement by the terms of which it was agreed that, in consideration of advancements made and to be made by Taylor for use in financing the manufacture and distribution of the carts, Watson would for a term of ten years give Taylor an undivided forty-nine per cent interest in and to the telescope feature. Notwithstanding the language contained in the agreement, it was the intention of the parties that Taylor should receive one-half of the profits derived from the invention but no interest in the patent rights. An application for a patent on the cart was filed and later the patent issued. While the application was pending, Watson—with the consent and assistance of Taylor—entered into an agreement with George Oliver O'Donnell, as trustee for Telescope Carts, Inc., to be thereafter incorporated. The agreement provided among other things that Watson thereby granted to the corporation the exclusive right, license, and privilege to manufacture, distribute, sell, develop, and use the telescope carts for and during the period of the application for letters patent, during the term for which letters patent were issued, and during any extension of such patent or patents. The corporation was organized and O'Donnell assigned to it all of his right, title, and interest in and to the agreement between himself and Watson. During 1950, Watson received from the corporation payment or payments under the contract in the aggregate amount of $78,442.75, out of which he paid Taylor $39,221.38. In their income tax return for the year 1950, Watson and his wife reported as ordinary income $39,221.37 which had been received from the corporation and paid the tax thereon. Within the statutory time, they filed a claim for refund in the amount of $7,450.04 upon the ground that the income received under the contract was part of the purchase price of the invention and therefore was subject to tax as long-term capital gain. The claim was not acted upon within six months after the date of its filing, and this action was filed to recover the asserted refund. In its findings of fact, the court found among other things that Watson held the invention relating to the carts for more than six months prior to the execution of the contract with O'Donnell; that he did not hold the invention primarily for sale to customers in the ordinary course of his trade or business; and that the agreement was a license agreement and did not constitute a sale of the invention. In its conclusions of law, the court concluded that for income tax purposes the contract did not constitute a sale of the invention; and that the income received from the corporation constituted ordinary income, not capital gain. Judgment was entered against the taxpayers, and they appealed.

It is a firmly accepted principle of law that if the patentee conveys by an instrument in writing the exclusive right to make, use, and vend the invention throughout the United States, or an undivided part or share of that exclusive right, or the exclusive right under the patent within a specified area within the United States, the conveyance constitutes an assignment of the patent, complete or partial as the case may be; and that a transfer short of that is not an assignment but a license. Waterman v. Mackenzie, 138 U.S. 252. In language too clear for doubt, the agreement into which Watson and O'Donnell entered expressly granted to Telescope Carts, Inc., the exclusive right to make, use, and vend the carts throughout the United States.

The agreement between Watson and O'Donnell was entitled "License Agreement," and in it the parties were referred to as "licensor" and "licensee," respectively. But nomenclature of that kind has little if any significance in resolving the question whether the instrument amounted to an assignment or was a license. The calling of the instrument a license agreement, and the denomination of the parties thereto as licensor and licensee, respectively, did not fix, limit, or qualify the scope and effect of the grant. The legal question whether the instrument constituted an effective assignment or was a license must be determined by considering together the several provisions contained in the instrument, not its title or the manner in which reference was made to the parties.

The agreement contained a provision relating to the termination of its exclusive character. The substance of the provision was that, in the event the corporation should after one year from the date of the agreement fail to make and sell 2,500 carts during any six-months period, the licensor should be free to license others to manufacture and sell carts. But that provision concerned itself exclusively with a condition subsequent. It did no more than provide that upon the occurrence of a stated event the grantor was empowered to terminate the exclusive right and title theretofore conveyed. It did not detract from the effectiveness of the agreement as constituting an assignment of the patent rights.

The contract contained a further provision that the rights of the licensee thereunder should not be assigned without the consent of the licensor having been obtained in writing. That precautionary provision was intended to protect the rights of the parties under the contract, not to proscribe, limit, or nullify their intent and purpose to vest immediately in the transferee the right to manufacture, sell, and use the carts throughout the life of the patent, as well as any extension or extensions thereof.

The agreement contained a provision for payment of royalties. That provision merely fixed the compensation to be paid as consideration for the transfer. It did not reserve to Watson any control over the patent or its use. It did not limit or qualify the scope of the grant. And since the agreement contained language vesting in the corporation the exclusive right to manufacture, sell, and use carts throughout the United States, the provision for payment of royalties did not change the nature of the transfer to a license.

The agreement contained two provisions relating to suits for infringement. The substance of one provision was that in the event a suit was filed charging that the manufacture and sale of carts designed by Watson constituted infringement of a prior patent, payment of royalties to Watson should be suspended during the pendency of the action; that in the event it should be judicially determined that such invention did not infringe, payment of the suspended royalties should be paid in a lump-sum; and that in the event it should be determined that the invention did infringe, payment of royalties under the agreement should cease. That provision concerned itself solely and exclusively with the question of royalties in the event of a suit or suits charging that the Watson invention infringed. It did not reserve to Watson or vest in him any property or proprietary rights in the invention. The other provision obligated Watson and the corporation to act jointly in resisting infringement of the Watson invention, and fixed the manner in which damages recovered for infringement should be divided between them. Without such a provision, the Telescope Carts, Inc., would have the right to institute and maintain in its own name an action for infringement of the patent and retain all damages recovered. *Waterman v. Mackenzie, supra.* And in the absence of a provision of that nature, Watson would have been under no obligation to institute and maintain alone or in conjunction with the company any action for infringement. The underlying reason for the insertion of that provision must have been that in the prosecution of such an action the presence and aid of the inventor would be of value in protecting the property and proprietary rights of the corporation in the invention and the patent covering it, and would also be of value in safeguarding the financial interest of the patentee in respect to continued payment of royalties. The provision was one designed to protect and safeguard such respective rights and interests. It was not intended to reserve to Watson any property or proprietary right in the invention which was at variance with an assignment to the corporation of the right to manufacture, sell, and use carts throughout the life of the patent.

The contract between Watson and O'Donnell constituted an assignment to the corporation of the invention relating to the collapsible carts. Such assignment amounted to a sale of a capital asset. And inasmuch as Watson held the invention for more than six months prior to the transfer, and did not hold it primarily for sale to customers in the ordinary course of his trade or business, the income which the taxpayers received in the form of royalties from the corporation constituted long-term gain as distinguished from ordinary income.

The judgment is reversed and the cause is remanded with directions to enter judgment for the taxpayers.

————————

Stern v. United States

164 F. Supp. 847 (E.D. La. 1958)

J. SKELLY WRIGHT, DISTRICT JUDGE:

This case concerns "Francis" the talking mule. Francis is a product of World War II. It was created by a lonely second lieutenant in the Pacific theater of operations who sometimes wondered whether there was anything in the Army lower than a second lieutenant. Francis convinced him there was. Now, seven motion pictures later, that second lieutenant, the taxpayer here, is claiming that the income from "Francis" is entitled to capital gains treatment under the Internal Revenue laws.

In 1933, after attending Harvard University, David Stern, III, was employed as a dramatic critic for the *Philadelphia Record*, a newspaper owned by his father. Beginning four months later, he became successively comptroller of the *Record*, classified advertising salesman, assistant classified manager, classified manager, promotion manager, and general manager. During the time that Stern was learning the business, he continued to serve the *Record* as part-time dramatic critic. In 1938 he became publisher of the *Courier-Post* newspapers in Camden, New Jersey. Throughout the prewar years, when Stern was a newspaper business executive, his hobby was writing. He wrote some stories and articles in his spare time, but he was unable to sell any of them.

In the spring of 1943, Stern enlisted as a private in the United States Army. He was later commissioned as a second lieutenant, and subsequently became co-officer in charge of the Central Pacific Edition of *Stars and Stripes*. While in the Pacific, Stern wrote some imaginary dialogue between a second lieutenant and an old Army mule, some of which he sold to *Esquire* for approximately $200. He also wrote several short stories while in the Army which he sold to magazines for $50 to $250.

After his release from the Army in 1946, Stern returned to Camden as publisher of the *Courier-Post* newspapers. In 1947 Stern's connection with the *Courier-Post* newspapers was terminated. He immediately entered negotiations to purchase a newspaper. While so doing and at the suggestion of a book publisher, he rewrote, in book form, all of the episodes about the talking mule, Francis. During this period he also wrote a sequel to "Francis," called "Francis Goes to Washington." It, too, was published by Farrar-Strauss, publisher of "Francis." In July 1949 Stern completed negotiations for the purchase of *The New Orleans Item* and took over the controlling interest and active management of the newspaper as its publisher. Since that date, he has devoted virtually his full time to the newspaper business as publisher.

On June 2, 1950 Stern sold to Universal Pictures Co., Inc., all of his "right, title and interest ... in and to ... that certain character known as 'Francis' conceived and created by" him, together with all of his rights to the two novels mentioned above and all of his rights to any contracts with respect to the properties conveyed. In consideration of this transfer, Universal agreed to pay him $50,000 plus 5% of the net profits from photoplays based on the character Francis, and 75% of all sums received by Universal under contracts for the use of licensing of the property. Payment of the $50,000 entitled Universal to a "commitment period" of two years within which to make a motion picture. Thereafter, and following release of each picture, Universal was entitled to additional commitment periods by paying a similar fixed consideration of $50,000 as to each picture or period. The contract further provided that "if purchaser shall elect not to pay fixed consideration with respect to any next succeeding commitment period ... the property shall revert to the seller," all rights in motion pictures produced to remain in Universal. Under this agreement, Universal produced six additional motion pictures in which the character Francis was used. Stern prepared the screen play for the first of these pictures but has had no connection whatever with the writing or production of subsequent pictures except occasionally and incidentally as a consultant. The novel, "Francis Goes to Washington," was not used for screen material.

Plaintiffs have reported as ordinary income for tax purposes all amounts received by them from the sale of the motion picture and publishing rights to the novel "Francis," for preparing a short screen treatment of the book, "Rhubarb," and income received under the agreement for writing screen plays. Only those amounts received from Universal for the character Francis have been treated by plaintiffs as capital gains, accrued during the years received. For the year 1950, the Internal Revenue Service originally accepted plaintiffs' treatment of this income as capital gains from the sale of the character Francis. In considering subsequent years, the Appellate Division of the Internal Revenue reopened the return for the year 1950 and ruled that income from the character Francis was not subject to capital gains treatment for the reason that the contract with Universal was not a sale of the character Francis, that if it were, Francis was property held by the taxpayer primarily for sale to customers in the ordinary course of his business and, further, under the provision of Section 210(a) of the Revenue Act of 1950, amending the provisions of Section 117(a)(1) of the Internal Revenue Code of 1939, 26 U.S.C.A. § 117(a)(1), the character Francis was similar to a copyright, a literary or artistic composition and, therefore, not a capital asset.

Taxpayer has paid the Government the asserted deficiencies in income taxes for the years 1950–53 resulting from the Commissioner's refusal to recognize his treatment of amounts received from Universal Pictures Company pursuant to the contract in suit as a long-term capital gain. Timely claims for refund have been filed and disallowed, after which disallowance this suit was instituted. Taxpayer's position here is the same as it has been since the filing of his original income tax returns. He states that his contract with Universal Pictures Company was a sale of the capital asset, Francis, not in the ordinary course of his business, and, consequently, he is entitled to capital gains treatment of the income received from that sale. The Government here takes the same position taken by the Appellate Division of Internal Revenue Service as well as the Commissioner in his disallowance of the claim for refund.

The question as to whether the taxpayer's contract with Universal Pictures is a sale will be considered first because if it is not a sale, it will be unnecessary to consider the other objections to capital gains treatment of the income made by the Government. It will be noted in the contract that Stern sold all of his interest in the books "Francis," and "Francis Goes to Washington," the character Francis, and all rights and pending contracts concerning them. The agreement makes reference to "the full and complete ownership in the property sold, transferred and granted to (Universal) hereunder." It declares that Stern "hereby sells, transfers and conveys … all right, title and interest" in the property to Universal and guarantees "the full benefit of (Universal's) full and complete ownership in the property." Obviously, the draftsmen of this contract intended that it be a sale and called it such. Apparently they were familiar also with the one case, Cory v. Commissioner of Internal Revenue, 2d Cir., 230 F.2d 941, which the Government cites as authority for its contention that this agreement is not a sale, because the language of the agreement leaves no doubt that Stern transferred his entire bundle of rights in all the Francis properties, together with rights of future exploitation, to Universal Pictures. Thus this agreement is different from the agreement under consideration in *Cory v. Commissioner, supra*, because there the agreement provided for "a transfer of a part of the cluster of rights" inhering in the taxpayer.

The Government's suggestion, without citation of authority, that the contract in suit is not a sale because it provided for contingent payments of indeterminate sums similar to royalties, and because the property reverted back to Stern if the fixed consideration for any period is not paid, cannot convert this contract of sale into a licensing agreement. Perhaps a sale which provides for contingent payments of indeterminate sums and reversion does violence to the doctrinaire concepts of what a sale should be. But the tax cases interpreting Section 117 of the Code have so long and so consistently held such contracts to be sales that the Internal Revenue Service itself in a recent ruling is now indicating its acquiescence in this classification.

The Government next contends that if the contract in suit is a sale, then the income therefrom is still not entitled to capital gains treatment because it was a sale of "property held by the taxpayer primarily for sale to customers in the ordinary course of his trade or business." Section 117(a)(1)(A), Internal Revenue Code of 1939. The resolution of this question depends on appraisal of the total factual situation. Unquestionably, under Section 117(a) of the Code, a taxpayer may have more than one business. Before any business can come within Section 117(a), however, it must be an "occupational undertaking which required the habitual devotion of time, attention or effort with substantial regularity." The criteria in making this determination are fully set forth in opinions by the Fifth Circuit so it would serve no useful purpose to repeat them here. Those cases do show that a court should not be quick to put a man in business under Section 117(a) simply because he has been successful in earning extra income through a hobby or some other endeavor which takes relatively small part of his time.

Here the taxpayer is a newspaper publisher and has been, with the exclusion of the war years, actively directing newspapers since 1938. Virtually his entire time has been given to that endeavor. As a hobby he has written a few short stories, some of which have been productive of small amounts of income. On two occasions he has written screen plays. He has created the character Francis and written two novels about it. This literary work has taken relatively little of his time. It was more or less a relaxation from his principal employment. Under the circumstances, it can hardly be said that the taxpayer created "Francis" to hold as "property held by the taxpayer primarily for sale to customers in the ordinary course of his trade or business." Section 117(a)(1)(A), IRC, 1939.

The Government makes much of the fact that in one of the schedules attached to taxpayer's return, he professes to be a writer. Even if the taxpayer were responsible for this statement, his literary license in this regard should not be allowed to affect the tax treatment accorded his income. Actually, the indication of Stern as a writer was the work of the accountant who prepared the return. It is further noted that the schedule on which the profession appears relates to income and expenses attendant his writing. On the first page of each return in the space provided for "Occupation," the word "Publisher" appears.

Finally, and unfortunately for the taxpayer, the Government's position on the 1950 amendment to the 1939 Code is well taken. That amendment excludes from capital gains treatment income from the sale of "a copyright; a literary, musical, or artistic composition; or similar property" held by "a taxpayer, whose personal efforts created such property." The purpose of this amendment is obvious. It is intended to deny capital gains treatment to income from the sale, by their creator, of literary, musical, or artistic compositions, or similar property. Prior to 1950, various rulings of the Internal Revenue Service had approved capital gains treatment of various literary, musical and artistic compositions, including books and radio programs. Congress determined to eliminate such treatment for such compositions. Hence the amendment.

The taxpayer contends that the character "Francis" is not covered by the amendment, that it is not subject to copyright, that it is not a literary, musical or artistic composition or similar property. He argues that he has paid his taxes at the regular rates on all his income from his writings. He states that the character "Francis" is an "intellectual conception" and that as such the income from the sale thereof is entitled to capital gains treatment.

The taxpayer cites several cases in support of his position that the character Francis is not subject to being copyrighted. And he spends much time in his brief arguing that the Internal Revenue Service itself has limited the words of the statute "or similar property" to property capable of being copyrighted. It is not necessary for this Court to appraise the taxpayer's citations, his argument on this point, or the counter citations and argument of the Government. It is this Court's view that the character Francis, irrespective of its susceptibility to copyright, is "a literary composition" and as such the income from the sale thereof is not entitled to capital gains treatment. The taxpayer concedes, as he must, that the novel, "Francis," in which the character Francis is the leading figure, is a literary composition, but he argues that Francis, the principal characterization in the book, is not. In this he is mistaken. The character Francis gets its definition and its delineation from the book. The literary description in the book composes the character. How can it be said that the book is a literary composition yet the main character delineated therein is not? A slice of the loaf is still bread. It would be absurd to attribute to Congress the intention, under the 1950 amendment, of covering whole literary compositions but not parts thereof, particularly in view of the catchall, "or similar property," which appears at the end of the amendment.

Without the literary description of Francis, his mannerisms and his manifestations, Francis would cease to exist. In any event, an amorphous Francis could hardly be called "property held by the taxpayer," the sale of which is entitled to capital gains treatment. Section 117(a)(1), IRC, 1939. If Francis is, as taxpayer suggests, an "intellectual conception," sans form and substance, existing in the mind alone, it is incapable of ownership and, therefore, of being "property held by the taxpayer." If Francis has sufficient form and substance to be considered property capable of ownership, this is so because of its literary composition.

The taxpayer is entitled to capital gains treatment on the income from the contract in suit for the year 1950 because the 1950 amendment to the Code does not apply to income received during that year. As to subsequent years, however, capital gains treatment of the income from the contract must be denied as proscribed by that amendment.

V. Related Matters

- **Section 1239 Ordinary Income.** Under section 1239, discussed in Chapter 19, any gain recognized on the sale of intellectual property, directly or indirectly, between related parties will be treated as ordinary income if such property is, in the hands of the transferee, subject to the allowance for depreciation provided in section 167. IRC § 1239(a). The purpose behind section 1239 is to prevent taxpayers from selling low-basis, high-value depreciable property to a related party, such as a controlled corporation, in order to step up the property's basis for depreciation purposes in the hands of the related transferee at the low cost of a capital gains tax to the transferor. Section 1239 applies to sales between related persons. Read IRC §§ 1239(b)–(c) for the definition of related persons. Further, section 1239 comes into play only when the property sold is, in the hands of the transferee, subject to the allowance for depreciation provided under section 167. Although patent applications are not depreciable, section 1239 specifically provides that patent applications are treated as depreciable for section 1239 purposes. IRC § 1239(e).

- **Section 1245 Recapture.** Section 1245, also discussed in Chapter 19, provides that gain recognized on the disposition of section 1245 property shall be reported as ordinary income to the extent of any depreciation or amortization deductions taken with respect to the property. IRC § 1245(a). Section 1245 property is defined as depreciable personal property, which includes both tangible and intangible personal property. IRC § 1245(a)(3); Treas. Reg. § 1.1245-3(b). Section 1245 encompasses intellectual property that is subject to the allowance for depreciation under section 167, as well as intellectual property that is subject to fifteen-year amortization under section 197 (because section 197 intangibles are treated as property subject to the allowance for depreciation under section 167). IRC § 197(f)(7). Intellectual property, the development costs of which were deducted under section 174, are not subject to section 1245 recapture. *See* Rev. Rul. 85-186, 1985-2 C.B. 84. Thus, gain attributable to intellectual property developments costs that were currently deducted under section 174 do not have to be recaptured as ordinary income.

Chapter 30

Assignment of Income

I. Assignment

Read: Internal Revenue Code: Skim §§ 1(g), (j)(4); 7872(a), (c)(1)–(2).

Treasury Regulations: None.

Text: Overview
Lucas v. Earl
Helvering v. Horst
Estate of Stranahan v. Commissioner
Related Matters

Complete the problems.

II. Problems

1. Bill Russell earns a substantial salary playing basketball for a team in the National Basketball Association. What are the tax consequences to Bill of the following events?

   (a) At the beginning of the season Bill directs the team to pay $300,000 to a bank to pay off the mortgage on his parent's home. *Bill is Taxed*

   (b) At the all-star game Bill wins the slam dunk contest and receives a Corvette Stingray worth $100,000. Prior to the contest Bill had promised his niece that she could have whatever he won.

   (c) Same as (b) except that under his contract with his agent, Perry Rogers, Perry was entitled to 10% of any prizes earned by Bill. Bill wrote Perry a check for $10,000.

   (d) Halfway through the season Bill declared that he had earned enough and asked the team to pay the remainder of his salary to the American Red Cross.

   (e) Same as (d) except that Bill told the team to give it to any charity they wished.

   (f) During the off season Bill works for a basketball apparel company making appearances at sports conventions which include paid autograph signing sessions. Under his agreement with his employer, the autograph fees are paid to the company.

2. J. Pierpont Morgan owns a building which is leased to a bank. The rent, $10,000 a month, is payable on the 1st day of each month. The rent is paid in advance.

How are Pierpont and his son, Rex, treated for tax purposes in the following circumstances?

(a) On March 1st Pierpont assigns Rex all rent from the building for the rest of the year.

(b) On March 1st Pierpont assigns Rex all rent from the building for the next five years.

(c) On March 1st Pierpont transfers the building and all future rent to Rex.

(d) On March 31st Pierpont transfers the building and all of the year's rent, including the January through March rent, to Rex.

(e) On March 1st Pierpont sells the right to the next three years of rent to Rex for $300,000 which represents the present value of the future payments.

3. Joseph Henry invented and patented a mechanism for communicating telepathically. He sold his patent to a major corporation in exchange for a royalty interest in the sales of the mechanism. Joseph then assigned half of his royalty interest to his nephew, George Phelps, and the other half to his nephew, Samuel Morse. Who is taxed on the royalty income?

4. Bret Maverick won the Powerburst lottery. This entitled him to twenty annual payments of $1,000,000 each. A year later he sold his interest to the remaining payout for one $15,000,000 payment. What is the character of his gain from that payment?

5. Arthur Miller wrote a play about the life of Greta Garbo. Betty Davis entered into a contract with Arthur with respect to the play. Arthur retained legal and equitable title to the play; however, the contract gave Betty the exclusive right to stage the play for five years. It also gave Betty the right to prohibit the production of the play into a film for the longer of five years or as long as the play was running on Broadway. Finally, the contract gave Betty the right to receive 30% of the net profits to star in the play for five years and 25% of the net profits to star in any film version of the play that was produced within five years. A little more than a year later, John Huston approached Arthur and Betty about the possibility of turning the play into a film without it ever being brought to the stage. Ultimately Arthur and Betty agreed to this proposal. Under the agreement between Arthur, Betty and John, the contract between Arthur and Betty was cancelled. In consideration for agreeing to the cancellation of the contract with Arthur, Betty received $3,000,000 from John. Of this amount, $1,000,000 was for giving up the exclusive right to stage the play, $1,000,000 was for giving up the right to prohibit the production of a film version of the play, and $1,000,000 was for agreeing to give up the right to receive 25% of the net profits for starring in the film version of the play. (John thought Betty was not right for the role.) Assuming that Betty had a zero basis in the contract with Arthur, what is the character of the income she received for cancelling the contract?

III. Overview

A. Introduction

Families often operate as a single economic unit. The happy family, like the Three Musketeers, may be "all for one and one for all." In contrast, the federal income tax is primarily levied on an individual basis. There are two major exceptions to this latter principle. The first is the joint filing permitted to married couples considered in Chapter 14. The second is the "Kiddie Tax" noted below.

Because of the progressive rate structure in section 1 of the Code, related taxpayers have some incentive to shift income among themselves in order to take advantage of the lower tax brackets more than once and, sometimes, to avoid the higher brackets altogether. For happy families this tax incentive may accord with their natural impulses. Consider the following example in illustration of these points.

Example: Income Splitting in a Two Bracket Income Tax. Assume an income tax with two rates. The first rate of 25% applies to all taxable income up to $50,000. The second rate of 50% applies to all taxable income over $50,000. In other words we have two tax brackets, a 25% bracket and a 50% bracket. Assume further that Taxpayer A has $100,000 of taxable income from her employment.

A's tax liability is $37,500:

Bracket 1: $50,000 × .25 =	$12,500
Bracket 2: $50,000 × .50 =	$25,000
Total Tax Due	$37,500

Assume that A has an adult daughter, B, living at home. B is a budding artist, but, as yet, has no income. If A could transfer half her income and the tax liability that goes with it to her daughter, it would reduce their aggregate tax liability from $37,500 to $25,000. This would avoid $12,500 of tax.

A's tax liability: $50,000 × .25 =	$12,500
B's tax liability: $50,000 × .25 =	$12,500
Total Tax Due	$25,000

In this second scenario the taxpayers have used the first bracket twice and have avoided the second bracket entirely. As long as A can count on her daughter to spend the money as A prefers, this is a very nice tax dodge. As we will see, however, a taxpayer's ability to engage in this sort of "assignment of income" has been substantially curtailed. The evolution of the law in this area has been long, complex, and is continuing. By and large it has been the courts, rather than Congress, who have sorted out the tax treatment of assigned income.

There are many strands of the court-made "assignment of income doctrine." We will focus on two of these strands: (1) assignments of earned income, and (2) assignments of income from property. We will also take note of assignments designed to convert ordinary income into capital gains. Whether the assignment is gratuitous or for adequate consideration often impacts its treatment. Another area of complexity is the role that community property law can play with respect to determining if there has been an assignment of income.

Note that the present day incentive to assign income from one related taxpayer to another is not quite as great as that in the hypothetical above. The present rate structure for ordinary income is relatively flat by historic standards. At present there are seven brackets for individuals ranging from 10% to 37%. *See* IRC § 1(a)–(d), (j). (The actual rate structure is more nuanced than this because of the phase out rules applicable to various tax benefits and due to the potential application of the alternative minimum tax.)

B. Assignments of Earned Income

1. The Basic Rule and the Community Property Twist

The foundational case on the assignment of income doctrine is *Lucas v. Earl*, which is included in the materials. The Supreme Court held that income is taxed to the person who earned it. This simple rule left many questions unanswered. For example, what if the earner is acting as the agent of another? Or, what if, by operation of law, the income belongs to another? Or what if the earner declines to accept the income? Though *Earl* did not answer these questions, the Court's reasoning provided some hints that subsequent cases embellished upon. Chief among these cases was Poe v. Seaborn, 282 U.S. 101 (1930), decided the same year as *Earl*. *Seaborn* involved the interaction between federal tax law and the community property law of the State of Washington. There, the Court held that half of a husband's earnings was taxed to his wife since by operation of law the earnings belonged to her from the instant they were earned. Though the husband had the authority to spend those earnings, his authority to act arose from an agency relationship rather than from his ownership of the earnings. Thus, income earned by an agent acting for a principal is taxed to the principal, at least when state law creates the agency relationship automatically.

The holding in *Seaborn* led to a significant disparity between the way the income of married couples was taxed in community property states and non-community property states. The community property couples got the benefit of income splitting. The non-community property couples did not. This was one of the reasons that Congress adopted the joint filing system that is in place today. Any married couple who jointly files is automatically treated for tax rate purposes as if each of the spouses earned half of their aggregate income. (But remember this comes at the cost of joint liability.) As a consequence of the joint filing regime, the *Earl/Seaborn* dichotomy is largely irrelevant in harmonious marriages.

The *Seaborn* rule can be a serious disadvantage in the contexts of separation and divorce. Consider both the tax and non-tax aspects of the situation described below.

Example: Community Property, Divorce, and Taxation. Spouses X and Y reside in a community property state. X earns $100,000 a year. Y earns $40,000 a year. Under *Seaborn*, if they file separate tax returns, each must report $70,000 of income.

Assume Y files for divorce on 2/1/Year 1 but no decree of divorce is entered until 1/1/Year 2. Assume further that state law provides that the community continues until the decree is entered. (Not all community property states' laws so provide.)

From 2/1/Year 1, X and Y live apart. Y buys a $15,000 car. X spends freely but acquires no assets. They have no agreement about support. Each lives off what she or he earns.

In Year 2, X reports $70,000 of Year 1 income and pays taxes on it. Y reports $40,000 of Year 1 income and pays taxes on it. The IRS comes along and says there is another $30,000 of income on which tax is owed. Who owes the tax? Quite possibly, it is Y.

To add insult to injury, X may own half of Y's new car under community property law.

It is useful to consider whether Y has a malpractice claim against Y's attorney if Y is held responsible for the taxes on $30,000 of X's earnings.

Practice Pointer

Every lawyer or accountant who practices in the areas of family law, estate planning, tax planning, or who handles property transactions involving married persons should have some familiarity with community property law. This is true even if the lawyer or accountant practices in a non-community property state since the client may have a community property history. Community property may retain its character as such even if the couple moves to a non-community property state. A lawyer or accountant should routinely ascertain whether the client has a community property history. Can you name the nine community property states?

There is a provision, section 66, that can provide relief from the hardship to the lesser earning spouse in cases like the one above. But it has rather limited application.

Domestic Partners: Subsequent to a change in California community property law that clarified the community status of income of registered domestic partners, the IRS has agreed that *Poe v. Seaborn* applies and requires that each partner must report one half of their combined incomes on his or her federal return. Priv. Ltr. Rul. 201021048 (May 5, 2010). For some analysis, see Patricia A. Cain, *Taxation of Domestic Partner Benefits: The Hidden Costs,* University of San Francisco Law Review, Forthcoming, Santa Clara Univ. Legal Studies Research Paper No. 6-11 (available on SSRN). *See also* Patricia A. Cain, *Planning for Same-Sex Couples in 2011*, ALI-ABA Estate Planning Course Materials Journal, Vol. 17, p. 5, June 2011 (available on SSRN).

2. More on Principals and Agents and a Note about Disclaimers

The IRS accepts that a person who earns a fee while acting on behalf of his employer and who, by prior agreement, endorses that fee over to his employer, is not taxable on those earnings. Rev. Rul. 74-581, 1974-2 C.B. 25. In the Service's view, it is essential that the obligation to transfer the funds to the employer arose before the act of earning occurred. The same holds true for disclaimers.

A disclaimer, in the immediate context, is an unconditional refusal to accept earnings to which one is entitled. If the person making the disclaimer does so before the right to receive the income has been fixed, she will not be taxed on the earnings. Rev. Rul. 66-167, 1966-1 C.B. 20. In order to qualify as unconditional, the disclaimant cannot direct the earnings to another. Commissioner v. Giannini, 129 F.2d 638 (9th Cir. 1942). Thus, for example, a disclaimant who refuses her Christmas bonus and asks that it be given to her mother remains taxable on the bonus if her request is granted.

3. The Teschner Twist

An interesting case that straddles the line between agency and the gratuitous assignment of earned income is Teschner v. Commissioner, 38 T.C. 1003 (1963) (nonacq.). In *Teschner*, a father entered a contest and won a valuable prize. By the terms of the contest the father was eligible to enter but, by virtue of his age, was ineligible to win. However, he was permitted in advance to designate a young person to receive the prize in the event he won. He chose his daughter. The question presented was whether father or daughter was taxable with respect to the prize. In a split decision, the Tax Court ruled that daughter must report the income. The majority distinguished *Lucas v. Earl* on the grounds that in *Teschner*, the father did not voluntarily give up the income to his daughter because he never had any right to it. The IRS has not acquiesced to this decision.

C. Assignments of Income from Property

1. Gratuitous Assignments

Normally one who owns a piece of property also owns the income from that property. In such cases it is obvious that the owner of the property is taxed on the income from the property. In the gift context this is an implicit message of the carryover basis rule of section 1015. But what if the owner of the property transfers the right to receive the income from the property to another person while retaining the property itself? Who is taxable on that income now? Generally speaking, if the assignment of the income from property is gratuitous, the owner of the property remains taxable on the income. Helvering v. Horst, 311 U.S. 112 (1940). How the court reached this result is worth studying first hand and the case is included in the materials.

A more nuanced question arose in Blair v. Commissioner, 300 U.S. 5 (1937). In *Blair*, the taxpayer inherited an income interest in trust for life. He had no rights to the trust principal. But, under federal tax law, he was taxed on the trust income distributable to him. Subsequently, he transferred an undivided portion of the income interest to his children and took the position that the children, not he, were henceforth taxable on that income. The IRS disagreed. The Supreme Court held that the assignment was successful in transferring the tax liability to the children. The underlying logic supporting this outcome is the lack of a differentiated retained interest. All Blair owned was an income stream and he gave part of that away. He did not retain the source of the income (indeed he never owned it). Note that the result would have been different had he assigned the income for a limited term such as a year. It is important that he gave up an *undivided* interest in *everything* he had. *See* Harrison v. Shaffner, 312 U.S. 579 (1941). The *Blair* analysis has been extended to the transfer of royalty interests in patents. *See* Heim v. Fitzpatrick, 262 F.2d 887 (2d Cir. 1959).

2. Grantor Trusts, the Kiddie Tax, and the Rate Structure for Entities

From the foregoing it should be apparent that income from property can be assigned to another person if one is willing to transfer the property to the assignee. This leaves some planning opportunities for more affluent members of society. Suppose, for example, that wealthy Grandfather wants to provide for the college education of Grandchild and simultaneously reduce his current income taxes. Grandfather could transfer income producing property to a trust for Grandchild's benefit and thereafter argue that Grandchild should be taxed on the income. Congress thought this planning opportunity was too generous and attacked it in three ways.

First, Congress established the grantor trust rules in sections 671–79. These rules provide that if a grantor sets up a trust but retains any of a number of different rights, including the right to revoke and certain rights of reversion, then the trust income remains taxable to the grantor. The second attack is that the rate structure applicable to entities such as trusts is less graduated than the rate structure for individuals. For example, the top tax rate for income taxed to trusts quickly reaches 37%. IRC § 1(e), (i) & (j). Thus, if the grantor trust rules do not apply, and, instead, the trust is taxed on income from the property that Grandfather transferred for Grandchild's benefit, there is still little or no income tax savings. Finally, if those rules do not apply, there is another attack known as the Kiddie Tax. *See* IRC § 1(g), (j)(4). With some exceptions, it effectively provides that the unearned (i.e., investment) income of children under the age of 18 is taxed at the tax rates for trusts and estates.

3. Assignments after Realization or Accrual

We have seen that generally an assignment of the property that produces the income will cause the assignee to become liable for the taxes on the income from the property. A significant caveat to this principle is that income that is already realized at the time of the assignment remains with the assignor for tax purposes. Suppose, for example, Mother negotiates the sale of a piece of real property at a substantial gain. Suppose further that after the contract has been executed but before the deed has been signed, Mother transfers a half interest in the property to Son. Thereafter Mother and Son convey the property to the buyer and each receive half the proceeds. Who is taxed on the gain? The answer is, Mother. *See* Salvatore v. Commissioner, 29 T.C.M. 89 (1960). Had Mother simply entered into an unenforceable oral agreement with the buyer before making the assignment to Son, the result would likely be different. Thus, one can see that this rule may function as a trap for the unwary or the poorly advised.

Just as realized income is taxed to the owner at the time of realization, so too is accrued income taxed to the person who owned the property at the time of accrual. Thus, for example, if Mother assigns to Daughter her fee simple interest in a rental property after $1,000 of rent has accrued, Mother will remain taxable on that rent even if it is paid to Daughter. Of course, any rent that accrues after the date of the assignment is taxed to Daughter.

4. Allocations of Basis for Gratuitous Assignments in Trust

Recall that bequeathed property takes a date of death fair market value basis under section 1014(a) and gifted property takes a carryover basis for gain purposes under section 1015(a). If the bequest or gift takes the form of a transfer into a trust with a life estate to one beneficiary and a remainder to another, how should that basis be divided between the beneficiaries? The answer is a bit complicated. Initially the basis is allocated between the life tenant and the remainderman in proportion to the fair market values of their interests. But this basis allocation has little utility from the life tenant's perspective. This is because the life tenant is not permitted to deduct any portion of his basis from the income distributions. IRC § 273. Moreover, as time passes, the basis allocable to each interest will shift as their relative values shift. Treas. Reg. § 1.1015-1(b). Thus, when the life tenant dies, the entire basis is allocated to the remainder interest. Even if the life tenant sells his interest, he is denied any of the basis to offset his gain. IRC § 1001(e)(1). There is an exception to this rule if the life tenant and the remainderman sell their entire interests to a third party in one transaction. IRC § 1001(e)(3). Thus, the only way for the life tenant to use basis to reduce the amount of gain allocated to him is through a joint sale with the remainderman.

As an aside, it is worth noting that at the time it is funded, the trust has the same basis in its assets as the aggregate bases of the life tenant and the remainderman. *See, e.g.*, Treas. Reg. §§ 1.1014-4(a), 1.1015-1(b). If the trust holds depreciable property, the depreciation deductions to which it is entitled will serve to reduce the taxable income of the trust. Thus, the life tenant who is taxed on the income distributed to him by the trust indirectly benefits from the basis inherent in its depreciable assets. Except for the brief treatment in Chapter 37 and a few scattered comments, the income taxation of trusts and estates and their beneficiaries is beyond the scope of this book. This area of tax law is governed by subchapter J (IRC §§ 641–91). There is a subtlety and brilliance to subchapter J that defies easy summary and none will be attempted here.

5. Anticipatory Assignments for Value

Thus far we have focused on assignments of income in the form of gifts. But what if a taxpayer *sells* the right to future income while retaining the property that produces the income? If your inclination is to treat this as a transaction governed by section 1001, you are on the right track. By definition one has a zero basis in pre-tax income.

Thus, if one sells the right to future income, one's amount realized is itself pure income. From this one can see that a sale of future income does not on its face raise the same tax avoidance concerns as a gratuitous assignment of income. Indeed it results in an acceleration of tax liability. Thus, the general rule is that a sale of future income will be respected for tax purposes. Still there are games to be played in this area, and there are many cases involving purported sales of future income that have been treated differently from the way in which the taxpayers would have preferred. *See, e.g.,* Mapco Inc. v. United States, 556 F.2d 1107 (Ct. Cl. 1977). The *Estate of Stranahan* case in the materials provides a helpful perspective on the matter.

Normally the sale price of future income will be less than the face amount of all future payments in order to account for the time value of money. We call this "discounting" to present value. Assuming the sale of future income is respected for tax purposes, the buyer takes a section 1012 cost basis in the income. When the full amount of the future income is paid, the buyer will have income determined by reference to the difference between basis and amount realized. Thus, as illustrated below, in the aggregate, the buyer and the seller will recognize the full amount of the future income.

Example: The Taxation of a Sale of Future Income. Alex is a cash method service professional with $100,000 of accounts receivable outstanding. Alex has a cash flow problem and agrees to sell the accounts receivable to Beatrice for their present value of $93,000. Alex, thus, has $93,000 of income on the sale and Beatrice takes a cost basis in the receivables of $93,000. When Beatrice collects the $100,000 from Alex's customers, she will have $7,000 of income. Between Alex and Beatrice all $100,000 of income from the receivables has been recognized. The character of Alex's income is ordinary since the accounts receivable are not capital assets in his hands. *See* IRC § 1221(a)(4). As to the character of Beatrice's income, see the discussion below and section 1234A.

D. Assignments Designed to Transmute Ordinary Income into Capital Gains

As you well understand by now, ordinary income is generally taxed at higher rates than long-term capital gains. It is not surprising then that taxpayers have long sought to transmute one into the other. A leading case in this area is Commissioner v. P.G. Lake Inc., 356 U.S. 260 (1958) (though its precise holding has since been reversed by statute). In *P.G. Lake,* an oil company sold a portion of its future income from wells in which it owned a working interest. It took the position that the sale of a portion of a capital asset produced a capital gain. The Supreme Court held that one who converts future ordinary income to present income will find that present income also to be ordinary. The retention of a continuing interest in the oil property was central to the Court's analysis. While this outcome may seem obvious, in truth, the matter is often quite difficult. This is because all that is needed under the statute in order to realize a capital gain is the sale or exchange of a capital asset. IRC § 1222. And, a capital asset, after all, includes a plethora of differing property rights. *See* IRC § 1221. *See also* Commissioner v. Ferrer, 304 F.2d 125 (2d Cir. 1962) (involving various play and film production rights). Thus, it has proven possible from time to time to sell what looks like ordinary income and receive capital gains treatment. Consider, for example, the case of Commissioner v. Brown, 380 U.S. 563 (1965). There the taxpayer sold a business to a tax exempt charity on an installment basis. The installment payments were payable solely out of the income of the business over a ten year period so that the charity bore no risk. The debt was secured by the assets of the business. During the early part of the post-sale period, the sellers continued to manage the business. The IRS argued that the sale was simply a mechanism for turning ordinary income into capital gains, but the Court held otherwise. The mere fact that the source of payment was the income of the business was deemed irrelevant. Instead the focus was on the actuality of the sale.

We note a couple of additional landmark cases to illustrate the richness of this area of law. In Hort v. Commissioner, 313 U.S. 28 (1941), the taxpayer received $140,000 from his tenant in exchange for the cancellation of their lease agreement. This amount was less than the present value of the future payments under the lease. The taxpayer argued that the lease was a capital asset that was being sold and therefore he suffered a capital loss. The IRS argued the payment was entirely ordinary income. The Court agreed with the government. The payment was a mere substitute for rent which, of course, is ordinary income. Further, since the seller retained the underlying income producing asset, he was entitled to no basis recovery on cancellation of the lease. Contrast *Hort* with Metropolitan Building Co. v. Commissioner, 282 F.2d 592 (9th Cir. 1960), in which a lessee agreed to sell its leasehold interest back to the lessor in order to permit a sublessee to lease directly from the building owner. The funds for the buyout actually came from the sublessee. Again, the government argued that the payment was a substitute for rent (this time arising from payments by sublessee to sublessor) and should be treated as ordinary income. The lessee/sublessor claimed a capital gain on sale of its lease. This time, the court agreed with the taxpayer. It reasoned that, since the lessee was selling everything it had, this was the sale of a capital asset. In some respects, this reasoning harkens back to the *P.G. Lake* case discussed above. The essential distinction between *Hort* and *Metropolitan* is that in *Hort* the taxpayer retained the income producing asset and in *Metropolitan* the taxpayer did not. This distinction is often decisive in these transmutation cases.

Sales of Lottery Winnings. A quite contemporary application of this branch of the assignment of income doctrine has arisen in the context of sales of future lottery installments. The courts have consistently held that such sales yield ordinary income rather than capital gains. *See, e.g.,* Womack v. Commissioner, 510 F.3d 1295 (11th Cir. 2007); Watkins v. Commissioner, 447 F.3d 1269 (10th Cir. 2006); United States v. Maginnis, 356 F.3d 1179 (9th Cir. 2004); Davis v. Commissioner, 119 T.C. 1 (2002). The essential logic for this outcome is that had the taxpayer simply collected the installments as they came due, the income would have been ordinary. From a consistency standpoint the accelerated payments should be treated the same way. But notice that unlike the *P.G. Lake* case there is no retained interest in the underlying asset. Doesn't this make the situation more like *Metropolitan*?

In this short section we have only grazed the surface of this topic. If you would like to learn more about the assignment of income doctrine as it applies to characterization of gains and losses, a good place to begin is the seminal article by Frank Lyon and James Eustice entitled *Assignment of Income: Fruit and Tree as Irrigated by the P.G. Lake Case*, 17 Tax Law Rev. 1 (1964).

E. The Special Case of Gift Loans

It is not unusual for family members to loan money to one another without charging any interest. Since money is always deemed to have value over time, this is the economic equivalent of an assignment (as a gift) of the interest that could have been earned. In cases of small intra-family gift loans, we might be inclined to say "so what?" However, completely ignoring this planning opportunity creates a large tax loophole for the wealthy. For example, suppose that Mother makes a $10,000,000 interest free loan to Son in order to start his own business. If the annual interest rate Mother could have charged a third party borrower is 5%, this is the equivalent of an assignment of $500,000 of interest income a year from Mother to Son. The Supreme Court recognized that under such circumstances a gift was taking place for gift tax purposes. *See* Dickman v. Commissioner, 465 U.S. 330 (1984). Thereafter, Congress codified the *Dickman* result and addressed the income tax significance of these gift loans in section 7872. In essence that section provides that Mother and Son are treated as though Mother made a gift of the "forgone interest" to Son and that Son subsequently paid the interest to Mother (measured by the *applicable federal rate* established by section 1274(d) compounded semi-annually and discussed in Chapter 26). Thus, Mother will have interest income under section 61 and Son may have an interest deduction under section 163.

Section 7872 has application not only to gift loans but also to other loans that may understate interest such as loans between employers and their employees and loans between corporations and their shareholders. Its operation is far more complex than has been described here. There is a de minimis exception for gift loans of less than $10,000.

F. Assignments of Income to Entities

Although this chapter emphasizes assignments of income within the family context, it is worth noting that taxpayers have often attempted to assign income to entities that they control. The highest individual marginal rate is 37%. As we will learn in Chapter 37, the corporate income tax rate is significantly lower—at only 21%. This creates an incentive for an individual to shift earned income to his or her controlled corporation. Assume for example that a lawyer, who is in the highest income tax bracket, provides services to a client. Before collecting from the client, the lawyer transfers the claim for the fee (account receivable in respect of services rendered) to a newly formed corporation in exchange for all the stock. Who is taxed when the company collects on the account receivable? If the company is taxed, the lawyer will have saved $1,600 in taxes ($3,700 − $2,100). The courts and the Service, however, have concluded that where there is a tax avoidance purpose for the transaction (which might be evidenced by the corporation not conducting an ongoing business), the assignment of income rule of *Lucas v. Earl* applies. *See, e.g.,* Rev. Rul. 80-198, 1980-2 C.B. 113; Johnson v. Commissioner, 78 T.C. 882 (1982), *aff'd,* 734 F.2d 20 (9th Cir. 1984). For the use of partnerships to assign income, see IRC §§ 704(e), 761(b) (under general rules defining a partnership, the parties must have joined together to carry on an active trade or business, financial operation, or venture). Here, the lawyer would have to include the receivable in income when received by the company. This example was a clear case of tax avoidance. But in many other cases involving the incorporation of an ongoing sole proprietorship, assignment of income principles will not apply. The rationale is that the change of business form from sole proprietorship or partnership to corporation has a basic business purpose and is not typically designed for deliberate tax avoidance. *See* Hempt Brothers, Inc. v. United States, 480 F.2d 1172 (3d Cir. 1974).

The decision to use a corporation for a *closely held business* must be weighed against many other considerations. For example, corporate profits, although taxed at a low 21% rate, are subject to a second tax when distributed as dividends to shareholders. Recall that qualified dividends are taxed at 20% for high income earners. These combined taxes (.21 + .20) produce an effective rate very close to the individual rate of 37%.

Congress has recently enacted a 20% deduction on qualified business income of sole proprietorships and pass-through entities such as partnerships and LLCs. IRC § 199A. For those who qualify, this means business income is effectively taxed at a top rate of 29.6% instead of 37% (.37 × .80). This may ultimately tip the scales toward use of a pass-through entity rather than a corporation. For further treatment of these issues, see Chapter 37. For present purposes, we mention section 199A because of its potential use by highly compensated individuals to package some of their income inside of passthrough entities in order to take advantage of the 20% deduction. The provision contains various guardrails to prevent this strategy because it is intended to chiefly benefit capital intensive businesses. Time will tell whether tax planners can find lawful mechanisms for taking advantage of section 199A even though their clients were not the intended beneficiaries of the provision. As this area of law develops, we can anticipate that there may be further debate on the fundamental question of whether income from capital deserves to be taxed at lower rates than income from labor.

IV. Materials

Lucas v. Earl

281 U.S. 111 (1930)

Mr. Justice Holmes delivered the opinion of the Court.

This case presents the question whether the respondent, Earl, could be taxed for the whole of the salary and attorney's fees earned by him in the years 1920 and 1921, or should be taxed for only a half of them in view of a contract with his wife which we shall mention. The Commissioner of Internal Revenue and the Board of Tax Appeals imposed a tax upon the whole, but their decision was reversed by the Circuit Court of Appeals. A writ of certiorari was granted by this Court.

By the contract, made in 1901, Earl and his wife agreed "that any property either of us now has or may hereafter acquire … in any way, either by earnings (including salaries, fees, etc.), or any rights by contract or otherwise, during the existence of our marriage, or which we or either of us may receive by gift, bequest, devise, or inheritance, and all the proceeds, issues, and profits of any and all such property shall be treated and considered and hereby is declared to be received, held, taken, and owned by us as joint tenants, and not otherwise, with the right of survivorship." The validity of the contract is not questioned, and we assume it to be unquestionable under the law of the State of California, in which the parties lived. Nevertheless we are of opinion that the Commissioner and Board of Tax Appeals were right.

The Revenue Act of 1918 imposes a tax upon the net income of every individual including "income derived from salaries, wages, or compensation for personal service … of whatever kind and in whatever form paid." § 213 (a). A very forcible argument is presented to the effect that the statute seeks to tax only income beneficially received, and that taking the question more technically the salary and fees became the joint property of Earl and his wife on the very first instant on which they were received. We well might hesitate upon the latter proposition, because however the matter might stand between husband and wife he was the only party to the contracts by which the salary and fees were earned, and it is somewhat hard to say that the last step in the performance of those contracts could be taken by anyone but himself alone. But this case is not to be decided by attenuated subtleties. It turns on the import and reasonable construction of the taxing act. There is no doubt that the statute could tax salaries to those who earned them and provide that the tax could not be escaped by anticipatory arrangements and contracts however skillfully devised to prevent the salary when paid from vesting even for a second in the man who earned it. That seems to us the import of the statute before us and we think that no distinction can be taken according to the motives leading to the arrangement by which the fruits are attributed to a different tree from that on which they grew.

Judgment reversed.

Helvering v. Horst

311 U.S. 112 (1940)

Mr. Justice Stone delivered the opinion of the Court.

The sole question for decision is whether the gift, during the donor's taxable year, of interest coupons detached from the bonds, delivered to the donee and later in the year paid at maturity, is the realization of income taxable to the donor.

In 1934 and 1935 respondent, the owner of negotiable bonds, detached from them negotiable interest coupons shortly before their due date and delivered them as a gift to his son who in the same year collected them at maturity. The Commissioner ruled that under the applicable § 22 of the Revenue Act of 1934, the interest payments were taxable, in the years when paid, to the respondent donor who reported his income on the cash receipts basis. The Circuit Court of Appeals reversed the order of the Board of Tax Appeals sustaining the tax. We granted certiorari because of the importance of the question in the administration of the revenue laws and because of an asserted conflict in principle of the decision below with that of Lucas v. Earl, 281 U.S. 111, and with that of decisions by other circuit courts of appeals.

The court below thought that as the consideration for the coupons had passed to the obligor, the donor had, by the gift, parted with all control over them and their payment, and for that reason the case was distinguishable from *Lucas* v. *Earl, supra*, and Burnet v. Leininger, 285 U.S. 136, where the assignment of compensation for services had preceded the rendition of the services, and where the income was held taxable to the donor.

The holder of a coupon bond is the owner of two independent and separable kinds of right. One is the right to demand and receive at maturity the principal amount of the bond representing capital investment. The other is the right to demand and receive interim payments of interest on the investment in the amounts and on the dates specified by the coupons. Together they are an obligation to pay principal and interest given in exchange for money or property which was presumably the consideration for the obligation of the bond. Here respondent, as owner of the bonds, had acquired the legal right to demand payment at maturity of the interest specified by the coupons and the power to command its payment to others, which constituted an economic gain to him.

Admittedly not all economic gain of the taxpayer is taxable income. From the beginning the revenue laws have been interpreted as defining "realization" of income as the taxable event, rather than the acquisition of the right to receive it. And "realization" is not deemed to occur until the income is paid. But the decisions and regulations have consistently recognized that receipt in cash or property is not the only characteristic of realization of income to a taxpayer on the cash receipts basis. Where the taxpayer does not receive payment of income in money or property realization may occur when the last step is taken by which he obtains the fruition of the economic gain which has already accrued to him. Old Colony Trust Co. v. Commissioner, 279 U.S. 716; Corliss v. Bowers, 281 U.S. 376, 378. Cf. Burnet v. Wells, 289 U.S. 670.

In the ordinary case the taxpayer who acquires the right to receive income is taxed when he receives it, regardless of the time when his right to receive payment accrued. But the rule that income is not taxable until realized has never been taken to mean that the taxpayer even on the cash receipts basis, who has fully enjoyed the benefit of the economic gain represented by his right to receive income, can escape taxation because he has not himself received payment of it from his obligor. The rule, founded on administrative convenience, is only one of postponement of the tax to the final event of enjoyment of the income, usually the receipt of it by the taxpayer, and not one of exemption from taxation where the enjoyment is consummated by some event other than the taxpayer's personal receipt of money or property. This may occur when he has made such use or disposition of his power to receive or control the income as to procure in its place other satisfactions which are of economic worth. The question here is, whether because one who in fact receives payment for services or interest payments is taxable only on his receipt of the payments, he can escape all tax by giving away his right to income in advance of payment. If the taxpayer procures payment directly to his creditors of the items of interest or earnings due him, see *Old Colony Trust Co.* v. *Commissioner, supra;* or if he sets up a revocable trust with income payable to the objects of his bounty, he does not escape taxation because he did not actually receive the money.

Underlying the reasoning in these cases is the thought that income is "realized" by the assignor because he, who owns or controls the source of the income, also controls the disposition of that which he could have received himself and diverts the payment from himself to others as the means of procuring the satisfaction of his wants. The taxpayer has equally enjoyed the fruits of his labor or investment and obtained the satisfaction of his desires whether he collects and uses the income to procure those satisfactions, or whether he disposes of his right to collect it as the means of procuring them.

Although the donor here, by the transfer of the coupons, has precluded any possibility of his collecting them himself, he has nevertheless, by his act, procured payment of the interest as a valuable gift to a member of his family. Such a use of his economic gain, the right to receive income, to procure a satisfaction which can be obtained only by the expenditure of money or property, would seem to be the enjoyment of the income whether the satisfaction is the purchase of goods at the corner grocery, the payment of his debt there, or such nonmaterial satisfactions as may result from the payment of a campaign or community chest contribution, or a gift to his favorite son. Even though he never receives the money, he derives money's worth from the disposition of the coupons which he has used as money or money's worth in the procuring of a satisfaction which is procurable only by the expenditure of money or money's worth. The enjoyment of the economic benefit accruing to him by virtue of his acquisition of the coupons is realized as completely as it would have been if he had collected the interest in dollars and expended them for any of the purposes named.

In a real sense he has enjoyed compensation for money loaned or services rendered, and not any the less so because it is his only reward for them. To say that one who has made a gift thus derived from interest or earnings paid to his donee has never enjoyed or realized the fruits of his investment or labor, because he has assigned them instead of collecting them himself and then paying them over to the donee, is to affront common understanding and to deny the facts of common experience. Common understanding and experience are the touchstones for the interpretation of the revenue laws.

The power to dispose of income is the equivalent of ownership of it. The exercise of that power to procure the payment of income to another is the enjoyment, and hence the realization, of the income by him who exercises it. We have had no difficulty in applying that proposition where the assignment preceded the rendition of the services, *Lucas* v. *Earl, supra; Burnet* v. *Leininger, supra,* for it was recognized in the *Leininger* case that in such a case the rendition of the service by the assignor was the means by which the income was controlled by the donor and of making his assignment effective. But it is the assignment by which the disposition of income is controlled when the service precedes the assignment, and in both cases it is the exercise of the power of disposition of the interest or compensation, with the resulting payment to the donee, which is the enjoyment by the donor of income derived from them.

This was emphasized in Blair v. Commissioner, 300 U.S. 5, on which respondent relies, where the distinction was taken between a gift of income derived from an obligation to pay compensation and a gift of income-producing property. In the circumstances of that case, the right to income from the trust property was thought to be so identified with the equitable ownership of the property, from which alone the beneficiary derived his right to receive the income and his power to command disposition of it, that a gift of the income by the beneficiary became effective only as a gift of his ownership of the property producing it. Since the gift was deemed to be a gift of the property, the income from it was held to be the income of the owner of the property, who was the donee, not the donor—a refinement which was unnecessary if respondent's contention here is right, but one clearly inapplicable to gifts of interest or wages. Unlike income thus derived from an obligation to pay interest or compensation, the income of the trust was regarded as no more the income of the donor than would be the rent from a lease or a crop raised on a farm after the leasehold or the farm had been given away. *Blair* v. *Commissioner, supra,* and cases cited. We have held without deviation that where the donor retains control of the trust property the income is taxable to him although paid to the donee.

The dominant purpose of the revenue laws is the taxation of income to those who earn or otherwise create the right to receive it and enjoy the benefit of it when paid. The tax laid by the 1934 Revenue Act upon income "derived from ... wages, or compensation for personal service, of whatever kind and in whatever form paid, ...; also from interest ..." therefore cannot fairly be interpreted as not applying to income derived from interest or compensation when he who is entitled to receive it makes use of his power to dispose of it in procuring satisfactions which he would otherwise procure only by the use of the money when received.

It is the statute which taxes the income to the donor although paid to his donee. *Lucas* v. *Earl, supra; Burnet* v. *Leininger, supra.* True, in those cases the service which created the right to income followed the assignment, and it was arguable that in point of legal theory the right to the compensation vested instantaneously in the assignor when paid, although he never received it; while here the right of the assignor to receive the income antedated the assignment which transferred the right and thus precluded such an instantaneous vesting. But the statute affords no basis for such "attenuated subtleties." The distinction was explicitly rejected as the basis of decision in *Lucas* v. *Earl.* It should be rejected here; for no more than in the *Earl* case can the purpose of the statute to tax the income to him who earns, or creates and enjoys it be escaped by "anticipatory arrangements however skillfully devised" to prevent the income from vesting even for a second in the donor.

Nor is it perceived that there is any adequate basis for distinguishing between the gift of interest coupons here and a gift of salary or commissions. The owner of a negotiable bond and of the investment which it represents, if not the lender, stands in the place of the lender. When, by the gift of the coupons, he has separated his right to interest payments from his investment and procured the payment of the interest to his donee, he has enjoyed the economic benefits of the income in the same manner and to the same extent as though the transfer were of earnings, and in both cases the import of the statute is that the fruit is not to be attributed to a different tree from that on which it grew. *See Lucas* v. *Earl, supra.*

Reversed.

Estate of Stranahan v. Commissioner

472 F.2d 867 (6th Cir. 1973)

PECK, Circuit Judge.

This appeal comes from the United States Tax Court, which partially denied appellant estate's petition for a redetermination of a deficiency in the decedent's income tax for the taxable period January 1, 1965 through November 10, 1965, the date of decedent's death.

The facts before us are briefly recounted as follows: On March 11, 1964, the decedent, Frank D. Stranahan, entered into a closing agreement with the Commissioner of Internal Revenue Service (IRS) under which it was agreed that decedent owed the IRS $754,815.72 for interest due to deficiencies in federal income, estate and gift taxes regarding several trusts created in 1932. Decedent, a cash-basis taxpayer, paid the amount during his 1964 tax year. Because his personal income for the 1964 tax year would not normally have been high enough to fully absorb the large interest deduction, decedent accelerated his future income to avoid losing the tax benefit of the interest deduction. To accelerate the income, decedent executed an agreement dated December 22, 1964, under which he assigned to his son, Duane Stranahan, $122,820 in anticipated stock dividends from decedent's Champion Spark Plug Company common stock (12,500 shares). At the time both decedent and his son were employees and shareholders of Champion. As consideration for this assignment of future stock dividends, decedent's son paid the decedent $115,000 by check dated December 22, 1964. The decedent thereafter directed the transfer agent for Champion to issue all future dividend checks to his son, Duane, until the aggregate amount of $122,820 had been paid to him. Decedent reported this $115,000 payment as ordinary income for the 1964 tax year and thus was able to deduct the full interest payment from the sum of this payment and his other income. During decedent's taxable year in question, dividends in the total amount of $40,050 were paid to and received by decedent's son. No part of the $40,050 was reported as income in the return filed by decedent's estate for this period. Decedent's son reported this dividend income on his own return as ordinary income subject to the offset of his basis of $115,000, resulting in a net amount of $7,282 of taxable income.

Subsequently, the Commissioner sent appellant (decedent's estate) a notice of deficiency claiming that the $40,050 received by the decedent's son was actually income attributable to the decedent. After making an adjustment which is not relevant here, the Tax Court upheld the deficiency in the amount of $50,916.78. The Tax Court concluded that decedent's assignment of future dividends in exchange for the present discounted cash value of those dividends "though conducted in the form of an assignment of a property right, was in reality a loan to [decedent] masquerading as a sale and so disguised lacked any business purpose; and, therefore, decedent realized taxable income in the year 1965 when the dividend was declared paid."

As pointed out by the Tax Court, several long-standing principles must be recognized. First, under Section 451 (a) of the Internal Revenue Code of 1954, a cash basis taxpayer ordinarily realizes income in the year of receipt rather than the year when earned. Second, a taxpayer who assigns future income for consideration in a bona fide commercial transaction will ordinarily realize ordinary income in the year of receipt. Commissioner v. P. G. Lake, Inc., 356 U.S. 260 (1958); Hort v. Commissioner, 313 U.S. 28 (1941). Third, a taxpayer is free to arrange his financial affairs to minimize his tax liability; thus, the presence of tax avoidance motives will not nullify an otherwise bona fide transaction.[3] We also note there are no claims that the transaction was a sham, the purchase price was inadequate or that decedent did not actually receive the full payment of $115,000 in tax year 1964. And it is agreed decedent had the right to enter into a binding contract to sell his right to future dividends.

The Commissioner's view regards the transaction as merely a temporary shift of funds, with an appropriate interest factor, within the family unit. He argues that no change in the beneficial ownership of the stock was effected and no real risks of ownership were assumed by the son. Therefore, the Commissioner concludes, taxable income was realized not on the formal assignment but rather on the actual payment of the dividends.

It is conceded by taxpayer that the sole aim of the assignment was the acceleration of income so as to fully utilize the interest deduction. Gregory v. Helvering, 293 U.S. 465 (1935), established the landmark principle that the substance of a transaction, and not the form, determines the taxable consequences of that transaction. *See also* Higgins v. Smith, 308 U.S. 473 (1940). In the present transaction, however, it appears that both the form and the substance of the agreement assigned the right to receive future income. What was received by the decedent was the present value of that

---

3. "As to the astuteness of taxpayers in ordering their affairs so as to minimize taxes, we have said that 'the very meaning of a line in the law is that you intentionally may go as close to it as you can if you do not pass it.' Superior Oil Co. v. Mississippi, 280 U.S. 390, 395–96. This is so because 'nobody owes any public duty to pay more than the law demands: taxes are enforced exactions, not voluntary contributions.'" Atlantic Coast Line v. Phillips, 332 U.S. 168, 172–73 (1947) (Frankfurter, J.).

income the son could expect in the future. On the basis of the stock's past performance, the future income could have been (and was[5]) estimated with reasonable accuracy. Essentially, decedent's son paid consideration to receive future income. Of course, the fact of a family transaction does not vitiate the transaction but merely subjects it to special scrutiny. Helvering v. Clifford, 309 U.S. 331 (1940).

We recognize the oft-stated principle that a taxpayer cannot escape taxation by legally assigning or giving away a portion of the income derived from income producing property retained by the taxpayer. Lucas v. Earl, 281 U.S. 111 (1930); Helvering v. Horst, 311 U.S. 112 (1940); *Commissioner v. P. G. Lake, Inc., supra*. Here, however, the acceleration of income was not designed to avoid or escape recognition of the dividends but rather to reduce taxation by fully utilizing a substantial interest deduction which was available.[6] As stated previously, tax avoidance motives alone will not serve to obviate the tax benefits of a transaction. Further, the fact that this was a transaction for good and sufficient consideration, and not merely gratuitous, distinguishes the instant case from the line of authority beginning with *Helvering v. Horst, supra*.

The Tax Court in its opinion relied on three cases. In Fred W. Warner, 5 B.T.A. 963 (1926), which involved an assignment by taxpayer to his wife of all dividend income respecting his 12,500 shares of General Motors Corporation stock, it was held the dividends were income to the taxpayer and were not diverted to the wife through the purported assignment. However, this was a mere gratuitous assignment of income since apparently the only consideration for the assignment was ten dollars. Alfred LeBlanc, 7 B.T.A. 256 (1927), involved a shareholder-father assigning dividends to his son for as long as the son remained with the father's corporation. The Court held that in effect the father postdated his assignment to the dates when he was to receive dividends and hence the dividends were income to the father. However, here again it is apparent that at the time of the assignment there was no consideration. In Trousdale v. Commissioner, 219 F.2d 563 (9th Cir. 1955), a taxpayer-partner attempted to convert future ordinary income into capital by selling his partnership interest. The Ninth Circuit determined that the sale of future partnership profits cannot be converted to capital gain but must be considered ordinary income. It is significant to note that the consideration for the assignment was recognized as ordinary income in the year the assignment was executed even though several outstanding accounts were apparently not collected in full until the following year.

Hence the fact that valuable consideration was an integral part of the transaction distinguishes this case from those where the simple expedient of drawing up legal papers and assigning income to others is used. The Tax Court uses the celebrated metaphor of Justice Holmes regarding the "fruit" and the "tree," and concludes there

---

5. It was determined that with the current dividend payment rate at that time of 50 cents per share per quarter, $115,000 represented the present value of the right to receive the assigned dividends of $4.60 per share discounted at the then prevailing interest rate of five percent.

6. By accelerating income into the year 1964, when it would be offset by the interest deduction, decedent could reduce his potential tax liability for the future years in which the dividends would be paid.

has been no effective separation of the fruit from the tree. Judge Cardozo's comment that "metaphors in law are to be narrowly watched, for starting as devices to liberate thought, they end often by enslaving it" (Berkey v. Third Avenue Railway Co., 244 N.Y. 84, 94, 155 N.E. 58 (1926)) is appropriate here, as the genesis of the metaphor lies in a gratuitous transaction, while the instant situation concerns a transaction for a valuable consideration.

The Commissioner also argues that the possibility of not receiving the dividends was remote, and that since this was particularly known to the parties as shareholders and employees of the corporation, no risks inured to the son. The Commissioner attempts to bolster this argument by pointing out that consideration was computed merely as a discount based on a prevailing interest rate and that the dividends were in fact paid at a rate faster than anticipated. However, it seems clear that risks, however remote, did in fact exist. The fact that the risks did not materialize is irrelevant. Assessment of the risks is a matter of negotiation between the parties and is usually reflected in the terms of the agreement. Since we are not in a position to evaluate those terms, and since we are not aware of any terms which dilute the son's dependence on the dividends alone to return his investment, we cannot say he does not bear the risks of ownership.

Accordingly, we conclude the transaction to be economically realistic, with substance, and therefore should be recognized for tax purposes even though the consequences may be unfavorable to the Commissioner. The facts establish decedent did in fact receive payment. Decedent deposited his son's check for $115,000 to his personal account on December 23, 1964, the day after the agreement was signed. The agreement is unquestionably a complete and valid assignment to decedent's son of all dividends up to $122,820. The son acquired an independent right against the corporation since the latter was notified of the private agreement. Decedent completely divested himself of any interest in the dividends and vested the interest on the day of execution of the agreement with his son.

The Commissioner cites J. A. Martin, 56 T.C. 1255 (1972), aff'd 469 F.2d 1406 (5th Cir. 1972), to show how similar attempts to accelerate income have been rejected by the courts. There taxpayer assigned future rents in return for a stated cash advance. Taxpayer agreed to repay the principal advanced plus a 7% per annum interest. These facts distinguish this situation from the instant case as there the premises were required to remain open for two years' full rental operation, suggesting a guarantee toward repayment. No such commitment is apparent here.

The judgment is reversed and the cause remanded for further proceedings consistent with this opinion.

V. Related Matters

- **IRC § 66.** As mentioned earlier, this section provides narrow relief from liability on community income. It will treat each spouse's earned income as separate for federal tax purposes if the spouses live apart the entire year, do not file a joint return, and no community income is transferred between the spouses.

- **IRC § 73.** This section establishes that a child's earned income is taxed to the child not the parent even when it is paid to the parent.

- **IRC § 1041.** The IRS has ruled that the assignment of income doctrine does not trump section 1041 when one spouse buys out the other's right to future pension income. Rev. Rul. 2002-22, 2002-1 C.B. 849. Thus the payee does not have income and the payor does not get a basis increase.

- **Assignments of Self Created Property.** Assignments of self created property, such as patents and copyrights, will cause the assignee to be taxed on the income therefrom. Rev. Rul. 54-599, 1954-2 C.B. 52.

- **IRC § 1286.** This section applies a rule different from *Horst* to "stripped bonds." When a donor strips a bond by giving away interest coupons, a portion of the donor's basis goes with the gift. The donee is taxed upon receipt of the payments for the coupons but can offset the basis received from the donor against the payments. Thus, from the donor's perspective, the assignment of income is partially effective. When the principal amount of the bond is repaid, the lost basis will cause the donor to have some income. In effect the interest component of the bond has been divided between the bond and the stripped coupons.

Chapter 31

Alimony and Support

I. Assignment

Read: Internal Revenue Code: §§ 71; 215(a)–(b). Skim §§ 166(a)–(b), (d); 212.

Treasury Regulations: §§ 1.71-1T(b) & (c).

Text: Overview
Related Matters

Complete the problems.

II. Problems

1. Henry Tudor and Catherine Aragon were married for several years and have two children, Elizabeth and Mary. In a year prior to 2019, Henry and Catherine begin living apart, and a decree of divorce was entered that directs Henry to pay Catherine $20,000 a year for five years or until her death, whichever is sooner. How are the payments treated for tax purposes in the following circumstances?

    (a) Henry makes the first year payment to Catherine in cash.

    (b) Henry makes the first year payment by transferring a car worth $20,000 to Catherine.

    (c) Same as (a) except that at the direction of the decree Henry pays off a $20,000 note secured by the car owned by Catherine.

    (d) Same as (c) except that Henry pays the note at Catherine's written request.

    (e) Same as (a) except that the Henry and Catherine have a written separation agreement that says the payments are not alimony.

    (f) Same as (a) except the decree directs that the payments shall be reduced by $5,000 per year for each child that achieves an earned income level of $10,000 or more per year.

    (g) Same as (f) except that in the first year, Henry has a liquidity problem and only pays $15,000.

2. Farid Es Sultaneh and S.S. Kresge divorced in 2014 (Year 1). (In 2014, there was a property settlement but no alimony was paid. In Years 2015–2017 (Years 2–4), Farid made cash payments to S.S. that met the definition for alimony in

section 71(b) in the following amounts: $120,000 (Year 2); $100,000 (Year 3); and $60,000 (Year 4).

(a) What are the tax consequences in Year 4 for Farid and S.S. resulting from these payments?

(b) Same as (a) except that S.S. remarries at the end of Year 3 and no payments are made in Year 4.

(c) Same as (a) except that the payments are a fixed portion of the rent from an office building owned by Farid.

III. Overview

A. Introduction

In an earlier chapter, we looked briefly at section 1041 which addresses the tax treatment of property transfers between spouses and between former spouses incident to divorce. In this chapter and the next, we are going to take a closer look at the tax consequences of divorce. Under state law, there are three possible ways to treat payments from one spouse to another as part of a divorce. A payment is either alimony, child support, or a property settlement. Historically, for tax purposes, alimony was ordinary income to the payee and was deductible by the payor. Child support was neither income to the payee nor deductible by the payor. Under past and present tax law, a property settlement is a non-recognition event for both parties and results in a transferred basis. A lawyer representing a party to a divorce needed to be alert to these differing tax treatments of payments and transfers because of the advantages and disadvantages that came with each designation. In this chapter we will look at alimony and child support.

One of the most revolutionary changes for individual taxpayers in The Tax Cuts and Jobs Act of 2017 (TCJA) was in the area of alimony. The TCJA permanently treats alimony as not income to the payee and non-deductible by the payor after 2018. The mechanism for this change was the complete repeal of sections 71 and 215 effective January 1, 2019, with respect to divorce and separation instruments executed on or after that date. This approach does leave sections 71 and 215 in place for divorce and separation instruments executed before that date. For this reason, we will discuss sections 71 and 215 in the present tense for the remainder of this chapter but recognize that for post-2018 divorces, sections 71 and 215 are repealed. The reader may be wondering at this point what law in the future will govern the tax treatment of transfers that are denominated as alimony or child support under state law. The short answer is that section 1041 will govern such transfers. Section 1041 is treated in detail in the next chapter.

The policy basis for the prospective repeal of the alimony deduction appears to be a concern that taxpayers could use the deduction to boost payments to the payee at no increased cost to the payor. This approach took advantage of the likelihood that the payor was in a higher tax bracket than the payee. Thus, the tax cost to the payee of reporting the income was less than the tax cost to the payor of reporting that same amount of income. For this reason, the payee might agree to treat the payment as alimony in exchange for an increase in the amount of the payment offered by the payor. Apparently, Congress saw this planning opportunity as an unwarranted tax subsidy. A counter argument might be that the deductibility of alimony created an incentive for the payor spouse to help the less well-off spouse get her or his life together after the trauma of divorce.

B. Alimony (Before 2019)

Section 71(a) provides for the inclusion of alimony or separate maintenance in the gross income of the payee spouse or former spouse. Section 215(a) provides for a deduction from gross income for the payor spouse or former spouse. The payor's deduction is measured by reference to the payee's inclusion. *See* IRC § 215(b). If the payor and payee are in the same tax brackets, this matching of income and deduction would be revenue neutral for the government. However, more typically, the payor is in a higher tax bracket than the payee; therefore, there is a reduction in the aggregate tax liability of the two people as compared with their aggregate tax liability in the absence of the alimony rule.

Whether a payment is alimony is to a significant degree a matter for negotiation between the parties. Within some limits then, the parties can decide who gets taxed on the income. It is a bargaining chip. Obviously the payor has an incentive to have any payment denominated as alimony rather than as child support or a property settlement since the first is deductible and the other two are not. As a practical matter the payor may have some leverage to force the payee to accept this designation since the payor often is wealthier or has more income than the payee. As we will see, section 71(f) seeks to restrain the parties from characterizing as alimony payments that are really property settlements. The definition of alimony in section 71(b) also acts as a restraint on this tendency.

1. Alimony Requirements

Section 71(b)(1) sets out specific criteria for a payment to constitute alimony for tax purposes. A *cash* payment is alimony if:

a. it is received under a "divorce or separation instrument";

b. it is not designated as a *non*-alimony payment;

c. it is made at a time when the payor and payee are not members of same household (if the divorce is final or there is a legal separation); and

d. there is no liability to make further payments after the death of the payee.

Note that by implication, a "divorce or separation agreement" includes a temporary support order. *See* IRC § 71(b)(2)(C). But the requirement that the spouses live apart does not apply to temporary support orders. Thus, a payment pursuant to a temporary support order can be alimony even if the spouses are still living under the same roof.

This may seem an arcane point but it is surprising how often divorcing spouses continue to live together for some period of time.

Note also that a "divorce or separation agreement" does not include informal agreements set forth in letters from one spouse's attorney to another. *See, e.g.,* Estate of Hill v. Commissioner, 59 T.C. 846 (1973) (disallowing alimony deductions for payments since letter did not constitute a written agreement).

2. Disguised Property Settlements: Section 71(f)

The most complex provision concerning alimony is section 71(f). This provision recaptures what otherwise qualifies for treatment as alimony so that the payor has gross income and the payee has a deduction in a later year. IRC §71(f)(1). It is intended to prevent property settlements from being characterized as alimony by discouraging "front-loading." Front-loading occurs when there are early large cash payments which dwindle in size over a short time, usually three years. The recapture occurs in the third year of post-separation payments, but it arises by reference to an analysis of first and second year post-separation payments. The clock does not begin to run on this analysis until the first year when alimony is paid. Thus, if the divorce occurs in Year 1 and the alimony begins in Year 3, Year 3 is the beginning year for calculating whether there is any recapture. IRC §71(f)(6).

The recapture amount is the sum of the "excess alimony payments" from the first post-separation year and the second post-separation year. IRC §71(f)(2). The recapture computation is performed in reverse order, that is, we calculate the second post-separation year excess alimony payments and then the first year excess alimony payments. This is because one needs to know the second year recapture amount (called the second year "excess payments") to compute the first year recapture amount. Both recapture amounts may be expressed formulaically.

Second Year Excess Payments (E.P.) Formula: IRC §71(f)(4)

$$\text{2nd yr E.P.} = \text{2nd yr pmts} - (\text{3rd yr pmts} + 15{,}000)$$

First Year Excess Payments Formula: IRC §71(f)(3)

$$\text{1st yr E.P.} = \text{1st yr pmts} - \left[\frac{(\text{2nd yr pmts} - \text{2nd yr E.P.} + \text{3rd yr pmts})}{2} + 15{,}000 \right]$$

There are some exceptions to the recapture rules for exigent circumstances such as the death or remarriage of the payee or the death of the payor. IRC §71(f)(5).

Example: Alimony Recapture. A divorce decree requires Alpha to pay Omega (in a form that satisfies section 71(b)) the following sums.

Year 1	$100,000
Year 2	50,000
Year 3	10,000

In each of the three years the payments are deductible by Alpha and includable in gross income by Omega. However, in the third year, there will be recapture of income by Alpha and a deduction by Omega of $92,500 computed as follows:

I. Year 2 Excess Payment: IRC § 71(f)(4).

$$\$25,000 = \$50,000 \text{ 2nd yr pmt} - (\$10,000 \text{ 3rd yr pmt} + \$15,000)$$

II. Year 1 Excess Payment: IRC § 71(f)(3).

$$\$67,500 = \$100,000 \text{ 1st yr pmt} - \left[\frac{(50,000 \text{ 2nd yr pmt} - 25,000 \text{ 2nd yr E.P.} + 10,000 \text{ 3rd yr pmt})}{2} + 15,000 \right]$$

III. Total Excess Payments for Years 1 & 2.

$$\begin{array}{r} \$25,000 \\ + \ \underline{\$67,500} \\ \$92,500 \end{array}$$

For Year 3, Alpha will report $92,500 of income (while also deducting the Year 3 payment of $10,000) and Omega will deduct $92,500 (while also reporting the Year 3 payment as income). Query: Is Omega's deduction an above the line deduction or an itemized deduction? Read carefully IRC § 71(f)(1)(B).

3. Indirect Payments

Payments of cash to someone other than the former spouse can be alimony if the other requirements of section 71(b) are met. *See* IRC § 71(b)(1)(A) (parenthetical language "on behalf of"). Thus, for example, payments on the mortgage of a house owned by the payee spouse can be alimony. The key is that the payment must satisfy an exclusive obligation of the payee spouse. Thus, payments on the mortgage of a house owned by the payor cannot be alimony even if the payee spouse resides in the house. *See* Treas. Reg. § 1.71-1T(b) Q&A 6.

4. Expenses to Obtain Alimony and to Defend against Those Claims

Case law has established that expenses incurred to obtain alimony are deductible under section 212(1) which authorizes deductions for ordinary and necessary expenses incurred "for the production or collection of income." *See* Ruth K. Wild, 42 T.C. 706 (1964). This makes sense because the income obtained will be taxable to the recipient under section 71(a). However, expenses incurred to defend against an alimony claim are not deductible. *See* Fleischman v. Commissioner, 45 T.C. 439 (1966). This outcome is more difficult to explain and discussion of it is deferred to Chapter 35.

C. Child Support

Payments denominated as child support are not deductible by the payor and are not included in the gross income of the payee. IRC § 71(c)(1). This is consistent with the tax treatment of payments in support of the children of non-divorced spouses. While it is possible to disguise child support payments as alimony there are a number of hurdles to prevent this characterization. One of these is the requirement that alimony must terminate upon the death of the payee. Normally one would not want child support to do this. Other hurdles to disguising child support as alimony are the rules of section 71(c) providing that payments which are reduced by the happening of *contingencies relating to the child* such as death, marriage or reaching a certain age are treated as child support. *See* Treas. Reg. § 1.71-1T(b) Q&A 17–18.

1. Failure to Pay

When a payor is obliged to pay both alimony and child support, any shortfall in meeting those obligations first reduces the alimony deemed paid. IRC § 71(c)(3). In other words the payor gets no alimony deduction until first fully satisfying the payor's child support obligation.

Payees who have been unable to collect child support have sometimes sought to deduct the unpaid amounts as non-business bad debts under section 166(d). However, a non-business bad debt is deductible only to the extent of the taxpayer's adjusted basis in the debt, and courts have been unwilling to find a basis in unpaid child support. *See* Diez-Arguelles v. Commissioner, 48 T.C.M. 496 (1984). This is true despite the fact that one can reasonably argue that the expenses of the payee spouse in supporting the child should create a basis in the arrears child support.

2. Expenses to Obtain Child Support

Legal fees incurred to collect child support have been held non-deductible on grounds similar to those for denying deduction of expenses associated with defending an alimony claim. McClendon v. Commissioner, T.C. Memo. 1986-416. This line of reasoning is discussed in Chapter 35.

IV. Materials

None

V. Related Matters

- **Dependency Exemption and Child Tax Credit**. Ordinarily the divorced parent with custody for the greater part of the year (the "custodial parent") is entitled to the dependency exemption for a minor child of the marriage. If the custodial parent waives the exemption *in writing*, the non-custodial parent may have the exemption.

IRC § 152(e). This means that the allocation of the exemption is a matter for negotiation. Currently, the dependency exemption amount is zero, so its real importance is related to the child tax credit. This is because the child tax credit goes to the parent who is entitled to the dependency exemption. *See* IRC §§ 24(a), (c)(1), 152(e)(1).

- **Substitute Payments.** If payments denominated as alimony cease upon the death of the payee but the payor is obliged to make substitute payments to another upon the death of the payee, none of the payments are alimony for federal tax purposes. *See* Hoover v. Commissioner, 102 F.3d 842 (6th Cir. 1996); Okerson v. Commissioner, 123 T.C. 258 (2004).

- **Palimony.** Court ordered payments to former lovers, sometimes called "palimony," may be categorized as payments for past services (taxable to the payee) or as property divisions. Green v. Commissioner, T.C. Memo 1987-503. Palimony arises from right of contract. *See* Marvin v. Marvin, 557 P.2d 106 (Cal. 1976). Voluntary payments to lovers are usually treated as gifts for tax purposes. *See* United States v. Harris, 942 F.2d 1125 (9th Cir. 1991).

Chapter 32

Transfers of Property between Spouses or Incident to Divorce

I. Assignment

Read: Internal Revenue Code: §§ 402(a), (e)(1)(A); 1041; 1223(2). Skim §§ 83(a)–(b); 301(a), (c)(1); 302(a), (b)(3), (d); 414(p)(1).

Treasury Regulations: §§ 1.1041-1T (b)–(d); 1.1041-2.

Text: Overview
Craven v. United States
Revenue Ruling 2002-22
Related Matters

Complete the problems.

II. Problems

1. Medea and Euripides were divorced in Year 1. What are the consequences of the following transactions?

   (a) In Year 1, pursuant to their divorce decree, Medea transferred to Euripides her half interest in a piece of investment land they had owned for years as community property. Her share of their basis was $50,000 and her interest was worth $250,000.

   (b) Same as (a) except that Euripides pays Medea $250,000 cash for her interest.

   (c) Same as (b) except that Euripides pays only $100,000 but assumes Medea's half of a $300,000 mortgage on the property.

   (d) Same as (b) except that the property transferred are zero basis accounts receivable from their closely held business.

   (e) What if in (a) Euripides immediately sold the land for $500,000 in cash to a third party?

   (f) Same as (a) except that Medea transferred the interest to Sophocles in satisfaction of a $250,000 debt that Euripides owed Sophocles.

2. Napoleon and Josephine started a successful software company, Jonapster, Inc., shortly after their marriage. They each owned 50% of the Jonapster stock with

each having a $10,000 basis in their respective blocks of stock. Fifteen years later they divorced. Assuming there are no agreements other than those described, what are the tax consequences to Josephine and Napoleon of the following transactions?

(a) Pursuant to the divorce instrument Napoleon sells his Jonapster stock to Josephine for $500,000.

(b) Pursuant to the divorce instrument Napoleon sells his Jonapster stock back to Jonapster for $500,000. Josephine had no obligation to buy the stock.

(c) The divorce instrument places a primary and unconditional obligation on Josephine to buy Napoleon's Jonapster stock for $500,000. However, the parties agreed that the funds for the buyout would come from Jonapster. Jonapster issued a check for $500,000 to Napoleon and Napoleon transferred his stock to Josephine.

(d) Same as (c) except that Napoleon transferred his stock to Jonapster.

3. Charybdis and Scylla, who are both age 60, were married for 35 years before divorcing. A major property interest acquired during the marriage is Scylla's deferred compensation retirement account. On the date of the divorce the account was worth $1,000,000. All of the funds in this account were contributed on a pre-tax basis and will be ordinary income to someone when distributed. Who will be taxed on the distributions described below?

(a) As part of the divorce it is agreed that when Charybdis reaches age 65, Scylla will begin making payments to Charybdis of $4,000 per month in settlement of Charybdis' claims against Scylla's retirement account. When Scylla and Charybdis reach age 65, Scylla begins receiving distributions of $8,000 per month from Scylla's retirement account. Scylla then pays $4,000 of that amount to Charybdis each month.

(b) As part of the divorce the judge enters a qualified domestic relations order (QDRO) equally dividing the retirement account into two retirement accounts, one for Scylla and one for Charybdis. When Scylla and Charybdis reach age 65 each begins receiving distributions of $4,000 per month from their respective retirement accounts.

III. Overview

A. Property Settlements

Generally, property transfers, other than gifts, trigger gain or loss recognition under section 1001. This was the general rule for the tax treatment of transfers between spouses or former spouses incident to divorce in an earlier era. *See* United States v. Davis, 370 U.S. 65 (1962). Today, however, property passing from one spouse to another or from one former spouse to another in settlement of their respective property rights has no immediate income recognition consequence for either party. As of 2019, all transfers of property, including cash, between spouses and between former spouses incident to divorce are governed by section 1041. This provision prevents recognition of gain or loss by the transferor. IRC § 1041(a). It also indirectly provides that the transferee has no income by specifying that the transfer is treated as a gift. IRC § 1041(b)(1). *See* IRC § 102(a). It further provides for a transferred basis *in all cases* for the transferee. IRC § 1041(b)(2). In this last respect, it differs from section 1015(a) which sometimes denies a transferred basis for loss recognition purposes. Note that the transferred basis also means that the transferee will tack onto the transferor's holding period. IRC § 1223(2). Though section 1041 is a relatively straightforward provision, it has many nuances, some of which are explored in this chapter.

B. Transfers Incident to Divorce

Any transfer of property between spouses is governed by section 1041. However, with respect to former spouses it only applies to transfers "incident to the divorce." IRC § 1041(a)(2). A transfer between former spouses is deemed incident to the divorce if it occurs within one year from the date on which the marriage ends or is "related to the cessation of the marriage." IRC § 1041(c). The regulations flesh out the meaning of this last phrase. In general, they provide that a transfer is related to the cessation of the marriage if it is pursuant to a divorce or separation instrument (as defined in section 71(b)(2)) and the transfer occurs within six years of the marriage's end. Treas. Reg. § 1.1041-1T Q&A 7. Annulments are treated as divorces for this and other section 1041 purposes. *Id.*

C. Transfers to Third Parties

Under limited circumstances a transfer of property to a third party can qualify for treatment under section 1041. Essentially, section 1041 will apply when either the divorce decree or a written agreement between the spouses authorizes a spouse or former spouse to make the payment on behalf of the other spouse or former spouse. Treas. Reg. § 1.1041-1T(c) Q&A 9. The effect is to grant non-recognition to the transferor spouse in the same way as if the transferor had made the transfer to the other spouse. Thereafter the non-transferor spouse is treated as if he or she had made a taxable transfer to the third party. Thus, normally transfers to third parties cause the deemed transferee spouse or former spouse to recognize gain or loss.

Example. The divorce decree requires that husband transfer stock worth $100,000 to wife. The stock has a basis of $40,000 in husband's hands. Pursuant to a written agreement with wife, husband transfers the stock to Bank X in satisfaction of wife's home mortgage. Pursuant to Treas. Reg. § 1.1041-1T(c) Q&A 9, husband will receive non-recognition treatment under section 1041(a). Wife will recognize $60,000 of gain on her deemed transfer of the stock to Bank X.

D. Incorporated Family Businesses

It is not uncommon for married couples to own businesses together. Often when such couples divorce one party (the remaining spouse) will buy out the other party's (the departing spouse's) interest in the business. Generally, section 1041 applies to such transactions in a straightforward fashion. But special problems can arise for buyouts in which the business is conducted as a corporation. There are basically three ways to structure the purchase of the departing spouse's stock: a straight purchase, a distribution combined with a purchase, or a redemption. Each of these forms requires a different analysis for tax purposes.

Straight Purchase. A straight purchase is a sale of the stock to the remaining spouse in which the remaining spouse uses his or her own funds for the purchase. This is a classic section 1041 transaction in which the departing spouse receives non-recognition and the remaining spouse takes a carry over basis.

Distribution Followed by Purchase. In this scenario, the funds for the purchase are distributed from the corporation to the remaining spouse who then transfers them to the departing spouse in exchange for the departing spouse's stock. Tax treatment of distributions are governed by section 301. Typically, the remaining spouse is treated as having dividend income. The purchase is treated as a section 1041 transaction. Thus, the remaining spouse gets taxed and the departing spouse gets non-recognition. Notice that despite recognizing income the remaining spouse gets no basis adjustment in the stock received from the departing spouse. IRC § 1041(b)(2). This tax payment without basis step up makes this an unappealing option to the remaining spouse.

Redemption. A redemption is a purchase of the shareholder's stock by the issuing corporation. Tax treatment of a redemption is governed by section 302. Normally, if the form of this transaction is respected, the departing spouse is treated as having engaged in a sale or exchange with the corporation. *See* IRC §§ 302(a) & (b)(3). Thus, section 1041 does not apply, and the departing spouse will recognize gain or loss. The remaining spouse is unaffected from a tax standpoint.

The first and second scenarios described above are taxed according to their forms. However, redemptions raise complexities that have taken some time to resolve. In a number of cases, the departing spouse argued successfully that section 1041 non-recognition applied even when he or she sold her stock back to the corporation. The *Craven v. United States* case in the materials illustrates the analysis that led to this result. The upshot of these cases was considerable uncertainty about the tax treatment of divorce-related redemptions.

Subsequent to the *Craven* case, the government promulgated Treasury Regulation § 1.1041-2. With some exceptions, the regulation provides that if the buyout is structured as a redemption of the departing spouse's stock, section 1041 will *not* apply. Treas. Reg. § 1.1041-2(a)(1). In other words, the form of the transaction will be respected for tax purposes. Thus, the redemption will usually be a gain or loss recognition event for the departing spouse. However, the regulation creates an exception to this general rule for a redemption that as a matter of law would be treated as a constructive distribution to the remaining spouse. Treas. Reg. § 1.1041-2(a)(2). The typical situation in which the law will imply a constructive distribution to the remaining spouse is when the redemption is carried out to satisfy the remaining spouse's "primary and unconditional obligation" to buy the shares from the departing spouse. *See* Treas. Reg. § 1.1041-2(d) ex. 1. If the constructive distribution exception applies, the transaction is treated as though the distribution was made to the remaining spouse who then buys the departing spouse's stock and surrenders it back to the corporation. In other words, it is the *remaining* spouse who is treated as having engaged in a redemption with the corporation. *See* Treas. Reg. § 1.1041-2(a)(2). Under this scenario the departing spouse will get non-recognition under section 1041. The remaining spouse's redemption will likely fail to qualify for sale or exchange treatment and instead will be treated as a dividend. *See* IRC § 302(d).

To complicate things further (but in a taxpayer friendly way), the regulation permits the parties to override both the main redemption rule and its constructive distribution exception by agreement. In other words, they can agree to flip flop the outcomes just described. *See* Treas. Reg. § 1.1041-2(c)(1), (2).

E. Assignment of Income Doctrine and Division of Pensions and Other Ordinary Income Rights

Often the spouses' pensions and retirement account rights are the most valuable assets of the marriage. Thus, proper division of these accounts upon divorce is vitally important. Typically under state law each spouse will own some portion of the other spouse's pension. In most cases pensions and retirement accounts are forms of deferred compensation that have not yet been taxed to the earner. Thus, a division of such an account could be viewed as an assignment of income from the earner spouse to the non-earner spouse. There was a time when the Service took the view that section 1041 did not apply to transfers of rights to ordinary income and, instead, the assignment of income doctrine applied unless a more specific statute controlled. However, the Service has begun to retreat from that position. See Revenue Ruling 2002-22 found in the materials. Note that for qualified pensions there is a specific provision that obviates any question of the assignment of income doctrine applying. Instead it makes clear that the payee is the one who is taxed. *See* IRC § 402(e)(1)(A).

A point of practical importance is that, under the Employee Retirement Income Security Act (ERISA), divisions of pensions and retirement accounts must be carried out through "qualified domestic relations orders" (QDROs). Otherwise they will not be respected by pension managers. QDROs have various technical requirements. *See* 29 U.S.C. § 1056(d). Failure to properly draft a pension division as a QDRO can have serious adverse consequences. *See, e.g.,* Hamilton v. Wash. State Plumbing & Pipefitting Indus. Pension Plan, 433 F.3d 1091 (9th Cir. 2005).

F. Policies Supporting Section 1041

Section 1041 rests on differing policy considerations for ongoing marriages and for failing marriages. In the case of ongoing marriages, the rationale for section 1041 is that the couple is a single economic unit and transfers between the spouses should thus be ignored. In the case of failed marriages the rationale is two fold. First, divorce is not an appropriate time to impose tax because to do so would impose a hardship and a potential trap at a time of crisis. Second, the former rules often led to inconsistent treatment by the parties that cost the government money or at least a lot of time in litigation. This happened when the transferor failed to report any gain but the transferee claimed a stepped up basis. Though section 1041 grants deferral it also establishes clear tax consequences upon a future transfer of the property by the transferee spouse.

IV. Materials

Craven v. United States

215 F.3d 1201 (11th Cir. 2000)

Cynthia Holcomb Hall, Senior Circuit Judge:

The United States appeals an order granting summary judgment in favor of Linda Craven ("Linda"). Linda had sued the Internal Revenue Service ("IRS") seeking a refund of certain proceeds she had received from her divorce settlement which she claimed were not taxable to her. [W]e affirm.

The following facts are undisputed by both parties: Linda married Billy Joe Craven ("Billy Joe") in 1966. In 1971, the couple started their own pottery business, in which they both worked. In 1975, Billy Joe incorporated the business under the name of Craven Pottery, Inc. ("the corporation"). The corporation was formed with Billy Joe owning 51% of the stock, Linda owning 47% of the stock, and the remaining 2% being owned by their two children at 1% each respectively. Billy Joe became the corporation's president.

Linda stopped working at the corporation in 1987, because of the souring of the Cravens' marriage. In 1988 the Cravens separated, and in 1989, Linda sued Billy Joe and the corporation for a divorce seeking damages against both Billy Joe and the corporation for misappropriation of her salary. Her requested relief consisted in a demand that the corporation be sold and that the proceeds be divided up amongst the shareholders.

In 1991, a divorce decree was entered into. This decree contained a settlement agreement between Billy Joe, Linda, and the corporation, and settled all matters between the parties. By terms of this agreement, Billy Joe and Linda agreed to divide their marital property. In relevant part, Linda agreed to sell to the corporation, and the corporation agreed to buy, her stock pursuant to a consent in lieu of special joint meetings of directors and shareholders of the corporation. The divorce was the sole reason for Linda's agreement to transfer the stock.

The corporation gave Linda a promissory note in the face amount of $4.8 million for her stock. Billy Joe guaranteed the note and expressly acknowledged that its terms were of "direct interest, benefit and advantage" to him. The note was payable in 120 equal monthly payments beginning in July 2000, together with the lump sum payments of $1 million each in June 2000, 2005, and 2010. The corporation had the option of electing to pay any amount due under the promissory note before its due date by paying its then present value, and such payments were to be applied in satisfaction of the lump sum payments first beginning with one due in 2010, next liquidating the payment due in 2005, then the one due in 2000, and lastly the monthly installments. In determining the present value of a payment, it was to be discounted from the due date to the date of payment by applying an annual interest rate of 7.5% as the discount rate. The stock redemption agreement between Linda and the corporation provided that the payments under the note were without stated interest, and that the corporation would send taxpayer Forms 1099-INT stating the amounts of interest imputed to her under 26 U.S.C. § 1272 ("§ 1272").

Four prepayments of the note were made, the first by Billy Joe in 1991 and the remaining three prepayments by the corporation in 1992, 1993, and 1998. Pursuant to the stock redemption agreement, the corporation filed Forms 1099-INT for the years 1992, 1993, and 1994, reflecting interest income imputed to Linda on the note. Linda did not report the imputed interest income on the note, nor did she report capital gains from the redemption of her stock in the corporation in her tax returns for 1992, 1993, and 1994. However, she filed disclosure statements taking the position that the redemption qualified for nonrecognition under 26 U.S.C. § 1041 (" § 1041").

After an audit, the IRS determined that the redemption did not qualify for nonrecognition treatment under § 1041 and that, consequently, Linda had capital gains based on the principal of the prepayments on the note. Linda paid the resulting tax, filed a timely claim for refund, and after that claim was denied, sued for the refund in federal district court.

The district court held that Linda qualified for nonrecognition under § 1041 because the redemption fell within the confines of Temp. Treas. Reg. § 1.1041-1T(c) (Q&A 9) ("Q&A 9") which states that under certain circumstances a transfer of property to a third party on behalf of a spouse (or former spouse) will qualify under § 1041. The district court reached this conclusion because the redemption came as a result of Billy Joe's obligation under Georgia law to equitably divide all marital assets. The district court noted that since Billy Joe had guaranteed the corporation's payment of the note, and since Billy Joe was, in effect, in complete control over the corporation, all arrangements made by Linda pursuant to the divorce settlement were to be considered "on behalf" of Billy Joe.

The central issue of this case is whether Linda can avoid recognition of gain on the redemption of her stock in Craven's Pottery, Inc. in accordance with a property settlement incident to a divorce.

The income tax consequences that would normally ensue from this transaction are clear when § 1041 does not apply. Where a redemption of stock completely terminates the shareholder's interest in the corporation, the Internal Revenue Code treats the redemption as a sale of stock. *See* 26 U.S.C. §§ 302(a) & (b)(3). The amount by which the payment of principal received by the shareholder from the sale of the stock exceeds the taxpayer's basis in the stock constitutes gain, which is ordinarily taxed as capital gain. *See* 26 U.S.C. § 1001(a). The IRS accordingly determined that, in this case, taxpayer had capital gains based on the principal of the prepayments made to her on the notes of $187,922 in 1992 and $285,709 in 1993.

Section 1041 provides a broad rule of nonrecognition for sales, gifts, and other transfers of property between one spouse (or former spouse) and another. It provides in relevant part, that:

> No gain or loss shall be recognized on a transfer of property from an individual to (or in trust for the benefit of) —
>
> (1) a spouse, or
>
> (2) a former spouse, but only if the transfer is incident to the divorce.

Thus, the provision is not limited to transfers in divorce, but also applies to conveyances between spouses who are not contemplating divorce. Under § 1041(b), property received in a transfer subject to § 1041 is excluded from the recipient's gross income as if it were a gift, even if the transfer is a cash sale or is made without donative intent as part of a contested divorce. The recipient takes a "carryover" basis for the property equal to the transferor's basis, even if it exceeds the value of the property at the time of the transfer.

Shortly after the enactment of § 1041, the Treasury department published a temporary regulation, which is still in effect, to provide guidance to taxpayers. The Ninth Question of 26 C.F.R. § 1.1041-1T, which is relevant to the present appeal, states in pertinent part:

> Q-9 May transfers of property to third parties on behalf of a spouse (or former spouse) qualify under § 1041?
>
> A-9 Yes. There are three situations in which a transfer of property to a third party on behalf of a spouse (or former spouse) will qualify under § 1041. The first situation is where the transfer to the third party is required by a divorce or separation instrument. The second situation is where the transfer to the third party is pursuant to the written request of the other spouse (or former spouse). The third situation is where the transferor receives from the other spouse (or former spouse) a written consent or ratification of the transfer to the third party.... In the three situations described above, the transfer of property will be treated as made directly to the nontransferring spouse

(or former spouse) and the nontransferring spouse will be treated as immediately transferring the property to the third party. The deemed transfer from the nontransferring spouse (or former spouse) to the third party is not a transaction that qualifies for nonrecognition of gain under § 1041.

An example of such an occurrence is where the husband owes a debt to a bank, and the wife, as part of the divorce settlement, transfers appreciated stock of her own directly to the bank in discharge of husband's debt. Such a transfer would fall within the first "situation" described in the regulation, *i.e.*, the transfer would be one "required by a divorce or separation instrument" and would be treated as made by the wife "on behalf of" the husband. Therefore, the stock would be deemed to go first from wife to husband in a nonrecognition transaction covered by § 1041, with husband acquiring a carryover basis in the stock, and then from husband to the bank, which would trigger gain to husband measured by the excess of the discharged debt over the carryover basis. The effect of this would be to preserve the element of gain, but to shift the incidence of the tax from wife to husband, "on behalf of" whom wife made the transfer to the "third party" bank.

Linda contends that her transfer of stock qualified for nonrecognition treatment under § 1041 as interpreted in Temp. Reg. § 1.1041-1T(c). She argues that the transfer of the stock to the corporation was done pursuant to her divorce agreement and therefore was on behalf of her former spouse within the language and purposes of the temporary regulations. The IRS disputes that the transfer was "on behalf of" Billy Joe so as to come within the regulation and shield Linda from recognizing gain. It is undisputed that the transfer occurred incidental to the Cravens' divorce. Therefore, the central question is whether the transfer was made by Linda "on behalf" of Billy Joe. Linda offered the district court three main reasons, which the district court agreed with, for why § 1041 would apply to her redemption of the stock: (1) because Georgia law obligates the equal distribution of marital assets pursuant to a divorce agreement, Linda was obligated to redeem her stock to the corporation; (2) Billy Joe was the guarantor of the corporation's payments that were due on the note, and because Georgia law makes guarantors jointly and severally liable for any debts incurred on the note, her redemption of the stock was "on behalf" of Billy Joe; and (3) because the corporation is a closely held one where, after the redemption, Billy Joe owned 98% of the stock, Linda's transfer was, in effect, to her husband.

In agreeing with Linda's arguments, the district court relied primarily on Arnes v. United States, 981 F.2d 456 (9th Cir.1992) ("*Arnes I*"). In *Arnes I*, the divorcing spouses, who each owned 50% of a corporation that ran a McDonald's franchise, were required to transfer the entire ownership to one of the spouses according to McDonald's policy. As a result, the divorce decree had one spouse sell her 50% stock interest to the corporation for a dollar amount which the other spouse guaranteed. The Ninth Circuit ruled that this transaction came within the confines of § 1041 because the redemption relieved the husband of an obligation to purchase his wife's stock and thereby conferred a benefit upon him. The district court in this case ruled the facts and analysis of *Arnes I* were squarely on point.

The *Arnes I* decision has been called into question as being factually and analytically flawed. *See* Blatt v. Commissioner, 102 T.C. 77 (1994) (reviewed by the court). *Blatt* explained the faulty reasoning of *Arnes I* by pointing out that the Ninth Circuit never identified where the obligation of the husband to buy the stock came from. Indeed, as the Tax Court held in a subsequent case, Arnes v. Commissioner, 102 T.C. 522, 528–29 (1994) ("*Arnes II*"), it was the corporation which was under the obligation to buy the wife's stock, and not the husband. Thus, the redemption was "on behalf" of the corporation, and not the husband, and § 1041 should not have been implicated as a result.

Fortunately, a recent Tax Court decision that came down after the district court reached its decision in this case, and after both parties had already completed their briefing before this Court, resolved the tension between *Blatt, Arnes I, Arnes II,* and the facts of this case. *See* Read v. Commissioner, [Current] Tax. Ct. Rep. (CCH) No. 53,736, at 3911 (Feb. 4, 2000) (reviewed by the court). The parties were aware of *Read* before oral argument because both submitted Federal Rules of Appellate Procedure 28(j) notices regarding this new case, and the matter was debated extensively at oral argument.

In *Read,* the Tax Court was confronted with facts that are basically identical to the ones at issue in this case. In that case, a husband ("H") and a wife ("W") owned all the voting, and virtually all of the non-voting stock of a corporation ("C"). When H and W divorced, pursuant to the divorce order, H elected to buy out W's shares in C by having C purchase W's stock, and by having C issue a promissory note to W bearing 9% interest for the balance of the purchase price. H then unconditionally guaranteed the payments by C to W in his individual capacity.

As in this case, the issue in *Read* was whether § 1041, as interpreted in Q&A 9, operated to deny recognition of the gain resulting to W on the transfer of her stock to C. The Tax Court held that under § 1041, the gain was not to be recognized for tax purposes. In interpreting the meaning of the term "on behalf" from Q&A 9, the Tax Court rejected the notion that under Q&A 9, § 1041 only applies if H had a "primary-and-unconditional-obligation" to purchase W's stock, stating that the "primary-and-unconditional-obligation" standard was "not an appropriate standard to apply in any case involving a corporate redemption in a divorce setting in order to determine whether the transfer of property by the transferring spouse to a third party is on behalf of the nontransferring spouse within the meaning of Q&A 9." *Id.* at 3921. The Tax Court noted that the "primary-and-unconditional-obligation" standard applies when the corporation pays H's debt for H and such payment is deemed a dividend to H. Rather, the Tax Court gave the term "on behalf" a plain meaning such as "in the interest of" or "as a representative of," and ruled that because W was acting under H's election as mandated by their divorce decree, W was acting "on behalf" of H and therefore fell within the rubric of § 1041 and Q&A 9.

Given the detailed and comprehensive analysis undertaken by the *Read* court, and the factual similarities between *Read* and this case, we find the *Read* result persuasive. As illustrated above, the meaning of the phrase "on behalf" reflects the notion that a transfer from A to C is treated for tax purposes as a transfer from A to B to C, when A is in fact transferring on behalf of B to C. *See e.g. Blatt,* 102 T.C. at 81; *Read,* [Current] Tax. Ct. Rep. at 3923. The facts of this case show that the transfer from Linda to the corporation squarely comports with this understood definition of "on behalf."

The three facts that place Linda within the framework outlined by the *Read* court are: (1) she was redeeming her stock pursuant to the divorce settlement; (2) Billy Joe guaranteed the note; and (3) in that note Billy Joe acknowledged that its terms were of "direct interest, benefit and advantage" to him. The first fact enumerated above would be enough on its own to qualify Linda's transfer to the corporation for nonrecognition under § 1041. The other two facts simply add strength to this conclusion. When the Cravens settled their divorce, they agreed to this redemption, and subscribed to a document that obligated Linda to transfer her stock to the corporation. In so doing, Linda was acting "on behalf" of Billy Joe because the divorce settlement reflected Billy Joe's wishes on the matter. Therefore, the Cravens' divorce settlement is akin to H's election in *Read,* which the *Read* court found decisive in its ruling that W was acting on H's behalf in transferring her stock to C. This implication is confirmed by Billy Joe's explicit action of guaranteeing the note in his individual capacity, something H did as well in *Read,* and expressing in the guarantee that such an action was in his "interest." "Interest" is exactly what precedent instructs us is the plain meaning of "on behalf" and we need not look any further to determine that Billy Joe's interest, as admitted by him and as evidenced by his agreeing to the divorce settlement, was being served by Linda's transfer of her stock to the corporation.

We hold that the proceeds of Linda's transfer to the corporation fit within the terms outlined by § 1041 and Q&A 9, and therefore qualify for nonrecognition. This holding follows the rationale behind the adoption of § 1041 because it "facilitates the division of a marital estate incident to divorce without taxation to the spouse who is withdrawing assets from the marital estate." *See Read* at 3926 (Colvin, J., concurring). As such, Congress' stated purpose of broadly applying § 1041 to transactions between divorcing spouses incident to their divorce is properly served.

AFFIRMED.

Revenue Ruling 2002-22

2002-1 C.B. 849

ISSUES

(1) Is a taxpayer who transfers interests in nonstatutory stock options and nonqualified deferred compensation to the taxpayer's former spouse incident to divorce required to include an amount in gross income upon the transfer?

(2) Is the taxpayer or the former spouse required to include an amount in gross income when the former spouse exercises the stock options or when the deferred compensation is paid or made available to the former spouse?

FACTS

Prior to their divorce in 2002, *A* and *B* were married individuals residing in State *X* who used the cash receipts and disbursements method of accounting.

A is employed by Corporation *Y*. Prior to the divorce, *Y* issued nonstatutory stock options to *A* as part of *A*'s compensation. The nonstatutory stock options did not have a readily ascertainable fair market value within the meaning of § 1.83-7 (b) of the Income Tax Regulations at the time granted to *A*, and thus no amount was included in *A*'s gross income with respect to those options at the time of grant.

Y maintains two unfunded, nonqualified deferred compensation plans under which *A* earns the right to receive post-employment payments from *Y*. Under one of the deferred compensation plans, participants are entitled to payments based on the balance of individual accounts. By the time of *A*'s divorce from *B*, *A* had an account balance of $100x under that plan. Under the second deferred compensation plan maintained by *Y*, participants are entitled to receive single sum or periodic payments following separation from service based on a formula reflecting their years of service and compensation history with *Y*. By the time of *A*'s divorce from *B*, *A* had accrued the right to receive a single sum payment of $50x under that plan following *A*'s termination of employment with *Y*. *A*'s contractual rights to the deferred compensation benefits under these plans were not contingent on *A*'s performance of future services for *Y*.

Under the law of State *X*, stock options and unfunded deferred compensation rights earned by a spouse during the period of marriage are marital property subject to equitable division between the spouses in the event of divorce. Pursuant to the property settlement incorporated into their judgment of divorce, *A* transferred to *B* (1) one-third of the nonstatutory stock options issued to *A* by *Y*, (2) the right to receive deferred compensation payments from *Y* under the account balance plan based on $75x of *A*'s account balance under that plan at the time of the divorce, and (3) the right to receive a single sum payment of $25x from *Y* under the other deferred compensation plan upon *A*'s termination of employment with *Y*.

In 2006, *B* exercises all of the stock options and receives *Y* stock with a fair market value in excess of the exercise price of the options. In 2011, *A* terminates employment with *Y*, and *B* receives a single sum payment of $150x from the account balance plan and a single sum payment of $25x from the other deferred compensation plan.

LAW AND ANALYSIS

Section 1041 and the assignment of income doctrine

Section 1041(a) provides that no gain or loss is recognized on a transfer of property from an individual to or for the benefit of a spouse or if the transfer is incident to divorce, a former spouse. Section 1041(b) provides that the property transferred is generally treated as acquired by the transferee by gift and that the transferee's basis in the property is the adjusted basis of the transferor.

Section 1041 was enacted in part to reverse the effect of the Supreme Court's decision in United States v. Davis, 370 U.S. 65 (1962), which held that the transfer of appreciated property to a spouse (or former spouse) in exchange for the release of marital claims was a taxable event resulting in the recognition of gain or loss to the transferor. *See* H.R. Rep. No. 432, 98th Cong., 2d Sess. 1491 (1984). Section 1041 was intended to "make the tax laws as unintrusive as possible with respect to relations between spouses" and to provide "uniform Federal income tax consequences" for transfers of property between spouses incident to divorce, "notwithstanding that the property may be subject to differing state property laws." *Id.* at 1492. Congress thus intended that § 1041 would eliminate differing federal tax treatment of property transfers and divisions between divorcing taxpayers who reside in community property states and those who reside in noncommunity property states.

The term "property" is not defined in § 1041. However, there is no indication that Congress intended "property" to have a restricted meaning under § 1041. To the contrary, Congress indicated that § 1041 should apply broadly to transfers of many types of property, including those that involve a right to receive ordinary income that has accrued in an economic sense (such as interests in trusts and annuities). *Id.* at 1491. Accordingly, stock options and unfunded deferred compensation rights may constitute property within the meaning of § 1041. *See also* Balding v. Commissioner, 98 T.C. 368 (1992) (marital rights to military pension treated as property under § 1041).

Although § 1041 provides nonrecognition treatment to transfers between spouses and former spouses, whether income derived from the transferred property and paid to the transferee is taxed to the transferor or the transferee depends upon the applicability of the assignment of income doctrine. As first enunciated in Lucas v. Earl, 281 U.S. 111 (1930), the assignment of income doctrine provides that income is ordinarily taxed to the person who earns it, and that the incidence of income taxation may not be shifted by anticipatory assignments. However, the courts and the Service have long recognized that the assignment of income doctrine does not apply to every transfer of future income rights. *See. e.g.,* Rubin v. Commissioner, 429 F.2d 650 (2d Cir. 1970); Hempt Bros., Inc. v. United States. 490 F.2d 1172 (3d Cir. 1974), *cert. denied*, 419 U.S. 826 (1974); Rev. Rul. 80-198 (1980-2 C.B. 113). Moreover, in cases arising before the effective date of § 1041, a number of courts had concluded that transfers of income rights between divorcing spouses were not voluntary assignments within the scope of the assignment of income doctrine. *See* Meisner v. United States, 133 F.3d 654 (8th Cir. 1998); Kenfield v. United States, 783 F.2d 966 (10th Cir. 1986); Scludze v. Commissioner, T.C.M. 1983-263; Cofield v. Koehler, 207 F. Supp. 73 (D. Kan. 1962).

In *Hempt Bros., Inc. v. United States*, the court concluded that the assignment of income doctrine should not apply to the transfer of accounts receivable by a cash basis partnership to a controlled corporation in a transaction described in § 351(a), where there was a valid business purpose for the transfer of the accounts receivable together with the other assets and liabilities of the partnership to effect the incorporation of an ongoing business. The court reasoned that application of the assignment of income doctrine to tax the transferor in such circumstances would frustrate the Congressional intent reflected in the nonrecognition rule of § 351(a). Accordingly, the transferee, not the transferor, was taxed as it received payment of the receivables. In Rev. Rul. 80-198, the Service adopted the court's position in *Hempt Bros.*, but ruled that the assignment of income doctrine would nonetheless apply to transfers to controlled corporations where there was a tax avoidance purpose.

Similarly, applying the assignment of income doctrine in divorce cases to tax the transferor spouse when the transferee spouse ultimately receives income from the property transferred in the divorce would frustrate the purpose of § 1041 with respect to divorcing spouses. That tax treatment would impose substantial burdens on marital property settlements involving such property and thwart the purpose of allowing divorcing spouses to sever their ownership interests in property with as little tax intrusion as possible. Further, there is no indication that Congress intended § 1041 to alter the principle established in the pre-1041 cases such as *Meisner* that the application of the assignment of income doctrine generally is inappropriate in the context of divorce.

Specific provisions governing nonstatutory stock options

Section 83(a) provides, in general, that if property is transferred to any person in connection with the performance of services, the excess of the fair market value of the property over the amount, if any, paid for the property is included in the gross income of the person performing the services in the first taxable year in which the rights of the person having the beneficial interest in such property are transferable or are not subject to a substantial risk of forfeiture, whichever is applicable. In the case of nonstatutory stock options that do not have a readily ascertainable fair market value at the date of grant, § 83 does not apply to the grant of the option, but applies to property received upon exercise of the option or to any money or other property received in an arm's length disposition of the option. *See* § 83(e) and § 1.83-7(a).

Although a transfer of nonstatutory stock options in connection with a marital property settlement may, as a factual matter, involve an arm's length exchange for money, property, or other valuable consideration, it would contravene the gift treatment prescribed by § 1041 to include the value of the consideration in the transferor's income under § 83. Accordingly, the transfer of nonstatutory stock options between divorcing spouses is entitled to nonrecognition treatment under § 1041.

When the transferee exercises the stock options, the transferee rather than the transferor realizes gross income to the extent determined by § 83(a). Since § 1041 was intended to eliminate differing federal tax treatment for property transferred or divided between spouses in connection with divorce in community property states and in non-community property states, § 83(a) is properly applied in the same manner in both contexts. Where compensation rights are earned through the performance of services by one spouse in a community property state, the portion of the compensation treated as owned by the non-earning spouse under state law is treated as the gross income of the non-earning spouse for federal income tax purposes. Poe v. Seaborn, 282 U.S. 101 (1930). Thus, even though the non-employee spouse in a non-community property state may not have state law ownership rights in nonstatutory stock options at the time of grant, § 1041 requires that the ownership rights acquired by such a spouse in a marital property settlement be given the same federal income tax effect as the ownership rights of a non-employee spouse in a community property state. Accordingly, upon the subsequent exercise of the nonstatutory stock options, the property transferred to the non-employee spouse has the same character and is includable in the gross income of the non-employee spouse under §83(a) to the same extent as if the nonemployee spouse were the person who actually performed the services.

The same conclusion would apply in a case in which an employee transfers a statutory stock option (such as those governed by §422 or 423(b)) contrary to its terms to a spouse or former spouse in connection with divorce. The option would be disqualified as a statutory stock option, see §§422(b)(5) and 423(b)(9), and treated in the same manner as other nonstatutory stock options. Section 424(c)(4), which provides that a §1041(a) transfer of stock acquired on the exercise of a statutory stock option is not a disqualifying disposition, does not apply to a transfer of the stock option. *See* H.R. Rep. No. 795, 100th Cong., 2d Sess. 378 (1988) (noting that the purpose of the amendment made to §424(c) is to "clarify[y] that the transfer of stock acquired pursuant to the exercise of an incentive stock option between spouses or incident to divorce is tax free").

CONCLUSION

Under the present facts, the interests in nonstatutory stock options and nonqualified deferred compensation that *A* transfers to *B* are property within the meaning of §1041. Section 1041 confers nonrecognition treatment on any gain that *A* might otherwise realize when *A* transfers these interests to *B* in 2002. Further, the assignment of income doctrine does not apply to these transfers. Therefore, *A* is not required to include in gross income any income resulting from *B*'s exercise of the stock options in 2006 or the payment of deferred compensation to *B* in 2011. When *B* exercises the stock options in 2006, *B* must include in income an amount determined under 83(a) as if *B* were the person who performed the services. In addition, *B* must include the amount realized from payments of deferred compensation in income in the year such payments are paid or made available to *B*. The same conclusions would apply if *A* and *B* resided in a community property state and all or some of these income rights constituted community property that was divided between *A* and *B* as part of their divorce.

HOLDINGS

(1) A taxpayer who transfers interests in nonstatutory stock options and nonqualified deferred compensation to the taxpayer's former spouse incident to divorce is not required to include an amount in gross income upon the transfer.

(2) The former spouse, and not the taxpayer, is required to include an amount in gross income when the former spouse exercises the stock options or when the deferred compensation is paid or made available to the former spouse.

V. Related Matters

- **Property Transfers Pursuant to Prenuptial Agreements.** Property transfers made prior to marriage pursuant to prenuptial agreements are outside the operation of section 1041. Most likely they are taxable events for the transferor rather than gifts.

See Farid-Es-Sultaneh v. Commissioner, 160 F.2d 812 (2d Cir. 1947). Typically one party transfers tangible or intangible property to the other in exchange for the other's agreement to waive any additional property claims in the event of divorce. It is apparently the Service's position that the party waiving any further claims does not have income at the time of the transfer and takes a date of transfer fair market value basis in the property. *See* Rev. Rul. 67-221, 1967-2 C.B. 63. If the agreement is signed before marriage but the transfers occur after the marriage, should section 1041 apply?

- **Unmarried Co-Habitants.** Transfers between unmarried persons living together are outside the operation of section 1041.

- **Deductibility of Expenses Relating to Property Settlements.** Generally speaking, expenses, including attorney's fees, incurred as part of a property settlement are non-deductible. The deductibility of attorney's fees is addressed in Chapter 35.

- **Social Security Aspects of Marriage and Divorce.** A spouse who does not work outside the home acquires social security rights by virtue of marriage to a working spouse. Generally the homemaker is entitled to social security benefits equal to half the amount to which his or her spouse is entitled. *See* 42 U.S.C. §402. This right to benefits is not affected by a divorce that occurs after more than ten years of marriage. However, remarriage before age sixty will terminate these benefit rights.

Chapter 33

Education Benefits and Costs

I. Assignment

Read: Internal Revenue Code: §§ 25A; 108(f); 117; 127; 132(d); 221; 222. Skim §§ 135; 529; 530.

Treasury Regulations: § 1.25A-5(e)(3); Prop. Treas. Reg. 1.117-6(c)(2), (d), Ex. 5.

Text: Overview
Revenue Ruling 2008-34
Related Matters

Complete the problems.

II. Problems

1. David Johnston is a geologist for a mining company who specializes in finding deposits of precious metals, especially gold. He holds a masters degree in geology. He takes evening courses at his local university in order to earn a doctorate in geology. His purpose in pursuing a doctorate is to obtain a position as a professor of geology. Professors are required to have a Ph.D.

   (a) May he deduct the costs of his doctorate as an ordinary and necessary business expense under section 162?

   (b) Same as (a) except that when he becomes a professor he plans to continue to work for industry as a part time consultant, a common practice among professors?

   (c) What if he does not plan to become a professor but believes that the added credential will allow him to establish his own consulting business instead of working as an employee for a single company?

   (d) What if he is pursuing his doctorate because his employer requires that he hold a doctorate in order to advance in the company?

2. The following eleven students are taking classes at State University Law School, which has a full-time J.D. program the tuition of which is $20,000 per year. Unless noted otherwise, assume that each student is enrolled full-time in Law School's J.D. program. Describe generally the tax consequences for each of the following:

(a) Amber, who has impressive academic credentials, receives a full tuition scholarship from Law School. Amber is not required to perform services to Law School as a condition of receiving the scholarship.

(b) Brad receives a full tuition scholarship from a reputable tax law firm. As a condition to receiving the scholarship, Brad agrees to work for the law firm after graduation. Brad has no previous relationship with the law firm.

(c) Chad is a long-time employee at Law School who is now pursuing a J.D. degree (in the school's part-time program). Because Chad has at least five years of continuous full-time employment with Law School, Chad receives a waiver benefit of 100% of the cost of tuition under Law School's Post Graduate Tuition Benefits Program. Chad is not engaged in teaching or research for Law School.

(d) Doug, who had a career before entering law school, has substantial savings that generate interest and dividend income. Doug pays his own tuition with some of his savings. Doug is not a dependent of any other taxpayer.

(e) Ed's parents pay Ed's tuition with a combination of previous income and current income savings. Ed is 22 years old and his parents properly claim him as a dependent.

(f) Fran pays her tuition with a $15,000 cash gift she received from Grandmother.

(g) Greg has no savings and receives no financial assistance to pay tuition. Greg thus borrows $8,500 in subsidized federal loans and the rest in private loans to attend law school. The interest on the federal loans is deferred, but Greg pays interest on the private loans each year.

(h) Henry has been awarded a $15,000 loan to pay tuition as part of Law School's Foundation's Loan Repayment Assistance Program. The loan, which is evidenced by a promissory note bearing adequate interest, will be forgiven provided he remains employed on a full-time basis in a public interest job.

(i) Irene, a full-time paralegal at a local tax law firm, receives a "forgivable loan" from her employer to attend Law School (in the school's part-time program). One of the terms of the forgivable loan contract is that Irene must work at least three years at the law firm after obtaining the J.D. degree or she will have to repay the borrowed funds with interest. The firm also agrees to pay Irene additional compensation in the year of discharge to help pay taxes owed on the income from discharge of indebtedness.

(j) Joy, a full-time paralegal at a local corporate law firm, merely "audits" two business law courses at Law School to enhance her business law knowledge. Joy is not enrolled in the J.D. program and plans to remain a paralegal. Joy's employer pays the tuition for these courses.

(k) Karen's tuition is paid from a distribution from the state's NextGen 529 College Investing Plan managed by Merrill Lynch. Karen's parents have been making contribution to the plan for a number of years in anticipation of Karen's attending law school.

III. Overview

Education has many beneficial aspects in life. It can broaden and deepen our understanding of the world in which we live. It can introduce us to lifelong friends. It can enhance our sense of community and enrich our inner landscapes. It can equip us to earn a decent living. Indeed, it is often an avenue to prosperity. To some it may seem like the only way out of poverty. It is no wonder, then, that many of us devote years beyond high school and large sums of money to obtaining associate, baccalaureate, professional, and other advanced degrees. Moreover, many of us continue to seek educational opportunities throughout our working lives and may even leave homemaking or the workforce in order to return to school as full time students. When we lose our jobs, or our marriage fails, or our children are out of the home, obtaining more education may seem the best (or only) career-planning move available.

Not only is education valuable to us as individuals, it also has value for society. A better educated citizenry may hope to have a higher standard of living. It is likely to be a more productive workforce and to add value in every endeavor to which it addresses itself. Or so we may believe. If we value education in our society, it makes sense that our government should assist its citizens in their efforts to obtain it. But what are the best mechanisms for such assistance? In kindergarten through high school and in our public colleges and universities, we directly subsidize the schools so that the immediate costs to the student are eliminated or reduced. But other, less direct, mechanisms are also available, and Congress has seized upon a number of them.

This chapter brings together a patchwork quilt of provisions addressing the income tax treatment of education. As will be described below, some education expenses are deductible as business expenses under section 162. More often, however, education is treated as a personal matter within the meaning of section 262 even though much of education may be devoted to preparing to enter a job or profession. In addition, the cost of education is often considered a capital expenditure within the scope of section 263 rather than as a current expense. To counter these principles of tax policy, Congress has enacted several provisions that allow either a deduction or a credit for educational expenses that are not otherwise deductible under section 162. Congress also has enacted varying exclusion provisions relating to scholarships and grants, employer-provided educational assistance, and educational savings. Many of these deductions, credits, and exclusions apply not only to the taxpayer, but also to the taxpayer's spouse and dependents. In what follows we briefly survey this area of law without attempting a detailed treatment.

A. Business Education

Education expenses are deductible under section 162 if they are incurred in order to maintain or improve skills in a trade or business in which the taxpayer is already engaged. Treas. Reg. § 1.162-5(a)(1). Education expenses are also deductible under section 162 if they are incurred to meet the requirements of one's employer or of one's profession as a condition to retention of employment. Treas. Reg. § 1.162-

5(a)(2). However, education expenses incurred to meet the minimum requirements for qualifying to engage in a trade or business are considered personal and are not deductible under section 162. Treas. Reg. § 1.162-5(b)(2). Nor does section 162 authorize a deduction for educational expenses incurred in order to enter a new trade or business. Treas. Reg. § 1.162-5(b)(3). For a case holding that a German lawyer could not deduct the cost of obtaining a J.D. from the University of San Diego Law School, *see* O'Connor v. Commissioner, T.C. Memo 2015-155.

B. Scholarships and Fellowships

The government and many colleges and universities offer aid to students in the form of grants and scholarships. Under certain conditions section 117(a) excludes from gross income these amounts received by a taxpayer to aid him or her in the pursuit of study or research. Prop. Treas. Reg. § 1.117-6(c)(3)(i). The taxpayer must be a degree candidate at an educational organization (i.e., an institution which maintains a regular faculty and curriculum). IRC §§ 117(a), 170(b)(1)(A)(ii). And the scholarship or fellowship grant must be used for qualified tuition and related expenses (i.e., tuition and fees for required books, supplies, and equipment, but not meals, lodging, and other personal expenses). IRC § 117(b); Prop. Treas. Reg. § 1.117-6(c)(2). The scholarship or fellowship must not represent payment for teaching, research, or other services (including future services) required of the student as a condition for receiving the scholarship or fellowship. IRC § 117(c); Prop. Treas. Reg. § 1.117-6(d).

Example. Student receives a $6,000 scholarship from University. As a condition to receiving the scholarship, Student performs research services for University. Other researchers who are not scholarship recipients receive $2,000 for similar services. $2,000 of the scholarship must be included in Student's gross income as wages, and $4,000 of the scholarship can be excluded under section 117(a) if used for qualified tuition and related expenditures. Prop. Treas. Reg. § 1.117-6(d), ex. 5.

C. Employer-Provided Educational Assistance

Employers sometimes provide educational assistance to their employees and their dependents. Absent an exclusion rule, the assistance would be considered taxable compensation to the employee. IRC § 61(a)(1). Employer-employee scholarships typically fail to qualify for exclusion under section 117(a), just discussed. *See* Bingler v. Johnson, 394 U.S. 741 (1969) (holding an employer-employee scholarship was taxable compensation). However, the Code contains other provisions that exclude some employer-provided educational benefits.

1. Qualified Tuition Reductions

An employee of an educational organization (or such employee's spouse or dependent child) who receives a tuition waiver or reduction in tuition for education at such organization (or another educational organization) may be entitled to exclude the benefit from gross income if certain requirements are satisfied. IRC § 117(d). The tuition reduction must be for education below the graduate level unless it is for a graduate student engaged in teaching or research activities. IRC § 117(d)(2), (5). And the tuition reduction must be available to employees so as not to discriminate in favor of highly compensated employees. IRC § 117(d)(3). As with the tax treatment of scholarship and fellowships, the tuition reduction must not represent payment for teaching, research, or other services required of the student to receive the tuition reduction. IRC § 117(c).

2. Educational Assistance Programs

Section 127 allows a taxpayer-employee to exclude up to $5,250 from gross income of amounts paid by any employer for education of the employee (tuition, books, and supplies, or an employer-provided educational course) at the undergraduate or graduate level. IRC § 127(c)(1) (the payment must not be for education involving sports, games, or hobbies). The employer-provided educational assistance program must be furnished pursuant to a program or written plan that does not discriminate in favor of highly compensated employees. IRC § 127(b). Employer-provided educational assistance that exceeds the $5,250 maximum, or that is otherwise disqualified under section 127, may nevertheless qualify for exclusion as a working condition fringe benefit. IRC § 132(j)(8).

3. Working Condition Fringe Benefits

Section 132(d) permits a taxpayer-employee to exclude from gross income employer-provided educational assistance if the taxpayer would have been entitled to deduct the education as a business expense under section 162 had the taxpayer paid for the education herself. Review Treas. Reg. § 1.162-5(a)–(b), discussed above.

D. Education Loans

Absent government grants, university scholarships, or employer-provided educational assistance, families must often borrow money to pay for college. Loans for education can come from a variety of sources: banks, retirement plans with loan features, home equity lines of credit, etc. As addressed early in the course, student loans are not included in gross income because of the obligation to repay the debt in full at some point in the future.

1. Deductibility of Interest

Recall from Chapter 11 that personal interest is generally not deductible. IRC § 163(h)(1). There is an important exception, however. Interest on loans used to pay for education may be deductible under section 221. IRC § 163(h)(2)(F). Under section 221, up to $2,500 of interest paid on higher education loans for cost of attendance (tuition, fees, room and board, and related expenses, less certain nontaxable educational benefits and qualified scholarships received) is deductible. IRC § 221(a), (d). The deduction is an above-the-line deduction. IRC § 62(a)(17).

The amount of loan interest that may be deducted under section 221 is phased out for taxpayers at moderate income levels, which are adjusted annually for inflation.

IRC § 221(b)(2), (f). For 2017, for example, the $2,500 maximum deduction began to phase out for taxpayers with modified adjusted gross income in excess of $65,000 ($135,000 for joint filers), and was completely phased out for taxpayers with modified adjusted gross income of $80,000 ($165,000 for joint filers). Rev. Proc. 2016-55, 2016-45 I.R.B. 707. When you graduate from school and begin paying back your student loans, will you benefit from section 221?

Interest on home equity loans is not deductible for tax years 2018 through 2025. IRC § 163(h)(3)(F). Prior to 2018, a taxpayer could deduct interest if a family got a home equity loan to pay for education costs. The maximum amount for "home equity indebtedness," however, was $100,000. *See* IRC § 163(h)(2)(D), (3).

2. Forgiveness of Student Loans

There are many different types of student loan forgiveness programs. As part of some income-based repayment programs, some federal student loan debt gets forgiven after a certain period of time. As part of its Federal Stafford Loan Forgiveness Program, the federal government will cancel all or part of an educational loan if the student performs certain volunteer work, or performs military service, or teaches or practices medicine in certain types of communities. Many educational organizations, such as non-profit law school foundations, have designed loan repayment assistance programs for graduates who pursue public service work.

Loan forgiveness is generally considered income to the borrower. IRC § 61(a)(12). There are exceptions. Section 108(f), for example, excludes discharged student loans if, among other things, the student whose loan is discharged works for a certain period of time "in certain professions." There is nothing in the Code explaining the meaning of this phrase. In *Moloney v. Commissioner*, the Tax Court stated in dicta that "[t]he term 'certain professions' to which section 108(f)(1) applies are medicine, nursing, and teaching." T.C. Summ. Op. 2006-53 n.5 (Apr. 17, 2006). Does this mean that section 108(f)(1) does not apply to a student who is performing work in the legal profession, a profession other than the ones mentioned? In Revenue Ruling 2008-34, included below, the Service clarified that law school loan forgiveness programs qualify for the section 108(f)(1) exception. The Service also clarified that a loan made under a law school's loan repayment assistance program that refinances the graduate's original student loan(s) meets the definition of "student loan" in section 108(f)(2).

Student loan debt discharge exclusion has been expanded to include discharges because of the student's death or total and permanent disability. IRC § 108(f)(5). The exclusion applies to discharges of *eligible* loans after 2017 and before 2026. Eligible loans is interpreted broadly, and includes certain private education loans. *See* IRC § 108(f)(5)(B).

E. Special Credits and Deduction for Qualified Tuition and Related Expenses

As discussed more fully in Chapter 15, Congress has enacted two provisions that permit some expenditures for higher education to be credited: the Hope Scholarship

Credit (a per student credit) and the Life Time Learning Credit (a per taxpayer credit). IRC § 25A. Recall that the 2015 PATH Act made permanent the previously temporary American Opportunity Tax Credit in section 25A(i). The American Opportunity Tax Credit modified the Hope Scholarship Credit in a number of favorable ways (e.g., the modified credit was increased to $2,500 and was made applicable to the first four years of college instead of just the first two).

The modified Hope Scholarship Credit (now known as the American Opportunity Tax Credit) and the Lifetime Learning Credit are mutually exclusive credits for qualified tuition and related expenses at an eligible institution of higher education for the taxpayer, the taxpayer's spouse, and the taxpayer's dependents. IRC § 25A(f)(1); Treas. Reg. § 1.25A-2(d)(2)(ii), (3). Any expenses satisfied by funds excluded from income under section 117 (qualified scholarships) or section 127 (educational assistance programs) cannot be credited. IRC § 25A(g)(2). However, tuition funded by gifts that are excluded under section 102 do qualify for the credits. IRC § 25A(g)(2)(C). And, expenses paid with loan proceeds are eligible for the credits in the payment year, not the year the loan is repaid. Treas. Reg. § 1.25A-5(e)(3). The total amount of combined credit under section 25A is subject to phase-out as the taxpayer's modified adjusted gross income rises above certain limits. IRC § 25A(d), (i)(4). The phase-out limits are adjusted for inflation. IRC § 25A(h)(2). Note that the American Opportunity Tax Credit is partially refundable in certain cases. IRC § 25A(i)(5).

Section 222 allows a deduction of up to $4,000 for qualified tuition and related expenses. The definition of qualified tuition and related expenses is borrowed from the Hope Scholarship Credit (now American Opportunity Tax Credit) and Lifetime Learning Credit. IRC § 222(d)(1). As with the education credits, the section 222 deduction is subject to income phase out rules. IRC § 222(b)(2). The deduction may not be used for qualifying expenses of an individual for whom either of the education credits is claimed. IRC § 222(c). Thus, a taxpayer must decide between the credit or the deduction. Any expenses satisfied by funds excluded from income under sections 117 or 127 cannot be deducted, but qualified expenses funded by gifts excluded under section 102 can. IRC § 221(d)(1). The deduction is above the line. IRC § 62(a)(18). It should be noted that the section 222 deduction was slated to expire at the end of 2017. However, it is described here because Congress has extended the life of this provision on more than one occasion and it may do so again.

F. Charitable Deduction for Tuition Payments to a Church School

Taxpayers generally cannot deduct as a charitable contribution any part of the tuition costs for their children's secular education, as the tuition payments typically do not exceed the value of the secular education their children receive in return. But what if the children attend a religious school, and part of their school day is spent on secular education and part is spent on religious education? Can taxpayers deduct that part of the tuition attributable to their children's religious education? In these cases, taxpayers are typically denied any charitable deduction for dual tuition payments, as they often have trouble showing that any dual tuition payments they may have made exceed the value of the secular education their children receive. Review *Sklar v. Commissioner*, 282 F.3d 610 (9th Cir. 2002), which is included in Chapter 20. However, as discussed in *Sklar*, in Revenue Ruling 93-73, 1993-2 C.B. 75, the Service declared obsolete an earlier ruling that had prohibited a charitable deduction for the costs of auditing, training, and other courses in the Church of Scientology. Thus, the possibility of treating contributions to a church for religious training as deductible gifts is not entirely foreclosed.

G. Saving for Higher Education

1. Section 135: Income from U.S. Savings Bonds to Pay Higher Education Costs

Section 135 was enacted to encourage the purchase of U.S. savings bonds to pay for higher education costs. The U.S. savings bonds, which are purchased at a discount for less than their face value, accrue interest yearly. When the bonds are cashed in (redeemed), gain attributable to interest earned on the bonds over the life of the bonds is excludable from gross income to the extent the bond proceeds are used on qualified higher education expenses (tuition and fees at an eligible educational institution for the taxpayer or taxpayer's spouse and dependents, but not, for example, expenses funded by scholarships, tuition reductions, employer-provided educational assistance, and expenses taken into account for purposes of the Hope Scholarship Credit (now American Opportunity Tax Credit) and the Lifetime Learning Credit under section 25A). IRC § 135(a), (c), (d). If the bond redemption proceeds in a given year exceed the qualified higher education expenses for the year, only a portion of the interest income is excluded based on the ratio of expenses to bond proceeds. IRC § 135(b)(1). The exclusion is subject to an income phase out. IRC § 135(b)(2). The phase out amounts are adjusted for inflation. IRC § 135(b)(2)(B).

2. Section 529: Qualified Tuition Programs

Many states and educational institutions have established programs that allow taxpayers to prepay or contribute to an account for paying education expenses of a designated beneficiary at an eligible educational institution. Section 529 authorizes saving after-tax dollars for education expenses in these qualified tuition programs which is then permitted to grow tax free until disbursement. IRC § 529(a), (c)(3). If the funds are used for "qualified higher education expenses" (defined broadly) there are no income tax consequences upon withdrawal. IRC § 529(c)(3)(B). If the funds are not used for qualifying expenses of a designated beneficiary, the earnings are taxable and a penalty will apply. IRC § 529(c)(3)(A), (c)(6). Interestingly, the Tax Cuts and Jobs Act of 2017 modified section 529 plans to allow such plans to distribute not more than $10,000 in expenses for tuition incurred during the taxable year in connection with the enrollment or attendance of the designated beneficiary at a public, private or religious elementary or secondary school. IRC § 529(c)(7), (e)(3). This limitation applies on a per-student basis, rather than a per-account basis. Thus, under the provision, although an individual may be the designated beneficiary of multiple accounts, that individual may receive a maximum of $10,000 in distributions free of tax, regardless of whether the funds are distributed from multiple accounts. Any excess distributions received by the individual would be treated as a distribution subject to tax under the general rules of section 529. (The $10,000 annual per student limitation does not apply to distributions to post-secondary school expenses.)

A beneficiary must be designated at the time of establishing the account. New designated beneficiaries may be added later without adverse consequences if they are members of the original designated beneficiary's family. IRC § 529(c)(3)(C). Not all qualified tuition programs are alike and a well advised purchaser will compare plans before buying. It should be noted that transfers to qualified tuition programs are gifts for gift tax purposes. However, they can qualify for the annual exclusion. IRC § 529(c)(2). For a discussion of the gift tax see Chapter 41.

3. Section 530: Coverdell Educational Savings Accounts

Like qualified tuition programs, educational savings accounts are designed to encourage savings to cover future education costs (elementary and secondary school expenses as well as post-secondary expenses). The tax treatment of education savings accounts under section 530 is similar to the tax treatment of qualified tuition programs under section 529, namely after-tax contributions are permitted to grow tax free and proceeds can be withdrawn tax free for qualified education expenses at eligible educational institutions. IRC § 530(a), (d)(2), (d)(4)(A). But there are some significant differences between the two provisions. For example, there is a ceiling ($2,000) on contributions to educational saving accounts, and this contribution ceiling is phased-out for high income taxpayers. IRC § 530(b)(1)(A), (c)(2). Section 529 plans, in contrast, generally have no federal contribution restrictions. In addition, educations savings accounts permit the withdrawing of money tax free for qualified elementary and secondary school expenses. IRC § 530(b)(2)(A)(ii), (b)(3). Section 529 plans do not.

H. Coordination Rules

There are various rules to coordinate the use of the deductions, credits and exclusions described above. In general, those coordination rules embody two principles of tax policy. First, expenditures to produce tax exempt income are not deductible or creditable. Second, no expenditure should reduce a person's tax liability twice even if it is deductible or creditable under more than one provision. For example, if an education expense is deductible under one provision (e.g., section 162), it is not deductible under another provision (e.g., section 222). *See* IRC §§ 221(e)(1), 222(c)(1). As further example, education costs funded by amounts excluded by section 117 (scholarships) and section 127 (employer-provided assistance) do not qualify for the Hope Scholarship Credit (now American Opportunity Tax Credit) or the Lifetime

Learning Credit. Similarly, education costs funded by amounts excluded by section 529 (qualified tuition programs) or section 530 (educational savings accounts) do not qualify for the education credits. IRC § 25A(g)(2). *See also* IRC § 25A(g)(5). *But see* IRC § 25A(g)(2)(C) (education costs funded by gifts excluded by section 102 do qualify for the education credits).

IV. Materials

Revenue Ruling 2008-34

2008-28 I.R.B. 76

ISSUE

Do the terms of a loan made under the Loan Repayment Assistance Program (LRAP) described below satisfy the requirements of § 108(f)(1) of the Internal Revenue Code, and is the LRAP loan a "student loan" within the meaning of § 108(f)(2)?

FACTS

A, an individual, attended law school and has student loan debt. Neither the loans nor the underlying loan documents addressed whether any of the indebtedness would be forgiven if *A* worked in a particular profession for a specified period of time.

A's law school offers a Loan Repayment Assistance Program (LRAP) to help reduce the student loan debt of graduates who engage in public service. The LRAP is designed to encourage graduates to enter into public service in occupations or areas with unmet needs. Under the LRAP, the law school makes loans that refinance the graduates' original student loan(s). To qualify for an LRAP loan, a graduate must work in a law-related public service position for, or under the direction of, a tax-exempt charitable organization or a governmental unit, including a position in (1) a public interest or community service organization, (2) a legal aid office or clinic, (3) a prosecutor's office, (4) a public defender's office, or (5) a state, local, or federal government office. The amount of the LRAP loan is based on the graduate's outstanding student loan debt and annual income. After the graduate works for the required period in a qualifying position, the law school will forgive all or part of the graduate's LRAP loan.

After *A* graduates from law school, *A* signs an LRAP promissory note and accepts the terms and conditions of the law school's LRAP loan. The LRAP loan provides that the indebtedness will be forgiven if *A* works for a certain minimum period of time in a qualifying law-related public service position.

LAW

Section 61(a) provides that gross income means all income from whatever source derived. Section 61(a)(12) provides that gross income includes income from the discharge of indebtedness.

Section 108(f)(1) provides that in the case of an individual, gross income does not include any amount which (but for § 108(f)) would be includible in gross income by reason of the discharge (in whole or in part) of any student loan if such discharge was pursuant to a provision of such loan under which all or part of the indebtedness of the individual would be discharged if the individual worked for a certain period of time in certain professions for any of a broad class of employers.

Section 108(f)(2) defines "student loan" for purposes of § 108(f) to include any loan to an individual to assist the individual in attending an educational organization described in § 170(b)(1)(A)(ii) made by (A) the United States, or an instrumentality or agency thereof, (B) a State, territory, or possession of the United States, or the District of Columbia, or any political subdivision thereof, or (C) certain tax-exempt public benefit corporations. The Taxpayer Relief Act of 1997 (1997 Act), Pub. L. 105-34, added § 108(f)(2)(D), which amended and expanded the definition of "student loan" to include loans made by the educational organizations themselves if the loans were made either:

(i) pursuant to an agreement with any entity described in subparagraph (A), (B), or (C) under which the funds from which the loan was made were provided to such educational organization, or

(ii) pursuant to a program of such educational organization which is designed to encourage its students to serve in occupations with unmet needs or in areas with unmet needs and under which the services provided by the students (or former students) are for or under the direction of a governmental unit or an organization described in section 501(c)(3) and exempt from tax under section 501(a).

The 1997 Act further amended § 108(f)(2) to provide that the term "student loan" includes any loan made by an educational organization described in section 170(b)(1)(A)(ii) or by an organization exempt from tax under section 501(a) "to refinance a loan to an individual to assist the individual in attending any such educational organization but only if the refinancing loan is pursuant to a program of the refinancing organization which is designed as described in subparagraph (D)(ii)."[1] The legislative history to the 1997 Act explains that, in the case of loans made or refinanced by educational organizations (and loans refinanced by certain tax-exempt organizations), the student's work must fulfill a "public service requirement." *See* H.R. Conf. Rep. No. 105-220, at 375–76 (1997).

ANALYSIS

The terms of *A*'s LRAP loan provide for loan forgiveness only if *A* works for a certain minimum period of time in a qualifying law-related public service position. This requirement is consistent with the requirement in § 108(f)(1) to work in certain professions for a certain period of time.

---

1. A technical correction clarified that gross income does not include amounts from the forgiveness of loans made by educational organizations and certain tax-exempt organizations to refinance *any* existing student loan (and not just loans made by educational organizations). *See* Pub. L. 105-206, § 6004(f)(1), and H.R. Rep. No. 356, 105th Cong., 1st Sess. 10 (1997).

Rev. Rul. 2008-34, 2008-28 I.R.B. 76, 2008 WL 2468948 (IRS RRU).

Additionally, the law school's LRAP is designed to encourage its students to engage in public service in occupations or areas with unmet needs. All of the positions listed in the LRAP are for, or under the direction of, a governmental unit or a tax-exempt charitable organization. Further, the LRAP loan was made to refinance *A*'s original student loans. Therefore, the LRAP loan meets the definition of a "student loan" in § 108(f)(2).

HOLDING

The terms of the loan made under the LRAP satisfy the requirements of § 108(f)(1), and the LRAP loan is a "student loan" within the meaning of § 108(f)(2).

V. Related Matters

- **Costs of an LL.M. in Taxation**. A lawyer who obtains an LL.M. in taxation is not deemed to have qualified for a new profession and thus the costs of the degree may be deductible under the principles addressed in Treas. Reg. § 1.162-5. However, it is necessary to have already entered practice in order to obtain this benefit. Thus, one who goes straight from a J.D. program to an LL.M. program may fail to qualify. *See* Ruehmann v. Commissioner, T.C. Memo 1971-157.

- **Educational Travel**. Section 274(m)(2) disallows deduction of expenses for travel as a form of education (such as when a French teacher travels to France to informally improve her language skills). However, this rule does not apply to the costs of travel that are simply part of obtaining an education the costs of which are otherwise deductible under section 162 (such as when a French teacher travels to France to study the French language at the Sorbonne). The general deductibility of business travel expenses is addressed in Chapter 7.

Chapter 34

Personal Injury Recoveries and Punitive Damages

I. Assignment

Read: Internal Revenue Code: §§ 104(a); 105(a)–(c), (e); 106(a).

Treasury Regulations: §§ 1.104-1(a)–(d).

Text: Overview
Private Letter Ruling 200041022
Amos v. Commissioner
Stadnyk v. Commissioner
Chief Counsel Advice Memorandum 201045023
Related Matters

Complete the problems.

II. Problems

1. Wyatt Earp sued Doc Holliday for injuries stemming from a hunting accident last year. While hunting for birds, Doc Holliday shot Wyatt Earp in the shoulder causing Wyatt to have a heart attack. Wyatt won and received an award of $500,000 allocated by the jury as follows: pain, suffering, and emotional distress ($250,000); medical expenses ($75,000); lost wages ($50,000); and punitive damages ($125,000).

   (a) What are the tax consequences to Wyatt as a result of the jury award?

   (b) Same as (a) except that Doc merely pointed his gun and shouted at Wyatt causing Wyatt to have a heart attack.

   (c) Same as (a) except that Doc poked his gun in Wyatt's back causing a severe bruise and causing Wyatt to have a heart attack.

2. Assume Wyatt Earp and Doc Holliday, in Problem 1, agree to settle the suit out of court. Doc agrees to pay Wyatt $400,000, which Wyatt insisted be allocated entirely to pain and suffering, in return for Wyatt's agreement not to defame Doc, publicize facts relating to the hunting accident, or assist in any criminal prosecution against Wyatt with respect to the hunting incident.

   (a) Why did Wyatt insist that the settlement award be allocated entirely to pain and suffering? Will the allocation be respected?

(b) What impact, if any, should Wyatt's agreement not to defame Doc, publicize facts relating to the incident, or assist in criminal prosecution have on the tax consequences of the settlement?

3. Bill Gates and Warren Buffet were the only customers transacting business at Celebrity Bank. Clyde Barrow, a masked man, came into the bank and ordered Bill and Warren to the ground at gun point in order to take cash from bank officials. Bill laid face down on the floor as instructed by the robber. Warren was slow to follow directions; as a result the robber forcibly grabbed Warren's arm and brought him to the ground and then tied his hands behind his back causing a severe bruise around his wrists. Bill and Warren were held hostage on the floor for over an hour until police were able to make an arrest. Bill and Warren, who were both traumatized by the incident, sued Clyde for false imprisonment, and each collected an unapportioned jury award of $50,000 for their emotional and physical distress. What are the tax consequences to Bill and Warren as a result of the award?

4. James Dean was in an automobile accident that caused permanent bodily injury. During the year, James paid total medical expenses of $9,000 and, as a result of his injury, was indemnified under two insurance policies (Policy A paid $7,000; Policy B paid $5,000). James took no deduction under section 213 for his medical expenses. To what extent are the insurance proceeds includible in James's gross income under each of the following:

(a) Policy A and Policy B are both James' personal health insurance policies. James paid the annual premiums for both.

(b) Policy A is James' employer's general health insurance policy and Policy B is his employer's comprehensive supplemental health insurance policy. James' employer paid the entire annual premiums for both policies.

(c) Policy A is James' employer's health insurance policy for which the employer paid the annual premium. Policy B is James' personal health policy for which he paid the annual premium.

III. Overview

Section 104 excludes from gross income compensation received for certain personal injuries and sickness. One justification sometimes offered for the exclusion is that a personal damage award makes a taxpayer whole and puts him in the same position he would have been in had the injury not occurred; in other words, a damage award is a return of "human capital" lost rather than an accession to wealth. This view is flawed in light of the fact that taxpayers do not have a basis in their human capital (e.g., their labor, reputation, and well-being). A better justification for the exclusion is compassion—those who suffer from personal injury or sickness have suffered enough and should not have to suffer additional harm by paying a tax liability as a result of their misfortune.

Section 104 identifies five areas of exclusion: (1) compensation under so-called "workmen's compensation acts," (2) damages on account of personal physical injury or physical sickness, (3) benefits under self-financed health and accident insurance policies, (4) disability pensions arising out of certain government service, and (5) disability income received by officials who are violently attacked outside the country. IRC § 104(a)(1)–(5). These exclusions are restricted by an "except" clause, the effect of which is to include in gross income reimbursement of medical expenses that were deductible in a prior year. For example, if a taxpayer incurred and deducted $1,000 of medical expenses in Year 1 that were reimbursed in Year 2, she would have to include in gross income the reimbursement to prevent her from enjoying a double tax benefit.

This chapter focuses mainly on the tax treatment of compensatory and punitive damages received on account of personal injuries and sickness, and amounts received under insurance policies.

A. Damages Received on Account of Personal Injuries or Sickness

Section 104(a)(2) excludes damages received "on account of personal physical injuries or physical sickness." The word "physical" was added in 1996 to eliminate confusion over the scope of the exclusion for nonphysical injuries incurred in connection with a taxpayer's employment or business. For example, courts and the Service had trouble defining the scope of the exclusion for damages received for injuries to professional reputation and for employment-related discrimination, such as sex, age, and gender discrimination. In Burke v. United States, 504 U.S. 229 (1992), the Supreme Court's first decision on section 104(a)(2), the Court held that payments received in settlement of a sex discrimination claim under Title VII of the Civil Rights Act of 1964 were not excludable, because the pre-1991 version of Title VII did not permit a wide-range of compensatory damages, but limited available remedies to back pay and equitable relief. Three years later, in Commissioner v. Schleier, 515 U.S. 323 (1995), the Supreme Court held that an award for back pay and liquidated damages received under the Age Discrimination in Employment Act was not excludable, because the damages were not "on account of" a personal injury. The *Schleier* Court held that damages are excludable when two, independent conditions are met: (1) they are received in a tort-like cause of action; and (2) they are received "on account of" a personal injury—an origin of the claim inquiry. Although both *Burke* and *Schleier* limited the scope of section 104(a)(2), Congress chose to restrict it further in 1996 by requiring that the personal injury or sickness be "physical." The 1996 amendments did not change the "on account of" language. [Note that Treas. Reg. § 1.104-1(c), which was amended in 2011, removes the first condition of *Schleier* (i.e., damages must be received in a tort-like cause of action).]

The insertion of the word "physical" proved more mischievous than was anticipated by raising two immediate questions. First, did it refer to the *cause* of the injury or to the *effect* of the injury, or, perhaps, to both? Second, if it referred to the cause did the causative action have to involve physical contact with the injured party? These questions still haunt the application of the provision but it is well settled that damages for non-physical injury or sickness that are "on account of" physical injury or sickness are excludable. Assume, for example, that a taxpayer is in an automobile accident, is physically injured, and as a result of that injury suffers medical expenses, lost wages, pain and suffering, and loss of consortium with his spouse. Any damages that the taxpayer *and his spouse* receive would be "on account of" his physical injuries (i.e., all damages flowed therefrom), and would thus be excludable. *See* H.R. Conf. Rep. No. 104-737 at 300 (1996) (stating that "if an action has its origin in a physical injury or physical sickness, then all damages (other than punitive damages) *that flow therefrom* are treated as payments received on account of physical injury or physical sickness whether or not the recipient of the damages is the injured party").

Neither the Code nor the regulations define what "physical" means, which is stunning considering the importance of the term. In Private Letter Ruling 200041022, included in the materials below, the Service attempted for the first time to provide guidance to taxpayers, stating "direct unwanted or uninvited physical contacts resulting in observable bodily harms such as bruises, cuts, swelling, and bleeding are personal physical injuries under section 104(a)(2)." Notice that the Service seems to be saying that both the cause and the harm must be physical in nature.

Keep in mind that section 104(a)(2) excludes any damages received "on account of" physical injury or sickness. Courts continue to struggle to determine what nexus between damages and physical injury is required to satisfy the "on account of" standard. In *Amos v. Commissioner* (a case involving former basketball player Dennis Rodman), included below, the Tax Court was faced with a settlement involving more than one ground for compensation and decided an allocation was in order. Did the court get it right?

The Code is explicit that "emotional distress" is not to be treated as a physical injury or sickness, except for related medical care expenses. IRC § 104(a) flush language. According to the legislative history, "physical symptoms" resulting from emotional distress (e.g., insomnia, headaches, and stomach disorders) are to be treated as emotional distress. H.R. Conf. Rep. No. 104-737 at 88 n.24 (1996). However, in Domeny v. Commissioner, T.C. Memo. 2010-9, the court allowed the exclusion for damages received by a multiple sclerosis sufferer whose condition was exacerbated by emotional distress she experienced in a hostile work environment. There was no unwanted physical contact involved. In Parkinson v. Commissioner, T.C. Memo. 2010-142, an employee who suffered from heart disease sued his employer for infliction of emotional distress that exacerbated his illness. Again there was no harmful physical contact. The tax court allocated half of the resulting settlement proceeds to physical injury and half to emotional distress and ruled that the physical injury half was excluded from income. Perhaps these outcomes are explained by the presence of "physical sickness" but they cast doubt upon the Service's physical contact requirement and seem to accept that physical harm is the deciding factor. They also make one wonder whether we can we truly distinguish between an emotional injury and physical injury? Is a stomach ache fundamentally different from a muscle ache? Is the trauma one might experience through the eyes and ears fundamentally different from the trauma one might experience through touch?

This is an evolving and confused area of the law. Two helpful efforts to explain and resolve the confusion are Morgan L. Holcomb, *Taxing Anxiety*, 14 FLA. TAX REV. 77 (2013) and Ronald H. Jensen, *When Are Damages Tax Free? The Elusive Meaning of "Physical Injury,"* 10 PITT. TAX REV. 87 (2013).

An interesting issue is whether false imprisonment damages should be excluded from gross income under section 104(a)(2). In *Stadnyk v. Commissioner,* included in the materials, the Sixth Circuit held that a taxpayer could not exclude damages received for false arrest, opining that mere physical restraint and physical detention are not physical injuries. But in Chief Counsel Advice Memorandum 201045023 the IRS advised that a wrongfully incarcerated person could exclude damages if that person suffered physical injuries or physical sickness while incarcerated. More recently Congress enlarged that outcome in section 139F which provides an exclusion for compensation for wrongful incarceration even where there is no physical injury. But section 139F does not apply to cases like *Stadnyk* since section 139F requires that the taxpayer have been convicted of a crime. *See* IRC § 139F(b)(1).

Planning Note

Lawyers should draft pleadings carefully with an awareness of the later potential tax consequences. For example, in a sexual harassment case, a plaintiff's lawyer should focus more on physical elements in the complaint (e.g., unauthorized touching, observable bodily harm, cuts, bruises), and stress that damages flowed from such physical injuries. In non-physical injury cases, if allowed by the court, lawyers should inform juries of the tax law treatment of any recovery so that juries may decide to increase the award to cover plaintiffs' taxes. Lawyers should document that they have advised clients when awards may be taxable.

B. Punitive Damages

In contrast to compensatory damages, which are designed to compensate victims, punitive damages are designed to punish the wrongdoer. Prior to 1996, the tax treatment of punitive damages was somewhat unsettled. Section 104(a)(2) provided specifically that no exclusion was available for punitive damages arising out of non-physical injury or sickness, but said nothing about excludability of punitive damages arising out of physical injury or sickness. In O'Gilvie v. United States, 519 U.S. 79 (1996), the Supreme Court held that such damages were not excludable under section 104(a)(2). In 1996, Congress amended section 104(a)(2) to clarify that punitive damages, whether or not related to a claim for damages arising out of physical injury or sickness, are not excludable from gross income.

Since punitive damages are clearly taxable, there is an incentive for taxpayers to allocate as much of a personal physical injury award to excludable compensatory damages as opposed to taxable punitive damages. A couple of points are worth raising about allocations. First, if the parties to a suit fail to allocate a settlement award, the Service and courts can make their own determination of appropriate allocation between the compensatory damage portion and the punitive damage portion, using the initial complaint to help in the determination. *See* Rev. Rul. 58-418, 1958-2 C.B. 18. Second, even if the parties make an allocation, the allocation may not be respected if it did not result from adversarial, arm's-length negotiation. *See* Robinson v. Commissioner, 102 T.C. 116 (1994) (refusing to uphold a non-adversarial allocation); McKay v. Commissioner, 102 T.C. 465 (1994) (upholding arm's-length allocation).

Planning Note

Lawyers should be mindful of the relevance of initial pleadings in justifying allocations in later settlements. It may be difficult to argue later that a settlement is 100% compensatory if the initial complaint asked for a lot of punitive damages. When allocating a settlement award, document the adversarial, arm's-length nature of the settlement.

C. Structured Settlements

Settlements in personal physical injury cases are typically paid in one of two ways. The recipient may receive a lump sum payment or agree to a *structured settlement* arrangement providing for periodic payments. Section 104(a)(2) makes no distinction between damages received as lump sums or as periodic payments. For example, if a plaintiff agrees to settle a personal physical injury claim for a lump sum payment of $100,000, the lump sum payment is excludable. If the plaintiff agrees to settle for five annual payments of $20,000, each payment is fully excludable. *See* Rev. Rul. 79-313, 1979-2 C.B. 75.

If a recipient prefers payments spread out over time, she is better off agreeing to a structured settlement arrangement rather than receiving a lump sum and then purchasing an annuity with a lump sum payment. If a recipient chooses to receive a lump sum payment, and then uses it to purchase an annuity contract providing for periodic payments, then a portion of each payment under the annuity contract is includable in income. More specifically, under section 72, each annual payment is partially excludable as tax-free recovery of the investment in the contract, and partially includable based on the expected return on the investment in the annuity contract. IRC § 72(b). In contrast, if a recipient agrees to a structured settlement arrangement with the defendant, each periodic payment received thereunder is fully excludable from income. IRC § 104(a)(2). Taxation of annuities is addressed more fully in Chapter 36.

As an alternative to making periodic payments directly to the plaintiff, a defendant may assign the liability for future periodic payments to a third party (e.g., an insurance company or other structured settlement company). The funds received by a structured settlement company for assuming the liability (and purchasing a "qualified funding asset") are excludable from the assignee's gross income, provided certain conditions are met. IRC § 130. Query: Why does the government choose to subsidize structured settlement arrangements?

D. Accident or Health Insurance Proceeds

Section 104(a)(3) excludes from gross income amounts received under self-financed accident and health insurance policies for personal injuries or sickness (even if such amounts exceed expenses actually incurred). Amounts received under employer-provided plans are not excludable under section 104(a)(3), but may be excludable under section 105. *See* Treas. Reg. § 1.104-1(d). Section 105(a) generally includes such amounts in income, but then sections 105(b) and 105(c) back out medical expense reimbursements and certain payments for permanent bodily injury and disfigurement (to the extent of medical expenses actually paid). Note the difference between sections 104(a)(3) and 105. The section 104(a)(3) exclusion pertaining to self-financed policies is not limited to actual expenses for medical care; the section 105(b) exclusion pertaining to employer-financed policies is so limited (in other words, the excess indemnification attributable to the employer's policy is includable in gross income). Query: What happens if a taxpayer is indemnified under both his personal insurance policy and his employer's insurance policy, and the total amount received under both policies exceeds total medical expenses? *See* Rev. Rul. 69-154, 1969-1 C.B. 46.

Section 106 excludes from an employee's gross income an employer's contributions to accident and health insurance plans or other payments to compensate or reimburse employees for injury or sickness. This treats all employees equally whether or not employers pay health benefits directly to employees or provide health benefits indirectly through the purchase of insurance.

IV. Materials

Private Letter Ruling 200041022

Oct. 13, 2000

Dear

This letter is in response to your request for a ruling submitted on behalf of A and her husband, B, regarding the tax treatment of a damage award they received pursuant to a settlement agreement with C. You request a ruling that the entire award will be excludable from A's and B's gross income under § 104(a)(2) of the Internal Revenue Code.

FACTS

C and C's corporation employed A in various capacities from date 1 through date 4. From date 2 through date 3, A was C's full-time driver and accompanied C on many trips. Early in this period, C acted in a friendly manner toward A. After a while, however, C began a slow progression of attempts to make sexual contact with A and made several suggestive or lewd remarks in A's presence. Also, early in this period,

C physically touched A but these contacts did not result in any observable bodily harm (*e.g.*, cuts, bruises, etc.) to A's body or cause extreme pain to A. Later, while on a road trip, C assaulted A causing what A represents was extreme pain (the "First Pain Incident"). After the First Pain Incident, A began to have headache and digestive problems, but two doctors could not find anything physically wrong. Your ruling request does not assert that these problems were due to the First Pain Incident or prior events. On a subsequent road trip, C also assaulted A, cutting her and biting her (the "First Physical Injury").

A became executive director of C's household around date 3. During this period, C physically and sexually assaulted A. In one assault, C cut A. As a result of another series of C's assaults, A suffered skin discoloration and swelling accompanied by extreme pain for which A received medical treatment from a doctor. On date 4, A terminated her employment with C.

A subsequently retained the services of a law firm, which presented C with a complaint. The complaint alleged that C inflicted emotional and physical harm on A. A's complaint asserted causes of action, including sex discrimination and reprisal under Statute, battery, and intentional infliction of emotional distress. The complaint also specifically requested leave to amend the complaint to add a claim for punitive damages for A's common law claims. The complaint does not refer to claims for interest. On date 5, C executed the Settlement Agreement with A and B under which C agreed to pay $z to settle all claims of A and B. The Settlement Agreement did not allocate the proceeds to any of the claims.

Statute permits claimants to sue for discrimination in employment on account of sex (including sexual harassment) and reprisal. Under sections x and y of Statute, a claimant may recover damages for mental anguish and suffering. Likewise, State law permits a claimant to recover damages for humiliation and disgrace in an action for assault and battery.

LAW AND ANALYSIS

Section 61 provides, in general, that gross income means all income from whatever source derived.

Section 104(a)(2) provides that except in the case of amounts attributable to (and not in excess of) deductions allowed under § 213 (relating to medical, etc., expenses) for any prior taxable year, gross income does not include the amount of any damages (other than punitive damages) received (whether by suit or agreement) on account of personal physical injuries or physical sickness.

Section 104 also provides that for purposes of § 104(a)(2), emotional distress shall not be treated as a physical injury. However, § 104 also provides that the preceding sentence shall not apply to an amount of damages not in excess of the amount paid for medical care (described in § 213(d)(2)(A) or (B)) that is attributable to emotional distress.

Section 1.104-1(c) of the Income Tax Regulations provides, in part, that the term "damages received (whether by suit or agreement)" means an amount received through prosecution of a legal suit or action based upon tort or tort type rights, or through a settlement agreement entered into in lieu of such prosecution.

In Commissioner v. Schleier, 515 U.S. 323 (1995), the Supreme Court of the United States ("Court") held that two independent requirements must be met for a recovery to be excluded from income under former § 104(a)(2).

- First, the underlying cause of action giving rise to the recovery must be "based upon tort or tort type rights." In United States v. Burke, 504 U.S. 229 (1992), the Court concluded that in order for the first requirement to be met the relevant cause of action must provide the availability of a broad range of damages, such as damages for emotional distress, pain, and suffering.

- Second, the damages must be received "on account of personal injuries or sickness." In *Schleier*, the Court illustrated the application of the second requirement by way of an example in which a taxpayer who is injured in an automobile accident sues for (1) medical expenses, (2) pain, suffering, and emotional distress that cannot be measured with precision, and (3) lost wages. The Court explained that the second requirement would be met for recovery of (1) the medical expenses for injuries arising out of the accident, (2) the amounts for pain, suffering and emotional distress, and (3) the lost wages as long as the lost wages resulted from the time in which the taxpayer was out of work due to the injuries sustained in the accident.

Rev. Rul. 85-97, 1985-2 C.B. 50, concerns a taxpayer who received damages in settlement of suit for injuries he suffered when he was struck by a bus. The taxpayer's complaint alleged that as a direct result of being struck by the bus he had been unable to pursue normal employment activities and had lost wages, had suffered and would continue to suffer great pain of body and mind and loss of earning capacity, and had incurred and would incur hospital and doctors' bills. The ruling concludes that the entire amount of the settlement received by the taxpayer was excludable from gross income as amounts received on account of personal injuries under former § 104(a)(2).

Section 1605 of the Small Business Job Protection Act of 1996 (the "1996 Act") restricted the exclusion from gross income provided by § 104(a)(2) to amounts received on account of personal *physical* injuries or *physical* sickness. [Emphasis added.] H.R. Conf. Rep. No. 737, 104th Cong., 2d Sess. 301 (1996), provides the following explanation of the amendment made by the 1996 Act:

> The House bill also specifically provides that emotional distress is not considered a physical injury or physical sickness. [FN 56] Thus the exclusion from gross income does not apply to any damages received (other than for medical expenses as discussed below) based on a claim of employment discrimination or injury to reputation accompanied by a claim of emotional distress. Because all damages received on account of physical injury or physical sickness are excludable from gross income, the exclusion from gross income applies to any damages received based on a claim of emotional distress that is attributable to physical injury or physical sickness. In addition, the exclusion

from gross income specifically applies to the amount of damages received that is not in excess of the amount paid for medical care attributable to emotional distress.

Footnote 56 of the Conference Report states, "It is intended that the term emotional distress includes symptoms (e.g., insomnia, headaches, stomach disorders) which may result from such distress." H.R. Conf. Rep. No. 737 at 301.

In this case State law actions under Statute and in battery permit recovery for a broad range of damages of the kind described in *Burke*, such as damages for emotional distress and humiliation. Thus, A and B received their damages in a settlement agreement that is in lieu of a suit or action based on tort or tort type rights within the meaning of § 1.104-1(c).

The term "personal physical injuries" is not defined in either § 104(a)(2) or the legislative history of the 1996 Act. However, we believe that direct unwanted or uninvited physical contacts resulting in observable bodily harms such as bruises, cuts, swelling, and bleeding are personal physical injuries under § 104(a)(2). *See* Black's Law Dictionary 1304 (Rev. 4th ed. 1968) which defines the term "physical injury" as "bodily harm or hurt, excluding mental distress, fright, or emotional disturbance."

In this case, C's uninvited and unwanted physical contacts with A prior to the First Pain Incident did not result in any observable harms (*e.g.*, bruises, cuts, etc.) to A's body or cause A pain. Further, it is not represented that the medical treatment that A received after the First Pain Incident for headaches and digestive problems were related to events that occurred with or prior to that incident. Thus, any damages A received for events occurring prior the First Pain Incident are not received on account of personal physical injuries or physical sickness under § 104(a)(2).

However, according to the representations submitted, A suffered several physical injuries within a relatively short period of time commencing with the First Physical Injury. Thus, under the facts of this case, damages A and B received under the Settlement Agreement for pain, suffering, emotional distress and reimbursement of medical expenses that are properly allocable to the period beginning with the First Physical Injury are attributable to and linked to the physical injuries A suffered and were received on account of personal physical injuries or physical sickness under § 104(a)(2).

Finally, damages A and B received under the Settlement Agreement that are properly allocable to punitive damages are includible in their gross income. A portion of damages received may be properly allocable to punitive damages notwithstanding that a settlement agreement is entered into prior to a jury's award of punitive damages.

HOLDING

Based strictly on the information submitted and each of the representations made, we conclude that—

(i) damages that A and B received under the Settlement Agreement that are properly allocable to events prior to the First Pain Incident are not received on account of personal physical injuries or physical sickness under § 104(a)(2) and are includible in their gross income under § 61; and

(ii) damages that A and B received under the Settlement Agreement for pain, suffering, emotional distress and reimbursement of medical expenses that are properly allocable to the period beginning with the First Physical Injury are excludable from their gross income under § 104(a)(2) except for amounts attributable to (and not in excess of) deductions allowed under § 213 (relating to medical, etc., expenses) for any prior taxable year; and

(iii) damages that A and B received under the Settlement Agreement that are properly allocable to punitive damages are includible in their gross income under § 61.

A copy of this letter should be attached to any income tax return to which it is relevant. Except as expressly provided in the preceding paragraph, no opinion is expressed or implied concerning the tax consequences of any aspect of any transaction or item discussed or referenced in this letter. A letter ruling will not ordinarily be issued because of the factual nature of the problem. Because the perception of pain is essentially subjective, it is a factual matter. Therefore, we cannot rule whether damages properly allocable to the First Pain Incident (a physical contact that did not manifest itself in the form of a cut, bruise, or other similar bodily harm) were received on account of personal physical injuries or physical sickness.

In addition, no opinion is expressed concerning the percentage of the damages received that is excludable from income under § 104(a)(2). The Service will not ordinarily issue a ruling whether an allocation of a settlement award (including a lump sum award) between back pay, compensatory damages, and punitive damages is a proper allocation for federal income tax purposes.

This ruling is directed only to the taxpayer(s) requesting it. Section 6110(k)(3) provides that it may not be used or cited as precedent. Temporary or final regulations pertaining to one or more of the issues addressed in this letter have not yet been adopted. Therefore, this letter ruling will be modified or revoked by the adoption of temporary or final regulations to the extent the regulations are inconsistent with any conclusion in the letter ruling.

Sincerely,

Heather C. Maloy Associate Chief Counsel (Income Tax & Accounting)

Amos v. Commissioner

T.C. Memo. 2003-329

CHIECHI, J.

Respondent determined a deficiency of $61,668 in petitioner's Federal income tax (tax) for 1997.

The only issue remaining for decision is whether the $200,000 settlement amount (settlement amount at issue) that petitioner received in 1997 in settlement of a claim is excludable under section 104(a)(2) from petitioner's gross income for that year. We hold that $120,000 is excludable and that $80,000 is not.

FINDINGS OF FACT

During 1997, petitioner was employed as a television cameraman. In that capacity, on January 15, 1997, petitioner was operating a handheld camera during a basketball game between the Minnesota Timberwolves and the Chicago Bulls. At some point during that game, Dennis Keith Rodman, who was playing for the Chicago Bulls, landed on a group of photographers, including petitioner, and twisted his ankle. Mr. Rodman then kicked petitioner.

On January 15, 1997, shortly after the incident, petitioner was taken by ambulance for treatment at Hennepin County Medical Center. Petitioner informed the medical personnel at that medical center that he had experienced shooting pain to his neck immediately after having been kicked in the groin, but that such pain was subsiding. The Hennepin County medical personnel observed that petitioner was able to walk, but that he was limping and complained of experiencing pain. The Hennepin County medical personnel did not observe any other obvious signs of trauma. Petitioner informed the Hennepin County medical personnel that he was currently taking pain medication for a preexisting back condition. The Hennepin County medical personnel offered additional pain medications to petitioner, but he refused those medications. After a dispute with the Hennepin County medical personnel concerning an unrelated medical issue, petitioner left Hennepin County Medical Center without having been discharged by them.

While petitioner was seeking treatment at Hennepin County Medical Center, he contacted Gale Pearson about representing him with respect to the incident. Ms. Pearson was an attorney who had experience in representing plaintiffs in personal injury lawsuits. After subsequent conversations and a meeting with petitioner, Ms. Pearson agreed to represent him with respect to the incident.

On January 15, 1997, after the incident and petitioner's visit to the Hennepin County Medical Center, petitioner filed a report with the Minneapolis Police Department. In the police report, petitioner claimed that Mr. Rodman had assaulted him.

On January 16, 1997, petitioner sought medical treatment at the Veterans Affairs (VA) Medical Center. The medical personnel at that medical center took X-rays of petitioner's back. Petitioner complained to the VA medical personnel about his groin area, but he did not advise them that he was experiencing any symptoms related to that complaint. The VA medical personnel determined that there was no swelling of, but they were unable to ascertain whether there was bruising around, petitioner's groin area. The VA medical personnel gave petitioner some pain medication and told him to continue taking his other prescribed medications. The VA medical personnel prepared a report regarding petitioner's January 16, 1997 visit to the VA Medical Center. That report indicated that, except for certain disk problems that petitioner had since at least as early as February 14, 1995, "the vertebrae are intact and the remaining disk spaces are normal."

Very shortly after the incident on a date not disclosed by the record, Andrew Luger, an attorney representing Mr. Rodman with respect to the incident, contacted Ms. Pearson. Several discussions and a few meetings took place between Ms. Pearson and Mr. Luger. Petitioner accompanied Ms. Pearson to one of the meetings between her and Mr. Luger, at which time Mr. Luger noticed that petitioner was limping. Shortly after those discussions and meetings, petitioner and Mr. Rodman reached a settlement.

On January 21, 1997, Mr. Rodman and petitioner executed a document entitled "CONFIDENTIAL SETTLEMENT AGREEMENT AND RELEASE." The settlement agreement provided in pertinent part:

> For and in consideration of TWO HUNDRED THOUSAND DOLLARS ($200,000), the mutual waiver of costs, attorneys' fees and legal expenses, if any, and other good and valuable consideration, the receipt and sufficiency of which is hereby acknowledged, Eugene Amos, on behalf of himself, his agents, representatives, attorneys, assignees, heirs, executors and administrators, hereby releases and forever discharges Dennis Rodman, the Chicago Bulls, the National Basketball Association and all other persons, firms and corporations together with their subsidiaries, divisions and affiliates, past and present officers, directors, employees, insurers, agents, personal representatives and legal counsel, from any and all claims and causes of action of any type, known and unknown, upon and by reason of any damage, loss or injury which heretofore have been or heretoafter may be sustained by Amos arising, or which could have arisen, out of or in connection with an incident occurring between Rodman and Amos at a game between the Chicago Bulls and the Minnesota Timberwolves on January 15, 1997 during which Rodman allegedly kicked Amos ("the Incident"), including but not limited to any statements made after the Incident or subsequent conduct relating to the Incident by Amos, Rodman, the Chicago Bulls, the National Basketball Association, or any other person, firm or corporation, or any of their subsidiaries, divisions, affiliates, officers, directors, employees, insurers, agents, personal representatives and legal counsel. This Agreement and Release includes, but is not limited to claims, demands, or actions arising under the common law and under any state, federal or local statute, ordinance, regulation or order, including claims known or unknown at this time, concerning any physical, mental or emotional injuries that may arise in the future allegedly resulting from the Incident.

* * *

> It is further understood and agreed that the payment of the sum described herein is not to be construed as an admission of liability and is a compromise of a disputed claim. It is further understood that part of the consideration for this Agreement and Release includes an agreement that Rodman and Amos shall not at any time from the date of this Agreement and Release forward disparage or defame each other.

It is further understood and agreed that, as part of the consideration for this Agreement and Release, the terms of this Agreement and Release shall forever be kept confidential and not released to any news media personnel or representatives thereof or to any other person, entity, company, government agency, publication or judicial authority for any reason whatsoever except to the extent necessary to report the sum paid to appropriate taxing authorities or in response to any subpoena issued by a state or federal governmental agency or court of competent jurisdiction. Any court reviewing a subpoena concerning this Agreement and Release should be aware that part of the consideration for the Agreement and Release is the agreement of Amos and his attorneys not to testify regarding the existence of the Agreement and Release or any of its terms.

* * *

It is further understood and agreed that Amos and his representatives, agents, legal counsel or other advisers shall not, from the date of this Agreement and Release, disclose, disseminate, publicize or instigate or solicit any others to disclose, disseminate or publicize, any of the allegations or facts relating to the Incident, including but not limited to any allegations or facts or opinions relating to Amos' potential claims against Rodman or any allegations, facts or opinions relating to Rodman's conduct on the night of January 15, 1997 or thereafter concerning Amos. In this regard, Amos agrees not to make any further public statement relating to Rodman or the Incident or to grant any interviews relating to Rodman or the Incident. * * *

It is further understood and agreed that any material breach by Amos or his attorney, agent or representative of the terms of this Agreement and Release will result in immediate and irreparable damage to Rodman, and that the extent of such damage would be difficult, if not impossible, to ascertain. To discourage any breach of the terms of this Agreement and Release, and to compensate Rodman should any such breach occur, it is understood and agreed that Amos shall be liable for liquidated damages in the amount of TWO HUNDRED THOUSAND and No/100 Dollars ($200,000) in the event such a material breach occurs. Amos agrees that this sum constitutes a reasonable calculation of the damages Rodman would incur due to a material breach.

It is further understood and agreed, that, in the event Rodman or Amos claim a material breach of this Agreement and Release has occurred, either party may schedule a confidential hearing before an arbitrator of the American Arbitration Association for a final, binding determination as to whether a material breach has occurred. If, after the hearing, the arbitrator finds that Amos has committed a material breach, the arbitrator shall order that Amos pay the sum of $200,000 in liquidated damages to Rodman. * * *

Amos further represents, promises and agrees that no administrative charge or claim or legal action of any kind has been asserted by him or on his behalf in any way relating to the Incident with the exception of a statement given by Amos to the Minneapolis Police Department. Amos further represents, promises and agrees that, as part of the consideration for this Agreement and Release, he has communicated to the Minneapolis Police Department that he does not wish to pursue a criminal charge against Rodman, and that he has communicated that he will not cooperate in any criminal investigation concerning the Incident. Amos further represents, promises and agrees that he will not pursue any criminal action against Rodman concerning the Incident, that he will not cooperate should any such action or investigation ensue, and that he will not encourage, incite or solicit others to pursue a criminal investigation or charge against Rodman concerning the Incident.

Petitioner filed a tax return for his taxable year 1997. In that return, petitioner excluded from his gross income the $200,000 that he received from Mr. Rodman under the settlement agreement.

In the notice that respondent issued to petitioner with respect to 1997, respondent determined that petitioner is not entitled to exclude from his gross income the settlement amount at issue.

OPINION

We must determine whether the settlement amount at issue may be excluded from petitioner's gross income for 1997. Petitioner bears the burden of proving that the determination in the notice to include the settlement amount at issue in petitioner's gross income is erroneous.

Section 61(a) provides the following sweeping definition of the term "gross income": "Except as otherwise provided in this subtitle, gross income means all income from whatever source derived." Not only is section 61(a) broad in its scope, Commissioner v. Schleier, 515 U.S. 323, 328 (1995), exclusions from gross income must be narrowly construed, id.; United States v. Burke, 504 U.S. 229, 248 (1992).

Section 104(a)(2) on which petitioner relies provides that gross income does not include:

> (2) the amount of any damages (other than punitive damages) received (whether by suit or agreement and whether as lump sums or as periodic payments) on account of personal physical injuries or physical sickness;

The regulations under section 104(a)(2) restate the statutory language of that section and further provide:

> The term "damages received (whether by suit or agreement)" means an amount received (other than workmen's compensation) through prosecution of a legal suit or action based upon tort or tort type rights, or through a settlement agreement entered into in lieu of such prosecution. [Sec. 1.104-1(c), Income Tax Regs.]

The Supreme Court summarized the requirements of section 104(a)(2) as follows:

> In sum, the plain language of § 104(a)(2), the text of the applicable regulation, and our decision in Burke establish two independent requirements that a

taxpayer must meet before a recovery may be excluded under § 104(a)(2). First, the taxpayer must demonstrate that the underlying cause of action giving rise to the recovery is "based upon tort or tort type rights"; and second, the taxpayer must show that the damages were received "on account of personal injuries or sickness." [*Commissioner v. Schleier, supra* at 336–337.]

When the Supreme Court issued its opinion in *Commissioner v. Schleier, supra,* section 104(a)(2), as in effect for the year at issue in *Schleier,* required, inter alia, that, in order to be excluded from gross income, an amount of damages had to be received "on account of personal injuries or sickness." After the Supreme Court issued its opinion in *Schleier,* Congress amended section 104(a)(2), effective for amounts received after August 20, 1996, by adding the requirement that, in order to be excluded from gross income, any amounts received must be on account of personal injuries that are physical or sickness that is physical. The 1996 amendment does not otherwise change the requirements of section 104(a)(2) or the analysis set forth in *Commissioner v. Schleier, supra;* it imposes an additional requirement for an amount to qualify for exclusion from gross income under that section.

Where damages are received pursuant to a settlement agreement, such as is the case here, the nature of the claim that was the actual basis for settlement controls whether such damages are excludable under section 104(a)(2). The determination of the nature of the claim is factual. Where there is a settlement agreement, that determination is usually made by reference to it. If the settlement agreement lacks express language stating what the amount paid pursuant to that agreement was to settle, the intent of the payor is critical to that determination. Although the belief of the payee is relevant to that inquiry, the character of the settlement payment hinges ultimately on the dominant reason of the payor in making the payment. Whether the settlement payment is excludable from gross income under section 104(a)(2) depends on the nature and character of the claim asserted, and not upon the validity of that claim.

The dispute between the parties in the instant case relates to how much of the settlement amount at issue Mr. Rodman paid to petitioner on account of physical injuries. It is petitioner's position that the entire $200,000 settlement amount at issue is excludable from his gross income under section 104(a)(2). In support of that position, petitioner contends that Mr. Rodman paid him the entire amount on account of the physical injuries that he claimed he sustained as a result of the incident.

Respondent counters that, except for a nominal amount (i.e., $1), the settlement amount at issue is includable in petitioner's gross income. In support of that position, respondent contends that petitioner has failed to introduce any evidence regarding, and that Mr. Rodman was skeptical about, the extent of petitioner's physical injuries as a result of the incident. Consequently, according to respondent, the Court should infer that petitioner's physical injuries were minimal. In further support of respondent's position to include all but $1 of the settlement amount at issue in petitioner's gross income, respondent contends that, because the amount of any liquidated damages (i.e., $200,000) payable by petitioner to Mr. Rodman under the settlement agreement was equal to the settlement amount (i.e., $200,000) paid to petitioner under that agreement, Mr. Rodman did not intend to pay the settlement amount at issue in order to compensate petitioner for his physical injuries.

On the instant record, we reject respondent's position. With respect to respondent's contentions that petitioner has failed to introduce evidence regarding, and that Mr. Rodman was skeptical about, the extent of petitioner's physical injuries as a result of the incident, those contentions appear to ignore the well-established principle under section 104(a)(2) that it is the nature and character of the claim settled, and not its validity, that determines whether the settlement payment is excludable from gross income under section 104(a)(2). In any event, we find below that the record establishes that Mr. Rodman's dominant reason in paying the settlement amount at issue was petitioner's claimed physical injuries as a result of the incident.

With respect to respondent's contention that Mr. Rodman did not intend to pay the settlement amount at issue in order to compensate petitioner for his physical injuries because the amount of liquidated damages (i.e., $200,000) payable by petitioner to Mr. Rodman under the settlement agreement was equal to the settlement amount (i.e., $200,000) paid to petitioner under that agreement, we do not find the amount of liquidated damages payable under the settlement agreement to be determinative of the reason for which Mr. Rodman paid petitioner the settlement amount at issue.

On the record before us, we find that Mr. Rodman's dominant reason in paying the settlement amount at issue was to compensate petitioner for his claimed physical injuries relating to the incident. Our finding is supported by the settlement agreement, a declaration by Mr. Rodman, and Ms. Pearson's testimony.

The settlement agreement expressly provided that Mr. Rodman's payment of the settlement amount at issue

> releases and forever discharges * * * [Mr.] Rodman * * * from any and all claims and causes of action of any type, known and unknown, upon and by reason of any damage, loss or injury * * * sustained by Amos [petitioner] arising, or which could have arisen, out of or in connection with * * * [the incident].

Mr. Rodman stated in Mr. Rodman's declaration that he entered into the settlement agreement "to resolve any potential claims" and that the settlement agreement was intended to resolve petitioner's "claim without having to expend additional defense costs." The only potential claims of petitioner that are disclosed by the record are the potential claims that petitioner had for the physical injuries that he claimed he sustained as a result of the incident. Furthermore, Ms. Pearson testified that Mr. Rodman paid the entire settlement amount at issue to petitioner on account of his physical injuries. As discussed below, Ms. Pearson's testimony that Mr. Rodman paid that *entire* amount on account of petitioner's physical injuries is belied by the terms of the settlement agreement. Nonetheless, her testimony supports our finding that Mr. Rodman's dominant reason in paying petitioner the settlement amount at issue was to compensate him for claimed physical injuries relating to the incident.

We have found that Mr. Rodman's dominant reason in paying petitioner the settlement amount at issue was to compensate him for his claimed physical injuries relating to the incident. However, the settlement agreement expressly provided that Mr. Rodman paid petitioner a portion of the settlement amount at issue in return for petitioner's agreement not to: (1) Defame Mr. Rodman, (2) disclose the existence or the terms of the settlement agreement, (3) publicize facts relating to the incident, or (4) assist in any criminal prosecution against Mr. Rodman with respect to the incident (collectively, the nonphysical injury provisions).

The settlement agreement does not specify the portion of the settlement amount at issue that Mr. Rodman paid petitioner on account of his claimed physical injuries and the portion of such amount that Mr. Rodman paid petitioner on account of the nonphysical injury provisions in the settlement agreement. Nonetheless, based upon our review of the entire record before us, and bearing in mind that petitioner has the burden of proving the amount of the settlement amount at issue that Mr. Rodman paid him on account of physical injuries, we find that Mr. Rodman paid petitioner $120,000 of the settlement amount at issue on account of petitioner's claimed physical injuries and $80,000 of that amount on account of the nonphysical injury provisions in the settlement agreement. On that record, we further find that for the year at issue petitioner is entitled under section 104(a)(2) to exclude from his gross income $120,000 of the settlement amount at issue and is required under section 61(a) to include in his gross income $80,000 of that amount.

We have considered all of the contentions and arguments of respondent and of petitioner that are not discussed herein, and we find them to be without merit, irrelevant, and/or moot.

Stadnyk v. Commissioner

367 Fed.Appx. 586 (6th Cir. 2010)

CLAY, CIRCUIT JUDGE.

Petitioners Daniel and Brenda Stadnyk appeal from the order entered by the United States Tax Court denying their petition for redetermination of a deficiency. For the reasons set forth below, we affirm the Tax Court's order.

Background

On December 11, 1996, Petitioners purchased a used 1990 Geo Storm from Nicholasville Road Auto Sales, Inc. ("Nicholasville Auto") for $3,430.00. Brenda Stadnyk tendered two checks to Nicholasville Auto as partial payment, check number 1080 for $100 and check number 1087 for $1,100, from a checking account with Bank One, Kentucky, N.A. ("Bank One"). After Petitioners drove approximately seven miles from the dealership, the car broke down. Petitioners spent $479.78 to repair the car. They attempted to call Nicholasville Auto about the Geo Storm, but their calls were ignored, placed on hold for long periods of time, and not returned.

Because of their dissatisfaction with the car, Mrs. Stadnyk contacted Bank One to place a stop payment order on check number 1087 for $1,100. Bank One's record of the stop payment order indicates "dissatisfied purchase" as the reason for the stop payment. However, Bank One incorrectly stamped the check "NSF" for insufficient funds and returned it to Nicholasville Auto. On February 4, 1997, Nicholasville Auto filed a criminal complaint against Mrs. Stadnyk for issuing and passing a worthless check in the amount of $1,100.

At approximately 6:00 p.m. on February 23, 1997, officers of the Fayette County Sheriff's Department arrested Mrs. Stadnyk at her home in the presence of her husband, her daughter, and a family friend, and transported her to the Fayette County Detention Center. She arrived at the detention center at approximately 6:30 p.m., and she was handcuffed, photographed, and confined to a holding area. At approximately 11:00 p.m., Mrs. Stadnyk was transferred to Jessamine County Jail, where she was searched via pat-down and use of an electric wand. Mrs. Stadnyk was required to undress to her undergarments, remove her brassiere in the presence of officers, and put on an orange jumpsuit. She was released on bail at approximately 2:00 a.m. on February 24, 1997. On April 23, 1997, Mrs. Stadnyk was indicted for "theft by deception over $300.00" based on the returned check marked for insufficient funds. These charges were later dropped.

Mrs. Stadnyk testified that she did not suffer any physical injury as a result of her arrest and detention. According to Mrs. Stadnyk, nobody put their hands on her, grabbed her, jerked her around, bruised her, or hurt her. As a result of the incident, Mrs. Stadnyk visited a psychologist every 1.5 to two weeks for approximately eight sessions. The cost of these sessions was covered by Mrs. Stadnyk's insurance and employer. Mrs. Stadnyk did not pay any out-of-pocket medical expenses for physical injury or mental distress as a result of the arrest and detention.

On August 25, 1999, Mrs. Stadnyk filed a Complaint against J.R. Maze, the owner of Nicholasville Auto, Nicholasville Auto, and Bank One. On July 5, 2000, she filed a First Amended Complaint, alleging that Bank One breached its fiduciary duty of care by improperly and negligently marking her check "NSF" for insufficient funds. Mrs. Stadnyk's First Amended Complaint also included the following claims against J.R. Maze and Nicholasville Auto: malicious prosecution, abuse of process, false imprisonment, defamation, and outrageous conduct. The First Amended Complaint repeated and incorporated by reference these allegations against Bank One.

On March 7, 2002, Mrs. Stadnyk entered into a mediation agreement with Bank One, under which Bank One agreed to pay Mrs. Stadnyk $49,000 to settle her claims and provide her with a letter of apology. In return, Mrs. Stadnyk agreed to dismiss her complaint against Bank One. The mediation agreement form stated that "Bank One shall pay the total sum of $49,000, by 3/15/02, by official check" and that "[t]he suit shall be dismissed with prejudice with each party to pay their own costs & fees." (App. at 206). It contained no language indicating the purpose for which the settlement was paid. On March 14, 2002, Bank One issued a check to Mrs. Stadnyk for $49,000, and on May 3, 2002, Mrs. Stadnyk's complaint against Bank One was dismissed with prejudice.

During the trial before the Tax Court, Mrs. Stadnyk testified that her attorney, the attorney for Bank One, and the mediator all advised her that the settlement proceeds would not be subject to income tax. Based on this advice, the Stadnyks did not report the $49,000 settlement on their 2002 Form 1040 income tax return, although Bank One issued Mrs. Stadnyk a Form 1099-MISC reporting the payment of the $49,000 settlement. On March 14, 2005, Respondent issued a notice of deficiency to Petitioners, after determining that Petitioners were liable for a tax deficiency of $13,119.00 and an accuracy-related penalty of $2,624.00 under Internal Revenue Code ("I.R.C.") §6662(a). Petitioners timely appealed to the Tax Court. On January 12, 2009, the Tax Court ruled in favor of Respondent with respect to the deficiency and in favor of Petitioners with respect to the penalty. On April 15, 2009, Petitioners filed a timely notice of appeal.

Discussion

Under I.R.C. §61(a), taxpayers are liable for all gross income, which is defined as "all income from whatever source derived." 26 U.S.C. §61(a). The Supreme Court has instructed that §61 "be construed liberally 'in recognition of the intention of Congress to tax all gains except those specifically exempted.'" Greer v. United States, 207 F.3d 322, 326 (6th Cir. 2000) (quoting Comm'r v. Glenshaw Glass Co., 348 U.S. 426, 430 (1955)). Accordingly, Mrs. Stadnyk's $49,000 settlement classifies as gross income under §61(a), and Petitioners can only avoid paying taxes on the damages award if it falls under an exclusion.

The exclusion from §61(a) at issue in the instant case is contained in §104(a)(2), which permits taxpayers to exclude from income "the amount of any damages received (whether by suit or agreement and whether as lump sums or as periodic payments) on account of personal physical injuries or physical sickness." 26 U.S.C. §104(a)(2). Under the 1996 Amendment, I.R.C. §104(a)(2) expressly limits the type of damages excludable from income to personal *physical* injuries or *physical* sickness and expressly states that emotional distress does not constitute a physical injury or sickness. Pub. L. No. 104-188, §1605(a), 110 Stat. 1755, 1838. Kentucky courts have defined false imprisonment as "any deprivation of the liberty of one person by another or detention for however short a time without such person's consent and against his will, whether done by actual violence, threats or otherwise." Grayson Variety Store, Inc. v. Shaffer, 402 S.W.2d 424, 425 (Ky. 1966). The tort of false imprisonment protects personal interest in freedom from physical restraint; the interest is "in a sense a mental one" and the injury is "in large part a mental one." Banks v. Fritsch, 39 S.W.3d 474, 479 (Ky. Ct. App. 2001).

During her deposition, Mrs. Stadnyk testified that she did not suffer any physical injury as a result of her arrest and detention. According to Mrs. Stadnyk, nobody carrying out her arrest or detention put their hands on her, grabbed her, jerked her around, bruised her, or hurt her. Petitioners' brief concedes that the actions of the police were proper and that Mrs. Stadnyk presumes that she was treated in the same manner as anyone else arrested for passing a bad check. Nothing in the record suggests that Mrs. Stadnyk suffered physical, as opposed to emotional, injuries as a result of Bank One's actions.

The Tax Court correctly noted that "[t]he damages sought by [Mrs. Stadnyk] against Bank One are stated in terms of recovery for nonphysical personal injuries: [e]motional distress, mortification, humiliation, mental anguish, and damage to reputation." (App. at 88). These are all emotional injuries, and are thus not excludable under § 104(a)(2). *See* Sanford v. Comm'r, 95 T.C.M. (CCH) 1618 (2008) (settlement award for emotional distress relating to sexual harassment and discrimination claims is not excludable); Polone v. Comm'r, 86 T.C.M. (CCH) 698 (2003) (settlement award for defamation claim is not excludable), *aff'd* 505 F.3d 966 (9th Cir.2007); Venable v. Comm'r, 86 T.C.M. (CCH) 254 (2003) (settlement payment for mental anguish and loss of reputation relating to malicious prosecution claim is not excludable), *aff'd* 110 Fed. Appx. 421 (5th Cir.2004).

However, despite Mrs. Stadnyk's testimony, Petitioners argue that Mrs. Stadnyk suffered a physical injury because "[p]hysical restraint and detention and the resulting deprivation of [Mrs. Stadnyk's] personal liberty is [itself] a physical injury ... that Mrs. Stadnyk endured for an eight hour period." (Pets.' Br. at 15.) Petitioners further argue that Mrs. Stadnyk suffered physical damages in addition to emotional damages because "to be falsely imprisoned, the person must first be physically restrained or held against their will" and "[t]hus the damages received from false imprisonment arise from the person's physical loss of their freedom and the mental suffering and humiliation that accompany this deprivation." (Pets.' Br. at 15.)

In other words, Petitioners are asking the Court to create a *per se* rule that every false imprisonment claim necessarily involves a physical injury, even though physical injury is not a required element of false imprisonment under Kentucky law. To be sure, a false imprisonment claim may cause a physical injury, such as an injured wrist as a result of being handcuffed. But the mere fact that false imprisonment involves a physical act-restraining the victim's freedom-does not mean that the victim is *necessarily* physically injured *as a result of* that physical act. In the instant case, Mrs. Stadnyk unequivocally testified that she suffered no physical injuries as a result of her physical restraint. Thus, Petitioners have failed to establish that Mrs. Stadnyk suffered from personal physical injuries or physical sickness.

In addition, the Supreme Court has construed the "on account of" phrase to require a direct causal link between the physical injury and the damages recovery in order to qualify for the income exclusion. *See Schleier,* 515 U.S. at 329–31. This direct causal connection must be more than a "but for" link, because a "but for" analysis would "bring virtually all personal injury lawsuit damages within the scope of the provision, since: but for the personal injury, there would be no lawsuit, and but for the lawsuit, there would be no damages." O'Gilvie v. United States, 519 U.S. 79, 82 (1996) (internal quotation marks omitted). Rather, the "on account of" phrase requires that the damages be awarded by reason of, or because of, a personal physical injury. *Id.* at 83. *See also Greer,* 207 F.3d at 327 (requiring that "the agreement was executed 'in lieu' of the prosecution of the tort claim and 'on account of' the personal injury"). Petitioners bear the burden of "present[ing] concrete evidence demonstrating the precise causal connection" between the personal physical injuries and the settlement payment. *Id.* at 334.

The settlement agreement does not include any express language of purpose. It only provides that "Bank One shall pay the total sum of $49,000" and that the "suit shall be dismissed with prejudice." (App. at 206). Petitioners' only evidence arguably supporting the purpose necessary for exclusion under § 104(a)(2) is Mrs. Stadnyk's testimony that her attorney, the attorney for Bank One, and the mediator all advised her that the settlement proceeds would not be subject to income tax. However, even assuming the attorneys did give her this advice, there is no evidence concerning the basis for the advice. The attorneys may have advised Mrs. Stadnyk based on any number of incorrect beliefs, such as the belief that all personal injury awards are excludable from income, as Petitioner argues here, or the belief that a physical injury was unnecessary. Given that the settlement agreement included no indication that Bank One paid the settlement on account of any physical injury and that all of Mrs. Stadnyk's damages were stated in terms of emotional distress, Petitioners have failed to offer any concrete evidence demonstrating a causal connection between any physical injury and the settlement award.

Thus, Petitioner's settlement award may not be excluded from taxation under § 104(a)(2).

Conclusion

Because the Tax Court properly found that Petitioners owe income taxes on the damages award received pursuant to their settlement with Bank One, we AFFIRM the Tax's Court's order.

V. Related Matters

- **Business Damages.** In determining the proper tax treatment of business damages, the question to be asked is: "In lieu of what were the damages awarded?" Raytheon Products Corp. v. Commissioner, 144 F.2d 100, 113 (1st Cir. 1944). Damages awarded for lost profits or income are taxable as ordinary income. Damages awarded for damage to property (e.g., injury to goodwill of a business) represent a return of capital and are tax free to the extent of basis in the property. To the extent such damages exceed basis in the damaged asset, the excess may be taxable as capital gains depending on the nature of the property. As can be seen, the taxability of proceeds depends on the origin and character of the claim which gives rise to the litigation.

- **Intellectual Property Litigation.** Damages for patent or copyright infringement represent the taxpayer's lost profits (royalties), and therefore are taxable as ordinary income. See, e.g., Mathey v. Commissioner, 177 F.2d 259 (1st Cir. 1949); Big Four Industries, Inc. v. Commissioner, 40 T.C. 1055 (1963), acq., 1964-2 C.B. 3. Damages for trademark infringement, in contrast, are for damage to the trademark and the goodwill associated therewith (injury to a capital asset rather than harm in the form of lost profits). Thus, such damages are included in gross income only to the extent they exceed basis in the damaged capital. *See, e.g.*, Inco Electroenergy Corp. v. Commissioner, 54 T.C.M. (CCH) 359 (1987).

• **Human Egg Donors.** The Tax Court recently concluded that a $20,000 payment received for service as a human egg donor did not constitute amounts received for sale of property. Nor was it excludable from income as a recovery for personal injuries under section 104(a)(2). Instead the payment was taxable as compensation income. Perez v. Commissioner, 144 T.C. 51 (2015).

Chapter 35

Attorney's Fees

I. Assignment

Read: Internal Revenue Code: §§ 162(a), (q); 212; 262; 263(a); 265(a)(1).

Treasury Regulations: §§ 1.212-1(e), (k)–(m); 1.262-1(b)(7); 1.263(a)-2(a), (c).

Text: Overview
Fleischman v. Commissioner
Commissioner v. Banks
Related Matters

Complete the problems.

II. Problems

1. Professor Langdell, who teaches litigation courses at a renowned law school, is quite litigious. This year, he paid attorney's fees in connection with several different lawsuits. Discuss the deductibility of the following attorney's fees paid. (None of the fees were paid under a contingency fee agreement.)

   (a) $15,000 in connection with a suit against a third party for personal physical injuries Professor Langdell sustained in a boating accident. Professor Langdell received $50,000 in compensatory damages.

   (b) $3,000 in connection with an action against his publisher to collect past due royalties from the sale of his copyrighted casebook.

   (c) $6,000 incurred to contest condemnation of his log cabin in Montana.

   (d) $2,000 paid for advice on the taxability of the compensatory damages received in (a) above.

   (e) $5,000 incurred to obtain a Private Letter Ruling from the IRS on the deductibility of his attorney's fees.

2. William Orange and Eva Eliver entered into a prenuptial agreement in Year 1 in which William agreed to transfer $500,000 of Google stock to Eva in which he had a basis of $200,000 in exchange for her agreement that she would ask for nothing more in the event of a divorce. William transferred the stock in Year 1 and they were married later that year. In Year 12, they divorced. As part of the divorce proceedings the prenuptial agreement was set aside as having been obtained

by fraud (since William grossly under represented his net worth to Eva). Eventually William agreed to pay Eva a substantial amount, part of which was in the form of alimony and part of which was a property settlement. Both parties incurred substantial attorneys fees for various aspects of the proceedings as follows:

William: $50,000 in defending the prenuptial agreement
           $10,000 in negotiating the alimony agreement
           $15,000 in negotiating the property settlement
           $12,000 in planning for the tax consequences of the divorce

Eva: $50,000 in attacking the prenuptial agreement
           $10,000 in negotiating the alimony agreement
           $20,000 in negotiating the property settlement

Which of the attorney's fees, if any, are tax deductible by the payor?

3. Farzana Chowdhury was forced to leave her job as a loan officer of Friendly Bank. Later, she hired an attorney under a contingent fee arrangement and filed a discrimination lawsuit against her former employer. This year, the parties settled the case for $1 million. Friendly Bank paid $600,000 to Farzana and $400,000 to Farzana's attorney pursuant to the attorney's fee agreement.

   (a) What is the proper tax treatment of the $400,000 attorney's fee?

   (b) Would it make a difference if Farzana's suit was against her ex-boyfriend for defamation?

III. Overview

A. Deductibility of Attorney's Fees and Other Litigation Costs

Section 162 allows a deduction for ordinary and necessary business expenses paid or incurred during the year in carrying on any trade or business, and section 212 allows a deduction for ordinary and necessary expenses paid or incurred during the year for the production or collection of income and for the management, conservation, or maintenance of property held for the production of income. Section 262 provides that no deduction shall be allowed for personal, living, or family expenses, and section 263 provides that no deduction shall be allowed for capital expenditures. Courts initially struggled with the appropriate standard to apply in determining whether attorney's fees and other litigation costs are deductible under sections 162 or 212 or nondeductible under sections 262 or 263. Courts considered whether the taxpayer's primary purpose in initiating or defending litigation should be controlling, or whether the outcome of the litigation should be a factor. It is now well-settled that the origin and character of the claim with respect to which litigation costs are incurred is the controlling test.

The "origin of the claim" test was originally created by the Supreme Court in United States v. Gilmore, 372 U.S. 39 (1963), and used to determine whether litigation costs were incurred in a business or profit-seeking context or whether the costs were personal. In *Gilmore*, the taxpayer attempted to deduct a portion of the legal fees he paid in a divorce proceeding — specifically that portion attributable to his attorney's efforts to keep ownership of certain closely-held stock (income-producing property) that his spouse had demanded in the divorce. The Supreme Court held the divorce proceeding and the costs thereof "stemmed entirely from the marital relationship," and hence were nondeductible personal expenses. The Court noted:

> [C]haracterization, as "business" or "personal" of the litigation costs of resisting a claim depends on whether or not the claim *arises in connection with* the taxpayer's profit-seeking activities. It does not depend on the *consequences* that might result to a taxpayer's income-producing property from a failure to defeat the claim.... [W]e resolve the conflict among the lower courts on the question before us in favor of the view that the origin and character of the claim with respect to which an expense was incurred, rather than its potential consequences upon the fortunes of the taxpayer, is the controlling basic test of whether the expense was "business" or "personal" and hence whether it is deductible or not.

The origin of the claim standard has also been used to determine whether litigation costs — even if incurred in a business or profit-seeking activity — are nondeductible capital expenditures. In Woodward v. Commissioner, 397 U.S. 572 (1970), the taxpayers, who owned a majority interest in a corporation, paid legal fees in an appraisal proceeding which arose in connection with the required purchase of a dissenting, minority shareholder's stock. Relying on its decision in *Gilmore*, the Supreme Court held that the origin of the claim that gave rise to the legal fees was the acquisition of stock and, thus, the fees should be capitalized:

> [A] standard based on the origin of the claim litigated comports with this Court's most recent ruling on the characterization of litigation expenses for tax purposes. In *United States v. Gilmore*, this Court held that the expense of defending a divorce suit was a nondeductible personal expense, even though the outcome of the divorce case would affect the taxpayer's property holdings, and might affect his business reputation. The Court rejected a test which looked to the consequences of the litigation, and did not even consider the taxpayer's motives or purposes in undertaking defense of the litigation, but rather examined the origin and character of the claim against the taxpayer, and found that the claim arose out of the personal relationship of marriage.

Review Treas. Reg. §§ 1.263(a)-2(a), -2(c) (giving as examples of capital expenditures the cost of acquiring property having a useful life substantially beyond the taxable year and the cost of defending or perfecting title to property); Temp. Treas. Reg. § 1.263(a)-2T(e). Review also Treas. Reg. § 1.212-1(k).

The origin of the claim test is not a purely mechanical test; it requires more than looking merely to the taxpayer's intent in filing the suit. One must also consider the issues involved, the nature and objectives of the litigation, the defenses asserted, the purposes for which the amounts claimed to be deductible were expended, the background of the litigation, and all facts pertaining to the controversy. *See* Boagni v. Commissioner, 59 T.C. 708, 713 (1973). The origin of the claim test has been used in a number of lower court cases. Read *Fleischman v. Commissioner*, included in materials below. *See also* Madden v. Commissioner, 514 F.2d 1149 (9th Cir. 1975), *rev'g* 57 T.C. 513 (1971) (requiring capitalization of legal fees incurred in contesting condemnation of property); Georator Corp. v. United States, 485 F.2d 283 (4th Cir. 1973) (requiring capitalization of legal fees incurred in resisting a petition to cancel registration of a trademark); Kellner v. Commissioner, T.C. Memo 1982-729 (requiring capitalization of legal fees incurred to establish title to assets in deceased spouse's estate). When attorney's fees must be capitalized, they are added to the basis of the related property.

For legal fees to be deductible under section 212(1), they must relate to the production or collection of *taxable* income—amounts includible in gross income. For example, damages received on account of non-physical injury are includible in gross income; as a result, attorney's fees to recover such damages are deductible under section 212 as expenses for the production of income.

Legal fees paid in connection with the production or collection of *tax-exempt* income are generally not deductible in order to prevent what would, in effect, be a double benefit—an exclusion and a deduction. Treas. Reg. § 1.212-1(e) (citing IRC § 265). For example, attorney's fees paid in connection with the receipt of damages on account of personal physical injury are nondeductible since such damages are excludable from gross income under section 104(a)(2). Likewise, attorney's fees paid in connection with the receipt of child support are nondeductible on the theory that child support is not taxable. *See* IRC § 71(c).

Legal or other professional fees paid or incurred in connection with the determination, collection, or refund of any tax are deductible under section 212(3). Treas. Reg. § 1.212-1(l). Fees for tax planning advice (advice concerning future transactions as opposed to consummated transactions) are also deductible. *See* Carpenter v. United States, 338 F.2d 366 (Ct. Cl. 1964); Rev. Rul. 89-68, 1989-1 C.B. 82 (permitting deduction for fees paid in connection with obtaining a private letter ruling). This includes legal fees and expenses for estate planning advice. *See* Merians v. Commissioner, 60 T.C. 187 (1973), acq., 1973-2 C.B. 2. Courts are split on whether section 212(3) is subject to the capital limitation of section 263. *See* Sharples v. United States, 533 F.2d 550 (Ct. Cl. 1976) (allowing a section 212(3) deduction for legal fees paid in contesting a tax liability which arose from a capital transaction); *but see* Honodel v. Commissioner, 722 F.2d 1462 (9th Cir. 1984) (disallowing a section 212(3) deduction for tax advice related to a capital acquisition).

If a legal fee is partially deductible and partially nondeductible, the taxpayer must allocate the fee between the deductible and nondeductible portions. *See* Treas. Reg. § 1.212-1(k) ("Attorneys' fees paid in a suit to quiet title to lands are not deductible;

but if the suit is also to collect accrued rents thereon, that portion of such fees is deductible which is properly allocable to the services rendered in collection of such rents."); Southland Royalty Co. v. United States, 582 F.2d 604 (Ct. Cl. 1978) (holding that portion of legal fees to construe royalty provisions of a mineral lease were deductible, but that portion incurred in seeking a declaratory judgment regarding taxpayer's rights to a twelve-year mineral lease were not deductible). Lawyer fee statements that make a reasonable and good faith allocation are typically respected.

B. Above or Below the Line Determination

Attorney's fees related to a trade or business (other than the trade or business of being an employee) that are deductible under section 162 are considered above-the-line deductions (i.e., are taken into account in computing adjusted gross income). IRC § 62(a)(1). Examples include expenses in preparing that portion of a tax return relating to the taxpayer's business, and attorney's fees in contesting tax deficiencies arising from the taxpayer's business.

Prior to 2004, all attorney's fees other than those described above were considered miscellaneous itemized deductions, subject to the section 67 limitation and the section 68 limitation. (Recall that the Tax Cuts and Jobs Act of 2017 (TCJA) eliminated miscellaneous itemized deductions for years 2018–2025.) Attorney's fees in this category included legal fees related to the trade or business of being an employee, deductible under section 162. McKay v. Commissioner, 102 T.C. 465 91994), rev'd on other grounds, 84 F.3d 433 (5th Cir. 1996). More significantly, this category included the broad range of legal fees deductible under section 212, or fees paid in connection with: (1) the production or collection of taxable income; (2) the management, conservation, or maintenance of property for the production of income; and (3) the determination, collection, or refund of any tax. Treating attorney's fees as miscellaneous itemized deductions had negative implications beyond the section 67 and section 68 limitations for taxpayers subject to the alternative minimum tax, since attorney's fees classified as miscellaneous itemized deductions are not allowable as deductions in computing the alternative minimum tax. *See* Hukkanen-Campbell v. Commissioner, 274 F.3d 1312 (10th Cir. 2001). In many cases, plaintiffs ended up paying more in attorney's fees and federal taxes than the damage awards they received.

The American Jobs Creation Act of 2004 provided much needed relief by amending section 62(a). Section 62(a)(20) provides an above-the-line deduction for attorney's fees and costs in connection with claims of "unlawful discrimination" and certain claims against the federal government. The amount that may be deducted above-the-line may not exceed the amount includible in the taxpayer's gross income for the taxable year on account of a judgment or settlement. Section 62(e) defines "unlawful discrimination" to include a number of specific statutes, any federal whistle-blower statute, and any federal, state, or local law "providing for the enforcement of civil rights" or "regulating any aspect of the employment relationship ... or prohibiting the discharge of an employee, the discrimination against an employee, or any other form of retaliation or reprisal against an employee for asserting rights or taking other actions permitted by law." The laundry list in section 62(e), which includes a catchall category, largely covers employment discrimination claims. However, it does not include all claims. Arguably, it does not include claims for defamation, invasion of privacy, false imprisonment, intentional infliction of emotional distress, and tortious interference with contract that occur outside the employment context. This has potentially grave consequences for plaintiffs because of the suspended deductibility of miscellaneous itemized deductions until 2026.

As further relief, Congress recently added section 62(a)(21), which provides an above the line deduction for attorney's fees related to whistleblower awards. However, the above the line deduction cannot exceed the income the plaintiff receives from the litigation in the same tax year.

C. Contingent Fees

In some lawsuits, plaintiffs will engage an attorney to represent them on a contingent fee basis. Under a typical contingent fee agreement, if a plaintiff recovers damages, a prearranged percentage of the damages will be paid to the attorney; if no damages are recovered, no fee is paid. An interesting issue is whether amounts paid to an attorney under a contingency fee agreement impact the amount of an award otherwise included in gross income. In other words, does the taxpayer have to include the entire amount of damages in income and then take a deduction for the portion paid to the attorney, or does the taxpayer exclude the portion of the recovery paid to the attorney and claim no deduction. Several courts held that, in a contingency fee arrangement, a taxpayer could not exclude that portion of the recovery paid directly to the attorney, but had to include the entire amount of damages in gross income and then claim a miscellaneous itemized deduction (subject to the two-percent floor) for that portion of the award paid to the attorney. [This was not a wash since, as noted above, no deduction is allowed for miscellaneous itemized deductions for purposes of the alternative minimum tax.] Other courts held that a taxpayer could exclude contingency fees paid directly to the attorney in some or all cases. The Supreme Court resolved this issue in *Commissioner v. Banks*, included in the materials below.

The *Banks* decision is significant in light of the 1996 amendments to section 104(a)(2), which cause an increasing number of damage awards to be taxable. (Recall from the previous chapter that section 104(a)(2) now excludes only non-punitive damages received on account of personal physical injuries or physical sickness.) The 2005 *Banks* decision is seemingly insignificant, however, in light of the 2004 amendments to section 62(a), which provide an above-the-line deduction for an increasing number of deductible attorney's fees. Indeed, the *Banks* Court noted that had section 62(a)(20) been in force, the case likely would not have arisen. Keep in mind, however, that *Banks* is still precedent for the contingent fee arrangements not eligible for an above-the-line deduction. As noted above, this includes claims for defamation, invasion of privacy, and tortious interference with contract — to name a few.

IV. Materials

Fleischman v. Commissioner

45 T.C. 439 (1966)

Simpson, Judge:

The Commissioner has determined a deficiency in the petitioner's income tax for 1962 in the amount of $725.60. The issue in this case is whether the petitioner may deduct legal expenses incurred in defending his wife's lawsuit to set aside their antenuptial contract.

FINDINGS OF FACT

Meyer J. Fleischman, the petitioner, is a physician in Cincinnati, Ohio. He reported his income on the cash method of accounting and filed his 1962 income tax return with the district director of internal revenue at Cincinnati, Ohio.

On February 25, 1955, petitioner entered into an antenuptial agreement with Joan Ruth Francis. That agreement was made in contemplation of marriage and provided:

> Now, Therefore, it is agreed between said parties that should said marriage terminate in the future through divorce or annulment that at said time of the granting of the annulment or divorce Party of the Second Part [Meyer] shall pay to Party of the First Part [Joan] the sum of Five Thousand ($5,000.00) Dollars in cash. In consideration of said payment the parties hereto agree and do hereby release and forever relinquish any and all claims to or interest of any kind in any property, whether real, personal or mixed which either party has now or may have during his or her lifetime or at their death, whether said interest should be by way of inheritance, distributive share, statutory exemptions or allowance, dower or otherwise, and each party agrees that all of each party's respective property upon death shall go to his or her devisees, legatees, other heirs, next of kin and/or assigns. The parties hereto agree to do such things and to deliver such instruments from time to time as may be necessary or desirable to carry into effect the foregoing agreement.

Petitioner and Joan R. Francis were married on February 26, 1955. On December 20, 1961, Joan filed for a divorce in the Court of Common Pleas, Division of Domestic Relations, Hamilton County, Ohio. In her suit for divorce the wife made the following prayer:

> Wherefore, plaintiff prays that she may be divorced from defendant Meyer J. Fleischman; that she be awarded temporary and permanent alimony; that during the pendency of this cause defendant Meyer J. Fleischman be enjoined and restrained from concealing, secreting and/or disposing of any property of any kind or type, and that defendant Rae Goldstein be enjoined and restrained during the pendency of this cause from paying over or delivering unto defendant Meyer J. Fleischman any property of any kind or type, in-

cluding but not limited to money, and from concealing, secreting and/or disposing of any property of the Fleischman Realty Company in her possession or under her control. That plaintiff be awarded a fair and equitable division of all properties, real and personal, of the defendant Meyer J. Fleischman, and for all such other and further relief to which she may be entitled in the premises, including her attorney fees and expenses.

On December 26, 1961, she filed another action in the Court of Common Pleas, Hamilton County, Ohio. The latter suit was instituted to set aside the antenuptial agreement and was necessary because the domestic relations division had no jurisdiction to declare the contract void and invalid. In her petition, she alleged that her husband had deceived her by false representations concerning the validity of the agreement, and that at the time of the agreement and at the time of filing suit she had no idea of the nature and extent of the defendant's property. She asserted that the provisions made for her under the agreement were grossly disproportionate to her husband's means.

A decree of divorce was entered on October 19, 1962. The suit to rescind and invalidate the antenuptial agreement was dismissed with prejudice on the plaintiff's application October 22, 1962.

Petitioner did not deduct the legal expenses incurred in connection with the divorce proceeding. Petitioner did deduct on his 1962 return $3,000 for legal expenses incurred in defending the suit to invalidate the antenuptial agreement signed on February 25, 1955. Respondent disallowed this deduction and determined a deficiency of $725.60. This deficiency is in issue here.

OPINION

The sole question in this case is whether petitioner is entitled to deduct $3,000 in legal expenses incurred in defending his wife's suit to set aside an antenuptial agreement.

We hold that he is barred from deducting these expenses by section 262 of the Internal Revenue Code of 1954 and the decision of the Supreme Court in United States v. Gilmore, 372 U.S. 39 (1963).

The petitioner's brief asserts first that his position was adequately set forth in the opinion of Carpenter v. United States, 338 F. 2d 366 (Ct. Cl. 1964). Second, he argues that Erdman v. Commissioner, 315 F. 2d 762 (C.A. 7, 1963), affirming 37 T.C. 1119 (1962), supports his position. Lastly, petitioner suggests that the litigation giving rise to the legal expenses here in issue did not grow out of the marriage relationship, but sprang from rights excluded from that relationship. The respondent has countered that the *Carpenter* case is distinguishable; that *Erdman* is inapposite; and that the suggested distinction between rights flowing from the marriage relationship and rights flowing from an antenuptial agreement is one of form and should be rejected. In the alternative, respondent urges that the expenses were incurred in defending title to property and should be capitalized, not allowed as a deduction.

We agree with all three of respondent's arguments and, therefore, do not reach his alternative proposition.

Petitioner's first contention, that his position is sustained by *Carpenter* is untenable. *Carpenter* involved a deduction for legal expenses paid for tax counsel in the course of a divorce proceeding. The court found these payments to be deductible under section 212(3) as an ordinary and necessary expense paid in connection with the determination of a tax. In Fleischman's case, there is no suggestion in the record that the legal expenses involved were for consultation and advice on tax matters. The stipulation clearly states that the expenses were incurred in defending a suit to set aside and declare void an antenuptial contract.

If petitioner means to rely on *Carpenter* to sustain his case under section 212(2) or 212(1), he is left with the liability that the case did not deal with those paragraphs. Paragraph (3) of section 212, as the *Carpenter* case holds, expresses a policy and has a meaning quite different from paragraphs (1) and (2). In fact, the court pointed out in *Carpenter* that the legal fees would not be deductible under section 212(2).

If petitioner cites *Carpenter* for the proposition that certain legal fees can be deducted even though incurred in connection with a divorce, he is certainly correct. This Court has so held in the case of Ruth K. Wild, 42 T.C. 706 (1964). The question in the case before us, however, is whether *these* legal expenses are deductible, and in resolving that issue, the *Carpenter* case is of no assistance.

The petitioner's second argument is that the case of *Erdman* v. *Commissioner* may be pertinent. We do not agree. *Erdman* concerned the deductibility of legal expenses incurred by taxpayers defending their title to property as beneficiaries of a testamentary trust. In the alternative, it was contended that the trust was entitled to deduct these expenses. This Court held that the attorney's fees were an expenditure of the trust, not of the taxpayer. In addition, the trust was not permitted to deduct the fee currently as it was charged to trust corpus, not income. Calvin Pardee Erdman, 37 T.C. 1119 (1962).

On appeal, the Seventh Circuit upheld the Tax Court on both grounds and added that the taxpayer's expenses were capital in nature, being in defense of title, and not deductible for that reason as well. *Erdman* v. *Commissioner, supra*. It is our view that the factual and legal issues in *Erdman* are so significantly different from those in this case that it is of no assistance in reaching our decision.

The expenditures in question are deductible, if at all, only under section 212. Since there is not the slightest indication in the record that the counsel fees concerned taxes, we do not consider this case under section 212(3). In addition, there is no support for the view that the petitioner incurred the legal expenses for the production or collection of income, nor does he argue that he did; therefore, section 212(1) is not raised. The petition alleges that the expense was for the preservation and protection of taxpayer's real property inherited from his mother. This leaves only the suggestion that the expenses are deductible under section 212(2) as paid for the management, conservation, or maintenance of property held for the production of income.

In approaching the issue thus presented, it is helpful to consider the general purpose and history of section 212. Prior to 1942, legal expenses were deductible only if the suit occasioning them was directly connected with or proximately related to the taxpayer's trade or business. Legal costs which were simply personal expenses were not deductible, although the line between personal and business expenses was sometimes difficult to draw.

Certain investment activities conducted by the taxpayer might generate taxable income; however, the expenses attributable to these activities were not deductible where the activities did not constitute a trade or business. Higgins v. Commissioner, 312 U.S. 212 (1941). In order to equalize the treatment of these expenses with business expenses, both of which produced taxable income, Congress added section 23(a)(2) to the 1939 Code by the Revenue Act of 1942 (56 Stat. 798, 819). That section provided as follows:

SEC. 23. DEDUCTIONS FROM GROSS INCOME.

In computing net income there shall be allowed as deductions:

(a) Expenses. —

* * *

(2) Non-trade or non-business expenses. — In the case of an individual, all the ordinary and necessary expenses paid or incurred during the taxable year for the production or collection of income, or for the management, conservation, or maintenance of property held for the production of income.

At the same time that Congress enacted section 23(a)(2), it also added sections 22(k) and 23(u) to the 1939 Code. In general, those sections required a divorced spouse to include alimony payments in her gross income and permitted the paying spouse to deduct the amounts paid from his taxable income. Thus, while the Congress increased the range of deductions by section 23(a)(2), it also provided for a new kind of taxable income to a divorced spouse. However, Congress left us with no guidance in the legislative history as to the relationship between the alimony provisions and section 23(a)(2).

Section 23(a)(2) was construed as enlarging the category of incomes with respect to which expenses were deductible. Deductions under that section were analogous to business expenses and were allowable or not in accordance with principles which had long controlled these expenses. McDonald v. Commissioner, 323 U.S. 57 (1944). In particular, legal expenses were allowable as investment expenses subject to the same limitations imposed on legal fees incurred in a trade or business. Trust of Bingham v. Commissioner, 325 U.S. 365 (1945).

Great difficulty was experienced in distinguishing deductible legal expenses from those which were purely personal. This Court found that a wife could deduct legal fees incurred to obtain alimony included in her gross income under the Revenue Act of 1942. Elsie B. Gale, 13 T.C. 661 (1949), affd. 191 F. 2d 79 (C.A. 2, 1951), acq. 1952-1 C.B. 2; Barbara B. LeMond, 13 T.C. 670 (1949), acq. 1952-1 C.B. 3. On the other hand, the husband's legal expenses were regarded as personal even if he was compelled to pay his wife's counsel fees, or if his income-producing property was threatened with sequestration to pay alimony. Lindsay C. Howard, 16 T.C. 157 (1951), affd. 202 F. 2d 28 (C.A. 9, 1953); Robert A. McKinney, 16 T.C. 916 (1951); Thorne Donnelley, 16 T.C. 1196 (1951).

The Supreme Court in construing the new section found that Congress did not intend to permit taxpayers to deduct personal, living, or family expenses. Lykes v. United States, 343 U.S. 118, 125 (1952). In applying this rationale, the Court stated as follows:

> * * * Legal expenses do not become deductible merely because they are paid for services which relieve a taxpayer of liability. That argument would carry us too far. It would mean that the expense of defending almost any claim would be deductible by a taxpayer on the ground that such defense was made to help him keep clear of liens whatever income-producing property he might have. * * * Section 23(a)(2) never has been so interpreted by us. It has been applied to expenses on the basis of their immediate purposes rather than upon the basis of the remote contributions they might make to the conservation of a taxpayer's income-producing assets by reducing his general liabilities. *See McDonald* v. *Commissioner, supra,* * * *

In 1963, the Court undertook to explain the application of this rationale to a husband's legal expenses incurred in a divorce action. United States v. Gilmore, 372 U.S. 39 (1963).

The taxpayer in *Gilmore* owned a controlling interest in three corporations. The dividends and salary from these companies were his major source of income. In a divorce proceeding, his wife alleged that much of this property was community property and that more than half of the community property should be awarded to her. The taxpayer incurred substantial legal expenses in the course of successfully resisting these claims. He sought to deduct the expenses attributable to his defense against his wife's property claims under section 23(a)(2) of the 1939 Code. The Supreme Court sustained the Government's contention that deductibility depended upon the origin and nature of the claim giving rise to the legal expenses, rather than upon the consequences of such a claim to income-producing property.

The Supreme Court reached this result for two basic reasons. First, the language of the statute "conservation of property" was said to refer to operations performed with respect to the property itself rather than the taxpayer's retention of ownership in it. Secondly, the Court examined the legislative history and discerned a congressional purpose to equalize treatment of expenditures for profit-seeking activities with those related to a trade or business. In order to achieve this result, any limitation or restriction imposed upon a business expense must be applied to section 23(a)(2) expenses. Among those restrictions was the rule, now embodied in section 262, that personal, living, or family expenses are not deductible. The characterization of litigation costs as personal or business depends upon whether the claim involved in the litigation arises in connection with the profit-seeking activities. A suit against a taxpayer must be directly connected with or proximately result from his business before it is a business expense. This being so, the "origin of claim" test used in the business deduction cases was selected as most consistent with the meaning of section 23(a)(2). The claim against the property in a divorce suit arises only from the marital relationship and is therefore personal. The wife's rights, if any, must have their source in the marriage.

Dispelling all doubts that the Supreme Court was passing only on community property claims was United States v. Patrick, 372 U.S. 53 (1963), decided the same day as *Gilmore*. The *Patrick* case dealt with a property settlement which was made prior to divorce and which was supposed to have preserved the husband's income-producing property. The Supreme Court found little or no difference between that situation and *Gilmore* where the issue concerned community property and the wife's claim to an award of more than her existing share of such property.

Gilmore was decided under the 1939 Code and *Patrick* under the 1954 Code. There was no suggestion in these cases that enactment of the 1954 Code changed the meaning of the statutory language. The 1954 Code divides the provisions formerly contained in section 23(a)(2) of the 1939 Code into two paragraphs. The first deals with expenses for the production of income, and the second with expenses for the management, conservation, or maintenance of property held for the production of income. In connection with section 212 (1) and (2), the legislative history specifically states that no substantive change from section 23(a)(2) of the Internal Revenue Code of 1939 was made. Thus, the Code simply puts in separate paragraphs what was once one sentence.

Scarcely had the *Gilmore* case been decided, when the Tax Court was again confronted with the issue of the deductibility of the wife's attorney fees expended to collect defaulted alimony payments. Jane U. Elliott, 40 T.C. 304 (1963), acq. 1964-1 C.B. (Part 1) 4. In accordance with prior law, the wife was allowed a deduction under section 212(1). The Court held that the legal fees in question were incurred for the production of her taxable income. *Gilmore* and *Patrick* were not cited in this opinion.

The following year the case of Ruth K. Wild, 42 T.C. 706 (1964), was presented for review by the whole Court. The wife sought a deduction for counsel fees under section 212(1) in reliance upon the *Elliott* case for expenses incurred in negotiating an alimony agreement and in hearings concerning this agreement. The respondent contended that *Gilmore* and *Patrick* required a contrary result since the expenses were attributable to a claim which was based on her marital rights and not on a profit-seeking activity. This Court distinguished *Gilmore* and *Patrick* upon the basis that both of those cases were decided under paragraph (2) of section 212 and the contention in the *Wild* case was that the legal fees were deductible under paragraph (1). The Commissioner's regulations permitting a deduction for legal costs attributable to the collection of taxable alimony had not been changed following the *Gilmore* decision. Neither had his acquiescence in *Elliott* been withdrawn. These two factors influenced the Court in holding that the wife could continue to deduct legal expenses related to alimony. Thus, she retained a deduction under section 212(1).

This Court has made it clear that the wife's deduction under section 212(1) is limited to expenses incurred in obtaining alimony includable in her gross income. There is no deduction for expenses related to property claims, even when incurred by the wife. Those claims grow out of the marital relationship and are covered by the rule in *Gilmore*.

Turning to the case at hand, both petitioner and respondent have argued the case under section 212(2). In order to prevail, the petitioner must demonstrate how his expenses differ from those in *Gilmore* and *Patrick*. We find that he has failed in this task.

Petitioner suggests that his expenses differ from those at issue in *Gilmore* because his were caused by a separate suit to rescind a contract. In Joan Fleischman's second suit, she alleged that the provisions of the antenuptial agreement were disproportionate to her husband's means at the time the agreement was made and at the time of suit. Simultaneously, she had a divorce suit pending requesting support payments. Viewed in its entirety, her effort was one directed at obtaining support payments greater than those provided in the antenuptial agreement. In part, her claim to greater rights was founded upon facts existing or arising during the marriage. In this respect her claim was not unlike that involved in the *Gilmore* case. There, the claim was that certain community property belonging one-half to the husband should be awarded to the wife because of wrongs committed during the marital relationship. The Supreme Court rejected any distinction between legal expenses related to the issue of whether assets were community property and those related to an award of such property. Both issues have a common origin. In both *Gilmore* and here, the wife was requesting an award of property and her right was founded only upon the consequences that State law attaches to marriage. In petitioner's case, his wife made no claim to specific property except as a source of payment, hence his position is even weaker than that of the taxpayer in *Gilmore*.

The fact that Fleischman's wife first had to file a separate suit to invalidate the antenuptial agreement is solely the result of the restricted jurisdiction of the Ohio divorce courts. That fact alone is not a sound basis for a distinction in the field of Federal taxation.

For ascertaining the source of claims giving rise to legal expenses, the Supreme Court suggested a "but for" test. If the claim could not have existed but for the marriage relationship, the expense of defending it is a personal expense and not deductible. Applying that test, it is clear that but for her marriage to petitioner, the wife could have no claim to the property sought to be protected.

In deciding that the antenuptial agreement in this case is not significantly different from a property settlement incident to a divorce, we are aided in our reasoning by *United States* v. *Patrick*. In that case, complicated property adjustments were required so that the husband could retain controlling interest in a publishing business owned jointly with his wife. The legal fees involved were spent arranging a transfer of various stocks, leasing real property, and creating a trust, rather than conducting divorce litigation. The Supreme Court found no legal significance in these differences from *Gilmore*. The Court found that the transfers were incidental to the litigation which had its origin in taxpayer's personal life. It could be argued that we should take a narrow view and say that the suit to set aside petitioner's antenuptial agreement concerned contract rights. However, that view ignores the fact that marital rights were the subject of this contract and the fact that the second lawsuit was intimately bound up with the divorce litigation. In *Patrick*, the settlement agreement stated that it settled "rights growing out of the marital relationship." In the case at hand, the agreement states that the parties desire to agree to a distribution of property should their marriage be dissolved by divorce or annulment. We can perceive little or no difference between the two agreements when the question of deducting legal expenses is in issue.

In conclusion, we find no significant distinction between this case and the *Gilmore* and *Patrick* cases, and accordingly, we hold that the legal expenses incurred by the petitioner are not deductible.

Decision will be entered for the respondent.

Commissioner v. Banks

543 U.S. 426 (2005)

Justice Kennedy delivered the opinion of the Court.

The question in these consolidated cases is whether the portion of a money judgment or settlement paid to a plaintiff's attorney under a contingent-fee agreement is income to the plaintiff under the Internal Revenue Code. The issue divides the courts of appeals. In one of the instant cases, Banks v. Commissioner, 345 F.3d 373 (2003), the Court of Appeals for the Sixth Circuit held the contingent-fee portion of a litigation recovery is not included in the plaintiff's gross income. The Courts of Appeals for the Fifth and Eleventh Circuits also adhere to this view. In the other case under review, Banaitis v. Commissioner, 340 F.3d 1074 (2003), the Court of Appeals for the Ninth Circuit held that the portion of the recovery paid to the attorney as a contingent fee is excluded from the plaintiff's gross income if state law gives the plaintiff's attorney a special property interest in the fee, but not otherwise. Six Courts of Appeals have held the entire litigation recovery, including the portion paid to an attorney as a contingent fee, is income to the plaintiff. Some of these Courts of Appeals discuss state law, but little of their analysis appears to turn on this factor. Other Courts of Appeals have been explicit that the fee portion of the recovery is always income to the plaintiff regardless of the nuances of state law. We granted certiorari to resolve the conflict.

We hold that, as a general rule, when a litigant's recovery constitutes income, the litigant's income includes the portion of the recovery paid to the attorney as a contingent fee. We reverse the decisions of the Courts of Appeals for the Sixth and Ninth Circuits.

I

A. Commissioner v. Banks

In 1986, respondent John W. Banks, II, was fired from his job as an educational consultant with the California Department of Education. He retained an attorney on a contingent-fee basis and filed a civil suit against the employer in a United States District Court. The complaint alleged employment discrimination in violation of 42 U.S.C. §§ 1981 and 1983, Title VII of the Civil Rights Act of 1964, as amended, 42 U.S.C. § 2000e *et seq.*, and Cal. Govt.Code Ann. § 12965 (West 1986). The original complaint asserted various additional claims under state law, but Banks later abandoned these. After trial commenced in 1990, the parties settled for $464,000. Banks paid $150,000 of this amount to his attorney pursuant to the fee agreement.

Banks did not include any of the $464,000 in settlement proceeds as gross income in his 1990 federal income tax return. In 1997 the Commissioner of Internal Revenue issued Banks a notice of deficiency for the 1990 tax year. The Tax Court upheld the Commissioner's determination, finding that all the settlement proceeds, including the $150,000 Banks had paid to his attorney, must be included in Banks' gross income.

The Court of Appeals for the Sixth Circuit reversed in part. It agreed the net amount received by Banks was included in gross income but not the amount paid to the attorney. The court held the contingent-fee agreement was not an anticipatory assignment of Banks' income because the litigation recovery was not already earned, vested, or even relatively certain to be paid when the contingent-fee contract was made. A contingent-fee arrangement, the court reasoned, is more like a partial assignment of income-producing property than an assignment of income. The attorney is not the mere beneficiary of the client's largess, but rather earns his fee through skill and diligence. This reasoning, the court held, applies whether or not state law grants the attorney any special property interest (*e.g.*, a superior lien) in part of the judgment or settlement proceeds.

B. Commissioner v. Banaitis

After leaving his job as a vice president and loan officer at the Bank of California in 1987, Sigitas J. Banaitis retained an attorney on a contingent-fee basis and brought suit in Oregon state court against the Bank of California and its successor in ownership, the Mitsubishi Bank. The complaint alleged that Mitsubishi Bank willfully interfered with Banaitis' employment contract, and that the Bank of California attempted to induce Banaitis to breach his fiduciary duties to customers and discharged him when he refused. The jury awarded Banaitis compensatory and punitive damages. After resolution of all appeals and post-trial motions, the parties settled. The defendants paid $4,864,547 to Banaitis; and, following the formula set forth in the contingent-fee contract, the defendants paid an additional $3,864,012 directly to Banaitis' attorney.

Banaitis did not include the amount paid to his attorney in gross income on his federal income tax return, and the Commissioner issued a notice of deficiency. The Tax Court upheld the Commissioner's determination, but the Court of Appeals for the Ninth Circuit reversed. In contrast to the Court of Appeals for the Sixth Circuit, the *Banaitis* court viewed state law as pivotal. Where state law confers on the attorney no special property rights in his fee, the court said, the whole amount of the judgment or settlement ordinarily is included in the plaintiff's gross income. Oregon state law, however, like the law of some other States, grants attorneys a superior lien in the contingent-fee portion of any recovery. As a result, the court held, contingent-fee agreements under Oregon law operate not as an anticipatory assignment of the client's income but as a partial transfer to the attorney of some of the client's property in the lawsuit.

II

To clarify why the issue here is of any consequence for tax purposes, two preliminary observations are useful. The first concerns the general issue of deductibility.

For the tax years in question the legal expenses in these cases could have been taken as miscellaneous itemized deductions subject to the ordinary requirements, 26 U.S.C. §§ 67–68, but doing so would have been of no help to respondents because of the operation of the Alternative Minimum Tax (AMT). For noncorporate individual taxpayers, the AMT establishes a tax liability floor equal to 26 percent of the taxpayer's "alternative minimum taxable income" (minus specified exemptions) up to $175,000, plus 28 percent of alternative minimum taxable income over $175,000. §§ 55(a), (b). Alternative minimum taxable income, unlike ordinary gross income, does not allow any miscellaneous itemized deductions. § 56(b)(1)(A)(i).

Second, after these cases arose Congress enacted the American Jobs Creation Act of 2004, 118 Stat. 1418. Section 703 of the Act amended the Code by adding section 62(a)(19) [now 62(a)(20)]. The amendment allows a taxpayer, in computing adjusted gross income, to deduct "attorney fees and court costs paid by, or on behalf of, the taxpayer in connection with any action involving a claim of unlawful discrimination." The Act defines "unlawful discrimination" to include a number of specific federal statutes, §§ 62(e)(1) to (16), any federal whistle-blower statute, § 62(e)(17), and any federal, state, or local law "providing for the enforcement of civil rights" or "regulating any aspect of the employment relationship … or prohibiting the discharge of an employee, the discrimination against an employee, or any other form of retaliation or reprisal against an employee for asserting rights or taking other actions permitted by law," § 62(e)(18). These deductions are permissible even when the AMT applies. Had the Act been in force for the transactions now under review, these cases likely would not have arisen. The Act is not retroactive, however, so while it may cover future taxpayers in respondents' position, it does not pertain here.

III

The Internal Revenue Code defines "gross income" for federal tax purposes as "all income from whatever source derived." 26 U.S.C. § 61(a). The definition extends broadly to all economic gains not otherwise exempted. Commissioner v. Glenshaw Glass Co., 348 U.S. 426, 429–430 (1955). A taxpayer cannot exclude an economic gain from gross income by assigning the gain in advance to another party. Lucas v. Earl, 281 U.S. 111 (1930); Helvering v. Horst, 311 U.S. 112, 116–117 (1940). The rationale for the so-called anticipatory assignment of income doctrine is the principle that gains should be taxed "to those who earned them," a maxim we have called "the first principle of income taxation." The anticipatory assignment doctrine is meant to prevent taxpayers from avoiding taxation through "arrangements and contracts however skillfully devised to prevent [income] when paid from vesting even for a second in the man who earned it." Lucas, 281 U.S. at 115. The rule is preventative and motivated by administrative as well as substantive concerns, so we do not inquire whether any particular assignment has a discernible tax avoidance purpose. As Lucas explained, "no distinction can be taken according to the motives leading to the arrangement by which the fruits are attributed to a different tree from that on which they grew." Ibid.

Respondents argue that the anticipatory assignment doctrine is a judge-made antifraud rule with no relevance to contingent-fee contracts of the sort at issue here. The Commissioner maintains that a contingent-fee agreement should be viewed as an anticipatory assignment to the attorney of a portion of the client's income from any litigation recovery. We agree with the Commissioner.

In an ordinary case attribution of income is resolved by asking whether a taxpayer exercises complete dominion over the income in question. *Glenshaw Glass Co.*, *supra*, at 431; *see also* Commissioner v. Indianapolis Power & Light Co., 493 U.S. 203, 209 (1990). In the context of anticipatory assignments, however, the assignor often does not have dominion over the income at the moment of receipt. In that instance the question becomes whether the assignor retains dominion over the income-generating asset, because the taxpayer "who owns or controls the source of the income, also controls the disposition of that which he could have received himself and diverts the payment from himself to others as the means of procuring the satisfaction of his wants." *Horst, supra*, at 116–117. *See also Lucas, supra*, at 114–115. Looking to control over the income-generating asset, then, preserves the principle that income should be taxed to the party who earns the income and enjoys the consequent benefits.

In the case of a litigation recovery the income-generating asset is the cause of action that derives from the plaintiff's legal injury. The plaintiff retains dominion over this asset throughout the litigation. We do not understand respondents to argue otherwise. Rather, respondents advance two counterarguments. First, they say that, in contrast to the bond coupons assigned in *Horst*, the value of a legal claim is speculative at the moment of assignment, and may be worth nothing at all. Second, respondents insist that the claimant's legal injury is not the only source of the ultimate recovery. The attorney, according to respondents, also contributes income-generating assets—effort and expertise—without which the claimant likely could not prevail. On these premises respondents urge us to treat a contingent-fee agreement as establishing, for tax purposes, something like a joint venture or partnership in which the client and attorney combine their respective assets—the client's claim and the attorney's skill—and apportion any resulting profits.

We reject respondents' arguments. Though the value of the plaintiff's claim may be speculative at the moment the fee agreement is signed, the anticipatory assignment doctrine is not limited to instances when the precise dollar value of the assigned income is known in advance. *Lucas, supra*. Though *Horst* involved an anticipatory assignment of a predetermined sum to be paid on a specific date, the holding in that case did not depend on ascertaining a liquidated amount at the time of assignment. In each of the cases before us, as in *Horst*, the taxpayer retained control over the income-generating asset, diverted some of the income produced to another party, and realized a benefit by doing so. As Judge Wesley correctly concluded in a recent case, the rationale of *Horst* applies fully to a contingent-fee contract. *Raymond v. United States*, 355 F.3d, at 115–116. That the amount of income the asset would produce was uncertain at the moment of assignment is of no consequence.

We further reject the suggestion to treat the attorney-client relationship as a sort of business partnership or joint venture for tax purposes. The relationship between client and attorney, regardless of the variations in particular compensation agreements or the amount of skill and effort the attorney contributes, is a quintessential principal-agent relationship. Restatement (Second) of Agency § 1, Comment *e* (1957) (hereinafter Restatement); ABA Model Rules of Professional Conduct Rule 1.3, and Comment 1; Rule 1.7, Comment 1 (2002). The client may rely on the attorney's expertise and special skills to achieve a result the client could not achieve alone. That, however, is true of most principal-agent relationships, and it does not alter the fact that the client retains ultimate dominion and control over the underlying claim. The control is evident when it is noted that, although the attorney can make tactical decisions without consulting the client, the plaintiff still must determine whether to settle or proceed to judgment and make, as well, other critical decisions. Even where the attorney exercises independent judgment without supervision by, or consultation with, the client, the attorney, as an agent, is obligated to act solely on behalf of, and for the exclusive benefit of, the client-principal, rather than for the benefit of the attorney or any other party. Restatement §§ 13, 39, 387.

The attorney is an agent who is duty bound to act only in the interests of the principal, and so it is appropriate to treat the full amount of the recovery as income to the principal. In this respect Judge Posner's observation is apt: "[T]he contingent-fee lawyer [is not] a joint owner of his client's claim in the legal sense any more than the commission salesman is a joint owner of his employer's accounts receivable." *Kenseth*, 259 F.3d, at 883. In both cases a principal relies on an agent to realize an economic gain, and the gain realized by the agent's efforts is income to the principal. The portion paid to the agent may be deductible, but absent some other provision of law it is not excludable from the principal's gross income.

This rule applies whether or not the attorney-client contract or state law confers any special rights or protections on the attorney, so long as these protections do not alter the fundamental principal-agent character of the relationship. Cf. Restatement § 13, Comment *b*, and § 14G, Comment *a* (an agency relationship is created where a principal assigns a chose in action to an assignee for collection and grants the assignee a security interest in the claim against the assignor's debtor in order to compensate the assignee for his collection efforts). State laws vary with respect to the strength of an attorney's security interest in a contingent fee and the remedies available to an attorney should the client discharge or attempt to defraud the attorney. No state laws of which we are aware, however, even those that purport to give attorneys an "ownership" interest in their fees, convert the attorney from an agent to a partner.

IV

The foregoing suffices to dispose of Banaitis' case. Banks' case, however, involves a further consideration. Banks brought his claims under federal statutes that authorize fee awards to prevailing plaintiffs' attorneys. He contends that application of the anticipatory assignment principle would be inconsistent with the purpose of statutory fee-shifting provisions. In the federal system statutory fees are typically awarded by the court under the lodestar approach, and the plaintiff usually has little control over the amount awarded. Sometimes, as when the plaintiff seeks only injunctive relief, or when the statute caps plaintiffs' recoveries, or when for other reasons damages are substantially less than attorney's fees, court-awarded attorney's fees can exceed a plaintiff's monetary recovery. Treating the fee award as income to the plaintiff in such cases, it is argued, can lead to the perverse result that the plaintiff loses money by winning the suit. Furthermore, it is urged that treating statutory fee awards as income to plaintiffs would undermine the effectiveness of fee-shifting statutes in deputizing plaintiffs and their lawyers to act as private attorneys general.

We need not address these claims. After Banks settled his case, the fee paid to his attorney was calculated solely on the basis of the private contingent-fee contract. There was no court-ordered fee award, nor was there any indication in Banks' contract with his attorney, or in the settlement agreement with the defendant, that the contingent fee paid to Banks' attorney was in lieu of statutory fees Banks might otherwise have been entitled to recover. Also, the amendment added by the American Jobs Creation Act redresses the concern for many, perhaps most, claims governed by fee-shifting statutes.

For the reasons stated, the judgments of the Courts of Appeals for the Sixth and Ninth Circuits are reversed, and the cases are remanded for further proceedings consistent with this opinion. *It is so ordered.*

V. Related Matters

- **Stock Appraisal Fees.** *Woodward v. Commissioner*, discussed above, held that costs associated with stock appraisal proceedings were nondeductible capital expenditures. Regulations under section 263, effective beginning 2004, clarify that such costs are to be capitalized. Treas. Reg. §§ 1.263(a)-4(b), -4(e)(5), Ex. 4, -5(e).

- **Confidential Sexual Harassment Settlements:** In the wake of a series of high profile scandals involving allegations of sexual harassment and the rise of the #metoo movement, Congress enacted section 162(q) denying deductions for payments to settle sexual harassment or abuse cases where the settlement agreement is made confidential. The attorney's fees in such cases are also non-deductible. The apparent intent of this provision is to encourage making such settlements public, perhaps to protect victims from serial harassers. A number of the more sensational cases involved allegations of repeated sexual harassment or abuse followed by repeated payments to keep the alleged victims silent. It seems the limitation on the deduction of attorney's fees applies to the payee as well as the payor of the settlement. If this is so, the payee will need to consider the terms of any settlement most carefully if the exclusion under section 104(a)(2) does not apply.

- **Intellectual Property Litigation.** With respect to intellectual property litigation cases, the precise nature of the particular intellectual property involved is important in determining the tax treatment of legal fees. In Urquhart v. Commissioner, 215

F.2d 17 (3d Cir. 1954), the Third Circuit held that legal fees incurred in a patent infringement action were deductible as ordinary and necessary expenses. In Danskin, Inc. v. Commissioner, 331 F.2d 360 (2d Cir. 1964), the Second Circuit held that legal fees incurred in a trademark infringement action were not deductible as ordinary and necessary expenses. Can you reconcile these two cases? Are there enough inherent differences in these intellectual property rights and remedies involved to justify differing tax treatment of legal fees in infringement actions? Is there an argument for treating all intellectual property infringement actions the same?

- **Criminal Litigation**. With respect to criminal (as opposed to civil) litigation, the deductibility of attorney's fees depends on the government's charges. Costs of defending prosecution charges involving profit-seeking activities (e.g., criminal charges of attempted bribery or criminal fraud charges brought under the Securities Act of 1933) are deductible. *See, e.g.*, Commissioner v. Tellier, 383 U.S. 687 (1966); O'Malley v. Commissioner, 91 T.C. 352 (1988). In contrast, costs of defending other charges (e.g., murder charges and assault and battery charges) are not deductible. *See, e.g.*, Nadiak v. Commissioner, 356 F.2d 911 (2d Cir. 1966); Hylton v. Commissioner, 32 T.C.M. 1238 (1973).

Chapter 36

Retirement Resources and Deferred Compensation

I. Assignment

Read: Internal Revenue Code: §§ 72(a)–(c)(1), (t)(1); 401(a)(1); 402(a); 403(a)(1); 691(a)(1); 1014(c). Skim: §§ 72(t)(2); 404(a); 408(a), (d)(1).

Treasury Regulations: None

Text: Overview
Revenue Ruling 80-248
Gee v. Commissioner
Related Matters

Complete the problems.

II. Problems

1. George and Grace Burns are a retired couple living in a valuable home on a pristine mountain lake. They plan to live there as long as they are able. George is 75 and Grace is 74. They have three adult children all of whom are fairly prosperous and who have children of their own. George and Grace have relatively little income in retirement. Their home is their most valuable asset. They would like to see the home remain in the family as recreational property for their descendants. Their children have indicated a willingness to help make this a reality by contributing financially to their parent's retirement. An estate planner has presented three alternatives for the family's consideration. The first is for the kids to simply make cash gifts to their parents with the expectation that the home will be left to them by will. The second is an installment sale of the home from the parents to the kids coupled with a lease of the home to the parents by the kids. The third is a reverse mortgage financed by the kids.

    (a) What income tax and non-tax advantages and disadvantages do you see with respect to these alternatives?

    (b) Do you see any ethical issues for the family's advisor?

2. Ray Milland bought a single life annuity for $400,000. Under the annuity contract, Ray will receive $32,000 a year for life. His life expectancy is 25 years.

(a) In the first year of the annuity payments, how much income will Ray have?

(b) How will Ray be taxed in Year 26?

(c) If Ray dies after twenty years, what is the effect of the annuity on his final tax return?

3. Warren Buffett is offered two alternative forms of deferred compensation in Year 1. The first alternative provides for a pre-tax payment of $10,000 invested tax-free in a trust account at 10% compounded annually for 7.2 years. After 7.2 years the funds in the trust account will be distributed to Warren and taxed to him. Under the second alternative, a post-tax payment of $6,000 ($10,000 pre-tax) will be invested tax-free in a trust account for 7.2 years, again at 10% compounded annually. After 7.2 years the funds in the trust account will be distributed to Warren without any further taxation.

(a) If under both alternatives the applicable tax rate is a flat 40%, what is Warren's after tax yield upon distribution of the accounts to him?

(b) Same as (a) except in Year 7 the applicable tax rate is 20%.

(c) Same as (a) except in Year 7 the applicable tax rate is 50%.

4. George Jones and Tammy Wynnette are a long time married couple who are now eligible for full Social Security benefits. George worked full time for forty years. Based on his earnings history George is entitled to $800 in monthly benefits. Tammy worked full time for forty years. Based on her earnings history Tammy is entitled to $1,500 in monthly benefits. Richard and Patricia Nixon are also a long time married couple. Richard worked full time for thirty years. Based on his earnings history Richard is entitled to $2,000 in monthly benefits. Patricia has no earnings history.

(a) What is the aggregate monthly Social Security benefit that George and Tammy are entitled to?

(b) What is the aggregate monthly Social Security benefit that Richard and Patricia are entitled to?

(c) Do you think the two outcomes above represent good policy?

5. Do you think that Social Security should have an actuarial component, that is, should people with longer life expectancies receive smaller monthly benefits?

III. Overview

In this chapter, we take a broad look at taxation and retirement planning. This is an extremely complex area of specialization for lawyers, managers, and accountants. We will not examine most of the tax rules here in detail. Instead we will seek to gain an overall appreciation of the strengths and weaknesses of the present system and the planning implications of those characteristics for the average person.

Traditionally retirees rely on three sources for support during retirement: personal savings, deferred compensation, and Social Security benefits. Families may provide a fourth source of support, and, in what may seem like a contradiction in terms, many retirees now work after retirement.

A. Savings

The United States has one of the lowest savings rates in the industrialized world. This is one reason that the retirement prospects for many Americans are not particularly rosy. To the extent that Americans do save, the most common investment is in their homes. This is not a bad idea since everyone needs shelter and since the reduced income level that many will experience at retirement makes paying a mortgage after retirement a challenging proposition. Moreover, as we have seen in Chapter 22, homes are tax favored investments since at least some of the gain upon the sale of one's residence is excludable from income under section 121. Moreover, upon death the persons inheriting the home, often one's children, will take a date of death fair market value basis under section 1014. From this it may be apparent that a basic tax and financial planning strategy is to structure one's mortgage to be paid off by retirement. Still, one who is planning for retirement should seek to build a nest egg independent of housing in order to maintain a level of financial solvency and liquidity. If one succeeds in doing so, the question then becomes how to preserve that solvency and liquidity for the remainder of one's life. Sometimes the answer is an annuity.

1. Annuities

An annuity is a contract between a contract owner and an obligor. The obligor is usually an insurance company. The contract calls for a stream of future payments to an annuitant, usually for life, received for an up front payment or payments to the obligor. An annuity can be for a single life or for multiple lives. A joint and survivor annuity is a common planning tool for married couples. An annuity can be for a term of years instead of for life. The amount of each payment to the annuitant is derived by an actuarial calculation that considers the life expectancy of the annuitant and the expected rate of return on the up front payment.

The taxation of annuities is governed by section 72. It provides for treating a portion of each payment received by the annuitant as a non-taxable return of basis and part as taxable income. In this context basis is called "investment in the contract." *See* IRC § 72(c)(1). The amount of basis recovery in each payment received is determined by reference to an "exclusion ratio" the numerator of which is investment in the contract and the denominator of which is the "expected return on the contract." IRC § 72(b)(1). The expected return on the contract is determined actuarially.

Exclusion Ratio

$$\frac{\text{Investment in the Contract}}{\text{Expected Return on the Contract}}$$

Return of Investment in Each Payment

$$\text{Payment} \times \frac{\text{Investment in the Contract}}{\text{Expected Return under the Contract}} = \text{Return of Investment}$$

If the annuitant out lives her life expectancy and, thus, fully recovers her investment in the contract, the full amount of all payments thereafter are taxable income. IRC § 72(b)(2). If the annuitant dies before recovering her full investment, the unrecovered investment amount is deductible on the decedent's final return. IRC §§ 72(b)(3) & (4).

To illustrate these points consider the following example:

Example. Balthazar pays $1,000,000 to an insurance company for an annuity contract. Monthly payments of $10,000 begin when Balthazar has life expectancy of 200 months (16 years, 8 months). Thus, the expected return on the contract is $2,000,000. For the first 200 months, half ($5,000) of each payment is non-taxable return of investment and half ($5,000) is taxable income.

$$\$10,000 \ (\text{pymt.}) \times \frac{1,000,000 \ (\text{Invtmt.})}{2,000,000 \ (\text{Exp. Rtn})} = \$5,000 \text{ Return of Investment}$$

If Balthazar outlives his life expectancy then in month 201 and thereafter the entire $10,000 payment is income since his investment has been fully recovered. If Balthazar dies after 192 months then his executor will be entitled to deduct the unrecovered investment of $40,000 (8 × $5,000) on Balthazar's final return.

An annuity contract can be inherited in some circumstances. For example, an annuity may be purchased by a person who dies prior to the beginning of the pay out period. Anything the successor in interest receives in excess of the investment in the contract is treated as income in respect of a decedent under section 691. Thus, the beneficiaries will not receive a basis step up under section 1014. *See* IRC § 1014(c). Instead they will step into the annuitant's shoes for tax purposes. *See* Rev. Rul. 2005-30, 2005-1 C.B. 1015.

2. Reverse Mortgages

The reverse mortgage is a potential retirement planning tool for those whose main savings vehicle is their home. Under this arrangement a lender, usually a bank, agrees to make monthly payments to a home owner in return for an ever growing share of the homeowner's equity. While a reverse mortgage resembles an installment sale, it is typically structured as a loan with deferred interest payments. The home is simply security for the loan. Thus, the payments do not trigger any gain recognition for the homeowner even if the limits of section 121 are exceeded. Revenue Ruling 80-248, included in the materials, addresses the treatment of the deferred interest payments by the cash basis borrower and lender. For a useful discussion of the pros and cons of reverse mortgages, *see* Dan Latona, *Reversing Course: Strengthening Consumer Protections for Reverse Mortgages*, 23 ELDER L.J. 417 (2016).

B. Retirement Plans

There are many types of retirement plans. They are characterized by reference to three overlapping dichotomies: employer funded versus individual funded, defined benefit versus defined contribution, and pre-tax contributions versus post-tax contributions. Many retirement plans ultimately become annuities.

1. Employer Funded Retirement Plans

Employer funded retirement plans fall into two broad categories, qualified plans and non-qualified plans. We will focus on qualified plans. These plans arise under the Employee Retirement Income Security Act of 1974 (ERISA). A plan is "qualified" when it is in compliance with government rules, primarily with respect to non-discrimination and financial set asides. In other words, such plans cannot discriminate in favor of highly compensated employees and they are obliged to partially fund their anticipated future obligations under the plan. In exchange for meeting these and other qualifications, the tax system confers an immediate tax deduction on the employer for those set asides and deferral of income to the employee until actual receipt of the compensation. This latter trait allows the funds that are set aside to grow tax free.

Before going further, non-qualified plans deserve a brief mention. Typically the reason for employing a non-qualified plan is to avoid the non-discrimination rules that apply to qualified plans. In other words non-qualified plans are used when the employer does not want to make the plan available to all of its employees. The cost to the employer of using a non-qualified plan is the loss of a current deduction. *See* IRC § 404(a)(5). However, under some non-qualified plans the employee may still get deferral of income under section 409A.

a. Defined Benefit and Defined Contribution Qualified Plans

An employer funded retirement plan may be either a "defined benefit" or a "defined contribution" plan. In either event the plan involves the creation of a trust to hold funds for the future well being of the employees. The chief distinction between the two types of plans is with respect to who bears the direct investment risk for the plan.

A defined benefit is a promise to pay from employer to employee. Under these plans the employer has accepted the risk that the funds set aside in trust to fund the plan may not grow rapidly enough to pay the full amount to which the employee is entitled upon retirement. The employee's entitlement is based on some sort of formula that gives weight to years of service and level of compensation. [A typical defined benefit plan can be described with a formula that takes years of service (e.g., 30 years) times a percentage (e.g., 2%) times the employee's highest annual compensation (e.g., $100,000) to yield an annual pension benefit ($30 \times .02 \times \$100,000 = \$60,000$).]

A defined contribution plan, on the other hand, is an investment trust account into which the employer and, sometimes, the employee place funds for which risk of loss is on the employee. Usually the employer will contribute a percentage of the employee's salary to the account in each pay period. (There are dollar caps applicable to all qualified plans.) A typical defined contribution trust account is invested in broad based mutual funds. Upon retirement or certain other events the employee is only entitled to as much money as is represented by the value of those investments.

b. Payout

Under both defined benefit and defined contribution plans the payout to the employee may be in the form of an annuity for life. If so, the rules of section 72 are often implicated. If the employee is married, often he or she will select a joint life annuity in order to protect his or her spouse. In the case of the defined contribution plan the annuity is purchased upon retirement with the funds in the account. If the account was funded with pre-tax dollars, the annuitant has no tax basis in the account. In other words, from a tax perspective the investment in the contract is zero. This means that the entire amount of the payments are taxable income to the annuitant as received. *See* IRC §§ 72(a), 402(a), & 403(a). If some post-tax dollars were used to fund the annuity, tax-free basis recovery is permitted on a statutory schedule. *See* IRC § 72(d). Some plans allow the employee to directly withdraw funds from the accounts. An employee who chooses not to annuitize the account upon retirement assumes the risk of running out of funds prior to death. As with the annuity, the pre-tax contributions and their earnings are taxable income to the employee as they are received.

Normally, distributions from defined benefit accounts do not begin until retirement. Distributions from defined contribution accounts cannot usually begin without penalty until the employee reaches age 59½. The penalty for early withdrawal is 10 percent of the distribution. *See* IRC § 72(t)(1) & (2)(A)(i).

c. Relative Merits of the Two Approaches

The modern trend in employer based retirement plans is toward defined contribution and away from defined benefit plans. This is probably an unfavorable development for most employees since the direct investment risk for their retirement planning is shifted to them and the payouts may be smaller. However, employees have not always fared well under defined benefit plans because many of those plans have been underfunded by insolvent employers. In recent years there have been a number of bankruptcies, most notably in the airline and steel industries, that have led to defined benefit pension plan defaults. When this happens there is a quasi-governmental entity, the Pension Benefit Guaranty Corporation (PBGC), that takes over responsibility for paying those pensions. The benefits paid by the PGBC may be less than those the employer had promised to pay.

The defined contribution plan carries direct investment risk for the employee but has certain advantages. These include portability, limited investment control, insulation from employer insolvency, and the ability to pass by inheritance in some cases. In the modern world it is common for employees to change jobs many times. With each job change the employee can keep the old investment account or "rollover" the old account in to an individual retirement account (described below). Moreover, most defined contribution plans will permit the employee a number of investment choices with respect to the contributions. These choices may range from very secure investments such as government bonds to higher risk equities. Since the employees own their investment accounts, they have some protection from employer insolvency as long as the account is not heavily invested in the employer's stock. If the funds in the account have not been used to buy an annuity, the account can be inherited by the employee's designated beneficiaries. Even if the account has been annuitized, it may have some inheritable value if the payout has not reached certain minimums. However, since the account is income in respect of a decedent (IRD) under section 691, the beneficiaries will not receive a basis step up under section 1014. *See* IRC § 1014(c). Instead they will step into the employee's shoes for tax purposes which means that the distributions will be ordinary income to them.

2. Individual Funded Retirement Accounts

Individuals have a number of options with respect to tax favored retirement planning through Individual Retirement Accounts (IRAs) and Cash or Deferred Arrangements (CODAs). *See, e.g.*, IRC §§ 408, 401(k). Functionally, IRAs and CODAs are similar, but CODAs are employer based and IRAs are not. Indeed, IRAs are primarily intended to benefit persons who lack adequate employer based retirement saving options. There are various annual limitations on how much money can be contributed to IRAs and CODAs. *See, e.g.*, IRC § 219(b)(1) & (5).

a. Pre-Tax Contribution Accounts

Like defined contribution plans, traditional IRAs and CODAs allow directing pre-tax dollars into investment accounts on a tax deferred basis. Again the taxpayer has a range of investment options. Both the IRA and the CODA are funded by the individual. In the case of the CODA an employee authorizes the employer to transfer a portion of the employee's compensation into the account. This sort of salary reduction agreement is sometimes called a "401(k) plan." This is a reference to the most prominent of the Code provisions that authorize these arrangements, but there are other Code provisions that authorize these accounts as well. *See, e.g.*, IRC § 403(b)(1)(E).

Like the defined contribution accounts, IRAs and CODAs are subject to a withdrawal penalty of 10 percent on most distributions made before the distributee has reached age 59½. However, there are a number of exceptions to this rule most notably for qualified education expenses and for first time home purchases. *See* IRC § 72(t)(2)(E) & (F). The case of *Gee v. Commissioner*, in the materials, illustrates how carefully one must apply these rules to avoid the penalty.

b. Post-Tax Contribution Accounts

It is permitted under some circumstances to fund IRAs and CODAs with post-tax dollars. *See, e.g.*, IRC § 408A. These are known as "Roth" accounts. The advantage of this less favored front end treatment is that neither the principal nor the earnings on these accounts are taxed upon distribution as long as the distributions occur more than five years after establishing the IRA and after the beneficiary has reached age 59½. Economically, the traditional IRA or CODA and the Roth IRA or CODA are equivalent if we assume identical yields on investment, constant tax rates, and that the distributee has no other income. But these assumptions are hardly safe ones. The marginal tax rate that applies to an individual is affected both by acts of Congress and by changes in his or her overall income level. In this context it is worth noting that, unlike the traditional account, the Roth account is not income in respect of a decedent. The designated beneficiary who inherits a Roth account will take it free of any income tax.

3. Retirement Planning and Time Value of Money

As noted earlier the defined benefit plan is on the decline and the defined contribution/IRA/CODA approach is on the rise. This shift of investment risk from the employer to the individual has enormous planning significance for the working person. This is because the timing of one's savings for retirement dramatically effects the amount of savings one can expect to have upon retirement. A small amount saved and invested early in one's life may have much greater retirement value than a large amount of money saved and invested late in life. This is because over a long span of time sensible monetary investments usually grow geometrically. The reader who is familiar with the Rule of 72 already understands this. The Rule of 72 is a way of describing how much time is needed to double one's investment at an assumed annual rate of return. The assumed annual rate of return (expressed as an interest rate) is divided into 72 to derive the doubling period. For example if the rate of return is 9% then the investment will double in value in 8 years (72 divided by 9 equals 8). Consider then what happens to the value of a $5,000 investment that doubles in value every 8 years.

Dollar Value at:

1/1 Year 1	5,000
1/1 Year 9	10,000
1/1 Year 17	20,000
1/1 Year 25	40,000
1/1 Year 33	80,000
1/1 Year 41	160,000

Observe that it is the change in value between Years 33 and 41 that matters most. Under a retirement system where the individual is the direct investor for his or her own retirement, the prudent person will save early and often. Do you think most worker's are doing this? If they are not, they may end up heavily dependent on the minimal support provided by Social Security.

C. Social Security

Social Security is a federal government program designed to provide a modest amount of income to the elderly, the disabled, and their dependents. The statutory framework for Social Security is set out at 42 U.S.C. §§ 401–33. This scheme is fleshed out in a complex set of regulations beginning at 20 C.F.R. § 404. Social Security provides well over one third of the income of the elderly in the United States. Indeed, a large majority of elderly Americans depend on Social Security payments for more than half of their income. The source of this support is a mandatory 12.4% payroll tax on earned income up to an inflation adjusted maximum that in 2018 was $128,400. Half of the tax is withheld from the worker's pay and half is the responsibility of the employer. But economists generally agree that the full economic burden of the tax falls on workers. In other words, if there were no Social Security tax, employers would pay 6.2% more in wages. Persons who are self employed pay the full 12.4% directly but get an income tax deduction for half of what they pay.

Benefits under Social Security are loosely tied to a worker's contributions to the system. But there is an important element of income redistribution built into the plan. Moreover, there is no actuarial component to benefits calculation. In other words benefits are not tied to life expectancy. Obviously, this advantages persons with greater life expectancies such as women and certain racial groups. In addition, the statutory scheme includes provisions for periodic cost of living adjustments (COLAs). In 2018 the average monthly benefit was $1,404, and the maximum monthly benefit was $2,788. The latest figures on benefits may be found at www.ssa.gov.

1. Eligibility

Anyone born in 1929 or later needs 40 Social Security credits to be eligible for retirement benefits. A person can earn up to four credits per year, so one needs to work in at least 10 years to become eligible for retirement benefits. A person receives credits based on earnings. Each year the amount of earnings needed for a credit is adjusted for inflation. In 2018, a person received one credit for each $1,320 of earnings, up to a maximum of four credits per year. (A person can also gain eligibility for Social Security benefits by being married for ten years to a person who is eligible.) One can elect to begin receiving permanently reduced benefits at age 62 but full benefits do not begin until age 65 or older. Higher starting ages for full benefits are being phased in for persons born in 1939 and later. Under current law persons born after 1959 will receive full benefits at age 67. Spouses and former spouses of qualified workers are entitled to their own benefits based on their own employment histories or 50% of their spouse's benefit whichever ever is greater. A surviving spouse is entitled to the greater of his own benefits or 100% of his spouse's benefits.

There are many nuances to the benefits election under Social Security and the decision of when and how to take benefits should not be made lightly. Coordination between spouses may often have significant advantages. For example, suppose that one spouse were eight years older than the other and was also a significantly higher earner than the younger spouse. It might make sense for the older spouse to wait until age 70 to begin drawing Social Security benefits while the younger spouse might start drawing reduced benefits in the same year upon reaching age 62. Their combined benefits might be sufficient in combination with their other retirement savings. When the older spouse dies, the younger spouse would step into the older spouse's higher benefit shoes for the rest of his or her life. Obviously, many factors, including their current states of health, can impact this decision-making process.

2. Income Tax Treatment of Benefits

In general Social Security benefits are not subject to income tax. There is a major exception to this rule with respect to the benefits of individuals whose adjusted gross income exceeds certain levels. *See* IRC § 86.

3. Pressures for Reform and Policy Choices Implicated

Social Security is a "pay as you go" system. Its current tax revenues are used to pay current benefits. Presently the system is running a surplus which is "invested" in government bonds. (In other words, the federal government is borrowing the excess Social Security funds and promising to repay them later with interest. This is a bit like borrowing from oneself.) As the baby boom generation retires the system will begin to operate at a deficit. For this reason some people urge that the system be reformed now. Potential approaches to reform include: raising Social Security taxes, reducing benefits, changing the COLA formula, raising the eligibility age, and changing the system from a defined benefit to a defined contribution type plan. This last approach has been touted as a way to give "ownership" of Social Security to workers. But keep in mind that it does so by shifting investment risk to the worker. As noted earlier this same shift is already occurring with respect to private pension plans. What happens to those persons whose investments perform poorly?

IV. Materials

Revenue Ruling 80-248

1980-2 C.B. 164

ISSUES

When is interest on a "reverse mortgage loan" includible in the gross income of a lender and deductible by a borrower under the circumstances described below?

FACTS

A state permits various kinds of lending institutions located within the state to make reverse mortgage loans to individuals who own their own homes, which they occupy as their principal residence. A reverse mortgage loan is secured by a mortgage on the borrower's principal residence. A reverse mortgage loan is one in which the lending institution commits itself to a principal amount, not to exceed 80 percent of the appraised value of the property, which is paid to the borrower in installments over a period of months or years. Repayment of the loan is due when the principal amount has been fully paid to the borrower, the residence that secures the loan is sold, the borrower dies, or the borrower ceases to use the home as the borrower's principal residence. The loan agreement may provide that interest will be added to the outstanding loan balance monthly as it accrues. The outstanding loan balance is the current amount of money owed by the borrower to the lending institution and includes the total of the installments paid by the lender to date, the total accrued interest if any to date, and any other charges, such as taxes and insurance, paid to date by the lender upon the borrower's failure to make such payment. The primary purpose of the reverse mortgage loan is to enable elderly persons with limited incomes to remain in their homes.

A lending institution made a reverse mortgage loan to an individual who qualified for such a loan. The loan agreement provides that interest will be added to the outstanding loan balance monthly as it accrues. Both the lender and the borrower use the cash receipts and disbursements method of accounting.

LAW AND ANALYSIS

(1) Section 451 of the Internal Revenue Code provides that the amount of any item of gross income is includible in the gross income for the taxable year in which received by the taxpayer, unless, under the method of accounting used in computing taxable income, such amount is to be properly accounted for as of a different period.

Section 1.451-(a) of the Income Tax Regulations provides that income is includible in gross income for the taxable year in which it is actually or constructively received by the taxpayer, unless it is includible in a different year in accordance with the taxpayer's method of accounting.

Section 1.451-2 (a) of the regulations provides that income although not actually reduced to a taxpayer's possession is constructively received by the taxpayer in the taxable year during which it is credited to the taxpayer's account, set apart for the taxpayer, or otherwise made available so that the taxpayer may draw upon it at any time, or so that the taxpayer could have drawn upon it during the taxable year if notice of intention to withdraw had been given. However, income is not constructively received if the taxpayer's control of its receipt is subject to substantial limitations or restrictions.

In this case, the loan agreement provides that interest will be added to the outstanding loan balance monthly as it accrues. However, this interest is not received by the bank, nor is it available to be drawn upon by the bank. Therefore, the bank is not in actual or constructive receipt of the interest when it is added to the outstanding loan balance.

(2) Section 163 (a) of the Code allows as a deduction all interest paid or accrued within the taxable year on indebtedness. [Eds. Note: Section 163 has since been amended to disallow a deduction for personal interest.]

Section 461 (a) of the Code provides that the amount of any allowable deduction shall be taken for the taxable year that is the proper taxable year under the method of accounting used in computing taxable income.

Section 1.461-1 (a) (1) of the regulations provides that, under the cash receipts and disbursements method of accounting, amounts representing allowable deductions shall, as a general rule, be taken into account for the taxable year in which paid.

If a taxpayer who uses the cash receipts and disbursement method of accounting owes interest on an obligation and gives a note to the creditor to cover the interest, the taxpayer has not paid the interest for federal income tax purposes. The payment occurs when the taxpayer pays the interest in cash or by transferring property.

HOLDINGS

The interest is includible in the lender's gross income when it is actually or constructively received by the lender and is deductible by the borrower when it is actually paid by the borrower. Actual or constructive receipt or payment does not occur when the interest is added to the outstanding loan balance. Therefore, the interest is neither includible in the lender's gross income nor deductible by the borrower at that time.

Gee v. Commissioner

127 T.C. No. 1 (2006)

KROUPA, Judge: Respondent determined a $97,789 deficiency in petitioners' Federal income tax for 2002.

The issue is whether a $977,888 distribution petitioner Charlotte Gee (petitioner) received in 2002 from an individual retirement account (IRA) she maintained only in her name, and which had been funded in part with a rollover from her deceased husband's IRA, is subject to the 10-percent additional tax on early distributions under section 72(t). We hold that the distribution is subject to the additional tax under section 72(t).

Background

This case was submitted to the Court fully stipulated under Rule 122. The stipulation of facts and the accompanying exhibits are incorporated by this reference, and the facts are so found. Petitioners resided in Bolivar, Tennessee, when they filed the petition.

Petitioner opened an IRA with PaineWebber in 1993. Her husband at the time, Ray A. Campbell, Jr. (Mr. Campbell), also opened an IRA with PaineWebber in 1993. Petitioner was married to Mr. Campbell when the IRAs were established and remained married until Mr. Campbell's death on June 21, 1998, at age 73.

Mr. Campbell was the sole owner of his IRA, account number MN 21719 17, and petitioner was the primary beneficiary. Petitioner was the sole owner of her IRA, account number MN 21712 17, when Mr. Campbell died.

Petitioner requested PaineWebber to distribute the entire balance in Mr. Campbell's IRA to her IRA at PaineWebber. PaineWebber distributed $1,010,988.38 to petitioner's separately owned IRA in July 1998 in the form of a direct rollover. Petitioner was age 51 at the time of the rollover.

Petitioner transferred her IRA funds in November 2000, then totaling $2,646,797.89, to SEI Private Trust Co. (SEI). In 2002, petitioner requested and received a $977,887.79

distribution from her IRA at SEI. Petitioner was under age 59½ in 2002 when she received the distribution.

Petitioners reported the IRA distribution on their joint Federal income tax return for 2002 but did not report or remit the 10-percent additional tax on early distributions. Petitioners attached a statement to their return stating that SEI had entered the wrong distribution code on the information return. The correct distribution code should have been for "a distribution of IRA for her deceased husband."

Respondent determined that, although the distribution would have been exempt from the 10-percent additional tax when it was made to petitioner's IRA upon Mr. Campbell's death, the funds became subject to the 10-percent additional tax when distributed to her from her own IRA.

Petitioners timely filed a petition with this Court contesting respondent's determinations in the deficiency notice.

Discussion

We are asked to decide whether petitioner is liable for the 10-percent additional tax on early distributions under section 72(t). Section 72(t) imposes a 10-percent additional tax on the amount of an early distribution from a qualified retirement account (as defined in section 4974(c)). See sec. 72(t)(1). Section 72(t)(2) provides for certain exceptions to the imposition of this 10-percent additional tax.

The parties agree that the only relevant exception is section 72(t)(2)(A)(ii), which provides that distributions "made to a beneficiary (or to the estate of the employee) on or after the death of the employee" are not subject to the 10-percent additional tax. Petitioner argues that the entire distribution she received from her IRA was an amount received on or after the death of Mr. Campbell. We note that this Court has not previously decided whether an IRA distribution retains its character as a distribution to a beneficiary "on or after the death of an employee" if the distribution is of funds that were rolled over to the IRA upon the employee's death.

Respondent argues that once petitioner as surviving spouse decided to maintain the funds in an account in her own name as owner of the IRA, she became the owner of the IRA "for all purposes of the Code," relying upon section 1.408-8, Q&A-5 and 7, Income Tax Regs. Petitioner counters that the funds from her deceased husband's IRA did not lose their character as funds from her deceased husband's IRA. Even though petitioner rolled over the funds from her deceased husband's IRA into her separate IRA, petitioner did not make any additional contributions after her husband died and also did not "redesignate" the account as her own. See sec. 1.408-8, A-5(b), Income Tax Regs. We agree with respondent.

We find that petitioner received the distribution from her own IRA, not from an IRA of which she was a beneficiary on or after the death of an employee. We further find that the source of the amount received, whether originating from her deceased husband's IRA or petitioner's own contributions, is irrelevant. We recognize that petitioner may not have technically redesignated the IRA as her own. She did not need to "redesignate" the IRA. The IRA was her previously existing account. We therefore find no merit to petitioner's argument that the rolled over funds retain their character because she did not redesignate her IRA.

Petitioner rolled over the entire amount received from her deceased husband's IRA into her own IRA. Petitioner is and was the sole owner of her separately created IRA. The distribution petitioner received was not occasioned by the death of her deceased husband nor made to her in her capacity as beneficiary of his IRA.

Petitioner cannot have it both ways. She cannot choose to roll the funds over into her own IRA and then later withdraw funds from her IRA without additional tax liability because the funds were originally from her deceased husband's IRA. Accordingly, once petitioner chose to roll the funds over into her own IRA, she lost the ability to qualify for the exception from the 10-percent additional tax on early distributions. The funds became petitioner's own and were no longer from her deceased husband's IRA once petitioner rolled them over into her own IRA. The funds therefore no longer qualify for the exception.

The section 72(t) tax discourages premature IRA distributions that frustrate the intention of saving for retirement. Dwyer v. Commissioner, 106 T.C. 337, 340 (1996); see also S. Rept. 93-383, at 134 (1974), 1974-3 C.B. (Supp.) 80, 213. To avoid the section 72(t) additional tax, petitioner must show that the IRA distribution falls within one of the exceptions provided under section 72(t)(2). She has not done so. Thus, the 10-percent additional tax under section 72(t) applies to the distribution petitioner received from her IRA in 2002.

We accordingly sustain respondent's determination in the deficiency notice that petitioners are liable for the $97,789 additional tax under section 72(t) for 2002.

V. Related Matters

- **Constructive Receipt and Economic Benefit Doctrines.** The cash method payee's income taxation with respect to deferred compensation arrangements that are outside the scope of the rules described in this chapter are primarily governed by the doctrine of constructive receipt. *See* Rev. Rul. 60-31, 1960-1 C.B. 174; Minor v. United States, 772 F.2d 1472 (9th Cir. 1985). The application of the economic benefit doctrine and of section 83 must also be considered. *See, e.g.,* Rev. Rul. 69-50, 1969-1 C.B. 140; Rev. Rul. 77-420, 1977-2 C.B. 172. For a sophisticated analysis of these issues, see Gregg D. Polsky & Brant J. Hellwig, *Taxing the Promise To Pay*, 89 Minn. L. Rev. 1092 (2005).

- **Life Insurance.** Life insurance proceeds are excluded from income in most circumstances. IRC § 101(a)(1). When life insurance proceeds are received as an annuity, the exclusion does not apply to the amount paid in excess of the face amount of the policy. IRC § 101(d). Life insurance proceeds may be collected tax free in advance of death in some cases where the payee is terminally or chronically ill. IRC § 101(g).

- **Medicare.** Medicare provides health insurance coverage for the elderly. It is partially funded with a payroll tax of 1.45% on the employer and 1.45% on the employee.

High-wage earners owe an additional 0.9% on earned income above certain thresholds.

- **IRAs and CODAs in Divorce.** Deferred compensation plans, IRAs, and CODAs are divisible assets in cases of divorce. Tax liability upon subsequent distributions usually passes to the transferee. *See, e.g.,* IRC § 408(d)(6). For a discussion of the use of Qualified Domestic Relations Orders (QDROs) in the divorce setting, see Chapter 32.

- **Saving for a Permanently Disabled Person:** Sometimes an aging parent may need to put a plan in place to care for a permanently disabled child. Congress recently enacted new section 529A in the Achieving a Better Life Experience (ABLE) Act. This provision authorizes a tax favored savings account for long-term disability care. This ABLE account resembles the 529 Account for college savings addressed in chapter 33. Tax benefits include the exclusion from gross income of earnings on such savings when the funds are used for the benefit of a person who became disabled before reaching age 26. Contributions to these accounts are also excluded from gift tax. The accounts, thus, provide a planning mechanism for parents and other family members to put aside resources for a disabled child. Distributions come out tax free as long as the funds are used for qualified expenses such as education or healthcare. Funds held in these accounts will not disqualify the beneficiary from need based government benefits such as Medicaid. For a detailed discussion see Stephanie R. Hoffer, *Making the Law More ABLE: Reforming Medicaid for Disability*, 76 Ohio State L.J. 1255 (2015).

Chapter 37

Overview of Entity Taxation

I. Assignment

Read: Internal Revenue Code: Skim §§ 11(a)–(b); 61(a)(7); 199A; 531; 541; 643(a); 651–652; 661–662; 671–679, 701–704; 705(a); 731(a); 752; 1361; 1366; 1367(a); 1368(b)(1); 1371.

Treasury Regulations: Skim §§ 1.704-1(b)(2)(iv); 301.7701-2(a), -3(a), -3(b)(1).

Text: Overview

Complete the problems

II. Problems

1. Three of your clients—Moe, Larry, and Curly—have just asked you for your advice. They are in the planning stages of a small shopping plaza project, and would like your recommendation on the appropriate form of entity to be used. The estimated cost of purchasing the land and constructing the shopping plaza is $3,000,000. Your clients' equity contribution will be $600,000, and the remainder of the estimated costs will be borrowed from a local bank. They estimate that the project will produce large tax losses in the first few years of operation, but some positive cash flow by the second year. Moe will take an active role in management, while Larry and Curly will take a passive role.

   (a) Would you recommend that a C corporation be used to own and operate the shopping plaza? Why or why not?

   (b) Assume that your clients have considered using either a limited partnership with Moe as the general partner, a limited liability company, or an S corporation. Which would you recommend and why?

   (c) For the entity recommended in (b), what steps would you take to ensure desired classification for tax purposes?

2. Mother creates a "simple trust" for the benefit of her two children Son and Daughter (the income beneficiaries) and her three grandchildren (the remainder beneficiaries). Under the terms of the trust, Trustee is required to distribute all of its income currently, including all realized capital gains, and may also distribute trust principal. In the current year, the trust has $25,000 of rental income and

$5,000 of long-term capital gains. In the current year, Trustee directs distributions from the trust of $30,000 to Son and $20,000 to Daughter. What is the proper tax treatment of the trust distributions?

III. Overview

This chapter offers a glimpse of the rules for taxing the income from property held indirectly through an entity. The tax treatment of corporations, partnerships, and trusts is an enormous field of study. Knowledge of this area is tremendously important to anyone who seeks to advise such entities and their owners. It is hoped that this chapter will provide the stimulus for further study.

It is well established that an owner of property is taxed on any income generated by that property. Helvering v. Horst, 311 U.S. 112 (1940). Accordingly, if an individual owns a group of assets that comprise a trade or business (e.g., a sole proprietorship), all income generated by the business is taxed to that individual. Most individuals prefer not to operate their businesses as sole proprietorships, but instead choose to operate through a business form of statutory creation. There are various non-tax reasons for this preference including: the ability to pool capital, centralized management, and limited liability. Entities often serve important estate planning functions as well. For example, parents may wish to prepare their children to take over a family business while keeping control for the near term. Transfers of minority stock or limited partnership interests can serve this purpose.

A variety of state-law entities are available, including the corporation, the limited partnership, the limited liability company, and the trust. As will be discussed, trusts are more often used for estate planning than for business planning. Tax considerations often play an important role in determining which entity to use.

A. Corporations

A corporation is a legal entity distinct from its owners. State law formalities must be met to create the legal entity. The corporation's owners (shareholders) own stock, which represents legal ownership and a stake in assets and future profits of the corporation. The corporation is solely responsible for its debts and obligations. Shareholders are not personally liable for debts of the corporation, unless they have entered into an agreement to the contrary (e.g., a personal guarantee). They are typically at risk to lose only their investment in the shares.

For federal tax purposes, every corporation formed under state corporate law is either a C corporation, taxed under the rules of subchapter C of the Code, or an S corporation, taxed under the rules of subchapter S of the Code.

1. C Corporations

Every corporation formed under state law that does not elect to be treated as an S corporation for federal tax purposes is a C corporation, taxed under the provisions of subchapter C of the Code. *See* IRC §§ 301–85. Almost all publicly traded stocks are in C corporations. A C corporation is a separate taxable entity distinct from its shareholders, and pays tax on the enterprise's taxable income. Though there are important differences, generally speaking a corporation determines its taxable income much the same way as an individual. For tax years beginning in 2018, the corporate income tax imposed by section 11(a) is a flat 21% of taxable income, which is significantly lower than the highest individual marginal rates. IRC § 11(b). Prior to 2018, a graduated corporate tax rate structure, with a top rate of 35%, existed. The Tax Cuts and Jobs Act (TCJA) eliminated the graduated rate structure and enacted a 21% flat rate to spur economic growth and jobs creation, and to make U.S. companies globally competitive. It should be noted that in addition to the federal income tax, a C corporation might also be subject to certain penalty taxes, noted below. The TCJA, however, repealed the corporate alternative minimum tax.

When a C corporation's income is distributed to shareholders as a dividend, the shareholders are taxed. IRC § 61(a)(7). Hence, the earnings of a C corporation are subject to two levels of tax — the first at the corporate level (21%) and the second at the shareholder level (maximum rate of 20% for "qualified dividends"). In light of the second level of tax for dividend distributions, there is a strong incentive for corporations to retain earnings. To prevent the accumulation of earnings for the purpose of avoiding the shareholder tax on dividend distributions, there are a couple of penalty taxes imposed by the Code. The personal holding company tax is imposed on closely held corporations with substantial amounts of undistributed passive income. *See* IRC § 541. The accumulated earnings tax is imposed on subchapter C corporations, that are not personal holding companies,that accumulate earnings for the purpose of avoiding the shareholder tax on dividend distributions. *See* IRC § 531. Both taxes are penalty taxes that must be paid in addition to the regular tax.

Not only do operating distributions result in two levels of tax in the C corporation context, so do liquidating distributions. This is because liquidation is treated as a gain recognition event at both the corporate and at the shareholder level. *See* IRC §§ 331 & 336.

Historically, the double tax on C corporation earnings, including the exit tax at liquidation, made the C corporation less attractive to *closely held businesses* — which would often choose to operate instead as partnerships or as S corporations for tax purposes. The significantly lower corporate tax rate, however, may influence the choice-of-entity decision for closely held businesses that previously chose to operate as pass-through entities, especially if they can employ strategies to avoid the second layer of tax at the shareholder level (e.g., leave earnings in the corporation in a way to avoid the penalty taxes discussed above, or leave earnings in the corporation until the shareholders die and their heirs get a basis stepped up to fair market value).

2. S Corporations

Certain qualified domestic corporations, newly formed under state law or preexisting, may elect to be treated as S corporations for federal tax purposes and, hence, taxed under the Code provisions of subchapter S, rather than the provisions of subchapter C. *See* IRC §§ 1361–77. The S corporation is one of the most frequently formed business entity today. An S corporation generally is not a separate taxpaying entity; rather income and deduction items are allocated to the individual shareholders and reported on their individual tax returns. Hence, S corporation income is taxed only once at individual shareholder rates rather than twice. Recall the top individual rate is now 37%.

Each owner's share of the corporation's income and deduction items is determined by reference to the owner's share of the corporation's stock. *See* IRC § 1366. Thus, for example, a person who owns 10 percent of an S corporation's stock will report and pay taxes on 10 percent of the corporation's taxable income. This is true without regard to whether that income is distributed. But the income allocated to the shareholder increases the shareholder's basis in his S corporation stock. IRC § 1367(a)(1). Any subsequent distribution from the S corporation is tax free to the shareholder as long as it does not exceed the shareholder's basis. IRC § 1368(b)(1).

When Congress lowered the tax rate applicable to C corporations from 35% to 21%, it was concerned about the negative impact on closely held businesses that operate as pass-through entities, such as partnerships, LLCs, and S corporations. Although not taxed at the entity level, pass-through income is automatically taxed to the individual owner at a potential top rate of 37%, which is significantly higher than the 21% flat rate applicable to C corporations. To level the playing field between C corporations and pass-through entities, Congress enacted section 199A of the Code, a temporary provision that applies to tax years beginning before 2026. It allows an individual to deduct 20% of his or her share of so-called "qualified business income" of a pass-through business entity. For top bracket individuals who qualify for this deduction, their share of pass-through income is effectively taxed at 29.6% instead of 37% (.37 × .80). Because the 20% deduction is immensely complicated, we reserve further treatment until the end of this chapter.

Example: S Corporation Taxation. A and B form S corporation ABS by each contributing $100,000 of cash. They each receive 100 shares of stock, with a tax basis of $100,000. IRC § 358(a). In Year 1, ABS earns $10,000 of net operating income, which is "qualified business income" eligible for the 20% deduction under section 199A at the shareholder level. Thus, at the end of Year 1, A and B will each be allocated $5,000 of ordinary income; but each will claim a 20% ($1,000) deduction under section 199A and pay tax on only $4,000 as a result of their share of ABS's business activity for the year. Each of their bases in their ABS stock will increase to $105,000. (Note that their bases increase by their allocable share of income, not by the 80% portion that is taxed.) If ABS distributes its $5,000 of earnings to A and $5,000 to B, they will have no further income. Their bases in their ABS stock will return to $100,000 each.

Only corporations that meet certain eligibility requirements may elect S corporation status. The eligibility requirements include: (1) an S corporation cannot have more than 100 shareholders; (2) only individuals (excluding nonresident alien individuals), estates, certain trusts, and tax exempt charitable organizations can be shareholders of an S corporation; and (3) an S corporation may not have more than one class of stock (e.g., cannot have preferred stock). IRC § 1361.

The rules of subchapter S do not address all aspects of the formation, operation, and liquidation of an S corporation. These large gaps are filled in by subchapter C. *See* IRC § 1371(a). Thus, it is vital to know the subchapter C rules if you serve as an advisor to an S corporation or its owners. In the next chapter we will look at the corporate formation rules of subchapter C.

In many respects, the S corporation tax rules resemble a simplified version of those for partnerships described below. The relative simplicity of S corporation tax rules are one of its main attractions both to their owners and to their tax advisors.

B. Unincorporated Businesses

1. *General Partnerships, Limited Partnerships, Limited Liability Partnerships, and Limited Liability Companies*

General Partnerships. A general partnership exists when two or more persons carry on as co-owners a business with the expectation of generating profits. A general partnership is a contractually-based, flexible business form that usually arises when two or more persons go into a business without much thought as to what their relationship is. Each partner is personally responsible for partnership debt and obligations. This unlimited personal liability is a significant drawback of the general partnership form. Some joint development arrangements and licensing arrangements run the risk of being treated as general partnerships, subject to federal and state rules governing partnerships, rather than purely contractual relationships. The parties should draft joint development agreements and licensing agreements with this in mind.

Limited Partnerships. Unlike a general partnership, which often arises in informal circumstances, a limited partnership is a creature of state law that must satisfy filing requirements to come into existence. A limited partnership has one or more general partners and one or more limited partners. General partners have unlimited personal liability for partnership debts and obligations. Limited partners are not liable for debts and obligations of the partnership as long as they do not participate in control of the business. A limited partner's liability is generally limited to the capital that he or she contributes to the business.

Limited Liability Partnerships. Another, more recent, creature of statute is the limited liability partnership (LLP). In an LLP, even general partners have limited liability (except for their own professional negligence).

Limited Liability Companies. A limited liability company (LLC) is a hybrid entity combining both corporate and partnership features. Despite being called a "company," an LLC is an unincorporated business entity formed under state law. Like a corporation and a limited partnership, an LLC can only be created by following state law requirements (i.e., filing articles of organization). LLC owners are known as members. There are no restrictions on the number or types of owners (as is the case with S corporations). All members of an LLC have limited liability protection regardless of their management activity. This is a significant advantage over the limited partnership form, wherein general partners have unlimited liability and limited partners may be personally liable if they participate in management.

As will be discussed below all of these unincorporated businesses most typically are treated as partnerships for federal tax purposes.

2. Tax Classification of Unincorporated Businesses

The Check-the-Box Rules. Treasury regulations permit most unincorporated business entities to elect, by "checking a box" on an election form, to be treated as either partnerships or corporations for federal income tax purposes. *See* Treas. Reg. § 301.7701-1 to -3. Specifically, under the check-the-box regulations, an unincorporated business entity with two or more members, can freely elect to be taxed as a corporation (taxed under subchapter C or, if eligible, under subchapter S) or a partnership (taxed under subchapter K — IRC § 701-77). Treas. Reg. § 301.7701-2(a), -3(a). An unincorporated entity with a single member, such as the single-member LLC, can freely elect to be a corporation (taxed under subchapter C or, if eligible, under subchapter S) or to be "disregarded" for tax purposes (i.e., activities are treated in the same manner as a sole proprietorship and reported on Schedule C of the Form 1040). *Id.* If an unincorporated business entity eligible to make an election fails to do so, a set of default rules applies. Under the default rules, an unincorporated entity with more than one owner will be taxed as a partnership (taxed under the rules of subchapter K); an unincorporated entity (LLC) with only one owner will be disregarded (taxed as a sole proprietorship). Treas. Reg. § 301.7701-3(b)(1). Because many unincorporated entities desire pass-through tax treatment, the default under the regulations, an election generally is unnecessary. The regulations set forth the procedures for making an election to be classified differently from the default result (for example, an LLC desiring to be taxed as a C or S corporation).

3. Tax Treatment of Partnership Income

If an unincorporated entity chooses to be taxed under the rules of subchapter K, the entity is not a separate taxable entity for federal income taxes, but rather is a pass-through entity. Under subchapter K, items of income, gain, loss, deduction, and credit are determined at the entity level, but then flow through to individual partners and are reported on their individual returns. *See* IRC §§ 701, 702 & 704. (Those items of income and deduction that have differential impacts, such as capital gains and section 1231 gains, flow through to each partner separately and then are reported on that partner's individual tax return. *See* IRC § 703.) The partner reports these items without regard to whether the partnership makes any distributions. The payback for this treatment is that distributions are generally tax free to the partners but will reduce the partners' bases in their partnership interests. IRC §§ 731(a) & 705(a).

As noted above in connection with S corporation income, partnership income may qualify for the 20% deduction applicable to "qualified business income" (QBI). IRC § 199A. If a partner or LLC member qualifies, he or she can deduct 20% of the QBI generated by the partnership or LLC. The deduction effectively lowers the tax rate applicable to this type of pass-through income. If a partner is in the 37% rate bracket, then QBI is taxed at 29.6% (.37 × .80). If a partner is in the 35% bracket, then QBI is taxed at only 28% (.35 × .80). The scope of QBI is addressed later. For present purposes, it does not include any guaranteed payment made by a partnership to a partner for payment of services.

Each partner's equity interest in the partnership is represented by a *capital account*. The regulations specify an elaborate scheme for keeping track of each partner's capital account. *See* Treas. Reg. § 1.704-1(b)(2)(iv). A very rough summary is set out below.

Maintaining a Partner's Capital Account

> **Cash or net FMV of property contributed by partner**
> **+ Partner's share of partnership income**
> **− Cash or net FMV of property distributed to partner**
> **− Partner's share of partnership losses**
> **Partner's Capital Account Balance**

There is a similar set of rules for keeping track of a partner's basis, known as *outside basis*, in his partnership interest. There are two main differences between the rules for adjusting capital accounts and the rules for adjusting outside basis. First, upon contribution and distribution of property, the partner's basis in the partnership is increased or decreased by the basis of the asset rather than its net value. IRC § 705(a). Second, a partner's share of the partnership liabilities is included in her basis in accordance with the *Crane* principle. IRC § 752. The partner's basis in the partnership is quite important to the partner for several reasons. We will note two here. First, distributions reduce basis, and cash distributions in excess of basis trigger gain recognition. *See* IRC § 731. Second, if a partnership has losses, each partner's share of those losses reduces that partner's basis. But the partner is *not* permitted to recognize his share of those losses to the extent they exceed his basis in the partnership. IRC § 704(d). From the foregoing we may summarize the adjustments to a partner's basis in the partnership as follows:

Maintaining a Partner's Outside Basis

> **Cash or basis of property contributed by partner**
> **+ Partner's share of partnership liabilities**
> **+ Partner's share of partnership income**
> **− Cash or basis of property distributed to partner**
> **− Any reduction in partner's share of liabilities**
> **− Partner's share of partnership losses**
> **Partner's Basis in the Partnership**

One important tax difference between a partnership and an S corporation is that partnership tax rules permit tax items to pass through to the partners on a non-pro rata basis if certain rules are followed. This means, for example, that the partnership's depreciation deductions can generally be allocated in a manner that is disproportionate to the partners' capital accounts. In order for such disproportionate allocations to be respected for tax purposes they must have *substantial economic effect*. *See* IRC § 704(b). This means among other things, that the allocations must be reflected in the partners' capital accounts. Thus, if we allocate a tax depreciation deduction to a partner, when the deduction is taken we will reduce both partner's basis in the partnership and the partner's capital account balance in a corresponding manner.

The various rules just described may be better understood by considering the following example:

Example: Partnership Taxation. A and B form general partnership AB by each contributing $100,000 of cash. They agree to share profits and losses equally except A is entitled to all depreciation deductions of the partnership. In Year 1, the partnership buys depreciable machinery for $100,000 and properly takes a $20,000 depreciation deduction. In Year 1, the partnership earns $30,000 of ordinary income disregarding the depreciation on the machinery. (Note: Because A and B exceed certain taxable income thresholds and the partnership is engaged in a "specified service trade or business," A and B are ineligible for the 20% deduction for qualified business income under section 199A. See the discussion below.)

In Year 1, both A and B will begin with a tax basis in the partnership and a capital account balance of $100,000. At the end of Year 1, A will report a $5,000 loss on her individual return as a result of her share of AB's business activity for the year. A's basis in the partnership and A's capital account balance will be reduced to $95,000. Since the partnership earned a profit from B's perspective, B will report $15,000 of income on B's individual return as a result of her share of AB's business activity for the year. B's basis in the partnership and capital account balance will increase to $115,000. The adjustments to outside basis and capital accounts may be summarized as follows:

A		B	
Outside Basis	Capital Account	Outside Basis	Capital Account
$100,000	$100,000	$100,000	$100,000
− 20,000 (Deprec.)	− 20,000 (Deprec.)		
+ 15,000 (Inc.)	+ 15,000 (Inc.)	+ 15,000 (Inc.)	+ 15,000 (Inc.)
$95,000	$95,000	$115,000	$115,000

There are two key points to note about these adjustments. First, if we assume that the tax depreciation and the economic depreciation are equal, then the combined capital account balances of A and B of $210,000 ($95,000 + $115,000 = $210,000) are equal to the net value of the partnership ($130,00 cash + $80,000 machinery = $210,000). Thus, the capital accounts keep track of the partners' individual and aggregate equity interests. Second, if we liquidate the partnership according to positive capital account balances (as we are required to do) then A would receive cash and property worth $95,000 and B would receive cash and property worth $115,000. When we consider the additional depreciation deduction that was awarded to A of $20,000 and the $15,000 of income that B reported, their ending economic and tax positions are exactly equal on a net basis. Thus, the disproportionate allocation of depreciation had a substantial economic effect. In other words, A got the tax benefit of the deduction and bore the economic cost that correlates to it. B bore the tax burden of reporting income and got the economic benefit of that income.

The rules for taxation of partnership income are highly nuanced and complex. The example above barely skims the surface. The partnership tax rules are also very flexible and afford many opportunities for tax planning. For this reason the partnership form is often selected for tax purposes. Any person who chooses to serve as an advisor to partnerships and their owners is well advised to study these rules closely. In a later chapter, we examine the tax rules that apply to formations of partnerships.

C. Trusts

1. Divided Ownership

Trusts are mechanisms by which legal and equitable title to property are divided. Legal title is placed with a *trustee*. Equitable title is lodged in one or more *beneficiaries*. The trustee stands in a fiduciary relationship to the beneficiaries of the trust and must manage the property for their benefit. The trust instrument (i.e., a written document executed according to the requirements of state law) establishes the relationship between the property and the interested parties. It guides the trustee's actions.

Trusts often serve as a mechanism for dividing ownership of property on a temporal basis. Thus, for example, one beneficiary may be the life tenant receiving the income from the trust and another beneficiary may be the remainderman who is entitled to receive the trust assets upon the death of the life tenant. The ability to divide property on a temporal basis is one reason trusts are commonly used for estate planning purposes. Suppose, for example, Mother has married for a second time and has children by her first marriage. Mother may wish to allow her present husband to reside in their residence after she dies. But she may wish for her children from her first marriage to benefit from the residence after her second husband dies. The use of a trust is one way to accomplish these goals by making the husband the life tenant and the children the remaindermen. The trustee might be a bank, lawyer, or other unrelated third party. Sometimes the trustee may be one of the beneficiaries.

2. The Tax Treatment of Trust Income

There are two main categories of trusts for tax purposes, grantor trusts and regular trusts.

Grantor Trusts. The grantor is the person who created the trust by transferring property to it. When the grantor maintains some degree of direct control over the trust after its formation the trust may be characterized as a grantor trust. The income from a grantor trust is usually taxed to the grantor as though the grantor owned the trust property directly. Whether the retained control is sufficient to cause this result is dictated by sections 671 through 679 of the Code. Some examples of retained rights that will trigger grantor trust treatment include: the right to revoke the trust, the right to change the beneficiaries, the right to a substantial reversion, and the right to borrow from the trust without adequate security. As mentioned in an earlier chapter, the grantor trust rules were originally enacted as a way of preventing assignments of income to trusts. Today these rules are utilized by estate planners to achieve a variety of income tax and estate and gift tax goals.

Regular Trusts. There are two kinds of regular trusts, simple trusts and complex trusts. Simple trusts are obliged to distribute all of their income currently. Complex trusts may accumulate their income. The tax treatment of both kinds of regular trusts (and estates) is controlled by subchapter J of the Code. *See* IRC §§ 641–91. Regular trusts are at least nominally taxpaying entities. But, in fact, income from the trust assets may be taxed to the trust or to the beneficiaries depending on whether the trust income is currently distributed to the beneficiaries. The mechanism for achieving this result is a deduction granted to the trust for distributions. *See* IRC §§ 651 & 661. Thus, if a trust distributes all of its income currently, its distribution deduction will reduce its taxable income to zero. So much of its current income as is distributed is then taxed to the recipient beneficiaries. *See* IRC §§ 652 & 662. Conversely, if a trust retains any of its income, the trust will report and pay taxes on the retained income.

Many complexities can arise in trust taxation the details of which are beyond the scope of this book. For example, how does one distinguish between distributions of income and distributions of trust principal? Or, if a trust has both capital gains and ordinary income, how does a beneficiary know the character of the distributions he or she is receiving? We have space here only to hint at the answers. The primary mechanism for answering these questions is the concept of *distributable net income* (DNI). *See* IRC § 643(a). DNI is essentially a trust's current taxable income prior to applying the distribution deduction rules. All distributions are deemed to be from DNI to the extent of DNI. The distributions are striped with their respective shares of DNI. This means, among other things, that the income has the same character in the beneficiary's hands as it did in the trust's. An example involving a simple trust may be helpful here.

Example: Tax Treatment of Distributions from a Simple Trust. Simple Trust (ST), managed by Trustee T, is required to distribute all of its income currently, including all realized capital gains. It may also distribute trust principal. In the current year, ST has $50,000 of rental income and $10,000 of long-term capital gains. Thus, ST has DNI of $60,000. A and B are the beneficiaries of ST. In the current year, T directs distributions from ST of $60,000 to A and $40,000 to B. Thus, the trust distributed $40,000 in excess of its income.

Since the trust distributed all of its current income, its distribution deduction will reduce its taxable income to zero. The trust will owe no taxes in the current year.

Since A received three fifths of the funds distributed, A is deemed to have received three fifths of the ordinary income ($30,000), three fifths of the long-term capital gain ($6,000), and three fifths of the principal distributed ($24,000). Since B received two fifths of the funds distributed, B is deemed to have received two fifths of the ordinary income ($20,000), two fifths of the long-term capital gain ($4,000), and two fifths of the principal distributed ($16,000). A and B will each report their respective shares of trust income on their current year tax returns. The income will have the same character in their hands as it did in ST's.

D. The Deduction for Qualified Business Income — Section 199A

As introduced earlier, when Congress reduced the top corporate income tax from 35% to 21%, it also provided temporary tax relief for certain owners of pass-through entities in the form of a 20% deduction on qualified business income. IRC § 199A. The 20% deduction can be taken only by non-corporate owners of certain sole proprietorships, partnerships, LLCs, and S corporations through 2025. C corporations and their shareholders do not qualify. The deduction is not an above the line deduction in arriving at adjusted gross income. IRC § 62(a). Further, it is not an itemized deduction, but it is available to itemizers and non-itemizers alike. IRC § 63(b)(3), (d)(3).

The 20% deduction applies only to "qualified business income," which generally is the net amount of qualified items of income, gain, deduction, and loss with respect to a U.S. trade or business. IRC § 199A(c). It does not apply to investment income. IRC § 199(c)(3)(B). And, it does not apply to compensation for services rendered. IRC § 199A(c)(4). Thus, if a shareholder-employee of an S corporation received from the corporation $50,000 in salary, a $3,000 allocable share of the company's investment income (capital gain and interest income), and a $25,000 allocable share of the company's net operating income, only $25,000 would *potentially* be eligible for the 20% deduction. We say "potentially" because availability of the deduction depends upon a number of factors, including the taxpayer's income level and the type of business conducted.

There are a number of rules and limitations, the application of which depends upon whether a taxpayer falls below certain taxable income thresholds — $157,500 (for single taxpayers) or $315,000 (for married couples filing jointly). These thresholds, which are determined without regard to the section 199A deduction, are indexed for inflation after 2018. As you will see below, when taxable income exceeds these thresholds, calculation of the deduction becomes more complicated.

1. Taxable Income of $157,500 or Less ($315,000 for Married Taxpayers)

For taxpayers with taxable income of not more than $157,500 ($315,000 for married couples), the deduction is 20% of qualified business income of any trade or business *other than a trade or business of providing services as an employee*. IRC § 199A(d)(1). This means that individuals working as employees are not eligible for the deduction.

(As noted in Chapter 30, some commentators predict this could lead to a significant shift in workplace arrangements—from employee-based arrangements to independent contractor-based relationships. Only time will tell.) In the case of partnerships, LLCs, and S corporations, the deduction applies at the individual owner level, and each partner or shareholder takes into account only her allocable share of the entity's net operating income. The deduction may not exceed 20% of the taxpayer's taxable income (determined without regard to the section 199A deduction) reduced by net capital gain (that is, taxable income made up of ordinary income and dividend income). IRC § 199A(a)(1)(B), (e)(1).

2. Taxable Income Greater Than $157,500 ($315,000 for Married Taxpayers)

For taxpayers with taxable income exceeding $157,500 ($315,000 for married couples), things get complicated as two independent limitations begin to phase in as income increases. The first is a limitation on the types of businesses that will qualify for the deduction. The second is a cap on the amount that can be deducted, determined either by reference to a percentage of W-2 wages paid by the business or by reference to a percentage of W-2 wages and the cost of depreciable property used in business. These limitations are fully phased in when a taxpayer's taxable income reaches $207,500 ($415,000 for married couples), indexed for inflation after 2018. Within the phase-in range, only a percentage of business income gets the deduction. To simplify things, we will discuss the two limitations as if they were fully phased in.

Under the first limitation applicable to high income earners, certain businesses ("specified service trades or businesses") are excluded from the deduction. IRC § 199A(d)(1)(A), (3). These include: (1) any business involving the performance of services in the fields of health, law, accounting, actuarial science, performing arts, consulting, athletics, financial services, or brokerage services; (2) any business the principal asset of which is the reputation or skill of one or more of its employees or owners; and (3) any business involving the performance of services consisting of investing and investment management, trading, or dealing in securities, partnership interests, or commodities. IRC § 199A(d)(2). This first limitation serves to prevent high income taxpayers from attempting to convert wages or other compensation for personal services to income eligible for the deduction. Businesses not mentioned above, such as engineering and architectural businesses, are not excluded if they otherwise qualify. Keep in mind, however, there is an independent wage-and-capital-based limitation that may still apply to such businesses.

Under the second limitation, high income taxpayers are subject to a cap on the amount that can be deducted. The cap is the *greater of*: (1) 50% of the W-2 wages paid by the business; or (2) 25% of the W-2 wages plus 2.5% of the unadjusted basis immediately after acquisition of all "qualified property." IRC § 199A(b)(2)(B). Qualified property means depreciable tangible property that is used in a qualified business to produce qualified business income, and that is still within its depreciable period (a period that ends on the later of the date 10 years after placed in service or the last day of the applicable recovery period that would apply under section 168). Land and intangible assets are not qualified property. IRC § 199(b)(6). (For partnerships and S corporations, these caps apply at the individual partner or shareholder level. The deduction cap applicable to an S corporation shareholder, for example, will be determined by reference to the shareholder's allocable share of the corporation's W-2 wages and unadjusted basis of qualified property.) IRC § 199A(f)(1)(A)(ii). The W-2 wage limitation is designed to apply to labor-intensive businesses, whereas the capital-based limitation is designed to apply to capital-intensive businesses. As you can see, the 20% deduction is not significant for service businesses or those that invest little in depreciable property. It does potentially benefit, as one example, pass-through entities engaged in manufacturing.

Even if a high income taxpayer can get past these alternative limitations, there is the overriding limitation based on taxable income. As with low income taxpayers, the section 199A deduction cannot exceed 20% of the excess, if any, of the taxpayer's taxable income over any net capital gain. IRC § 199A(a)(1)(B), (e)(1).

3. Example

Taxpayer (who is single and in the top 37% bracket) holds a 100% ownership interest in an S corporation that operates a widget-making business. The S corporation buys a widget-making machine for $200,000 and places it in service in 2018. The S corporation, which has one employee who earns $30,000, generates $100,000 of net operating income in 2018. Will Taxpayer be entitled to a 20% ($20,000) deduction under section 199A? If Taxpayer's taxable income were under $157,500, he would be allowed a deduction of $20,000. However, because Taxpayer's taxable income (determined without regard to the section 199A deduction) exceeds $157,500 (i.e., he has lots of taxable income from sources unrelated to the S corporation), we must see if one of the two alternative constraints apply. He will not be subject to the limitation for "specified service businesses" because a widget-making business is not the type of business excluded for high income taxpayers. He will, however, be subject to the wage and capital-based limitation. The limitation is the *greater of* (1) 50% of Taxpayer's share of W-2 wages paid by the corporation, here $15,000, or (2) the sum of 25% of Taxpayer's share of W-2 wages paid by the corporation ($7,500) plus 2.5% of Taxpayer's $200,000 unadjusted basis of the machine immediately after its acquisition: $200,000 × .025 = $5,000, here $12,500. Taxpayer's deduction under section 199A is capped at $15,000.

Though you may be inclined to think otherwise, we have treated section 199A lightly here. It is a complex provision that is more comprehensible after one has studied the tax treatment of business entities. For that reason, its full study is more fitting in a business tax course than an individual income tax course.

E. Business Planning with Entities

Choice of Entity. As noted at the outset, there are many non-tax reasons for using entities for business planning purposes, limited liability being chief among them. The choice of entity in any particular case is likely to be driven by both tax and non-tax considerations. Historically, most advisers steered their clients away from the C corporation in a closely held situation because of the potential adverse tax consequences. Recall from above that income of a C corporation is subject to "double taxation." Income is taxed first at the corporate level and then again when corporate dividend payments are made. Many advisors, however, are reconsidering the use of C corporations after Congress drastically reduced the corporate tax rate to 21%. However, the impact of the section 199A 20% deduction on qualified business income of pass-through entities must also be assessed. For clients who qualify for the deduction, a pass-through entity may still be the preferred choice. Whether to choose an S corporation or a partnership or an LLC requires consideration of many other factors.

S corporations are often used in service enterprises because of certain payroll tax advantages. S corporations are not used, however, if there is a desire to use disproportionate allocations of tax items such as depreciation. Moreover, liquidation of an S corporation can trigger gain recognition in situations where no gain need be recognized in the partnership context. The partnership is often the tax entity of choice for small businesses. But this still leaves many choices since general partnerships, limited partnerships, limited liability partnerships, and limited liability companies can all be partnerships from a tax perspective. How do we choose among them?

The limited liability company might seem like the obvious choice in most situations since it confers complete insulation from personal liability for its members. The difficulty is that, since it is a newer form of entity, less is known about how it works in a variety of tax and non-tax contexts. For this reason many tax professionals will persist in recommending a more traditional form such as the limited partnership.

Combined and Multiple Entities. Many business owners choose to combine business entities. For example, a common business combination is a limited partnership in which the sole general partner is a corporation (or limited liability company) and the limited partners are shareholders (or members) of the general partner. The reason for using an LLC as the general partner is to obtain limited liability for all participants.

Using multiple entities to segregate assets or activities can also have its advantages. Chiefly this is done to insulate one activity or group of assets from liabilities associated with another activity or group of assets. For example, a law or accounting firm may place its office building in one LLC and operate its firm out of another LLC with the operating LLC paying rent to the holding LLC. This offers some protection against losing the building due to a malpractice claim against one of the partners. This has the further utility that the entry of new partners into the operating LLC does not require the transfer or sale of an interest in the building to those new partners. They simply acquire no interest in the holding LLC.

F. Estate Planning with Entities

Estate planning is the process by which individuals make arrangements for their property and personal needs during disability and after death. It is a complex area of legal specialization that draws on a diverse body of law (e.g., property, wills, trusts, insurance, and, of course, taxes). Often there is more than one option for organizing and disposing of a client's property and the estate planning lawyer's job is to help the client choose the plan that minimizes overall tax costs and maximizes the amount of property to be distributed to beneficiaries. When considering the tax costs of estate plans, one must consider not only the income taxes pertinent to estate planning, but also the federal estate and gift taxes (the subject of Chapter 41).

1. Trusts

Trusts are a typical component of an estate plan. For example, any person who plans to leave property to a person who may be a minor at the time the transfer takes effect will want to consider a trust as a property management vehicle. The same is true for someone who wishes to provide for a seriously disabled person. As noted earlier, any time the transferor wishes to divide property interests on a temporal basis a trust is called for. Thus, for example, a child who wishes to provide for her parent in the event that the child predeceases the parent may put property in trust with a life interest in the parent and the remainder passing to someone else such as the child's children. These non-tax reasons for the use of trusts may be augmented by tax reduction motives that are beyond the scope of this chapter. Suffice it to say that there are a rich variety of estate planning devices employing trusts that are designed especially to reduce estate, gift, and income taxes. These include split interest charitable trusts, life insurance trusts, spousal life interest trusts, and a number of grantor retained interest trusts.

2. Closely Held Corporations

There are many challenges associated with closely held business interests from an estate planning perspective. For many shareholders of closely held corporations, for example, their stock represents a sizeable portion of their estate, yet it is the least liquid asset. Lack of liquidity to enjoy retirement or to pay estate taxes at death is usually caused by lack of a defined market for the stock or because the taxpayer wants to keep the stock within the family. Small business interests, especially minority interests, are also difficult to value absent a value controlling agreement.

One solution to liquidity and valuation problems is a buy-sell agreement, which typically provides that either the corporation or the remaining shareholders will purchase the stock of a retired or deceased shareholder. Buy-sell agreements need to be properly structured, especially to establish value of stock for estate tax purposes. Conditions prescribed by section 2703 are typically considered in a separate course on estate and gift taxation. Buy-sell agreements are usually funded with life insurance policies.

Congress has enacted partial solutions to the liquidity problems associated with closely held stock. Section 6166, for example, allows executors to make installment payments of federal estate tax attributable to closely held interests, provided the value of the closely held interests exceeds 35% of the decedent's gross estate. *See* IRC § 6166. For other partial relief provisions, see IRC §§ 303, 2032A, 6161.

3. Family Limited Partnerships

Family Limited Partnerships (FLPs) have been popular estate planning tools for gifting assets while retaining control over them. In a typical FLP, parents transfer an asset to a limited partnership. In the partnership, the general partner(s) will often own 1% of equity and the limited partner(s) will own 99% of equity. The parents may retain the general partnership interest (either individually or in a limited liability vehicle, such as an LLC or S corporation), and subsequently gift the limited partnership interests to their children. If done properly, the parents can transfer their property (and income attributable to it) to their children at a low gift tax cost, while retaining considerable control of the asset.

At the heart of the FLP plan are *valuation discounts*. Substantial discounts are frequently allowed in valuing the gifted limited partnership interests on account of their minority interest status and their lack of marketability. The FLP permits donors to discount the value of gifts to donees that otherwise might not be discounted if made outright to them. In addition to gift tax implications, there are income tax implications to the FLP. As noted earlier, limited partnerships are pass-through entities, meaning income from partnership property passes through and is taxed to the individual partners. If parents/donors own a 1% interest, they're taxed on 1% of the partnership income. If children/donees own 99% of the partnership, then they're taxed on 99% of the partnership income. As you can see, the limited partnership can shift income from parents to children whose income tax rates may be as low as 10% or 12%. Note, however, that sections 704(e) and 761(b) prescribe certain requirements that must be met before a limited partner will be considered a partner for federal tax purposes.

The government has used different approaches in attacking FLPs and the valuation discounts they produce. Recent tools, such as section 2036 and proposed regulations under section 2704, are beyond the scope of this chapter.

Chapter 38

Corporate Formations

I. Assignment

Read: Internal Revenue Code: §§ 351(a)–(b); 357(a), (c); 358(a), (d)(1); 362(a); 368(c); 1032(a). Skim §§ 83(a)–(b); 1223(1)–(2); 1245(b)(3).

Treasury Regulations: §§ 1.351-1(a)(1); 1.358-2(b)(2).

Text: Overview
Revenue Ruling 64-56
Revenue Ruling 74-477
Related Matters

Complete the problems.

II. Problems

1. Gary Cooper, Ernest Hemingway, and Ingrid Bergman decide to form Highcountry Corporation to operate a flyfishing, skiing, and horseback riding resort near Sun Valley, Idaho. What are the tax consequences of this formation under the following circumstances?

   (a) Gary contributes investment land worth $1,000,000 in which he has a basis of $500,000. Ernest contributes $1,000,000 in cash. Ingrid, who is a rancher, contributes livestock held as inventory and an easement granting unlimited grazing and recreational access to 10,000 acres of nearby forest and range land owned by a third party. The livestock are worth $200,000 and have an aggregate basis of $300,000. The easement is worth $800,000 and has a basis of $400,000. Each of them receives 300 shares of Highcountry common stock in exchange for their transfers.

   (b) Same as (a) except that each receives 200 shares of common stock valued at $500,000 and 100 shares of preferred stock also valued at $500,000.

   (c) Same as (a) except that Gary's land is worth $1,100,000. To equalize the deal he receives $100,000 of cash in addition to the stock.

   (d) Same as (c) except that Gary's basis in the land is $1,050,000.

   (e) Same as (a) except that Gary, Ernest, and Ingrid each receives 270 shares of stock worth $1,000,000 and Averil Harriman, an expert fly fisher and guide, receives 90 shares worth $300,000 of fully vested stock in exchange for agreeing to manage Highcountry for ten years.

(f) Same as (e) except that each of the four owners receive 225 shares worth $1,000,000.

(g) Same as (a) except that Gary's land is worth $1,100,000 and is transferred subject to a $100,000 mortgage which Highcountry assumes.

(h) Same as (g) except that the land is worth $1,600,000 and is subject to a $600,000 mortgage which Highcountry assumes.

(i) Same as (a) except that Ernest only contributes $900,000 of cash but also contributes secret fly tying knowledge that is worth $100,000. This fly tying knowledge produces fishing flies of such superior design that even beginning fly fishers catch lots of fish.

III. Overview

From a non-tax perspective, a corporation is formed by complying with formalities of state law in such respects as promulgation of articles of incorporation, the election of officers and directors, and so forth. From a tax perspective the formation of a corporation is essentially a sale or exchange between a corporation and its founding shareholders. The shareholders transfer cash or other property to the corporation and take back stock in the corporation. The corporation issues its stock for the cash or property received from the shareholders. Normally each party is deemed to give and receive property of equal value. Thus, in the absence of overriding rules, section 1001 would cause each party to recognize gain or loss. However, with good reason, Congress has chosen to treat corporate formations as non-recognition events under certain circumstances. As will be detailed below, the tax rules with respect to corporate formations bear a strong similarity to the like kind exchange rules studied in Chapter 24. The basic pattern is the grant of non-recognition of gain or loss but at the price of a carry over basis in the property acquired in the formation. The justification for this approach is two fold. First, non-recognition fosters *capital formation*, that is, the pooling of money and other productive assets. In a capitalist society capital formation is a good thing since it generates economic activity leading to profits for investors and jobs for employees. Second, current gain recognition may be unfair in that the investor may have simply changed the form but not the substance of her investment. This second point is readily understood in the context of conversion of an ongoing business from a sole proprietorship to a corporation. To all outward appearances the business may be no different after formation than it was before.

A. A Cautionary Note and a Statement of Relevance

The traditional corporation is commonly called a "C corporation" in tax lingo because the rules for its tax treatment are found in subchapter C of the Internal Revenue Code. *See* IRC §§ 301–85. Almost all publicly traded stocks are in C corporations. Over the years it has become increasingly rare to form a *closely held* business as a C corporation. In major part this is because of the double tax on corporate earnings described in the last chapter. Instead most closely held businesses operate as partnerships or as S corporations for tax purposes. (In this context keep in mind that most limited liability companies (LLCs) are partnerships for tax purposes.) As noted in the previous chapter, however, the recent reduction in the corporate tax rate (to 21%) may cause many closely businesses to rethink the corporate form. Many aspects of the tax treatment of S corporations and their shareholders are addressed in subchapter S of the Internal Revenue Code. *See* IRC §§ 1361–77. However, those tax aspects of S corporations not addressed in subchapter S are still subject to the rules of subchapter C. For example, the subchapter C formation rules apply to S corporation formations. Thus, subchapter C has continuing relevance for small businesses even though it is no longer advisable in many cases to form a new business as a C corporation.

B. The Fundamental Rules

The key operative provision in most corporate formations is section 351. It prevents recognition of gains and losses by the transferors when property is contributed *solely* for stock of a corporation if afterwards the transferors are in "control" of the corporation. IRC § 351(a). Money is property for this purpose. Rev. Rul. 69-357, 1969-1 C.B. 101. Not even the depreciation recapture rules will override section 351(a) in most cases. *See* IRC § 1245(b)(3). The transferor takes a basis in the stock received equal to her basis in the property and cash given up. IRC § 358(a)(1). If the transferor receives more than one class of stock the basis is allocated between classes based on their relative values. Treas. Reg. § 1.358-2(b)(2). If the property given up by the transferor was capital gain property or section 1231 property, the transferor can tack the property's holding period to the stock's holding period. IRC § 1223(1).

The provision that grants the corporation non-recognition is section 1032(a). This is important because normally the corporation will have a zero basis in its own stock. But rather than being obliged to take a zero basis in the property received for the stock, the corporation takes the transferor's basis in the property. IRC § 362(a). (Note: If the transferor has a net built in loss on the property contributed, the corporation must reduce its basis by the amount of the net built in loss. There is a provision that will permit the corporation to take a full carryover basis if the transferor agrees to take a fair market value basis in the stock. IRC § 362(e)(2)(C).) It also receives tacking of holding periods. IRC § 1223(2).

Example. Andy owns a patent on some computer hardware that he purchased for $50,000 as a business investment. He decides to incorporate. He does so by contributing the patent (now worth $200,000) in exchange for all of the stock of the corporation. Andy will recognize no gain on the transfer (IRC § 351(a)) and will take a $50,000 basis in the stock (IRC § 358(a)(1)). His holding period for the stock includes his holding period for the patent. IRC § 1223(1). The corporation will recognize no gain on the transfer (IRC § 1032(a)) and will take a $50,000 basis in the patent (IRC § 362(a)). The corporation's holding period for the patent includes Andy's holding period. IRC § 1223(2).

C. Some of the Nuances

1. Who Is a "Person"?

Section 351 can apply to any transferor who is a "person." For this purpose a person can include trusts, estates, partnerships, and corporations as well as individuals. Treas. Reg. § 1.351-1(a)(1). *See* IRC § 7701(a)(1).

2. What Does "Control" Mean, and How Is "Immediately After" Measured?

In order for section 351 to apply, the transferors of property have to be in "control" of the corporation "immediately after" the transfers. Control means that the transferors own at least eighty percent of each class of stock that is issued and outstanding. IRC § 368(c). *See also* Rev. Rul. 59-259, 1959-2 C.B. 115; Treas. Reg. § 1.351-1(a)(1). The requirement in section 351 that control must exist "immediately after" the property transfers has been construed to mean that the various transfers need not occur simultaneously, but should be pre-planned and must occur with "expedition consistent with orderly procedure." Treas. Reg. § 1.351-1(a)(1). Thus, where several persons are forming a corporation, there is some allowance for normal delays in making the various transfers.

3. What Happens if Stock Is Received for Services?

Section 351 only grants non-recognition for transfers of "property" for stock. Thus, a person who receives stock for services is outside of the operation of section 351. *See* IRC § 351(d)(1); Treas. Reg. § 1.351-1(a)(1)(i). The shareholder who receives stock for services has compensation income measured by the value of the stock. IRC § 61. It is ordinary income in the year in which the interest in the stock becomes vested unless the shareholder elects to take it into income earlier. IRC § 83. The service shareholder's basis in the stock is its tax cost, that is, its fair market value on the date it is taken into income. IRC § 1012.

Even though the service shareholder recognizes income on receipt of the stock, the corporation still does not recognize gain or loss. Treas. Reg. § 1.1032-1(a) (last sentence). Depending on the nature of the services the corporation will either capitalize the cost or take a current deduction.

The transfer of stock for services during formation poses a risk to the other shareholders since only transferors of property are included in the control group for purposes of the 80% control requirement. Obviously one way to avoid this is by transferring less than twenty percent of the stock for services. There is a leniency rule that provides that if a service provider puts up at least ten percent property for his stock, all of his stock can be counted for purposes of the control test. Rev. Proc. 77-37, 1977-2 C.B. 568. *See also* Treas. Reg. § 1.351-1(a)(1)(ii).

D. Receipt of Boot

For various reasons a contributing shareholder may receive cash or other property in addition to stock in the corporation as part of the formation. Just as with like kind exchanges we refer to this other property as "boot." If boot is received by the transferor, realized gain (but not loss) is recognized by the transferor to the extent of the boot's value. IRC § 351(b). In other words the transferor will recognize the *lesser* of gain realized or boot received. If the boot is cash the transferor's basis in her stock is decreased to the extent of the cash received and increased to the extent of the gain recognized. IRC § 358(a)(1). If the boot is property other than cash, the transferor's basis in the stock is reduced by the value of the boot received and increased by the gain recognized. The non-cash boot will take a fair market value basis. IRC § 358(a)(2).

The corporation's basis in the property it receives from the transferor is increased by the amount of gain recognized by the transferor. IRC § 362(a) (flush language).

Example. Assume Aretha forms a corporation. Aretha contributes to the corporation a song copyright she has owned for 3 years with an adjusted basis of $80,000 and a fair market value of $100,000. She receives back from the corporation 40 shares of stock worth $80,000 and $20,000 of cash. (Don't worry about the source of the cash.)

Aretha will recognize $20,000 of gain since the boot she received is equal to her realized gain. IRC § 351(b). Her basis in her stock is $80,000 (her beginning basis of $80,000 minus $20,000 of cash received plus $20,000 of gain recognized). IRC § 358(a)(1). The corporation's basis in the copyright is $100,000 (Aretha's original $80,000 basis plus the $20,000 of gain she recognized). IRC § 362(a). Note that both Aretha and the corporation will tack holding periods. IRC §§ 1223(1) & (2).

E. Transfers of Liabilities

We learned earlier in this book when considering the *Crane* case that acquisition indebtedness is included in basis and, concomitantly, relief of indebtedness is included in amount realized. Thus, under a section 1001 analysis, relief of indebtedness can generate realized gain. In the chapter on like kind exchanges we saw that relief of indebtedness is treated as cash received for basis and boot purposes. The question then becomes whether under section 351, transfer of a liability to the corporation (assumption of a liability by the corporation for a shareholder) is like the receipt of cash boot. Code section 357 skirts a middle course between complete non-recognition and recognition. If property is transferred to the corporation subject to a liability not in excess of the transferor's basis, no gain is recognized. IRC § 357(a). The cost for this non-recognition is that the transferor's basis in his stock is reduced by the amount of the liability. IRC § 358(d)(1). In short, the liability is not treated as boot for gain recognition purposes but is treated as boot for basis purposes. Thus, the gain arising from the debt relief is only deferred not forgiven.

If the liability exceeds the transferor's basis, then the transferor recognizes gain to the extent of the excess. IRC § 357(c)(1). If the transferor recognizes gain under this rule his ending basis in his stock is always zero because it is reduced by the amount of cash deemed received.

The corporation's basis is the transferor's plus the amount of gain, if any, recognized by the transferor. IRC §362(a).

Example. Althea and Bao form a corporation. Althea contributes land worth $100,000 (with a basis of $50,000) subject to a liability of $20,000 (which the corporation assumes) and receives 80 shares of stock. Bao contributes equipment worth $120,000 (with a basis of $80,000) subject to a $110,000 liability (which the corporation assumes) and receives 10 shares of stock.

	AB	FMV	LIAB	STOCK
A	50	100	20	80
B	80	120	110	10

Althea recognizes no gain since her debt relief does not exceed her basis. IRC § 357(a). Her basis in her stock is $30,000 ($50,000 beginning basis minus $20,000 debt relief). IRC §§ 358(a) & (d). The corporation takes a $50,000 basis in the land. IRC § 362(a).

Bao recognizes $30,000 of gain, the amount by which his debt exceeds his basis. IRC § 357(c)(1). His basis in the stock is zero ($80,000 beginning basis plus $30,000 of gain recognized minus $110,000 of debt relief). IRC §§ 358(a), (d). The corporation takes a $110,000 basis in the equipment ($80,000 beginning basis plus $30,000 of gain recognized). IRC § 362(a).

F. Conclusion

The formation of new corporations, especially S corporations, is an everyday matter in the world of business. From the foregoing it should be apparent that a working knowledge of tax principles governing corporate formations is essential to anyone who participates in such formations as a lawyer, accountant, investor, or business manager. While this chapter outlines the income tax basics of such formations there are many more details that we have left out that would be included in a text on corporate income tax law. In such a book the reader would also encounter a thorough treatment of the tax treatment of the ongoing operations of a corporation as well as the treatment of such matters as liquidations and mergers. Part of this chapter's purpose is to show why one might want to study such a text. The tax law is ubiquitous. It follows the flow of money and property through the hands of individuals and businesses from beginning to end. Those persons who choose to enter of the world of commerce while maintaining an attitude of indifference or conscious disregard of the tax law do so at some peril.

IV. Materials

Revenue Ruling 64-56

1964-1 C.B. 133

The Internal Revenue Service has received inquiries whether technical "know-how" constitutes property which can be transferred, without recognition of gain or loss, in exchange for stock or securities under section 351 of the Internal Revenue Code of 1954.

The issue has been drawn to the attention of the Service, particularly in cases in which a manufacturer agrees to assist a newly organized foreign corporation to enter upon a business abroad of making and selling the same kind of product as it makes. The transferor typically grants to the transferee rights to use manufacturing processes in which the transferor has exclusive rights by virtue of process patents or the protection otherwise extended by law to the owner of a process. The transferor also often agrees to furnish technical assistance in the construction and operation of the plant and to provide on a continuing basis technical information as to new developments in the field. Some of this consideration is commonly called "know-how." In exchange, the transferee typically issues to the transferor all or part of its stock.

Section 351 of the Code provides, in part, as follows:

(a) GENERAL RULE. — No gain or loss shall be recognized if property is transferred to a corporation by one or more persons solely in exchange for stock or securities in such corporation and immediately after the exchange such person or persons are in control (as defined in section 368 (c)) of the corporation. For purposes of this section, stock or securities issued for services shall not be considered as issued in return for property.

Since the term "know-how" does not appear in section 351 of the Code, its meaning is immaterial in applying this section, and the Service will look behind the term in each case to determine to what extent, if any, the items so called constitute "property ... transferred to a corporation ... in exchange for stock."

The term "property" for purposes of section 351 of the Code will be held to include anything qualifying as "secret processes and formulas" within the meaning of sections 861 (a) (4) and 862 (a) (4) of the Code and any other secret information as to a device, process, etc., in the general nature of a patentable invention without regard to whether a patent has been applied for (see G.C.M. 21507, C.B. 1939-2, 189; Wall Products Inc. v. Commissioner, 11 T.C. 51, at 57 (1948), acquiescence, C.B. 1949-1, 4; Ralph L. Evans v. Commissioner, 8 B.T.A. 543 (1927)), and without regard to whether it is patentable in the patent law sense. Other information which is secret will be given consideration as "property" on a case-by-case basis.

The fact that information is recorded on paper or some other physical material is not itself an indication that the information is property. See, for example, Harold L. Regenstein, et ux. v. Commissioner, 35 T.C. 183 (1960), where the fact that a program for providing group life insurance to Federal Government employees was transmitted in the form of a written plan did not preclude a finding that the payment for the plan was a payment for personal services.

It is assumed for the purpose of this Revenue Ruling that the country in which the transferee is to operate affords to the transferor substantial legal protection against the unauthorized disclosure and use of the process, formula, or other secret information involved.

Once it is established that "property" has been transferred, the transfer will be tax-free under section 351 even though services were used to produce the property. Such is generally the case where the transferor developed the property primarily for use in its own manufacturing business. However, where the information transferred has been developed specially for the transferee, the stock received in exchange for it may be treated as payment for services rendered. *See Regenstein, supra*, where the taxpayer developed a plan for selling insurance which he ultimately sold to certain insurance companies. The court held that the consideration received was payment for services.

Where the transferor agrees to perform services in connection with a transfer of property, tax-free treatment will be accorded if the services are merely ancillary and subsidiary to the property transfer. Whether or not services are merely ancillary and subsidiary to a property transfer is a question of fact. Ancillary and subsidiary services could be performed, for example, in promoting the transaction by demonstrating and explaining the use of the property, or by assisting in the effective "starting-up" of the property transferred, or by performing under a guarantee relating to such effective starting-up. Compare Raymond M. Hessert v. Commissioner, Tax Court Memorandum Opinion, entered October 31, 1947, and Arthur C. Ruge, et ux. v. Commissioner, 26 T.C. 138, at 143 (1956), acquiescence, C.B. 1958-2, 7. Where both property and services are furnished as consideration, and the services are not merely ancillary and subsidiary to the property transfer, a reasonable allocation is to be made.

Training the transferee's employees in skills of any grade through expertness, for example, in a recognized profession, craft, or trade is to be distinguished as essentially educational and, like any other teaching services, is taxable when compensated in stock or otherwise, without being affected by section 351 of the Code. However, where the transferee's employees concerned already have the particular skills in question, it will ordinarily follow as a matter of fact that other consideration alone and not training in those skills is being furnished for the transferor's stock.

Continuing technical assistance after the starting-up phase will not be regarded as performance under a guarantee, and the consideration therefor will ordinarily be treated as compensation for professional services, taxable without regard to section 351 of the Code.

Assistance in the construction of a plant building to house machinery transferred, or to house machinery to be used in applying a patented or other process or formula which qualifies as property transferred, will ordinarily be considered to be in the nature of an architect's or construction engineer's services rendered to the transferee and not merely rendered on behalf of the transferor in producing, or promoting the sale or exchange of, the things transferred. Similarly, advice as to the lay-out of plant machinery and equipment may be so unrelated to the particular property transferred as to constitute no more than a rendering of advisory services to the transferee.

The transfer of all substantial rights in property of the kind hereinbefore specified will be treated as a transfer of property for purposes of section 351 of the Code. The transfer will also qualify under section 351 of the Code if the transferred rights extend to all of the territory of one or more countries and consist of all substantial rights therein, the transfer being clearly limited to such territory, notwithstanding that rights are retained as to some other country's territory. See Lanova Corporation v. Commissioner, 17 T.C. 1178 (1952), acquiescence, C.B. 1952-1,3.

The property right in a formula may consist of the method of making a composition and the composition itself, namely the proportions of its ingredients, or it may consist of only the method of making the composition. Where the property right in the secret formula consists of both the composition and the method of making it, the unqualified transfer in perpetuity of the exclusive right to use the formula, including the right to use and sell the products made from and representing the formula, within all the territory of the country will be treated as the transfer of all substantial rights in the property in that country.

The unqualified transfer in perpetuity of the exclusive right to use a secret process or other similar secret information qualifying as property within all the territory of a country, or the unqualified transfer in perpetuity of the exclusive right to make, use and sell an unpatented but secret product within all the territory of a country, will be treated as the transfer of all substantial rights in the property in that country.

Revenue Ruling 55-17, C.B. 1955-1, 388, is modified to remove the implication that payments for the rights described there as "know-how" will be treated as royalty income without regard to the factors applied here to determine whether such rights constitute property.

Nothing hereinbefore stated should be construed as limiting in any way the effective operation of other sections of the Internal Revenue Code upon transactions between domestic and related foreign corporations. See, for example, sections 367, 482, and 1491.

Revenue Ruling 74-477

1974-2 C.B. 116

A, an individual, proposes to transfer property to X corporation solely in exchange for all of the outstanding voting common stock of X. Pursuant to the agreement between A and X, appraisal fees, legal fees, and shipping and packaging expenses, incurred by A in connection with the transfer will be paid or assumed by X, These expenses are bona fide expenses directly relating to the transfer by A of property to X.

Held, under section 357 (a) of the Code, X may assume such liabilities that arise out of the transfer of the property. Such expenses paid or assumed by X will not be considered as "boot" received by A under section 351 (b) of the Code. However, any bona fide expenses of X paid by A will be treated as a contribution by A to the capital of X.

V. Related Matters

- **Allocation of Boot Among Assets Transferred.** When a shareholder contributes more than one asset and receives stock and boot, some complexities arise as to how to allocate the boot to the various assets contributed. These complexities are addressed in Revenue Ruling 68-55, 1968-1 C.B. 140.

- **Tax Avoidance Provision.** Section 357 has a provision designed to prevent a taxpayer from manipulating the boot leniency rule. *See* IRC § 357(b).

- **Accounts Payable.** Liabilities, such as accounts payable, that give rise to a deduction when paid are disregarded for section 357 and section 358 purposes. IRC §§ 357(c)(3), 358(d)(2).

- **Effect of Issuance of Promissory Note.** There is some authority for the proposition that one can avoid the operation of section 357(c) by contributing one's own note for the excess liability. *See* Perrachi v. Commissioner, 143 F.3d 487 (9th Cir. 1998); Lessinger v. Commissioner, 872 F.2d 519 (2d Cir. 1989). The Service has not acquiesced to these decisions.

- **Contribution of Personal Use Property.** When personal use property is contributed to a corporation, the basis used is the lesser of cost or fair market value for loss purposes. Treas. Reg. 1.165-7(a). (This makes sense since the loss would not have been deductible had the taxpayer sold the personal use property at a loss.)

- **Organizational Expenditures.** A corporation may elect to deduct immediately up to $5,000 of "organizational expenditures," and amortize the balance over 180 months beginning with the month in which the corporation begins business. IRC § 248.

Chapter 39

Partnership Formations

I. Assignment

Read: Internal Revenue Code: §§ 705(a); 721; 722; 723; 731(a)(1); 733; 752(a)–(b); 1223(1)–(2); 1245(b)(3). Skim §§ 83(a)–(c); 704(c)(1)(A); 707(a)(2)(B); 709; 724.

Treasury Regulations: §§ 1.704-1(b)(2)(iv)(b); 1.721-1(b). Skim §§ 1.752-1, -2, -3.

Text: Overview
McDougal v. Commissioner
United States v. Frazell
Related Matters

Complete the problems.

II. Problems

1. Henry Adams (A) and Fulgencio Batista (B) are planning to organize a general partnership, Xerxes (X), to engage in the operation of a fishing camp in northern Maine. A will contribute to X a tract of lake front property, and B will contribute $200,000 of cash to be used in the construction of a lodge. The land has a fair market value of $200,000, and A's adjusted basis is $100,000. X will issue to both A and B a general partnership interest representing a 50% interest in the capital, profits, and losses of X in exchange for the contributions.

    (a) What are the tax consequences to A, B, and X upon formation of the partnership? Your analysis should address gain realization, gain recognition, inside basis, outside basis, holding period, and capital account balances.

    (b) Same as (a) except that A's land is worth $210,000. In order to equalize the contributions of the two partners, X, as part of the transaction, distributes to A $10,000 of the $200,000 of cash contributed by B.

    (c) Same as (b) except that A's adjusted basis for the land is $5,000.

    (d) Same as (a) except that A's land is subject to a nonrecourse liability of $120,000, and B contributes cash of $80,000. Assume that the partnership interest each receives has a fair market value of $80,000 because X has a net worth of $160,000 (i.e., $280,000 of assets and a $120,000 liability).

    (e) Same as (a) except that A did not own any land to contribute to X. A contributed instead a "letter of intent" in exchange for his partnership interest. The letter of intent recited that A and a landowner had begun negotiations to finance and construct a lodge, with the landowner providing a favorable land lease and loan. A assigned to X the agreement to lease and loan commitment and agreed to continue negotiations.

(f) Same as (a) except that B did not contribute cash. Instead B receives his 50% capital interest in the partnership in exchange for his agreement to manage the business for five years.

III. Overview

As discussed in Chapter 37, unincorporated business entities possess unique state law characteristics. A *general partnership* exists when two or more persons carry on a business with the expectation of generating profits. No formal filing requirements are necessary. Each partner in a general partnership is personally responsible for partnership debts and obligations. A *limited partnership* is a creature of state law that must satisfy filing requirements to come into existence. A limited partnership has one or more general partners and one or more limited partners. General partners have unlimited personal liability for partnership debts and obligations. Limited partners, in contrast, are not liable for debts and obligations of the partnership as long as they do not participate in the control of the business. A *limited liability company* (LLC) is a hybrid entity combining both corporate and partnership features. Despite being called a company, an LLC is an unincorporated business entity formed under state law. Like a corporation and a limited partnership, an LLC can only be created by satisfying state law filing requirements. All members of an LLC have limited liability protection regardless of their management activity. This is a significant non-tax advantage over the limited partnership form, wherein general partners have unlimited liability and limited partners may be personally liable if they participate in management.

Although unincorporated businesses possess different state law characteristics, they are generally treated as partnerships for federal income tax purposes. Under the tax rules governing the operations of partnerships, found in subchapter K of the Internal Revenue (§§ 701–777), a partnership is not a separate taxable entity for federal income tax purposes, but rather, is a pass-through entity. This means that items of income, gain, loss, deduction, and credit are determined at the entity level, but then flow through to individual partners and are reported on their individual returns.

As with corporate formations, Congress has generally chosen to treat partnership formations as non-recognition events. Non-recognition fosters the formation of partnerships, something that should not be impeded by taxes. Non-recognition also recognizes that a partner who has transferred property in exchange for a partnership interest has not changed her economic position—the partnership interest is substantially a continuation of the partner's old investment still unliquidated.

A. The Fundamental Rules

The key operative provision in most partnership formations is section 721. It provides that no gain or loss shall be recognized by a *partner* upon a contribution of property to the partnership in exchange for a partnership interest. Section 721 parallels section 351, its corporate tax counterpart, in that a contribution must qualify as "property" and that property must be "exchanged" for an ownership interest in the new entity. Section 721 differs from section 351 in several respects. For example, section 721 does not have a "control" requirement. Thus, any contribution of property in exchange for a partnership interest, no matter how small, will generally be nontaxable.

If section 721 applies to a contribution of property to a partnership, the reporting of gain or loss realized is postponed to a later year—for example, when the partnership interest received on formation is later sold or disposed of in a taxable transaction. Gain or loss is preserved by generally giving the partner the same basis in the partnership interest acquired (known as "outside basis") as he or she had in the property given up in the exchange. IRC § 722. A partner's outside basis represents the partner's *post-tax* investment in the partnership, and is later adjusted upward for the partner's share of profits and downward for the partner's share of deductions. IRC § 705. Since a partner's basis in the partnership interest is determined by reference to the partner's basis in property given up, the partner's holding period for the partnership interest received generally includes the holding period of the property given up. IRC § 1223(1).

Consistent with the tax treatment of corporations that issue stock for property, *partnerships* do not recognize gain or loss when they issue partnership interests in exchange for money or property. IRC § 721. A partnership that receives property in exchange for its partnership interests in a nontaxable formation steps into the shoes of the transferor. Thus, a partnership's basis in any property received in a section 721 exchange (known as "inside basis") is the same as the transferor partner's basis. IRC § 723. The partnership's holding period in such property includes the holding period of the transferor partner. IRC § 1223(2).

The tax rules governing basic partnership formations can be illustrated with the following simple example.

Example 1. Andy and Bob decide to form a 50-50 partnership that will develop real estate. Andy, contributes $100,000 in cash in exchange for a 50% partnership interest worth $100,000. Bob contributes a tract of land with an adjusted basis of $30,000 and an agreed value of $100,000, in exchange for a 50% partnership interest worth $100,000. Andy has no gain or loss realized since he contributes cash (i.e., the value of the interest received equals the basis of the cash contributed). Andy's basis in his partnership interest ("outside basis") is $100,000, and his holding period for the partnership interest begins with the exchange. Bob has a realization event since he transfers appreciated property in exchange for different property—a partnership interest. Although Bob's gain realized is $70,000 (amount realized of $100,000, the fair market value of the partnership interest received, minus adjusted basis of $30,000 in the land transferred), none of it is recognized pursuant to section 721. Bob's basis in his partnership interest ("outside basis") is $30,000, and his holding period for his partnership interest includes his holding period for the land. IRC §§ 721, 722, 1223(1). The partnership recognizes no gain with respect to the cash and land received in exchange for the partnership interests issued. The partnership's basis in the land ("inside basis") is $30,000, the same basis Bob had, and the partnership's holding period for the land includes Bob's holding period. IRC §§ 721, 723, 1223(2).

B. Some of the Nuances

1. What Happens if a Partnership Interest Is Received for Services?

An important requirement for non-recognition treatment under section 721, as with section 351, is that "property" must be transferred. Although there is no statutory definition of property for purposes of section 721, the Service and the courts have been guided by analogous interpretations under section 351. For purposes of both provisions, the term is defined broadly and embraces money, goodwill and other intangibles. *See* Rev. Rul. 64-56, 1964-1 C.B. 133 (ruling that the transfer of all substantial rights in technical know-how (trade secrets) will be treated as a transfer of property for purposes of section 351). *See also* United States. v. Stafford, 727 F.2d 1043 (11th Cir. 1984) (finding that a letter of intent embodying favorable loan and lease commitments secured through the efforts of the contributing partner was property for purposes of section 721).

Although the term property has been broadly construed, it does not include services rendered to a partnership. As a general rule, a partner who receives a partnership interest in exchange for services must report as ordinary income the value of the partnership interest received. IRC § 61. It is sometimes difficult to value certain partnership interests. The receipt of a *capital interest* (an interest in the current value of the partnership) for services provided to or for the benefit of a partnership should be currently taxable as compensation since a capital interest is easy to value. Treas. Reg. § 1.721-1(b)(1). *McDougal v. Commissioner*, a case included below, addresses the tax consequences to a partner who receives a capital interest in exchange for past services rendered. (Note: Whether the receipt of a *profits interest* (an interest only in future profits) for services rendered should be taxable has been the subject of much litigation, since profits interests are difficult to value. *See, e.g.,* Campbell v. Commissioner, 943 F.2d 815 (8th Cir. 1991); Diamond v. Commissioner, 492 F.2d 286 (7th Cir. 1974). The treatment of profits interests is beyond the scope of this chapter.)

Sometimes it is difficult to determine the extent to which a mixed contribution of property and services qualifies as "property" for purposes of section 721. Read *United States v. Frazell*, included in the materials below.

2. What Happens if a Partnership Later Sells Contributed Property?

Taxpayers have historically formed partnerships to shift income to other partners and to alter the character of gains and losses with respect to contributed property. The Code now contains several rules that prevent the shifting of income and the conversion of gains and losses through contributions of property to new or existing partnerships.

As a general rule, a partner's allocable share of partnership gain or loss is determined by the partnership agreement. IRC §704(a). This general allocation rule would easily allow the shifting of pre-contribution gains or losses among the partners. The congressional response is found in section 704(c)(1)(A), which requires the partnership to allocate pre-contribution gain or loss solely to the contributing partner. Using the example above, assume Andy and Bob agree to allocate profits according to their equal 50% interests in the partnership. If the partnership subsequently sold the land contributed by Bob, the partnership agreement would allocate the $70,000 gain equally to Andy ($35,000) and Bob ($35,000). In other words, one-half of the gain would be allocated to Andy even though the entire gain was attributable to the period when Bob held the property. Section 704(c)(1)(A) prevents any pre-contribution gain from being shifted to Andy. Bob will be allocated the entire $70,000 gain. Other built-in gain rules (IRC §§704(c)(1)(B), 737) are beyond the scope of this chapter.

As a general rule, the character of gain or loss recognized by a partnership on the sale of property is determined at the partnership level, without regard to the prior status of the property in the hands of the contributing partner. This general rule is subject to an exception. Under section 724, the character of gain or loss on the disposition of certain contributed property (e.g., unrealized receivables, inventory items) is determined by reference to the character of such property in the hands of the contributing partner. In other words, the pre-contribution character of the contributed property is preserved. Using the example above, assume Bob, who contributed real property at formation, was a dealer in land (inventory in his hands). Although the land is a capital asset in the partnership's hands, the partnership would recognize ordinary income on a later sale—the same character that Bob would have recognized if he had sold the land prior to the partnership formation.

C. Receipt of Boot

Although section 721 does not have a "solely in exchange" for requirement, a partner who receives money in addition to receiving a partnership interest at formation may have to report some gain. Under section 731, a partner generally recognizes no gain on a distribution of cash. However, if the cash distribution exceeds a partner's adjusted basis in his or her partnership interest (which is determined by reference to the adjusted basis of the property contributed), then the excess is treated as gain from the sale or exchange of a partnership interest. IRC §731. Taxation is deemed appropriate when a cash distribution exceeds a partner's outside basis, since the partner is apparently receiving something more than previously taxed income or a return of capital. In contrast to this rule for boot distributions of cash, no gain or loss is recognized on boot distributions of property.

Gain recognized by a partner as a result of a boot distribution of cash is typically characterized as capital gain unless the partnership has a lot of inventory or accounts receivable. IRC §§ 741, 751. The partner's adjusted basis in the partnership interest must be reduced, but not below zero, by the amount of the distribution. IRC § 733.

Let's illustrate the boot distribution rules.

Example 2. Same as Example 1, above, except that Bob's land was worth $110,000 instead of $100,000, and Bob received a 50% partnership interest valued at $100,000 and cash of $10,000 to equalize the exchange. Bob realizes gain of $80,000 ($110,000 AR minus $30,000 AB). No gain is recognized upon *receipt of the partnership interest.* IRC § 721. His initial basis in the partnership interest is $30,000. IRC § 722. No gain is recognized upon *receipt of cash* because the cash did not exceed his initial outside basis of $30,000. His basis in the partnership interest, however, is reduced by the $10,000 boot distributed to $20,000. Assuming a hypothetical sale the next day of Bob's partnership interest, Bob would realize gain of $80,000 (fair market value of the partnership interest of $100,000 minus adjusted basis of partnership interest of $20,000). Thus, the initial gain realized at formation has been preserved. [Note that this example ignores the potential application of the so-called "disguised sales" rules.]

D. Transfers of Liabilities

Many partnership formations involve the contribution of encumbered property by a partner. To determine the impact of liabilities at formation, we must look to section 752, which governs the treatment of partnership liabilities in several transactions including formations. Consistent with the *Crane* case, section 752(b) treats a partnership's assumption of a partner's liabilities as if it were a cash distribution by the partnership to the partner, and section 752(a) treats an increase in a partner's share of partnership liabilities as if it were a cash contribution by the partner to the partnership. The regulations under section 752 provide for netting of the two figures to determine the ultimate net deemed cash distribution or contribution. Treas. Reg. § 1.752-1(f). A net deemed cash distribution is treated as boot and taxable under section 731 to the extent the deemed distribution exceeds the partner's basis in the partnership interest (which is determined by reference to the adjusted basis of the property contributed). See above discussion of section 731.

Under this framework, a partner who contributes encumbered property may have to recognize gain at formation. The amount of gain depends on the amount of partner liabilities assumed by the partnership (deemed cash distribution), and the partner's share of partnership liabilities (deemed cash contribution). The regulations under section 752 provide a mechanism for allocating partnership liabilities among all the partners. In general, a partner's share of partnership liabilities for purposes of section 752 depends on the status of the partner (general or limited) and the nature of the liability (recourse or nonrecourse). *See* Treas. Reg. § 1.752-2 (providing a partner's share of recourse debt equals the portion of the debt for which the partner bears the economic risk of loss); Treas. Reg. § 1.752-3 (providing a partner's share of nonrecourse debt generally equals the partner's share of partnership profits).

Lets illustrate this.

Example 3. Andy and Bob decide to form a 50-50 partnership that will develop real estate. Andy contributes $50,000 in cash in exchange for a 50% partnership interest worth $50,000. Bob contributes a tract of land, with an adjusted basis of $30,000 and an agreed value of $100,000, in exchange for a 50% partnership interest worth $50,000. The land is subject to a $50,000 liability, which the partnership assumes at formation. Andy has no gain or loss, his basis in his partnership interest ("outside basis") is $50,000, and his holding period for the partnership interest begins with the exchange. Bob's gain realized is $70,000 (amount realized of $100,000, the fair market value of the partnership interest received and the amount of liabilities assumed by the partnership, minus adjusted basis of $30,000 in the land transferred). Bob received a partnership interest and also had a net decrease in liabilities (deemed distribution). First, no gain is recognized for receipt of the partnership interest pursuant to section 721. Bob's initial basis in his partnership interest ("outside basis") is $30,000, and his holding period for his partnership interest includes his holding period for the land. IRC §§ 721, 722, 1223(1). Next, is any gain recognized as a result of liability relief? Bob is relieved of an individual debt of $50,000 (deemed distribution), but, as an equal partner, he is allocated a share of that debt in the amount of $25,000 (deemed contribution). The deemed distribution, therefore, is really only $25,000, the net decrease in liabilities. Because the deemed cash distribution of $25,000 does not exceed Bob's initial outside basis of $30,000, Bob has no gain as a result of the debt relief. IRC § 731. His basis in his partnership interest, however, is reduced by $25,000 to $5,000. IRC § 705(a). Andy's basis in his partnership interest is increased from $50,000 to $75,000 in order to reflect his share of the liability. IRC § 752. [Note this example ignores the potential application of the disguised sales rules. IRC § 707(a)(2)(B).]

E. Capital Accounts

It is important to keep track of a partner's outside basis—adjusted basis in his or her partnership interest—for several reasons. Cash distributions are tax free to the extent of the partner's outside basis. IRC § 731. A partner can deduct his or her allocable share of partnership losses only to the extent of his or her outside basis. IRC § 704(d). Outside basis will also dictate the amount of gain or loss on the disposition of a partner's interest. Outside basis is a device used to continue the historic tax aspects of a partnership interest. Recall that a partner's initial outside basis equals the adjusted basis of property contributed at formation.

As discussed in Chapter 37 a "capital account" must also be maintained for each partner according to regulations under section 704. Treas. Reg. § 1.704-1(b)(2)(iv). In contrast to basis, capital accounts measure the economic (rather than tax) relationship among the partners. Created by the partnership agreement, a capital account begins with a partner's contribution, and is adjusted throughout the life of the partnership for further contributions, distributions, and allocable shares of income and loss. At any point in time, a capital account represents a partner's equity in the partnership and identifies what he would be entitled to receive upon liquidation of his partnership interest.

Recall that a partner's initial outside basis equals the adjusted basis of contributed property. IRC § 722. A partner's initial capital account, in contrast, begins with the net fair market value of contributed property. Treas. Reg. § 1.704-1(b)(2)(iv). Using Example 1 above to illustrate, the following figures represent the outside basis and capital accounts for Andy and Bob:

	Andy		Bob	
	Outside Basis	Capital Account	Outside Basis	Capital Account
	$100,000	$100,000	$30,000	$100,000

Note that we book the land contributed by Bob at fair market value to give Bob full credit for the value of his contribution. Both Andy and Bob begin with equal capital accounts reflecting their 50-50 partnership arrangement. If the partnership were to liquidate shortly after formation, selling off its only asset (the land contributed by Bob), it would have $200,000 in cash to distribute to the partners in accordance with their positive capital account balances; $100,000 would go to Andy, and $100,000 would go to Bob.

IV. Materials

McDougal v. Commissioner

62 T.C. 720 (1974)

FAY, JUDGE.

F. C. and Frankie McDougal are husband and wife, as are Gilbert and Jackie McClanahan. Each couple filed joint Federal income tax returns for the years 1968 and 1969 with the district director of internal revenue in Austin, Tex. Petitioners were all residents of Berino, N. Mex., when they filed their petitions with this Court.

F. C. and Frankie McDougal maintained farms at Lamesa, Tex., where they were engaged in the business of breeding and racing horses. Gilbert McClanahan was a licensed public horse trainer who rendered his services to various horse owners for a standard fee. He had numbered the McDougals among his clientele since 1965.

On February 21, 1965, a horse of exceptional pedigree, Iron Card, had been foaled at the Anthony Ranch in Florida. Title to Iron Card was acquired in January of 1967 by one Frank Ratliff, Jr., who in turn transferred title to himself, M. H. Ratliff, and John V. Burnett (Burnett). The Ratliffs and Burnett entered Iron Card in several races as a 2-year-old; and although the horse enjoyed some success in these contests, it soon became evident that he was suffering from a condition diagnosed by a veterinarian as a protein allergy.

When, due to a dispute among themselves, the Ratliffs and Burnett decided to sell Iron Card for whatever price he could attract, McClanahan (who had trained the horse for the Ratliffs and Burnett) advised the McDougals to make the purchase. He made this recommendation because, despite the veterinarian's prognosis to the contrary, McClanahan believed that by the use of home remedy Iron Card could be restored to full racing vigor. Furthermore, McClanahan felt that as Iron Card's allergy was not genetic and as his pedigree was impressive, he would be valuable in the future as a stud even if further attempts to race him proved unsuccessful.

The McDougals purchased Iron Card for $10,000 on January 1, 1968. At the time of the purchase McDougal promised that if McClanahan trained and attended to Iron Card, a half interest in the horse would be his once the McDougals had recovered the costs and expenses of acquisition. This promise was not made in lieu of payment of the standard trainer's fee; for from January 1, 1968, until the date of the transfer, McClanahan was paid $2,910 as compensation for services rendered as Iron Card's trainer.

McClanahan's home remedy proved so effective in relieving Iron Card of his allergy that the horse began to race with success, and his reputation consequently grew to such proportion that he attracted a succession of offers to purchase, one of which reached $60,000. The McDougals decided, however, to keep the horse and by October 4, 1968, had recovered out of their winnings the costs of acquiring him. It was therefore on that date that they transferred a half interest in the horse to McClanahan in accordance with the promise which McDougal had made to the trainer. A document entitled "Bill of Sale," wherein the transfer was described as a gift, was executed on the following day.

Iron Card continued to race well until very late in 1968 when, without warning and for an unascertained cause, he developed a condition called "hot ankle" which effectively terminated his racing career. From 1970 onward he was used exclusively for breeding purposes. That his value as a stud was no less than his value as a racehorse is attested to by the fact that in September of 1970 petitioners were offered $75,000 for him; but after considering the offer, the McDougals and McClanahan decided to refuse it, preferring to exploit Iron Card's earning potential as a study to their own profit.

On November 1, 1968, petitioners had concluded a partnership agreement by parol to effectuate their design of racing the horse for as long as that proved feasible and of offering him out as a stud thereafter. Profits were to be shared equally by the McDougals and the McClanahans, while losses were to be allocated to the McDougals alone.

OPINION

Respondent contends that the McDougals did not recognize a $25,000 gain on the transaction of October 4, 1968, and that they were not entitled to claim a $30,000 business expense deduction by reason thereof. He further contends that were Iron Card to be contributed to a partnership or joint venture under the circumstances obtaining in the instant case, its basis in Iron Card at the time of contribution would have been limited by the McDougals' cost basis in the horse, as adjusted. Respondent justifies these contentions by arguing that the transfer of October 4, 1968, constituted a gift.

In the alternative, respondent has urged us to find that at some point in time no later than the transfer of October 4, 1968, McDougal and McClanahan entered into a partnership or joint venture to which the McDougals contributed Iron Card and McClanahan contributed services. Respondent contends that such a finding would require our holding that the McDougals did not recognize a gain on the transfer of October 4, 1968, by reason of section 721, and that under section 723 the joint venture's basis in Iron Card at the time of the contribution was equal to the McDougals' adjusted basis in the horse as of that time.

We dismiss at the outset respondent's contention that the transfer of October 4, 1968, constituted a gift, and we are undeterred in so doing by the fact that petitioners originally characterized the transfer as a gift, Bogardus v. Commissioner, 302 U.S. 34 (1937). A gift has been defined as a transfer motivated by detached and disinterested generosity, Commissioner v. Duberstein, 363 U.S. 278 (1960). The presence of such motivation is belied in this instance by two factors. The relationship of the parties concerned was essentially of a business nature, and the transfer itself was made conditional upon the outcome of an enterprise which McDougal had undertaken at McClanahan's suggestion and in reliance upon McClanahan's ability to render it profitable. These factors instead bespeak the presence of an arm's-length transaction.

With respect to respondent's alternative contention, we note firstly that the law provides no rule easy of application for making a determination as to whether a partnership or joint venture has been formed but rather directs our attention to a congeries of factors relevant to the issue, of which none is conclusive.

A joint venture is deemed to arise when two or more persons agree, expressly or impliedly, to enter actively upon a specific business enterprise, the purpose of which is the pursuit of profit; the ownership of whose productive assets and of the profits generated by them is shared; the parties to which all bear the burden of any loss; and the management of which is not confined to a single participant.

While in the case at bar the risk of loss was to be borne by the McDougals alone, all the other elements of a joint venture were present once the transfer of October 4, 1968, had been effected. Accordingly, we hold that the aforesaid transfer constituted the formation of a joint venture to which the McDougals contributed capital in the form of the horse, Iron Card, and in which they granted McClanahan an interest equal to their own in capital and profits as compensation for his having trained Iron Card. We further hold that the agreement formally entered into on November 1, 1968, and reduced to writing in April of 1970, constituted a continuation of the original joint venture under section 708(b)(2)(A). Furthermore, that McClanahan continued to receive a fee for serving as Iron Card's trainer after October 4, 1968, in no way militates against the soundness of this holding. See sec. 707(c), and sec. 1.707-1(c), example 1, Income Tax Regs. However, this holding does not result in the tax consequences which respondent has contended would follow from it. See sec. 1.721-1(b)(1), Income Tax Regs.

When on the formation of a joint venture a party contributing appreciated assets satisfies an obligation by granting his obligee a capital interest in the venture, he is deemed first to have transferred to the obligee an undivided interest in the assets contributed, equal in value to the amount of the obligation so satisfied. He and the obligee are deemed thereafter and in concert to have contributed those assets to the joint venture.

The contributing obligor will recognize gain on the transaction to the extent that the value of the undivided interest which he is deemed to have transferred exceeds his basis therein. The obligee is considered to have realized an amount equal to the fair market value of the interest which he receives in the venture and will recognize income depending upon the character of the obligation satisfied. The joint venture's basis in the assets will be determined under section 723 in accordance with the foregoing assumptions. Accordingly, we hold that the transaction under consideration constituted an exchange in which the McDougals realized $30,000, United States v. Davis, 370 U.S. 65 (1962); Kenan v. Commissioner, 114 F.2d 217 (C.A. 2, 1940), affirming 40 B.T.A. 824 (1939).

In determining the basis offset to which the McDougals are entitled with respect to the transfer of October 4, 1968, we note the following: that the McDougals had an unadjusted cost basis in Iron Card of $10,000; that they had claimed $1,390 in depreciation on the entire horse for the period January 1 to October 31, 1968; and that after an agreement of partnership was concluded on November 1, 1968, depreciation on Iron Card was deducted by the partnership exclusively.

[Pre-1984] section 704(c) allows partners and joint venturers some freedom in determining who is to claim the deductions for depreciation on contributed property. As is permissible under the statute, petitioners clearly intended the depreciation to be claimed by the common enterprise once it had come into existence, an event which they considered to have occurred on November 1, 1968. Consistent with their intent and with our own holding that a joint venture arose on October 4, 1968, we now further hold that the McDougals were entitled to claim depreciation on Iron Card only until the transfer of October 4, 1968. Thereafter depreciation on Iron Card ought to have been deducted by the joint venture in the computation of its taxable income.

In determining their adjusted basis in the portion of Iron Card on whose disposition they are required to recognize gain, the McDougals charged all the depreciation which they had taken on the horse against their basis in the half in which they retained an interest. This procedure was improper. As in accordance with section 1.167(g)-1, Income Tax Regs., we have allowed the McDougals a depreciation deduction with respect to Iron Card for the period January 1 to October 4, 1968, computed on their entire cost basis in the horse of $10,000; so also do we require that the said deduction be charged against that entire cost basis under section 1016(a)(2)(A).

As the McDougals were in the business of racing horses, any gain recognized by them on the exchange of Iron Card in satisfaction of a debt would be characterized under section 1231(a) provided he had been held by them for the period requisite under section 1231(b) as it applies to livestock acquired before 1970. In that as of October 4, 1968, Iron Card had been used by the McDougals exclusively for racing and not for breeding, we do now hold that they had held him for a period sufficiently long to make section 1231(a) applicable to their gain on the transaction. This is the case although the McDougals may have intended eventually to use Iron Card for breeding purposes.

The joint venture's basis in Iron Card as of October 4, 1968, must be determined under section 723 in accordance with the principles of law set forth earlier in this opinion. In the half interest in the horse which it is deemed to have received from the McDougals, the joint venture had a basis equal to one-half of the McDougals' adjusted cost basis in Iron Card as of October 4, 1968, i. e., the excess of $5,000 over one-half of the depreciation which the McDougals were entitled to claim on Iron Card for the period January 1 to October 4, 1968. In the half interest which the venture is considered to have received from McClanahan, it can claim to have had a basis equal to the amount which McClanahan is considered to have realized on the transaction, $30,000. The joint venture's deductions for depreciation on Iron Card for the years 1968 and 1969 are to be determined on the basis computed in the above-described manner.

When an interest in a joint venture is transferred as compensation for services rendered, any deduction which may be authorized under section 162(a) (1) by reason of that transfer is properly claimed by the party to whose benefit the services accrued, be that party the venture itself or one or more venturers, sec. 1.721-1(b)(2), Income Tax Regs. Prior to McClanahan's receipt of his interest, a joint venture did not exist under the facts of the case at bar; the McDougals were the sole owners of Iron Card and recipients of his earnings. Therefore, they alone could have benefited from the services rendered by McClanahan prior to October 4, 1968, for which he was compensated by the transaction of that date. Accordingly, we hold that the McDougals are entitled to a business expense deduction of $30,000, that amount being the value of the interest which McClanahan received. Respondent has contended that a deduction of $30,000 would be unreasonable in amount in view of the nature of the services for which McClanahan was being compensated. But having found that the transaction under consideration was not a gift but rather was occasioned by a compensation arrangement which was entered upon at arm's length, we must reject this contention. See sec. 1.162-7(b)(2), Income Tax Regs.

United States v. Frazell

335 F.2d 487 (5th Cir. 1964)

TUTTLE, CHIEF JUDGE.

On February 9, 1951, William Frazell, a geologist, entered into a contract with the N. H. Wheless Oil Company, a partnership, and W. C. Woolf, under which Frazell was to check certain areas to determine whether potentially productive oil and gas properties might be procured there. He was to recommend those properties he found suitable to Wheless and Woolf, and upon their joint approval, he was to attempt to acquire such properties, taking title thereto in the names of Wheless and Woolf in equal shares. In return for these services, Frazell was to receive "a monthly salary or drawing account," plus expenses, and specified interests in the property acquired. It was agreed, however, "that Frazell shall not be entitled to, nor shall he be considered as owning, any interest in said properties until such time as Wheless and Woolf shall have recovered their full costs and expenses of said properties" including the amounts paid out to Frazell.

The arrangement proved successful, and it was evident in the early part of 1955 that Wheless and Woolf would fully recover their costs and expenses by the end of November of that year. In April 1955, the 1951 contract was terminated, and by contract dated April 20, 1955, all the properties acquired under the earlier arrangement were transferred to the W.W.F. Corporation, a Delaware corporation formed specifically to acquire these properties in return for the issuance of debentures to Wheless and Woolf and of stock to Wheless, Woolf, and Frazell. Frazell received 6,500 shares of W.W.F. stock (13% of the total issued), having a fair market value of $91,000.00, but he included no part of this amount in his 1955 income tax return. The Commissioner ruled that the $91,000.00 should have been included in income and assessed a deficiency, which Frazell paid under protest and seeks to recover here.

Frazell contends that he received the W.W.F. stock in a tax-free exchange within the terms of section 351(a), Internal Revenue Code of 1954. The district court agreed that section 351(a) is applicable in this case. This was said to follow from that court's finding that the 1951 contract created a "joint venture" among the three participants. We take no issue with the trial court's finding of fact in this matter, but it does not follow from the categorization of the 1951 arrangement as a "joint venture" that the April 1955 transactions resulted in no taxable income to Frazell.

It is fundamental that "compensation for services" is taxable as ordinary income under the Internal Revenue Code of 1954. I.R.C. §61(a)(1). This principle applies whether the one compensated for his services is an employee receiving a salary, fees, or commission (ibid.), one receiving corporate securities (I.R.C. §351(a)), or a "service partner" receiving an interest in the partnership. (I.R.C. §721; Treas.Reg. §1.721-1(b)(1)).

The regulation pertaining to partnerships provides that:

> [T]he value of an interest in such partnership capital so transferred to a partner as compensation for services constitutes income to the partner under section 61. The amount of such income is the fair market value of the interest in capital so transferred ... at the time the transfer is made for past services.... The time when such income is realized depends on all the facts and circumstances, including any substantial restrictions or conditions on the compensated partner's right to withdraw or otherwise dispose of such interest.

This rule would have been directly applicable had the 1951 contract continued in effect through November 1955, the date on which Wheless and Woolf would have fully recovered their costs in the venture. The contract made in clear that Frazell would "not have the right to dispose of any rights which may accrue to him" before those costs were recovered. But after November, he would have received a largely unrestricted interest in about 13% of the partnership properties. That this interest was primarily, if not entirely, in return for Frazell's services to the enterprise is undisputed. Thus, so much of the interest Frazell was to receive in November 1955 as could be attributed to his services for the oil venture would have been ordinary income to him in the year of receipt.

The fact that the contract was terminated prior to November 1955 should have no effect on the tax consequences of Frazell's arrangements. The transactions of April 1955 may be viewed in either of two ways: (1) If Frazell's partnership interest became possessory immediately upon the termination of the 1951 contract, so much of that interest received as compensation for services was taxable to him under the rule of Treasury Regulation § 1.721(b)(1). Thereafter, the transfer of his interest for W.W.F. stock was tax-free under section 351(a). (2) If the $91,000.00 of W.W.F. stock was given in substitution for the partnership interest originally contemplated, so much of that stock received in compensation for services was taxable to Frazell under section 351(a). As either view of the 1955 transactions results in ordinary income to Frazell there is no reason for us to split hairs and choose between them.

This is not to say that the full $91,000.00 is ordinary income. The trial court found that, just as Wheless and Woolf contributed large amounts of capital, "Frazell supplied to the venture a very valuable oil map which was his private property." 213 F.Supp. at 461. Indeed the record shows that prior to entering into the 1951 contract Frazell had acquired several maps which apparently proved very helpful to the work of the venture. Among the reasons given by Mr. Wheless for desiring to employ Frazell was that "he had accumulated maps, geological data and various information that was valuable to the arrangement that it would have taken a long time for someone else just moving into the territory to accumulate." And Frazell himself testified that he "had contributed considerable information and maps which resulted in the discovery and production of oil...." Although it is clear that the greater part of the 13% interest received by Frazell was received as compensation for services, the court's finding and the cited testimony suggest that some part of that interest might have been received in return for "property;" namely, the maps. That part of the property Frazell received in 1955 attributable to his contribution of maps is not taxable in 1955 no matter whether we view the interest received as a partnership interest vesting on the termination of the 1951 contract (I.R.C.1954 § 721) or as shares of W.W.F. stock given in substitution therefor. (I.R.C.1954 § 315(a)). See Treas.Reg. § 1.351-1(2), example 3; Mertens, The Law of Federal Income Taxation, vol. 6, § 35.37, pp. 108–09.

Before the nonrecognition rule can be applied to the maps in this case, however, two factual determinations must be made: (1) Did Frazell contribute the maps in question to the oil venture or did he keep them as his own personal property? (2) If he contributed them to the venture, what was their value at the time they were contributed?

The judgment is therefore reversed and the case remanded to the district court to determine whether the maps introduced at the original trial were contributed by Frazell to the oil venture created by the 1951 contract. If the court finds that the maps were so contributed, it shall determine their value as of the time of their contribution. Such part of $91,000.00 as exceeds the value of the maps as determined by the trial court is properly taxable to Frazell as ordinary income.

Reversed and remanded.

V. Related Matters

- **Accounts Receivable.** Accounts receivable are treated as property for purposes of section 721. Accounts payable are not treated as liabilities for purposes of section 752. Therefore, a partner will have no constructive distribution of cash, potentially taxable under section 731, when a partnership assumes an account payable at formation. In accordance with section 704(c) principles, the contributing partner will have income when the account payable is collected by the partnership and a deduction when the account payable is paid by the partnership. Rev. Rul. 88-77, 1988-2 C.B. 128.

- **Disguised Sales.** When a partner transfers money or other property to a partnership and the partnership makes a related transfer of money or other property back to that partner, the two transfers may be treated as a taxable sale or exchange of property between the partnership and the partner. IRC § 707(a)(2)(B). Detailed regulations help determine when a contribution and related distribution should be recast as a taxable sale or exchange, as opposed to a tax free contribution under section 721 followed by a tax free distribution under section 731. Treas. Reg. § 1.707-3.

- **Organization Expenses.** As a general rule, a partnership cannot immediately deduct organization and syndication expenses. IRC § 709(a). However, the partnership may elect to deduct up to $5,000 of certain qualified "organizational expenses," and amortize the rest over 180 months. IRC § 709(b).

Chapter 40

Overview of International Income Taxation

I. Assignment

Read: Internal Revenue Code: Skim §§ 199; 482; 861; 862; 864; 865; 871; 881; 882; 901–908; 911; 1441; 1442. Skim also §§ 59A; 245A; 250; 951A; 965.

Treasury Regulations: None.

Text: Overview
Boulez v. Commissioner
Related Matters

Complete the Problems.

II. Problems

1. Explain whether the following amounts received by Jacques Marchiel, a citizen and bona fide resident of the United States, are U.S. source income or foreign source income:

   (a) $500 dividend from ABC, Inc.—a domestic corporation.

   (b) $1,000 dividend from XYZ, Inc.—a French corporation.

   (c) $1,200 interest on a loan to his brother, Louis, who is a U.S. citizen residing in France.

   (d) Same as (c) except Louis is a citizen of France and not a U.S. citizen.

   (e) $20,000 rent from a duplex owned by Jacques and located in the United States.

   (f) $20,000 rent from a duplex owned by Jacques and located in France.

2. Pleides, Inc., a foreign corporation, transferred to Andromeda, Inc., a U.S. corporation, the exclusive right to use Pleides's patented process within the United States for an amount equal to five percent of net profits Andromeda earns from the process. Pursuant to the assignment, Pleides received $50,000 this year. What is the source of this amount?

3. Maurice Debussy is a famous French conductor. He resides in Paris when he is not on tour. Maurice has recorded several CDs and owns copyrights in those recordings. Maurice is very particular about owning all copyrights in his recordings. Recently, OMD (Online Music Digital), a New York corporation, approached

Maurice with a lucrative proposal wherein Maurice would conduct a group of musicians and record 10 new CDs in exchange for a total of $3.0 million in royalties to be paid in installments over two years. All the recording activities would occur at OMD's studio located in New York City. According to the proposal, Maurice would assign all copyrights in the new CDs to OMD. What will be the U.S. income tax consequences of Maurice's future income?

4. Borkenstick, Inc., a domestic manufacturing corporation with a branch plant located in Germany, realized $300 million of taxable income from its U.S. activities and $200 million of taxable income (exclusive of German taxes) from its German activities. What is Borkenstick's U.S. tax liability assuming the United States has a flat corporate income tax rate of 30% and Germany has a flat corporate income tax rate of 50%?

5. Multinational Corp., a very important client, has just learned about a transfer pricing dispute between the IRS and a major pharmaceutical company, and is concerned about section 482 allocations. You have been asked the following questions: What is the root of the transfer pricing problem? Is there anything that can be done to avoid transfer pricing disputes?

III. Overview

Many of the themes we have studied apply to international transactions as they do in domestic transactions. For instance, U.S. income tax rules that determine *what* is included in gross income, *when* income must be reported, and *who* is responsible for reporting income generally apply to international transactions. An additional query, however, is added in connection with international transactions: *Where*, in a geographical sense, is an item income? To answer this question, source rules become very important, particularly when determining whether foreign persons are subject to U.S. income tax.

The United States has the power to tax U.S. citizens, resident aliens, and domestic corporations (collectively, U.S. persons) on their worldwide income, regardless of where they are or where their property is located. Cook v. Tait, 265 U.S. 47, 55–56 (1924). Non-resident aliens and foreign corporations, on the other hand, are generally taxed only on U.S. source income, not worldwide income. The Code sets forth bright line rules for determining whether a non-citizen is a resident or non-resident alien. IRC § 7701(b). The test for determining whether a corporation is a domestic corporation or foreign corporation is easy because one must look only to where the corporation was created or organized. IRC § 7701(a)(3)–(4).

Although the United States has the power to tax U.S. persons on their worldwide income, it generally cedes the right to tax foreign source income (income derived from sources outside the United States) to the foreign country where the income is generated. Under the Code, taxes paid to a foreign jurisdiction may qualify for a deduction or credit against U.S. tax liability. Under some tax treaties, the U.S. tax assessed on foreign source income may be reduced or eliminated altogether.

This chapter introduces the major concepts of international taxation from the perspective of the United States. It focuses on the basic rules regarding U.S. taxation of U.S. persons on their foreign activities and U.S. taxation of foreign persons on their U.S. activities. The critical role of tax treaties is also considered.

A. Taxation of Foreign Income of U.S. Persons

1. General Taxing Rules

United States persons (citizens, resident aliens, domestic corporations) may derive income from sources outside the United States (i.e., foreign source income). For example, a U.S. citizen may receive compensation for providing services in a foreign country, or a domestic corporation may receive royalties for licensing intellectual property overseas. The U.S. tax treatment of U.S. persons who directly conduct foreign business operations is relatively straightforward. United States persons engaged in activities abroad are generally taxed on their worldwide income (income earned in the United States as well as income earned in a foreign country) under the rates specified in either section 1 (individual citizens and resident aliens) or section 11 (domestic corporations). *But see* IRC §911 (providing a limited exclusion from gross income for income earned abroad), discussed more fully below.

Historically, a U.S. person that conducted foreign business operations through a foreign corporation or other foreign entity was generally subject to U.S. tax on the foreign source income when the income was repatriated to the United States (e.g., through a dividend distribution to the U.S. shareholder). Under this scheme, U.S. persons could seemingly defer tax on corporate income as long as that income remained within the foreign corporation and was not distributed to the U.S. person.

To thwart the benefits of deferral, Congress has enacted various safeguards. One anti-deferral regime is known as the Controlled Foreign Corporation (CFC) provisions. IRC §§ 951–964. If a foreign corporation is a *controlled foreign corporation* at any time during the taxable year, each *U.S. shareholder* shall include in his or her gross income (as a deemed distribution) the shareholder's pro rata share of the corporation's *Subpart F income*. IRC §951(a). *See* IRC §§957(a) (defining a CFC), 951(b) (defining a U.S. shareholder), 952 (defining Subpart F income). In other words, if a CFC exists, U.S. shareholders are treated as receiving a current distribution out of certain income of the CFC, and are subject to current taxation.

Subpart F income is generally income that is easily movable and subject to low rates of foreign tax. One type of subpart F income is "foreign personal holding company income," which includes income received by a CFC from passive investments, such as dividends, interest, rents, and royalties. IRC §954(c). An exception exists for rents and royalties that are generated from an active business, and another exception exists for rents and royalties from a related party in the same country as the CFC ("same party exception"). IRC §954(c)(2)(A). Another type of subpart F income is "foreign base company sales income," which is income received by a CFC attributable to goods purchased from or sold to a related party (i.e., U.S. parent company) where the CFC's country of organization is not the origin or destination of the goods. IRC § 954(d). An exception exists if the CFC itself manufactures the property. Treas. Reg. § 1.954-3(a)(4). There are other exceptions to subpart F income in addition to those noted here. For example, there is a "high tax exception," under which an item of income is excluded if the effective rate of tax imposed on the income by a foreign country is greater than 90% of the maximum rate of U.S. tax.

Exceptions to subpart F income, such as the "same country exception" and the "manufacturing exception" make it relatively easy to avoid subpart F of the Code. Indeed, many U.S. companies have avoided subpart F of the Code by utilizing creative tax planning structures, many involving offshore subsidiaries that hold intellectual property, to reduce their worldwide taxes. The Tax Cuts and Jobs Act (TCJA) made several fundamental changes to the taxation of multinational companies to curtail use of these aggressive tax minimization strategies. While these new provisions are too complex for detailed treatment in this book, it is worth highlighting a few.

To encourage U.S. companies not to lodge their foreign earnings outside the United States, the TCJA adopted a 100% deduction for dividends received from foreign subsidiary corporations. IRC § 245A (providing a dividends received deduction for the foreign-source portion of dividends received from a foreign subsidiary). This change moves the United States from a "worldwide tax system" closer to a "territorial tax system" for earnings of foreign subsidiaries that are not subpart F income. (The TCJA also created a special deduction for certain foreign-derived intangible income, a welcome incentive for companies to locate intangible property in the United States. IRC § 250. This new provision in effect grants the benefit of a reduced tax rate to a new class of income earned directly by a U.S. corporation (foreign derived intangible income)).

In addition to the above *carrot* measures, the TCJA adopted a number of *stick* measures to limit aggressive tax minimization strategies. It adopted a minimum tax on "global intangible low-taxed income" (GILTI). IRC § 951A. Thus, in addition to retaining current subpart F of the Code (which immediately taxes certain classes of income discussed above), the TCJA subjects a new, very broad, class of income (GILTI) to immediate taxation at a reduced rate. The TCJA also adopted a "Base Erosion Anti-Abuse Tax" (BEAT), an anti-base erosion measure that imposes a minimum tax on certain deductible payments, such as royalties, to a foreign affiliate. IRC § 59A.

2. The Foreign Tax Credit

As discussed, U.S. persons are subject to U.S. tax on income earned in a foreign country. That income may be taxable in the foreign country as well. To provide relief from this double taxation, the United States generally allows U.S. persons to offset U.S. taxes with the income taxes paid in the foreign country. This is accomplished by applying a credit for foreign income taxes paid to any foreign country against U.S. income tax owed on the same income. IRC §§ 901–908. The Code also allows a deduction for foreign income taxes IRC § 164(a). A taxpayer is not allowed to take both a deduction and a credit for the same foreign income tax and must choose between the two. IRC § 275(a)(4). In most cases, U.S. persons will elect to take the foreign tax credit over the deduction because a credit offsets taxes on a dollar for dollar basis whereas the benefit of a deduction depends on the taxpayer's tax rate.

The amount of the foreign tax credit equals the amount of any income taxes paid or accrued during the taxable year to any foreign country or to any possession of the United States. IRC § 901(b). The foreign tax credit is subject to an important limitation found in section 904. The limitation is determined by multiplying the U.S. tax (determined prior to the credit) by a fraction, the numerator of which is foreign taxable income and the denominator of which is the taxpayer's worldwide taxable income. The formula is depicted by the following equation:

Foreign Tax Credit Limit Formula

$$\text{Credit Limit} = \text{U.S. Tax} \times \frac{\text{Foreign Taxable Income}}{\text{Worldwide Taxable Income}}$$

The purpose of this limitation is to prevent foreign income taxes from reducing U.S. income taxes on U.S. source income. For example, assume that a U.S. domestic corporation earns income of $10,000 from activities in a foreign country and $20,000 of income from U.S. sources. If the U.S. tax rate is a flat 30% and the foreign tax rate is a flat 50%, then the U.S. tax liability on the $30,000 of worldwide income would be $9,000. Without the limitation discussed above, the domestic corporation could credit the $5,000 of foreign taxes paid against the U.S. tax liability, resulting in a net U.S. tax liability of $4,000 (an effective rate of 20% rather than 30%). To prevent the foreign taxes of $5,000 from reducing U.S. income taxes on U.S. source income, the foreign tax credit is limited and cannot exceed a percentage of the U.S. tax (with the percentage being the corporation's foreign source income divided by worldwide income). In other words, applying the formula above, the maximum credit equals $3,000 [$9,000 × ($10,000/$30,000)] rather than the $5,000 paid to the foreign government. If this limitation prevents taxes from being immediately credited, the excess creditable taxes ($2,000 in the example) may be carried back one year and carried forward ten years with an eye always on the limitation. IRC § 904(c).

Recall from above that the TCJA provided a 100% deduction for the foreign source portion of the dividends received from the foreign subsidiary corporations. To avoid providing a double tax benefit, the TCJA also provided that no foreign tax credit or deduction is allowed for any foreign taxes paid with respect to the deductible portion of the dividend. IRC § 245A(d).

3. Foreign Earned Income Exclusion

Section 911(a) allows certain citizens and residents of the United States living abroad to elect to exclude foreign wages from U.S. gross income. The maximum amount of foreign earned income that may be excluded is $80,000, indexed for inflation (the exclusion for 2018 was $104,100). Section 911(a) also allows an individual to exclude amounts paid by his employer for housing. The maximum housing exclusion is 30% of the maximum amount of the foreign earned income exclusion. To claim the foreign earned income exclusion, an individual must meet one of two qualifications tests: a bona fide residence test (reside for a period that includes a full calendar year), or a physical presence test (reside at least 330 full days in a 12-month period).

B. Taxation of U.S. Income of Foreign Persons

Non-U.S. persons (non-resident alien individuals and foreign corporations) may derive income from within the United States (i.e., U.S. source income). The U.S. taxation of foreign individuals and corporations is not as all encompassing as the taxation of U.S. persons doing business abroad. This is because non-U.S. persons, unlike U.S. persons, are not subject to U.S. taxation on their worldwide income. They are generally taxed only on U.S. source income. The applicable rate structure imposed on non-U.S. persons depends on the type of income involved.

1. Taxation of Business Income

a. In General

Under the Code, non-treaty, non-U.S. persons are taxed on most U.S. business income in the same manner that U.S. persons are. In other words, a non-U.S. person engaged in a trade or business in the United States is taxed under the graduated rates of either section 1 (in the case of non-resident alien individuals) or section 11 (in the case of foreign corporations) on taxable income that is effectively connected with the conduct of the trade or business within the United States. IRC §§ 871 (b) (non-resident alien individuals), 882 (foreign corporations). The Code attempts to define two terms of art necessary to determine the taxation of U.S. business income derived by non-U.S. persons: (1) *engaged in a trade or business* in the United States and (2) income *effectively connected* with the conduct of a trade or business within the United States (sometimes referred to as *effectively connected income*). IRC § 864.

b. Treaty Exceptions

The statutory concepts of *engaged in a trade or business* and *effectively connected income* that appear in the Code are replaced with thresholds much higher when there is an applicable income tax treaty. Tax treaties impose a *permanent establishment* requirement rather than an *engaged in a trade or business* requirement and an *attributable to* requirement rather than an *effectively connected* requirement. Under the treaty concepts, if a non-U.S. person lacks a permanent establishment in the United States, the business income is generally exempt from U.S. tax. If a non-U.S. person has a permanent establishment in the United States, then *business profits* that are *attributable to* the *permanent establishment* are generally subject to U.S. tax.

The term *permanent establishment* is typically defined in the relevant treaty and is usually equated with a fixed place of business, such as a factory or office through which business is carried on. The term *business profits* generally includes income derived from the active conduct of a trade or business and may include income, such as royalties, that may be exempt from U.S. tax under another treaty provision. The term *attributable to* generally refers to that income which is derived from the permanent establishment (i.e., the income was generated by the assets or activities of the permanent establishment).

2. Taxation of Non-Business Income from U.S. Sources

a. "Fixed or Determinable, Annual or Periodical" (FDAP) Income

Under the Code, non-treaty, non-U.S. persons are generally subject to a flat tax of 30% (as opposed to the graduated rates of sections 1 or 11) each taxable year on the amount of non-business income received from sources within the United States, but only to the extent the amount received is not effectively connected with the conduct of a trade or business within the United States. IRC §§ 871(a), 881(a). The 30% flat tax is imposed on *fixed or determinable annual or periodical* income received, including passive income such as interest, dividends, rents, and royalties. This category of income is sometimes known by its acronym, FDAP. Gain from the sale of property may be treated as royalty income if payments are contingent on the property's productivity, use, or disposition. IRC § 871(a)(1)(D). The 30% tax on fixed or determinable income is applied on a gross basis without any deductions for costs incurred in producing the income. For the tax collection mechanism, see IRC §§ 1441, 1442 (requiring the withholding and remitting of the 30% tax to the Service).

b. Treaty Exceptions

Most tax treaties impose a lower rate on non-business income than the 30% statutory rate. Furthermore, some treaties completely exempt certain income, such as royalties, from tax altogether. Thus, royalties derived by a foreign licensor from the United States may either be exempt from U.S. taxation or subject to a rate lower than 30% (typically 15%). Under most treaties, gains from the sale of property by a non-U.S. person are not taxed by the U.S., but are taxed only in the foreign jurisdiction. However, under some treaties the United States may reserve the right to tax gains from the sale of property if payments are contingent on the productivity, use, or disposition of the property.

C. Source Rules

For non-U.S. persons, it is important to determine whether items are sourced inside or outside the United States because non-U.S. persons are taxed only on U.S. source income—with the applicable rate structure depending on whether the income is business income (i.e., effectively connected income) or non-business income (i.e., fixed or determinable annual or periodical income). Although the source rules with respect to U.S. persons seem irrelevant (because U.S. persons are taxed on worldwide income), they are important for obscure reasons. As described above, the U.S. source rules become relevant for U.S. persons in the calculation of the foreign tax credit.

Specifically, the foreign tax credit is available only for foreign taxes paid with respect to foreign source income.

The Code contains rules that determine the source of income. IRC §§ 861–865. These source rules are broken into categories of income (e.g., compensation, interest, dividends, rents royalties, sales of real property interests, and sales of personal property). The Code also contains rules for the allocation of deductions (e.g., sourcing of interest and research and development expenses).

1. Income Source Rules

Interest-Residence of Payor. The source of interest income depends on the residence or place of incorporation of the obligor. IRC §§ 861(a)(1), 884(f)(1)(A). Accordingly, interest arising from debts of resident alien individuals and domestic corporations is sourced in the United States. An exception (providing for foreign source) exists if 80% of the U.S. obligor's income is derived from an active foreign business.

Dividends-Residence of Payor. As with the interest source rule, the source rule for dividends is generally the residence of the payor. IRC §§ 861(a)(2), 884(a). Thus, dividends received from a domestic corporation are considered U.S. source income. Dividends received from a foreign corporation are foreign source income. An exception exists if a foreign corporation has a substantial United States business nexus. IRC § 861(a)(2)(B).

Personal Services Compensation — Place of Performance. The source rule for personal services compensation is simple. If services are performed in the United States, then the compensation is U.S. source income regardless of the residence of the payor; if compensation is paid for services performed outside of the United States, the compensation is foreign source income. IRC § 861(a)(3). There is a de minimis exception, under which compensation is given a foreign source if a non-U.S. service provider is only temporarily present in the United States and earns $3,000 or less. IRC § 864(b). The time period set forth in the Code, 90 days, is typically extended by tax treaties.

Rents and Royalties—Place of Use of Property. Rents and royalties are generally sourced according to the situs of the use of the property giving rise to the income. IRC § 861(a)(4). For example, if an intellectual property licensee uses the intellectual property in its U.S. trade or business, the royalties are U.S. source income even if the intellectual property was developed overseas and the royalties are paid overseas pursuant to a contract signed overseas. *See* Rev. Rul. 68-443, 1968-2 C.B. 304 (holding that the source of royalties paid with respect to the use of a trademark is the country in which the products bearing the trademark are ultimately used and where the trademark is protected); Rev. Rul. 72-232, 1972-1 C.B. 276 (holding that royalties paid for the use of a foreign copyright for text books printed in the United States but sold solely in the foreign country is sourced outside the United States). *See also* Rohmer v. Commissioner, 14 T.C. 1467 (1950) (holding that the source of a copyright royalty is the place where the copyrighted material is consumed and protected by copyright law).

Real Estate—Location of Real Estate. With respect to real estate dispositions, the situs of the real property is the critical factor. Gain from the sale of real property located in the United States is considered U.S. source income; conversely, gain from the sale of real property located outside the United States is considered foreign source. IRC § 861(a)(5).

Non-Inventory Personal Property—Residence of Seller. The source of gain from the sale of non-inventory personalty depends on the residence of the seller rather than where title passes. IRC § 865. The source of gain from the disposition of an intangible asset depends on the nature of the sale. If the sale proceeds are contingent on the productivity, use, or disposition of the property by the purchaser, the proceeds are treated as royalties and, hence, sourced according to where the property is used. IRC §§ 861(a)(4), 865(d). If the sale proceeds are not contingent, then any gain is sourced according to the seller's residence. IRC § 865(a). For purposes of the source rules, residency is determined by where an individual has a *tax home*, which is generally the individual's regular or principal place of business. *See* IRC § 865(g). Thus, in the case of non-contingent sales, gain from the sale of intangible property by an individual with a tax home in the United States is sourced in the United States, and gain from the sale of such property by an individual who does not have a tax home in the United States is sourced outside the United States. [Note: The source rule for sales of inventory property focuses on the jurisdiction in which title passes and not the residence of the seller. *See* IRC § 861(a)(6). *But see* IRC § 863(b) (providing income from inventory produced in the U.S. and sold outside the U.S. (or vice versa) is sourced on the basis of the production activities).]

2. Deduction Allocation and Apportionment Rules

Non-business income (FDAP income) of a non-U.S. person is generally taxed at a flat 30% rate (or lower treaty rate) on a gross basis with no allowance for deductions. However, business income (income that is effectively connected with the conduct of a U.S. trade or business) of a non-U.S. person is generally taxed under the graduated rates of sections 1 or 11, with proper allowances for deductions. In other words, the Code allows deductions only where the deductions are effectively connected with a U.S. trade or business.

As with income, it is important to identify the source of deductions as either U.S. source deductions or foreign source deductions. The Code and the regulations prescribe rules for the allocation and apportionment of expenses, losses, and other deductions for taxpayers. *See, e.g.,* Treas. Reg. § 1.861-17(a)(14) (providing allocation rules for research and development expenditures). These rules, which are the same for both foreign and U.S. persons, are beyond the scope of this chapter.

D. The Role of Treaties

The United States has entered into numerous tax treaties with foreign countries in order to ameliorate possible double taxation and to clarify which treaty country retains the right to tax certain classes of persons and certain items of income in connection with cross-border transactions. There are general treaty provisions that govern the taxation of business profits. There are also treaty provisions that govern the taxation of non-business profits. For instance, most tax treaties exempt royalties from tax or, in the alternative, impose a rate lower than the 30% statutory rate set forth in the Code. Therefore, royalties derived by a foreign licensor from the United States may be either exempt from U.S. taxation or may be subject to a lower treaty rate—typically 15%.

When a statute (such as the Internal Revenue Code) and a treaty conflict, both cannot be supreme, and one must give way. Generally, when the Code and a treaty provision conflict, the later adopted controls. Of course, if there is a statute and a treaty on the same subject, effect should be given to both if possible. If a treaty and a later statute relate to the same subject, courts will try to construe them in a way that is consistent with the intent of each and that results in the absence of conflict between the two. Therefore, only if it is determined that there is an actual conflict between a tax act and treaty will the later-in-time rule operate.

E. Section 482: Transactions between Related Parties

Related parties (such as a domestic parent corporation and its wholly owned foreign subsidiary corporation) should engage in transactions at arm's length to ensure the proper reporting of taxable income. To help achieve that goal, section 482 authorizes the Commissioner to reallocate gross income, deductions, credits, or allowances among commonly controlled entities in order to ensure that taxpayers clearly reflect income attributable to related party transactions, and to prevent the avoidance of taxes with respect to such transactions. As stated by the regulations, the purpose of section 482 is to place a controlled taxpayer on a tax parity with an uncontrolled taxpayer by determining the true taxable income of the controlled taxpayer. Treas. Reg. § 1.482-1(a)(1). In determining the true taxable income of a controlled taxpayer, the standard to be applied is that of a taxpayer dealing at arm's length with an uncontrolled taxpayer. Treas. Reg. § 1.482-1(b)(1). For a classic section 482 case in which the government won, see E.I. Du Pont de Nemours and Company v. United States, 608 F.2d 445 (Ct. Cl. 1979).

The regulations under section 482 provide several methods for determining an arm's length price for the transfer or use of property. Treas. Reg. § 1.482-4(a). The *comparable uncontrolled transaction method*, for example, evaluates whether the amount charged for a controlled transfer of property was arm's length by reference to the amount charged in a comparable uncontrolled transaction. Treas. Reg. § 1.482-4(c)(1). For two cases applying the comparable uncontrolled price method, see United States Steel Corp. v. Commissioner, 617 F.2d 942 (2d Cir.1980), and Bausch & Lomb v. Commissioner, 933 F.2d 1084 (2d Cir.1989). The government has issued numerous regulations under section 482.

Example. U.S. Parent Co., a major manufacturer of soft contact lenses, formed a subsidiary corporation in Ireland (Foreign Sub). U.S. Parent granted Foreign Sub a nonexclusive license to manufacture and sell contact lenses using U.S. Parent's technology, in exchange for a royalty of 5% of Foreign Sub's net contact lens sales. Under section 482, the Service may argue that the 5% royalty rate is unreasonable and should be higher to reflect an arm's length consideration.

The Service offers taxpayers, through its Advance Pricing Agreement (APA) Program, the opportunity to reach an agreement, before filing a tax return, on the appropriate transfer pricing method to be applied to related party transactions at issue. An APA involves not only an agreement between the taxpayer and the Service, but also an agreement between the United States and one or more foreign tax authorities that the transfer pricing method is correct to assure the taxpayer that income will not be subject to double taxation by the United States and the foreign government.

IV. Materials

Boulez v. Commissioner
83 T.C. 584 (1984)

KORNER, JUDGE:

Respondent determined a deficiency in petitioner's individual income tax for the calendar year 1975 in the amount of $20,865.61. After concessions, the issue which we are called upon to decide is whether certain payments received by petitioner in the year 1975 constitute sale "royalties" and are therefore exempt from tax by the United States, or whether said payments constitute compensation for personal services and are therefore taxable by the United States.

OPINION

Petitioner contends that the payments to him in 1975 by CBS, Inc. were not taxable by the United States, because they were "royalties." Respondent contends that the payments in question were taxable to petitioner by the United States because they represented compensation for personal services performed in the United States by petitioner.

Acknowledging that the provisions of the [applicable] treaty take precedence over any conflicting provisions of the Internal Revenue Code, we must decide whether the payments received by petitioner in 1975 from CBS, Inc. constituted royalties or income from personal services. This issue, in turn, involves two facets:

> (1) Did petitioner intend and support to license or convey to CBS Records, and did the latter agree to pay for, a property interest in the recordings he was engaged to make, which would give rise to royalties?

> (2) If so, did petitioner have a property interest in the recordings which he was capable of licensing or selling?

The first of the above questions is purely factual, depends upon the intention of the parties, and is to be determined by an examination of the record as a whole, including the terms of the contract entered into between petitioner and CBS Records, together with any other relevant and material evidence.

The second question—whether petitioner had a property interest which he could license or sell—is a question of law.

We will examine each of these questions in turn.

1. THE FACTUAL QUESTION

By the contract entered into between petitioner and CBS Records in 1969, as amended, did the parties agree that petitioner was licensing or conveying to CBS Records a property interest in the recordings which he was retained to make, and in return for which he was to receive "royalties?"

The contract between the parties is by no means clear. On the one hand, the contract consistently refers to the compensation which petitioner is to be entitled to receive as "royalties," and such payments are tied directly to the proceeds which CBS Records was to receive from sales of recordings which petitioner was to make. Both these factors suggest that the parties had a royalty arrangement, rather than a compensation arrangement, in mind in entering into the contract. We bear in mind, however, that the labels which the parties affix to a transaction are not necessarily determinative of their true nature, and the fact that a party's remuneration under the contract is based on a percentage of future sales of the product created does not prove that a licensing or sale of property was intended, rather than compensation for services.

On the other hand, the contract between petitioner and CBS Records is replete with language indicating that what was intended here was a contract for personal services. Thus, paragraph 1. [of the contract] clearly states that CBS Records was engaging petitioner "to render your services exclusively for us as a producer and/or performer. It is understood and agreed that such engagement by us shall include your services as a producer and/or performer." Paragraph 3. of the contract then requires petitioner to "perform" in the making of a certain number of recordings in each year. Most importantly, in the context of the present question, paragraph 4. of the contract makes it clear that CBS considered petitioner's services to be the essence of the contract: petitioner agreed not to perform for others with respect to similar recordings during the term of the contract, and for a period of five years thereafter, and he was required to "acknowledge that your services are unique and extraordinary and that we shall be entitled to equitable relief to enforce the provision of this paragraph 4."

Under paragraph 5. of the contract, it was agreed that the recordings, once made, should be entirely the property of CBS Records, "free from any claims whatsoever by you or any person deriving any rights or interests from you." Significantly, nowhere in the contract is there any language of conveyance of any alleged property right in the recordings by petitioner to CBS Records, nor any language indicating a licensing of any such purported right, other than the designation of petitioner's remuneration as being "royalties." The word "copyright" itself is never mentioned. Finally, under paragraph 13. of the contract, CBS Records was entitled to suspend or terminate its payments to petitioner "if, by reason of illness, injury, accident or refusal to work, you fail to perform for us in accordance with the provisions of this agreement."

Considered as a whole, therefore, and acknowledging that the contract is not perfectly clear on this point, we conclude that the weight of the evidence is that the parties intended a contract for personal services, rather than one involving the sale or licensing of any property rights which petitioner might have in the recordings which were to be made in the future.

2. THE LEGAL QUESTION

Before a person can derive income from royalties, it is fundamental that he must have an ownership interest in the property whose licensing or sale gives rise to the income. [T]his Court held that in order for a payment to constitute a "royalty," the payee must have an ownership interest in the property whose use generates the payment.

It is clear, then, that the existence of a property right in the payee is fundamental for the purpose of determining whether royalty income exists.

Did the petitioner have any property rights in the recordings which he made for CBS Records, which he could either license or sell and which would give rise to royalty income here? We think not.

In spite of change in the law in 1971, however, petitioner's contractual relationship with CBS Records went on as before. Neither the amendment to that contract of 1971, nor the further amendment in 1974, made any reference to the change of the copyright laws, nor modified the basic contract in any respect which would be pertinent to the instant question. We conclude, therefore, that the parties saw no need to modify their contract because they understood that even after the Sound Recording Amendment of 1971, petitioner still had no licensable or transferable property rights in the recordings which he made for CBS Records, and we think this was correct.

The Copyright Act of 1909, even after its amendment by the Sound Recording Amendment of 1971, describes the person having a copyrightable interest in property as the "author or proprietor," 17 U.S.C. sec. 9, and further provides that "the word 'author' shall include an employer in the case of works made for hire." 17 U.S.C. sec. 26. The above is a statutory enactment of the long-recognized rule that where a person is employed for the specific purpose of creating a work, including a copyrightable item, the fruits of his labor, carried out in accordance with the employment, are the property of his employer. The rule creates a rebuttable presumption to this effect, which can be overcome by express contractual provisions between the employee and the employer, reserving to the former the copyrightable interest.

Here, the petitioner, a musical conductor of world-wide reputation, was employed to make recordings for CBS Records, and in doing so, was to exercise his peculiar and unique skills in accordance with his experience, talent, and best judgment. In these circumstances, we do not think that petitioner was an "employee" in the common law sense, but rather was an independent contractor, with the same relationship to CBS Records as a lawyer, an engineer, or an architect would have to his client, or a doctor to his patient. This, however, provides no grounds for distinction, since the "works for hire" rule applies to independent contractors just as it does to conventional employees.

In the instant case, the application of the works for hire rule means that petitioner had no copyrightable property interest in the recordings which he created for CBS Records, even after 1971. Petitioner was engaged for the specific purpose of making the recordings in question; his contract with CBS Records reserved no property rights in the recordings to him, and indeed made it specific that all such rights, whatever they were, were to reside in CBS Records. Under these circumstances, we do not think that petitioner has overcome the statutory presumption of the works for hire rule, nor that he has shown that he had any property interest in the recordings, either before 1971 or thereafter, which he could either license or sell to CBS Records so as to produce royalty income within the meaning of the treaty. This conclusion, in turn, reinforces our belief, which we have found as a fact, that the contract between petitioner and CBS Records was one for the performance of personal services.

V. Related Matters

- **OECD's Base Erosion and Profit Shifting (BEPS) Project.** Base erosion due to profit shifting is not merely a U.S. concern but is also a large problem in many other countries that do not have low tax rates. There is statistical and anecdotal evidence that foreign-based multinationals engage in the same income-shifting strategies as U.S. based multinationals. In 2015, the OECD delivered a number of concrete action plan recommendations to help address the problems of income shifting. It is the most important development in cross-border taxation in decades. It will be interesting to see how nations respond to the OECD's BEPS recommendations. We will likely see incomplete and uneven adoption by OECD member countries. Indeed, the TCJA changes highlighted in the Overview were passed swiftly by Congress without regard to OECD recommendations. Some predict that non-uniform adoption and enforcement of international tax law will only create new loopholes to be exploited.

Chapter 41

Overview of Estate and Gift Taxation

I. Assignment

Read: Internal Revenue Code: §§ 2001(a)–(c); 2010; 2056(a); 2501; 2503(b); 2505(a). Skim §§ 2601–2613; 2631–2641; 2642(c); 2651(e)(1).

Treasury Regulations: None.

Text: Overview

Complete the problems.

II. Problems

In the problems that follow please ignore the inflation adjustments called for by section 2010(c) and, instead, assume that the basic exclusion amount is a flat $10,000,000. You may also assume that the annual exclusion under section 2503(b) is $15,000.

1. In the current year, Captain Kurtz passed away with a gross estate of $12,100,000. His debts and the costs of administering his estate totaled $100,000. What is his estate's estate tax liability under the following circumstances?

   (a) The captain had made no taxable gifts during life. Under his will everything passed to his children, Conrad and Jim.

   (b) Same as (a) except that the captain had made adjusted taxable gifts of $1,000,000.

   (c) Same as (a) except that the captain leaves $2,000,000 to his wife, Medea, and $10,000,000 to his children.

2. Mary Todd has four children and ten grandchildren. This year she made outright gifts of $10,000 in cash to each of these fourteen people. These were her only gifts. What is her "total amount of gifts" within the meaning of section 2503(a)? *See* IRC § 2503(b)(1).

3. In the current year, Mata Hari gave $11,015,000 to her grandson, Hermann Goering. What are Mata's transfer tax consequences under the following circumstances?

   (a) Her son Adolf, Hermann's father, is still living at the time of the gift. Mata has her full section 2505 tax credit remaining and she allocates $6,000,000 of her GSTT exemption to the gift. She requires Hermann to pay any GSTT on the transfer.

(b) Same as (a) except that Adolph is no longer living.

(c) Same as (a) except that Mata had made a taxable gift of $500,000 in a prior year.

III. Overview

A. Introduction

Throughout this book we have approached various topics within federal taxation with differing degrees of specificity in order to emphasize important points while avoiding information overload. This chapter is the broadest treatment in the book because it surveys an important but quite distinct area of federal taxation, the gratuitous transfer taxes. The purpose of this chapter is give the reader a sense of the structure and operation of these taxes without belaboring the details. Estate and gift taxation and estate planning are fields worthy of full scale study and many books address them in detail.

There are three federal gratuitous transfer taxes: the estate tax (IRC §§ 2001–2058), the gift tax (IRC §§ 2501–2524), and the generation skipping transfer tax (GSTT) (IRC §§ 2601–2664). You may never have heard of the last one. Suffice it to say at this point that it is a tax designed to prevent estate and gift tax avoidance on a generation of transfer tax by the simple device of skipping a generation, e.g., by leaving one's estate to one's grandchildren rather than to one's children.

1. Why Have Such Taxes?

The transfer taxes are excise taxes on the privilege of giving away one's property to another person. Some people question the fairness and logic of taxing such transfers. There is no absolute justification for these taxes, any more than there is an absolute justification for the income tax, the property tax, or the sales tax. The estate tax probably came into being because death is such a clearly identifiable event that it made taxation relatively easy. Also, dead people are less inclined to resist taxation than most others. The simple fact is that nearly all forms of taxation arise first because of the need to fund the government. "Taxes are the price we pay for a civilized society," Justice Holmes said. Even so, the forms of taxation a nation adopts do say something about its values. An estate tax makes sense in the context of a nation, such as the United States, that does not honor hereditary offices. We do not believe in privilege by birth. The American ideal, if not the reality, is that all women and men are created equal and that the opportunity to gather wealth should exist for everyone in equal measure. In this context the estate tax may be seen as an effort to prevent the aggregation of much of the nation's wealth, and the corresponding power, in the hands of a relatively few families. (This also explains the use of graduated rates.) How well the transfer taxes work to accomplish that goal is a matter of debate. Compared to the income tax, the transfer taxes raise very little revenue. However, they are sometimes credited with encouraging substantial gifts to charities. As a final policy point, we should remember the basis step up rules of section 1014. If we were to repeal the transfer taxes, would it make sense to leave section 1014 on the books?

2. Who Pays the Transfer Taxes?

Very few people are affected by the gratuitous transfer taxes. An unmarried decedent's estate of less than $10,000,000 escapes any federal estate tax if the decedent made no lifetime taxable gifts. Thus a married couple could easily pass $20,000,000 in property to their children tax free. With judicious planning much larger sums could be transferred free of estate or gift tax. A few of the major planning techniques are discussed below.

B. Transfer Tax Theory

There are six basic principles thought to be embodied in a good transfer tax.

1. It should apply to all property a person can transfer.

2. There should be no difference in treatment between inter vivos and testamentary transfers.

3. Each transfer should be taxed only once.

4. The tax should be imposed at least once each generation.

5. Valuation rules should account for the different ways in which property can be divided.

6. Illiquidity relief should be liberally provided.

Most of these rules derive from a higher principle of tax theory: a tax should be economically neutral. In the present context this means the tax result should be the same no matter how the taxpayer chooses to transfer her property. Thus, she will choose the most rational approach to meet her goals. Neutrality is a general principle of tax theory that is often honored in the breach. The transfer taxes are no exception. The interaction between the transfer taxes and the income tax basis rules is a good illustration of failed neutrality. There is a strong bias in the system in favor of holding appreciated property until death rather than transferring it during life because of the basis step up for bequests afforded by section 1014. Recall that appreciated property given away during life takes a carryover basis under section 1015.

C. The Estate Tax in Outline

The estate tax is borne by a decedent transferor's estate. It is computed by determining the "gross estate" (like gross income in the income tax) and taking certain deductions to derive the "taxable estate." The tax rate schedule is applied to the taxable estate. The resulting tentative tax liability is then reduced by the "unified credit" to arrive at a final tax owed.

The Conceptual Structure of the Estate Tax

Gross Estate
− Deductions
Taxable Estate
× Rate
Tentative Tax
− Unified Credit
Tax Owed

The actual computation is significantly more complicated because the estate tax is integrated with the gift tax and because of the nominally progressive rate structure embodied in section 2001(c). The apparent progressivity of that rate structure is misleading. In essence the estate tax rate is a flat 40% of the fair market value of that portion of the taxable estate that is not shielded by the unified credit.

1. The Gross Estate

The "gross estate" is a non-intuitive concept since it includes many things in addition to property the decedent owned at death. Moreover, significant valuation issues can also arise. The gross estate usually must be valued at its fair market value as of the date of death of the person whose estate is being taxed. IRC §2031(a).

The gross estate consists of (primarily) 10 categories of property:

1. Property owned at death. §2033
2. Certain property transferred near death. §2035
3. Property which was transferred before death but over which the transferor retained some right of enjoyment. §2036
4. Property which was transferred before death but enjoyment of which was conditioned upon surviving the donor. §2037
5. Revocably transferred property. §2038
6. Certain annuities. §2039
7. Certain jointly held property. §2040
8. Property over which the decedent held a general power of appointment. §2041
9. Certain life insurance proceeds on the decedent's life. §2042
10. Certain property in which the decedent held a life interest received from his spouse. §2044

We will not examine these inclusion rules in any detail. But it is useful to understand that the gross estate can consist of many things beyond the decedent's probate estate. Clearly the completion of an estate tax return or the development of an estate plan for a wealthy person are not tasks for the uninformed.

2. The Taxable Estate

The taxable estate consists of the sum of the items just noted reduced by certain deductions. These are:

1. Creditor's claims and expenses of the estate. § 2053

2. Casualty losses during administration. § 2054

3. Charitable deduction. § 2055

4. Marital deduction. § 2056

The charitable deduction correlates in many respects with the same deduction for income tax purposes and has many technical limitations, especially for split interest transfers. The deduction for gifts between spouses also requires a further comment. This deduction rests on the idea that a married couple is a single economic unit and, thus, gifts between spouses should be ignored for transfer tax purposes. But not every gift between spouses qualifies for the deduction. Gifts of lifetime or term interests must be carefully structured in order to qualify. *See* IRC § 2056(b)(7). The marital deduction is a commonly used estate planning tool.

3. The Rate Structure

The rate structure for both the estate tax and the gift tax is set out in section 2001(c). *See also* IRC § 2502(a). The maximum rate under that provision is 40%.

4. The Unified Credit

The unified credit is the device that allows estates of less than $10,000,000 to go untaxed. It is set out in section 2010. The term "unified" refers to the way in which the credit's operation is integrated into a similar gift tax credit found in section 2505. The two credits are of equal amounts and both are annually adjusted for inflation since 2011. The two credits are unified in one important respect. The use of the gift tax credit has the effect of reducing the available estate tax credit. Thus, for example, a $500,000 taxable inter vivos gift means that a decedent's estate can only shelter $9,500,000 of property from taxation by use of the estate tax unified credit.

The mechanics of the unified credit are a bit tricky. The statutes establish what is called an "applicable exclusion amount" of $10,000,000 for the estate tax and for the gift tax. *See* IRC §§ 2010(c), 2505(a). The applicable exclusion amount is adjusted for inflation after year 2011. The "applicable credit" is the amount of tax that would otherwise be owed on a transfer of the applicable exclusion amount under the section 2001(c) rate structure.

A complicating factor is that under certain circumstances, a decedent's unused applicable exclusion amount can be used by the decedent's surviving spouse. *See* IRC § 2010(c). Thus, for example, if a husband dies having used only $7,000,000 of his applicable exclusion amount, his wife may be entitled to use his remaining applicable exclusion amount of $3,000,000 in addition to her own basic exclusion amount of $10,000,000 (remembering that these numbers are adjusted for inflation).

D. The Gift Tax in Outline

The gift tax serves to back up the estate tax. Without a gift tax one could avoid tax on transfers from one generation to the next by the use of inter vivos gifts. Its structure is similar to that of the estate tax. Its provisions relating to such things as powers of appointments, charitable gifts, and inter-spousal transfers tend to mirror those of the estate tax. However, it does have a few unique rules some which we will note below.

In Chapter 4, we considered the *Duberstein* case which held that for income tax purposes a gift must arise out of "detached and disinterested generosity." This is not the rule in the gift tax context. Instead a gift occurs when there is a transfer of property for less than full and adequate consideration. *See* Treas. Reg. § 25.2511-1(g)(1). In order for a gift to be complete for gift tax purposes the donor must give up "dominion and control" over the property. Treas. Reg. § 25.2511-2(b). Thus, a transfer of property to a revocable trust, for example, is not a completed gift and is not currently taxable. If the trust makes distributions or later becomes irrevocable, the gift tax is triggered at that time.

The gift tax is levied on the transferor (donor). The rates are established by section 2001(c). *See* IRC § 2502(a). Although an annual return is used, all gifts since 1932 are used to compute the tax rate. Thus, earlier years' gifts push current gifts into higher tax brackets. If you find this confusing, be patient. Computing the estate and gift taxes is developed further in a moment.

1. The Annual Exclusion

The first $10,000 of a present interest gift to anyone is excluded from the gift tax. IRC § 2503(b). (This number is adjusted for inflation and is currently $15,000.) This is known as the "annual exclusion" and, as its name describes, it arises anew each year. Thus, one can make gifts year after year with no gift tax consequences as long as the amount given to any particular person does not exceed the annual exclusion limit. This is an obvious planning opportunity. For example, a person can make gifts to her children and grandchildren over a span of years in order to spend down her estate to a level where little or no estate tax will apply when she dies. There are several nuances to the annual exclusion. Spouses may double their available exclusion by treating one another's gifts to third parties as being made half by each even though only one spouse actually made the gift. IRC § 2513. Gifts in trust to minor children can qualify if they meet certain terms. *See* IRC § 2503(c). Certain payments for education and for medical care for another are also excluded if made directly to the provider. IRC § 2503(e).

2. Special Valuation Rules

Valuation poses serious problems in the administration of both the estate and the gift taxes. Well advised taxpayers often slice and dice their property interests in ways that make the value of property highly debatable and hire experts who will testify that the form in which an interest is held reduces it value for transfer tax purposes. For example, a taxpayer may put his property inside a limited partnership and then give away minority interests to his children. Arguably the minority interests are worth less for gift tax purposes than the underlying assets since the limited partner has no control and since the interest may not be readily marketable. Much of the litigation in the estate and gift tax area concerns the value of transferred property interests.

There are a few statutorily adopted valuation rules that attempt to shore up the gift tax against various efforts at tax planning. These rules are found in sections 2701 through 2704. Section 2701 relates to transfers of interests in a corporation or partnership. Section 2702 relates to transfers into a trust. Section 2703 relates to buy-sell agreements, and section 2704 relates to certain lapsing rights and restrictions. We will not analyze these provisions here. We simply observe their existence as a cautionary note for would be estate planners.

E. Computing the Estate and Gift Taxes

The manner of computing both the estate tax and the gift tax is based on the assumption of a highly progressive rate structure. As we have noted, currently that assumption is not valid. Nonetheless the statutory architecture remained in place and is useful to understand.

Both computations employ a "stacking" concept. That is, in each computation we stack all prior gratuitous transfers beneath the ones that are presently being taxed. Then we compute a tax on the sum of those transfers past and present. Thus the prior transfers push the current transfers into higher tax brackets. We avoid taxing the prior transfers more than once by backing out the prior years' taxes from the current liability.

1. The Estate Tax Computation

Not only is the estate tax computation complicated by the use of stacking, but it is also complicated by the fact that inter vivos gifts can reduce the amount of the unified credit that is available at death. The way the statutes arrive at these two results is set out on the following page.

Estate Tax Computation Worksheet with Statutory Cross-References

1. Gross Estate (2031-44)   _____
2. Total Deductions
3.   Marital (2056)   _____
4.   Charitable (2055)   _____
5.   Casualties (2054)   _____
6.   Debts (2053)   _____
7.   Others   _____
8.   TOTAL   − _____
9. Taxable Estate (2051, 2001(b)(1)(A))   _____
10. Adjusted Taxable Gifts (2001(b)(1)(B))   + _____
11. Tentative Taxable Estate   _____
12. Apply 2001(c) rate   × rate _____
13. Tentative Estate Tax (2001(b)(1), (c))   _____
14. Total Taxable Gifts   _____ (2001(b))
15. Apply 2001(c) rate   × rate _____
16. Gross Gift Tax   _____ (2001(b)(2))
17. Unified Credit   − _____ (2505)
18. Gift Tax Payable (2001(b)(2))   − _____
19. Pre-Credit Estate Tax   _____
20. Unified Credit (2010)   − _____
21. Net Estate Tax Liability   _____

Notice that lines 9 (taxable estate) and 10 (adjusted taxable gifts) are added together before the tentative tax is computed on the sum using the section 2001(c) rate schedule. This is what is designed to push the estate into the higher tax brackets. Then line 18 backs out the gift tax on the prior years' gifts to avoid double taxing them. Finally the tax liability is reduced by the unified credit at line 20 to arrive at the final liability.

For many people the most confusing thing about this computation is that the unified credit gets deducted twice; once at line 17 and again at line 20. The line 17 deduction is the gift tax unified credit, and the line 20 deduction is the estate tax unified credit. Is the credit being allowed twice? The answer is no. The key to understanding this is to observe that the line 17 deduction *reduces* the line 18 amount which is then deducted from the tentative tax. In other words the first use of the credit reduces a tax reduction. Only the second use of the credit reduces the estate tax liability.

2. The Gift Tax Computation

The gift tax computation is less complex but still daunting.

Gift Tax Computation Worksheet with Statutory Cross-References

1.	<u>Current gross gifts</u>	_____
2.	− <u>Exclusions</u> (2503(b), (c), (e) & 2513)	− _____
3.	Total amount of gifts (2503(a))	_____
4.	− <u>Deductions</u> (e.g. 2523 (marital deduction))	− _____
5.	Current taxable gifts (2503(a))	_____
6.	+ <u>Prior years' taxable gifts</u>	+ _____
7.	Total tentative taxable gifts	_____
8.	× <u>Rate</u> (2502(a)(1), 2001(c))	× rate _____
9.	Tentative tax (2502(a)(1))	_____
10.	− <u>Tax on prior years' gifts</u> (2502(a)(2) (Pre-credit))	_____
11.	Gift tax liability before credit	_____
12.	− <u>Unused unified credit</u> (2505(a))	− _____
13.	Current gift tax liability	_____

Notice in this computation that on line 10 the prior years' tax is deducted from the tentative tax liability without reduction for the prior use of the unified credit. Then when the unified credit is deducted on line 12 only so much of the unified credit as was not used in prior years is deducted. The reason for doing the computation this way is that we use the current year tax rate schedule to determine the tentative tax even if the rate schedule was different in prior years. But we use the actual amount for prior use of the unified credit to determine how much unified credit remains available in the current year.

F. The Generation Skipping Transfer Tax (GSTT)

We noted earlier that as a matter of theory an ideal gratuitous transfer tax should apply once each generation. The generation skipping transfer tax (GSTT) is designed to foster that requirement. It is an excise tax on the transfer of property to a person who is more than one generation below the generation of the transferor. The tax is, in the main, a device for closing the loophole that exists in the estate and gift taxes for transfers of property from one generation to another without any tax. To understand this consider the two following examples:

Example 1. Grandfather dies leaving $20,000,000 to Father who lives off the income but not the principal. Father dies leaving the $20,000,000 to Granddaughter (Father's daughter, Grandfather's granddaughter).

Example 2. Grandfather dies leaving $20,000,000 in trust to Father for life, remainder to Granddaughter.

The first example results in the estate tax being applied twice, once when Grandfather dies and again when Father dies. In the second example the termination of Father's life estate does not trigger any estate or gift tax since he was not the transferor. Thus, in the absence of the GSTT, the $20,000,000 would pass from Grandfather to Granddaughter with only one application of transfer tax. Under the GSTT when Father dies the termination of the trust will trigger the GSTT which will be borne by the trust.

1. The Triggering Event

The GSTT is triggered by any one of three events: (1) a direct skip, (2) a taxable distribution, or (3) a taxable termination. A direct skip is a transfer subject to estate or gift tax to a "skip person." IRC § 2612(c). A skip person is a natural person who is two or more generations below the transferor. IRC § 2613(a)(1). In addition, a trust is a skip person if all interests in the trust are held by skip persons or if no one other than a skip person can receive a distribution from the trust after the transfer creating the trust. IRC § 2613(a)(2). A taxable distribution is a distribution from a trust to a skip person (other than a taxable termination or a direct skip). IRC § 2612(b). A taxable termination is the termination of any interest held in trust unless after the termination the interest is held by a non-skip person or unless after the termination there can be no distributions from the trust to a skip person. IRC § 2612(a).

2. Generation Assignment

Generation assignment is a mechanical process. For lineal descendants of the transferor, you simply count generations (e.g., a grandchild is two generations below a grandparent.) IRC § 2651(b)(1). The spouses of lineal descendants are assigned to the descendant's generation. IRC § 2652(c)(2).

Unrelated transferees are assigned generations according to the following rules: (1) If the transferee is not more than 12? years younger than the transferor, he is assigned to the transferor's generation; (2) If more than 12? years younger but not more than 37? years younger than the transferor, the transferee is assigned to one generation below the transferor; and (3) Each 25 years thereafter the transferee is assigned to a new generation. *See* IRC § 2651(d). A spouse is assigned to the transferor's generation so there is no GSTT on a transfer between spouses no matter what their ages. IRC § 2651(c)(1).

3. Deceased Parent Rule

There are a number of special rules to iron out the wrinkles. One important rule is that a descendant whose parents are deceased at the time of the transfer that creates the descendant's interest moves up to the parent's generation. IRC § 2651(e); Treas. Reg. § 26.2612-1(a)(2). Thus, for example, a gift from a grandparent to a grandchild is not a direct skip if the grandchild's parent is dead.

4. The Taxable Amount and Tax Liability

The amount against which the tax is levied varies somewhat depending upon several factors including whether it arises out of a direct skip, taxable distribution, or taxable termination. But basically the amount is the fair market value of the property interest passing to the skip person (*see* IRC §§ 2621–2623) valued as of the time of the transfer. *See* IRC § 2624(a).

The transferee is liable for the tax on a taxable distribution. The trustee is liable for the tax on a taxable termination. The transferor is liable for the tax on a direct skip. IRC § 2603. Where there is a direct skip, the GSTT paid by the transferor is treated as part of the gift for gift tax purposes. IRC § 2515.

5. The Exemption

There is an exemption from the GSTT equal to the inflation-adjusted applicable exclusion amount under section 2010(c) ($11,200,000 in 2018). The transferor may allocate the exemption to any particular transfers she chooses. IRC § 2631. There are special rules for designating how the exemption is used in the absence of a specific election by the transferor. IRC § 2632. Basically, inter vivos direct skips are allocated first and, at death, direct skips are allocated ahead of trusts created which may result in taxable terminations or distributions. IRC §§ 2632(b) & (c).

If the exemption amount is allocated to a trust, the trust keeps that exemption throughout its existence until there is a gift tax or an estate tax applied to the trust. At that point the new decedent or donor is treated as the transferor for GSTT purposes. Moreover, if the amount of the exemption that is allocated to the trust is less than the value of the trust, there will still be some tax liability at various junctures. It is generally advisable to make trusts either wholly exempt from GSTT or wholly non-exempt. In other words, if the transfers into trust exceed the available exemption amount, two or more trusts should be created, one that is exempt and one that is not exempt. This greatly simplifies management and tax planning down the road.

The importance of the exemption for a select group of wealthy people cannot be over emphasized. Those who can afford to tie up significant wealth in an irrevocable trust can avoid all transfer taxes for many generations by establishing dynastic trusts in states that do not have a rule against perpetuities. These trusts are more commonly established in states such as South Dakota and Delaware that also do not have a state income tax.

6. The Annual Exclusion

Inter vivos transfers that would otherwise be subject to the GSTT receive the benefit of the section 2503 annual exclusions. *See* IRC §§ 2642(c), 2611(b), 2612(c)(1). This is an important planning device since one can make annual gifts to grandchildren or to grandchildrens' trusts without attracting the GSTT.

7. The Tax Computation

The GSTT is computed by multiplying "the applicable rate" times "the taxable amount." IRC § 2602.

GSTT = Applicable rate × Taxable amount

This is not as simple as it sounds because the applicable rate must be derived through a number of computational steps.

The applicable rate is the product of the "maximum federal rate" and "the inclusion ratio" for the transfer. IRC § 2641(a).

Applicable rate = Maximum federal rate × Inclusion ratio

The maximum federal rate is the highest marginal rate imposed by section 2001(c) (40%). IRC § 2641(b).

The inclusion ratio with respect to the transfer is the excess of 1 over "the applicable fraction" determined for the trust from which the transfer is made or, in the case of a direct skip, the applicable fraction determined for the skip. IRC § 2642(a)(1).

Inclusion ratio = 1 − Applicable fraction

The applicable fraction is a fraction the numerator of which is the amount of the GST exemption provided by section 2631 which has been allocated to the trust or to the direct skip. The denominator of the applicable fraction is generally the value of the property transferred. IRC § 2642(a)(2)(B).

$$\text{Applicable fraction} = \frac{\text{GST exemption allocated to trust or direct skip}}{\text{Value of the property transferred}}$$

From the foregoing it should be evident that the applicable rate cannot be determined until the inclusion ratio is known. In turn, the inclusion ratio cannot be determined until the applicable fraction is known. Therefore, we must first derive the applicable fraction, then the inclusion ratio and then the applicable rate. This process is illustrated below.

8. Illustration of the GSTT's Application

Assume Grandmother decides to make an inter vivos gift of $1,015,000 to Grandson. This is a direct skip because it is a gift subject to gift tax to a person assigned to a generation two generations below Grandmother. Therefore, it is potentially subject to the GSTT. (This assumes that Grandson's parent who is a lineal descendant of Grandmother is still living.) Grandmother elects to assign $250,000 of her exemption amount to the direct skip. She also applies her section 2505 unified credit to the entire gift.

The annual exclusion is available for this gift. This reduces the amount potentially subject to GSTT to $1,000,000.

The applicable fraction with respect to this direct skip is ¼.

$$\frac{1}{4} = \frac{250,000}{1,000,000}$$

The inclusion ratio is ¾.

$$\frac{3}{4} = 1 - \frac{1}{4}$$

The applicable rate is 30%.

$$40\% \times \frac{3}{4} = 30\%$$

The amount of GSTT owed on the transfer is $300,000.

$1,000,000 (the taxable amount) × 30% = $300,000.

If Grandmother pays the GSTT on the transfer, that is deemed a further gift for gift tax purposes.

Notice that had Grandmother elected to use $1,000,000 of her GSTT exemption on the direct skip there would have been no GSTT liability. This is because the applicable fraction would have been 1 (the numerator and the denominator would both have been $1,000,000) and thus the inclusion ratio would have been zero (1 − 1 = 0). Thus the applicable rate would have been zero as well because any number multiplied by zero is zero.

9. Conclusion

The generation skipping transfer tax is designed to be a powerful impediment to the use of such transfers for tax avoidance purposes. The annual exclusion and the exemption amount ameliorate this effect in many cases. The exemption amount can be used in a dynastic trust to create a perpetually exempt trust that will benefit generation after generation.

IV. Materials

None

V. Related Matters

None

Chapter 42

Tax Practice and Procedure

I. Assignment

Read: Internal Revenue Code: Skim §§ 6001; 6011; 6072(a)–(b); 6081(a)–(b); 6151; 6161; 6201; 6203; 6212; 6213; 6303; 6321; 6322; 6323; 6330; 6331; 6501(a), (c)(1)–(3), (e)(1)(A); 6502; 6503; 6851; 6861; 7429; 7430; 7502; 7602(a)(1). Skim §§ 6662(b)(6) & 7701(o).

Treasury Regulations: None.

Text: Overview
Form 870, Waiver of Restrictions on Assessment and Collection of Deficiency in Tax and Acceptance of Overassessment
Form 872, Consent to Extend Time to Assess Tax
Form 872-A, Special Consent to Extend the Time to Assess Tax
Form 1040X, Amended U.S. Individual Income Tax Return
Form 4868, Application for Automatic Extension of Time to File U.S. Individual Income Tax Return
Form 9465, Installment Agreement Request
Related Matters

Complete the Problems.

II. Problems

1. Frida Kahlo, a single individual who uses the cash method and calendar year, received from her employer in Year 1 a salary of $75,000 and an all-expense paid vacation as additional compensation.

    (a) What is the deadline for filing Frida's Year 1 tax return?

    (b) Can Frida receive an extension of time for filing her return?

    (c) What should Frida do if she does not have the money to pay the tax due at the time of filing?

    (d) Assume Frida filed her return on April 15, Year 2, but did not report the vacation as additional compensation based on her employer's statement that the trip was not includable in her gross income. What should Frida do if she later learns that the value of the trip was includable in income as compensation? If Frida does nothing, when is the last day the IRS may assess additional tax with respect to the Year 1 return?

(e) Assume Frida filed her return on April 15, Year 2, and reported the vacation as gross income on her Year 1 tax return. Frida estimated the trip was valued at $2,000, and reflected that amount on her return. In Year 4, the IRS audited Frida's return and determined that the correct value of the trip, includible in gross income, was $75,000, resulting in additional taxes due. What options are available to Frida?

(f) Same as (e). Assume that Frida did not agree with the audit examiner's proposed adjustments and decided to take advantage of the IRS appeals process in hopes of reaching a mutually acceptable settlement as to the correct value of the trip. Because the statute of limitations on assessment is about to expire, the Appeals Officer has recently asked Frida to extend the statute of limitations. Should Frida agree? If so, should the extension be made on Form 872 or Form 872-A?

(g) Same as (f). Assume that Frida and the IRS Appeals Division do not reach an agreement, and the IRS mails Frida a notice of deficiency on February 15, Year 5. What should Frida do now? Does Frida have the option of petitioning to have her case heard as a small tax case? What happens to the statute of limitations on assessment once a notice of deficiency is issued?

(h) Same as (g). Assume that Frida litigated in Tax Court and lost (the decision became final on May 15, Year 7). Frida subsequently ignored the IRS notice and demand for payment. Can the IRS levy on Frida's wages to collect the tax due? Can the IRS barge into her house and take her clothing, jewelry, and other personal effects?

III. Overview

A. Tax Returns

The federal income tax system is a "voluntary compliance" system requiring taxpayers to file timely annual tax returns and to pay their tax due. IRC §§ 6001, 6011. To promote and enforce voluntary compliance, the government: (1) collects information from employers and other payers to verify income shown on taxpayers' returns; (2) requires employers to withhold and remit taxes throughout the year (and self-employed taxpayers to make estimated tax payments); and (3) audits a certain percentage of tax returns each year.

Individuals and C corporations must file their income tax returns by the fifteenth day of the fourth month (typically April 15th) following the close of the taxable year. IRC § 6072(a). Partnerships and S Corporations must file their income tax returns by the fifteenth day of the third month (typically March 15th) following the close of the taxable year. IRC § 6072(b). Most taxpayers still file their returns by mail. *See* IRC

§ 7502 (providing that timely mailing equals timely filing). An increasing number of taxpayers, however, file their returns electronically (through tax preparation software, various Web sites, and tax professionals). An individual may obtain an automatic six-month extension by filing Form 4868 before the return due date. IRC § 6081(a). For corporate filing extensions, see IRC § 6081(b) and Form 7004. If an individual discovers a mistake on a return already filed, she should amend the return by filing Form 1040X. *See* Badaracco v. Commissioner, 464 U.S. 386 (1984) (holding that the original return, and not the accepted return, counts for statute of limitation purposes).

Payment of tax is due by the last day the tax return is due regardless of filing extensions. In other words, an extension of time for filing does not extend the time for making payment. IRC § 6151. If a taxpayer is unable to pay tax when due, there are some options. Upon a showing of "undue hardship," a taxpayer may be granted an extension of time for payment. IRC § 6161; *see* Form 1127. In addition, a taxpayer may be eligible to enter into an installment agreement with the IRS to pay in installments. *See* Form 9465, included below.

Penalties may be imposed for late filing and for late payment of tax. The penalty for late filing or failure to file is generally 5% of the net tax due per month up to 25%. IRC § 6651(a)(1). The penalty for late payment is generally .5% of the net tax due per month up to 25%. IRC § 6651(a)(2). If both penalties apply, the failure to pay penalty reduces the amount of the failure to file penalty. The late filing and late payment penalties may be avoided if the taxpayer shows that the failure to file or pay was due to reasonable cause and not willful neglect.

B. The Examination Process and Settlements

Congress has granted the IRS broad authority to audit tax returns to encourage taxpayers to report their income and expense items correctly. *See* IRC § 6201 (authorizing the IRS to make inquiries, determinations, and assessments of all taxes); IRC § 7602(a)(1) (granting authority to "examine any books, papers, records, or other data which may be relevant" to determine the correctness of tax returns). The IRS has various methods for determining which tax returns are audited. For example, the IRS uses a secret computer formula to classify tax returns as to their error potential. Further, the IRS has an aggressive information return matching program to make sure taxpayers report the right amount of wages (Form W-2) and investment (Form 1099) income. Each year, only a limited number of returns are selected for audit. The extent of the so-called "audit lottery" has varied over time.

There are different ways in which an audit may be conducted. Correspondence audits typically involve simple issues and are conducted through the mail. Office audits involve more complex issues and are conducted at the IRS office closest to the taxpayer's residence. Field audits typically involve business returns and are conducted at the taxpayer's place of business.

At the conclusion of an audit, the examiner may propose no change in the taxpayer's tax liability. Alternatively, the examiner may propose adjustments to the taxpayer's liability, in which case the taxpayer must decide whether to agree with or contest the proposed adjustments. If the taxpayer agrees with, or reaches a mutually acceptable agreement with the examiner, the taxpayer generally signs Form 870 and pays the deficiency. If, however, the taxpayer does not agree with the examiner, the IRS will issue a preliminary notice of deficiency (30-day letter), which permits the taxpayer to file a written protest and request IRS appeals consideration. The IRS appeals process allows taxpayers and the IRS to resolve tax disputes quickly and inexpensively. Appeals officers have a lot of flexibility in resolving or compromising issues based on the "hazards of litigation." Indeed, the mission of the IRS appeals process is to reach a fair and impartial resolution of tax controversies without litigation, and a large majority of appeals cases do get settled.

If a taxpayer and the appeals division reach a mutually acceptable settlement, they generally memorialize that settlement in Form 870-AD. If they cannot reach an agreement, and there is still a tax deficiency after the appeals process, the IRS issues a notice of deficiency (90-day letter) under section 6212. Once the IRS issues the notice of deficiency, the taxpayer's recourse is to pay the tax or litigate the matter.

C. Tax Litigation

As noted in Chapter 1, the taxpayer has choices regarding the forum in which to litigate tax issues. The taxpayer may first pay the asserted deficiency and commence a refund action in either the U.S. District Court or U.S. Claims Court. Alternatively, the taxpayer may file a petition with the Tax Court for a redetermination of the proposed deficiency. IRC § 6213.

Several factors should be considered in selecting the proper forum. The availability of funds is often a key factor in deciding which forum to use. The only way to litigate in the U.S. District Court and the U.S. Claims Court is to first pay the asserted tax deficiency. This forces many taxpayers to litigate in the Tax Court, the only forum in which a taxpayer may litigate a disputed tax claim without first having to pay the asserted deficiency. Other factors include: (1) the prior precedential decisions of the three trial courts and their relevant appellate courts; (2) whether the taxpayer wants a jury trial, which is available only in the district court; (3) the expertise of the Tax Court judges in deciding tax matters; and (4) the level of discovery required in each trial court, with discovery in Tax Court being much less extensive than in district court. *See* T.C. Rule 70 (noting discovery in Tax Court is often achieved through informal consultations and communications).

Section 7430 authorizes the court to award the taxpayer attorney's fees and other costs incurred by the taxpayer if: (1) the taxpayer prevails, and (2) the IRS's position was not substantially justified. For a taxpayer to get an award of attorney's fees, the taxpayer must have exhausted all administrative remedies with the IRS (e.g., request an Appeals conference and submit a written protest) before litigating the issue.

D. Assessment Process

The IRS cannot collect tax without first "assessing" it, a term used to describe the IRS's formal recording of a tax liability. IRC § 6203. As a general rule, the IRS must assess tax within three years of when the return was filed. IRC § 6501(a). The statute of limitations is six years if a tax return reflects a substantial omission of items (i.e., an omission from gross income of "an amount properly includible therein which is in excess of 25% of the amount of gross income stated in the return"). IRC § 6501(e)(1)(A). *See* United States v. Home Concrete & Supply, LLC, 132 S. Ct. 1836 (2012) (holding an understatement of gross income attributable to an overstatement of basis in sold property is not an omission from gross income that triggers the extended six-year assessment period); *but see* IRC § 6501(e)(1)(B)(ii) (legislatively repealing the *Home Concrete* ruling). The statute of limitations is unlimited if the taxpayer files no return, a false return, or a fraudulent return. IRC § 6501(c)(1)–(3). *See* Badaracco v. Commissioner, 464 U.S. 386 (1984) (holding that an unlimited statute of limitations applies if the taxpayer files a fraudulent return but then files an amended, nonfraudulent return).

There are different types of assessments:

Summary Assessments. The IRS has the power to summarily assess and collect any unpaid tax shown to be due in a taxpayer's voluntarily submitted tax return. IRC § 6201(a).

Deficiency Assessments. If the IRS wishes to assess a deficiency in taxes, it must first send the taxpayer a notice of deficiency (90-day letter), which gives the taxpayer 90 days to decide whether to agree with or to contest the asserted deficiency in Tax Court. IRC § 6212, 6213. The IRS is prohibited from assessing tax during the 90-day period following issuance of the statutory notice (the prohibited period); and if the taxpayer contests the deficiency by filing a petition with the Tax Court, the prohibited period is continued and the statute of limitations is tolled until the Tax Court's decision becomes final. IRC §§ 6213(a), 6503(a). Note: If a taxpayer agrees with the asserted deficiency and signs a Form 870, the IRS is allowed to immediately assess tax. During an audit or during the IRS appeals process, the IRS may ask the taxpayer for an extension of the statute of limitations on assessments. Extensions can be made on Form 872 (fixed-date consent) or Form 872-A (open-ended consent). Query: Why would a taxpayer ever agree to extend the statute of limitations?

Jeopardy Assessments. Jeopardy assessments permit immediate assessment of taxes if the IRS believes that assessment or collection will be jeopardized by delay. IRC § 6851, 6861. Jeopardy assessments are typically made if the IRS believes that the taxpayer's financial solvency is imperiled or that the taxpayer is planning to depart quickly from the United States or is planning to hide or transfer property placing it beyond the reach of the government. Treas. Reg. §§ 1.6851-1; 301.6861-1. Congress has enacted an expedited administrative and judicial review process for jeopardy assessments. IRC § 7429.

E. Tax Collection Process

Within sixty days of tax assessment, the IRS issues a notice and demand for payment, which opens the door to collection remedies provided in the Code. IRC § 6303. If a taxpayer fails to pay the assessed amount after a notice and demand for payment, the federal tax lien attaches to the taxpayer's property. IRC § 6321. The unpaid tax results in a "lien in favor of the United States upon all property and rights to property, whether real or personal, belonging to the taxpayer," a phrase that has been construed liberally. The federal tax lien is automatically perfected and is valid against the taxpayer and certain other parties (i.e., has priority over certain competing interests). The federal tax lien, however, is not perfected (valid) against bona fide purchasers and certain classes of creditors (e.g., mechanic's lienors or judgment lien creditors) until a Notice of Federal Tax Lien is properly filed. With respect to these classes of creditors, the interest that is perfected first has priority. It should be noted that section 6323(b) lists several types of interests that qualify for "super priority status" and are entitled to priority regardless of when the interest arises. Some require that the holder have no actual knowledge of the federal tax lien. Once a federal tax lien arises, it lasts until the liability is satisfied or the statute of limitations on collections (ten years after date of assessment) has expired. IRC §§ 6322, 6502.

A federal tax lien does not automatically result in the collection of a tax liability. The IRS must enforce the lien through an appropriate collection device (e.g., an administrative collection remedy or a judicial avenue).

One collection device is the federal tax levy, which requires a third party to pay to the IRS amounts which he or she owes to the taxpayer. *See* IRC § 6331(a) (identifying which property is subject to levy). For example, if the IRS issues a Notice of Levy on Wages, Salary, and Other Income (Form 668-W) to the taxpayer's employer, the employer must surrender to the IRS a portion of taxpayer's wages (part of the wages are exempt from levy under the Code). A levy on salary continues until the tax is paid or the IRS releases the levy. IRC §§ 6331(e), 6343. Certain property is exempt from levy (e.g., minimum amount of wages, clothing, certain furniture, personal effects, certain tools of a business). IRC § 6334(a), (d). The taxpayer's principal residence is also exempt in certain cases (e.g., small deficiency cases). IRC § 6334(a)(13), (e). The IRS cannot levy during the period an installment agreement is in effect. The IRS must also serve proper notice of its intent to levy and provide notice and opportunity for a hearing. IRC §§ 6330, 6331(a), (d).

Under its levy authority, the IRS can also seize property held by the taxpayer or a third party. IRC § 6331(b). The IRS must, however, send a notice of seizure; and before entering premises to seize assets, it must obtain a writ of entry from a federal district court.

In addition to the administrative collection remedies (liens and levies), the government can bring suit in federal district court to collect the tax liability. IRC §§ 7401–7403. The IRS typically uses the courts for collection when the tax due is large.

Offer in Compromise. If a taxpayer is unable to pay a tax liability in full, and an installment agreement is not an option, the taxpayer may be able to take advantage of the Service's "offer in compromise" program. Through this program, the Service may settle or "compromise" a tax liability by accepting less than full payment whenever either (1) doubt as to liability exists or (2) doubt as to collectibility exists. *See* IRC § 7122. A taxpayer submits an offer on Form 656. While the offer is being processed, the Service usually suspends collection.

F. Providing Tax Advice and Opinions

Tax lawyers are subject to a variety of rules when advising a client with respect to a tax return position or when giving written tax advice and opinions. The main sets of authorities governing tax opinions are: (1) general professional ethics rules; (2) Treasury Department Circular 230; and (3) the Code and Regulations.

1. General Professional Ethics Rules

Tax lawyers are expected to follow state codes of professional conduct, which are often based on ABA model rules. *See, e.g.*, ABA Model Rules 1.2(d) & 2.1. In ABA Formal Opinion 314 (Apr. 27, 1965), the American Bar Association concluded that an attorney may advise a client to take favorable tax return positions as long as there is a "reasonable basis" for the positions. In ABA Formal Opinion 85-352 (July 7, 1985), the American Bar Association reconsidered and revised this Opinion, and concluded that an attorney may advise a client to take favorable tax return positions "if the lawyer has a good faith belief that those positions are warranted in existing law or can be supported by a good faith argument for an extension, modification or reversal of existing law." To satisfy the "good faith" test, the lawyer does not have to believe that the client's position will ultimately prevail if challenged; however, there must be some "realistic possibility of success" if the matter is litigated—generally there must be a one-third chance of success.

2. Circular 230

The Treasury Department is authorized to regulate CPAs, lawyers, and other representatives practicing before it. 31 U.S.C. § 330. Those regulations are set forth in Treasury Department Circular No. 230, which provides a broad set of rules regulating many aspects of tax practice. The rules in Circular 230 are mandatory and are enforced by the Treasury Department.

Circular 230 once required the same "realistic possibility of success" standard with respect to tax return positions that is required under the ethics rules discussed above. Today, however, Circular 230 (amended in 2014) takes a "reasonableness" approach. It requires, among other things, that the practitioner base all written advice on reasonable factual and legal assumptions, exercise reasonable reliance on representations, statements, and findings, and use reasonable efforts to identify and ascertain the facts relevant to the written advice. Circular 230, § 10.37. A practitioner must not take into account the possibility that a tax return will not be audited or that an issue will not be raised on audit. *Id.* § 10.37(a)(2)(v).

3. Code and Regulations (Statutory Penalties)

The Code and regulations contain a variety of rules that a practitioner who renders tax opinions should be aware of, including the section 6662 *substantial understatement penalty* (which clients wish to avoid) and the section 6664 *tax return preparer penalty* (which return preparers wish to avoid).

Section 6662 imposes a penalty on taxpayers for substantial understatement of tax liability. It can be avoided if: (1) facts are adequately disclosed and a "reasonable basis" exists for the position taken by the taxpayer; or (2) there is or was "substantial authority" for the position taken by the taxpayer. If the lawyer cannot conclude that a position is supported by substantial authority, she should advise the client of the penalty that the client may suffer and of the opportunity to avoid such penalty by adequate disclosure.

Section 6694 imposes penalties on those who prepare tax returns taking positions that may not be legally supported. For undisclosed positions, section 6694 requires a tax return preparer to have "substantial authority" for the tax treatment of the position. For disclosed positions, new section 6694 requires the tax return preparer to have a "reasonable basis" for the tax treatment of the position.

Note that the realistic possibility of success standard under the ethics rules, discussed above, is a lesser standard than the "substantial authority" test, but greater than the "reasonable basis" test, of sections 6662 and 6664.

IV. Materials

Form **870** (Rev. March 1992)	Department of the Treasury—Internal Revenue Service **Waiver of Restrictions on Assessment and Collection of Deficiency in Tax and Acceptance of Overassessment**	Date received by Internal Revenue Service

Names and address of taxpayers *(Number, street, city or town, State, ZIP code)* | Social security or employer identification number

Increase (Decrease) in Tax and Penalties

Tax year ended	Tax	Penalties		

(For instructions, see back of form)

Consent to Assessment and Collection

I consent to the immediate assessment and collection of any deficiencies *(increase in tax and penalties)* and accept any overassessment *(decrease in tax and penalties)* shown above, plus any interest provided by law. I understand that by signing this waiver, I will not be able to contest these years in the United States Tax Court, unless additional deficiencies are determined for these years.

YOUR SIGNATURE HERE ➤		Date
SPOUSE'S SIGNATURE ➤		Date
TAXPAYER'S REPRESENTATIVE HERE ➤		Date
CORPORATE NAME ➤		
CORPORATE OFFICER(S)	Title	Date
SIGN HERE ➤	Title	Date

Catalog Number 16894U   Form **870** (Rev. 3-1992)

Name of Taxpayer:

Identification Number:

Form 870 page 2   **Instructions**

General Information

If you consent to the assessment of the deficiencies shown in this waiver, please sign and return the form in order to limit any interest charge and expedite the adjustment to your account. Your consent will not prevent you from filing a claim for refund *(after you have paid the tax)* if you later believe you are so entitled. It will not prevent us from later determining, if necessary, that you owe additional tax; nor extend the time provided by law for either action.

We have agreements with State tax agencies under which information about Federal tax, including increases or decreases, is exchanged with the States. If this change affects the amount of your State income tax, you should file the required State form.

If you later file a claim and the Service disallows it, you may file suit for refund in a district court or in the United States Claims Court, but you may not file a petition with the United States Tax Court.

We will consider this waiver a valid claim for refund or credit of any overpayment due you resulting from any decrease in tax and penalties shown above, provided you sign and file it within the period established by law for making such a claim.

Who Must Sign

If you filed jointly, both you and your spouse must sign. If this waiver is for a corporation, it should be signed with the corporation name, followed by the signatures and titles of the corporate officers authorized to sign. An attorney or agent may sign this waiver provided such action is specifically authorized by a power of attorney which, if not previously filed, must accompany this form.

If this waiver is signed by a person acting in a fiduciary capacity *(for example, an* executor, *administrator, or a trustee)* Form 56, Notice Concerning Fiduciary Relationship, should, unless previously filed, accompany this form.

Catalog Number 16894U   Form **870** (Rev. 3-1992)

Form **872** (Rev. July 2014)	Department of the Treasury-Internal Revenue Service **Consent to Extend the Time to Assess Tax**	In reply refer to: TIN

_____
_____
(Name(s))

taxpayer(s) of _____
_____
(Address)

and the Commissioner of Internal Revenue consent and agree to the following:

(1) The amount of any Federal _____ tax due on any return(s) made by or
(Kind of tax)

for the above taxpayer(s) for the period(s) ended
_____
_____

may be assessed at any time on or before _____ . If a provision
(Expiration date)

of the Internal Revenue Code suspends the running of the period of limitations to assess such tax, then, when, under the Internal Revenue Code, the running of the period resumes, the extended period to assess will include the number of days remaining in the extended period immediately before the suspension began.

(2) The taxpayer(s) may file a claim for credit or refund and the Service may credit or refund the tax within 6 months after this agreement ends, except with respect to the items in paragraph (4).

(3) Paragraph (4) applies only to any taxpayer who holds an interest, **either directly or indirectly,** in any partnership subject to subchapter C of chapter 63 of the Internal Revenue Code.

(4) Without otherwise limiting the applicability of this agreement, this agreement also extends the period of limitations for assessing any tax (including penalties, additions to tax and interest) attributable to any partnership items (see section 6231 (a)(3)), affected items (see section 6231(a)(5)), computational adjustments (see section 6231(a)(6)), and partnership items converted to nonpartnership items (see section 6231(b)). Additionally, this agreement extends the period of limitations for assessing any tax (including penalties, additions to tax, and interest) relating to any amounts carried over from the taxable year specified in paragraph (1) to any other taxable year(s). This agreement extends the period for filing a petition for adjustment under section 6228(b) but only if a timely request for administrative adjustment is filed under section 6227. For partnership items which have converted to nonpartnership items, this agreement extends the period for filing a suit for refund or credit under section 6532, but only if a timely claim for refund is filed for such items.

(5) This Form contains the entire terms of the Consent to Extend the Time to Assess Tax. There are no representations, promises, or agreements between the parties except those found or referenced on this Form.

Your Rights as a Taxpayer

You have the right to refuse to extend the period of limitations or limit this extension to a mutually agreed-upon issue(s) or mutually agreed-upon period of time. **Publication 1035, Extending the Tax Assessment Period,** provides a more detailed explanation of your rights and the consequences of the choices you may make. If you have not already received a Publication 1035, the publication can be obtained, free of charge, from the IRS official who requested that you sign this consent or from the IRS' web site at www.irs.gov or by calling toll free at 1-800-TAX-FORM (1-800-829-3676). Signing this consent will not deprive you of any appeal rights to which you would otherwise be entitled.

(Space for signature is on the back of this form and signature instructions are attached)

Catalog Number 20755I	www.irs.gov	Form **872** (Rev. 7-2014)

TIN	Period Ending		Expiration Date

SIGNING THIS CONSENT WILL NOT DEPRIVE THE TAXPAYER(S) OF ANY APPEAL RIGHTS TO WHICH THEY WOULD OTHERWISE BE ENTITLED.

YOUR SIGNATURE HERE ➔

(Date signed)

(Type or Print Name)

I am aware that I have the right to refuse to sign this consent or to limit the extension to mutually agreed-upon issues and/or period of time as set forth in I.R.C. § 6501(c)(4)(B).

SPOUSE'S SIGNATURE ➔

(Date signed)

(Type or Print Name)

I am aware that I have the right to refuse to sign this consent or to limit the extension to mutually agreed-upon issues and/or period of time as set forth in I.R.C. § 6501(c)(4)(B).

TAXPAYER'S REPRESENTATIVE SIGN HERE ➔
(Only needed if signing on behalf of the taxpayer.)

(Date signed)

(Type or Print Name)

I am aware that I have the right to refuse to sign this consent or to limit the extension to mutually agreed-upon issues and/or period of time as set forth in I.R.C. § 6501(c)(4)(B). In addition, the taxpayer(s) has been made aware of these rights.

If this document is signed by a taxpayer's representative, the Form 2848, Power of Attorney and Declaration of Representative, or other power of attorney document must state that the acts authorized by the power of attorney include representation for the purposes of Subchapter C of Chapter 63 of the Internal Revenue Code in order to cover items in paragraph (4).

CORPORATE NAME ➔

CORPORATE OFFICER(S) SIGN HERE ➔

(Type or Print Name)   _(Title)_   _(Date signed)_

➔

(Type or Print Name)   _(Title)_   _(Date signed)_

I (we) am aware that I (we) have the right to refuse to sign this consent or to limit the extension to mutually agreed-upon issues and/or period of time as set forth in I.R.C. § 6501 (c)(4)(B).

INTERNAL REVENUE SERVICE SIGNATURE AND TITLE

(IRS Official's Name - see instructions)   _(IRS Official's Title - see instructions)_

(IRS Official's Signature - see instructions)   _(Date signed)_

Catalog Number 20755I   www.irs.gov   Form **872** (Rev. 7-2014)

	Department of the Treasury-Internal Revenue Service	In reply refer to
Form **872-A** (Rev. February 2005)	**Special Consent to Extend the Time to Assess Tax**	Taxpayer Identification Number

_____
(Name(s))

Taxpayer(s) of _____
(Number, street, city or town, state, zip code)

and the Commissioner of Internal Revenue consent and agree as follows:

(1) The amount of any Federal_____ tax due on any return(s) made by or for the
(Kind of tax)

above taxpayer(s) for the period(s) ended _____
may be assessed on or before the 90th (ninetieth) day after: (a) the date on which a Form 872-T, *Notice of Termination of Special Consent to Extend the Time to Assess Tax,* is received by the division operating unit of the Internal Revenue Service having jurisdiction over the taxable period(s) at the address provided in paragraph (4) below or the address designated by the division operating unit in a Form 872-U, *Change of IRS Address to Submit Notice of Termination of Special Consent to Extend the Time to Assess Tax,* which address will supersede the address provided in paragraph (4) below; or (b) the Internal Revenue Service mails Form 872-T to the last known address of the taxpayer(s); or (c) the Internal Revenue Service mails a notice of deficiency for such period(s); except that if a notice of deficiency is sent to the taxpayer(s), the time for assessing the tax for the period(s) stated in the notice of deficiency will end 60 days after the period during which the making of an assessment is prohibited. A final adverse determination subject to declaratory judgment under sections 7428, 7476, or 7477 of the Internal Revenue Code will not terminate this agreement.

(2) This agreement ends on the earlier of expiration date determined in paragraph (1) above or the assessment date of an increase in the above tax or the overassessment date of a decrease in the above tax that reflects the final determination of tax and the final administrative appeals consideration. An assessment or overassessment for one period covered by this agreement will not end this agreement for any other period it covers. Some assessments do not reflect a final determination and appeals consideration and therefore will not terminate the agreement before the expiration date. Examples are assessments of: (a) tax under a partial agreement; (b) tax in jeopardy; (c) tax to correct mathematical or clerical errors; (d) tax reported on amended returns; and (e) advance payments. In addition, unassessed payments, such as amounts treated by the Service as cash bonds and advance payments not assessed by the Service, will not terminate this agreement before the expiration date determined in (1) above. This agreement ends on the date determined in (1) above regardless of any assessment for any period includable in a report to the Joint Committee on Taxation submitted under section 6405 of the Internal Revenue Code.

(3) This agreement will not reduce the period of time otherwise provided by law for making such assessment.

(4) This agreement may be terminated by either the taxpayer or the Internal Revenue Service with the use of Form 872-T which is available from the division operating unit of the Internal Revenue Service considering the taxpayer's case. For a termination initiated by the taxpayer to be valid, the executed Form 872-T must be delivered to one of the following addresses or the address designated by the division operating unit considering the taxpayer's case in a Form 872-U, which address will supersede the address below:

If **MAILING** Form 872-T, send to: If **HAND CARRYING** Form 872-T, deliver to:

(5) The taxpayer(s) may file a claim for credit or refund and the Service may credit or refund the tax within 6 (six) months after this agreement ends.

(Signature instructions and space for signature are on the back of this form)   www.irs.gov   Catalog Number 20760B Form **872-A** (Rev. 2-2005)

Your Rights as a Taxpayer

You have the right to refuse to extend the period of limitations or limit this extension to a mutually agreed-upon issue(s) or mutually agreed-upon period of time. Publication 1035, *Extending the Tax Assessment Period*, provides a more detailed explanation of your rights and the consequences of the choices you may make. If you have not already received a Publication 1035, you can obtain one, free of charge, from the IRS official who requested that you sign this consent or from the IRS' web site at www.irs.gov or by calling toll free at **1-800-829-3676**. Signing this consent will not deprive you of any appeal rights to which you would otherwise be entitled.

	Date signed
Your signature here I am aware that I have the right to refuse to sign this consent or to limit the extension to mutually agreed-upon issues and/or period of time as set forth in I.R.C. §6501(c)(4)(B).	
Spouse's signature I am aware that I have the right to refuse to sign this consent or to limit the extension to mutually agreed-upon issues and/or period of time as set forth in I.R.C. §6501(c)(4)(B).	Date signed
Taxpayer's Representative signature I am aware that I have the right to refuse to sign this consent or to limit the extension to mutually agreed-upon issues and/or period of time as set forth in I.R.C. §6501(c)(4)(B). In addition, the taxpayer(s) has been made aware of these rights.	Date signed

(You must also attach written authorization as stated in the instructions below.)

Corporate Officer's signature
I (we) am aware that I (we) have the right to refuse to sign this consent or to limit the extension to mutually agreed-upon issues and/or period of time as set forth in I.R.C. §6501(c)(4)(B).

Authorized Official signature and title *(see instructions)*	Date signed
Authorized Official signature and title *(see instructions)*	Date signed

INTERNAL REVENUE SERVICE SIGNATURE AND TITLE

Division Executive name *(see instructions)*	Division Executive title *(see instructions)*

BY

Authorized Official signature and title *(see instructions)*	Date signed

Instructions

If this consent is for income tax, self-employment tax, or FICA tax on tips and is made for any year(s) for which a joint return was filed, both husband and wife must sign the original and copy of this form unless one, acting under a power of attorney, signs as agent for the other. The signatures must match the names as they appear on the front of this form.

If this consent is for gift tax and the donor and the donor's spouse elected to have gifts to third persons considered as made one-half by each, both husband and wife must sign the original and copy of this form unless one, acting under a power of attorney, signs as agent for the other. The signatures must match the names as they appear on the front of this form.

If this consent is for Chapter 41, 42, or 43 taxes involving a partnership, only one authorized partner need sign.

If this consent is for Chapter 42 taxes, a separate Form 872-A should be completed for each potential disqualified person or entity that may have been involved in a taxable transaction during the related tax year. See Revenue Ruling 75-391, 1975-2 C.B. 446.

If you are an attorney or agent of the taxpayer(s), you may sign this consent provided the action is specifically authorized by a power of attorney. If the power of attorney was not previously filed, you must include it with this form.

If you are acting as a fiduciary *(such as executor, administrator, trustee, etc.)* and you sign this consent, attach Form 56, *Notice Concerning Fiduciary Relationship*, unless it was previously filed.

If the taxpayer is a corporation, sign this consent with the corporate name followed by the signature and title of the officer(s) authorized to sign.

Instructions for Internal Revenue Service Employees

Complete the Division Executive's name and title depending upon your division:

- Small Business and Self-Employed Division = Area Director; Director, Specialty Programs; Director, Compliance Campus Operations, etc.
- Wage and Investment Division = Area Director; Director, Field Compliance Services.
- Large and Mid-Size Business Division = Director, Field Operations for your industry.
- Tax Exempt and Government Entities Division = Director, Exempt Organizations; Director, Employee Plans; Director, Federal, State and Local Governments; Director, Indian Tribal Governments; Director, Tax Exempt Bonds.
- Appeals = Chief, Appeals.

The appropriate authorized official within your division must sign and date the signature and title line.

Form **872-A** (Rev. 2-2005)

Form 1040X

(Rev. January 2017)

Department of the Treasury—Internal Revenue Service

Amended U.S. Individual Income Tax Return

▶ Information about Form 1040X and its separate instructions is at *www.irs.gov/form1040x.*

OMB No. 1545-0074

This return is for calendar year ☐ 2016 ☐ 2015 ☐ 2014 ☐ 2013

Other year. Enter one: calendar year ____ **or** fiscal year (month and year ended): ____

Your first name and initial	Last name	Your social security number
If a joint return, spouse's first name and initial	Last name	Spouse's social security number
Current home address (number and street). If you have a P.O. box, see instructions.	Apt. no.	Your phone number

City, town or post office, state, and ZIP code. If you have a foreign address, also complete spaces below (see instructions).

Foreign country name	Foreign province/state/county	Foreign postal code

Amended return filing status. You must check one box even if you are not changing your filing status. **Caution:** In general, you can't change your filing status from joint to separate returns after the due date.

☐ Single
☐ Married filing jointly
☐ Married filing separately
☐ Head of household (If the qualifying person is a child but not your dependent, see instructions.)
☐ Qualifying widow(er)

Use Part III on the back to explain any changes

Full-year coverage.
If all members of your household have full-year minimal essential health care coverage, check "Yes." Otherwise, check "No." (See instructions.)
☐ Yes ☐ No

Income and Deductions		**A. Original amount** or as previously adjusted (see instructions)	**B. Net change**—amount of increase or (decrease)—explain in Part III	**C. Correct amount**
1	Adjusted gross income. If net operating loss (NOL) carryback is included, check here ▶ ☐ **1**			
2	Itemized deductions or standard deduction **2**			
3	Subtract line 2 from line 1 **3**			
4	Exemptions. **If changing, complete Part I on page 2 and enter the amount from line 29** **4**			
5	Taxable income. Subtract line 4 from line 3 **5**			
Tax Liability				
6	Tax. Enter method(s) used to figure tax (see instructions): **6**			
7	Credits. If general business credit carryback is included, check here ▶ ☐ **7**			
8	Subtract line 7 from line 6. If the result is zero or less, enter -0- **8**			
9	Health care: individual responsibility (see instructions) **9**			
10	Other taxes **10**			
11	Total tax. Add lines 8, 9, and 10 **11**			
Payments				
12	Federal income tax withheld and excess social security and tier 1 RRTA tax withheld (**If changing,** see instructions.) **12**			
13	Estimated tax payments, including amount applied from prior year's return **13**			
14	Earned income credit (EIC) **14**			
15	Refundable credits from: ☐ Schedule 8812 Form(s) ☐ 2439 ☐ 4136 ☐ 8863 ☐ 8885 ☐ 8962 or ☐ other (specify): **15**			

16	Total amount paid with request for extension of time to file, tax paid with original return, and additional tax paid after return was filed	**16**
17	Total payments. Add lines 12 through 15, column C, and line 16	**17**

Refund or Amount You Owe

18	Overpayment, if any, as shown on original return or as previously adjusted by the IRS	**18**
19	Subtract line 18 from line 17 (If less than zero, see instructions.)	**19**
20	**Amount you owe.** If line 11, column C, is more than line 19, enter the difference	**20**
21	If line 11, column C, is less than line 19, enter the difference. This is the amount **overpaid** on this return	**21**
22	Amount of line 21 you want **refunded to you**	**22**
23	Amount of line 21 you want **applied to your** (enter year): _____ estimated tax ▪ **23**	

Complete and sign this form on Page 2.

For Paperwork Reduction Act Notice, see instructions.   Cat. No. 11360L   Form **1040X** (Rev. 1-2017)

Form 1040X (Rev. 1-2017)   Page **2**

Part I	**Exemptions**

Complete this part **only** if you are increasing or decreasing the number of exemptions (personal and dependents) claimed on line 6d of the return you are amending.

See *Form 1040 or Form 1040A instructions* and *Form 1040X instructions.*

			A. Original number of exemptions or amount reported or as previously adjusted	**B. Net change**	**C. Correct number or amount**
24	Yourself and spouse. **Caution:** If someone can claim you as a dependent, you can't claim an exemption for yourself	24			
25	Your dependent children who lived with you	25			
26	Your dependent children who didn't live with you due to divorce or separation	26			
27	Other dependents	27			
28	Total number of exemptions. Add lines 24 through 27	28			
29	Multiply the number of exemptions claimed on line 28 by the exemption amount shown in the instructions for line 29 for the year you are amending. Enter the result here and on line 4 on page 1 of this form. .	29			

30   List **ALL** dependents (children and others) claimed on this amended return. If more than 4 dependents, see instructions.

(a) First name Last name	**(b)** Dependent's social security number	**(c)** Dependent's relationship to you	**(d)** Check box if qualifying child for child tax credit (see instructions)
			☐
			☐
			☐
			☐

Part II	**Presidential Election Campaign Fund**

Checking below won't increase your tax or reduce your refund.

☐   Check here if you didn't previously want $3 to go to the fund, but now do.
☐   Check here if this is a joint return and your spouse did not previously want $3 to go to the fund, but now does.

Part III	**Explanation of changes.** In the space provided below, tell us why you are filing Form 1040X.

▶ Attach any supporting documents and new or changed forms and schedules.

Remember to keep a copy of this form for your records.

Under penalties of perjury, I declare that I have filed an original return and that I have examined this amended return, including accompanying schedules and statements, and to the best of my knowledge and belief, this amended return is true, correct, and complete. Declaration of preparer (other than taxpayer) is based on all information about which the preparer has any knowledge.

Sign Here
▶

Your signature	Date	Spouse's signature. If a joint return, **both** must sign.	Date

Paid Preparer Use Only
▶

Preparer's signature	Date	Firm's name (or yours if self-employed)	
Print/type preparer's name		Firm's address and ZIP code	
PTIN	☐ Check if self-employed		
		Phone number	EIN

For forms and publications, visit IRS.gov.   Form **1040X** (Rev. 1-2017)

Form **4868**

Department of the Treasury
Internal Revenue Service (99)

Application for Automatic Extension of Time
To File U.S. Individual Income Tax Return

▶ Information about Form 4868 and its instructions is available at *www.irs.gov/form4868*.

OMB No. 1545-0074

2016

There are three ways to request an automatic extension of time to file a U.S. individual income tax return.

1. You can pay all or part of your estimated income tax due and indicate that the payment is for an extension using Direct Pay, the Electronic Federal Tax Payment System, or using a credit or debit card. See *How To Make a Payment,* on page 3.
2. You can file Form 4868 electronically by accessing IRS *e-file* using your home computer or by using a tax professional who uses *e-file*.
3. You can file a paper Form 4868 and enclose payment of your estimate of tax due.

It's Convenient, Safe, and Secure

IRS *e-file* is the IRS's electronic filing program. You can get an automatic extension of time to file your tax return by filing Form 4868 electronically. You'll receive an electronic acknowledgment once you complete the transaction. Keep it with your records. Don't mail in Form 4868 if you file it electronically, unless you're making a payment with a check or money order (see page 3).

Complete Form 4868 to use as a worksheet. If you think you may owe tax when you file your return, you'll need to estimate your total tax liability and subtract how much you've already paid (lines 4, 5, and 6 below).

Several companies offer free e-filing of Form 4868 through the Free File program. For more details, go to IRS.gov and click on *freefile*.

Pay Electronically

You **don't** need to file Form 4868 if you make a payment using our electronic payment options. Your extension will be automatically processed when you pay part or all of your estimated income tax electronically. You can pay online or by phone (see page 3).

E-file Using Your Personal Computer or Through a Tax Professional

Refer to your tax software package or tax preparer for ways to file electronically. Be sure to have a copy of your 2015 tax return—you'll be asked to provide information from the return for taxpayer verification. If you wish to make a payment, you can pay by electronic funds withdrawal or send your check or money order to the address shown in the middle column under *Where To File a Paper Form 4868* (see page 4).

File a Paper Form 4868

If you wish to file on paper instead of electronically, fill in the Form 4868 below and mail it to the address shown on page 3.

For information on using a private delivery service, see page 4.

Note: If you're a fiscal year taxpayer, you must file a paper Form 4868.

General Instructions

Purpose of Form

Use Form 4868 to apply for 6 more months (4 if "out of the country" (defined on page 2) and a U.S. citizen or resident) to file Form 1040, 1040A, 1040EZ, 1040NR, 1040NR-EZ, 1040-PR, or 1040-SS.

Gift and generation-skipping transfer (GST) tax return (Form 709). An extension of time to file your 2016 calendar year income tax return also extends the time to file Form 709 for 2016. However, it doesn't extend the time to pay any gift and GST tax you may owe for 2016. To make a payment of gift and GST tax, see Form 8892. If you don't pay the amount due by the regular due date for Form 709, you'll owe interest and may also be charged penalties. If the donor died during 2016, see the instructions for Forms 709 and 8892.

Qualifying for the Extension

To get the extra time you must:

1. Properly estimate your 2016 tax liability using the information available to you,

2. Enter your total tax liability on line 4 of Form 4868, and

3. File Form 4868 by the regular due date of your return.

⚠ **CAUTION** *Although you aren't required to make a payment of the tax you estimate as due, Form 4868 doesn't extend the time to pay taxes. If you don't pay the amount due by the regular due date, you'll owe interest. You may also be charged penalties. For more details, see Interest and Late Payment Penalty on page 2. Any remittance you make with your application for extension will be treated as a payment of tax.*

You don't have to explain why you're asking for the extension. We'll contact you only if your request is denied.

Don't file Form 4868 if you want the IRS to figure your tax or you're under a court order to file your return by the regular due date.

▼ DETACH HERE ▼

Form **4868**

Department of the Treasury
Internal Revenue Service (99)

Application for Automatic Extension of Time
To File U.S. Individual Income Tax Return

For calendar year 2016, or other tax year beginning ____ , 2016, ending ____ , 20 ____ .

OMB No. 1545-0074

2016

Part I Identification			
1 Your name(s) (see instructions)			
Address (see instructions)			
City, town, or post office	State	ZIP Code	
2 Your social security number	3 Spouse's social security number		

Part II Individual Income Tax

4 Estimate of total tax liability for 2016 . .	$	
5 Total 2016 payments		
6 **Balance due.** Subtract line 5 from line 4 (see instructions)		
7 Amount you're paying (see instructions) . ▶		
8 Check here if you're "out of the country" and a U.S. citizen or resident (see instructions) . . . . . ▶ ☐		
9 Check here if you file Form 1040NR or 1040NR-EZ and didn't receive wages as an employee subject to U.S. income tax withholding . . . . ▶ ☐		

For Privacy Act and Paperwork Reduction Act Notice, see page 4.

Cat. No. 13141W

Form **4868** (2016)

When To File Form 4868

File Form 4868 by April 18, 2017. Fiscal year taxpayers file Form 4868 by the original due date of the fiscal year return.

Taxpayers who are out of the country. If, on the regular due date of your return, you're out of the country and a U.S. citizen or resident, you're allowed 2 extra months to file your return and pay any amount due without requesting an extension. Interest will still be charged, however, on payments made after the regular due date, without regard to the extension. For a calendar year return, this is June 15, 2017. File this form and be sure to check the box on line 8 if you need an additional 4 months to file your return.

If you're out of the country and a U.S. citizen or resident, you may qualify for special tax treatment if you meet the bona fide residence or physical presence tests. If you don't expect to meet either of those tests by the due date of your return, request an extension to a date after you expect to meet the tests by filing Form 2350, Application for Extension of Time To File U.S. Income Tax Return.

You're out of the country if:

• You live outside the United States and Puerto Rico and your main place of work is outside the United States and Puerto Rico, or

• You're in military or naval service on duty outside the United States and Puerto Rico.

If you qualify as being out of the country, you'll still be eligible for the extension even if you're physically present in the United States or Puerto Rico on the regular due date of the return.

For more information on extensions for taxpayers out of the country, see Pub. 54, Tax Guide for U.S. Citizens and Resident Aliens Abroad.

Form 1040NR or 1040NR-EZ filers. If you can't file your return by the due date, you should file Form 4868. You must file Form 4868 by the regular due date of the return.

If you didn't receive wages as an employee subject to U.S. income tax withholding, and your return is due June 15, 2017, check the box on line 9.

Total Time Allowed

Generally, we can't extend the due date of your return for more than 6 months (October 16, 2017, for most calendar year taxpayers). However, there may be an exception if you're living out of the country. See Pub. 54 for more information.

Filing Your Tax Return

You can file your tax return any time before the extension expires. Don't attach a copy of Form 4868 to your return.

Interest

You'll owe interest on any tax not paid by the regular due date of your return, even if you qualify for the 2-month extension because you were out of the country. The interest runs until you pay the tax. Even if you had a good reason for not paying on time, you will still owe interest.

Late Payment Penalty

The late payment penalty is usually ½ of 1% of any tax (other than estimated tax) not paid by April 18, 2017. It is charged for each month or part of a month the tax is unpaid. The maximum penalty is 25%.

The late payment penalty won't be charged if you can show reasonable cause for not paying on time. Attach a statement to your return fully explaining the reason. Don't attach the statement to Form 4868.

You're considered to have reasonable cause for the period covered by this automatic extension if **both** of the following requirements have been met.

1. At least 90% of the total tax on your 2016 return is paid on or before the regular due date of your return through withholding, estimated tax payments, or payments made with Form 4868.

2. The remaining balance is paid with your return.

Late Filing Penalty

A late filing penalty is usually charged if your return is filed after the due date (including extensions). The penalty is usually 5% of the amount due for each month or part of a month your return is late. The maximum penalty is 25%. If your return is more than 60 days late, the minimum penalty is $205 (adjusted for inflation) or the balance of the tax due on your return, whichever is smaller. You might not owe the penalty if you have a reasonable explanation for filing late. Attach a statement to your return fully explaining your reason for filing late. Don't attach the statement to Form 4868.

How To Claim Credit for Payment Made With This Form

When you file your 2016 return, include the amount of any payment you made with Form 4868 on the appropriate line of your tax return.

The instructions for the following line of your tax return will tell you how to report the payment.

• Form 1040, line 70.
• Form 1040A, line 46.
• Form 1040EZ, line 9.
• Form 1040NR, line 66.
• Form 1040NR-EZ, line 21.
• Form 1040-PR, line 11.
• Form 1040-SS, line 11.

If you and your spouse each filed a separate Form 4868 but later file a joint return for 2016, enter the total paid with both Forms 4868 on the appropriate line of your joint return.

If you and your spouse jointly file Form 4868 but later file separate returns for 2016, you can enter the total amount paid with Form 4868 on either of your separate returns. Or you and your spouse can divide the payment in any agreed amounts.

Specific Instructions

How To Complete Form 4868

Part I—Identification

Enter your name(s) and address. If you plan to file a joint return, include both spouses' names in the order in which they will appear on the return.

If you want correspondence regarding this extension to be sent to you at an address other than your own, enter that address. If you want the correspondence sent to an agent acting for you, include the agent's name (as well as your own) and the agent's address.

If you changed your name after you filed your last return because of marriage, divorce, etc., be sure to report this to the Social Security Administration before filing Form 4868. This prevents delays in processing your extension request.

If you changed your mailing address after you filed your last return, you should use Form 8822, Change of Address, to notify the IRS of the change. Showing a new address on Form 4868 won't update your record. You can download or order IRS forms at *www.irs.gov/formspubs.*

If you plan to file a joint return, enter on line 2 the SSN that you'll show first on your return. Enter on line 3 the other SSN to be shown on the joint return. If you're filing Form 1040NR as an estate or trust, enter your employer identification number (EIN) instead of an SSN on line 2. In the left margin, next to the EIN, write "estate" or "trust."

IRS individual taxpayer identification numbers (ITINs) for aliens. If you're a nonresident or resident alien and you don't have and aren't eligible to get an SSN, you must apply for an ITIN. Although an ITIN isn't required to file Form 4868, you'll need one to file your income tax return. For details on how to apply for an ITIN, see Form W-7 and its instructions. If you already have an ITIN, enter it wherever an SSN is requested. If you don't have an ITIN, enter "ITIN TO BE REQUESTED" wherever an SSN is requested.

 An ITIN is for tax use only. It doesn't entitle you to social security benefits or change your employment or immigration status under U.S. law.

Part II—Individual Income Tax

Rounding off to whole dollars. You can round off cents to whole dollars on Form 4868. If you do round to whole dollars, you must round all amounts. To round, drop amounts under 50 cents and increase amounts from 50 to 99 cents to the next dollar. For example, $1.39 becomes $1 and $2.50 becomes $3. If you have to add two or more amounts to figure the amount to enter on a line, include cents when adding the amounts and round off only the total.

Line 4—Estimate of Total Tax Liability for 2016

Enter on line 4 the total tax liability you expect to report on your 2016.

- Form 1040, line 63.
- Form 1040A, line 39.
- Form 1040EZ, line 12.
- Form 1040NR, line 61.
- Form 1040NR-EZ, line 17.
- Form 1040-PR, line 6.
- Form 1040-SS, line 6.

If you expect this amount to be zero, enter -0-.

Make your estimate as accurate as you can with the information you have. If we later find that the estimate wasn't reasonable, the extension will be null and void.

Line 5—Estimate of Total Payments for 2016

Enter on line 5 the total payments you expect to report on your 2016.

- Form 1040, line 74 (excluding line 70).
- Form 1040A, line 46.
- Form 1040EZ, line 9.
- Form 1040NR, line 71 (excluding line 66).
- Form 1040NR-EZ, line 21.
- Form 1040-PR, line 11.
- Form 1040-SS, line 11.

For Forms 1040A, 1040EZ, 1040NR-EZ, 1040-PR, and 1040-SS, don't include on line 5 the amount you're paying with this Form 4868.

Line 6—Balance Due

Subtract line 5 from line 4. If line 5 is more than line 4, enter -0-.

Line 7—Amount You Are Paying

If you find you can't pay the amount shown on line 6, you can still get the extension. But you should pay as much as you can to limit the amount of interest you'll owe. Also, you may be charged the late payment penalty on the unpaid tax from the regular due date of your return. See *Late Payment Penalty* on page 2.

Line 8—Out of the Country

If you're out of the country on the regular due date of your return, check the box on line 8. "Out of the country" is defined on page 2.

Line 9—Form 1040NR or 1040NR-EZ Filers

If you didn't receive wages subject to U.S. income tax withholding, and your return is due June 15, 2017, check the box on line 9.

How To Make a Payment

Making Payments Electronically

You can pay online with a direct transfer from your bank account using Direct Pay, the Electronic Federal Tax Payment System, or by debit or credit card. You can also pay by phone using the Electronic Federal Tax Payment System or by debit or credit card. For more information, go to *www.irs.gov/payments.*

Confirmation number. You'll receive a confirmation number when you pay online or by phone. Enter the confirmation number below and keep it for your records.

Enter confirmation number here ▶ _____

Note: If you use an electronic payment method and indicate the payment is for an extension, you don't have to file Form 4868. You should pay the entire estimated tax owed or you could be subject to a penalty. Your extension will be automatically processed when you pay part or all of your estimated income tax electronically.

Pay by Check or Money Order

- When paying by check or money order with Form 4868, use the appropriate address in the middle column under *Where To File a Paper Form 4868* on page 4.

- Make your check or money order payable to the "United States Treasury." Don't send cash.

- Write your SSN, daytime phone number, and "2016 Form 4868" on your check or money order.

- Don't staple or attach your payment to Form 4868.

Note: If you e-file Form 4868 and mail a check or money order to the IRS for payment, use a completed paper Form 4868 as a voucher. Please note with your payment that your extension request was originally filed electronically.

No checks of $100 million or more accepted. The IRS cannot accept a single check (including a cashier's check) for amounts of $100,000,000 ($100 million) or more. If you're sending $100 million or more by check, you'll need to spread the payments over two or more checks with each check made out for an amount less than $100 million. The $100 million or more amount limit **does not** apply to other methods of payment (such as electronic payments), so please consider paying by means other than checks.

Form 4868 (2016)   Page **4**

Where To File a Paper Form 4868

If you live in:

If you live in:	And you're making a payment, send Form 4868 with your payment to Internal Revenue Service:	And you're not making a payment, send Form 4868 to Department of the Treasury, Internal Revenue Service Center:
Alabama, Georgia, Kentucky, New Jersey, North Carolina, South Carolina, Tennessee, Virginia	P.O. Box 931300 Louisville, KY 40293-1300	Kansas City, MO 64999-0045
Connecticut, Delaware, District of Columbia, Maine, Maryland, Massachusetts, Missouri, New Hampshire, New York, Pennsylvania, Rhode Island, Vermont, West Virginia	P.O. Box 37009 Hartford, CT 06176-7009	Kansas City, MO 64999-0045
Florida, Louisiana, Mississippi, Texas	P.O. Box 1302 Charlotte, NC 28201-1302	Austin, TX 73301-0045
Alaska, Arizona, California, Colorado, Hawaii, Idaho, Nevada, New Mexico, Oregon, Utah, Washington, Wyoming	P.O. Box 7122 San Francisco, CA 94120-7122	Fresno, CA 93888-0045
Arkansas, Illinois, Indiana, Iowa, Kansas, Michigan, Minnesota, Montana, Nebraska, North Dakota, Ohio, Oklahoma, South Dakota, Wisconsin	P.O. Box 802503 Cincinnati, OH 45280-2503	Fresno, CA 93888-0045
A foreign country, American Samoa, or Puerto Rico, or are excluding income under Internal Revenue Code section 933, or use an APO or FPO address, or file Form 2555, 2555-EZ, or 4563, or are a dual-status alien, or are a nonpermanent resident of Guam or the U.S. Virgin Islands	P.O. Box 1302 Charlotte, NC 28201-1302 USA	Austin, TX 73301-0215 USA
All foreign estate and trust Form 1040NR filers	P.O. Box 1303 Charlotte, NC 28201-1303 USA	Cincinnati, OH 45999-0048 USA
All other Form 1040NR, 1040NR-EZ, 1040-PR, and 1040-SS filers	P.O. Box 1302 Charlotte, NC 28201-1302 USA	Austin, TX 73301-0045 USA

Private Delivery Services

You can use certain private delivery services designated by the IRS to meet the "timely mailing as timely filing/paying" rule for tax returns and payments. These private delivery services include only the following.

• DHL Express: DHL Express 9:00, DHL Express 10:30, DHL Express 12:00, DHL Express Worldwide, DHL Express Envelope, DHL Import Express 10:30, DHL Import Express 12:00, and DHL Import Express Worldwide.

• United Parcel Service (UPS): UPS Next Day Air Early AM, UPS Next Day Air, UPS Next Day Air Saver, UPS 2nd Day Air, UPS 2nd Day Air A.M., UPS Worldwide Express Plus, and UPS Worldwide Express.

• Federal Express (FedEx): FedEx First Overnight, FedEx Priority Overnight, FedEx Standard Overnight, FedEx 2 Day, FedEx International Next Flight Out, FedEx International Priority, FedEx International First, and FedEx International Economy.

The private delivery service can tell you how to get written proof of the mailing date.

 Private delivery services can't deliver items to P.O. boxes. You must use the U.S. Postal Service to mail any item to an IRS P.O. box address.

Privacy Act and Paperwork Reduction Act Notice. We ask for the information on this form to carry out the Internal Revenue laws of the United States. We need this information so that our records will reflect your intention to file your individual income tax return within 6 months after the regular due date. If you choose to apply for an automatic extension of time to file, you're required by Internal Revenue Code section 6081 to provide the information requested on this form. Under section 6109, you must disclose your social security number or individual taxpayer identification number. Routine uses of this information include giving it to the Department of Justice for civil and criminal litigation, and to cities, states, the District of Columbia, and U.S. commonwealths and possessions for use in administering their tax laws. We may also disclose this information to other countries under a tax treaty, to federal and state agencies to enforce federal nontax criminal laws, or to federal law enforcement and intelligence agencies to combat terrorism. If you fail to provide this information in a timely manner or provide incomplete or false information, you may be liable for penalties.

You aren't required to provide the information requested on a form that is subject to the Paperwork Reduction Act unless the form displays a valid OMB control number. Books or records relating to a form or its instructions must be retained as long as their contents may become material in the administration of any Internal Revenue law. Generally, tax returns and return information are confidential, as required by Internal Revenue Code section 6103.

The average time and expenses required to complete and file this form will vary depending on individual circumstances. For the estimated averages, see the instructions for your income tax return.

If you have suggestions for making this form simpler, we would be happy to hear from you. See the instructions for your income tax return.

Form 9465

(Rev. December 2013)
Department of the Treasury
Internal Revenue Service

Installment Agreement Request

▶ Information about Form 9465 and its separate instructions is at *www.irs.gov/form9465*.
▶ If you are filing this form with your tax return, attach it to the front of the return.
▶ See separate instructions.

OMB No. 1545-0074

Tip: If you owe $50,000 or less, you may be able to establish an installment agreement online, even if you have not yet received a bill for your taxes. Go to IRS.gov to apply to pay online. **Caution:** *Do not file this form if you are currently making payments on an installment agreement or can pay your balance in full within 120 days. Instead, call 1-800-829-1040. Do not file if your business is still operating and owes employment or unemployment taxes. Instead, call the telephone number on your most recent notice. If you are in bankruptcy or we have accepted your offer-in-compromise, see* **Bankruptcy or offer-in-compromise,** *in the instructions.*

Part I

This request is for Form(s) (for example, Form 1040 or Form 941) ▶ _____ and for tax year(s) (for example, 2012 and 2013) ▶ _____

1a Your first name and initial _____ Last name _____ | **Your social security number** _____

If a joint return, spouse's first name and initial _____ Last name _____ | **Spouse's social security number** _____

Current address (number and street). If you have a P.O. box and no home delivery, enter your box number. _____ | Apt. number _____

City, town or post office, state, and ZIP code. If a foreign address, also complete the spaces below (see instructions) _____

Foreign country name _____ | Foreign province/state/county _____ | Foreign postal code _____

1b If this address is new since you filed your last tax return, check here . . . . ▶ ☐

2 Name of your business (must be no longer operating) _____ | Employer identification number (EIN) _____

3 Your home phone number _____ Best time for us to call _____ | **4** Your work phone number _____ Ext. _____ Best time for us to call _____

5 Name of your bank or other financial institution: _____ | **6** Your employer's name: _____

Address _____ | Address _____

City, state, and ZIP code _____ | City, state, and ZIP code _____

7 Enter the total amount you owe as shown on your tax return(s) (or notice(s)) . . . . | **7** | _____

8 Enter the amount of any payment you are making with your tax return(s) (or notice(s)). See instructions | **8** | _____

9 Subtract line 8 from line 7 and enter the result . . . . | **9** | _____

10 Enter the amount you can pay each month. Make your payments as large as possible to limit interest and penalty charges. **The charges will continue until you pay in full. If no payment amount is listed on line 10, a payment will be determined for you by dividing the balance due by 72 months** . . | **10** | _____

11 Divide the amount on line 9 by 72 and enter the result . . . . | **11** | _____

• If the amount on line 10 is less than the amount on line 11 and you are unable to increase your payment to the amount on line 11, complete and attach Form 433-F, Collection Information Statement.

• If the amount on line 10 is equal to or greater than the amount on line 11 but the amount you owe is greater than $25,000 but not more than $50,000, you must complete either line 13 or 14, if you do not wish to complete Form 433-F.

• If the amount on line 9 is greater than $50,000, complete and attach Form 433-F, Collection Information Statement.

12 Enter the date you want to make your payment each month. **Do not** enter a date later than the 28th ▶ _____

13 If you want to make your payments by direct debit from your checking account, see the instructions and fill in lines 13a and 13b. This is the most convenient way to make your payments and it will ensure that they are made on time.

▶ **a** Routing number _____

▶ **b** Account number _____

I authorize the U.S. Treasury and its designated Financial Agent to initiate a monthly ACH debit (electronic withdrawal) entry to the financial institution account indicated for payments of my Federal taxes owed, and the financial institution to debit the entry to this account. This authorization is to remain in full force and effect until I notify the U.S. Treasury Financial Agent to terminate the authorization. To revoke payment, I must contact the U.S. Treasury Financial Agent at **1-800-829-1040** no later than 14 business days prior to the payment (settlement) date. I also authorize the financial institutions involved in the processing of the electronic payments of taxes to receive confidential information necessary to answer inquiries and resolve issues related to the payments.

14 If you want to make your payments by payroll deduction, check this box and attach a completed Form 2159, Payroll Deduction Agreement . . . . ☐

Your signature _____ | Date _____ | Spouse's signature. If a joint return, **both** must sign. _____ | Date _____

For Privacy Act and Paperwork Reduction Act Notice, see instructions. | Cat. No. 14842Y | Form **9465** (Rev. 12-2013)

V. Related Matters

- **Interest on Underpayments and Overpayments of Tax.** Taxpayers must pay interest to the IRS on underpayments of tax. The underpayment rate is 3% over the federal short-term rate. IRC § 6621(a). Interest accrues from the original return due date, without regard to extensions, to the date payment is received by the IRS. IRC § 6601, 6161. If a taxpayer overpays tax, the taxpayer is entitled to receive interest on the overpayment. The overpayment rate is the same as the underpayment rate. IRC § 6611.

- **Penalties: In General.** Accuracy-related and fraud penalties, codified in sections 6662–6664, may be imposed on underpayment of tax attributable to: negligence or disregard of rules and regulations; substantial understatement of income tax; substantial valuation misstatement; and fraud. Stacking of the penalties is prohibited. Treas. Reg. § 1.6662-2(c). A taxpayer may be able to avoid these penalties by showing there was reasonable cause for the return position and that the taxpayer acted in good faith. IRC § 6664(c); Treas. Reg. § 1.6664-4(a).

- **Negligence Penalty.** The *negligence penalty* is imposed at the rate of 20% of that portion of an underpayment of tax attributable to negligence or disregard of rules and regulations (a facts and circumstances determination). IRC § 6662(b)(1). "Negligence" means a failure to make a reasonable attempt to comply with tax laws (i.e., a failure to do what a reasonable and prudent person would do under like circumstances). *See* Treas. Reg. § 1.6662-3(b)(1). "Disregard of rules and regulations" includes any careless, reckless, or intentional disregard of rules and regulations, which include the Internal Revenue Code, temporary and final Treasury Regulations, revenue rulings, and certain IRS notices. IRC § 6662(c); Treas. Reg. § 1.6662-3(b)(2) (defining the terms "careless, reckless, and intentional").

- **Substantial Understatement Penalty.** The *substantial understatement penalty* is imposed at the rate of 20% of that portion of an underpayment of tax attributable to a substantial understatement of income tax due. IRC § 6662(b)(2). An understatement is substantial if it exceeds 10% of the tax required to be shown or $5,000, whichever is greater. IRC § 6662(d)(1)–(2). The understatement is reduced if the taxpayer has substantial authority for the taxpayer's position or the taxpayer sufficiently discloses the relevant facts affecting the taxpayer's position and there is a reasonable basis for the position. Treas. Reg. § 1.6662-4.

- **Substantial Valuation Misstatement Penalty.** For income tax purposes, the accuracy-related penalty for *substantial valuation misstatements* is 20% of the underpayment of tax attributable to a substantial valuation misstatement, which exists if the value or adjusted basis of property claimed on the tax return is 150% or more of the correct value or basis. IRC § 6662(b)(3), (e)(1). The penalty increases to 40% if the underpayment is attributable to a "gross" valuation misstatement, which exists if the value or basis of any property on a return is 200% or more of the correct value or basis. IRC § 6662(h). For estate and gift tax purposes, the 20% penalty applies to valuation understatements (the property's value reported on the estate or gift tax return is 65% or less of the correct value); the penalty increases to 40% if the property's value is grossly understated (i.e., the property's value reported on the return is 40% or less of the correct value).

- **Fraud Penalty.** The *fraud penalty* is imposed at the rate of 75% of the portion of the underpayment of tax which is attributable to fraud (i.e., intentional wrongdoing). IRC § 6663(a). Note that if any portion of the underpayment of tax is deemed attributable to fraud, the entire underpayment is treated as attributable to fraud, except with respect to any portion of the underpayment that the taxpayer establishes, by a preponderance of the evidence, is not attributable to fraud. A list of "badges of fraud" are included in the IRS's Internal Revenue Manual. IRM 20.1.5.12.1.

- **Transactions Lacking Economic Substance.** In 2010, Congress amended section 6662 to include penalties for understatements attributable to any disallowances of claimed tax benefits arising from transactions lacking economic substance. IRC § 6662(b)(6). This codification of the court-made "economic substance doctrine" is sought to be clarified in section 7701(o). The statute provides, in part, that a "... transaction shall be treated as having economic substance only if—(A) the transaction changes in a meaningful way (apart from Federal income tax effects) the taxpayer's economic position, and (B) the taxpayer has a substantial purpose (apart from Federal income tax effects) for entering into such transaction." IRC § 7701(o)(1). In practice, determining whether a transaction has economic substance has often proved a knotty problem.

Table of Internal Revenue Code Sections

647

Table of Treasury Regulations

Table of Administrative Pronouncements

The excerpted pronouncements are listed in bold type. The pages on which the excerpted pronouncements begin are also in bold type.

Table of Cases

The excerpted cases are listed in bold type. The pages on which the excerpted cases begin are also in bold type.

Index